The Idiot

"The real nineteenth-century prophet was
Dostoevsky, not Karl Marx."
Albert Camus

"Dostoevsky gives me more than any
scientist, more than Gauss!"
Albert Einstein

"The only psychologist from whom I
have anything to learn."
Friedrich Nietzsche

The novels of Dostoevsky are seething whirlpools,
gyrating sandstorms, waterspouts which hiss and boil
and suck us in. They are composed purely and wholly
the stuff of the soul. Against our wills we are drawn in,
whirled round, blinded, suffocated, and at the same
time filled with a giddy rapture. Out of Shakespeare
there is no more exciting reading."
Virginia Woolf

ONEWORLD CLASSICS

The Idiot

Fyodor Dostoevsky

ONEWORLD
CLASSICS

ONEWORLD CLASSICS LTD
London House
243-253 Lower Mortlake Road
Richmond
Surrey TW9 2LL
United Kingdom
www.oneworldclassics.com

The Idiot first published in 1869
This translation first published by Oneworld Classics Limited in 2010
Translation, Apparatus and Notes © Ignat Avsey, 2010

Front cover image © Getty Images

Printed in Great Britain by CPI Cox & Wyman, Reading, Berkshire

ISBN: 978-1-84749-150-3

Contents

Fyodor Dostoevsky (1821–81)

Mikhail Andreyevich
Dostoevsky, Fyodor's father

Maria Fyodorovna
Dostoevskaya, Fyodor's mother

Mikhail Mikhailovich
Dostoevsky, Fyodor's brother

Maria Dmitrievna
Dostoevskaya, Fyodor's first wife

Anna Grigoryevna Dostoevskaya,
Fyodor's second wife

Apollinaria Suslova,
Fyodor's mistress

The Mariinsky Hospital in Moscow, where
Dostoevsky was born in 1821

The Dostoevskys' dacha in Darovoye (above), the apartment where
Dostoevsky lived from 1861 to 1863 (bottom left), and which housed the
offices of his journal *Vremya* (bottom right)

The Idiot

Part One

1

A T ABOUT NINE IN THE MORNING at the end of November in melting
snow, the Warsaw train was steaming fast towards St Petersburg. It
was so damp and foggy that the dawn light struggled to break through;
nothing much was visible out of the windows ten paces either side of
the track. Some passengers were homeward bound from abroad, but
the third-class carriages were particularly crowded, in the main, with
small-town, short-distance business travellers. All were, as is usual on
such journeys, dog-tired and bleary-eyed; all were freezing cold with
pallid faces to match the fog.

In one of the third-class compartments by the window two people
had found themselves opposite each other from the small hours: both
were young, travelling light; neither was too smartly dressed; both had
rather distinctive features and – finally – both were ready to enter into
conversation. Had either of them been aware of what it was that united
them, they'd have wondered how it was that pure chance had brought
them face to face in this third-class compartment of the Warsaw-St
Petersburg train. One was short, about twenty-seven, with almost jet-
black, wavy hair, and small, grey but fiery eyes. His nose was flat and
wide, his cheekbones high; his thin lips were permanently curled into an
arrogant, mocking, well-nigh malevolent smirk; his brow, however, was
high and well formed, and more than made up for the ungainly, jutting
lower part of his face. What was most remarkable about this face though
was its deathly pallor, lending the young man an emaciated look even
despite his rather powerful build; along with everything else, he exuded
an ardour that bordered on anguish and did not accord at all well with
his arrogant, almost truculent smile and the impudent smugness of his
gaze. He was warmly dressed in a lined, black, wide-fitting sheepskin
that kept him warm through the night, whereas his fellow traveller
had endured the full rigour of a damp Russian November night totally
unprepared. All the latter man wore was a fairly wide, coarse cloak
with a huge hood, as is not infrequently worn by travellers wintering
in distant parts, in Switzerland or even northern Italy, but something

hardly designed for a journey such as that from Eydtkuhnen* to St Petersburg. What was suitable and perfectly adequate for Italy was not nearly sufficient for Russia. The wearer of the cloak and hood was also about twenty-six or -seven, slightly taller than average, with a very fair complexion, a good head of hair, sunken cheeks and a sparse, barely noticeable, very pale goatee beard. His eyes were large, sky-blue and intense; his gaze was calm and brooding, suffused with that strange glow which some people immediately recognize as a sure symptom of the falling sickness. On the whole, however, his face was pleasant, fine and lean, but drained of colour, especially now that it was livid with cold. On his knees he cradled a pathetic little bundle, fashioned from a piece of worn, faded raw-silk fabric, evidently comprising all his worldly possessions. He wore a pair of thick-soled boots with cross-laced gaiters – all very un-Russian. His dark-haired travelling companion in the lined sheepskin, partly from want of anything better to do, took all this in and, smiling that indiscreet smile which so often betrays man's delight in the discomfort of others, finally enquired, "Feeling the cold, eh?" And he jerked his shoulders.

"Indeed," the other replied with extreme readiness, "and, surprisingly, it's thawing. I hate to think what it's like when it's freezing! I had no idea it could be so cold here in Russia. Comes as quite a shock."

"Are you from abroad, or what?"

"Yes, from Switzerland."

"Ha! Some people!…" The man made a whistling sound and burst out laughing.

A conversation ensued. The alacrity and candour with which the fair-haired young man in the Swiss cloak took to answering all the prying, indiscreet and at times obviously idle questions of his swarthy interlocutor was nothing short of remarkable. In the process, he openly admitted that he had not been back to Russia for a long time – over four years – and that he'd been sent abroad for health reasons, with some strange nervous ailment like the falling sickness or St Vitus's dance, with nervous contractions and spasms. Listening to him, the dark-haired man smirked a few times, particularly broadly when, in answer to his question, "And did they cure you?" the blond man replied, "No, not really."

"Ha! I thought as much," the dark man observed cuttingly, "but you paid through the nose, and we here trust that lot."

"You're quite right!" a badly dressed passenger, something like a lowly copy clerk, sitting nearby, butted in; he was a strongly built man of about forty, red-nosed, with a face marked by blotches. "The truth is, they suck the lifeblood out of us Russians!"

"Oh, how wrong you are, gentlemen, as far as I'm concerned anyway," the patient from Switzerland hastened to observe in a mild and conciliatory tone. "Of course, I'm in no position to argue because I don't know how it is with other people, but my doctor gave all he had to help me with my fare and besides he supported me for close on two years at his own expense."

"There was no one else to pay, is that it?" the swarthy man enquired.

"Yes, Mr Pavlishchev, who funded me, died two years ago. I wrote to General Yepanchin's spouse, a distant relative of mine, but received no reply. So I simply upped sticks and came over."

"Over where?"

"You mean, where am I going to stay?... I must say, I still don't know... but..."

"It's yet to be arranged!"

Both men burst out laughing.

"Is that bundle all you have?" the swarthy man asked.

"I bet it is," the red-nosed clerk observed, utterly pleased with himself, "and that he has nothing in the luggage compartment – poverty of course is not the end of the world, but there you go..."

As it turned out, that was very much the case. The fair-haired young man made no bones about it, and owned up immediately with the utmost readiness.

"All the same, your bundle is not to be written off entirely," the clerk continued after they had all had their fill of laughter (remarkably, the owner of the bundle too began to laugh in the end at the mere sight of them, which added to the general merriment), "and though I wouldn't mind betting that it isn't stuffed with your rolls of gold napoleons* or *fredericks,* or even our very own Dutch ducats,* which is all too easy to conjecture just from the state of those gaiters over your foreign-looking boots, all the same... combine it with a putative relative, such as Madame la Générale Yepanchina, and your bundle immediately becomes a totally different proposition, unless of course you're wrong in styling her as your relative, which too is always possible in consequence of – shall we say – absent-mindedness... engendered by, let's say... too fertile an imagination, an in itself quite human trait if you ask me."

"Oh, you're perfectly right again," the fair-haired young man responded, "my mistake – she is altogether too distant to qualify as a relative. As a matter of fact, I was not at all surprised when there was no reply. I never really expected one."

"Just wasted postage. Hm... at least you're honest and above board about it, which is commendable! Hm... as for General Yepanchin, of course I know him, he's pretty well known. And the late Mr Pavlishchev, who maintained you in Switzerland, I knew him too, assuming of course it was Nikolai Andreyevich Pavlishchev, because there were two – cousins. The other one still resides in the Crimea, and as for Nikolai Andreyevich, he was a respectable gentleman, well connected too, and in his time the owner of four thousand souls—"

"Quite right, he was called Nikolai Andreyevich Pavlishchev," the young man said, and gave the know-all nosy parker an intent, probing look.

Such inquisitive gentlemen are an almost universal occurrence, in certain circles that is. They know everything, all their restless mental inquisitiveness and prying faculties are without exception directed to one goal only, this of course in the absence of any more important interests or preoccupations as a thinker of today might have put it. The word "everything", it must be said, has to be understood in a very restricted sense: where so-and-so works, whom he knows, what he's worth, where he was a governor, if at all, whom he was married to, how much his wife brought in, who his first and second cousins were, and so on and so forth. For the most part these individuals walk about ragged at the elbow and subsist on seventeen roubles per month. People of whom they know every last detail would never suspect what the force motivating these gentlemen was; all the same, having procured their knowledge – a truly encyclopaedic one, it must be owned – they are well pleased with themselves; they are filled with self-respect and even the joy of supreme spiritual contentment. To be sure, the practice is most enticing. I have observed men of learning, men of letters, poets, politicians, who all strove for and attained, in this well-nigh scientific pursuit, their highest aspirations and personal fulfilment, to the point that they owed their entire careers to it.

During the course of this conversation the swarthy young man kept yawning and glancing aimlessly out of the window, obviously wishing the journey would come to an end. He was self-absorbed to the point of being distracted and even odd; now he listened, now he didn't; he looked about vacantly, and laughed at the most inappropriate moments without rhyme or reason.

"May I enquire, whom do I have the honour of?..." the blotchy man enquired, turning to the fair-haired young man with the bundle.

"Prince Lev Nikolayevich Myshkin," the young man responded with complete alacrity.

"Prince Myshkin? Lev Nikolayevich? Now you have me," the clerk replied in puzzlement. "As a matter of fact I've never heard of him. I don't mean the name, it's sure to be in Karamzin's *History*,* it's just that these days one hardly comes across any Myshkins, no one ever hears of any."

"That's very true," the Prince replied immediately. "There are no more Myshkins these days, apart from me. I think I'm the last of them. As for the past, some of my family were indeed of peasant stock. My father, incidentally, happened to be an army man, a sub lieutenant, with a military upbringing. I'm not entirely sure how it is that Madame Yepanchina came to be a Myshkin, also the last of her line, if you follow my line, so to speak..."

"Ha ha ha, I like the way you doubled up your lines!" the clerk remarked with a broad grin.

The swarthy young man could not forbear a smile either, whereas the fair one appeared to be taken totally by surprise for having managed to come up with a pun, albeit a pretty weak one.

"You know, it was quite unintentional on my part," he tried to make up for it at last, very sheepishly.

"Never mind, never mind," the clerk rubbed it in good humouredly.

"And did you do any studying with this professor of yours?" the dark-haired man asked suddenly.

"Yes... I did—"

"I never studied a thing in my life."

"Well, it was nothing much, just bits and pieces," the Prince added as though apologizing. "Due to my illness I was in no fit state to undertake a regular course of studies."

"Do you know the Rogozhins?" the dark-haired man asked abruptly.

"No, I can't say I do. I know very few people in Russia. Are you Mr Rogozhin by any chance?"

"Yes, I am Rogozhin, Parfyon."

"Parfyon Rogozhin? Would that be the Rogozhins who—" the clerk was about to launch forth pompously.

"Yes, it would, yes," the swarthy man cut him off in exasperation, never having addressed him previously, taking care to speak to the Prince only.

"Well... I never!" the clerk exclaimed, dumbfounded, his eyes nearly popping out in amazement as his face dissolved into something ingratiating and submissive, verging on the awestruck. "So you're the son of that same Semyon Rogozhin, of venerable ancient lineage, who died not a month ago leaving behind a round two and a half million?"

"And how the deuce do you know he left two and a half million?" the dark-haired man interposed, not deigning even to look at the clerk now. "It beats me" (he winked at the Prince) "what these people hope to gain by their toadying! But it's true, my father died, and a month later here I am on my way back from Pskov without a penny to my name! Neither my brother, a right scoundrel, nor mother breathed a word, informed me of anything or sent me anything! Treated me like a dog! I lay a month on my sickbed in Pskov."

"And now there's a cool million and a bit at the very least waiting for you. Oh, Lord!" the clerk clasped his hands in agitation.

"Can anyone tell me, please, what business it is of his?" Rogozhin again nodded at him in angry irritation. "Don't you realize, you're not going to get a single copeck from me even if you do a handstand right here in front of me."

"And I will, I will."

"Look at him! I won't give you anything, nothing at all, you can dance for a week in front of me for all the good it'll do you."

"Don't then! It'll serve me right! Don't give me a thing, but I'll dance all the same! I'll leave my wife, my small children, just to dance in front of you. Flattery gets you everywhere!"

"Get lost!" Rogozhin said in disgust. "Five weeks ago," he continued, turning to the Prince, "I, like you, with just a bundle on my back, ran away from my father to my aunt's in Pskov, where I went down with a fever, and lo and behold the old boy went and died on me in my absence. An apoplectic fit! God rest his soul, but he came within an ace

10

of killing me at the time! Believe me, Prince, as God is my witness, if I hadn't scarpered, I'd have been done for."

"You must have really incensed him!" the Prince observed, looking at the millionaire in the sheepskin with unfeigned curiosity. But even if there was something curious in a man with a million-rouble inheritance, the Prince was intrigued and fascinated by something else besides. As for Rogozhin, he too for some reason was only too willing to talk to the Prince, even though his wish to converse appeared not to be motivated by any deep spiritual need, but seemed rather mechanical; more the result of distraction and agitation than inner compulsion – just so as to have something to look at and keep his tongue wagging. He still appeared to be feverish, or at least in early convalescence. As for the clerk, he hovered around Rogozhin and hung on his every word with abject sycophancy.

"Incensed, yes, he was incensed all right, and perhaps with reason," Rogozhin replied, "but it was my brother who got my dander up. I don't blame my mother, she's old, set in her ways, reads the Church Calendar* and has no mind of her own. Whatever anybody says, goes. But why didn't he let me know in time? Can anyone tell me that? True enough, I was comatose at the time. They say there was a telegram, and who should get it but my aunt. The woman's been widowed these past thirty years, and is surrounded from dawn to dusk by a gaggle of church-going biddies and holy fools.* She's half-sorceress, half-nun herself. The telegram put her in a right old tizzy, and off she ran with it unopened to the copper's shanty, where she left it. It was only thanks to Vasily Vasilych Konev, who wrote to me, bless him, that I got wise to everything. Under cover of night my brother had snipped all the heavy gilt tassels off the coffin pall. "They're worth a fortune!" he says. I could have had him packed off to Siberia for that, it's sheer sacrilege. Listen, eyesore!" he turned to the clerk. "Is it sacrilege legally?"

"Sacrilege, yes of course, it's sacrilege," the clerk confirmed at once.

"Hanging offence?"

"On the nearest lamp-post, straight away! No questions asked!"

"They think I'm still ill," Rogozhin continued, addressing the Prince, "but without a word, I got up from my sickbed, caught the train on the quiet, and here I come, dear brother Semyon Semyonych! Open up the gate! You were setting the old man against me, that I know. But that

I also upset the old boy mightily over Nastasya Filippovna is equally true. And that's all down to me. No one else is to blame."

"Over Nastasya Filippovna?" the clerk repeated obsequiously, as though adding two and two together.

"You know nothing about it!" Rogozhin snapped at him impatiently.

"And what if I do?" the clerk replied triumphantly.

"A likely story! There's no end of women by that name! And if you want to know my opinion, you're an arrogant, misbegotten swine! I knew it," he said, turning to the Prince, "sooner or later some such nasty piece of work was bound to cross my path."

"Well, perhaps I really do know, sir!" the clerk bustled. "Lebedev knows everything. It's all very well for you to reproach me, kind sir, but what if I were to prove it to you? Wouldn't she be the same Nastasya Filippovna because of whom your father belaboured you with a stout stick, she being the selfsame Miss Barashkova, a well-born lady indeed, perhaps of princely stock in a manner of speaking, but certainly well in with a certain Mr Totsky, Afanasy Ivanovich, a highly distinguished gentleman, landowner and the veritable father of all capitalists, chairman of any number of companies and organizations, and the esteemed General Yepanchin's bosom pal…"

"My word," Rogozhin seemed genuinely surprised, "the man really knows something, dammit!"

"He does indeed! Lebedev knows it all. My dear sir, I've even been in contact with old Alexander Likhachev for close on two months, also following the death of his father. We explored every establishment in town, every nook and cranny, so that in the end it reached a stage where Lebedev was simply indispensable to him. Now the man's languishing in the debtors' jail, but back then I even had occasion to make the acquaintance of Nastasya Filippovna, and not only her – what were they all called?… Armance, Coralie, Princess Patskaya, I got to know a whole bunch of them."

"Nastasya Filippovna!" Rogozhin exclaimed, his lips whitening and twitching, as he darted a stern look at Lebedev. "Do you mean she's with Likhachev?…"

"N-n-nothing to get upset about! N-nothing! Nothing at all!" Lebedev began to backtrack hurriedly in nervous agitation. "Likhachev hasn't got a chance in hell! Totsky is the only one. Of an evening he's usually ensconced in his private box at the Bolshoy or the French Theatre. Let the gentlemen officers talk their hearts out amongst themselves, but even they can't prove anything. All they can do is point and say, 'There, that's that selfsame Nastasya Filippovna!' and that's all. As for anything else – not a sausage! Cross my heart."

"That's exactly how it is," Rogozhin confirmed with a grim scowl. "Zalyozhev said the same thing. I remember, Prince, I was crossing the Nevsky at the time in my father's shabby old coat and she was stepping out of a shop, straight into a coach. I nearly died. Zalyozhev happened to be passing by, full of airs and graces, a lorgnette in his eye, and there was I in my greasy peasant boots, reeking of sour cabbage soup. 'She's not for you, my lad,' he reckons. 'She's quality. They call her Nastasya Filippovna, surname Barashkova, and she lives with Totsky, who doesn't know quite what to do with her now. He's reached the ripe old age of fifty-five and wants to marry the foremost beauty in all St Petersburg.' That's when he told me that I could see her that same day sitting in her private box at a ballet at the Bolshoy. If I'd mentioned to my old man about going to the ballet, he'd have killed me on the spot! However, I sneaked out for an hour or so, and had a good look at her. Couldn't sleep a wink that night. Next morning the old man, God rest his soul, gave me two loan bonds worth five thousand roubles each to sell, to pay seven and a half to the Andreyevs at their office and deliver the balance directly into his hands – he'd be waiting for me. I sold the bonds, took the money, but gave the Andreyev office a miss, and made a beeline for the jeweller's, where I blew the lot on a pair of diamond earrings, each stone the size of a nut. I was four hundred short, I left my name, and they trusted me. I went straight to Zalyozhev with the earrings. 'Come on, let's go to Nastasya Filippovna's!' I said. We set off. I can't remember where we were going, what was ahead, what was either side of me, or how we got there, it's a complete blank. But she received us both in her sitting room. At the time I didn't identify myself. Zalyozhev simply said, 'This is from Parfyon Rogozhin, he saw you at the theatre last night. Be so gracious as to accept this as a memento.' She undid the wrapping, had a look, and smiled: 'Thank your friend Mr Rogozhin for his thoughtfulness.' She made a graceful nod with her head, and left. I ask you, why didn't I die there and then! If I went there in the first place, it was because I didn't expect to come out of it alive! But what needled me most was the thought that that scoundrel Zalyozhev had taken all the glory. I'm hardly God's gift to women, dressed like a tramp, standing there dumbstruck, staring at her wide-eyed, dying of embarrassment, but he's your real toff, dressed to the nines according to the latest fashion, hair curled and oiled, fresh looking, chequered necktie – never lost for a word, and full of answers to everything. He puts me in the shade entirely! 'You watch your step!' I said to him when we left. He laughed it off. 'I'd like to see what you'll have to say to your father, Semyon Parfyonych.' I had a good mind to jump in the river there and then without even going home, but then I thought better of it. 'Well, so what!' And slunk back home with my tail between my legs."

"My, oh my!" the clerk continued to play the fool, twitching in every limb and winking at the Prince. "If I knew my Semyon Parfyonych right, he'd send you to kingdom come for ten, never mind ten thousand roubles."

The Prince studied Rogozhin intently, who seemed to have gone even paler than before.

"That he would!" Rogozhin said. "What's it to you? He got wise to everything in no time," he continued, addressing the Prince, "and then Zalyozhev went blabbing about it all over the town. The old man locked me in upstairs, and read the riot act to me. 'That's just to begin with,' he reckons, 'but I'll be back to kiss you goodnight before dark.' Guess what? The old devil went straight to Nastasya Filippovna's, bowed deep to her, cried his eyes out and implored her to have mercy on him. She brought the little box out at last. 'Here, take your earrings, old man. They're ten times as valuable to me now that I know what it cost Parfyon to get them. Give Parfyon Semyonych my regards and thank him for me.' Meanwhile, with my mother's blessing, I cadged twenty roubles from Sergey Protushin and set off for Pskov by rail. Got there in a stinking fever. The old church biddies nearly did for me with their incantations, and there was I sozzled, plastered, blotto, but I still had it in me to crawl round the taverns of the town on my last legs, blowing all I had, and ended up lying in the street senseless till the morning, wracked with fever and covered in dog bites. I don't know how I ever survived."

"Well, well, well," the clerk exulted, rubbing his hands in glee. "It'll be Nastasya Filippovna's turn now. The earrings are nothing! It's the reward she'll bestow for them—"

"If you just say another word about Nastasya Filippovna," Rogozhin exclaimed, gripping him by the hand tightly, "I swear, I'll horsewhip you even though you are a pal of Likhachev."

"If you do, you won't send me packing! Whip me, go ahead, you'll remember me all the better for that... There you are, we've arrived!"

True enough, the train was pulling into the station. Even though Rogozhin had said that he had departed on the quiet, there were already several people waiting for him. They were shouting and waving their caps about.

"I see Zalyozhev's here too!" Rogozhin muttered, looking at the crowd with a triumphant, somewhat hostile smile. Suddenly he turned towards the Prince. "Prince, I find it strange, but I've come to like you. Maybe it's down to the mood of the moment, but then I met him (he pointed at Lebedev) too at the same time, and I feel nothing for him. Come and see me, Prince. We'll get rid of these gaiters of yours. I'll dress you up in the best fur coat there is, fit you out with a tailcoat, a white waistcoat or whatever kind you wish, stuff your pockets full of money, and... we'll go and call on Nastasya Filippovna! Will you come?"

"Say yes, Prince Lev Nikolayevich!" Lebedev urged fervently and persuasively. "This is the chance of a lifetime! Don't let it slip!..."

Prince Myshkin rose to his feet, stretched out his hand cordially and said with deference, "I shall be delighted to come and am very happy you have found my company agreeable. If I can manage it, I might perhaps come this very day. Because, let me be frank, I too have come to like you, especially after your story about the diamond earrings, though I liked you from the first, earrings or no earrings, and in spite of your gruffness. Many thanks for the offer of the clothes and the fur coat, because really I shall soon be in need of both. As for money, I must confess, I have hardly anything at the moment."

"There'll be money enough by nightfall, there will! Be sure to come!"

"There will, there will," the clerk echoed, "even before nightfall, there will!"

"How about the fair sex, Prince? Are you much of a ladies' man? Might as well tell me now!"

"Me, n-n-no! You see... Perhaps you're not aware, but as a result of my illness, I've had no contact with women."

15

"If that's so, Prince," Rogozhin exclaimed, "you are truly a holy man, one of God's favoured!"

"God's favoured indeed," the clerk affirmed.

"Well, come along then, you creep," Rogozhin said to Lebedev, and they all left the carriage.

Lebedev was triumphant. The noisy crowd moved off in the direction of the Voznesensky Prospect. The Prince's way lay towards the Liteiny. It was raw and dank. The Prince asked passers-by for directions. It was about three versts to where he wanted to go, and he decided to take a cab.

2

G ENERAL YEPANCHIN was the owner of a house close by the Liteiny Prospect, on the side of the Preobrazhensky Cathedral. As well as this splendid residence, five-sixths of which were let out, he had another spacious house in Sadovaya Street, which also brought in a huge income. Besides these two houses, he had on the very edge of St Petersburg a large, very profitable estate; and there was also a factory somewhere or other in the district. In times gone by, General Yepanchin, as everybody knows, dabbled in the wine trade. More recently, he took pride in being a very influential member on the board of several established public companies. He had the reputation of being very wealthy, very enterprising and very well connected. In some quarters, not least in the government department in which he worked, he had become totally indispensable. And yet it was also common knowledge that General Yepanchin had no formal education and came from a humble military background, which of course could not but redound to his honour; but the General, though undoubtedly a highly gifted man, was not without his foibles, and was not particularly pleased if these were ever alluded to. But that he was gifted and worldly-wise, there could be no doubt whatsoever. For instance, he knew instinctively never to overreach himself – in fact, where necessary, to vacate the scene altogether – and the thing that people valued him for in particular was his artlessness, the knack of always knowing his place.

If only these judges of his character had a mere inkling of what sometimes went on deep in the soul of Ivan Fyodorovich, who knew his place so well!

Though he was well versed and practised in worldly affairs, and not devoid of unusual natural gifts, it suited him best to present himself as the executor of other people's ideas, rather than the promulgator of his own, "to serve *sans* servility"* and – in line with modern trends – even to parade his Russianness, but one with a human face. There had been some amusing anecdotes on this score; but for all that, the General always took them, even the most scurrilous ones, in good part; incidentally, luck always seemed to favour him, particularly at cards, and he played for high stakes, deliberately not only not concealing this allegedly trifling weakness of his, but indulging it to the full for all the benefits it frequently bestowed upon him. He kept mixed company, but his predilection was for the cream of society. As to his future prospects, he was more than sanguine: everything would come in its season and its time. Regarding his age, the General was, as it were, at the very peak, that is a round fifty-six, when life *in earnest* just begins. He looked healthy and fit: his teeth, though not too white, were strong; his build squat and sturdy; his mien businesslike at work in the mornings, relaxed and happy after hours at cards or at His Highness's. In a word, life for His Excellency, the General, was just a bowl of cherries!

The General was blessed with a flourishing family. Admittedly, there were some problems in that department, but for the most part it had already long been the focal point of all his most cherished hopes and aspirations. And, true enough, what could be dearer and nearer than one's family? What could be a better mainstay than one's own flesh and blood? The family comprised his wife and three grown-up daughters. He had married early, while still a subaltern, a girl almost his own age, distinguished neither by beauty nor education, who brought him only fifty souls* which, however, happened to be the basis of his subsequent good fortune. The General never regretted his early marriage, never referred to it as the result of the infatuation of impulsive youth, but respected his spouse so much and was sometimes so much in awe of her that it could easily pass for love. The lady herself was from the princely Myshkin line which, though not particularly illustrious, went back a long way and of which she was duly proud. It so happened that in earlier days a certain patron of hers, incidentally one of those whose patronage did not cost him a copeck, took an interest in the young couple. He opened the door to future prospects for the young officer and aided his path, although a wink and a nod would have

17

sufficed just as well. With a few exceptions, the couple's long-standing marriage knew no discord. In the very first years of their marriage the General's Lady, as a born princess and the last of her line, but perhaps due to personal accomplishments too, had contrived to find some very influential patronesses. Subsequently, relying on her husband's wealth and professional status, she began to adjust fully to the elevated circles in which she moved.

In the past few years, the three daughters – Alexandra, Adelaida and Aglaya – had matured and blossomed visibly. Though they were styled plain Yepanchins, on the mother's side they were titled; they had sizeable dowries and their father's career promised to be meteoric, but – and this is rather important – their most brilliant asset was their beauty, not excepting Alexandra, who was already twenty-five. The middle one was twenty-three, and the youngest, Aglaya, had just turned twenty. This baby sister was in fact exceptionally attractive, and was beginning to enjoy a great deal of admiring attention from all quarters. Besides, all three were gifted, intelligent and had a good upbringing. It was generally known that all three were very close and supportive of one another. There was even talk of some kind of a pact on the part of the elder two to benefit the youngest – the undisputed idol of the household. In society they liked to keep themselves to themselves and not be forward in any way. No one could accuse them of being arrogant or opinionated, and yet it was common knowledge that they lacked nothing in pride and could well stand up for themselves. The eldest was musical, the middle one painted exceedingly well – which fact hardly anyone became aware of for many years until quite recently, and fortuitously at that. In a word, the reports that circulated about them were highly complimentary. But they had their detractors too. Some people for instance were aghast at the number of books the threesome had read. Marriage was not their chief priority. They cultivated the company of some people, but only in moderation. This was all the more remarkable, considering the natural bent and ambition of their father.

It was already approaching eleven o'clock when the Prince rang the General's doorbell. The General resided on the first floor, and occupied rooms which were far from ostentatious, but in keeping with his status. The door was opened by a liveried valet, and there ensued a protracted conversation, from the very start of which the Prince and his little bundle were subjected to a great deal of suspicious scrutiny. Finally, in response to his repeated and clear-cut assurances that he was indeed Prince Myshkin and that he must, come what may, see the General on a pressing business matter, the mistrustful servant conducted him into a small lobby, right next to the waiting room that adjoined the study, and handed him over to another servant, a valet, on morning shift, charged with announcing visitors to the General. He was fitted out in tails, was over forty and had a sour mien; being at his master's beck and call somehow lent the man a great sense of self-importance.

"Please wait in the waiting room, and leave your bundle here," he said, with slow deliberation, making himself comfortable in his chair and casting disapproving glances at the Prince, who had settled right next to him, clutching his little bundle.

"If it's all right with you," the Prince said, "I'd rather wait here than on my own over there."

"You can't stay in the lobby, because you're a visitor, a personal caller. Is it the General himself you want to see?" Evidently, the valet could not bring himself to admit such a caller, and therefore decided to repeat his question.

"Yes, I'm here on a business matter..." the Prince returned.

"I am not asking what the purpose of your call is – my duty is just to announce you. But, as I said, I am not doing it without the secretary."

The man was evidently consumed with mistrust. The Prince was too unlike the usual run of day-to-day visitors, and although the General was obliged to see the strangest assortment of people at the appointed hour almost daily, on business that would have inured the valet to the oddest of them, he nevertheless hesitated even though his instructions for admission were somewhat flexible. The secretary's mediation was indispensable.

"Are you really... from abroad?" he finally enquired somewhat irresolutely, and stopped. Perhaps he intended to ask, "Are you really Prince Myshkin?"

"Yes, I've come straight from the station. I have a feeling you wanted to ask if I really am Prince Myshkin, but were too polite to do so."

"Hm..." the valet grunted, rather taken aback.

"I assure you, I told you the truth, and you should have no qualms about it. As to my appearance and this bundle, I can explain. My circumstances at present are very reduced indeed."

"Hm. That's not what I'm worried about, as it happens. It's my duty to announce you, and the secretary will come shortly, unless... Well, that's the point, 'unless'. You haven't come to trouble the General for money, if I may be so bold as to ask?"

"Oh no, you needn't worry about that at all. I have other business."

"I beg your pardon, but I was going by your appearance. You must wait for the secretary. The General himself is now in conference with a colonel, but the secretary is due shortly... the company's."

"Well, if it's going to be a long wait, may I ask if I could smoke here somewhere? I have my pipe and tobacco with me."

"S-smoke?" The valet gazed at him with astonished disdain as though he had misheard him. "Smoke? Certainly not, and I am surprised to hear you ask such a thing. Really!..."

"Oh, I didn't mean in this room. I quite understand. I'd be happy to go wherever's convenient. I've not had a smoke for the last three hours, and I'm dying for one now. Still, if that's the rule of the house..."

"What shall I do with you?" the valet mumbled involuntarily. "To begin with, you shouldn't be here at all. You should be sitting in the waiting room, being a visitor, and I shall be answerable... Anyhow, are you hoping to stay here permanently or something?" he added, casting another sidelong glance at the Prince's bundle, which continued to arouse his unease.

"No, I'm not, even if I were invited to, I wouldn't. I only came to introduce myself, that's all."

"What do you mean, introduce yourself?" the valet enquired in utter astonishment. "Why is it then you first said you were on business?"

"Well, not really! That is, there is a specific matter in the way of advice if you like, but my main mission is to convey my respects, because I am Prince Myshkin, and the General's Lady is the last of the Myshkins in the feminine line, and apart from us two, there are no more Myshkins left."

"So you're related too?" the valet exclaimed almost in alarm.

"Well that's as may be. At a stretch you might, of course, say we're related, but then again it's so distant, it's hardly worth mentioning. I once appealed to the General's Lady by letter from abroad, but she didn't reply. All the same, I thought I'd better get in touch on my return. I'm explaining all this to you now so as to put your mind at rest, because I can see you're still uneasy. Just say it's Prince Myshkin, and that in itself should explain the reason for my visit. If they see me – all well and good, if not – equally so, perhaps. Only I don't think they could refuse an audience. I'm sure the General's Lady would as a matter of course want to see the elder and last remaining male representative of her line, inasmuch as she takes particular pride in her lineage, or so I've heard."

The Prince's arguments seemed straightforward enough; but the more straightforward they were, the more outlandish they sounded in the circumstances, and the experienced valet could not but conclude that what could easily pass man to man, was totally inappropriate man to servant. And since servants are far sharper than their masters give them credit, the valet immediately concluded that there were two possibilities: either the Prince was some kind of a knight of the road and had come expressly to seek charity, or a Simple Simon with no self-respect, because no normal nobleman with any self-respect would spend his time sitting in a lobby talking about his personal affairs to a servant; in either case there loomed the danger of subsequently being held answerable for him.

"I think you had better step into the waiting room after all," he observed as authoritatively as he could.

"Had I sat there in the first place," the Prince said with a hearty laugh, "I'd not have been able to explain anything to you at all, and you'd still have been worried stiff looking at my cloak and bundle. Perhaps there's no need to wait for the secretary. Why not just go and announce me yourself?"

"I cannot announce someone like you without the secretary. Besides, His Excellency expressly gave orders not to be disturbed while he is in conference with the Colonel. Only Gavrila Ardalionych can enter unannounced."

"Is that a clerk?"

"Gavrila Ardalionych? No, he's employed by the company as a freelance. But why don't you at least leave your bundle here?"

"That's just what I was thinking. If you don't mind, I'll do just that. And you know, I'd better take my coat off too."

"I should think so, you can hardly go in with that coat on."

The Prince got up, hurriedly took off his cloak to reveal a rather smart jacket, of good quality though slightly the worse for wear. A steel fob chain passed across his waistcoat. At the end of it was a silver Swiss watch.

Though the Prince was certainly not all there – the valet no longer entertained any doubts on that score – the General's employee did not deem it proper to continue a personal conversation with him; besides, he struck him as really quite likeable, in his own way, of course. For the most part, however, the valet's feelings were mixed, but markedly inclined towards a strong and unmitigated exasperation.

"And when does the General's Lady receive visitors?" the Prince asked, resuming his former place.

"That I wouldn't know. She has no fixed hours, depends on the person. Her dressmaker may be admitted as early as eleven. Gavrila Ardalionych too is allowed in ahead of others, sometimes even for breakfast."

"You keep your rooms warmer here than is customary abroad in winter," the Prince observed. "But then it's warmer there outside, whereas indoors it's almost unbearably cold for us Russians."

"Haven't they got any heating?"

"Yes they have, but the houses are built differently, I mean the windows and stoves."

"Hm! And how long have you been travelling?"

"Four years. But I stayed mainly in one place in the country."

"Do things seem strange to you here?"

"I suppose they do. You might not believe me, but it's a wonder I haven't forgotten my Russian. There I am talking to you now and I can't help feeling, 'I'm not making a bad job of it.' Maybe that's why I can't stop talking. Truly, since yesterday I've not been able to speak Russian enough."

"Hm! Hm! Did you live in St Petersburg before?" Quite despite himself the valet found it impossible not to maintain such a cordial and agreeable conversation.

"In St Petersburg? Hardly at all, only in passing. And I knew nothing of the place before, and now there are so many new things going on that, I hear, even those who knew what it was like previously have to start all over again. There's much talk about the courts here."

"Ahem!... The courts. The courts, yes, yes, the courts. And what about over there, is there more justice in the courts, or not?"

"I don't know. I heard a lot of good things about ours. For one thing, we haven't got capital punishment."*

"And they have, have they?"

"Yes. I saw it in France, in Lyons. Schneider took me there."

"They hang them, do they?"

"No, in France they chop their heads off, as a rule."

"Do they scream?"

"Good Lord, no! It only takes a second. They lay the condemned out flat, and a broad blade – they call it a guillotine – comes down heavily, powerfully... the head flies off in the blink of an eye. The worst part is the preliminaries. When the sentence is read out, the machine is set up, the prisoner is bound, taken up the scaffold, that's the awful bit! People come running to gape, even women, though they try to discourage them from looking."

"None of their business!"

"Quite! Quite! The suffering of it all!... The condemned man I saw was an intelligent, fearless, powerful chap, getting on in years, by the name of Legros. Well, I tell you, you don't have to believe me, he was walking up the scaffold – crying, white as a candle. Is that possible? Isn't that dreadful? How can one cry from fear? It never occurred to me that anyone other than a child could cry from fear – and this a man who has never cried in his life, a man of forty-five. What was going on in his soul at the time, what torment was it being subjected to? It was being violated, there's no other word for it! It is written, 'Thou shalt not kill.' So, because he killed, he must be killed? No, that won't do. It's been a month, and I can still see it all. I've had countless dreams."

As he talked, the Prince became more animated and his pale cheeks flushed slightly, though he kept his voice down as before. The valet observed him with compassionate interest and listened with rapt attention; he was clearly a man with imagination and a reflective mind.

"It's as well that the suffering is not so great," he remarked, "if the head is severed so quickly."

"There you've said it!" the Prince responded fervently. "Everyone makes the same observation, and the machine – the guillotine – was invented for that very purpose. But it occurred to me then – supposing it's actually worse? You may find this strange and ridiculous, but if you stop and think about it there may be something in it. Just think – torture, the resulting suffering and injuries, the pain – it's all physical, and a distraction from the mental agony. As a result, right up to the moment of death, one only has one's physical injuries to contend

23

with. But what if the greatest pain is not in injuries, but rather in the knowledge that in an hour, in ten minutes, then in half a minute, finally *now* – this instant – you'll be decapitated, and that'll be the end of you as a human being, and that it's irrevocable. *Irrevocable*, mark you! As you put your head under the blade, and you hear the swish from above, that fraction of a second is the most terrifying of all. You know, it's not just my imagination, many people have said as much. I'm so convinced of this that I'll be frank with you. To punish murder by death is an immensely worse crime than the original murder. Death by edict is far more gruesome than normal murder. He who faces death in the dead of night on the highway, or wherever, still clings to the hope right up to the final moment that he'll survive. There have been cases when, even after a man's throat had been cut, he still didn't lose hope, but tried to escape or pleaded for mercy. Whereas here, that sweetener of death – one's last hope – is taken away in advance. The sentence has been passed, and the knowledge that it is irrevocable is the greatest torture of all, and there can be none greater in the world. Stand a soldier in front of a cannon and shoot point-blank at him, and he will continue to hope, but read out to the same soldier the *irrevocable* sentence of death, and he will either go out of his mind or begin to cry. Who will claim that human nature can endure such torment without loss of sanity? What is the reason for such abuse – outrageous, senseless, pointless? Perhaps there is a man who has been condemned, made to suffer, and later told, 'Go, you've been reprieved!' Perhaps such a one could provide an answer. Christ spoke of this agony and terror. No, man must not be subjected to such outrage!"

Though the valet could not have put all this quite like the Prince, he took in most of it as was to be seen by the transformed expression on his face.

"If you really must have a smoke," he said, "I don't see why not, only if you're quick about it. You must be here when you're called. See that door under the stairs? Go through, and you'll find a boxroom on the right where you can have your smoke, only don't forget to open the window, it's against the rules…"

But the Prince was too late to have his smoke. A young man with a bunch of papers in his hand entered the antechamber. The valet began to help him off with his fur coat. The young man looked askance at the Prince.

"This gentleman, Gavrila Ardalionych," the valet began deferentially, but with a note of familiarity, "tells me that he is a Prince Myshkin and the Lady's relation. He has just arrived by rail from abroad and that bundle he is holding is the only…"

The Prince did not hear the rest, because the valet lowered his tone to a whisper. Gavrila Ardalionych listened attentively and kept looking at the Prince with great curiosity. Finally, he stopped listening and rather abruptly turned towards the Prince.

"You are Prince Myshkin?" he asked with the utmost politeness and cordiality. He was very good-looking, about twenty-eight, slim, blond, above average height, with a goatee beard, and intelligent, very handsome features. Only his smile, however welcoming, was somewhat too refined; his pearl-white teeth just a little too even to be true; and the look in his eyes, despite their welcoming lustre and lively sparkle, was just a shade too sharp and inquisitive for comfort.

"That's not the way he is when he's alone," the Prince thought to himself, "and I doubt if he ever laughs."

The Prince repeated hurriedly as best he could almost verbatim what he had previously told Rogozhin and later the valet. Gavrila Ardalionych seemed to recall something.

"Was it you by any chance," he asked, "who sent a letter, was it from Switzerland, to Lizaveta Prokofyevna?"

"Yes, it was."

"In that case she should remember who you are. You have come to see His Excellency? I'll announce you directly… He will be free shortly. Only… would you mind waiting in the waiting room… Why is the gentleman here?" he asked the valet sharply.

"He wanted to stay here…"

The door to the study opened suddenly and a military man with a portfolio emerged, talking loudly as he took his leave.

"Is that you, Ganya?" a voice from the study called. "Come here a moment, please!"

Gavrila Ardalionych, with a nod at the Prince, disappeared through the door of the study.

A couple of minutes later the door opened again and Gavrila Ardalionych in a clear and cordial tone bade the Prince come in.

3

G ENERAL IVAN FYODOROVICH YEPANCHIN stood in the middle of his study and regarded the Prince with the utmost curiosity as he entered. He even took a step or two towards him. The Prince approached and introduced himself.

"So," the General responded, "how can I help you?"

"It's nothing urgent. All I wanted was to introduce myself. I'd hate to disturb you as I know you've already got a lot of prior engagements... But I've just got off the train... from Switzerland..."

A faint smile crossed the General's features; he thought awhile, then paused and thought again, frowned, measured his visitor once more up and down, pointed firmly to a chair, took a seat himself diagonally opposite and turned to the Prince with a show of impatient expectation. Ganya stood in one corner of the study by a writing desk sorting through some papers.

"On the whole I tend not to have an awful lot of time for social calls," the General said. "But, as no doubt, you have a specific reason, in this case—"

"That's just what I was afraid of," the Prince interjected, "that you would read into my visit some kind of ulterior motive. But, I assure you, apart from the pleasure of making your acquaintance, I have no other personal reason."

"The pleasure is all mine, of course, but life is not like that. Pleasures apart however, there are the odd duties, you know... Besides, I still fail to see what it is we have in common... that is, the reason..."

"Quite so, there is no reason, nor, I must admit, have we much in common. Being a Myshkin, the same as your wife, is neither here nor there, it goes without saying. I understand. However, that is the only reason I have. You see, it's four years since I was last in Russia. And I was not altogether of sound mind when I left! I knew precious little then, and much less now. I need some kind people to advise me. As a matter of fact, there is something I wanted to discuss, but have no idea whom to turn to. It occurred to me way back in Berlin, 'Why not start with them, after all we're as good as related. Perhaps we could be useful to one another – they help me, I help them, provided we can get along.' And from what I've heard, you are easy to get along with."

"I'm very flattered, I'm sure," the General interposed, somewhat astonished. "And may I enquire, where are you staying?"

"Nowhere as yet."

"So you've come here straight from the station. And… you've brought your personal effects with you, have you?"

"The only baggage I have is a small bundle with a change of clothes, nothing more. I usually carry it about with me. I'll look for a room in the evening."

"So you still intend to get a room?"

"Yes, of course."

"I was afraid for a moment you planned to stay here."

"That could only be on your invitation. However, even if you were to invite me, I assure you I wouldn't stay, not for any specific reason… but merely because it wouldn't be in my character…"

"Well, it's as well that I didn't invite you, nor do I intend to. Permit me, though, Prince, to clear up the matter once and for all. Since it's well understood that our family ties amount to next to nothing, and though of course the loss is entirely mine, wouldn't it be best if—"

"I just got up and left," the Prince said, rising to his feet with a spontaneously hearty laugh, notwithstanding the rather awkward situation in which he presently found himself. "Honest to goodness, General, though I had no idea what people were like here, or how they behaved, I was pretty sure this is precisely how it would end between us. Who knows, perhaps that's just as well… Incidentally, I never got a reply to my letter… Well, goodbye, and my apologies for having disturbed you."

The Prince's expression was so benign and so open that the General suddenly paused, and completely and instantaneously changed his attitude.

"Look here, Prince," he said in an altered tone of voice. "I certainly don't know you, but Lizaveta Prokofyevna may well want to have a look at her relative… Stay here a moment – that is, if you are not pressed for time."

"Indeed I'm not. Time is something I have in abundance." The Prince immediately deposited his soft round hat on the table. "Frankly, I had an idea that Lizaveta Prokofyevna might perhaps recall that I wrote to her. When I was waiting in the other room, your valet suspected I had come to ask for charity. I take it you are pretty strict about that here.

But that is not at all what I'm after. I just want to meet people, that's all. Only, I fear, I have been a nuisance, and that does worry me."

"Look here, Prince," the General said with a jolly smile, "if you really are what you seem to be, it would indeed be a pleasure to make your acquaintance. Only, you understand, I'm a busy man and there's always something to attend to, something to sign; His Excellency is probably expecting me even as we speak, then off to the department, so that in the end however well disposed I may be towards people... the deserving ones of course... but... Well, that said, I'm sure you've been well brought up and... Incidentally, how old are you, Prince?"

"Twenty-six."

"Ah, I took you to be much younger."

"Yes, they say I look young for my years. Besides, I'll soon learn not to trouble you, because I myself value my privacy... And, finally, it would seem, we have little in common on the face of it... what with one thing and another, it would probably be most unlikely that we had anything significant to bind us, though to be sure, I don't really believe that, because very often it only seems that way, whereas in reality there's plenty... it's just that people are so lazy, they like to pigeon-hole one another on sight, and not bother to delve any further... But I expect I'm being a bore. You seem to—"

"May I be so bold as to ask, have you any property? Or, perhaps, you intend to take up some gainful employment? Please excuse my being so..."

"Not at all, I can quite see the point of your question. As things stand I have no property, neither do I have any skills... that is, as things stand, though I'd like to. So far I have subsisted on other people's means. My medical supervisor and teacher in Switzerland, Professor Schneider, covered my travelling expenses... just about, so that now all I have left is a few copecks. However, there is something I wanted to bring up and seek advice on, but—"

"So, tell me, how do you intend to support yourself right now, and what are your immediate plans?" the General interrupted him.

"I'd like to get some work."

"I'm glad to hear it. And so... what about any skills, aptitudes such as would bring in the wherewithal? I'm sorry to..."

"Oh, don't apologize. No, I don't think I have any particular abilities or skills. You see, I have been in bad health and have not had the benefit of a proper education. As to earning my bread—"

28

The General again interrupted him and continued with his questioning. The Prince again went over everything he had said before. It turned out the General had heard of and even been personally acquainted with the late Pavlishchev. Why Pavlishchev had taken an interest in his upbringing, the Prince himself was at a loss to explain – well, maybe because he had been friendly with his late father. The Prince was left an orphan at quite an early age, and continued to live in the country, where the fresh air was beneficial for his health. Pavlishchev put him in the care of relatives, an aged landowning couple; to begin with he was looked after by a governess, then a tutor; he explained that though he remembered the circumstances of his past, he could make little sense of them. The frequent fits of his illness had reduced him almost to an idiot (he used the very word "idiot"). Finally, he recounted that one day Pavlishchev had met in Berlin one Schneider, a Swiss professor who, at his medical establishment in the canton of Valais, dealt with precisely such ailments, namely idiocy and insanity, by the application of his own remedial methods such as cold baths and physical exercises, not neglecting at the same time his patients' educational needs; that Pavlishchev had sent him to Switzerland about five years ago and had died three years later, suddenly, without having provided for him; that Schneider had continued to keep and treat him for a further two years; that he had not managed to effect a complete cure, but had nevertheless helped him a lot, and that finally, following a particular incident, had at the Prince's own request sent him back to Russia.

The General was not a little surprised. "And you know no one, absolutely no one in Russia?" he asked.

"Right now no one, but I hope... incidentally, I have a letter—"

"At least," the General interrupted him, having missed the reference to the letter, "have you been trained in anything, and won't your illness prevent you from performing, say, some not too taxing duties for a potential employer?"

"Oh, surely not. As for employment, I'd be extremely interested if only to see for myself exactly what I'm capable of. As for my studies these past four years, they were regular enough, based on the Professor's own system but, how shall I say, lacked continuity. All the same I managed to read a great number of Russian books."

"Russian books? I take it then you know the language and can write without making mistakes?"

"Quite so."

"Splendid! And what about your handwriting?"

"My handwriting is excellent!" the Prince said with enthusiasm. "Actually, that is my strong point. Even if I say so myself, I'm a bit of a calligrapher. Why don't you let me demonstrate?"

"That's very kind of you. In fact, it would serve a useful purpose… And your enthusiasm is absolutely disarming, Prince. You're very charming, to be sure."

"I can't help admiring your writing implements. What a lovely collection of pencils and pens, and the paper is of such high quality… And what a lovely office you have! I know that picture. It's a Swiss landscape. I'm positive the artist drew it from nature, and I'm sure I've seen the place – it's in the canton of Uri…"

"That may well be so, though it was bought here. Ganya, give the Prince some paper. Here's paper and pens for you. At this side table, please! What's that?" the General asked suddenly, turning to Ganya who was in the act of handing him a large photographic portrait that he produced from his briefcase. "I say, Nastasya Filippovna! Did she give it to you herself, I mean personally?" the General asked excitedly with undisguised curiosity.

"She gave it to me just now when I went to wish her many happy returns. I had asked her for one a long time ago. I'm not sure if it wasn't a hint at my turning up empty handed, without a present, on such an occasion," Ganya remarked with a mean smile.

"Not at all!" the General cut in with conviction. "You do get some strange ideas! She's not like that… she's not acquisitive. And, anyway, what could you give her? You'd need thousands! Unless you gave her your own portrait? Incidentally, she hasn't asked you for one so far, has she?"

"Not so far. And perhaps never will. You haven't forgotten, Ivan Fyodorovich, about tonight? You're one of the guests of honour."

"No, no, I shan't forget, I'll be there. It goes without saying – her birthday, twenty-five years old! Hm!… Listen, Ganya, you might as well know, prepare yourself. She promised Afanasy Ivanovich and me that she'll give her final word tonight – yes or no! So, be ready!"

Ganya was caught unawares to the extent that he lost a little colour.

"Did she really say that?" he asked with a tremor in his voice.

"Day before yesterday she gave her word. Both of us prevailed upon her so much so that she eventually relented. Only she asked not to reveal it to you beforehand."

The General looked hard at Ganya, whose embarrassment was evidently not to his liking.

"You will recall, Ivan Fyodorovich," Ganya said hesitantly, his voice drained of all confidence, "that she gave me full freedom not to decide at least until she made up her own mind, and even then I'd have the last word—"

"You don't... you don't really mean to say that you—" the General interjected in dismay.

"I didn't mean anything."

"Dammit, think what you're doing to us!"

"I'm not backing out at all. Perhaps you misunderstood me—"

"Not backing out? I should think not!" the General exclaimed, giving full vent to his displeasure. "This is not a question of your *not backing out*, but of your readiness, the enthusiasm, the delight with which you will welcome her proposal... What's the situation at home?"

"You may well ask! At home, everything is under control, only Father, as usual, keeps acting the fool. If you ask me, he's turned into a total disgrace. I don't even speak to him; all the same I keep him firmly in hand, and, if it weren't for mother, I really would have shown him the door. Mother, of course, doesn't stop crying, and I told them in no uncertain terms that I'm master of my own fate and insist that people in the house should... take heed of what I say. At least that's what I spelt out loud and clear to my sister, in other's presence."

"I'm still baffled, my friend," the General mused pensively, his shoulders hunched and his arms outspread a little. "When Nina Alexandrovna called the other day, remember? She was all moans and groans. 'What's the matter?' I said to her. It turned out, they felt it meant *disgrace* to them. What disgrace, may I ask? Who can reproach Nastasya Filippovna with anything? That she'd been living with Totsky? But that's sheer nonsense, especially in the circumstances! 'You'd not allow your daughters to associate with her, would you?' she said to me. Well, well, well! That's Nina Alexandrovna all over for you! I mean, how is it she can't understand, can't appreciate—"

"Her own position?" Ganya finished for the General, who was temporarily lost for words. "She does. Don't be angry with her. Incidentally,

I made it clear to the two of them at the time to keep out of other people's affairs. Nevertheless, everything hangs on her final word in our household. Once she pronounces it tonight, that'll be that."

The Prince, sitting as he did in the corner over his calligraphy test, could not help overhearing the whole of this exchange. He applied the finishing touches, went up to the table and held out the sheet of paper.

"So this is Nastasya Filippovna?" he said, after glancing at the portrait with intense curiosity. "She is so lovely!" he immediately added with ardour. The portrait did indeed show a woman of exceptional beauty. She was taken in a black silk dress of a very simple but elegant cut; her hair, apparently dark brown, was gathered in a simple fashion; the eyes deep-set, dark, the brow pensive; her expression passionate, somewhat haughty. The outlines of her face were on the hard side and, if anything, rather pale... Ganya and the General looked at the Prince in astonishment...

"What do you mean, Nastasya Filippovna?" the General asked. "How is it you already know Nastasya Filippovna?"

"Yes, barely twenty-four hours in Russia, and I already know the foremost beauty," the Prince responded and immediately recounted his story of the meeting with Rogozhin in all its particulars.

"Well I never!" the General, after hearing the story, again proclaimed in undisguised agitation, and looked searchingly at Ganya.

"Some other impropriety, I shouldn't wonder," Ganya mumbled, also somewhat nonplussed. "A rich boy painting the town red. I heard about him."

"To be sure, I heard about him too," the General chimed in. "Nastasya Filippovna told me the whole story of the earrings. However, we're up against something different now. It may well be a matter of a million... and passion – sordid passion, I admit, but passion all the same. It's well known what these gentlemen are capable of once they're intoxicated!... Hm!... I just hope there won't be any scandal!" the General concluded reflectively.

"You're concerned about the million?" Ganya snapped back.

"And you're not, I suppose?"

"What did you make of him, Prince?" Ganya suddenly addressed him. "Is he all right or just some kind of a mountebank? Your personal opinion!"

Ganya was all wound up as he posed this question. It was as if some special idea had flared up in his mind and shone in his eyes. The General, on the other hand, who was truly and sincerely worried, glanced askance at the Prince, but without expecting to hear anything revelatory.

"I don't know how to say this," the Prince replied, "but I too felt there was a great deal of passion in him, unwholesome passion. And he struck me as pretty unwholesome himself. I wouldn't be surprised if he ended up in his sickbed over the next few days, especially if he were to start living it up."

"Really? Was that your impression?" the General pursued the idea.

"Yes, indeed."

"We don't have to wait days to have a scandal on our hands," Ganya said with a wry smile. "There may be one before the day is out."

"Hm!... Of course... That goes without saying," the General said. "But then it all depends on how the mood takes her."

"I'm sure you know what she's like sometimes, don't you?"

"What if I do?" the General flared up excitedly. "Listen to me, Ganya, don't you be too contrary with her tonight and try, as it were, you know, not to upset... in a word, don't rub her up the wrong way... Hm!... Why are you screwing up your mouth so? Listen, Gavrila Ardalionych, it would be to the point, very much to the point, to ask ourselves what it is that motivates us. You see, as far as my own interests go in this matter, they have already been well catered for. Come what may, I'll ensure that things work out my way. Totsky didn't hem and haw when he took his decision, and the same goes for me too. And so, if I am concerned about anything, it's only your interests. Be fair, do you mistrust me or something? It goes without saying, you're... you're... in a word, no fool, and I've staked a lot on you... and, in the circumstances that is... that is—"

"Not to be sneezed at," Ganya again finished for the General with a caustic smile on his lips, which he no longer made any attempt to conceal. He regarded the General with febrile, puffed-up eyes, apparently wanting the latter to be in no doubt as to what he, Ganya, thought. The General flushed and flared up.

"Not to be sneezed at, there you go!" he responded, looking hard at Ganya. "You're a funny man, Gavrila Ardalionych! You are, it occurs to me, glad this merchant fellow has turned up as it's a way out for yourself. Whereas it is precisely at this juncture that one ought to have gone about the business with the utmost intelligence. It's all a question of sizing up the situation... and of being mutually honest and frank, or else... one should have forewarned other parties in order to avoid compromising them, the more so since there was always plenty of time for this, as indeed there is even now," the General furrowed his brows significantly, "despite the fact that it's now only a matter of a few hours... Can you see what I'm driving at? Can you? So, do you want to go ahead or don't you, which is it? If you don't, you only have to say so, and on your way. No one is detaining you, Gavrila Ardalionych, no one is pushing you into a trap, if it is indeed a trap that you fear."

"I want to," Ganya said softly but firmly, and lowered his eyes in glum silence.

The General was satisfied. He had lost his temper, and was visibly contrite that he had gone too far. He suddenly turned to the Prince, and the troubled thought that the Prince had witnessed and heard everything flashed across his face. But his fears were immediately dispelled. One look at the Prince was quite sufficient for that.

"I say!" the General exclaimed, looking at the specimen of calligraphy offered by the Prince. "This is true craftsmanship! And of a rare kind! Take a look, Ganya, such talent!"

On a thick sheet of vellum the Prince had written in old Russian script: "Signed in his own hand by the humble Abbot Pafnuty."

"This," the Prince explained with the utmost enthusiasm and animation, "is the authentic signature of the Abbot Pafnuty, copied from a fourteenth-century manuscript. They all wrote in an excellent hand, those abbots and bishops of ours, and with what taste and diligence! I don't suppose you have a Pogodin* edition about, General, do you? Then I wrote this example in another hand, a round French script belonging to the last century. There were several different types of writing about, depending on the designation – here's something in an ordinary scribe's hand, copied from a real sample (I used to have one). You must agree it's rather curious. Just look at these rounded Ds and As. I applied the French style to the Russian lettering and it turned out rather well. Here is another beautiful, unusual script; note this sentence: 'Diligence conquers all.' It's the Russian administrative, or more precisely, a military clerk's script. A petition to an important ٮ٭sonage would be penned thus, the lettering is rounded, rather fine, wouldn't you say? The black ink makes it particularly striking. I've rather gone to town on these flourishes and curlicues – hardly the stuff of professional calligraphers, you might say, but all in all, you must agree, it lends it character, it embodies the very essence of the daredevil military scrivener – an urge to let rip, but the uniform collar is much too tight about the neck, parade-ground discipline on a page of writing – isn't it just marvellous! I came across a sample of this not so long ago, quite by accident, and where, would you think? In Switzerland of all places! Well, and here's your common-or-garden plain old English script: this is sheer beauty, the ultimate in elegance, every letter a pearl, an exquisite gem. We now come to this, a variation on a theme – French, let me add. I copied it from a French travelling salesman. It's essentially the same English script all over, only the downward strokes are a shade thicker and bolder, but what a difference in tone! Observe too that the ovals are now virtual circles, but most importantly, the flourishes are back in use – what a thing these flourishes are! They can make or break the whole effect. If one can get the flourishes right, if one can find the right proportions, the result is devastating, mouth-watering."

"I say, you speak like an expert," the General observed with a laugh. "You seem to be more than just a calligrapher, you're a veritable artist, and no mistake! What do you say, Ganya?"

"Astonishing!" Ganya said. "Especially on top of such disarming awareness of one's mission," he added sarcastically.

"You may laugh, but you have a splendid career before you," the General said. "You've no idea the kind of people you'll be writing documents to for us now! You can command a salary of thirty-five roubles per month straight off. That said, it is already half-past twelve," he concluded with a glance at his watch. "To business, Prince. I for one have to hurry, and we may not have a chance to meet today. So, take a seat for a moment. As I already explained, I shan't be able to receive you at all frequently, but I do sincerely wish to help you in some small way, small – you understand, with the barest essentials; as for the rest it'll be entirely up to you. I should be able to settle you in some office or other, nothing strenuous, but conscientiousness will be the order of the day. Now to the rest. In the family home of this my friend here Gavrila Ardalionovich Ivolgin, whom I had the pleasure of introducing to you, his mother and sister have made available two or three furnished rooms which they are letting out on full board to tenants with excellent recommendations. No doubt Nina Alexandrovna will be happy to accept my recommendation. As for you, Prince, this will be a real find. First, you will have company, that is, you will reside in the bosom of a family, because the way I see it, you ought not to be on your own in such a city as St Petersburg. Nina Alexandrovna, Gavrila Ardalionovich's mother, and his sister Varvara Ardalionovna, are ladies whom I respect beyond measure. Nina Alexandrovna is the wife of Ardalion Alexandrovich, a general *à la retraite*, my former companion-at-arms, with whom however due to force of circumstances I no longer associate, which in no way prevents me from holding him in, so to speak, considerable regard. I am putting all this to you, Prince, to make it clear that I am as it were giving you my personal recommendation, which in a manner of speaking is tantamount to vouching for you. The terms are as reasonable as can be expected and, I trust, your salary will soon suffice to meet them. Of course, a man must have some pocket money, and I hope you will not take it amiss if I tell you that it were best if you avoided pocket money, I mean having money about your person altogether. I say this just by looking at you. But as your purse is quite empty right now, let me therefore as a gesture of goodwill offer you these twenty-five roubles. No doubt we shall settle up before long, and if you are the sort of earnest and sincere person that you seem to be, I foresee no difficulties between us on this score. If you are wondering why I am so concerned about you, suffice it to say I have my reasons. You shall know them in due course. You see, I am being quite open and frank with you. I hope, Ganya, you will not object to the Prince lodging in your house?"

"Oh, on the contrary!" Ganya responded politely but guardedly. "Mother will be well pleased, I'm sure…"

"So far, I seem to remember, you've managed to let out one room only. What was his name again, Ferd… Fer…"

"Ferdyshchenko."

"Yes, yes. I don't much like this Ferdyshchenko of yours. A sordid buffoon, if you ask me. It's simply beyond me why Nastasya Filippovna encourages him so much! Is he really her cousin as he insists?"

"Not at all, it's all a big joke! No more cousin than I am."

"To hell with him! Well, what do you say, Prince, is it a deal?"

"Thank you very much, General, you have been most kind to me, the more so since I never even asked for it. I say in all humility that I had no idea where I would sleep tonight. It is true, of course, that I had been invited by Mr Rogozhin."

"Rogozhin? No thank you! I would in all sincerity advise you as a father, or if you prefer, friend, to keep away from that gentleman. My advice is stick to the family I'm settling you in."

"Since you have been so kind to me," the Prince began, "perhaps you might care to look at this. I've a letter here—"

"Sorry, can't stop now," the General interrupted him, "I've completely run out of time. I'll just tell Lizaveta Prokofyevna about you, if she wants to see you now (don't worry, I know how to get round her), then if I were you I'd do my level best to get into her good books, because Lizaveta Prokofyevna could prove to be a very useful ally. You bear the same name, don't you? If she's unable to see you now, don't take it amiss, simply try another time. And you, Ganya, have a look at these accounts I've been poring over with Fedosyev just now. We mustn't forget about them…"

The General left the room, and so the Prince never had the opportunity to come to the matter that he had been attempting to broach for the fourth time. Ganya lit a cigarette and offered the Prince one; he took it, but kept quiet, not wishing to be a nuisance, and continued to gaze around the study. Ganya hardly looked at the sheet of paper covered in figures to which the General had drawn his attention. He was flustered; his whole bearing – the way he smiled, gazed about, his preoccupied air – became uncomfortably oppressive for the Prince after the two found themselves alone. Suddenly he approached the Prince, who at that moment was again looking at Nastasya Filippovna's portrait.

"So, you like that kind of woman, Prince?" he asked, staring hard at the Prince. There was a note of intense purposefulness in his voice.

"She is very striking!" the Prince replied. "And I'm sure her life story is quite remarkable. Her expression looks happy enough, but there's a lot of suffering there, wouldn't you say? It's in her eyes, these cheekbones, these rings under her eyes almost to the cheeks. There's pride here, a terrible pride, and I'm not sure whether she is a good person or not. Would that she were! Everything could be redeemed!"

"The question is, would *you* be prepared to marry such a woman?" Ganya persisted, continuing to gaze excitedly at the Prince.

"I cannot marry anyone, I am ill," the Prince said.

"What about Rogozhin?"

"Yes, of course, I think he'd marry her, tomorrow if he were able. Yes, he'd marry her all right, and come the following week, he'd knife her."

No sooner had the Prince said this than Ganya shuddered so violently that the Prince was hardly able to suppress an involuntary exclamation.

"What's wrong?" he said, grabbing hold of Ganya's hand.

"Your Highness! His Excellency bids you attend on Her Excellency," the valet announced from the doorway. The Prince followed in the valet's footsteps.

4

THE THREE YEPANCHIN GIRLS were all in full bloom and in their prime; they were tall, buxom with exquisite shoulders, full figures and strong, almost masculine, arms. In consequence of their health and vigour they enjoyed a healthy appetite, and liked to indulge it. Their mother, Lizaveta Prokofyevna, was sometimes not best pleased with this but, as with many of her attitudes which, despite all outward show of respect on the part of her daughters, had lost their formerly incontestable authority to the extent that they were time and again seriously challenged by the young ones, the General's Lady deemed it prudent to preserve her dignity and give in graciously. True, her character all too often did not yield to her better judgement, and with the passage of years Lizaveta Prokofyevna became more and more capricious and short-tempered, turning into something of an eccentric, but with a compliant and well-disciplined husband who supported her and bore with fortitude all her excesses and pent-up ire, family harmony was never seriously put at risk.

It must be owned that the General's Lady was no laggard at table herself, and usually at half-past twelve would sit down with her daughters to a copious lunch that could easily pass for a dinner. Prior to that, while still in bed, the young ladies would already have imbibed at precisely ten o'clock a cup of coffee immediately on waking. It was an arrangement they had introduced and clung to tenaciously. At half-past twelve a table would be laid in the small dining room next to mother's quarters and, time permitting, the General himself would sometimes join this intimate family repast. Besides tea, coffee, various cheeses, honey, butter, special pancakes (some of Lizaveta Prokofyevna's particular favourites), cutlets and so on, the menu would also include a piping hot, rich bouillon. On the morning on which our story began, the whole family had gathered in the small dining room awaiting the General's arrival for about half-past twelve. Had he been a minute late, he would have been sent for; however, he arrived punctually. On approaching his spouse to bid her good morning and to kiss her hand, he noticed something quite unusual in her features. And although he had vague intimations the night before that that was precisely what would happen in consequence of a certain "vicissitude" (as he himself put it), and had agonized over it even as he was falling asleep, he nevertheless felt his courage quail afresh. His daughters approached to kiss him. Again nothing untoward that he could put his finger on! All the same there was something unusual in the air. It is true, the General had through a variety of circumstances been put on the defensive lately; but, calling upon his reserves of experience and shrewdness as a veteran paterfamilias, he immediately took full charge of the situation.

We hope it will not unduly detract from the flavour of our story if we digress here to make a few observations in order to establish a clear and unambiguous depiction of the relationships and circumstances in which we find the Yepanchin family at the very outset of our tale. As we have already remarked just now, the General, though not particularly well educated – in fact a "self-taught man", as he himself liked to put it – was nonetheless an experienced and shrewd head of the household. Incidentally, he had once and for all firmly resolved never to press his girls into an early marriage; that is, not to nag them or bore them with undue asseverations of paternal love and concern for their happiness as so often and inevitably occurs even in the most prudent of families with an abundance of eligible daughters. He even managed to persuade Lizaveta Prokofyevna to agree, which of course was no easy matter inasmuch as it was contrary to all her natural tendencies; but the General's arguments were extremely persuasive and based on self-evident facts. Given a completely free rein, the prospective brides would, so his argument ran, come to their senses, and things would take off apace because it would be on a voluntary basis without any tantrums or undue fastidiousness; all that was required of the parents was to keep a sharp and above all secretive eye to forestall any outlandish choice or unnatural tendency and, after seizing the right moment, to come forth with all manner of assistance, and guide the course of events in a positive direction. A by no means insignificant consideration was the fact that the family's wealth and social standing was growing from year to year by leaps and bounds, as were the marriage prospects of the three sisters. But in the midst of all these inexorable facts, there arose another factor: the eldest of them, Alexandra, quite unexpectedly caught the family unprepared (as inevitably happens in such cases) and turned twenty-five. Almost simultaneously Afanasy Ivanovich Totsky, a man from the highest circles of society, with the best possible connections and immense wealth, once more evinced a long-standing desire to get married. He was about fifty-five, thoroughly refined in character and of exquisite good taste. He wished to marry well, and prided himself as a leading connoisseur of feminine beauty. Since he had already been for some time on an extraordinarily close footing with the General, their ties being strengthened all the more by a number of mutual financial transactions, he saw fit to turn to the General with a friendly request for guidance and advice whether or not he might seek the hand of one of his daughters. From that moment life's calm and peaceful course in the Yepanchin family was disturbed in no uncertain manner.

As already mentioned, the unquestioned beauty of the threesome was the youngest, Aglaya. But even Totsky with his unbounded selfishness knew full well that this was no match for him and that he should look elsewhere. Perhaps blind love and a most ardent friendship between the sisters distorted matters somewhat; but Aglaya's fate, from the vantage point of the elder two, was with the utmost sincerity imagined as nothing short of paradise on earth. Aglaya's future husband had to be the acme of all accomplishments and perfection itself, not to mention his wealth of course. They had, and this without indulging in any lengthy discussions, decided if need be to sacrifice themselves in favour of their younger sibling; Aglaya's share of the dowry was expected to be huge by any standards. The parents knew about this agreement between the two elder sisters, and therefore when Totsky asked for advice, they had not the slightest doubt that one of them would not refuse to accede to their wishes, the more so since Afanasy Ivanovich could not be expected to raise any issues over the dowry. As for Totsky's proposal, the General with his broad experience of life took it very seriously. Totsky himself, in view of a variety of extraordinary circumstances, continued to play a very cautious hand by no more than sounding the matter out, and in consequence the parents, too, imparted to their daughters no more than the vaguest of surmises. Their response, though not definitive, was nevertheless reassuring, indicating that the eldest, Alexandra, would not be altogether loath to accept. Though resolute in character, Alexandra was a very kind soul, sensible and very compliant; she felt she could even summon a certain enthusiasm for the match, and were she to give her word, she would keep it faithfully. She did not care for ostentation, and not only would not bring about any radical changes or upheaval, but could make life sweeter and more benign. Outwardly she was very attractive, though not stunningly so. What could be better for Totsky?

And yet the whole matter proceeded at a snail's pace. By mutually amicable agreement the General and Totsky were to avoid any formal or irreversible commitments. Even the parents avoided being totally open with their daughters, which eventually led to a certain amount of friction. The General's Lady, Madame Yepanchina, became manifestly irritable, and this was not insignificant. The fly in the ointment was one particularly awkward and bothersome incident from the past which threatened to bring the whole scheme crashing down about their ears.

This awkward and bothersome incident (as Totsky himself referred to it) had taken place a very long time before, some eighteen years or so. One of Afanasy Ivanovich's most magnificent estates in central Russia abutted directly onto a farm belonging to a poverty-stricken smallholder. This smallholder, an ex-army officer of good stock, by the name of Philip Alexandrovich Barashkov, and of a family lineage somewhat more distinguished than Totsky's, was a walking disaster. Being up to his neck in debt and with a heavy mortgage hanging over him, he had yet managed by a superhuman effort, working like a slave, to bring his affairs to some state of normality. At the least sign of success, his elation knew no bounds. Brimming with the joys of life and blithe hope, he left his farm on one occasion to go for a few days to the county town to meet and, God willing, settle up with one of his principal creditors. On the third day after his arrival in town, the steward of his blighted farmstead came galloping to him on horseback, his face scorched and his beard singed, to announce that his property had burnt down the day before, at noon precisely; his wife was dead but his children had survived. Used as he was to the vicissitudes of fortune, this however was too much even for Barashkov; he went out of his mind and a month later died of fever. The burnt-down house, along with the land and those bonded peasants who had not run away to lead the life of beggars, were sold to cover the debts; his two daughters – little girls of six and seven – were magnanimously taken care of by Afanasy Ivanovich Totsky. They were lodged with Afanasy Ivanovich's German-born steward, a retired clerk with numerous children of his own. Soon only the elder, Nastasya, remained, the younger one having died of whooping cough; shortly after that Totsky, who for the most part resided abroad, forgot about both of them. Some five years later Afanasy Ivanovich happened to be passing by his estate one day and he noticed in his country house, in the family fold of his German steward, a remarkably comely child, a girl of about twelve, lively, pleasant, intelligent and with the makings of a real beauty. In this regard Afanasy Ivanovich never erred. On this occasion he stayed on the estate only a few days, but he managed to make all the necessary arrangements; the girl's upbringing underwent a remarkable about-turn. A respectable, elderly governess was employed, experienced in the art of schooling young ladies; she was Swiss, well educated and able to offer not only the French language but other subjects too. She took up residence in the country house, and little Nastasya's tuition commenced in all earnestness. Precisely four years later the tuition came to an end; the governess left, and a lady arrived to take Nastasya with her. She was also an estate owner, and a neighbour of Totsky's, but in a another, distant part of the country, and she took Nastasya with full power of attorney from him. In the small hamlet where they moved there happened to be a snug, newly built timber cottage, remarkably tastefully appointed, the hamlet itself being rather aptly named Lucky. The lady brought Nastasya straight to this cosy little cottage and as she herself, a childless widow, lived only a verst away, she decided to take up residence there too. Soon an elderly housekeeper made her appearance, and was joined shortly by a young, experienced chambermaid. Musical instruments were found in the cottage, a splendid collection of books for women readers, paintings, reproductions, pencils, paintbrushes, paints, a wonderful horn, and a fortnight later Afanasy Ivanovich himself turned up... From then on he began to show an unusual predilection for this remote rural residence nestling in a distant corner of the wide-open steppe. He made a habit of subsequently dropping in every summer; stayed there for up to two, sometimes even three months; and so passed a considerable period of time, four happy years in all, peacefully and gracefully, leaving behind only the best of memories.

It so happened that one fine day at the beginning of winter, about four months after one of Afanasy Ivanovich's regular summer visits to Lucky, which on this occasion lasted a mere fortnight, word – or more precisely, rumour – reached Nastasya Filippovna that Afanasy Ivanovich was to get married to a wealthy society beauty in St Petersburg, forming a substantial and brilliant match. Subsequently this rumour proved not quite accurate in some particulars. The marriage even at the time was only prospective and nothing had yet been confirmed; all the same it caused an extraordinary upheaval in Nastasya Filippovna's soul. She suddenly displayed remarkable resolve and totally unexpected character traits. Without further ado she left her cottage and turned up in St Petersburg like a bolt from the blue at Totsky's, and what's more completely alone. The latter was much taken aback, and was about to reason with her; but almost from the first it became patently clear that he needed to alter completely his manner of speaking, his choice of words, his tone, his genteel and gracious platitudes that had formerly been used to such effect, his argumentation – in short, everything but everything had to go! The woman who now faced him was a different person, quite unlike the one he had known hitherto, whom only the previous July he had parted from in his remote country cottage.

This new woman, it turned out, knew and understood breathtakingly much – in fact, so much that it was a cause of wonderment where she had picked up such a lot of information, and had developed such clear-cut notions. (Surely not from that collection of books!) Moreover, she even had a good grasp of legal matters, and had deep-seated views if not of the world, then at least of how certain matters are arranged in it; finally, her character was not the same as before. There was no trace of that timid bashful schoolgirl who one moment could melt your heart with her indecisive skittishness and coyness only to withdraw into herself the next, saddened, dejected, perplexed, mistrustful, troubled and inclined to tears. No, the one who now laughed straight in his face and taunted him mercilessly, was an altogether different woman who took pleasure in announcing that she never harboured anything but the deepest contempt for him in her heart, contempt that bordered on revulsion from the first moment she had set eyes on him. She announced that she was perfectly indifferent to whom or when he married, but all the same she had come to upset his arrangements, and this out of spite simply because that's how she was inclined and would see to it there was no other outcome: "Well, if only to have a jolly good laugh at your expense, simply because it's my turn to laugh now."

At least she gave no further reason as to what else might have been on her mind. But all the time that the new Nastasya Filippovna mocked him and continued her diatribe, Afanasy Ivanovich kept weighing the matter up, trying as far as possible to put his disjointed thoughts in order; he listened with the greatest of care and took well-nigh two weeks to make up his mind; but two weeks later his mind was made up. The point was that at the time Afanasy Ivanovich was nearly fifty, enjoyed universal respect and was deeply set in his ways. His position in the world and society was firmly established. As behoves any highly respectable man, he valued his peace and creature comforts above all else in the world. Not the slightest disturbance or deviation was to be tolerated in what had taken a lifetime to bring to such perfection. That said, Totsky's experience and deep insight into human nature suggested to him immediately and accurately that the person he had to deal with was quite out of the ordinary, that she was not just full of empty threats, and, most importantly, that she would not baulk at anything because she appeared to be as reckless as they come and not amenable to any blandishments. Here was a case of a complete spiritual and emotional mess – some kind of romantic resentment, directed at God knows who or what, some kind of insatiable contempt that had exceeded all bounds – in a word, something highly grotesque and unbecoming in polite society, to encounter which was the worst punishment to befall any respectable gentleman. It goes without saying that, bearing in mind Totsky's wealth and connections, one could well imagine some small, totally unattributable "accident" happening, that could have put a stop to all further trouble. On the other hand it was also evident that Nastasya Filippovna was quite incapable of causing any serious harm even if she went to a court of law; neither could she provoke any kind of serious scandal, simply because she could always be so easily put in her place. But this would apply only if Nastasya Filippovna were to behave as might any woman in such cases – within the due limits of propriety. But this was precisely where Totsky's perspicacity came into its own. He was able to surmise that Nastasya Filippovna herself understood full well how little damage she could inflict upon him through the courts, and that she had her sights on something quite different and... her sparkling eyes were sufficient testimony of that. She had set everything at naught, her own safety above all. It took a great deal of sagacity and discernment for this sceptical and cynical man to appreciate this premonition fully and to conclude at that moment that she had long ceased to care about anything. Nastasya Filippovna was ready to bring herself down irrevocably, drag herself through the salt mines of Siberia just to tread underfoot the man whom she detested above all else in the world. Afanasy Ivanovich was always the first to admit that he was something of a coward, or, to put it another way, highly conservative. For instance, had he suspected that he would be murdered at the altar on his wedding day or that something else highly untoward, ridiculous and unpleasant like that would occur, he would of course have taken fright, but not so much because he'd be killed, or his blood spilt, or that he'd suffer the indignity of someone publicly spitting in his face and so on and so forth, but because it would all occur in such an unbecoming and unpleasant manner. But this is precisely what Nastasya Filippovna was counting on, even though she hadn't said so in so many words; he also knew that she had studied him well and that he held no secrets for her, and consequently knew where she could hurt him most. Also, since the marriage was still very much in the planning stage, Afanasy Ivanovich drew in his horns and gave in to Nastasya Filippovna.

This decision was prompted by one other factor: he just could not get over how different Nastasya Filippovna had become. Formerly she had been just a comely girl, whereas now... Totsky kept blaming himself that for four years he had looked but seen nothing. Of course, both parties had inwardly undergone unexpected changes. He recalled, however, instances from the past too when strange ideas had come to him occasionally just on looking into her eyes. It was as though he were gazing into a dark, unfathomable abyss. The eyes looked back questioningly, without yielding any of their own secrets. In the past couple of years he was often astonished at the change in the colouring of Nastasya Filippovna's complexion. She would often grow very pale and – strange to say – seemed all the more beautiful for that. Totsky, like all gentlemen who had sown their wild oats liberally, regarded this tasty morsel as easy pickings; lately, however, he had begun to revise his notions. Come what may, he had made up his mind the previous spring to marry off Nastasya Filippovna advantageously and generously at the first opportunity to some level-headed, respectable suitor, resident in some district other than his own. (My goodness, how viciously and cruelly Nastasya Filippovna now laughed at this!) But the wheel had turned, and Afanasy Ivanovich, attracted by the changed circumstances, had an idea he could take advantage of this woman a second time round. He decided to set her up in St Petersburg and surround her with luxury and comfort. If not one thing, then the other! Dammit, one could still cut a dash with such a fine woman in certain circles. Afanasy Ivanovich laid a lot of store by his reputation in this regard.

Five years of this life in St Petersburg had passed and in the meantime naturally a lot of things became clear. Afanasy Ivanovich's position was not enviable; the worst of it was that, having funked it once, he was forever ruing the day. He was afraid – of what he could not imagine – he was simply afraid of Nastasya Filippovna. At one stage, in the first two years, he even had the idea that Nastasya Filippovna was herself willing to marry him, but would not break her silence due to her inordinate pride, and was stubbornly expecting him to make the proposal. Such a notion appeared far-fetched; Afanasy Ivanovich winced and tried to think of a solution. To his no small and somewhat unpleasant surprise (such is the nature of man!) he discovered, in consequence of an unexpected occurrence, that even if he were to propose, he would be rejected. It took him some time to come to terms with this. He could think of only one explanation: the pride of an affronted and singular woman had reached such proportions that it was far more pleasant for her to pour out her bile in a refusal, rather than settle her affairs once and for all and attain the unattainable. It was particularly regrettable that Nastasya Filippovna had got the upper hand in the affair. She could not be bought off either, even at a very high price, and though she accepted the luxury that was offered to her, she lived rather modestly but had not managed to put anything by in the five years. Afanasy Ivanovich, to shatter his fetters decided on a clever ruse: he would by stealth and ingenuity tempt her with various solutions; but the most apparently ideal suitors – counts, hussars, foreign-embassy secretaries, poets, novelists, even left-wing politicians

– made no impression upon Nastasya Filippovna, as though in place of a heart she had a lump of rock and her feelings had withered and died long ago. For the most part she led a secluded life; she read, she even studied, and she loved music. She had only a few acquaintances. She associated mainly with some impoverished and eccentric female clerks, one or two actresses and some old crones, and was very fond of the large family of a respectable teacher where she herself was appreciated and welcomed. Quite often of an evening five or six people, no more, would gather at her place. Totsky was a frequent and punctual guest. Lately, not without some difficulty, General Yepanchin had made her acquaintance. About the same time, but without the slightest trouble, a young clerk named Ferdyshchenko, a very unpleasant foul-mouthed and bibulous buffoon with pretensions to joviality, managed to do likewise. Her circle also included an odd young man answering to the name of Ptitsyn, who was demure, tidy, well-groomed, and had started from penury and become a moneylender. Finally, Gavrila Ardalionovich too appeared on the scene... In the end Nastasya Filippovna acquired a strange reputation. Her beauty was celebrated everywhere, but that was all; no one could lay claim to have got anywhere with her, no one could pin anything on her. Her reputation, her education, her polished manners, her wit, all combined to confirm Afanasy Ivanovich in his resolve to carry out a certain plan. It was from this moment on that General Yepanchin himself began to take an active and vital part in the proceedings.

When Totsky turned to him for friendly advice regarding one of his daughters, he also at the same time made a clean breast of things. He confessed that he would *not baulk at any means* of securing his freedom; that he would not be content even if Nastasya Filippovna herself were to declare that she was ready to leave him in peace; that words were not enough for him, that he needed cast-iron guarantees. They put their heads together and decided to act in concert. At first it was agreed to approach the matter with the utmost discretion, to play upon the most delicate of sentiments. They both arrived at Nastasya Filippovna's, and Totsky straight away began by expostulating the full horror of his position; he put the blame completely upon his own shoulders; he frankly admitted that he was unable to excuse himself for his initial dastardly treatment of her because he was an incorrigible sensualist and could exercise no control over his actions, but that he now intended to get married, and the fate of a decent, respectable marriage was in her hands; in short, that everything hung on her decision. Then general Yepanchin took over in his capacity as a father, and he spoke with conviction; he eschewed all sentimentalities; he confirmed that he accepted without demur her right to decide Afanasy Ivanovich's fate; he delicately alluded in passing to his own integrity, pointing out that the fate of his daughter, nay of two daughters, depended on her decision. To Nastasya Filippovna's question, what was actually expected of her, Totsky, with his usual natural candour, admitted that he had been so traumatized over the past five years that he would be unable even now to find any peace of mind until and unless Nastasya Filippovna were to enter into matrimony herself. He immediately added that such a request on his part would, of course, be odd if he did not have some cogent reasons for it. He had noticed and was able to establish firmly that a young man from a very good background and excellent family in which he was still residing, namely Gavrila Ardalionych, himself a welcome guest at her house, had long since been madly in love with her and would, of course, be ready to lay down his life for the mere prospect of gaining her affections. Gavrila Ardalionych had personally confided this to Afanasy Ivanovich some considerable time past in all friendship and with the full candour of his youthful heart, and let him know that Ivan Fyodorovich himself, who patronized the young man, had also been privy to this all along. Finally, unless he, Afanasy Ivanovich, was very much mistaken, the young man's love for her was no secret to her either, and she regarded it with some sympathy. Of course no one found it more difficult to speak on this subject than he. But if Nastasya Filippovna were willing to see in him not just a selfish desire to settle his own fate but a genuine goodwill towards her, she would immediately realize that he had long been discomfited, nay pained, at the sight of her solitude. She had got stuck in a dreadful morass without prospects of a better life which, however, beckoned her strongly with all the blandishments of love and family happiness, and the promise of new horizons; yet, as things stood, she was wasting her – some would say unique – gifts, feeling sorry for herself, indulging herself in a kind of contemplative romanticism unworthy of her intellect and good nature. Having once more repeated that it was more difficult for him than for anyone else to speak about this, he concluded that he lived in the hope that Nastasya Filippovna would not treat him with contempt if he were to come up with a genuine offer of seventy-five thousand roubles to provide for her future needs. By way of explanation, he added that in any event this sum of money had already been earmarked for her in his will; in a word, this was not to be regarded as a sweetener of some sort... and, let's face it, why should he not be pardoned and excused for his natural yearning to somehow salve his conscience, and so on and so forth? In short, he resorted to all the arguments that are commonly used in such cases. Afanasy Ivanovich spoke at length and for some considerable time, not failing to omit, as it were in passing, one curious detail, that this allusion to the seventy-five thousand roubles was the first he had ever made and that even Ivan Fyodorovich – here and now present – had no inkling of it; *no one* had!

Nastasya Filippovna's reply came as a complete surprise to both friends.

Not only was there not a trace of her former derision, her enmity and hatred, her ridicule, the mere memory of which till now had sent shivers down Totsky's spine, but on the contrary, she appeared to be overjoyed at the opportunity of finally being able to talk over the matter with someone in a friendly and civilized manner. She admitted that she had long wanted to ask for friendly counsel but was held back by her pride, but now that the ice had been broken, nothing was more welcome to her. At first with a wistful smile, but then laughing out loud and clear, she declared that her stormy-petrel days were over; that she had long since changed her erstwhile attitude almost completely, and that even though at heart she was still her former self, she had perforce to reconcile herself to many an unpalatable fact; what had been done was water under the bridge; what had passed, had passed; and it was quite unnecessary for Afanasy Ivanovich to relive the past with such trepidation. Here she turned to Ivan Fyodorovich, and with the utmost respect announced that she had heard a great deal about his daughters and regarded them with the highest respect and admiration. The very thought of being – in whatever small way – of use to them, filled her with pride and pleasure. It was true that she found her present situation difficult and tiresome, extremely tiresome; Afanasy Ivanovich had divined her aspirations; she wanted to resurrect herself, if not in the romantic, then certainly in the family sense, and conscious of a new vista opening; but as to Gavrila Ardalionych, there was really nothing she could say. Yes, she had an idea he loved her; she felt she could reciprocate his love if only she could trust the strength of his attachment; but he was very young, even if he was sincere; a decision was not easy. Incidentally, she liked him most of all for his industry and the fact that he was the family's only breadwinner. She had heard that he was ambitious, proud, was striving for a career and personal advancement. She had also heard that Nina Alexandrovna Ivolgin, Gavrila Ardalionych's mother, was an excellent and highly respectable lady; that his sister, Varvara Ardalionovna was a remarkably energetic young lady; she had heard a great deal about her from Ptitsyn. She had heard that both of them were putting a very brave face on their adversity; she would have dearly liked to make their acquaintance, but the question remained whether they would be happy to receive her into the family fold. On the whole, she had nothing to say against the possibility of such an alliance, but it was a matter which still called for a great deal of reflection; she would prefer not to be hurried. As regards the seventy-five thousand – Afanasy Ivanovich need not have any qualms about it. She well understood the value of money, and would of course be happy to accept it. She was most grateful to Afanasy Ivanovich for his discretion in not mentioning it to the General, never mind Gavrila Ardalionych; however, what harm would there be in him knowing it in advance? She had no need to be ashamed of this money as a prospective member of the family. In any case, she owed nobody any apology, and made no bones about this. She would never marry Gavrila Ardalionych until she was absolutely convinced that neither he, nor any of the members of his family, harboured any grudge against her. At all events, she felt she had no reason to feel any sense of guilt, and that it would be far better if Gavrila Ardalionych were in possession of the full facts as to just how she had subsisted these five years in St Petersburg, in what relationship she was with Afanasy Ivanovich and how little capital she had succeeded in putting by during this time. Finally, even if she were to accept the money, it would not be as compensation for the shameful loss of her maidenhood – for which she was not to blame – but simply as a recompense for a wrecked life.

In the end she worked herself up into such a state expounding all this (to be sure, this was only natural), that General Yepanchin was well pleased and concluded that the matter was settled. However, the once bitten Totsky was not so sure, and still suspected a snake in the grass.

Nevertheless, talks began; the key point on which the two friends had based their plan, namely the possibility of Nastasya Filippovna's being attracted to Ganya, began to emerge ever more clearly and tellingly, such that in the end even Totsky began to believe in the possibility of a successful outcome. In the meantime, Nastasya Filippovna and Ganya had managed to talk to each other; very few words were exchanged, as though her modesty was in jeopardy. However, she did not discourage his love for her, but made it abundantly clear that she was in no way prepared to tie herself down; that right up to the wedding day (if such were to take place), she reserved the right, even at the eleventh hour, to say "no"; that Ganya on his part was empowered to feel equally free. Inevitably Ganya soon learnt that his family's opposition to this union, and to Nastasya Filippovna personally – the cause of much family strife – was known in great detail to Nastasya Filippovna; she herself never alluded to the matter, although increasingly he expected her to do so. There is of course much else that one might have inferred from all the stories and circumstances relating to the engagement and negotiations; but we have exceeded ourselves already, the more so since some of the circumstances were at the time no more than vague rumours. For instance, that Totsky was supposed to have learnt from somewhere that Nastasya Filippovna had entered into some vague and clandestine negotiations with the Yepanchin girls – a totally preposterous notion. On the other hand, another rumour to which he was prepared to lend credence, and which inspired holy dread in him, was that Nastasya Filippovna had apparently somehow surmised to a high degree of certainty that Ganya's sole reason for marriage was money; that Ganya himself was at heart a low, greedy, small-minded, resentful and boundlessly self-seeking scoundrel; that even though he had in the past passionately yearned for Nastasya Filippovna, after he detected that there was an attempt to take advantage of this nascent and mutual passion by selling her to him in the shape of a legitimate spouse, he began to hate her as his worst nightmare. Passion and hatred had curiously melded in his soul, and even though after much agonized heart-searching, he had given his consent to marry the "shameful" woman, he nevertheless swore to take revenge upon her and make her pay dearly, as he himself was alleged to have put it. It would seem that Nastasya Filippovna was aware of all this and was secretly plotting something of her own. Totsky had taken such a fright

51

at this that he stopped confiding his fears even to Yepanchin. Still, there were moments when he, weakling that he was, would occasionally perk up and take heart; for instance, he found particular cause for jubilation when Nastasya Filippovna finally promised the two friends that on the evening of her birthday celebrations she would make her final announcement.

But alas, a strange and utterly outlandish rumour concerning Ivan Fyodorovich himself appeared steadily to gain ever more currency and conviction. At first sight, nothing appeared to make sense. It was difficult to credit that Ivan Fyodorovich, at his venerable age, with his enormous intellect and thorough knowledge of life and so on and so forth, should himself have fallen for Nastasya Filippovna's charms – and this, madly, to the exclusion of everything else, with an all-consuming passion. It was difficult to tell what it was he was basing his hopes on. Perhaps even on Ganya's own cooperation? Totsky at least suspected something of the sort; he suspected some kind of a tacit, mutually advantageous pact between Ganya and the General. It is well known, of course, that a man in the throes of passion, especially when advanced in years, is liable to become completely blind, and nurture hope where none whatever exists; worse still, he is liable to lose all sense of proportion and behave like a silly child, even if he should be a veritable fount of wisdom in all other respects. It was common knowledge that as a present for Nastasya Filippovna's birthday, the General had put by a fabulous pearl necklace costing an enormous sum, and laid great store by this present even though he knew Nastasya Filippovna's lack of interest in such blandishments. On the eve of Nastasya Filippovna's birthday his excitement knew no bounds, but he managed to conceal it skilfully. It was precisely these pearls that attracted the particular attention of his spouse. True enough, Lizaveta Prokofyevna had for some considerable time been aware of a certain frivolity in her husband's behaviour and had by and large learnt to live with it; but this particular matter could not be allowed to pass; the rumour of the pearls interested her very much. The General had got wind of this; some words had been exchanged; he anticipated a massive showdown and lived in trepidation. It was for this reason that he felt most reluctant on the morning on which we began our story to return to the bosom of the family for lunch. Even before the Prince had turned up, he had planned to make an excuse and avoid the occasion.

To "avoid" for the General often meant simply to make himself scarce. Of all days, he wanted this one, especially the evening, to pass triumphantly and without any problems. And lo and behold, here was the Prince. "A veritable godsend!" the General thought to himself as he entered into the presence of his spouse.

5

THE GENERAL'S LADY was proud of her lineage. One can only imagine what it was like for her to discover that the last scion of her family, this Prince Myshkin, of whom she had already heard something, was no more than just a pitiable idiot without two copecks to rub together, currently doing the rounds as a beggar. The General laid it on a bit thick precisely so as to increase the effect and divert her attention as much as possible.

In difficult situations Lizaveta Prokofyevna tended to roll her eyes and, leaning back in her chair somewhat, would stare ahead vaguely without uttering a word. She was a rather tall woman, the same age as her husband. Her dark hair, though still luxuriant, was going grey; her nose was aquiline, her build sinewy; she had sunken, livid cheeks and thin drooping lips. She had a high, elongated forehead, and the ability at will to lend her rather large grey eyes an appearance of extreme consternation. At one time she had let herself be taken in by the belief that her glance had a certain extraordinary effect, and this had become a firm conviction.

"To see him? You want me to see him? What? Right now?" and the General's Lady rolled her eyes as she regarded her much-perturbed husband.

"No need to put yourself out in any way whatsoever, my dearest – that is, if you are disposed to receive him at all," the General hastened to qualify. "He's a veritable child, pathetic even. He suffers from some sort of fits. He's newly arrived from Switzerland, just off the train, dressed rather oddly, after the German fashion, and to cap it all without a copeck to his name, quite literally. He was almost in tears. I gave him twenty-five roubles, and have a mind to find him a job as a clerk in our office. And you, *mesdames*, I trust will ply him with some comestibles because I've a feeling he hasn't eaten—"

"You surprise me," the General's Lady pursued her line, "not eaten and fits! What sort of fits?"

"Oh, they don't occur that often, and he's just like a child really, but he's educated all right. I was going to ask you, *mesdames*," he said, again turning to his daughters, "to put him through his paces, I'd like to know what he is capable of."

"Put – him – through – his – paces?" the General's Lady drawled, and in utter consternation began to roll her eyes from her daughters to her husband and back again.

"Oh, my dearest, don't take it so seriously... anyway, it's up to you. All I had in mind was to give him a little bit of support and take him under our wing, almost as an act of charity."

"Take him under our wing? From Switzerland?!"

"Switzerland is neither here nor there. But, I repeat, it's up to you – my point being that, first of all, he shares our name, perhaps he's a cousin, and secondly, he's got nowhere to lay his head. I rather thought you might be, in a manner of speaking, interested, seeing as he's family."

"Of course, *Maman*, if he doesn't stand on ceremony," the eldest, Alexandra, observed. "Besides, he must be awfully hungry after such a journey. He could well do with a meal if he has no one to turn to."

"I tell you, he's just like a child. You could play blind man's buff with him."

"Blind man's buff! Explain yourself!"

"Oh, *Maman*, please stop pretending," Aglaya interrupted irritably.

Adelaida, the playful middle sister, could contain herself no longer and burst out laughing.

"Call him in, Papa, *Maman* agrees," Aglaya decided to settle the matter. The General rang the bell and asked to have the Prince summoned.

"But only if we tie a napkin round his neck when he sits down at table," the General's Lady decreed. "Call Fyodor, or better still, Mavra... to stand behind his back and keep an eye on him while he's eating. I hope he's not violent in his fits! And doesn't wave his arms about."

"On the contrary, he's well brought up and has excellent manners. A bit on the clumsy side, perhaps... Aha, here he is! May I introduce the last of the Myshkins, a namesake, and maybe a cousin – make him welcome, put him at his ease. They're just about to start lunch, Prince, do me the honour, make yourself at home... as for me, you must excuse me, I'm awfully late, I have to hurry—"

"We all know where to," the General's Lady observed grandly.

"I have to hurry, I do apologize, I'm running late! Show him your albums, *mesdames*, let him write something in them. He's such a calligrapher, simply marvellous! A real talent! You should see how he can do old-style handwriting, '*Abbot Pafnuty has hereto appended his signature*'... Well, goodbye then."

"Pafnuty? Abbot?" Lizaveta Prokofyevna exclaimed with aggrieved insistence as her husband attempted to make his getaway. "Stay, I say, please stay – where are you off to, and who is this Pafnuty?"

"Yes, of course, my dearest, there was such an abbot in olden times... and I must be off to the Count's, he's been expecting me for some time now, and the main point is, he made the appointment himself... Prince, au revoir!"

The General withdrew hurriedly.

"A count, a likely story!" the General's Lady remarked acerbically and turned her exasperated gaze upon the Prince. "Where were we then?" she began, straining irritably to gather her thoughts. "You were saying! Oh yes, so what about this abbot?"

"*Maman*!..." Alexandra exclaimed, and Aglaya even stamped her foot.

"Don't interfere, Alexandra Ivanovna!" Lizaveta Prokofyevna cut her short. "I too want to know. Take a seat, Prince, this chair, facing me – no, here, in the sun where there's more light, so that I can see you. So, what about this abbot?"

"Abbot Pafnuty," the Prince replied with a serious and attentive mien.

"Pafnuty? Sounds fascinating. Well, so what about him?"

The General's Lady fired her questions impetuously, quickly, brusquely, not shifting her gaze from the Prince, and when the Prince replied, she nodded in unison with his every word.

"The Abbot Pafnuty lived in the fourteenth century," the Prince began, "he was head of a monastery on the Volga, in the present-day Kostroma region. He was famed for his piety. He visited the Golden Horde* and helped to settle day-to-day matters. There was a document with his signature, and I saw a facsimile of it. I liked the hand and learnt to copy it. When the General asked for a specimen of my handwriting to find me suitable employment, I wrote down a number of sentences in various styles, amongst them '*Abbot Pafnuty has hereto appended his signature*', in the Abbot's own hand. The General seemed very pleased, which is why he mentioned it."

"Aglaya," the General's Lady said, "remember: Pafnuty, or better still, write it down, or I'm bound to forget it. To be sure, I thought it would be more interesting. Where then is this signature?"

"I think it was left on the General's desk in his study."

"To be sent for forthwith!"

"Why don't I write it out again for you, if you would allow me?"

"Of course, *Maman*," Alexandra said, "but let's have our lunch first, we're famished."

"Very well," the General's Lady decided. "Come, Prince. You are hungry, are you not?"

"Yes, right now I am very hungry, and I am most obliged to you."

"It's very good that you are courteous, and I'm glad to note that you're not at all... the crackpot we've been led to believe you were. Come. Sit here, facing me," she fussed, getting the Prince to sit where she wanted after they entered the dining room. "I want to look at you. Alexandra, Adelaida, serve the Prince. He's hardly... ill at all, wouldn't you say? Perhaps no need for the napkin after all... Prince, would you like a napkin tied while you eat?"

"When I was about seven, they would tie a napkin for me, but now I keep my napkin on my knees when I eat."

"And so you should. What about your fits?"

"My fits?" the Prince sounded a little surprised. "I don't have many fits these days. But then who knows, they say the climate here will be bad for me."

"There's nothing wrong with the way he speaks," the General's Lady observed, turning to her daughters, with a nod after every word the Prince said. "I hardly expected it. It seems therefore it's all just a pack of lies, as per usual. Help yourself, Prince, and tell me, where were you born, where were you educated? I want to know everything. I'm very interested in you."

The Prince thanked her, and while eating with considerable appetite, again began to recount what he had already gone over a number of times earlier that morning. Lizaveta Prokofyevna grew more and more pleased. The young ladies also listened quite attentively. They went over their kith and kin; it transpired the Prince knew his lineage fairly well, but no matter how hard they tried, no direct relationship could be established between him and the General's Lady. Two generations back there appeared to be some connection, but nothing after that. However, this discussion was just what the General's Lady, who hardly ever got an opportunity to talk about her family history however much she'd have liked to, needed, so that she left the table in a state of high spirits.

"Let us retire to the drawing room," she said, "and we'll have our coffee there. It's our common room, as it were," she said, leading the way, "or simply my little guest room, where we congregate when we're alone, and each one of us gets on with her own business. Alexandra – that's her, my eldest – plays the piano, reads and sews. Adelaida paints portraits or landscapes (never finishes any of course). As for Aglaya, she sits, and does nothing. I don't seem to be able to manage anything either. Everything ends in failure. Well, here we are. Sit down, Prince, here by the fireplace. I want to hear what you have to say for yourself. I need to be absolutely sure, and when I see Princess Belokonskaya, the old lady, I want to be able to tell her the whole story. And make sure you hold the girls' attention too. Well, go on then."

"*Maman*, it's easier said than done," Adelaida observed, having in the meantime set up her easel, taken her brushes and, holding her palette, begun to copy a landscape from a reproduction that she had started a long time ago. Alexandra and Aglaya sat down on a small sofa and, with hands folded, prepared to listen. The Prince observed that attention was being focused on him from all quarters.

"I wouldn't be able to say a thing if I were ordered around like that," Aglaya observed.

"Why not? What's so strange about it? Why shouldn't he tell us something? He's got a tongue in his head. I want to know if he can tell a story. It doesn't matter what. Tell us what you think of Switzerland, your first impressions. You'll see, he'll make a splendid start in a moment."

"It made a very strong impression—"

"There, there," Lizaveta Prokofyevna in her eagerness butted in, "he's started, I told you."

"Why don't you at least let him speak, *Maman*," Alexandra begged her. "This Prince is probably a thorough rogue, rather than an idiot," she whispered to Aglaya.

"You're probably right, I've had my suspicions from the start," Aglaya replied. "It's rather mean of him to act a role. What is he after?"

"At first it made a very strong impression on me," the Prince repeated. "After I was taken from Russia and travelled through various German towns, I just observed things in silence, and I even remember not asking any questions. This was after a series of violent and agonizing bouts of illness, for whenever it got worse and the frequency of the fits increased, I sank into a complete torpor, lost my memory completely, and though my mind continued to function, the logical thought processes seemed to break down. I could not connect more than two or three ideas in sequence. That's as I recall it. When the fits abated, however, I recovered my strength and vitality as now. I remember I was overcome with unbearable despondency, and was close to tears. I was in a constant state of amazement and disquiet. I was particularly concerned that everything was *foreign* to me. That much I could comprehend. Things foreign had a devastating effect upon me. I came out of this stupor; I remember the evening we reached Switzerland, when pulling into Basle, I was awoken by the braying of an ass in the market square. The ass took me completely by surprise and I was thoroughly delighted, such that all of a sudden everything in my head seemed to become clear."

"An ass? How curious!" the General's Lady remarked. "On second thoughts, nothing curious at all, one of us may yet fall in love with an ass," she went on, darting an angry glance at her daughters who were convulsed with laughter. "Happened in mythology. Continue, Prince."

"Ever since, I've been terribly fond of asses. I feel I have a soft spot for them. I started to enquire about them, because formerly I hadn't taken much notice of them, and I immediately realized that it's a wonderfully useful animal – plodding, strong, patient, cheap and hardy. And because of this ass I suddenly got to like the whole of Switzerland, so that all my former despondency was gone in a trice."

"That is all very fascinating, but the ass is neither here nor there. Let's change the subject. Why are you laughing, Aglaya? And you too, Adelaida? It was a perfectly reasonable story about the ass. The Prince had seen it himself, and what have you seen, I'd like to know? You've never been abroad!"

"I've seen an ass, *Maman*," Adelaida said.

"And I've heard one," Aglaya echoed. All three again burst out laughing. The Prince joined in.

"This is not very nice of you," Lizaveta Prokofyevna remarked. "You must excuse them, Prince, they're good girls really. I battle with them all the time, but I love them all the same. They're flighty, frolicsome and quite mad."

"Why?" the Prince enquired with a laugh. "In their place I wouldn't have missed the opportunity myself. And still I insist that an ass is a good and useful creature."

"And would you rate yourself as a good man, Prince? I'm simply curious," the General's Lady asked.

There was again laughter all round.

"This confounded ass again! I had put him right out of my mind," the General's Lady exclaimed. "Believe me, Prince, I was not casting—"

"...any aspersions? Oh, I believe you wholeheartedly."

And the Prince carried on laughing.

"I am glad you are taking it so well," the General's Lady said. "I can see you are a kind-hearted young man."

"Sometimes not so kind-hearted," the Prince replied.

"But I am kind-hearted," the General's Lady declared unexpectedly, "I'm always kind-hearted and, if you will, that is my only failing, because one ought not to be kind-hearted all the time. I'm often angry with that lot there, with Ivan Fyodorovich especially, but the worst of it is that the more angry I am, the more kind-hearted I become. Just before you came, I got awfully angry and pretended that I was both incapable and unwilling to understand anything. I am like that occasionally, just like a child. Aglaya gave me a scolding. Thank you, my dear. Still, this is all nonsense. I'm not as stupid as I look, or as my daughters make me out to be. I have a pretty strong character and like to call a spade a spade. And this is without any malice. Come here, Aglaya, kiss me, well... no more sentimentalities," she added after Aglaya had tenderly kissed her on her lips and on her hand. "Do continue, Prince, perhaps this time you'll come up with something more exciting than an ass."

"I still don't understand how anyone can be expected to tell a story just like that out of the blue," Aglaya remarked. "I'd never know what to say."

"But the Prince will, because the Prince is extraordinarily clever, at least ten times cleverer than you, perhaps a dozen. I hope you'll have enough sense to realize that, young lady. Prove it to them, Prince. Carry on! But leave the ass out of it this time. So, what else apart from an ass have you seen abroad?"

"That was clever about the ass," Alexandra observed. "The Prince spoke very well about his sorry state, and about how he began to see everything in a new light after an external shock. I've always been fascinated by how people go mad and then get better again. Especially if it all happens suddenly."

"True enough! True enough!" the General's Lady affirmed. "I can see that you too can show intelligence sometimes. Well, enough laughing! I think you were saying something about the Swiss countryside, Prince, well?"

"We arrived in Lucerne, and I was taken on the lake," the Prince said. "I could admire its beauty, but at the same time I felt awfully sad."

"Why?" Alexandra asked.

"I'm not sure. Such sights always unsettle and depress me when I first come across them. I can sense the beauty, but it unnerves me. To be sure, all this was at the height of my illness."

"That's as may be, but I'd very much like to have a look for myself," Adelaida said. "I can't wait for us to go abroad. It's two years already I've been looking for a suitable subject to paint:

> East and South have long
> since been described
> and their praises sung*...

Will you find me a subject to paint, Prince?"

"I know nothing of these things. The way I see it, you just take a look and start painting."

"I can't just 'take a look'."

"Why are you speaking in riddles? I don't understand anything!" the General's Lady cut in. "What does it mean, can't 'take a look'? You've got eyes, go ahead and look. If you haven't learnt to look here, you're not going to learn abroad. I'd rather, Prince, you told us how you went about looking."

"Yes, please," Adelaida added. "The Prince must surely have acquired the knack of looking when abroad."

"I don't know. I was there for health reasons. I don't know if I acquired the knack of looking. But I know that I was very happy nearly all of the time."

"Happy! You know how to be happy?" Aglaya exclaimed. "So how can you say you hadn't acquired the knack of looking? You should be able to teach us."

"Please teach us," Adelaida said with a laugh.

"I can't teach you anything," the Prince responded also with a laugh. "I spent nearly all my time abroad in a Swiss village, only rarely venturing elsewhere, and then for the most part locally. So what can I teach you? At first I simply found myself more engaged with life, then I soon started feeling better. Eventually, each succeeding day was precious for me and, as time passed, this feeling only intensified, till there was no mistaking it. I used to go to bed very content, and would get up even more so. And why – is rather difficult to explain."

"And so you didn't want to go anywhere, you weren't tempted anywhere?" Alexandra asked.

"To begin with, at the very start, yes, I was tempted, and was very restless. I never stopped thinking what would become of me, what fate had in store for me, at times it got almost unbearable. You know, this tends to happen, especially in solitude. There was a waterfall, nothing big, but it was on a high cliff, almost perpendicular, and ended in a fine, thread-like stream – white, lots of spray and rather noisy. It was a huge drop, but from my house it didn't seem like that. It was about half a verst away, but seemed no more than fifty paces. I liked to listen to it at night, and that was when I got really restless. At other times I'd go out at midday into the mountains and stop somewhere halfway up a slope, surrounded by pines, huge, old, smelling of resin. Higher up the cliff there'd be the ruins of a medieval castle; down below, our village, barely visible, all in bright sunshine, under an azure sky, not a sound anywhere. It was then that I'd feel I was being summoned somewhere, and I had the impression that if I were to carry on straight, and keep walking on and on beyond that line where the sky meets the earth, all would be resolved, and a new life would commence a thousand times more vigorous and tumultuous than ours. I always dreamt of a large town such as Naples, full of palaces, noise, thunder, vitality... Funny the things one dreams of! And later I realized that even within prison walls one can have a great life."

"I read just that in my reader when I was twelve," Aglaya said.

"That's all philosophy," Adelaida remarked, "you're a philosopher and have come to instruct us."

"You may be right," the Prince smiled. "Perhaps I really am a philosopher and, who knows, I may well be minded to instruct... This may well be so, indeed it may."

"And your philosophy is no better than Evlampiya Nikolayevna's," Aglaya chimed in, "a widow of an impoverished clerk, who goes around begging. Her only aim in life is to get things on the cheap, the cheaper the better; all she talks about is copecks, and, mark you, she has money, a real slyboots. The same goes for your great life within prison walls, and for that matter, for your four-year-long happiness in the village too for which you sold out your city of Naples, probably at a profit, even if it was only a matter of a few copecks."

"I could take issue regarding prison life," the Prince said. "I happened to hear the story of a man who spent about twelve years in prison. He was one of my professor's patients, receiving treatment. He suffered from fits, was often restless, he would cry and once even attempted suicide. His life in prison was sad, but, I assure you, by no means worthless. All he had for friends was a spider and a little sapling that had sprung up outside his cell window... But I think I'd better tell you about another meeting I had last year with a man. It was a rather strange case – strange, in that such cases occur very seldom. This man had once been led to the scaffold, together with others, and the death sentence by firing was read out to him for a political crime. About twenty minutes later it was commuted to a lesser form of punishment. However, in the intervening twenty minutes, or at least quarter of an hour, between the two sentences, he was fully convinced that in a few minutes he'd be dead. I was terribly keen to listen to him when he reminisced about what went on in his mind at the time, and I often urged him to talk about it. He recollected everything with extraordinary clarity, and said that he would never forget anything that happened. About twenty paces from the scaffold, surrounded by a crowd of people and some soldiers, three posts were dug in the ground because there were others under a similar sentence. The first three were led to the posts, tied fast, the execution garb – a long white cloak – was draped over them, white hoods were pulled down over their eyes to prevent them seeing the rifles, then a file of soldiers lined up in front of each post. The man who told me this story was the eighth in line, consequently he expected to be in the third group to be led to the posts. The priest did the rounds with a cross. By then he had no more than five minutes left to live. He recounted that those five minutes were like an eternity for him, a priceless treasure. He felt that in those five minutes he would be able to live so many lives that it was quite unnecessary to think about the final moment, such that he was even able to apportion them appropriately. He allotted enough time to say goodbye to his friends – this would take about two minutes, then two minutes to think back on his own life for the last time, and then the rest to cast one last look around. He recalled very well that that was just how he apportioned the time and managed to complete all three pledges. He was going to his death at the age of twenty-seven, strong and in the full bloom of health. Saying goodbye to his friends, he recalled that he had asked one of them a fairly mundane question and was very keen to hear the answer. After he had said goodbye to his friends, came the two minutes *to think back on his own life*. He knew precisely what he was going to think about. He just could not wait to see clearly and distinctly how it could be that here he was alive and well, and in three minutes he would be *quite another thing*, a someone or a something else – what exactly? Where exactly? He strove to resolve all this in his mind in those two minutes! Not far off was a church, its gilt dome shining resplendent in the brilliant sunshine. He recalled staring fixedly at the dome and the rays reflected from it. He couldn't tear his eyes from the rays. He imagined them to be his new incarnation, and that in three minutes he would somehow fuse with them... The uncertainty and revulsion of what was imminently in store were agonizing. But in his own words nothing was more insupportable than the persistent notion, 'What if I were not to die! What if I were to have my life back again – a whole infinity! And all would be mine! I'd make every moment last for ages, nothing would be wasted, every moment would be accounted for, everything would be taken care of!' He confessed that eventually this thought incensed him so much that he wished they would hurry up and shoot him."

The Prince suddenly fell silent. Everyone expected him to continue and draw a conclusion.

"Have you finished?" Aglaya asked.

"What? Oh yes, I have," the Prince said, coming out of a short reverie.

"Why on earth did you tell us all this?"

"I don't know… it came to mind… as we talked…"

"You're very mercurial," Alexandra observed. "You probably meant to show that nothing is trivial, and that a mere five minutes may sometimes be worth a whole fortune. All this is fine, but, if I may, what of this friend of yours who told you about such torments… you said he was reprieved? It follows therefore he was granted his coveted 'eternal life'. So what did he do with this fortune in the end? Did he account for every moment of it?"

"Oh no, he confided in me – I asked him this very question. It all went wrong, and he squandered many a precious moment."

"There you are, doesn't it demonstrate to you that it's impossible to live and account for every single moment? One way or another it's just not feasible."

"Not feasible one way or another," the Prince repeated. "That's how I too argued… All the same I'm not altogether convinced—"

"You mean to say, you hope you can spend your life more wisely than everybody else?" Aglaya asked.

"Yes, that too has crossed my mind."

"And still does?"

"Yes… it does," the Prince replied, still looking at Aglaya with a calm and even meek smile on his face. But the next moment he burst out laughing again, and looked at her full of merriment.

"I admire your modesty!" Aglaya snapped back almost irritably.

"You are very brave, I must say. There you are laughing away – as for me, I was so moved by his story that I dreamt about it later, about those very five minutes…"

Once again he looked seriously, searchingly at his listeners.

"You're not angry with me about something?" he asked suddenly in evident confusion, but nevertheless looking everyone in turn straight in the eye.

"Why should we be?" the three girls cried out in unison.

"Well, because I seem to be preaching all the time…"

There was general laughter again.

"If you're angry, there's no need to be," he said. "I know very well that I haven't lived enough and have precious little understanding of life at large. Perhaps my way of speaking may strike people as odd sometimes…" And he stopped in utter embarrassment.

"If, as you claim, you have been happy, it means you've had more experience of life, not less. Why then pretend and apologize?" Aglaya began belligerently. "And you should have no qualms about preaching to us. That doesn't mean at all that you're setting yourself above us. There's enough quietism in you to fill a hundred years with happiness. Show you an execution, or a little finger, and you'd come out with the same laudable opinion about both and, what's more, remain happy. That's one way to get by in life, I suppose."

"Why so angry, pray tell me?" the General's Lady was quick to respond, keeping a close eye on the speakers. "And what are you talking about? I can't understand. Finger? What finger? Utter balderdash! The Prince makes perfect sense, it's just that he's a little sad. Why are you disheartening him? He was quite cheerful when he started, now he's completely crestfallen. Look at him."

"Don't worry, *Maman*. Pity, Prince, you never saw an execution. I'd have had a question to put to you."

"I did see an execution," the Prince replied.

"You did?" Aglaya exclaimed. "I should have guessed! This makes all the difference. If you saw an execution, how can you say you led a happy life all the time? Now then, was I right or not?"

"Did they really execute someone in your village?"

"I saw it in Lyon. I went there with Schneider. One was underway when we arrived."

"Well, did you like it a lot? Did you find it edifying, instructive?" Aglaya asked.

"I didn't like it at all, and afterwards I was a little unwell – but I must admit, I was fascinated, I couldn't tear my eyes away."

"Nor would I have," Aglaya said.

"They don't like it at all when women come to watch, such women even get into the papers later."

"It goes without saying that if they reckon it's not for women, they must necessarily regard it (and consequently justify it) as being meant for men only. A wonderful piece of logic. And I suppose you are of the same mind of course, aren't you?"

"Tell us about the execution," Adelaida interrupted.

"I'd rather not just now…" the Prince replied with a frown, visibly embarrassed.

"Don't be so mean," Aglaya chided him.

"No, it's because I've just been describing this execution to someone else."

"Describing it to whom?"

"To your manservant, while I was waiting—"

"What manservant?" they all enquired in a chorus.

"The one who sits in the lobby, with slightly grey hair, reddish complexion. I was sitting there before being admitted to Ivan Fyodorovich."

"How odd," the General's Lady observed.

"The Prince is a democrat," Aglaya remarked trenchantly. "Well, if you confided in Alexei, surely you can tell us."

"I simply must hear it," Adelaida insisted.

"As a matter of fact," the Prince turned to her, perking up a little (he seemed to bounce back quickly and trustfully), "I really thought, when you asked for a subject to paint, of suggesting the face of a condemned man a minute or so before the guillotine blade falls – when he's still standing on the scaffold, about to lie down on the board."

"The face? Just the face?" Adelaida asked. "What a weird subject, and what sort of a picture would that be?"

"I don't know, but, why not?" the Prince persisted. "I recently saw one like that in Basle.* I'd very much like to describe it to you… some day I will… It left a powerful impression on me."

"You can tell us about the Basle picture later, I'm sure," Adelaida said, "as for now, describe for us the scene of the execution. Just as you see it, could you? What should the face look like? Just the face? What sort of a face?"

"Precisely a minute before death," the Prince began eagerly, carried away by his recollection, and apparently oblivious of everything else, "just after he had mounted the short steps and set foot on the scaffold. Here he glanced in my direction. I looked into his face and it all became clear to me… I don't quite know how to describe it! I really wish someone, perhaps you, would paint it! Yes, best of all you! I thought at the time that the picture would be absolutely enthralling. You see, nothing must be left out of what had gone before. He had been in prison and wasn't expecting the execution for at least another week. He had been counting on the usual formalities, that the warrant papers had to be sent somewhere and wouldn't be back for another week. And suddenly quite by chance the procedure was shortened. At five in the morning he was still asleep. It was the end of October. At five it's still cold and dark. The prison warden came in, softly, accompanied by guards, and touched him gently on the shoulder. The prisoner raised his head, leant on his elbow – the light dazzled him. 'What's going on?' – 'The execution is at ten.' Having just woken up, he didn't want to believe it. He began to argue that the death warrant wasn't due for another week. But once he had shaken off sleep completely, he stopped answering and fell silent – that's how the story goes anyway. Then he said, 'It's difficult when it's all so sudden...' and he fell silent again, and would not say anything more. Well, the next three or four hours were spent on the usual things: the priest; the breakfast, which comes with wine; boiled beef and coffee (pure mockery, if you ask me! The cruelty of it! On the other hand, to be honest, the innocent souls do it out of the goodness of their hearts, and regard it as philanthropy); then the toilet. (I take it you know what toilet for the condemned means?) Finally he is driven through the town to the place of execution... I think here too the impression is that one will live for ever while the journey is in progress. I can just imagine what must have been going through his head on the way: 'It's all a long way off yet, I've three more streets to live; when we come to the end of this one, there'll be another one, and then the next with the baker's on the right... it'll be ages before we reach the baker's!' There are people everywhere, shouting, noise, ten thousand faces, ten thousand pairs of eyes – all this has to be endured, and with it the thought, 'There's ten thousand of them, but not one is to be executed, whereas I will be!' These are the preliminaries. A series of steps leads up to the scaffold. At the bottom he suddenly burst into tears, yet he was a strong, manly fellow, a hardened criminal, by all accounts. A priest was constantly at his side, in the tumbrel too, repeating something over and over that hardly penetrated the man's consciousness, and when it did, only for a second. I presume it was like that. Finally, he began to ascend the steps. His feet were bound, therefore his movements were awkward. The priest, by the looks of it a sensible man, stopped talking and just kept presenting the crucifix to his lips. He was pale at the foot of the steps, but after mounting them, turned as white as a sheet, almost literally. His legs must have been getting stiff and giving way under him, and he was nauseous – as though his windpipe was being constricted and this caused a tickling in his throat. I wonder if you have ever experienced this in a state of fear or in some critical situation, when your mind while still fully alert has lost all power of control. I suppose if threatened with an imminent disaster, say a roof caving in, you'd want to cower down passively and shut your eyes – come what may!... It was precisely at these moments of helplessness that the priest would hastily, in silence, with a hurried gesture, thrust the crucifix right up to his lips – a small, silver thing – repeatedly, without let-up. And as soon as it touched his lips, he'd open his eyes, perk up for a few seconds and his legs would begin to move. He'd kiss the crucifix avidly, unceasingly, as though to stock up, just in case, as for a journey, but it's unlikely that he felt any kind of religious experience at the time. And so, right up to the stretcher-board... It's strange, but people hardly ever faint in these final moments! On the contrary the mind is very much alert and the head is pulsating with life, on, on and on, like an engine at full speed. I imagine various thoughts pulsating too, in fragments, ridiculous, irrelevant mostly. 'That chap staring – he's got a wart on his head. The lower button on the executioner's coat's gone rusty...' and all the time you know precisely what's going on around you. There's one particular bit you just can't get out of your mind, that you can't shut out or even avoid, it's always there and everything is centred on it and revolves around it. And to think that that's how it'll be till the last split second when the head is already on the block, waiting and... *taking it all in*, suddenly becoming aware of the swish of metal! Be sure you'll hear it! If it'd been me, I'd have been listening out for it and would have heard it! It would only have been for one insignificant fraction of a second, but I'd have heard it! And imagine, people still debate about whether for a second or so the severed head continues to be aware that it has been severed – just think of that! And what if it's five seconds!... Show the scaffold so that only the last tread of the steps is visible. The condemned has placed his foot on it, one can see his head, his face is as white as a sheet, the priest is holding forth the crucifix, his livid lips are there to meet it eagerly, and he's *watching*, and – *taking it all in*. The crucifix and the head – there's your picture. The faces of the priest, the executioner, his two assistants and a few heads and some pairs of eyes below – all that should be depicted in the background, enveloped in a mist as it were... That's how I picture it."

The Prince fell silent and looked at everyone.

"This is, to be sure, a far cry from quietism," Alexandra spoke under her breath.

"Well, tell us now how you fell in love," Adelaida said.

The Prince looked at her in astonishment.

"Listen," Adelaida hurried on, "you still owe us the description of the Basle painting, but right now, I want to hear how you fell in love. Don't deny it, you were in love, weren't you? Besides, as soon as you start speaking, you stop being a philosopher."

"Each time you come to the end of a story, you get embarrassed about what you've said," Aglaya suddenly observed. "Why is that?"

"Really, this is too silly, I must say," the General's Lady cut in sharply, looking indignantly at Aglaya.

"I agree." Alexandra confirmed.

"Pay no attention to her, Prince," the General's Lady said. "She's saying it deliberately out of some kind of spite. It's certainly not that she's been badly brought up. Don't be put out by their teasing. They're probably up to some prank, but I know they're very fond of you already. I know their faces."

"I know their faces too," the Prince said emphatically.

"Really?" Adelaida enquired with curiosity.

"What do you know about our faces?" the other two asked with eagerness.

But the Prince kept his silence and preserved a serious mien. Everyone awaited his answer.

"I'll tell you some other time," he said gently and firmly.

"You're determined to intrigue us, aren't you?" Aglaya exclaimed, "and look how solemn you are!"

"Very well then," Adelaida was quick off the mark again, "if you're such a connoisseur of faces, you must surely have been in love. I'm right, am I not? Come on, out with it!"

"I have not been in love," the Prince replied just as gently and firmly, "I've... known happiness of another kind."

"What? How?"

"All right then, I'll tell you," the Prince continued as though lost in thought.

6

" THERE YOU ARE," the Prince began, "all looking at me now with such expectation that, were I to let you down, I dare say you'd never forgive me. No, I'm joking," he hastened to add with a smile. "The place... was full of children, and I was always surrounded by them, just children. They were from the village, a whole crowd of them, all attending the same school. I didn't teach them, oh no, not at all, there was a teacher for that, one Jules Thibaut. Sometimes I'd take over, but mostly I just happened to be about, and that's how I spent the four years. I needed nothing else. I was perfectly frank with them, holding nothing back. Their parents and relatives took it in bad part because in the end the children couldn't do without me and kept crowding around me, and the form master eventually became my worst enemy. I made many enemies there, and all because of the children. Even Schneider used to pick on me. And what was it they were afraid of? A child may be told anything – anything! I was always astonished at how wrong adults were about children, mothers and fathers included. Nothing must be concealed from children under the pretext that they're too small to be told. What an unfortunate and wretched idea! Children are quick to notice that parents look upon them as too immature and lacking in understanding, whereas they understand everything. The grownups don't realize that even when faced with the most difficult problems, a child may make a very important contribution. My God! When a lovely little bird regards you trustingly and good-humouredly, wouldn't it be wicked to deceive it? I call them little birds, because there's nothing more wonderful in the world than a little bird. It was mainly on account of one incident that the villagers turned on me... Thibaut was simply jealous of me. At first he just shook his head and wondered how it was that children would follow everything I said to them and nothing of what he said. Then he ridiculed me when I pointed out to him that rather than us being able to teach them anything, they could teach us. I shall never understand how, being in constant contact with them as he was, he could bring himself to slander me! Children are the balm of life... Schneider had a patient, a most unfortunate creature. His case was so sad that it hardly bears thinking about. He was being treated for madness. To my mind he wasn't mad at all, he merely suffered dreadfully – that's all that was wrong with him. And if only you knew what in the end our children came to mean to him... But I'd better come to this man later. Now I'll tell you how it all started. The children didn't like me at first. I struck them as being so big and always clumsy. I know I'm not handsome... besides, one couldn't get away from the fact that I was a foreigner. At first the children laughed at me and in the end even started throwing stones after they'd seen me kiss Marie. And I only ever kissed her once... No, don't laugh," the Prince intervened hurriedly to check his listeners' suppressed smiles, "there was nothing amorous in it. If only you knew how pathetic she was, you too would have taken pity on her, as I did. She came from the village. Her mother was quite an old woman. One of the two windows in their tiny, run-down house was partitioned óff, and she was allowed, by permission of the village council, to sell pieces of string, cotton, tobacco, bars of soap all for mere pennies, which is how she got by. She was ill and her legs were swollen, obliging her to lead a sedentary life. Marie was her daughter, about twenty, weak and thin. She had been suffering from consumption for a good while already, all the same she went out every day to do heavy housework – scrub floors, launder, sweep courtyards, tend cattle. A passing French travelling salesman seduced her and took her away with him, but a week later abandoned her by the roadside and vanished on the sly. Begging along the way, she came back home, dirty, in rags, her shoes down at heel. She'd been walking a whole week, had slept rough and caught a bad cold. Her legs were covered in sores, her hands swollen and chapped. She had never been particularly good-looking, only her eyes were calm, kind and innocent. She was terribly quiet. Once, before this incident happened, she broke into a song during her work and, I remember, everyone was surprised and began to laugh: 'Marie's singing! Listen! She's started to sing!' This embarrassed her terribly and from then on she never sang again in her life. At the time people were still kind to her, but after she returned, sick and distraught, no one had any pity for her any more. They're very cruel over there! Their attitude is most intolerant in such cases. Her mother was the first to scold and denounce her: 'You've dishonoured me!' And indeed she was the first to expose her daughter to ridicule. When the villagers heard that Marie was back, they all came running to have a look at her, and nearly the whole village ended up in the old woman's hut – old men, children, womenfolk, young girls in an eager crowd. Marie was lying on the floor at the old woman's feet, hungry, dishevelled and in tears. When the villagers entered, she buried her face in her tousled hair and pressed herself hard against the floor. Everybody regarded her with disgust. The old men railed against her and admonished her, the young ones laughed, the women scolded and reproached her, making out she was some kind of despicable creature. Her mother allowed all this to happen, looked on and nodded with approval. She was herself very ill at the time and at death's door. Two months later she did indeed pass away. She knew she was going to die, nevertheless she wouldn't think of reconciliation with her daughter and wouldn't even talk to her, keeping her out of the room and hardly feeding her. Her feet had to be bathed regularly in warm water. Marie saw to it and nursed her every day. The old woman accepted all this without a kind word. Marie endured everything, and I later discovered after I had got to know her that she accepted all this without protest and regarded herself as a very low form of life. When the old woman became totally incapacitated, the other womenfolk in the village started coming in turn to look after her – that's the way they do it there. Marie was then deprived of food altogether, and unlike before, no one in the village would give her any work either. She was almost spat on, and the men, judging by the filth they said to her, had stopped regarding her as a woman. Occasionally, drunks on Sundays would throw coins straight at her feet for fun, and Marie would pick them up in silence. She had then already started to cough up blood. In the end her rags became so threadbare that it was no longer proper to show herself like that in the village. She had been walking barefoot ever since the day of her return. It was at this stage that a crowd of mainly school children – some forty or more – began to tease her and even throw mud at her. She turned to the cowherd, offering to look after his cows, but he chased her away. Then she began to tend the animals without his leave for days on end. The cowherd noticed that this was actually in his interest, and he accepted her and sometimes even gave her leftovers from his lunch, some bread and cheese. However, on her mother's death, the pastor in church felt no compunction in shaming Marie publicly. Marie stood by the coffin just as she was in her rags and wept. A large crowd had gathered to see her cry and walk behind the coffin. Then the pastor – still a young man with an ambition to become a great preacher – turned to everyone and pointed at Marie. 'There is the one who is responsible for the death of this worthy lady.' (A lie, of course, since she had been ill these two years past.) 'She stands before us not daring to look up, because she has had the finger of God upon her. There you see her in rags and barefoot – a lesson to those who lose their virtue! Who is she? She is her daughter!' and so forth all in this vein. And imagine, with most of them this perfidy went down well.

"But then... things took an unexpected turn. The children came to her defence, because by this time they were already on my side and loved Marie. This is how it happened. I wanted to do something for her – she was in great need of money, but I didn't have a penny. I had a small diamond pin and sold it to a dealer, who went from village to village trading in old clothes. He gave me eight francs though it was worth a full forty. It was some time before I managed to catch Marie on her own – at last I chanced to meet her outside the village near a hedge on a small mountain track behind a tree. I gave her the eight francs and told her to look after them because I had no more to give her, and then I kissed her and told her not to think that I had some base motive, and that I kissed her not because I was in love with her, but because I pitied her and thought her not to blame from the start, but merely unfortunate. I wanted to comfort and convince her at the same time that she shouldn't have such a low opinion of herself, but I don't think she understood me. I noticed this immediately, although she hardly said a word and stood, her eyes downcast, deeply embarrassed. When I stopped speaking she kissed my hand, and I at once took her hand and wanted to kiss it, but she withdrew it hurriedly. At that moment a whole crowd of children burst upon us. I later found out that they'd already been spying on me for some time. They began to whistle, clap their hands and laugh, and Marie fled. I wanted to say something, but they threw stones at me. That same day everyone came to know about it, the whole village. Everything again collapsed around Marie's ears. She became an even greater object of dislike. I even heard she was to be tried and punished. Thank God, however, it never came to that. But the children wouldn't let up for a moment after that: they mocked her worse than ever and threw lumps of mud at her. They chased her everywhere – no matter how hard she'd run with her weak chest, fighting for breath, they'd be after her, shouting and abusing her. Once I even took them on in a fight. Then I tried to reason with them, I spoke to them every day, whenever I could. Sometimes they'd stop to listen, but the verbal abuse continued. I spoke to them of Marie's ill fortune, and eventually they stopped and would disperse in silence. Little by little we began to converse. I concealed nothing from them, I told them everything. They listened with great curiosity and soon their pity for her had been reawakened. On meeting her, some would say a friendly hello. It's their custom to bow and say hello to one another irrespective of whether they are acquainted or not. I can imagine what a surprise this was for Marie. On one occasion two girls took some food to her and came back to tell me. They said Marie burst into tears, and that they loved her very much now. Soon everyone loved her, and me along with her. They began to visit me quite often and every time begged me to tell them stories. I believe I was a good storyteller, because they loved listening to me. Subsequently, I studied and read for the sole purpose of being able to recount it all to them afterwards, and in the three years that followed I did just that. When I was subsequently held to account – by, for instance, Schneider – people asked why I spoke with them as with adults, concealing nothing, and I replied that to lie would have been unworthy, that they knew everything anyway no matter how secretive one was with them, and if they tried to discover things by themselves, it might be sordid, whereas coming from me it would not be. One only needed to recall one's own childhood. They were not convinced... I had kissed Marie two weeks before her mother's death. By the time the pastor spoke, all the children were already on my side. I spoke to them immediately and explained what I thought of the pastor's attitude. They were all angry with him for this, and some even went and broke his windows with stones. I stopped them, because that was going too far, but the news soon spread throughout the village, and it was at this stage that they began to accuse me of having corrupted the children. Then the villagers found out that all the children loved Marie, and they took fright. But Marie was happy enough. The children were even forbidden to see her, but they ran to her on the quiet to where the cattle were grazing, which was quite far, about half a verst from the village. They brought her treats, while some came merely to embrace, kiss and tell her, '*Je vous aime, Marie!*' before dashing straight back. Marie nearly lost her reason at such unexpected good fortune. She had not imagined it in her wildest dreams. She was both happy and embarrassed, but the children were most eager, especially the girls, to run to her and say that I loved her and talked to them about her a lot. They told her that I had kept nothing from them, and that now they were sorry for her, loved her dearly and would always continue to do so. Then, they'd come dashing to me to say that they'd just seen Marie, and that she sent me her regards. Of an evening I'd go to the waterfall, a place completely secluded from the villages, surrounded by poplars, and the children would join me there, some by stealth. I believe my love for Marie was a source of great fascination for them, and about this alone, in all my time in the village, I deceived them. I did not attempt to dissuade them from their belief that I loved Marie, that I was in love with her, while in fact I was merely sorry for her. I could see plainly that they wanted it to be as they had imagined it and decided amongst themselves, and I kept quiet and pretended they had guessed correctly. And it's wonderful how discreet and gracious these little souls were. Incidentally, they couldn't quite understand how their kindly Léon could be so fond of Marie who walked about so badly dressed and barefoot. Imagine, they obtained shoes for her, and stockings, and underwear, and even some kind of frock. How they did it, I've no idea. They banded together. When I tried to question them, they merely laughed merrily, and the girls clapped their hands and kissed me. Occasionally I too would go to see Marie on the quiet. She was becoming very ill and could hardly walk. In the end she could no longer help the cowherd much, but she'd still go out with the herd every morning. She'd sit apart. Near a sheer, almost vertical, rock face there was a ledge. She'd settle into one tight corner on a stone and sit there almost motionless all day, from early morning till it was time for herding in the cattle. She was so weak with consumption that she even kept her eyes shut for the most part, dozing, her head against the rock and breathing heavily. Her face was emaciated, like a skeleton, and there were beads of sweat on her brow and temples. That's how I always used to find her. I used to come to visit her briefly, and didn't want to be seen. On seeing me, she'd give a start, open her eyes and start kissing my hands. I didn't withdraw them because for her it was an intense pleasure. All the time I was there, she'd tremble and cry. Sometimes she'd attempt to speak, but it was difficult to make out what she was saying. She was as if demented, in a state of agitation and euphoria. Sometimes children would accompany me. They'd position themselves nearby as though on guard duty against someone or something, and this gave them untold pleasure. When the time came for us to leave, Marie would again resume her solitary motionless pose, eyes shut, her head leaning against the rock wall. Perhaps she was just dreaming. One morning she could no longer go out to the herd and remained in her empty house. The children found this out and one by one they all came to see her that day. She had taken to her bed in the empty house, and for two days running she was looked after by the children alone, but when the news spread in the village that Marie was actually dying, old women from the village began to call on her to watch over and look after her. They had probably relented towards her; in any case the children were now free to go as they pleased, nor were they told off for it as previously. Marie continued in a somnolent state, but was restless in her sleep. Her coughing was getting quite dreadful. The old crones tried to shoo the children away, but they kept running up to the window, however briefly, merely to say, '*Bonjour, notre bonne Marie!*' The moment she heard it, she would immediately, without heeding the women, try to prop herself up in bed on her elbow, and nod her head in recognition and gratitude. They brought her treats as usual, but she hardly ate anything. It was thanks to them, I assure you, that she died a happy death. It was thanks to them that she forgot her dismal fate, as though through them she had been granted absolution, because right up to the very end she regarded herself as a great criminal. Like little birds they fluttered their wings against her window and called out each morning, '*Nous t'aimons, Marie!*' She died very soon. I thought she'd live much longer. On the eve of her death, just before sunset, I called on her. I think she recognized me, and I shook her hand for the last time. How emaciated it was! The next morning I was told she was dead. The children could not be held back. They decorated her entire coffin with flowers and set a garland on her head. The pastor no longer heaped shame upon her in church, and in any case only a few people came to her funeral, and those that did, merely out of curiosity. But when it came to carrying the coffin, the children rushed forward in a crowd. As they couldn't manage it themselves, they merely helped as they followed the coffin and cried. Since then Marie's little grave has been constantly tended by the children. They deck it out with flowers each year and have planted rose bushes around it. But after the funeral the whole village began to persecute me on account of the children. The main leaders were the pastor and the schoolmaster. The children were under strict orders not to have any dealings with me, and Schneider even took it upon himself to see to that. Nevertheless we did communicate, by sign language, at a distance. They used to send me little notes. Eventually things settled down and it was fine: I managed to get even closer to the children because of this victimization. In the final year I nearly made it up completely both with Thibaut and the pastor, whereas Schneider had a lot to say and argued with me about my flawed 'system' with the children. What system, I ask you? In the end Schneider came up with a very curious observation – this was shortly before my departure – he said he was firmly convinced that I myself was a complete child, that I merely had the build and features of an adult, but that as regards my spiritual make-up, my character and perhaps even mental development, I was not an adult and would remain so were I to live to sixty. I laughed outright. He was quite wrong, because how could I be taken for a child? But I must concede one thing, I really don't like mixing with people, adults, grown-ups – I noticed this long ago – I don't like it, because I'm no good at it. No matter what they say to me, how kind they are, I'm never comfortable with them, and I'm terribly glad whenever I can return to my friends, and my friends have always been children, but not because I myself am a child, but simply because I have always been drawn to children. At the very beginning of my stay in the village – the time I used to withdraw alone for solace into the mountains – especially at midday, when wandering on my own, I'd occasionally come across a noisy, unstoppable crowd, running home at the end of the lessons, with their satchels and slates, shouting, laughing, larking about, and my whole heart would suddenly go out to them. I don't know how to put it, but I began to experience some kind of a powerful feeling of happiness every time I met them. I'd stop and laugh with joy at the sight of their bouncing, darting little legs, at the boys and the girls running together, at their laughter and their tears (because many of them would already have managed to have a fight, burst into tears, make up again and continue their games, all before they reached home), and I'd then forget all my sorrows. Later, for the next three years, I could never understand why people should ever feel sad. My whole life there was centred round the children. It never occurred to me that I should have to leave the village, it never entered my mind that one day I should return to Russia. I always expected to stay there, but finally I saw that, after all, Schneider could not keep on supporting me. And then this rather important matter cropped up which made Schneider himself urge me to leave and take on responsibility for me here. I'll have to look into it and seek advice. Perhaps my lot will improve, but all that is by the by and of no importance. The main thing is that my life has already suffered a great change. I have left much behind, too much. It's all over now.

"I sat in the railway carriage and thought, 'Now I'm on my way to meet some people. I may perhaps know nothing at all, but a new life has begun.' I have promised myself to play my part fairly and resolutely. I may find it wearisome and difficult to deal with people. I've resolved to begin by being polite and open with everyone – surely no one can expect anything more of me. Perhaps here too people will take me for a child – let them! For some reason everyone also takes me for an idiot. Of course, there was a time when I was so ill that I could really be taken for an idiot. But what kind of idiot am I now if I'm aware that I'm being taken for an idiot? When I enter a room, I say to myself, 'They take me for an idiot, but nevertheless I'm *compos mentis*, and they don't realize it...' I often think this. When I stopped in Berlin and received some letters from the children who had already managed to write to me, I suddenly understood how much I really loved them. It was very difficult opening that first letter! How they grieved to see me go! A month before they had started repeating, '*Léon s'en va, Léon s'en va pour toujours!*' We used to gather every evening at the waterfall and talk about how we were going to part. Sometimes it was as much fun as before. Only when we dispersed for the night, they would hug me warmly and closely, which had never happened before. Some would pop in to see me on the quiet, individually, merely in order to embrace me and kiss me in private, not in front of the others. When that time came for me to set off, everybody, but everybody, came to the station. The railway station was about a verst from the village. They tried to hold back their tears, but many could not help themselves and wept out loud, especially the girls. We hurried so as not to be late, but someone or other would invariably rush out of the crowd, fall round my neck in the middle of the road, twine his little arms around me and kiss me, holding up the whole procession. And though time was short, everybody would stop and wait till the leave-taking was over. After I got into the carriage and the train began to move, they all called out 'Hurrah!' and stood there until the carriage was out of sight. And I too stared back... You know, when I first entered this room and looked at your kind faces – I now make a point of looking closely into people's faces – and heard your voices, it was my very first moment of joy since those days. In fact it occurred to me that perhaps I really am lucky – I know only too well one doesn't often come across people that one takes to immediately, but I met you almost as soon as I had left the carriage. I know very well that it's embarrassing to talk about one's feelings, but here I am talking about them, and I'm not embarrassed. I am an unsocial person, and shall probably not visit you again for a long time. I beg you not to misinterpret this. I said it not because I don't value you, and please don't imagine I've been offended in any way. You asked me about your faces, and what I can say about them. I'll be only too glad to do so. You, Adelaida Ivanovna, have a cheerful face, the most genial of the three. You are not only very attractive, but anyone looking at you is bound to say, 'She has the face of a kind sister.' You deal with people as they come – plainly and directly, but you can soon take accurate soundings of their hearts too. That's my opinion, anyway, for what it's worth. Your face too, Alexandra Ivanovna, is wonderful and very sweet, but perhaps you have a secret sorrow. At heart you are without a shadow of doubt exceptionally kind, but you are not brimming with joy. There's a touch of Holbein's Dresden Madonna* in you. Well now, there you have it. What do you make of my powers of divination? You yourselves endowed me with them. As for your face, Lizaveta Prokofyevna," he suddenly turned to the General's Lady, "as regards your face, I don't just think, I'm simply certain that despite your age, for better or for worse, you're a complete child through and through. I hope you don't mind my saying that? You know how highly I think of children, don't you? And, please, don't imagine that it was just foolish talk on my part about your faces. No, not at all! I could well have my own reason for it."

7

AFTER THE PRINCE HAD STOPPED, everyone regarded him with merriment, even Aglaya, but most of all Lizaveta Prokofyevna.

"So we've been subjected to an examination, have we?" she exclaimed. "No doubt, my dear ladies, you thought you'd take the poor dear under your wing, whereas he has turned the tables on you, letting it be known, what's more in advance, that we shouldn't expect him here too often. He's made a fool of the lot of us, of Ivan Fyodorovich especially, and I'm jolly glad of it. Well done, Prince: you realize, of course, it was you who were to be examined. As for what you said about my face, you're perfectly right – I am a child, and I know it. I knew it well before you ever came along, but you took the words out of my mouth. I think our characters are a perfect match, and it pleases me no end. The only difference is you're a man and I'm a woman, and have not been to Switzerland, otherwise we're the same."

"I wouldn't be too sure," Aglaya exclaimed, "the Prince said that he had an ulterior motive and it wasn't just idle talk."

"That's right, that's right," the others joined in.

"Don't delude yourselves, my dears, he may turn out smarter than the rest of us put together. You'll see. But why is it you never said a word about Aglaya, Prince? Aglaya wants to know, and so do I."

"I can't say anything now. Later."

"Why? Don't you find her remarkable?"

"Oh, indeed, I do. You are remarkably beautiful, Aglaya Ivanovna. You are so lovely, your beauty inspires fear."

"Is that all? What about her personality?" the General's Lady persisted.

"Beauty is very difficult to judge. I'm not ready for it yet. Beauty is a mystery."

"This would indicate that you have set Aglaya a riddle," Adelaida said. "Go ahead and solve it, Aglaya. But isn't she a picture, Prince, what do you say?"

"Indeed!" the Prince responded ardently, with an admiring sideglance at Aglaya. "Almost as good as Nastasya Filippovna, although there's a world of difference!..."

They all looked at one another.

"Like who-o-o?" the General's Lady intoned. "What do you mean Nastasya Filippovna? Where have you seen Nastasya Filippovna? What Nastasya Filippovna?"

"Gavrila Ardalionych was showing her portrait to Ivan Fyodorovich just now."

"What, he brought her portrait to Ivan Fyodorovich?"

"For him to have a look. Nastasya Filippovna gave Gavrila Ardalionych her portrait as a keepsake today and he brought it along."

"I want to see it!" the General's Lady flared up. "Where is this portrait? If she gave it to him, he must still have it, and he of course must still be in the study. He always comes to work on Wednesdays and never leaves before four. Call Gavrila Ardalionych at once! No, no need, I've no particular desire to see him. Be so good, Prince, dear: go to the study, ask him for the portrait and fetch it here. Tell him we want to have a look at it, I beg you."

"He's not at all bad, but rather odd," Adelaida remarked after the Prince had left the room.

"Yes, too much so," Alexandra agreed, "even verging on the ridiculous." Both appeared to leave something unsaid.

"I must say, that thing about our faces was pretty smart, no flies on him," Aglaya said. "He buttered us all up, including you, *Maman*."

"Don't be facetious, please!" the General's Lady exclaimed. "It was no flattery on his part, but I'm flattered."

"Do you think he was trying to be clever?" Adelaida asked.

"He's not as naive as he looks."

"There you go!" the General's Lady said in a temper. "If you ask me, you lot are even more ridiculous than he is. He may be naive, but he's no fool, not to put too fine a point on it. And nor am I."

Making his way to the study, the Prince reflected ruefully that by rights he shouldn't have mentioned the portrait. "But... perhaps, it was just as well that I did..." A strange idea was beginning to haunt him, but it was much too vague.

Gavrila Ardalionych was still sitting in the study, immersed in his documents. It really looked as if he was earning his salary with the company. He became very flustered when the Prince asked for the portrait and recounted how they had found out about it.

"Damn! Why couldn't you have kept your mouth shut!" he exclaimed angrily. "You know nothing... Idiot!" he muttered under his breath.

"It's my fault, I just didn't think. It cropped up in the course of the conversation. I said that Aglaya was almost as beautiful as Nastasya Filippovna."

Ganya asked to hear more. The Prince obliged. Ganya cast him another derisive glance.

"The man's obsessed with her—" he muttered and stopped in mid-flow to think. He was visibly agitated. The Prince reminded him about the portrait.

"Listen, Prince," Ganya said suddenly as though struck by an unexpected thought, "I've an enormous favour to ask... But I really don't know..."

He hesitated awkwardly; he appeared to be in a quandary and struggling with himself. The Prince waited in silence. Ganya once more measured him with an inquisitive, searching look.

"Prince," he began again, "in view of a totally bizarre turn of events... comical too... and one for which I'm not responsible... well, but that's by the by – I am, so it seems to me, being blamed by the ladies, with the result that for some time past now I've not been inclined to show myself in their presence uninvited. Right now I desperately need to see Aglaya Ivanovna. I've jotted down a few words just in case," (a small folded piece of paper suddenly appeared in his hands) "and I don't know how the deuce to pass it to her. You wouldn't, Prince, by any chance agree to hand it to her, but only to Aglaya Ivanovna personally – that is to say, so that no one else would see it – if you know what I mean? God knows there's no great secret in this, nor anything that... but... would you?"

"I'd rather not," the Prince replied.

"Oh, Prince," Ganya implored, "it's a dire necessity. Perhaps she'll reply... Believe me, I'd never have turned to you except in the direst of need... Who else can I entrust it to?... It's so important... I can't tell you how important it is for me..."

Ganya was overtaken with dread in case the Prince refused him, and tried to catch his eye with obsequious timidity.

"All right, I'll give it to her."

"But only so that nobody sees it," Ganya pleaded, overjoyed, "and – there's another thing, Prince – I can, can't I, rely on your word of honour?"

"I'm not going to show it to anyone if that's what you mean," the Prince said.

"The note is not sealed, but..." Ganya in his agitation let slip an obvious indiscretion, and broke off, embarrassed.

"Oh, I'm not going to read it," the Prince said curtly, took the portrait and left.

Ganya, left on his own, buried his head in his hands.

"One word from her, and I... and I, really, may well break it all off!..."

In his state of anxiety and expectation he could no longer settle back at his desk and began to pace up and down the room.

The Prince walked back, lost in thought; the errand rankled with him and so did the fact of Ganya writing to Aglaya Ivanovna. But two doors away from the drawing room he suddenly stopped as though recollecting something, glanced around, went up to a window nearer the light, and began to look at Nastasya Filippovna's portrait.

He strained to perceive the hidden trait in it which had so astonished him on first viewing. The memory of it had stayed with him, and he was eager to check his first impression. The remarkable beauty of this face, and something else besides, created an even greater impact upon him this time round. Unbounded pride and disdain, verging on hatred, were etched in this face, and yet at the same time there was also something confiding and surprisingly spontaneous there; these contrasts seemed to evoke in the onlooker something akin to compassion. The blinding beauty was almost unbearable, the beauty of a pale face, almost sunken cheeks and flaming eyes; an extraordinary beauty! The Prince viewed it for about a minute, then gave a start, brought the portrait hurriedly to his lips and kissed it. By the time he entered the room, his face was perfectly calm and composed.

But he had hardly stepped into the dining room (leading to the drawing room), when he bumped into Aglaya Ivanovna as she was coming out. She was on her own.

"Gavrila Ardalionych asked me to give you this," the Prince said, handing her the note.

Aglaya stopped, took the note and measured the Prince with an odd look. There was not a shadow of embarrassment in her eyes, only perhaps a hint of surprise, which was provoked more by the Prince himself than anything else. Aglaya's look appeared to demand an explanation from him – however did he become involved in this matter with Ganya? Her demeanour was cool and haughty. They stood facing each other for a few seconds; finally a faint look of derision flitted across her features; she gave a little smile and brushed past him.

For a little time without uttering a word the General's Lady studied Nastasya Filippovna's portrait with some scorn, holding it most demonstratively at arm's length from her eyes.

"Yes, not bad," she said at last, "not bad at all. I have seen her twice, but only from a distance. Is this your kind of beauty?" she suddenly addressed the Prince.

83

"Yes... this kind..." the Prince replied under some strain.

"That is to say, precisely this kind?"

"Precisely this kind."

"May I know why?"

"In this face... there's a lot of anguish..." the Prince said abstractedly as though talking to himself rather than in reply to the question.

"Perhaps you're just raving, my dear sir?" the General's Lady concluded and threw the portrait contemptuously aside on the table.

Alexandra picked it up, Adelaida approached her; they both stared at it. At that moment Aglaya came back into the room.

"It's overpowering!" Adelaida exclaimed suddenly, devouring the portrait with her eyes over her sister's shoulder.

"What did you say?" Lizaveta Prokofyevna enquired sharply. "What is overpowering?"

"Such beauty is – overpowering," Adelaida said fervently. "Such beauty can turn the world upside down!" And she walked back to her easel, lost in thought.

Aglaya gave the portrait merely a fleeting glance, frowned, puckered her lower lip and sat down at a distance, her arms folded.

The General's Lady rang the bell.

"Call Gavrila Ardalionych!" she said to the servant who answered her summons. "He is in the study."

"*Maman*!" Alexandra exclaimed emphatically.

"I want to say a couple of words to him – and that's that!" the General's Lady snapped back, brooking no opposition. She was clearly annoyed. "You see, Prince, nothing is ever out in the open in this house any more. Secrets are all the rage now! It's what's expected these days, it's the latest fad! How silly! And this in a matter which calls for the utmost frankness, clarity and honesty. Marriage contracts are in the air, and I don't like them one little bit..."

"*Maman*, what do you mean?" Alexandra again hastened to intervene.

"What is it now, my dear daughter? Are you telling me you like them? And if the Prince hears of it, so what, we're friends. I am at any rate his friend. God seeks good people, he has no use for evil and greedy ones – especially capricious ones, who decide one thing today, and say the reverse tomorrow. Do you follow me, Alexandra Ivanovna? They tell me, Prince, I'm an eccentric, but I wasn't born yesterday. The heart's

the thing, the rest is junk. You have to have brains too, of course...
perhaps, brains come before everything. No need to smile, Aglaya, I
know what I'm talking about. A fool with a good heart and no brains
is no better than a fool with brains and no heart. It's been tried and
tested. I'm a fool with a good heart and no brains, and you're a fool
with brains and no heart. That's why we're both unhappy and have to
grin and bear it."

"What exactly is it that makes you so unhappy, *Maman*?" Adelaida
said pointedly, the only one of the company who so far had managed
to retain her good temper.

"First and foremost, you, my learned daughters," the General's Lady
snapped back, "and as that in itself is quite enough, there's no need
to labour the point. Too much flapdoodle all round. I'd like to see
how you two (I'm leaving Aglaya out of it) will come out of it with all
your verbiage, and whether you, my worthy Alexandra Ivanovna, will
find happiness with your much respected gentleman?... A-ha!..." she
exclaimed, as Ganya appeared in the doorway. "Here comes another
marriage broker. How do you do!" she replied in response to Ganya's
cordial bow, but without inviting him to take a seat. "You are getting
married, are you not?"

"Married?... What?... To whom?..." the flustered Gavrila Ardalionych mumbled. He was absolutely flabbergasted.

"Are you entering into matrimony, I'm asking you, if that turn of
phrase is preferable to you?"

"N-no... I... n-no," Gavrila Ardalionych prevaricated, blushing with
shame. He cast a fleeting glance at Aglaya, sitting nearby, and averted
his eyes forthwith. Aglaya kept his cringing figure firmly in view, coldly
and calmly.

"No? You said 'no'?" the implacable Lizaveta Prokofyevna went on.
"Very well. I shall remember that this day, Wednesday morning, in
reply to my question, you said 'no'! It is Wednesday today, is it not?"

"I believe it is, *Maman*," Adelaida replied.

"No one ever knows what day it is. And the date?"

"Twenty-seventh," Ganya replied.

"Twenty-seventh? That's good to know. Well, goodbye, I believe you
are snowed under with work, whereas I have to get ready and leave. Do
take your portrait with you. Give my regards to the unfortunate Nina
Alexandrovna. Au revoir, my dear Prince! Don't forget to look in before

long, and I'll make sure to call on old Belokonskaya to tell her about you. And listen, my angel, I really believe it was God who brought you to St Petersburg from Switzerland specially for me. You may well have other business here, but principally you came for my sake. That's precisely how God sought to arrange it. Au revoir, my dear. Alexandra, be a darling, come and see me later."

Ganya, nonplussed, pained and annoyed, took the portrait from the table and addressed the Prince with a wry smile. "Prince, I'm going home now. If you haven't changed your mind to stay with us, I will take you there. You don't even know the address."

"Wait, Prince," Aglaya said, getting up abruptly, "you must write for me in my album. Father said you're a calligrapher. I'll fetch it directly..." And she left.

"Goodbye, Prince, I'm going too," Adelaida said.

She shook the Prince's hand warmly, gave him a sweet, cheerful smile, and also left.

"It was you!" Ganya gave vent to his anger, turning on the Prince as soon as the others had gone out: "It was you who couldn't keep your mouth shut about my getting married!" he muttered under his breath, his features distorted with rage and his eyes flashing venomously. "You pathetic, miserable little chatterbox."

"I assure you, you're mistaken," the Prince replied calmly and cordially.

"You overheard Ivan Fyodorovich say that everything will be settled at Nastasya Filippovna's tonight, and you passed it on! You're lying! They had no other way of knowing it! There's no one else in hell who could have told them, except you! Didn't the old girl imply as much?"

"You know best who told them or what was implied, I didn't breathe a word of it."

"Did you pass on my note? Answer me!" Ganya, bursting with impatience, interrupted him. But at that very moment Aglaya came back, and the Prince had no time to reply.

"Here you are, Prince," Aglaya said, placing the album on a little side table, "choose a page and write me something. Here's a pen, it's quite new. Do you mind if it's a steel one? I heard calligraphers won't use steel ones."

Talking to the Prince, she appeared not to notice Ganya's presence. But while the Prince was adjusting the pen, looking for a suitable page and getting ready, Ganya went to the fireplace, where Aglaya stood close to the Prince on his right, and in a quavering, hesitant voice said, speaking almost into her ear:

"A word, a single word from you – and I'll be saved."

The Prince turned abruptly and looked at them both. Ganya's face portrayed genuine despair; it would appear he had pronounced these words without thinking, recklessly. Aglaya regarded him a few seconds with the same unruffled wonderment as she had previously regarded the Prince, and for a moment it seemed that this wonderment, this incomprehension, was harder for Ganya to take than the most devastating contempt.

"So what should I write?" the Prince asked.

"I'll dictate to you," Aglaya said, facing him. "Are you ready? Please write, 'I don't go in for bargaining.' Now enter the day and the month. Let me see."

The Prince passed her the album.

"Splendid! You have done an excellent job! You have a marvellous hand! Thank you. Au revoir, Prince... On second thoughts," she added as though recollecting something, "come with me, I want to give you a keepsake."

The Prince followed her, but in the dining room, Aglaya stopped.

"Read this," she said, handing him Ganya's note.

The Prince took the note and looked at Aglaya in puzzlement.

"Look, I know you have not read it and cannot be the confidant of that man. Go on, I want you to read it."

The note appeared to have been written in haste:

My fate will be decided today, I'm sure you know in what way. Today I shall be obliged to give my word irrevocably. I've no right to your sympathy and dare not entertain any hopes; but you spoke a word once, one word only, and this word illuminated the awful darkness of my life, and has turned into a beacon for me. Say another such word now – and you will save me from calamity! Tell me, 'Break everything off,' and I shall, this very day. Oh, how little it should cost you to say that! For me these words would only be a token of sympathy and pity for me – only, only! And nothing more, nothing! I shall not delude myself with any kind of hope, because I'm not worthy of it. But your words would enable me again to reconcile myself to my poverty, and resign myself to my desperate situation joyfully. I shall accept the challenge, I shall glory in it, I shall emerge from it with my strength restored!

Send me a message of compassion (only of compassion, I beg you!). Do not be offended by the insolence of the despairing, of one in desperate straits, simply because he has had the audacity to make one last bid to save himself from ruination.

– G.I.

"This man insists," Aglaya said sharply, after the Prince had finished reading, "that the words 'Break everything off' would not compromise or bind me in the least, and gives me, as you can see, a written guarantee thereof by way of this very note. Note how naively he has stressed certain words here and there, and how crudely obvious is his ulterior motivation. Incidentally, he knows that were he to call everything off, of his own volition, without waiting for my reply and without even telling me about it, without any expectations, my feelings towards him would have changed, and I might perhaps have become his friend. He knows this perfectly well! But he is petty – he knows it, and yet he dare not. He knows, and he still wants a guarantee. He is incapable of relying on trust. He wants, rather than a hundred thousand roubles, to be assured regarding my feelings. As for the word to which he refers at the beginning of the note as having apparently illuminated his life, he's simply lying. I merely felt sorry for him once. But he's arrogant and brazen with it. In a flash he saw a chance for himself. I noticed it at once. Ever since he has been trying to ensnare me. He's doing so now. But enough! Take this note and give it back to him, immediately you leave the house, it stands to reason, not before."

"And what should I tell him in reply?"

"Nothing, of course, that goes without saying. That's the best reply of all. I take it you are planning to lodge with him, are you not?"

"On Ivan Fyodorovich's own recommendation," the Prince said.

"Be careful, I warn you. He will not forgive you, now that you're returning the note to him."

Aglaya shook the Prince's hand lightly, and left. Her face was serious and overcast; she did not even smile as she gave a quick nod in parting.

"I'll just pick up my bundle," the Prince said to Ganya, "and we'll go."

Ganya stamped his foot with impatience. His face was livid with rage. At last they walked out on to the street, the Prince carrying his bundle.

"And the reply? Where's the reply?" Ganya challenged him. "What did she say to you? Did you give her the letter?"

Without a word the Prince handed him his note back. Ganya was dumbfounded.

"What? My note!" he exclaimed. "The man didn't even give it to her! Oh, I should have known! D-damn you... Now I can see why she was so noncommittal! So how is it you didn't give it to her, oh, dammit..."

"I beg your pardon, quite the reverse, I managed to give her your note almost immediately after you gave it to me, and precisely as you instructed me to. It was back in my possession, because Aglaya Ivanovna gave it back to me just now."

"When? When did she give it back to you?"

"As soon as I had finished writing in her album and when she asked me to follow her. Surely you heard! We went into the dining room, she gave me the note, told me to read it and to give it back to you."

"To re-ea-d it?" Ganya yelled out almost at the top of his voice. "To read it! And did you?"

And he again stopped thunderstruck in the middle of the pavement, open-mouthed.

"Yes, just now."

"And it was she, she herself who gave it to you to read? Was it?"

"It was, and believe me I wouldn't have read it without her invitation."

For about a minute Ganya hesitated, desperately struggling to make sense of something, but he suddenly exclaimed, "That's impossible! She couldn't have asked you to read it! You're lying! You read it yourself!"

"I'm telling you the truth," the Prince replied in the same even-tempered tone, "and believe me, it pains me that this is having such an adverse effect upon you."

"But, you wretched man, did she at least say something to you? She must have said something!"

"Yes, of course."

"Speak, I tell you, speak, oh, hell!..."

And Ganya stamped the pavement a couple of times with his galosh-clad right foot.

"As soon as I read it, she told me you were trying to entrap her. That you'd have liked to compromise her so that, armed with renewed prospects, you could with impunity turn your back on the other chance of collecting a cool hundred thousand roubles. That had you done it without striking any bargains with her, had you broken everything off of your own accord, not seeking any guarantees from her, she would perhaps have become your friend. That's all, to be sure. Oh yes, when I asked after I'd already got the note back, what was her reply, she answered that no reply was the best reply of all – if my memory serves me right. Excuse me if I can't recall her exact words. I merely repeat what I understood her to say."

Ganya was overcome with rage and it burst forth uncontrollably.

"Aha! So that's it!" he fulminated. "My messages are to be discarded unceremoniously! Really! She won't bargain – well, I will! And we'll see! I'm not finished yet… we'll see!… I'll make her fall into line!…"

He fumed, grew pale, foamed at the mouth; he waved his fist about. Thus they walked on for a few paces. He paid no regard whatsoever to the Prince as though he were all alone, and his companion a mere cipher. But suddenly something must have dawned on him, and he stopped short.

"But how," he turned to the Prince all of a sudden, "how could you – an idiot," he added under his breath, "suddenly be drawn into such a confidence a bare two hours after your first meeting? How?"

Of all the emotions, jealousy was the only one that had as yet not assailed him. It now stung him to the quick.

"That's something I can't explain to you," the Prince replied.

Ganya looked at him furiously. "So she called you into the dining room to confide in you? Wasn't there something she meant to give you?"

"That's precisely what I thought."

"But what the blazes for? How did you manage to win them over? What's so special about you? Look here," he rattled on desperately. Everything about him at that moment was at sixes and sevens, in a disordered mess; he vainly tried to gather his thoughts. "Look here, you couldn't by any chance, could you, somehow try to recall and tell me verbatim what it was precisely you were talking about there, right from the very beginning? Think back, what was it you said?"

"Nothing could be easier," the Prince replied, "when I first entered and after I'd introduced myself, we talked about Switzerland."

"To hell with Switzerland!"

"Then about the death penalty..."

"The death penalty?"

"Yes, I was making a point... after that I told them about the three years I spent there, and the life story of an unfortunate villager..."

"Damn the unfortunate villager! What else?" Ganya ranted furiously.

"I mentioned Schneider's views of my character and that he persuaded me—"

"Schneider can go to blazes, a pox on him and his views! What else?"

"Let me see, then in the course of the conversation I started talking about faces, or should I say, facial expressions, and I made the point that Aglaya Ivanovna was nearly as beautiful as Nastasya Filippovna. That's where I inadvertently mentioned the portrait..."

"But did you not repeat, I hope you didn't repeat what you heard back in the study! Did you, or did you not?"

"I told you before, I did not."

"So, how in hell?... Wait! Perhaps Aglaya showed the note to the old girl?!"

"Rest assured, no. I was there all that time, and she didn't have the opportunity."

"Perhaps you missed something... Oh!" he exclaimed in the throes of despair. "You damned idiot! You can't even recall what happened!"

Ganya, not encountering any opposition, got carried away completely. A little more, and he would have started tearing his hair out. But it was precisely his fury which blinded him; otherwise he'd long have noticed that this "idiot", whom he so berated, was really remarkably quick on the uptake, skilful and discerning in his narration. But then something unexpected occurred.

"Let me tell you, Gavrila Ardalionych," the Prince said suddenly, "formerly I was so ill that I could really have been taken for an idiot. But now I'm fully recovered, and therefore I find it rather unpleasant to be called an idiot to my face. Although I could excuse you, in view of your mishaps, but in your distress you made a couple of sallies against me. I resent it very much, especially the cavalier way in which you did it, and since we're now at a crossroads, wouldn't it be better if we went our separate ways – you to the right, I to the left. I have twenty-five roubles on me and I should be able to find a room."

Ganya was dumbstruck and he blushed with shame.

"I'm terribly sorry, Prince," he exclaimed impetuously, passing from aggressive to highly affable, "for goodness' sake, I beg your pardon! You can see what a mess I'm in! You still hardly know a thing, but if you knew everything, you'd certainly have made some allowances for me. Though, I don't deserve it, of course…"

"Oh, no need to take it so seriously," the Prince hastened to assure him. "I can see how upset you are and that's why you are so intemperate. Think nothing of it, and let's go to your place. I'm perfectly happy…"

"No, I can't leave it like this," Ganya thought to himself as he darted angry glances at the Prince, walking beside him. "The cunning fox has managed to wheedle everything out of me, and then dropped his mask… There's more to it. We'll soon see! Everything will come out into the open, everything, everything! This very day!"

They had reached the house.

8

GANYA'S ROOMS, six or seven in all, were on the second floor, up a rather neat, spacious and bright flight of stairs; they were mostly on the small side and, it has to be owned, very plain, but all the same pretty much beyond the means of an office clerk with family responsibilities even if he was in receipt of two thousand roubles annually. The fact is, these premises, which the Ivolgins had moved into barely two months previously, could be maintained only by taking lodgers on full board, a plan advocated and argued for by Ganya's mother Nina Alexandrovna and sister Varvara Ardalionovna, who wished to prove their worth by contributing to the household income. Ganya hemmed and hawed, and found the idea of having lodgers utterly objectionable; he felt it compromised him in society where he liked to cut a certain dash as a young man with brilliant prospects. All these deals and concessions with fate, this need to scrimp and save – were running spiritual sores for him. For some considerable time past he had shown a disproportionate and unreasonable tendency to fly off the handle at the slightest trifle, and even if he occasionally agreed on a strictly temporary basis to concede or capitulate, it was only because he had already firmly made up his mind to turn over a new leaf and introduce all-round changes in his life with the least possible delay. But at the same time these changes, this very remedy on which he had staked everything, was itself fraught with not inconsiderable problems – problems the solution to which threatened to be even more burdensome and disagreeable than anything he had experienced before.

The whole place was divided by a passageway leading directly from the entrance hall. To one side were the quarters assigned to respectable lodgers with letters of recommendation; in addition, on the same side of the passageway at its far end, adjoining the kitchen, was the fourth room, rather more cramped than the rest, occupied by the head of the household, ex-General Ivolgin himself. He slept on a broad settee, and was expected to enter and leave the apartment only via the kitchen and the tradesmen's stairs. In this same room also lived Gavrila Ardalionych's thirteen-year-old younger brother, Kolya, a high-school student. There he did his homework and slept on a very old, narrow, foreshortened little couch, a torn sheet spread under him, discharging his main duty of looking after and waiting upon his father, who was more and more dependent on outside help. The Prince was allocated the middle room of the three. The first on the right was occupied by Ferdyshchenko, and the third on the left was still vacant. But Ganya first took the Prince into the family quarters. These consisted of a hall, doubling up when necessary as a dining room or a sitting room, which, to be sure, was a sitting room only in the mornings, but later in the day turned into Ganya's study and bedroom; and finally, a third room, cramped and always locked shut; this was Nina Alexandrovna's and Varvara Ardalionovna's bedroom. In a word, space was at a premium here; but all Ganya could do was to rage impotently. Even though he was, and made every effort to be civil to his mother, it was apparent at first glance that he was a proper family despot.

Nina Alexandrovna was not alone in the dining room, but was with Varvara Ardalionovna; they both appeared to be knitting something and conversing with a visitor, Ivan Petrovich Ptitsyn. Nina Alexandrovna seemed about fifty, with a thin, drooping face and prominent dark rings under her eyes. She had a somewhat woebegone and sickly air about her, but her face and eyes were pleasant enough; on first encounter she immediately exuded a commendable seriousness and genuine dignity of character. Despite her careworn appearance, there was something steadfast and even resolute about her. She was dressed very demurely, in dark colours, more befitting a much older person; but her behaviour, manners and speech spoke of a lady who had been accustomed to move in the very best circles.

Varvara Ardalionovna was a girl of about twenty-three, of average height, a rather bony build and a face which, though lacking great beauty, had that mysterious quality of being nonetheless irresistibly comely and attractive. She was very much like her mother, even in dress habits, rejecting all attempts at flattery. The look in her grey eyes could at times be scintillatingly merry and kindly, but tended to be more often than not sombre and pensive – too much so, especially lately. Her face also exuded steadfastness and resoluteness, much like her mother's, at times to an even greater degree. Varvara Ardalionovna was rather quick tempered and her brother had reason to be wary of her. And so had their present visitor Ivan Petrovich Ptitsyn. He was a soberly dressed gentleman of about thirty, with pleasant but on occasion rather overly refined manners. A reddish-brown goatee spoke of him as a man not in government employ.* His conversation was absorbing and sensible, but he preferred to keep his silence. He was not impartial towards Varvara Ardalionovna, and did not hide his feelings. Varvara Ardalionovna was friendly enough with him, but when it came to certain of his questions, she demurred, and as a matter of fact, resented them; Ptitsyn, however, took it all in good part. Varvara Ardalionovna was not unkind to him, and had lately begun to take him into her confidence. It was common knowledge that he sought to make money by investing for quick profit in more or less safe financial schemes. With Ganya he was on especially good terms.

Responding to Ganya's substantial but disjointed introduction, in the course of which he greeted his mother curtly, failed to acknowledge his sister altogether and immediately led Ptitsyn out of the room, Nina Alexandrovna addressed a few friendly words to the Prince and bade Kolya, who had just happened to peer round the door, to take him to the middle room. Kolya was a boy with a cheerful and rather pleasant countenance, and graced with an open and trusting manner.

"Where is your baggage?" he asked, conducting the Prince into the room.

"I've a little bundle. It's in the hall."

"I'll bring it in. We've only Cook and Matryona, that's all the servants we have, so I help out as well. Varya keeps an eye on everything, and she's never satisfied. Ganya says you're just back from Switzerland, is that so?"

"Yes."

"Is it nice there?"

"Very."

"Mountains?"

"Yes."

"I'll go and fetch your bundle now."

Varvara Ardalionovna entered.

"Matryona will make up your bed in a minute. Have you a suitcase?"

"No, just a little bundle. Your brother's gone for it. It's in the hall."

"There's no bundle there, except this thing. Where did you put it?" Kolya asked as he came back in.

"Yes, that's all there is," the Prince responded, taking hold of the bundle.

"Oh, good! I thought Ferdyshchenko might have helped himself to it."

"Don't talk nonsense," Varya admonished him; even with the Prince she maintained a clipped, barely polite, tone of voice.

"*Chère Babette*,* I'm not your Ptitsyn, you could be less grumpy with me."

"I could give you a good hiding, that's what I could, you silly little boy. If you need anything, ask Matryona. Dinner is at half-past four. You can eat with us, or in your room, as you like. Come along, Kolya, you mustn't disturb the gentleman."

"Aye, aye, milady!"

In the doorway they bumped into Ganya.

"Is father at home?" Ganya asked Kolya and, on receiving an affirmative response, whispered something in his ear.

Kolya nodded and followed Varvara Ardalionovna out of the room.

"One thing, Prince, I quite forgot to tell you, what with all these… goings-on. A favour of sorts, I'd be most grateful – only if this wouldn't prove too taxing – please, don't blether about what happened between me and Aglaya, and equally, not a word *there* about anything you're sure to discover here, which you will, you will. Hang it all... Try to control yourself at least for the day."

"I assure you I blethered far less than you imagine," the Prince said with some irritation in response to Ganya's remonstrances. Their relationship was going from bad to worse.

"I've just about had enough from you today. Please do as I ask you."

"You might also reflect, Gavrila Ardalionych, what obligation was I under, and why shouldn't I have mentioned the portrait? After all, you didn't ask me not to, did you?"

"This room is just awful," Ganya observed, looking about with displeasure, "it's dark and the windows look out onto the backyard. In every respect your presence here is most untimely... Well, on second thoughts, it's not my business. It's not me that runs this place."

Ptitsyn popped his head round the door and beckoned Ganya. The latter turned his back on the Prince and left hurriedly despite the fact that there was clearly something else he wanted to say, but was too embarrassed to begin. Besides, he had disparaged the room, possibly inadvertently, and was feeling bad about it.

No sooner had the Prince washed his face and spruced himself up than the door opened and a new figure made its appearance.

He was a man of about thirty, rather tall, broad-shouldered and with a massive mop of curly, reddish hair. He had a fleshy, ruddy face, thick lips, a large flat nose and narrow, deep-set, mocking eyes that appeared to wink ceaselessly. There was something distinctly arrogant about his attitude. His personal attire was not of the cleanest.

At first he opened the door only enough to poke his head in. This part of him spent a good five seconds taking in the room; then the door began to open further, slowly revealing the rest of his figure on the threshold, but the visitor still stayed out of the room, continuing to survey the Prince obliquely. Finally, he shut the door, approached, sat down on a chair, took the Prince firmly by the hand and made him sit down on a settee, diagonally opposite.

"Ferdyshchenko," he said with a hard, questioning look directed at the Prince.

"Yes, and?" the Prince replied, almost laughing.

"Lodger," Ferdyshchenko said, looking as before.

"You'd like to introduce yourself, would you?"

"What's the use!" the visitor sighed, ruffling his hair and fixing his eyes on a distant corner of the room. "Have you got any money?" he asked suddenly.

"A little."

"How little?"

"Twenty-five roubles."

"Let's have a look."

The Prince produced the twenty-five-rouble note and held it out to Ferdyshchenko. He unfolded it, inspected it, then turned it over and brought it up to the light.

"It's a curious thing," he said, as though lost in thought, "why should they turn brown? Sometimes these twenty-five-rouble notes tend to go awfully brown, while others, just the opposite, tend to fade. Take it."

The Prince took the note. Ferdyshchenko got up.

"I came to warn you. First, never lend me money, because you can bet your bottom penny I shall ask you to."

"All right."

"Do you intend to pay rent here?"

"I do."

"But I don't. Thank you. My door's the first on the right, have you seen it? Try not to call on me too often. But I will keep dropping in, don't worry. Have you seen the General?"

"No."

"Have you heard him?"

"Of course, not."

"Well, you will. You see, he asks even me to lend him money! *Avis au lecteur.** Goodbye. What a name to have, Ferdyshchenko! How can one put up with it?"

"Why not?"

"Goodbye."

And he moved towards the door. The Prince learnt subsequently that this gentleman was a self-appointed joker, but that his jokes invariably misfired. He made a bad impression on some people, and this genuinely bothered him, but nevertheless he did not desist. In the doorway he managed to pull himself together a little as he bumped into another gentleman on the way in; stepping aside for this new visitor, he gave one or two cautionary winks behind his back and thus, in spite of everything, managed to make a rather effective exit.

The new arrival was tall, about fifty-five or even more, rather corpulent, with purplish-red fleshy, sagging cheeks, framed by thick grey sideboards, whiskered and with large, somewhat bulging eyes. He would have been quite imposing, but for something distinctly sordid, untidy, even bedraggled about him. He wore an old frockcoat, threadbare at the elbows, and his shirt front too was soiled – a homely touch no doubt. Round him there was a distinct whiff of vodka, but all in all he cut a striking figure, somewhat mannered in the all too studied attempt to call attention to himself. The gentleman, smiling affably, approached the Prince with unhurried steps, and without saying a word took his hand; holding it firmly in his, he continued to gaze in the Prince's eyes for some little while as though recalling long forgotten features.

"I was right! It's him!" he said softly, but solemnly. "The spitting image! What was that, I thought, did I hear a familiar, a dear, name mentioned, and I recalled my forfeited past… Prince Myshkin?"

"Your servant."

"General Ivolgin, retired and ill-starred. Your name and patronymic, if I may be so bold?"

"Lev Nikolayevich."

"Yes, yes! My childhood friend, Nikolai Petrovich's son, childhood friend indeed!"

"My father's name was Nikolai Lvovich."

"Lvovich," the General corrected himself, but without haste, with perfect composure as though he knew it all along, and it was a mere slip of the tongue. He sat down and, taking hold of the Prince's hand, bade him take a seat next to him. "I dangled you on my knee."

"Is that so?" the Prince asked. "My father has been dead these past twenty years."

"Yes. Twenty years. Twenty years and three months. We went to school together. I went straight into the military…"

"Yes, my father was in the military too, a sub lieutenant in the Vasilevsky Regiment."

"Correction, Belomorsky. He was transferred to Belomorsky just before he died. I was there paying my last respects. Your mother…"

The General paused in painful recollection.

"Yes, six months later she too died, of a common cold," the Prince said.

"No, not of a cold. Not of a common cold, take the word of an old veteran. I was there and I buried her. Of grief for her Prince, not of a common cold, my dear sir. Y-yes, how well I remember the Princess herself! Those were the days! Because of her, the Prince and I, lifelong friends, nearly ended up murdering each other."

The Prince listened with mounting amusement.

"I was passionately in love with your dear mother when she was yet being wooed... by my friend. The prince got to know about it and was shocked. He comes to me one morning, seven it was. 'Get up!' I started dressing, slowly. Not a word spoken on either side. I realized what was the matter. He produced two guns from his pocket. At point-blank range. No witnesses. What's the use of witnesses if five minutes later we'll be sending each other to perdition! We loaded the guns, stuck the barrels into each other's chests, eyeball to eyeball. Suddenly, tears gushed from our eyes, our hands shook. Both, both, together! Well, it naturally gave way into a long embrace, magnanimity on both sides. The Prince called out, 'She's yours!' I cried, 'She's yours!' Yes, where were we?... Are you... staying here?"

"Yes, for a little while, possibly," the Prince said with a slight stutter.

"Prince, Mama wants you to come," Kolya said, popping his head into the room. The Prince was about to get up, but the General laid the palm of his right hand on his shoulder and gently but firmly pressed him back.

"As your father's true friend, let me tell you, sir," the General said, "I am, as you can well see, the victim of a tragic catastrophe, but I was never tried! Never! Nina Alexandrovna is an exceptional lady. Varvara Ardalionovna, my daughter, is an exceptional daughter! Through force of circumstances, we are obliged to let out accommodation – the indignity of it! I, who could well have been the Governor General!... But you are always welcome. And yet, there's a tragedy being played out in my household."

The Prince regarded him with interest and puzzlement.

"A marriage is in the offing, a most unusual marriage. Marriage between a woman of easy virtue and a young man with prospects of becoming a gentleman-in-waiting. This woman is to be brought into this house, my wife's and daughter's family residence. But while I have a breath of life in me, this will not happen! Over my dead body, let them step over me!… Ganya and I are no longer on speaking terms. I avoid him. I caution you in advance. If you choose to stay here, you'll be a witness to everything anyway. But you're my friend's son, and I'm entitled to expect…"

"Prince, I beg you, come to the sitting room," Nina Alexandrovna called, appearing at the doorway in person.

"Imagine, my dear," the General exclaimed, "it turns out I nursed the Prince in my arms!"

Nina Alexandrovna cast a reproachful glance at him and looked inquisitively at the Prince, but did not utter a word. The Prince followed her out; no sooner had they entered the sitting room and sat down than the General too entered. Nina Alexandrovna, who had started to communicate something to the Prince hurriedly and in low tones, stopped talking immediately and, visibly vexed, buried her face in her knitting. The General may have noticed her vexation, but he did not betray himself, and remained in excellent high spirits.

"My friend's son!" he exclaimed, addressing Nina Alexandrovna. "And so unexpected! I'd stopped thinking about it long ago. But, my dear, do you really not remember the late Nikolai Lvovich? You too met him in… Tver, if my memory serves me."

"I've no recollection of anyone called Nikolai Lvovich. Was that your father?" she asked the Prince.

"Yes. But, as I recall, he died in Yelisavetgrad, not Tver," the Prince observed delicately. "I heard this from Pavlishchev…"

"He died in Tver," the General insisted, "he was transferred to Tver shortly before his death, even before the onset of his illness. You, Prince, were still too young to remember either the transfer or the journey. Pavlishchev could well be wrong, though he was an excellent man."

"Did you know Pavlishchev?"

"There weren't many like him. But I was there when your father died. I gave him my blessing on his deathbed—"

"But my father died in police custody," the Prince observed again, "even though I never was able to establish why. He died in hospital."

"Oh, that was in the private Kolpakov case, and I vouch for it, your father would have been acquitted."

"Really? Are you perfectly sure?" the Prince enquired with especial curiosity.

"It stands to reason!" the General vociferated. "The court rose without coming to a decision. The case was unprecedented! Nay, mysterious! Sub lieutenant and company commander Larionov lies dead. The Prince is temporarily appointed his locum. So far so good. Private Kolpakov commits theft – he pilfers a pair of boots from a friend, sells them and gets drunk on the proceeds. Good. The Prince – note well, all this took place in front of the Sergeant Major and the Corporal – gives Kolpakov a dressing-down and threatens to have him flogged. Kolpakov returns to his quarters, lies down on his bunk and in a quarter of an hour dies. Excellent! But this is not all, not by a long chalk. Be that as it may, Kolpakov is buried. The Prince draws up a report, and Kolpakov is duly struck off the roll. You'd say, what could be better? But precisely six months later, on a military parade, Private Kolpakov, as though nothing had happened, turns up in the third company of the second battalion of the Novozemlyansky infantry regiment, of the same brigade and the same division! How about that?"

"Really!" the Prince exclaimed in astonishment.

"That is not right, it's a mistake!" Nina Alexandrovna intervened suddenly, looking almost ruefully at the Prince. "*Mon mari se trompe.*"*

"But my dearest, '*se trompe*' is easily said, but how would you solve such a case? Everybody was in a quandary. I'd have been the first to say '*qu'on se trompe*'. But unfortunately I witnessed it all myself and served on the investigative commission. All identification parades proved that it was the very same Kolpakov who six months previously had been interred at an ordinary military funeral to the roll of drums. A truly unprecedented case, well-nigh inconceivable, I agree, but—"

"Father, your dinner is ready," Varvara Ardalionovna announced, coming into the room.

"Ah, that's wonderful, splendid! I've worked up quite an appetite... But as to the case, it's remarkable, positively fraught..."

"The soup will go cold again," Varya remarked moodily.

"I'm coming, I'm coming," the General muttered on his way out. "And despite all investigations..." one could still hear him insisting.

"I'm afraid you'll have to make many allowances for Ardalion Alexandrovich if you choose to stay with us," Nina Alexandrovna said. "But he is unlikely to be much of a nuisance to you. As a matter of fact, he eats alone. You must agree all people have their failings and their… idiosyncracies, not least those who look utterly normal. There is one thing I shall be especially grateful for. If ever my husband should turn to you for the rent, please tell him you have already paid me. This is not to say of course that anything paid to Ardalion Alexandrovich would not be credited to your account, but it is only in the interests of good housekeeping… What is it, Varya?"

Varya had entered the room and without a word spoken, handed Nastasya Filippovna's portrait to her mother. With a start Nina Alexandrovna regarded it with some trepidation, before succumbing to an overwhelming expression of bitterness. Finally she raised a quizzical pair of eyes at Varya.

"A personal present to him from her," Varya said. "They plan to settle it all tonight."

"Tonight!" Nina Alexandrovna repeated mutely in a voice drained of hope. "Well then? This is the end of all doubting and hoping, the portrait says it all… Did he give it to you himself, incidentally?" she added in some amazement.

"You know we've hardly exchanged a word for over a month. I got it all from Ptitsyn, and the portrait was lying there on the floor by the table. I picked it up."

"Prince," Nina Alexandrovna suddenly turned to him, "there was something I wanted to ask you, which in fact is why I invited you here, have you known my son long? I seem to remember he said you only just arrived today from somewhere."

The Prince gave a brief account of himself, omitting the major part. Nina Alexandrovna and Varya heard him out.

"I am not asking you for anything about Gavrila Ardalionych," Nina Alexandrovna observed, "you must be quite clear about that. If there's something he'd rather not confide in me, I wouldn't pry behind his back. I only ask because of what he himself said a little while back in your presence, and what he said to me after I asked him about you when you'd gone. He said, 'He knows everything, there's no need to stand on ceremony with him!' What did he mean by that? That is, I'd like to know, to what extent…"

Ganya and Ptitsyn entered unexpectedly and Nina Alexandrovna immediately fell silent. The Prince stayed in his chair next to her, but Varya took a few steps sideways. Nastasya Filippovna's portrait lay for all to see, right in front of Nina Alexandrovna on her worktable. Catching sight of it, Ganya frowned, picked it up from the table with distaste and casually flung it across the room on to his desk.

"Today, Ganya?" Nina Alexandrovna asked suddenly.

"Today what?" Ganya started, and immediately took the Prince to task. "Ah, I should have known!… Listen, are you sick or something? What's eating you? Can't you get it into your head, Your Highness—"

"It's my fault, Ganya, no one else's," Ptitsyn interrupted.

Ganya looked at him in disbelief.

"Look, it's better that way, Ganya, the more so when you consider that the matter is at an end," Ptitsyn muttered, and moved towards the table where he sat down, produced a piece of paper covered in pencil writing, and began to study it closely. Ganya stood dejectedly, nervously anticipating a family scene. It did not even occur to him to apologize to the Prince.

"If everything is at an end, Ivan Petrovich is quite right," Nina Alexandrovna said, "don't make faces, please, and don't fret, Ganya. I'm not going to question anything you don't want to talk about yourself, and I assure you I've become completely reconciled, take my word for it, and stop fretting."

She said this without interrupting her work and seemed superficially calm and collected. Ganya was somewhat surprised and he continued to regard her in wary bafflement, waiting for her to make herself clearer. Family scenes had exacted a heavy toll on him. Nina Alexandrovna noticed this wariness and added with a bitter smile, "You still distrust me. Don't worry, there will be no more tears or entreaties, not from my side anyway. All I want is for you to be happy, and you know that. I'm resigned to fate, but in my heart I shall always be with you, whether we are together or apart. Of course, I can speak only for myself. You cannot expect the same from your sister—"

"Ah, her again!" Ganya burst out, regarding his sister with hatred and derision. "Mother dear! I swear to you again as I'd already given you my word previously, no one will ever dare to show you lack of respect while I live or while I'm here. I'll see to it whoever passes across our threshold—" Ganya was so enthused that there was something like reconciliation and genuine tenderness in his eyes.

"I've never been concerned about myself, Ganya, you know that. I've never been pained or worried on my own account all this time.

They say, the matter will be settled between you today. What will be decided?"

"She promised," Ganya replied, "she will announce at her place tonight if she's willing or not."

"We've kept off this topic for close on three weeks, and that was all to the good. Now that everything's coming to an end, I have only one question to put to you: how could she give you her consent or even her portrait if you don't love her? Have you really chosen, a woman of such... such..."

"...accomplishments, perhaps?"

"That's not the word I was looking for. Could you really have pulled the wool over her eyes to such an extent?" Her voice shook with indignation.

Ganya reflected a little and with no attempt to hide his derision, remarked, "You've allowed yourself to get carried away, Mother dear, the way you've always worked yourself into a state. You promised there'll be no questions or reprimands, and yet they've started already! Why don't we just leave it all, really. That's what you wanted to do anyway, wasn't it?... I shall never ever leave you. Anybody else would have run a mile from such a sister – look at her staring at me now! Let's not go on and on! I was so happy just now... And what makes you think I'm deceiving Nastasya Filippovna? As for Varya, it's up to her – enough! And I'll say that again – enough is enough!"

Ganya was getting more and more agitated and was aimlessly pacing up and down the room. Such discussions were always a sore point for all the members of the family.

"I told you," Varya said, "that if she comes here, I'm leaving, and I'll stick to my word too."

"Out of bloody-mindedness!" Ganya shouted. "Out of bloody-mindedness you won't even get married! Why are you sneering at me so? I couldn't care a fig, Varvara Ardalionovna! If you like, why don't you carry out your threat now? I'm seriously fed up with you! What! You've decided to leave us at last, Prince?" he called out, seeing that the latter had got to his feet.

The exasperation in his voice had reached the pitch where a person begins to take pleasure in it, succumbs to it involuntarily and allows it to overwhelm him whatever the consequences. The Prince hesitated in the doorway to think of something to say, but one glance at his tormentor's face told him that all that was needed was one last straw to break the camel's back, and he left without saying a word. A few minutes later he could tell by the voices issuing from the sitting room that with his departure the conversation had grown even more heated and unrestrained.

He crossed the entrance hall into the passageway leading to his room. As he went past the front door by the stairs, he realized there was someone outside frantically tugging at the bell cord, but something must have jammed because the bell was moving from side to side but there was no sound. The Prince turned the lock, opened the door and recoiled – facing him was Nastasya Filippovna. He recognized her immediately from the portrait. On seeing him her eyes flashed indignantly; she quickly went into the entrance hall and, pushing past him abruptly and letting her fur coat slip from her shoulder, she called out angrily, "If you're too lazy to fix the bell, you should at least have been sitting in the hall to let visitors in. There, he's dropped my coat now, fool!"

Her fur coat really lay in a heap on the floor; Nastasya Filippovna, not waiting for the Prince to help her out of it, had flung it into his hands without looking back as she walked past him, and he had failed to catch it.

"You ought to be sacked. Go and announce me!"

The Prince was about to say something, but his confusion was such that he was incapable of uttering a single word and, still clutching the fur coat which he had picked up off the floor, he headed for the sitting room.

"Not with my fur coat, for heaven's sake! Why've you got the coat? Ha-ha-ha! Are you mad, or what?"

The Prince turned back and stared at her wide-eyed; when she laughed – he too smiled back, but was still tongue-tied. In the first few seconds, when he was opening the door, he was pale; now there was a rush of blood to his face.

"What sort of an idiot are you?" Nastasya Filippovna exclaimed, indignantly, stamping her foot. "Where do you think you're going? Whom are you going to announce?"

"Nastasya Filippovna," the Prince mumbled.

"How do you know my name?" she enquired quickly. "I've never seen you before! Go ahead, announce me... What's all the shouting about?"

"They're having a quarrel in there," the Prince replied and headed for the sitting room.

He entered at a rather critical moment; Nina Alexandrovna had all but forgotten that she had reconciled herself to everything and had come out in defence of Varya. Ptitsyn too was standing at Varya's side, no longer fingering his pencil-covered scrap of paper. Varya, far from being cowed herself, was no shrinking violet; but her brother's slurs had become ever more abusive and intolerable. On such occasions she was wont to stop arguing altogether and just stand and stare derisively at her brother. This tactic, as she well knew, could exasperate him to the utmost limit. It was precisely at this moment that the Prince opened the door and announced, "Nastasya Filippovna!"

9

THE WHOLE COMPANY fell silent on the instant. Everyone stared at the Prince in utter disbelief, unable to get over the shock. Ganya stood petrified with fear.

Nastasya Filippovna's arrival, especially at that instant, was the strangest and most ill-timed surprise ever. Suffice to say that it was Nastasya Filippovna's first visit; till then she had been so haughty that when talking to Ganya she expressed no desire to get to know his relations, and lately had stopped even mentioning them as though they did not even exist. Though this suited Ganya well to some extent, a very unpalatable conversation thereby being avoided, in his heart he took note of her haughtiness. He expected taunts and innuendos directed at members of his family – that he was prepared to face, but never a personal visit. He was aware that she knew full well what was going on in his household as a result of their engagement and what his family's attitude to it was. Her calling on him, *now*, after presenting him with her portrait and on her birthday, the day she had promised to decide his fate, was tantamount to being that decision.

The consternation with which everyone regarded the Prince was short-lived. Nastasya Filippovna herself appeared in the doorway and on entering the room, again gave the Prince a gentle push.

"At last I managed to get through... what's the matter with your doorbell?" she said in good humour, putting out her hand to Ganya, who had scurried forward to meet her. "You should see your face, it's a real sight! Won't you introduce me, please..."

Ganya, at a total loss, introduced her to Varya first, and before shaking each other's hands, the two exchanged some odd glances. Nastasya Filippovna laughed and hid behind a mask of joviality; but Varya would have no pretence and stared ahead with gloomy determination, not even a shadow of a smile gracing her lips as conventional politeness alone might have decreed. Ganya nearly died; there was no time, or point, in trying to appeal to his sister, and he simply darted her such a withering glance that she immediately understood the gravity of the situation. At this juncture she seemed to have decided to relent towards him and smiled faintly at Nastasya Filippovna. (Deep down the members of this family still loved one another.) Nina Alexandrovna, whom Ganya in his confusion had introduced after his sister and, what is more, had presented to Nastasya Filippovna, instead of vice versa, saved the situation briefly. But Nina Alexandrovna had barely opened her mouth to say what a pleasure it was for her, when Nastasya Filippovna, not waiting for her to finish, turned to Ganya abruptly and, taking a seat (without invitation) on a little sofa in a corner by the window, exclaimed, "So where is your study then? And... where are the lodgers? You do have lodgers, don't you?"

Ganya blushed terribly and opened his mouth to say something, but Nastasya Filippovna added, "Where would you put the lodgers here, I wonder? You haven't even got a study. Does it pay?" she suddenly addressed Nina Alexandrovna.

"It's quite hard work," she replied. "Of course, it does bring in something. To be sure, we have only recently—"

But Nastasya Filippovna had again stopped listening. She looked at Ganya, and in a fit of laughter observed, "What's happened to your face? Oh my God, I've never seen anything like it!"

It took a few seconds for her to stop laughing with no signs of Ganya's features relaxing; only gradually did his numbness, his comical incoordination ease off; but he was still extraordinarily pale, and his lips remained set in a rictus, in which state he was incapable of pronouncing a single word, his eyes all the while staying glued to the face of his lady visitor, who continued her merry laugh.

There was another observer, who as yet had also not shaken off his bewilderment at the sight of Nastasya Filippovna, but who, though in his consternation he remained stuck in the doorway, could not help noticing the pallor and the ominous transformations in Ganya's face. This observer was the Prince. He took an involuntary step forward as though in panic.

"Have some water," he whispered to Ganya. "And for goodness' sake stop staring so..."

It was clear he said this without any forethought, without any ulterior motivation, simply as it came to him on the spur of the moment, but his words had the most extraordinary effect. It seemed as though Ganya wanted to heap all his pent-up anger upon the Prince. He grabbed him by the shoulder in silence and looked at him hard, vengefully and with hatred, as though unable to articulate a single word. In the general confusion, Nina Alexandrovna let out a shriek; Ptitsyn, disturbed, took a step forward, and Kolya and Ferdyshchenko, who had just appeared in the doorway, stopped in amazement; only Varya continued to eye the scene in sullen expectation. She remained standing, close by her mother, her arms folded on her chest.

But Ganya came to his senses the moment he had committed this gaffe, and gave a nervous laugh. He pulled himself together.

"Come, Prince, are you a doctor, or something?" he called out as merrily and good-naturedly as he could. "You gave me quite a turn. Nastasya Filippovna, may I introduce you to this most esteemed individual, never mind that I got to know him myself only this morning."

Nastasya Filippovna looked at the Prince with astonishment.

"Prince? Is he a Prince? Imagine, in the entrance hall I took him for a flunkey and sent him off to announce me! Ha-ha-ha!"

"What's the problem, what's the problem!" Ferdyshchenko intervened, hurriedly moving closer, happy that people had cheered up. "None at all – *se non è vero...*"*

"I nearly gave you a telling off, Prince. Forgive me, please. Ferdyshchenko, how come you're here, and at such an hour? I was hoping at least I wouldn't run into you. Who? What prince? Myshkin?" she double-checked with Ganya, who was still holding the Prince by the shoulder.

"Our lodger," Ganya repeated.

It was clear the Prince was being touted as some curio that had turned up conveniently at an awkward moment. He was almost being forced upon Nastasya Filippovna and he thought he clearly heard the word "idiot" whispered behind his back by way of explanation, most likely by Ferdyshchenko.

"Tell me, why did you not put me right then, after I made such an awful... mistake with regard to you?" Nastasya Filippovna continued as she went on surveying the Prince from head to foot in the most blatant manner; she was dying for an answer and quite convinced that it would be sufficiently silly to afford an excuse for some more mirth.

"I was taken by surprise, seeing you so unexpectedly..." the Prince muttered.

"And how did you know it was me? Where had you seen me previously? Funny, I do have the feeling I've seen you before somewhere! And do tell me, why did you get so flustered? What's so flustering about me?"

"My, oh my!" Ferdyshchenko said, continuing his clowning. "Answer her! Oh my God, the things I could have said in answer to such a question! Go on... You disappoint me, Prince!"

"You're so right," the Prince replied with a laugh. "I had seen your portrait and it bowled me over," he continued, turning to Nastasya Filippovna. "After that I talked with the Yepanchins about you... and early this morning, before I arrived in St Petersburg, in the train, I heard a lot about you from Parfyon Rogozhin... Also, I was thinking about you when I was opening the door for you, and there you were suddenly standing in front of me.

"And how did you know it was me?"

"By your portrait and—"

"And what else?"

"And because that's just how I imagined you... I too have a feeling I've seen you somewhere."

"Where? Where?"

"I'm sure I've seen your eyes somewhere... but it couldn't have been! I'm only imagining it... I've never been here before. Perhaps in a dream..."

"Well, Prince, you take the biscuit!" Ferdyshchenko declared for all to hear. "I withdraw my *se non è vero*! To be sure... to be sure, though, this is all because of his innocence!" he added ruefully.

The Prince's voice was unsteady and faltering, and he paused once or twice, breathing short. He was in a state of the utmost agitation. Nastasya Filippovna was regarding him with curiosity, but she had stopped laughing. At this very instant a new, stentorian voice suddenly resounded on the edge of the little crowd that had gathered closely round the Prince and Nastasya Filippovna, and which now suddenly split up. Nastasya Filippovna stood face to face with the head of the household, General Ivolgin himself. He was dressed in tails and a clean shirt, and his moustache had been freshly dyed...

This was altogether too much for Ganya. Self-seeking and vain to the point of hypochondria; having been yearning desperately for the past two months for some grounds to assert his propriety and good name; sensing that he was just a tiro on the stage of life who might turn tail any moment; having screwed up his courage for an out-and-out confrontation in his own house, where he was a prime despot, but too cowardly to bring it about in front of Nastasya Filippovna, who had beaten him squarely on all counts and still continued to dominate him to the very last; an "over-anxious pauper" as Nastasya Filippovna herself put it; an armchair avenger who'd sworn to pay her back cruelly one day and at the same time naively comforted himself in his heart of hearts that he'd settle everything and reconcile all contradictions – this man now had to drain the bitterest cup of all, and, what's more, at such a time! And then to cap it all, one more unforeseen and terrible ordeal for a vainglorious person to endure – the blushes over his father within the walls of his family home! "Is the prize itself worth it all in the end!" flashed through Ganya's mind.

What happened next was the stuff of nightmares; it sent shivers down his spine and made his hair stand on end – his father finally met Nastasya Filippovna! Sometimes he was wont to play a cruel joke on himself, deliberately teasing and provoking himself in an attempt to picture the General at the wedding ceremony, but he could never bring himself to see the scene through to the end. Perhaps he exaggerated the problem out of all proportion, but this is always the case with vainglorious people. In these two months he had had ample time to ponder the matter and come to a decision, and to promise himself that, come what may, he would bring his parent to heel, be it only temporarily, and if possible even spirit him out of St Petersburg, irrespective of whether his mother agreed to it or not. When Nastasya Filippovna had made her entry ten minutes previously, he had been so taken aback that he had completely forgotten about the possibility of Ardalion Alexandrovich appearing on the scene, and had consequently not taken any precautions. And all of a sudden here was the General, large as life, and what's more, dressed up in tails, and precisely when Nastasya Filippovna was hell bent on showering him and his family members with all manner of taunts (he did not have a shadow of doubt that that's what she meant to do). And, anyway, what was her present visit all about, if not that? Had she come to make friends with his mother and sister, or to insult them both under his own roof? But judging by the stance both parties had adopted, there was no more room for doubt. His mother and sister sat there, sidelined, looking utterly shamed, whereas Nastasya Filippovna had evidently even forgotten that they were in the same room as her… And if she carried on like that, she obviously had her own policy to pursue!

Ferdyshchenko took charge of the situation and brought the General to Nastasya Filippovna.

"Ardalion Alexandrovich Ivolgin," the General said with dignity, smiling and bowing, "an unfortunate old campaigner and paterfamilias, happy to welcome into its fold so charming a—"

He failed to finish; Ferdyshchenko hurriedly brought a chair behind him, and the General, slightly unsteady on his legs in his postprandial state, slumped, or rather, fell into it, but without the least trace of embarrassment. Sitting as he was directly opposite her and arching his back in gratification, he slowly brought her fingers to his lips with deliberate gallantry. The General was not one to get easily flustered. In outer appearance, apart from some indefinable shabbiness, he was still reasonably presentable, and was well aware of this. He had formerly moved in the best of circles, from which he had been finally excluded only two or three years before. It was from that time that he had without restraint abandoned himself to some of his weaknesses; but he had lost none of his skilful, pleasant ways. Nastasya Filippovna, of course, appeared to be delighted at his appearance in the room; she knew of him already by hearsay.

"I heard that my son—" Ardalion Alexandrovich began.

"Yes, your son! And you're a fine father, I must say! Why do I never see you at my place? Are you hiding yourself, or is your son hiding you? You of all people could have paid me a visit without compromising anybody."

"Children of the nineteenth century and their parents—" the General made another attempt at speaking.

"Nastasya Filippovna!" Nina Alexandrovna said in a loud voice. "Be so good as to excuse Ardalion Alexandrovich for a minute, he is wanted on business."

"But of course! I had heard so much about him, I was dying to see him for myself! Business? What business? I thought he was retired? You won't leave me, General, will you?"

"I give you my word he will be back, but right now he is need of rest."

"Ardalion Alexandrovich, I'm told you are in need of rest!" Nastasya Filippovna exclaimed, frowning and displeased, like a spoiled little brat deprived of her favourite toy. The General entered into the spirit of it and decided to play the clown to the last.

"My dear! My dear!" he said petulantly with his hand upon his heart and a solemn look at his spouse.

"Mother dear, wouldn't it be best if you left us?" Varya asked out loud.

"No, Varya, I shall stay to the bitter end."

Nastasya Filippovna could not but have heard both the question and answer; however, her merriment only increased as a result. She immediately again showered the General with questions, and five minutes later he was in the best of moods, holding forth to bursts of laughter all round.

Kolya tugged at the Prince's coat.

"Couldn't you at least take him out of the room! Couldn't you? Please!" And there were tears of indignation in the poor boy's eyes. "This is too bad of you, Ganya!" he added under his breath.

"I was really on the best of terms with General Ivan Fyodorovich Yepanchin," Ivolgin gushed in response to Nastasya Filippovna's questions. "He, I and the late Prince Lev Nikolayevich Myshkin, whose son I had hugged just now after a gap of twenty years, were inseparable, so to speak, a threesome – Athos, Porthos and Aramis.* But, alas, one is in his grave, brought down by slander and a bullet, the other – yours truly – is still fending off slander and bullets—"

"Bullets?" Nastasya Filippovna exclaimed.

"They're lodged here in my chest, since the siege of Kars,* and when there's a turn in the weather, I feel them. In all other respects I lead the life of a philosopher: I walk, stroll, play draughts in my café like a bourgeois who's turned his back on things, and I read *L'Indépendance.**

But I've broken with our Porthos, the General Yepanchin, after an incident with a lapdog two years ago at a railway station, I've broken with him entirely."

"A lapdog? How fascinating!" Nastasya Filippovna enquired with added interest. "With a lapdog? And did you say at a railway station?..." she threw in as an afterthought.

"It's a fatuous story, not worth the trouble. It was Princess Belokonsky's Governess, Mrs Smith, who started it all, but... it's not worth going into."

"But I insist!" Nastasya Filippovna cried enthusiastically.

"I've not heard this either!" Ferdyshchenko remarked. "*C'est du nouveau.*"

"Ardalion Alexandrovich!" Nina Alexandrovna's pleading voice was heard once more.

"Papa, you're wanted!" Kolya called out.

"It's a stupid story, won't take long to tell," the General began, well pleased with himself. "Two years ago, that's right! Maybe less, just after the opening of the new *** railway line, I (already in mufti), while trying to sort out some very important paperwork in connection with my delegation of duties, took a ticket, first class. I got in, took my seat and lit up. That is, I carried on smoking, I had lit up a bit earlier. I was all alone in the compartment. Smoking is neither prohibited nor encouraged – half-and-half, as per usual. Well, and depending on your general aspect. The window was down. Suddenly, just before the whistle, two ladies and a lapdog rushed in to occupy the seat directly opposite, in a tearing hurry. One, in a most flamboyant turnout, everything sky-blue; the other, more modestly dressed, in a black silk frock with a pelerine. Not at all bad-looking, uppity, speaking English. I'm, of course, minding my own business, smoking. That is, it did occur to me, however, I carried on regardless, inasmuch as the window was open, and it was all blowing out. The doggie, the size of my fist, jet black, white paws, cute little thing, was curled up in the lap of the lady in sky-blue. Silver collar, of course, with a tag. I'm as cool as a cucumber. Then I begin to notice the ladies are not best pleased – with my cigar – it goes without saying. One trained a lorgnette on me, tortoiseshell. I pretend not to notice – after all, they've not said a single word! If only they'd said something, given a warning, asked me – there is such a thing as human speech! Instead, not a sound... Suddenly – and this,

113

I tell you, without the least warning, that is without the very least, as though she'd lost her reason – the sky-blue one grabs my cigar and – out of the window. The train's hurtling along, I'm absolutely stunned. The woman's wild, wild as they come, but, to be sure, full-bodied, well endowed, tall, blonde, fresh-complexioned (too fresh), eyes sparkling furiously. Without a word, I put out my hand to the little bitch and with the utmost politeness, with exquisite good manners, I take the creature by the scruff of its neck between my finger and thumb, and out she goes through the window after the cigar! She just managed a tiny yelp! The train goes on at a pace—"

"You absolute monster, you!" Nastasya Filippovna yelled out, laughing her head off and clapping her hands like a little girl.

"Bravo, bravo!" Ferdyshchenko seconded. Ptitsyn, who did not relish the General's arrival either, smirked too. Even Kolya burst out laughing and cried, "Well done!"

"And I was right, I was right, thrice right!" the General went on triumphantly, "because if there's no smoking cigars in trains, there shouldn't be any dogs either."

"Bravo, Papa!" Kolya called out, elated. "Excellent! I'd have done just the same, that's for sure!"

"Well, what about the young lady?" Nastasya Filippovna would not relent.

"The lady? Well, she's at the bottom of it all," the General continued with a frown, "without a word being said and with no warning whatsoever, she gives me a resounding clip round the ear! A wild woman, totally untamed!"

"And what did you do?"

The General looked down, raised his eyebrows, hunched his shoulders, tightened his lips, spread out his arms, paused, and said, "I got carried away!"

"Was it hard? Did you strike her hard?"

"Heavens, not hard at all! There was an uproar all right, but not hard, trust me. I only once raised one arm to defend myself, only to defend myself. But Satan himself must have been waiting in the wings. The sky-blue one turned out to be English, a governess or some kind of a family friend of Princess Belokonskaya, and the one in black was one of the elder Belokonsky sisters, an old maid of about thirty-five. And it's well known on what terms Madame Yepanchina is with the Belokonsky house. All the princesses were up in arms, tears and lamentation all round for the beloved animal, six princesses screaming and screeching in chorus, the English woman joining in – the end of the world! Naturally, I paid a visit of repentance, begged forgiveness, wrote a letter, which was rejected. I was turned away, the letter was sent back unopened, a complete break with the Yepanchins, ostracism, exile!"

"One moment, please, there's something not quite right here!" Nastasya Filippovna suddenly interjected. "Five or six days ago I read in *L'Indépendance* – and I take *L'Indépendance* regularly – an exactly similar story! And when I say exactly the same, I mean exactly the same! It occurred on one of the Rhineland railways – between a Frenchman and an Englishwoman. There was the same cigar, a lapdog flung out of the window, and it also all ended just like in your story, down to the sky-blue frock!"

The General blushed unbearably; Kolya too blushed and buried his face in his hands; Ptitsyn abruptly turned to face the other way. Ferdyshchenko alone laughed uncontrollably. Ganya, it goes without saying, was dying a thousand deaths.

"I assure you," the General stuttered, "it all happened to me too—"

"Papa really had an unpleasant encounter with Mrs Smith, the Belokonsky governess," Kolya proclaimed, "I can remember."

"What! Exactly like it?" persisted the implacable Nastasya Filippovna.

"The same incident at opposite ends of Europe, correct in every detail, down to the sky-blue dress! I'll send you my copy of *L'Indépendance belge*."

"Mark you," the General persisted, "it happened two years previously—"

"Well, there is that!" Nastasya Filippovna was simply rolling with laughter.

"Father, I need a couple of words with you in private," Ganya said in an unsteady, disconsolate voice, his hand absent-mindedly resting on his father's shoulder. Unbounded hatred shone in his eyes.

At the same instant the doorbell in the entrance hall resounded with unusual loudness, threatening to break loose from its fastenings. The expectation was of an unusual visitor. Kolya rushed out to open the door.

10

T HE ENTRANCE HALL suddenly filled with people and noise; the way it felt from the sitting room was that more and more people were streaming in from the forecourt. Several voices were shouting and speaking at cross-purposes; it was audible on the stairs – the door to which, it seemed, remained ajar. It was to be no ordinary visit. Everyone in the sitting room exchanged glances. Ganya rushed into the adjoining room; there were people there too.

"Ah, here he is, Judas!" called out a voice that sounded familiar to the Prince. "How do you do, you rogue!"

"That's him all right!" another voice chimed in.

The Prince now recognized the first as belonging to Rogozhin, the second, to Lebedev.

Ganya remained in the doorway, speechless and as though stupefied, making no attempt to prevent any of about a dozen people, headed by Parfyon Rogozhin, from entering. It was a very motley crowd, and not only motley, but plain raucous. Some entered with their greatcoats and fur coats on, straight off the street. It must be said, no one was actually blind drunk, but all were well primed. They all appeared to be in need of one another's company to make the entrance; singly no one would have dared, but in a crowd they all appeared to egg one another on. Even Rogozhin, at the head of the crowd, trod warily, but he was intent on something and seemed brooding and anxiously preoccupied. His entourage formed a supporting throng or, more accurately, a supporting gang. Included was the coiffured Zalyozhev; he'd left his fur coat in the entrance hall and made a showy, posturing entry, accompanied by two or three like gentlemen, seemingly of the mercantile fraternity. There was another one, in what looked like a military greatcoat; also, an exceedingly fat little man, who never stopped laughing, and next to him was a huge taciturn fellow of enormous girth, who appeared to place great reliance on the size of his fists. The party also included a medical student and a shifty little Pole. From the stairs two female forms were trying to peer into the room, but could not quite pluck up the courage to enter; Kolya shut the door in their faces and bolted it.

"Hello, Ganya my lad, you damned scoundrel! I bet you're surprised to see Parfyon Rogozhin!" Rogozhin blurted out, stopping in the sitting room doorway and confronting Ganya. But at this instant he spotted Nastasya Filippovna right in front of him. It would seem it had never occurred to him he might meet her here, because the sight of her had an astonishing effect upon him; he went so pale that his lips turned blue. "So it's true, is it!" he said softly as though speaking to himself and looking totally lost. "The end!... Well... Let's hear what you have to say for yourself now!" he hissed, looking at Ganya in a towering rage. "Well... eh!..."

He was breathless and articulating his words with difficulty. His eyes suddenly fell upon Nina Alexandrovna and Varya and his embarrassment briefly overrode his anger. Behind him crowded the inebriated Lebedev, who followed him like a shadow, then came the student, the gentleman with the fists, Zalyozhev, bowing left and right, and last of all the fat little chap, who did not want to be left out. The presence of the ladies had a somewhat restraining influence upon them all and, it seemed, cramped their style and prevented them just in time from shouting and letting rip, after which the presence of ladies would have counted for very little.

"What? You here too, Prince?" Rogozhin observed abstractedly, somewhat surprised to come upon the Prince. "Still in your gaiters, e-eh?" he exclaimed with a sigh, but the very next moment he was already oblivious of the Prince as his eyes focused on Nastasya Filippovna, who seemed to attract him like a magnet.

She also regarded the visitors with alarm and curiosity.

Suddenly Ganya took the initiative.

"I beg your pardon, what's all this about?" he spoke in a loud voice, surveying the whole company, but addressing Rogozhin in the main. "Don't forget, gentlemen, you're in a private house. My mother and sister are here—"

"We can see that your mother and sister are here," Rogozhin returned through gritted teeth.

"Indeed, we can see that your mother and sister are here," Lebedev confirmed.

The gentleman with the ready fists, who took this as a sign that things were about to commence, began to grunt.

"There now!" Ganya's voice suddenly jumped an octave higher to rather incongruous effect. "First, may I please ask you all into the next room, and secondly, I don't at all recognize—"

"My word, he doesn't recognize!" Rogozhin mocked, standing his ground. "You don't recognize Rogozhin, do you?"

"I believe I did meet you somewhere, but—"

"I like that, 'meet you somewhere'! What about the two hundred roubles of my father's money I lost to you just three months ago, only he died without being any the wiser? You lured me into it and Kniff did the rest. Now do you recognize me? Ptitsyn was there! If I was to pull three roubles out now you'd crawl on all fours three times round the town and back, that's what you're like. You're a nasty piece of work! I've come specially to buy you off, out of my petty cash. You needn't worry about the way I look... my boots... I've money, boy, lots of it, I'll say jump and you'll jump, the lot of you! Name your price!" Rogozhin worked himself up more and more into a state of intoxication. "Look here, Nastasya Filippovna!" he called out. "Have a heart, tell me one thing – are you going to marry him or not?"

Rogozhin's question came as from one at his wits' end with nothing to lose, addressing an idol who had condemned him to death. He awaited the answer in mortal fear.

Nastasya Filippovna measured him with a derisively haughty glance, but after looking at Varya, at Nina Alexandrovna and more attentively at Ganya, she suddenly changed her tone.

"Nothing of the sort, what's come over you? Whatever makes you ask?" she responded softly and gravely with a note of surprise.

"Really? Really?" Rogozhin exclaimed in an ecstasy of joy. "Is that so?! And I was told... My word! Well I never!... Nastasya Filippovna! They told me you'd got engaged to that there Ganya! What, to him? I couldn't believe it! I said so at once! I shall buy him out for a hundred roubles, lock, stock and barrel; give him a thousand, well, three, to get shot of him, and he'll abscond on the eve of the wedding and leave the bride all to me. Am I not right, Ganya, you skunk! You would take three thousand, wouldn't you? Here they are, here! All I need is your signature. I said I'll buy you out, and I will!"

"Get out of here, you're drunk!" Ganya yelled out, alternately changing colour from red to white.

This was followed by an outburst of several voices. Rogozhin and his men had long been waiting for such a pretext. Lebedev lent over to whisper something purposefully into Rogozhin's ear.

"You're right, pen-pusher!" Rogozhin returned. "You're right, you drunken sot! All right, here goes. Nastasya Filippovna!" he exclaimed, looking at her like one demented, quailing and suddenly heartened to the point of arrogance. "Here's eighteen thousand!" And he flung before her on the table a packet wrapped in white paper, tied crosswise with a piece of string. "Here... and there'll be more!"

He stopped short, his courage failing him.

"No no no!" Lebedev interposed in hushed tones, visibly frightened; it was likely that he was aghast at the magnitude of the sum, and had initially suggested much less.

"No, pal, you're wrong," Rogozhin suddenly cut him off with a shudder under Nastasya Filippovna's blazing gaze, "you're stupid and you haven't got a clue where you are, and I'm no better. Blast! The more fool me for having listened to you," he added in deeply repentant tones.

After a long look at Rogozhin's mortified countenance, Nastasya Filippovna burst into laughter.

"Eighteen thousand, for me? There's the true yokel in you straight away!" she said with dismissive disdain and was about to get up from the sofa in order to depart. Ganya observed the scene with bated breath.

"Forty thousand, I tell you! Eighteen's nothing!" Rogozhin cried out. "Ivan Ptitsyn and the Bishop promised forty by seven o'clock. Forty thousand! On the nail!"

The proceedings were beginning to take on an unseemly tone, but Nastasya Filippovna would not leave and continued to play-act as though bent on mischief. Nina Alexandrovna and Varya also got to their feet with fear on their faces as to where all this would lead; Varya affected defiance but Nina Alexandrovna was visibly pained; she was shivering and on the verge of fainting.

"All right then – a hundred! I'll raise a hundred thousand this very day! Ptitsyn, can you help? Go on, you'll make a packet!"

"You're mad!" Ptitsyn suddenly hissed, coming up close hurriedly, and grabbing Rogozhin by the arm. "You're drunk, they'll have the law on you! Can't you see where you are?"

"Drink talking," Nastasya Filippovna said mockingly.

"I'm telling the truth! I'll have all the money before the evening's out," Rogozhin called out in an outburst of euphoria. "Ptitsyn, you damn loan shark, charge anything you want, but get me a hundred thousand by the evening. I mean business!"

"I say, this is too much!" Ardalion Alexandrovich Ivolgin, suddenly losing his temper, challenged Rogozhin with grim determination. This unexpected outburst on the part of the old man, who had hitherto kept his silence, was not devoid of comedy. There were guffaws of laughter.

"Look, who's that?" Rogozhin joined in. "Come and join me, Granddad, there'll be drinks for you!"

"This is altogether too much!" Kolya wailed, dying of shame and frustration.

"Is there really no one here," Varya called, shaking all over, "to get rid of this hussy for us?"

"So I'm a hussy, am I?" Nastasya Filippovna returned with light-hearted derision. "And like a fool I came to invite them to my place tonight! You can now see, Gavrila Ardalionych, what sort of a reception your sister's giving me!"

For a few moments, following his sister's desperate plea, Ganya remained speechless; but, on seeing that this time Nastasya Filippovna really was preparing to leave, he grabbed his sister by the arm like one demented.

"What have you done?" he shouted, with looks that threatened to kill. He looked confused and not quite master of his actions.

"What have I done?" Varya exclaimed again triumphantly, looking full of defiance at her brother. "Where is all this leading to? I suppose you'd want me to ask her pardon for insulting your mother and coming here to defame your family, you base man?"

They stood face to face glowering at each other for a few seconds. Ganya had still not let go of her arm. Varya tried to wrench herself free once or twice with all her strength, but being unsuccessful, and totally beside herself, she spat at her brother full in the face.

"What a girl!" Nastasya Filippovna exclaimed. "You've chosen well, Ptitsyn, I congratulate you!"

Totally enraged, and taking no account of his action, Ganya took a powerful swing at his sister. The blow would surely have landed on her face, but another hand suddenly reached out to restrain him.

The Prince now stood between him and his sister.

"That's enough!" the Prince said firmly, also shaking all over as after a severe shock.

"Are you never going to stop interfering!" Ganya bellowed, seeing red and, letting go of Varya's arm, with his free hand he delivered a resounding slap across the Prince's face.

"Oh!" Kolya exclaimed, burying his head in his hands. "Oh, my God!"

There were gasps all round. The Prince went pale. He gave Ganya a weird, accusatory glance; his lips, distorted by a strange and quite inappropriate smile, were trembling in a vain effort to formulate a response.

"I don't care about myself... but... not her... I won't allow it!..." he said at last softly; but then something seemed to give way in him; he turned away from Ganya, buried his face in his hands, went over to a distant corner and, with his face to the wall, said in a faltering voice, "One day you will really come to regret this!"

Ganya was truly crushed. Kolya hugged the Prince and comforted him; everyone – Rogozhin, Varya, Ptitsyn, Nina Alexandrovna, even the aged Ardalion Alexandrovich, crowded round the Prince in sympathy.

"It's nothing, it's quite all right!" the Prince mumbled as he faced everyone in turn, still smiling that awkward smile of his.

"And he will regret it!" Rogozhin cried. "You will regret it, Ganya, offending such an innocent lamb! Prince, my friend, leave them all, turn your back on them and come with me! You'll see what Rogozhin is like with people he cares for!"

Nastasya Filippovna too was most astonished at what Ganya had done and at the Prince's response. Her customary pale and reflective features, so out of keeping with her recent mask of assumed frivolity, were now racked by a new sentiment; and yet, she appeared not to want to reveal it, and the mischievous smile tried to make a comeback.

"I'm sure I've seen his face somewhere!" she suddenly observed, in all seriousness this time, recalling quite unexpectedly her previous question.

"And you're not even ashamed! Surely you're nothing like you make yourself out to be. I'm convinced of that!" the Prince suddenly cried, with heartfelt reproach.

Nastasya Filippovna showed surprise; she smiled as though masking something else under her smile, and with a somewhat hesitant glance at Ganya, made as if to leave the room.

121

But halfway, she turned back, approached Nina Alexandrovna with quick steps, took her hand and brought it to her lips.

"He is quite right, I am not like that at all," she whispered, her words faltering with emotion and her face flushed red; she then turned on her heel and left the room so quickly that no one realized quite why she had turned back. All anyone saw was that she had whispered something to Nina Alexandrovna and at most kissed her hand. However, Varya saw and heard everything and she followed Nastasya Filippovna with her eyes full of surprise.

Ganya came to and with a start rushed off after Nastasya Filippovna, but she had already left. He caught up with her on the stairs.

"I'll find my own way out!" she called out. "Au revoir, see you tonight! Make sure you come, mind!"

He retraced his steps, lost in thought, confused; he was thoroughly perplexed, much more so than previously. He couldn't get the Prince out of his mind either... He was so abstracted that he hardly noticed Rogozhin and his men shuffling past him and even jostling him in the doorway as they hurriedly followed Rogozhin out of the apartment. Everybody seemed to be expressing an opinion forcibly, arguing some point. Rogozhin was close on Ptitsyn's heels, insisting on something with great urgency.

"Not your day, Ganya, was it?" Rogozhin called out in passing.

Ganya looked at them both with alarm.

11

THE PRINCE LEFT THE SITTING ROOM and shut himself up in his room. He was immediately joined by Kolya, who began to comfort him. The poor lad could not help being solicitous.

"You did well to leave," he said, "they're going to be at one another's throats more than ever now, and that's how it is every day here, and all because of this Nastasya Filippovna."

"There are lots of running sores in this house, Kolya," the Prince observed.

"Yes, sores, that goes without saying. We brought it upon ourselves. But I've got a friend, and he's even more miserable. Do you want to meet him?"

"I do indeed. Your friend, you say?"

"Yes, almost. I'll explain it all later... Don't you think Nastasya Filippovna is gorgeous? I've never managed to see her till now, not for want of trying. She's just stunning. I wouldn't have minded if Ganya had gone for her out of love. But why is he taking money, that's what bothers me!"

"Yes, I can't say I like your brother much."

"No wonder! Especially after... You know, I don't really have much time for the conventional attitude in such cases. Some madman or a fool, or some out-and-out brute in a state of madness delivers a slap in the face, and the person in question is dishonoured for life, and can't redeem the offence except with blood, or unless the offender grovels before him on his knees. As far as I'm concerned this is weird and unreasonable. Lermontov's drama *The Masquerade* is based on this. And – if you ask me – it's silly. That is, it doesn't make sense. But then he wasn't much more than a child when he wrote it."

"I like your sister very much."

"She gave him as good as she got, spitting in his face. She's got guts, our Varya has! I'm sure you wouldn't have spat, but not because of cowardice. Talk of the Devil! I knew she'd come. She's a dear, even though she has her faults."

"What are you doing here?" Varya challenged her brother. "Go along, see to your father. I'm sorry he's bothering you, Prince!"

"No, not at all, quite the contrary."

"My older sister is on her hobby horse, if there's one thing I hate... Incidentally, I was sure father would go off with Rogozhin. He's probably sorry for himself now. Perhaps I should go and see him after all," Kolya added as he left the room.

"Thank God I've managed to take Mummy back to her room, and there've been no fresh incidents. Ganya is deeply shocked and withdrawn. Small wonder!... It'll be a lesson for him. I came to thank you and ask you, Prince, have you ever met Nastasya Filippovna before?"

"No, never."

"So how did you know to say to her directly that she's 'not like that'? And you seemed to be right. It turns out she is probably really not like that at all. But then I don't think I'll ever fathom her out! Of course, she was bent on giving offence, that's plain enough. I've heard loads of strange things about her from the past. But if she came to invite us, why did she have to be so beastly to Mother? Ptitsyn knows her very well, but he says there was no way of telling what she was going to get up to. And the way she spoke to Rogozhin?... That's not the way to talk if one has the least self-respect, in the house of your... Mama is also very worried about you."

"No need!" the Prince said with a shrug.

"And how readily she obeyed you..."

"Obeyed in what way?"

"You said she should be ashamed, and she changed instantly. You have an influence on her, Prince," Varya added with a shadow of a smile.

The door opened and Ganya entered quite unexpectedly.

"Prince, it was awful of me," he said with feeling, "forgive me, old chap." His expression was pained. The Prince regarded him with astonishment and took a while to reply. "Forgive me, please forgive me!" Ganya insisted. "If you like, I'll kiss your hand – well?"

The Prince was very surprised, and, not saying a word, he embraced him. They kissed each other in all sincerity.

"I'd never have imagined you were like that!" the Prince observed at last, his chest heaving. "I thought you wouldn't be... capable."

"To humble myself, you mean?... And what made me suppose you were an idiot! You are capable of perceiving what no one else ever will. I'd have liked to talk to you, but... better not!"

"Here's someone else you ought to ask pardon of," the Prince said, pointing to Varya.

"No, she's one of the enemy. Believe me, Prince, I've tried many a time. Forgiveness is not the done thing here!" Ganya declared fervently, and he turned away from Varya.

"Yes, I will forgive!" Varya said suddenly.

"And you will accept Nastasya Filippovna's invitation for tonight?"

"I will, if you tell me to, only be reasonable – how can I possibly go there after all this?"

"But she's not like that. You know, she's just play-acting! Leading us up the garden path?" Ganya retorted with a malicious laugh.

"I know she may be play-acting, but to what end? All the same, Ganya, think, what does she take you for? All right, so she kissed Mother's hand. Maybe that's part of her game, but she also mocked you! That's not worth seventy-five thousand roubles, trust me, my dear brother! I still believe in you, that's why I'm speaking to you. Look, why don't you stay away yourself tonight? Be careful! This is going to end in tears!" Having said this, Varya left the room, deeply upset.

"They're all like that!" Ganya said with a smirk. "And do they really imagine I don't know any of this myself? I know it all much better than they do."

Having said this, Ganya took a seat on the sofa, apparently intending to prolong his visit.

"If you know it all yourself," the Prince enquired rather diffidently, "how is it you chose such a difficult path for yourself, seeing that she's really not worth the seventy-five thousand?"

"I'm not talking about that," Ganya muttered. "Well, anyway, tell me, what do you think, I want your opinion above all – is this 'difficult path' worth seventy-five thousand or not?"

"To my mind, not."

"I should have guessed. And to marry on these terms would be shameful?"

"Very."

"Well then, you might as well know I will marry, now more certainly than ever. I may have had my doubts before, but not any more! No, don't say a word! I know what you're going to say…"

"I don't think you do! What I find astonishing is your immense confidence—"

"In what? What confidence?"

"That Nastasya Filippovna will necessarily agree to tie the knot with you, and secondly, even if she did, that the seventy-five thousand would immediately end up in your pocket. That said, there may of course be lots that I'm not privy to."

Ganya leant heavily in the direction of the Prince.

"There's no 'maybe' about it!" he said. "Why else would I have taken all this upon me?"

"I think it happens time and time again – people marry money, and it stays in the wife's hands."

"N-no, it's not going to be like that with us… There… there are circumstances," Ganya muttered, his expression changing from pensive to alarmed. "And as regards her decision, there's not the least doubt about it," he added hurriedly. "What makes you think she will refuse me?"

"I can only judge by what I've seen. There, Varvara Ardalionovna said the same thing—"

"Ha! They just don't know what to say. And as for Rogozhin, she laughed at him, that much I saw, don't worry. I couldn't help it. At first I had my doubts, but then I saw it. Or perhaps by the way she treated Mother, Father and Varya?"

"And you."

"Perhaps. But it's more a case of primeval feminine antagonism. She's very short-tempered, vengeful and proud. Like an office clerk who's been passed over for promotion! She wanted to demonstrate all her contempt for them... and to me too. That's the way it is, I don't deny it... Still, she will marry me. You've no idea to what lengths she may be driven by vanity. Now she looks down upon me for accepting money so that she, someone else's former mistress, may be palmed off on me, and has no idea that someone else might have taken even greater advantage of her. He'll have latched on to her and started befuddling her with all kinds of progressive and liberal notions about women's rights and the rest, and she would have been putty in his hands. He'll have sucked up to her, self-opinionated fool that she is (it's all so easy, you know!), that it's on account of the purity of her heart and her erstwhile suffering that he was asking for her hand, but in actual fact it would have been only for her money. I'm not being favoured because I can't be two-faced, more's the pity. And what is it she's up to herself if not the selfsame thing? So why berate me and play all these games? Because I myself refuse to give in and choose to show some mettle. Well, we'll see!"

"Were you really in love with her before?"

"I was at first. Well, that'll do... There are women who are fit only to be mistresses, nothing else. I'm not saying that she was my mistress. If she behaves, so will I. If she causes trouble, I'll leave her at once, but I'll keep the money. I don't want to be a laughing stock, anything but a laughing stock."

"If there's one thing," the Prince observed tentatively, "Nastasya Filippovna strikes me as being rather sensible. Why should she, with so much heartache in prospect, allow herself to be trapped? Surely she could find someone else to marry. That's what intrigues me."

"This is where her scheming comes in! There's a good deal you don't know in all this, you see... and, besides, she's convinced I love her to distraction, I swear to you and, you know, I'm firmly convinced that she too loves me, in her own way that is, it's more like love-hate. She'll treat me as her underling all our lives long (that may well be what she wants most of all), but will love me all the same after her own way. I tell you, she's a typical Russian in this. Well, she's in for a surprise from me. That scene with Varya was quite unpremeditated, but to my advantage. She has just seen and been able to assure herself of my fidelity and that I'll break all my ties for her sake. So you see, we're not so foolish after all. Incidentally, I hope you don't take me for an idle chatterbox? Prince, old chap, it may indeed be extremely foolish of me to confide in you like this. But it's precisely because you're the first decent person I've come across that I've latched on to you so. I trust you don't bear me any grudges for what I did, eh? This is perhaps the first time in years that I've spoken frankly. There's a dearth of honest people here. Ptitsyn's the most honest of the lot. Do you find it funny, or what? Scoundrels prefer the company of honest people – does that surprise you? For your knowledge I am… To be honest though, I don't think I am a scoundrel at all, what's your honest opinion? Why is it that following her example everyone calls me so? And, would you believe it, following both examples, I'm beginning to regard myself a scoundrel too! Now that takes the biscuit!"

"I'd never call you a scoundrel," the Prince said. "There was a time I thought you were bad, and suddenly you redeemed yourself. Hence the moral – don't judge prematurely. Now I can see that not only are you not bad, but one can't even accuse you of being spoilt. As I see it, you're simply a plain ordinary man in every sense of the word, with no originality to speak of."

Ganya gave him a malevolent little smile, but did not say a word. The Prince saw that his appraisal had not gone down well, felt a pang of embarrassment and also fell silent.

"Has father been asking you for money?" Ganya suddenly enquired.

"No."

"He will. Don't give him any! Imagine, there was a time he was a perfectly decent person. He mixed with the best of people. And how soon they all go to pot, these decent old people! All one needs is a slight change in circumstances, and all that was there formerly is gone in a puff of smoke. Formerly he never fibbed to the same extent, I assure you. Formerly he was just too excitable, and – you can see the result of that! Of course it's the demon drink to blame. Do you know, he keeps a mistress? So he's not just a petty fibber any more. I just can't understand how Mother puts up with it. Has he ever told you about the siege of Kars? Or how the left bay of his troika suddenly began to speak? Yes, it's come to that."

And Ganya suddenly began to roll with laughter.

"Why are you looking at me like that?" he asked.

"I was surprised that you can laugh so heartily. You still haven't lost the child's innocent laughter. Just now you said, 'I'll kiss your hand if you wish,' that's just how a child would have spoken. It shows you are still young at heart. And all of a sudden you start lecturing on this nonsense and the seventy-five thousand. Really it was all so gross and inappropriate."

"And what do you conclude from this?"

"That you're being a little bit inconsiderate perhaps. Wouldn't it be best to stop and think first? And it may well be that what Varvara Ardalionovna was saying is true after all."

"I see, we're into morality now! That I'm still immature, I wouldn't argue about," Ganya interrupted with fervour, "the fact alone that I'm engaged with you in this conversation is proof enough. I realize I'm sleepwalking into all this," he continued, "if I hadn't been, I'd have tripped up, that's for sure. I'm driven by passion, by the call of the heart, because I mean to make money. No doubt you think that as soon as I lay my hands on the seventy-five thousand, I'll buy myself a four-in-hand. Nothing of the sort, I'll start wearing my threadbare old tailcoat and cancel all my club connections. Not too many of our people in commerce can stand the heat, I mean to. It's all about standing firm to the end! Ptitsyn spent seventeen years sleeping rough, he peddled penknives in the street and built things up from nothing. Now he's got a cool sixty thousand but it's come through sheer hard graft! Well, I'll bypass all this graft and have a head start. In fifteen years' time they'll say, 'Look, there's Ivolgin, the King of the Jews.'" You tell me that I lack originality. Remember, my dear Prince, that there's nothing more offensive than to tell a man of our times and background that he lacks originality, lacks character and has nothing distinguishing about him. You didn't even deign to rate me as a proper scoundrel and, you know, I was ready kill you for that! You insulted me worse than Yepanchin, who thinks me (without any question, without any inducements, through the goodness of my heart alone) capable of selling my wife to him! This has long been a sore point with me, and I want money. Having made money, know you this – I shall be a highly original person. Money has that vile and detestable property that it can even bestow talent. And it will continue to be thus till the end of the world. You will tell me that this is childishness or, at the very least, daydreaming – well, that's no skin off my nose, but the mission will be accomplished regardless. I'll see things through to the end. *Rira bien, qui rira le dernier.** Why should Yepanchin offend me so? Is it because I make him angry? No! It's merely because I'm so insignificant. But, if I… Still, enough of that, it's time. I'll drop in some time again. You'll be comfortable here. You'll be one of the family. But, make sure you don't let the side down. I have a hunch we'll either be friends, or bitter enemies. What do you think, Prince: if I had kissed your hand (as I genuinely intended to), would I have subsequently become an enemy of yours?"

"Most assuredly, only not for ever, you subsequently wouldn't have been able to keep it up and would have pardoned me," the Prince concluded on reflection and with a hearty laugh.

"I say, you're a sly one. Hell, you've introduced a bit of venom even here. Who knows, perhaps you are my enemy after all? By the way, ha-ha-ha! I quite forgot, am I right in thinking that Nastasya Filippovna is very much to your liking, eh?"

"Yes, she… is!"

"Are you in love?"

"N-no."

"And yet you blush and there's suffering on your face. Well, all right, all right, I shan't mock. Au revoir. And do you know, she is charitable – it's hard to believe, isn't it? Do you think she lives with that Totsky? Not at all! And this has been so for quite some time now. And have you noticed, she is terribly awkward and at times awfully unsure of herself? Really. It is precisely women of that sort that like to dominate. Well, goodbye!"

Ganya left in a positively carefree mood and in much better spirits than when he came in. The Prince remained motionless for about ten minutes, immersed in thought.

Kolya again popped his head round the door.

"I'm not hungry, Kolya. I had a good meal at the Yepanchin's."

Kolya entered the room and gave the Prince a note. It was from the General, folded and sealed. By Kolya's face one could see how difficult it was for him to deliver the errand. The Prince read it, got up and took his hat.

"It's just a stone's throw away," Kolya was at pains to conceal his embarrassment. "He's sitting there now with a bottle. And however did he manage to get credit there? That's what I don't understand. Prince, I beg you, don't tell anyone afterwards that I passed the note to you! The number of times I swore not to pass these notes on, but I do it for pity's sake. And another thing, don't take any nonsense from him, simply give him some small change, and let that be the end of the matter."

"I had an idea myself, Kolya; I need to see your father... something's cropped up... Let's go..."

12

THEY DIDN'T HAVE FAR TO GO. Kolya led the Prince into a billiard room-cum-café hard by the Liteiny Prospect, where on the ground floor, entering straight from the street, and over to the right, was a private room in which Ardalion Alexandrovich, as a long-standing customer, was already seated at the table with a bottle before him, and actually holding a copy of *L'Indépendance belge*. He was expecting the Prince; as soon as he saw him, he laid the paper aside and launched into a fervent long-winded discourse of which the Prince, as it turned out, hardly understood a word, because the General was already more than a little drunk.

"I haven't got ten roubles," the Prince cut him off, "all I have is twenty-five. Why don't you change it and give me fifteen, otherwise I'll be penniless myself."

"Oh, have no fear. And rest assured, this very instant..."

"Besides, there's something I want to ask you, General. Have you ever been to Nastasya Filippovna's?"

"Me? Have I ever been to her place? You're asking me? On numerous occasions, my dear friend, on a whole lot of occasions!" the General exclaimed in an outburst of self-confident triumphant irony. "But in the end I myself called a halt, because of my reluctance to encourage an indecent relationship. You saw for yourself, you witnessed what happened this morning. I did everything a father could do – a humble, tolerant father. Now, however, a different sort of father will take centre stage, and then – we shall see, we shall see whether a venerable old veteran will put an end to an intrigue, or whether a shameless coquette will wheedle her way into a noble household."

"And I came expressly to enquire if you could not introduce me tonight as an acquaintance at Nastasya Filippovna's? I need to be there come what may. It's urgent, but I've no idea how to go about it. I was introduced, but she didn't actually invite me. She is holding a grand soirée tonight. I'm quite ready, as it happens, to flout the usual conventions and even put up with ridicule as long as I can gain access."

"That's exactly what I was thinking about, my young friend," the General called out enthusiastically, "it's not this piffling matter I summoned you for!" he continued, slipping the money through his fingers and letting it slide into his pocket, "I called you especially to make up a twosome for a visit to – nay, descent on – Nastasya Filippovna! General Ivolgin and Prince Myshkin! See what she says to that! This will be my opportunity, under the guise of good manners, to declare my will at last – more indirectly than directly, but it'll be as good as directly. After that it'll be up to Ganya what to do next, whether I'm a venerable father and... so to speak... and so on, or... But come what may! Yours is a highly promising idea. We'll set out at nine, there's still bags of time."

"Where does she live?"

"Far from here, near the Bolshoy Theatre, Mytovtsova's house, almost in the Square itself, on the first floor... It's not going to be a large party, even though it is her birthday, and it'll end early..."

The evening was wearing on; the Prince still sat, listened and waited as the General started on countless anecdotes, none of which he finished. The General asked for another bottle and took an hour over it, then a third, and polished that off too. In between he managed to recount half his life story. Finally the Prince got up and declared he could not wait any longer. The General drank the last dregs from the bottle, got up and headed for the exit, none too steadily. The Prince was desperate. He was annoyed with himself for having been so trusting. In fact his trust extended only in so far as he wanted the

General to effect an introduction to Nastasya Filippovna's even at the risk of provoking some incident, but he never expected the General to reach such a sorry state; the latter was completely drunk, he talked incessantly with gusto and tear-soaked eyes. It all revolved round the fact that in consequence of the foul behaviour of every member of his family, everything was going to rack and ruin and it was high time to put a stop to it. They finally emerged on the Liteiny Prospect. It was still thawing; a persistent dismal warmish breeze stirred on every street corner; carriage wheels slid through the mud; horses' hooves cut through the slush, finding the paved surface underneath with a thud; crowds of wet and cheerless pedestrians scurried about aimlessly on the pavements. They encountered the occasional drunk.

"Do you see those rows of lit windows?" the General said. "My comrades live there, whereas I, I, the most decorated and the most unfavoured of them all, I am obliged to trudge to the Bolshoy Theatre on my way to the abode of a woman of dubious reputation! A man who has thirteen bullets lodged in his chest... you don't believe me? And yet it was solely because of me that Pirogov sent a telegram to Paris and left the besieged Sebastopol briefly,* and Nélaton,* the French Physician-at-Court, secured for himself a free pass in the name of science into besieged Sebastopol to examine me. The Chiefs of Staff were informed: 'Ah, it's Ivolgin, the one with the thirteen bullets!...' That's the talk one heard, my dear sir! Do you see that house over there, Prince? It's where my old pal, General Sokolovich lives in the bosom of his numerous and worthy family. That house, then another three on the Nevsky and a couple more on Morskaya – and there you have the whole circle of my acquaintances, of my personal acquaintances, that is. Nina Alexandrovna has long reconciled herself to the circumstances. I however continue to reminisce... and, as it were, repose in the refined social circle of my erstwhile friends and subordinates, who to this day continue to respect me. This General Sokolovich (it's been some time since I've paid him a visit and saw Anna Fyodorovna)... you know, my dear Prince, once one ceases to entertain, a neglect of others sets in involuntarily. That said... hm... I have a feeling you don't believe me... To be sure, why not introduce the son of the best friend of my childhood days into this charming family home? General Ivolgin and Prince Myshkin! You will see a most charming girl, not just one; two or even three, the pride and joy of our city and society – charm, education, commitment... the feminist issues, poetry – all in all a felicitous and many-splendoured amalgam, and that's on top of a dowry of at least eighty thousand roubles in ready cash for each, which would not come amiss, never mind the femininist issues... in a word, I simply must and am duty bound to introduce you. General Ivolgin and Prince Myshkin!"

"What, now? But you've forgotten—" the Prince was about to retort.

"Don't worry, don't worry, I haven't forgotten, follow me! Here, up this splendid flight of stairs. I'm surprised there's no commissionaire about, but... it's a holiday, the commissionaire must be on leave. The drunkard should have been sacked. This Sokolovich, I'll have you know, is beholden to me for every stroke of fortune in his private and public life, to me and me alone and to no one else, but... we've arrived."

The Prince no longer protested against the visit and followed the General obediently so as not to irritate him, in the blithe hope that General Sokolovich and all his family would little by little dissolve like a mirage and prove to be mere figments of the imagination, and they would then be able to retrace their steps as though nothing had happened. But, to his horror, he was beginning to lose hope. The General climbed the staircase as if he really was on home ground, offering a running commentary of a biographical and topographical nature that betokened an accurate knowledge of the facts. At last, on the second floor, at the door of a magnificent apartment where the General was reaching for the doorbell, the Prince made his final decision to run; however, something caught his eye and he stopped.

"You've made a mistake, General," he said, "on the door it says Kulakov, whereas you want Sokolovich."

"Kulakov?... Kulakov doesn't ring a bell. This is Sokolovich's flat and I'm ringing Sokolovich's bell. Kulakov be damned... There, someone's coming."

The door really opened. A servant appeared and announced that their lordships were out.

"How unfortunate, how very unfortunate, this is indeed a stroke of bad luck!" Ardalion Alexandrovich repeated a number of times ruefully. "Tell them, my dear fellow, that General Ivolgin and Prince Myshkin wished to pay their profound respects and very much, very much regret that..."

At this moment another face looked out from the interior, probably that of the housekeeper, perhaps even governess, a lady of about forty, in a sombre attire. On hearing the names of General Ivolgin and Prince Myshkin, she approached tentatively, but full of curiosity.

"Maria Alexandrovna is not at home," she said, giving the General an especially searching look, "she and the young lady, Alexandra Mikhailovna, have gone to visit Grandmother."

"So Alexandra Mikhailovna is out too. Oh God, what awful bad luck! And imagine, madam, bad luck seems to follow me always! Please convey my regards, and for Alexandra Mikhailovna a reminder... in a word, convey to her my most heartfelt longing for that which she herself longed for on Thursday night to the strains of the Chopin ballad – she will know... My profound respects! General Ivolgin and Prince Myshkin!"

"I shall bear it in mind, sir," the lady said, inclining her head politely.

As they descended the stairs, the General, his fervour still not abated, continued to deplore that they had found nobody in and that the Prince had to forgo the opportunity of such a delightful acquaintanceship.

"You know, my dear chap, I am a bit of a poet at heart, have you noticed? To be sure, to be sure... I have the feeling we went to the wrong place entirely," he concluded unexpectedly. "The Sokoloviches, I now recall, live somewhere else entirely, and as far as I know, they're in Moscow now. Yes, I made a mistake, but... it can't be helped."

"There's only one thing I'd like to know," the Prince enquired despondently, "should I stop relying on you altogether and make my own way?"

"Stop relying? Make your own way? For heaven's sake why, when for me this is the most challenging assignment ever, and destined to play such a crucial role in the fate of my whole family? But, my young friend, you do not know Ivolgin. Whoever says 'Ivolgin', says 'rock'. You can rely on Ivolgin as on a rock, that's how they referred to me in the detachment in which my service career began. I just need to pop in while we're here into a house, my soul's sanctuary for many years now, following all the trials and tribulations..."

"You want to go back home?"

"No, I want to look up Mrs Terentyeva, the widow of Captain Terentyev, an erstwhile subordinate of mine... and even friend. Here, in the widow's house, my soul revives and it is where I take my personal and family grievances... And as today I bear a particularly heavy moral burden, I'd—"

"It seems I've made an awful mistake," the Prince muttered, "just by troubling you in the first place. Besides which you're now... Goodbye!"

"But I can't, I simply can't let you go now, my young friend!" the General snapped back. "The widow, the mother of a family, touches in me those chords which reverberate through my whole being. A call on her will be a matter of no more than five minutes. In this house – and I as good as live here – they don't stand on ceremony. I'll just have quick wash and smarten myself up, and then we'll take a cab straight to the Bolshoy Theatre. I assure you, I need you for the rest of the evening... This is the house, we're here already... Ah, Kolya, it's you? Tell me, is Marfa Borisovna in, or have you just arrived?"

"Oh no," Kolya, whom they ran into at the house gate, responded, "I've been here for ages, to see Ippolit, he's worse, he hasn't been up this morning. I've just been down to the shop to get a pack of cards. Marfa Borisovna is expecting you. Only, Papa, you should take a look at yourself!..." Kolya concluded, looking closely at his father's bearing and carriage. "Well, let's go then!"

The meeting with Kolya obliged the Prince to follow the General to Marfa Borisovna too, but he did not intend to remain there more than a few minutes. The Prince needed to see Kolya; as for the General, he'd resolved to part company with him, and was sorry he'd ever had anything to do with him. They used the tradesmen's stairs to go all the way up to the third floor.

"You want to introduce the Prince?" Kolya asked on the way.

"Yes I do, Kolya. General Ivolgin and Prince Myshkin, but, tell me... how is Marfa Borisovna?..."

"You know, Papa, it's better you didn't go at all! She'll kill you! You haven't shown up for three days, and she's expecting money from you. Why did you ever promise her any? You're always like that! Now you have to deal with it yourself."

On the third floor they stopped at a low door. The General was visibly perplexed and was urging the Prince to lead the way.

"I'll stay here," he mumbled, "I want it to be a surprise..."

135

Kolya entered first. A woman of about forty, heavily rouged and powdered, in slippers, a short jacket, her hair done in little plaits, looked out and the General's intended surprise went for nought. No sooner had the woman caught sight of him than she screamed.

"There he is, the worthless, obnoxious man, I had a nasty premonition!"

"Do let's enter, this is not serious," the General muttered in a continued effort to smile.

But it was serious. They had hardly entered and crossed the low, unlit entrance hall leading into a narrow front room, furnished with half a dozen wicker chairs and a couple of small gaming tables, than the woman resumed in her plaintive, apparently well-practised falsetto, "How is it you are not the least little bit ashamed, you barbarous monster, my family's blight, you unfeeling ogre! You robbed me, you sucked me dry, and still it's not enough for you! How much longer must I put up with this, you shameless disgusting man!"

"Marfa Borisovna, Marfa Borisovna! This... is Prince Myshkin. General Ivolgin and Prince Myshkin," the General mumbled in his state of confusion and embarrassment.

"Would you believe it," the Captain's widow suddenly turned to the Prince, "would you believe it, this shameless person has not spared my poor fatherless children! He's robbed me of everything, he's cleaned the house out, he's sold and pawned everything, he's left me with nothing. What will I do with your promissory notes, you devious, reprehensible man? Answer me, you snake in the grass, answer me, you greedy swine! How will I feed my little ones? Here he is, so sozzled he can't stand up any more... What have I done to deserve this, you vile, despicable cheat? Answer me!"

But the General was beyond all that.

"Marfa Borisovna, twenty-five roubles... all I can with the help of a high-minded friend. Prince! I've made a dreadful mistake! But such is... life... As for now... please excuse me, I feel weak," the General carried on, standing in the middle of the room and bowing left and right, "I feel faint, excuse me! Lena! Fetch me a cushion... my darling!"

Lena, an eight-year-old girl, immediately dashed off to fetch a cushion, which she placed on the hard, decrepit, buckram-covered settle. The General slumped down, probably with the intention of continuing his oration, but no sooner had he come into contact with it than he leant over, turned his face to the wall, and was fast asleep in an instant. Marfa Borisovna ceremoniously and despondently gestured the Prince towards a chair by the gaming table, sat down opposite, propping up her cheek with her hand and, sighing deeply without speaking a word, rested her eyes on the Prince. Three small children, two girls and a boy, Lena being the eldest, went up to the table, put their arms on it and also fixed their eyes on the Prince. Kolya came in from another room.

"I'm very glad I met you here, Kolya," the Prince addressed him. "I wonder if you could help me? I need to be at Nastasya Filippovna's without fail. I had asked Ardalion Alexandrovich originally, but as you see he's fallen asleep. Please take me there because I don't know my way around here at all. To be sure, I have the address, by the Bolshoy Theatre, Mrs Mytovtsova's house."

"Nastasya Filippovna, if you want to know, never lived near the Bolshoy Theatre, nor has Father ever been at her place. I'm surprised you took him at his word. She lives by Vladimirskaya Street at the Five-Ways Junction, which is not too far from here. Do you want to go now? It's half-past nine. I'll gladly take you there."

The Prince and Kolya set off immediately. Alas, the Prince had no money for a cab, and they had to go on foot.

"I wanted to introduce you to Ippolit," Kolya said, "he's the eldest son of the Captain's widow and he was in the other room. He's been in bed all day, feeling ill. But he is a bit odd, very quick to take offence, and I had an idea he'd feel awkward if he came out to see you under the circumstances… it's different for me, because I've a father, whereas he has a mother, and there's the difference, there's no dishonour for a man in that sort of situation. But maybe there's no such variation between the sexes. Ippolit is a splendid fellow, but he's got some weird ideas."

"You said he has consumption?"

"Yes, I think so, he'd be better off dead. If I were him, I'd definitely want to die. He'd hate to leave his brothers and sisters, those tiny tots. If we could, if we had the money, we'd have rented some lodgings and left our families behind. We dream of it. And do you know, when I told him what happened to you, he really lost his temper. He said that anyone who puts up with a slap in the face and doesn't fight a duel is a scoundrel. I must say, he's very much on edge, I've stopped contradicting him. So, Nastasya Filippovna invited you along at the drop of a hat?"

"The trouble is, she didn't!"

"So how come you're going?" Kolya exclaimed, coming to an abrupt halt in the middle of the pavement, "and… and dressed as you are, to a formal occasion?"

"Honestly, I don't know. If they let me in – all well and good, if they don't – so much the worse. As for my clothes – what's to be done?"

"Have you any business to be there? Or is it simply *pour passer le temps* in 'polite society'?"

"No, to be sure… that is, there is a business matter… it's difficult for me to explain, but—"

"Well, whatever it may be is up to you, my main concern is that you shouldn't be drawn to the reception just to enjoy the company of fancy women, generals and moneylenders. If that were so, pardon me, Prince, I'd have ridiculed you and held you in contempt. There are so few decent people about, there's no one to look up to. In the end one is obliged to look down upon the lot, but they don't like it. Varya's the first. And have you noticed, Prince, everyone's an adventurer these days! It's especially true of Russia, our beloved motherland. And how did all this come to be so? I haven't got a clue. You'd have thought everything was rock solid, but look what's happened! Everyone's talking and writing about it all over. They make a fuss about it. They all like to make a lot of fuss. The parents are the first to go back on their principles and then blush at their morals of yesterday. Take that father in Moscow who tried to persuade his son to stop at *nothing* in acquiring money. It was in the papers. Take my father, the General! What has become of him, I ask you? But you know what, I think my father is an honest man. I swear he is! He just needs to pull his socks up and stop drinking. Honestly! I feel sorry for him. But I'm afraid to open my mouth, because they'll all laugh. Honestly, I feel sorry for him. The rest are just too clever by half. Moneylenders one and all! Ippolit thinks there's nothing wrong with moneylenders, he says it's as it should be, they're part of the economic boom and bust, some kind of an ebb and flow, or something to that effect. I hate it when he speaks like that, but he's embittered. Imagine, his mother gets money from the General and lends it out to him at a high rate. It's pretty scandalous! But do you know that my mother, that is, Nina Alexandrovna, helps Ippolit out with money, items of clothing, underwear, the lot, and to some extent even the other children via Ippolit, because they're awfully neglected. Varya also helps."

"There you are, and you thought there were no honest and strong people about, just moneylenders. But there they are, the strong people, your mother and Varya. Wouldn't you say that to help under such circumstances is a sign of moral strength?"

"Varya is just too full of herself and she wants to show off so as to keep up with Mother. As for Mother... I really respect her. Yes, I respect and approve of what she does. Even Ippolit thinks so, and he's the resentful one. He made fun to begin with and said it was unbecoming of my mother, but now he's not so sure. Hm! So you call it moral strength, do you? I'll bear it in mind. Ganya knows nothing of this, but he'd call it self-indulgence."

"Ganya doesn't know, you say? It seems to me there's a great deal that Ganya doesn't know yet," the Prince couldn't help saying, lost deep in thought.

"You know, Prince, I like you very much. What happened back then between you will soon have faded from my mind."

"The feeling's mutual, Kolya."

"Listen, how do you plan to survive? I'll soon find some work and will earn something. Why don't the three of us – you, Ippolit and me – rent lodgings and live together? Father can then come and visit us."

"I'd be delighted. But we must wait and see. At the moment I'm very... very upset. What? Are we here? This is the house, is it?... What a splendid entrance! And a doorman too! Well, Kolya, I don't know what will come of it."

The Prince looked totally lost.

"Tell me about it tomorrow! Chin up! I wish you all the best, because I'm totally on your side! Goodbye. I'm going back to the house, and will tell Ippolit everything. Don't worry about not being admitted, because you will be! She's quite a character. Up these stairs, on the first floor. The doorman will show you."

13

As he climbed the stairs, the Prince did his best to keep his spirits up. "The worst case of all," he thought, "would be if she turned me away, or thought something bad of me, or if she let me in, but laughed in my face... But, never mind!" And true enough, in the event he was able to dismiss these fears. But as to why he was going in the first place and what he was going to do there, he had no satisfactory answers. Even if he could by some stroke of good fortune have found an opportunity to tell Nastasya Filippovna, "Don't marry this man, don't ruin your life, he doesn't love you, only your money, he said so himself, and so did Aglaya Yepanchina, which I've now come to tell you," this would hardly have been the right and proper thing to do under the circumstances. There was yet one more unresolved question, which was so fundamental that the Prince was even afraid to contemplate it; he shied away from it and dared not consider it; he blushed and shuddered at the very thought of it. But the upshot of it all was that in spite of all his fears and misgivings, he entered the building and asked for Nastasya Filippovna.

Nastasya Filippovna occupied a medium-size, but splendidly appointed, apartment. During the five years she'd lived in St Petersburg there was a time at the beginning when Afanasy Ivanovich was particularly unsparing with his money for her; he was still counting on her love and expected to entice her, in the main, by creature comforts and luxury, knowing full well how easy it was to get used to luxury and how difficult it was to do without it subsequently once it had become a necessity. In this respect Totsky remained true to the good old tradition which paid the highest regard possible to the invincible might of sensual attraction. Nastasya Filippovna did not spurn comfort; on the contrary, she enjoyed it, but – and this could not but appear surprising – would not be a slave to it, as though she could give it up at the drop of a hat; once or twice she even made a point of stating this, which did not best please Totsky. To be sure, there was a lot about Nastasya Filippovna which displeased Afanasy Ivanovich, even to the point of contempt. Quite apart from the gracelessness of the people whom she sometimes attracted, and was by nature inclined to attract, she had one or two other strange foibles; she evinced an uncouth combination of contrary inclinations, an ability to nurture and exhibit predilections which could not be associated with, or expected from, someone with claims to respectability and refinement. In truth, if Nastasya Filippovna had, for example, in the name of good taste and sophistication, pretended some such charming and disarming fact as not to know that peasant women were not in the habit of wearing fine cambric underwear such as she was, Afanasy Ivanovich would have been simply delighted. It was to such ends that Totsky, who was most knowledgeable in such matters, had sought to direct the whole of her early upbringing in line with his own scheme; alas, however, the results turned out to be most unexpected. Nonetheless, there remained something indefinably alluring about Nastasya Filippovna, which never ceased to baffle Afanasy Ivanovich, and continued to exercise him even now, long after all his earlier designs on her had come to nothing.

The Prince was greeted by a maid (Nastasya Filippovna's domestic staff were all female) and, to his surprise, she listened perfectly calmly to his request to see the lady of the house. Neither his dirty boots, nor his wide-brimmed hat, nor his cloak, nor even his dismayed looks, produced the slightest hesitation on her part. She helped him out of his cloak, invited him to step into a side room and set off to announce him.

Nastasya Filippovna's house party was made up of her usual entourage. If anything, there were fewer people present than in previous years on such occasions. The two principal guests were of course Afanasy Ivanovich Totsky and Ivan Fyodorovich Yepanchin; both were in fine form, but both were under a hidden cloud on account of their thinly veiled concern regarding the promised announcement relating to Ganya. There was of course Ganya himself – also very gloomy, withdrawn almost to the point of being unsociable, skulking mostly in the background, refusing to join in, not saying a word. He hadn't had the courage to bring Varya along, but Nastasya Filippovna never even mentioned her; although as soon as she had greeted him, she recalled the incident with the Prince. The General, who knew nothing of it, immediately pricked up his ears. At that point Ganya with perfect equanimity gave a terse, matter-of-fact, though very frank, account of all that had happened, and said that he'd already been to ask the Prince's pardon. Moreover, he did not fail in all earnestness to mention that someone had, goodness only knows why, declared the Prince to be an idiot, but that he disagreed with this totally and, it went without saying, considered him to be a man of perfect sense. Nastasya Filippovna heard him out with great attention and kept a close eye on Ganya while he spoke, but the conversation soon turned to Rogozhin, who had played such a crucial part that morning and in whom both Afanasy Ivanovich and Ivan Fyodorovich evinced a close interest. It transpired that Ptitsyn was the one with the most vital information on Rogozhin, having attempted till almost nine o'clock that evening to secure a deal for him. Rogozhin had insisted that he must have a hundred thousand roubles that very day. "Of course he was drunk," Ptitsyn observed, "but, difficult though it may be, he'll probably get his hundred thousand in the end, though maybe not all at once and not right today. There are several people working on it, for instance there's Kinder, Trepalov and the Bishop. They can charge any interest they like, in his drunken state and in the first flush of excitement…" Ptitsyn concluded. All this news was greeted with curiosity, by and large morbid; Nastasya Filippovna kept her silence, evidently wishing to keep her cards close to her chest. General Yepanchin appeared to take everything to heart more than anyone else. The pearl which he had presented to her in the morning was accepted with gracious reserve, followed by an all too ambiguous smile. Of all the guests Ferdyshchenko alone was in devil-may-care festive spirits, laughing loudly and uncontrollably at the slightest pretext in his self-appointed role of jester. Afanasy Ivanovich, normally a subtle and accomplished raconteur, who in former times was the life and soul of any party, was now clearly out of spirits and, what's more, betrayed a totally unaccustomed diffidence. The rest of the guests, who were by no means numerous (an incongruous, frail-looking elderly schoolmaster; a taciturn, incredibly shy young fellow, whom nobody had ever seen before; a spirited lady of about forty, evidently an actress; and a much younger, exceedingly well and opulently dressed, stunningly beautiful woman, also with nothing to say for herself) were not calculated to enliven the proceedings.

Under the circumstances the Prince's arrival was a welcome distraction. The announcement of his name provoked a mild commotion and a few suppressed smiles, especially as the amazement registered on Nastasya Filippovna's features indicated she had had no intention of inviting him. But after the initial surprise was over, Nastasya Filippovna suddenly evinced so much warmth that the majority immediately prepared to meet the uninvited guest with laughter and good cheer.

"It all stems from his innocence, I'd say," Ivan Fyodorovich Yepanchin observed. "On the whole it'd be wrong to encourage such tendencies, but as things stand, there's really no harm in his turning up here however bizarre the manner. He may liven up our party at least from what I know of him."

"But it's him foisting himself upon us!" Ferdyshchenko immediately came back.

"Your point being?" the General, who detested Ferdyshchenko, asked drily.

"That he should pay his entrance fee," was the reply.

"Well, Prince Myshkin is no Ferdyshchenko, I'm glad to say," the General snapped back, unable to reconcile himself to the idea of being in the same room as Ferdyshchenko and on an equal footing.

"Tut, tut, General, don't be too hard on Ferdyshchenko," he replied with a smile. "I'm a privileged guest."

"Why privileged?"

"On a previous occasion I had the honour of explaining this to the community at large in great detail. I'll repeat it again for Your Highness's sake. As Your Highness may have noticed, all people have wit, but I have none. By way of a concession I've been granted a special dispensation to speak the truth, since it's generally accepted that the truth is spoken only by those who are devoid of wit. Besides, I'm a vengeful person, and this also on account of having no wit. I'll endure any offence humbly, but only until the offender's fortunes take a turn for the worse – and that's just the point at which I strike back, the point at which I take my revenge, one way or another. I hit, as Ivan Petrovich Ptitsyn would say, below the belt, something which he of course would never do himself. Do you recall the fable 'The Lion and the Donkey'? Well, that's the way it is, it's all about the two of us."

"I sense you've overstepped the mark again, Ferdyshchenko!" the General said, his hackles rising.

"What are you on about, Your Highness!" Ferdyshchenko parried, sensing an opening, and having been waiting for just such an opportunity. "Don't you worry, Your Highness, I know my place, even if I said that you and I are the Lion and the Donkey, the role of Donkey of course falls to me, whereas Your Highness is the Lion. How does it go now?

> The mighty Lion, terror of the plain,
> With age perceived his powers wane.*

As for me, Your Highness, I'm the Donkey."

"I couldn't agree more," the General acquiesced triumphantly.

All this of course was banter of the crudest sort, but traditionally Ferdyshchenko was free to play the jester.

"Yes, the only reason I'm tolerated here," Ferdyshchenko once admitted, "is precisely because I speak in such a manner. Else, why should the likes of me be admitted? It all stands to reason. How may Ferdyshchenko, such as he is, be set alongside a refined gentleman like Afanasy Ivanovich? There's only one explanation, the two are set alongside each other merely to show how utterly ridiculous the pairing is."

But odd though it all was, it sometimes struck home, which was much to Nastasya Filippovna's liking. Those who wished to be in her company were obliged to put up with Ferdyshchenko. It was perhaps his most discerning realization that his acceptance at her place was assured from the very first when his presence proved to be a thorn in Totsky's side. Ganya for his part became the very martyr at the hands of Ferdyshchenko, who aimed barbed shafts at him. In this Ferdyshchenko proved himself to be very useful to Nastasya Filippovna.

"And I suggest the Prince begin the proceedings by singing the latest popular song to us," Ferdyshchenko proposed, leering slyly at Nastasya Filippovna to see her reaction.

"I should think not, Ferdyshchenko," she returned drily, "and please behave yourself."

"Aha! If he is the new favourite, I bow out…"

But Nastasya Filippovna got up without paying attention to him and went to welcome the Prince.

"I'm sorry," she said, coming up to the Prince, "I was too distracted when we first met to invite you along, and I'm delighted you are now giving me the opportunity to thank and congratulate you on your resolution."

While speaking, she looked at the Prince intently, trying to unravel his motivation.

The Prince may well have wanted to say something in response to her warm words, but he was so taken by her and so overwhelmed that he was utterly speechless. Nastasya Filippovna noticed this with delight. That evening she was in all her finery and the effect was stunning. She took him by the arm and went to introduce him to the guests. As they were about to enter the drawing room, the Prince stopped suddenly and, barely able to control his agitation, whispered hurriedly, "You are perfection itself... your complexion, your figure... it is impossible to imagine anything better... I so wanted to come here... I... forgive me..."

"Don't apologize," Nastasya Filippovna laughed, "or it will spoil all the originality and spontaneity. I'm beginning to see why people say you're not like others. So, you think I'm perfection itself, is that right?"

"Yes."

"You may be a good judge of character, but this time you're wrong. I will remind you of this before the night is out..."

She introduced the Prince to her guests, the majority of whom had already met him. Totsky immediately said something complimentary. The atmosphere became livelier, everyone began to talk at the same time and there was laughter all round. Nastasya Filippovna bade the Prince sit next to her.

"I don't think that there's anything unusual at all in the Prince coming here!" Ferdyshchenko's voice rang out above everyone else's. "It all speaks for itself and makes perfect sense!"

"Yes indeed, it all speaks for itself and makes perfect sense," Ganya, who had hitherto kept his silence, suddenly echoed. "I have kept a close watch on the Prince all along from the very instant when he first set eyes on Nastasya Filippovna's portrait on Ivan Fyodorovich's desk. I remember an idea struck me later in the day, which I now regard as a certainty, and to which, incidentally, the Prince himself owned up."

Ganya said this in all seriousness, without a hint of frivolity; there was even a note of melancholy in his voice, which created a somewhat odd impression.

"I did no such thing," the Prince replied, blushing, "I merely replied to your question."

"Well spoken, well spoken!" Ferdyshchenko called out. "If it's not sincere, at least it's clever."

There was a loud explosion of laughter.

"Keep your voice down, Ferdyshchenko," Ptitsyn said in a low voice with manifest displeasure.

"And judging by the fact that the Prince is blushing like a coy young maiden in consequence of a harmless joke, I conclude that, being a decent young man, he nurtures nothing but the most praiseworthy sentiments in his heart." Thus suddenly piped up, or more accurately stammered,

145

the toothless seventy-year-old schoolmaster, who hadn't said a word till then and from whom no one expected to hear anything at all in the course of the whole evening. This caused even more laughter. The septuagenarian, flattering himself that it was his superior wit that had brought on the laughter, joined in lustily as he surveyed the company, but ended up in a paroxysm of coughing, so that Nastasya Filippovna, who for some reason was inordinately fond of all such old eccentrics of either sex, holy fools included, began fussing over him, and ordered a cup of tea to be brought. She asked the maid to fetch a mantilla, which she wrapped round her shoulders, and then had the fire stoked up with a few more logs. In reply to her question as to what the time was, the maid informed her that it was already half-past ten.

"Ladies and gentlemen, would you like some champagne?" Nastasya Filippovna suddenly enquired. "I have it ready and waiting. It might add to the merriment. Please don't stand on ceremony."

This invitation, especially couched in such terms that it was, came as somewhat of a surprise; everyone knew what a stickler for etiquette Nastasya Filippovna had been at all her previous soirées. On the whole, the party was indeed getting merrier, but not quite as expected. The offer of the wine was not turned down, however; the first to accept was the General, then the boisterous lady, followed by the doddering old man, by Ferdyshchenko and finally by everybody else. Totsky too picked up his glass, hoping to impart an additional note of harmony to what appeared to be a new phase in the proceedings and to endow it with humour and jocularity. Ganya was the only one who abstained from drinking. Nastasya Filippovna, who also helped herself to a glass, announcing that she intended to drink three in the course of the evening, was unsettled and abrupt in her responses, which ranged from unprovoked hysterical mirth to intervals of pensive, almost gloomy, silence, but gave no other clues as to her real state of mind. Some suspected she had a fever; eventually it was noted that she seemed to be on tenterhooks, impatient and abstracted, waiting for something to occur, often glancing up at the clock.

"You appear to have a slight fever," the boisterous lady observed.

"Not just a slight one," Nastasya Filippovna replied, "a full-blown fever. That's why I wrapped my mantilla round my shoulders." She was as pale as ever, only now she appeared to be suppressing violent shivering too.

A wave of disquiet ran through the assembled company.

"Perhaps we should allow the lady of the house to rest?" Totsky observed, casting glances at Ivan Fyodorovich.

"Not on your life, gentlemen! I insist you all stay put. Your presence is particularly important for me tonight," Nastasya Filippovna declared emphatically. And as almost all the guests already knew that a very important announcement was in the offing, this lent a great deal of weight to her words. The General and Totsky exchanged glances once again; Ganya shifted uneasily in his chair.

"Why don't we play a little party game?" the boisterous lady suggested.

"I know a brilliant one," Ferdyshchenko chimed in. "It has only ever been played once in the world, and not very successfully at that."

"What was that?" the boisterous lady enquired.

"A group of us once got together, well we'd had a few, as is often the case, and suddenly someone suggested that each one of us, sitting as we were at the table, should recount something personal, something he well and truly believed to be the most disgraceful of all his acts. It had to be the truth, mind, above all, the truth, no lying!"

"Very odd," the General said.

"Absolutely, Your Highness, but that's what was so attractive about it."

"A hilarious idea," Totsky said, "but it makes sense – boasting turned on its head."

"Maybe that's just what was needed, Afanasy Ivanovich."

"A game like that would more likely bring on tears than laughter," the boisterous lady observed.

"Absolute rubbish, quite ridiculous," Ptitsyn piped up.

"And how did it go?" Nastasya Filippovna enquired.

"Not well at all, rather badly in fact. They all had their say, of course, after a fashion, some spoke the truth and, would you believe it, they even enjoyed it, but then everybody became shy, it was too much for them! All in all, however, we had a good time, in a way."

"This should be great fun!" Nastasya Filippovna enthused. "Why not have a go, ladies and gentlemen! Things are flagging a bit. If each one of us were to agree to tell something... of that kind... voluntarily, of course, no one should feel obliged, well? It might just work! At least it's something different!..."

147

"A brilliant idea!" Ferdyshchenko affirmed. "Ladies, of course, are let off. We shall draw lots as previously! Good, good, good! Anyone who doesn't want to participate is excused, but how thick-skinned have you got to be to do that! Let's have your names please, gentlemen, put them in my hat, the Prince will draw them. The rule couldn't be simpler, to recount the worst episode in your life – nothing could be easier, gentlemen! You'll see! If anybody runs into difficulties, I'm here to help!"

No one thought much of the idea. Some frowned, others smiled knowingly; there was the odd half-hearted protest, as from Ivan Fyodorovich, who was loath to contradict Nastasya Filippovna in her enthusiasm for this bizarre idea. Nastasya Filippovna was always wilful and obstinate in her predilections, if she chose to give voice to them, however trivial and capricious they might be. Just then she was highly excited, ebullient, she laughed convulsively, fitfully, especially at Tostsky's pained protestation. Her dark eyes lit up, her pale cheeks flushed. The desolate, hangdog expressions on people's faces seemed to encourage her; perhaps she was taken by the very cynicism and effrontery of the concept. Some were convinced she had some special plan up her sleeve. Be that as it may, people began to come forward, driven partly by curiosity, partly by mischief. Ferdyshchenko was in his element.

"But what if it's something quite out of order... in front of ladies?" the young man spoke for the first time, diffidently.

"So you keep quiet about it, unless you've run out of acceptably risqué stories," Ferdyshchenko returned. "It stands to reason, young man!"

"My problem is to know which one of my misdemeanours is the worst," the boisterous lady chimed in.

"Ladies are not obliged to participate," Ferdyshchenko reiterated, "but voluntary inspired contributions are always welcome. Gentlemen, if they are totally disinclined, will not be coerced either."

"So how can anyone prove that I won't lie?" Ganya asked. "But if I were to lie, the whole point of the game would be lost. And who could resist lying? It's a foregone conclusion."

"Just seeing how a person would go about concealing the truth should be exciting enough. As for you, my dear Ganya, I wouldn't worry about the odd lie, your very worst act is already common knowledge.

Just think, ladies and gentlemen," Ferdyshchenko suddenly exclaimed, bursting with excitement, "how we shall all manage to look into one another's eyes tomorrow for instance after hearing all the stories!"

"But this is quite unprecedented! Are you really serious, Nastasya Filippovna?" Totsky asked indignantly.

"Nothing ventured, nothing gained!" Nastasya Filippovna retorted with a smile.

"Hold on, Mr Ferdyshchenko, how can you expect to turn this into a *petit jeu*?" Totsky continued, getting more and more agitated. "I assure you such jiggery-pokery will not pass muster. You admitted yourself it all fell flat the previous time."

"What do you mean, it fell flat? I told my story of how I filched three roubles. I just stood up and came out with it!"

"No doubt. But was there really any chance you told it in such a way that people believed you? Gavrila Ardalionovich was quite right that any suggestion of insincerity would immediately kill everything stone dead. Truth here may be arrived at only by accident in a peculiar mood of braggadocio *de mauvais goût* that is totally inappropriate, indeed unthinkable, in present company."

"You're a fine one, Afanasy Ivanovich! I simply can't get over it!" Ferdyshchenko exclaimed. "Imagine, ladies and gentlemen: by his remark that I wouldn't have been capable of recounting my thievery piece with credibility, Afanasy Ivanovich is very subtly letting it be known that I wouldn't have been capable of stealing (after all it's not on to mention such things out loud) although in his heart of hearts he is firmly convinced that Ferdyshchenko has all the makings of a thief! But to business, gentlemen, I have all your names here, and yours too, Afanasy Ivanovich, which means, no one has declined! Prince, to business!"

The Prince without saying a word dipped his hand in the hat and drew out the first lot – Ferdyshchenko; the second – Ptitsyn; third – the General; fourth – Afanasy Ivanovich; fifth – his own; sixth – Ganya's, and so on. The ladies had not participated.

"Oh God, what rotten luck!" Ferdyshchenko exclaimed. "I was hoping the Prince would be first, the General second. Thank God, however, at least Ivan Petrovich Ptitsyn is after me, and that's a blessing. Well, ladies and gentlemen, it of course behoves me to set the example, but the thing that saddens me most of all at this moment is that I'm so insignificant and have nothing to recommend me. I've no title to speak of either, so who cares what misdemeanour Ferdyshchenko had got up to? And where shall I begin? It's a veritable *embarras de richesses*. You wouldn't want me to tell you about the three roubles again, would you, unless it were to prove to Afanasy Ivanovich that one doesn't necessarily have to be a thief to commit a theft."

"I give you this, Mr Ferdyshchenko, you've finally convinced me that for some there can be no greater pleasure than to rake up their past misdeeds even though no one asked for it... But... I beg your pardon, Mr Ferdyshchenko, don't let me stop you."

"Get on with it, Ferdyshchenko," Nastasya Filippovna commanded irritably and impatiently, "you rant too much!"

Everyone was aware that after her latest burst of convulsive laughter she had suddenly become dispirited, bitter and irritable. All the same, she persisted stubbornly and tenaciously, causing Afanasy Ivanovich untold suffering. Ivan Fyodorovich did not make life easy for him either. He just sat there with his glass of champagne without a care in the world, perhaps turning over in his mind a story he'd tell when his turn came.

14

"I'VE NOT AN OUNCE OF WIT IN ME, Nastasya Filippovna, that's why I can't keep my mouth shut," Ferdyshchenko proclaimed as he prepared to tell his story. "If I had as much of it as Afanasy Ivanovich or Ivan Petrovich, I wouldn't have stirred from my seat all night and would have kept perfectly quiet just as Afanasy Ivanovich and Ivan Petrovich are doing. Prince, allow me to ask you what you think, my view being that there are far more thieves in this world than honest people, and that there's no one who would not have stolen anything. That's just my opinion, but I in no way conclude from this that absolutely everyone's a thief, although, honest to goodness, I'm often sorely tempted. What's your opinion?"

"Pooh, how silly!" Darya Alexeyevna remarked. "It's sheer nonsense to suppose that everyone must have stolen something, it's not possible. I've never stolen anything ever!"

"You haven't stolen anything, Darya Alexeyevna, but what will the Prince say who's just gone all red?"

"I think you're telling the truth," the Prince said, who had indeed blushed for some reason, "but you exaggerate too much."

"And have you yourself ever stolen anything?"

"Hell! This is getting absolutely ridiculous! Come to your senses, Ferdyshchenko," the General intervened.

"It's all very simple," Darya Alexeyevna went on, "as soon as it came to the point, you were too embarrassed to continue and now you're taking advantage of the Prince, seeing that he's so defenceless."

"Ferdyshchenko, either get on with your story, or shut up if you're only interested in yourself!" Nastasya Filippovna said sharply and irritably. "You would try the patience of a saint!"

"I'm coming to it, Nastasya Filippovna. But if the Prince has owned up, because I insist that the Prince has as good as owned up, then what would anybody else (mentioning no names) have said if ever he wanted to tell the truth sometime? As for me, ladies and gentlemen, there's precious little more to add – it's all very mundane, silly and sordid. But I assure you I'm not a thief. How I came to steal, I've no idea. It was a couple of days ago, on Sunday, at Semyon Ivanovich Ishchenko's country residence. He was having a dinner party. After the meal the men drank some wine. I had an idea I'd ask Marya Semyonovna, his daughter, to play something on the piano. As I made for her room, over in a corner I spotted a green three-rouble note on her desk, probably left out for household expenses. Not a soul in the room. I took the note and put it in my pocket, what for? No idea. What came over me? – I can't explain. I just hurried back to the table and sat down. I must say I was pretty anxious as the seconds ticked by, but I kept talking nineteen to the dozen, made people laugh with my jokes. After that I joined the ladies. About half an hour later the loss was discovered and the housemaids were questioned. Suspicion fell on one of the girls, Darya. I feigned enormous interest and concern and remember that when Darya broke down completely, I tried to persuade her to own up, vouching with my life for Marya Semyonovna's kindness, and this in everybody's presence and for all to hear. Everyone just stared, whereas I was as pleased as Punch that I was sermonizing with the note safely in my pocket. I blew the three roubles that same night in a restaurant. I went in and asked for a bottle of wine. I had never before asked for just a bottle and nothing else to follow. I couldn't wait to spend the money. There were no pangs of conscience to speak of either before or after.

I don't suppose I'd do that sort of thing again, but it's up to you if you believe me or not. Well, that's all there is to it."

"Only that's unlikely to be the worst of your misdeeds," Darya Alexeyevna remarked contemptuously.

"That was more of a psychological aberration than a misdeed," Afanasy Ivanovich observed.

"What about the maid?" Nastasya Filippovna asked with unconcealed revulsion.

"The maid was sent packing the very next day. How else? They don't stand for nonsense in that house."

"And you went along with it?"

"I like that! Was I expected to come forward and give evidence against myself?" Ferdyshchenko responded with a short burst of forced laughter. It must be said that he was somewhat taken aback by the very unfavourable reaction of the audience to his story.

"How disgusting!" Nastasya Filippovna exclaimed.

"This takes the biscuit! You want to hear the worst thing a man has ever done and expect him to smell of sweet roses! Men's worst actions are bound to be disgusting as we are now about to hear from Ivan Petrovich Ptitsyn. Not everything that shines is gold and should be taken at face value, never mind a splendid carriage with four-in-hand. A splendid carriage is one thing, but by what means?"

In a word, Ferdyshchenko lost his composure completely and suddenly, his features distorted, went on the offensive, blindly overstepping the mark. Strange as it may seem, it was quite possible he expected an altogether different reaction to his tale; Ferdyshchenko was by nature much given to this "counterfeit braggadocio *de mauvais goût*", as Totsky had put it.

Nastasya Filippovna fairly shuddered with anger and looked hard at Ferdyshchenko, who took fright and went as quiet as a mouse, realizing that he had gone a step too far.

"Perhaps we should call it a day?" Afanasy Ivanovich Totsky remarked slyly.

"It's my turn, but I shall claim my right not to speak," Ptitsyn said firmly.

"You don't want to?"

"I can't, Nastasya Filippovna. Anyway this type of *petit jeu* is not my cup of tea at all."

"General, it would appear your turn is next," Nastasya Filippovna turned to Ivan Fyodorovich, "if you too were to back out, everybody else would follow suit and that would be that, which would concern me personally, because at the end of it all I was planning to recount an incident from my own life, but only after you and Afanasy Ivanovich have had your say, because I'd be looking to you two for inspiration," she concluded with a laugh.

"Oh well, if you too promise to participate," the General exclaimed with gusto, "I'm ready to let you have my whole life story! In truth, while waiting my turn, I already prepared my piece—"

"I can tell just by looking at His Highness what consummate literary skill has gone into the composition of his little story," Ferdyshchenko, still smarting from the recent put-down, remarked sarcastically with an ill-humoured smile playing about his lips.

Nastasya Filippovna darted a glance at the General and could not suppress a brief smile. But it was clear that a feeling of disquiet and irascibility was welling up in her. Totsky, when he heard her promise to tell a story of her own, went weak at the knees with fright.

"Like many another man, ladies and gentlemen," the General began, "I too in the course of my life have happened to commit acts somewhat lacking in discretion. The most curious thing, however, is the short incident I'm now about to relate, which I regard as the very worst in my life. This goes back some thirty-five years. Every time I think of it, I've never been able to rid myself of a certain, as it were, harrowing sensation. In essence, the matter was exceedingly trivial. I was a mere ensign in the army and had to toe the line. All the same, you know how it is, an ensign – a hot-blooded young blade, but as poor as a church mouse. My batman at the time, Nikifor, was an attentive, solicitous chap; he pinched and scraped on my behalf wherever he could by fair means or foul, light-fingered as they come, he'd whip anything he could lay his hands on – all for my benefit. As trustworthy and honest a fellow as you could wish for! Of course I kept him on a tight rein, but I was fair with it. We happened to be garrisoned in a small town. I was quartered in a little house on the outskirts belonging to a sub lieutenant's widow, as it happened. She was getting on for eighty or thereabouts, poor thing. The miserable little timber house she owned was decrepit and ramshackle, and she was so poor, she didn't even have a maid. But what was remarkable, she'd had very many relatives in her time. However, as the years went by some died, others left, yet others forgot about her altogether. As for her husband, she'd buried him about forty-five years previously. Some three years before that she also had a niece living with her, hunchbacked, embittered, a veritable witch. People said she even bit the old woman's finger once, but then she too died, so that for the past three years the old woman had to cope completely on her own. I was bored to death staying in her house, and she was so silly you couldn't get any sense out of her. She ended up stealing a prize cockerel I kept. It was a shady affair that still hasn't been cleared up to this day, but it had to be her. We fell out over that cockerel, and seriously at that, but just then, by coincidence, I was billeted, as soon as I applied, at the opposite end of the town with a large family, headed by a fellow with an enormous beard. I can still remember him. Nikifor and I moved in, and were jolly glad to leave the old hag behind. Three days or so went by, I returned from exercises, and Nikifor reported to me, 'We shouldn't have left our tureen behind at the previous landlady's. I've nothing to serve the soup in.' I was flabbergasted of course: 'What, what do you mean, how come our tureen was left behind?' Nikifor expressed some surprise and went on to report that as we were leaving, the landlady had refused to hand over our tureen on the grounds that since I'd broken her very own earthenware pot, she was keeping the tureen in exchange for the pot, and that apparently I myself had made her that offer. Such a damnable trick on her part pushed me to the very brink, it sent my blood racing, I leapt to my feet and rushed over to her place. I arrived there, you can imagine, quite beside myself. There she was sitting in a corner of the passageway all on her own as though keeping out of the sunlight, her hand propping up her cheek. I went for her, you know, hammer and tongs, 'You old this that and the other!' You know how it goes in Russian. Only looking at her, I had a strange feeling – there she was sat on the floor, her face turned towards me, eyes bulging, not saying a word, swaying, I fancied, ever so weirdly from side to side. I stood back, staring hard at her, and spoke to her – no reply. I hesitated. Flies were buzzing around me, the sun was setting, silence. Utterly shocked, I at last turned back to go home. Before I reached home I was summoned to the Sergeant Major; from there I had to go to the company quarters, so that by the time I got home it was already dark. And the first thing Nikifor says to me: 'Do you know, sir, our landlady has given up the ghost.' 'When?' I asked. 'Tonight, about an hour and a half ago.' That means she was passing away just as I was giving her a piece of my mind. You know, I was so shocked, I didn't know what to do. I couldn't get her out of my mind, she came to me in my sleep. I'm not superstitious, but I went to church three days later to attend her funeral. In a word, as time goes by, I think more and more about her. It's not the end of the world, but the memory is difficult to shake off. What's at the bottom of it all, I often think to myself? Firstly, a woman is, so to speak, a human being, as is nowadays readily acknowledged, and there she was, keeping her body and soul together for years and years, finally starting to go downhill. At one time she had had children, a husband, a family, relatives, everything around her was, as it were, hustle and bustle, fun and games, so to speak, and suddenly – a complete turnaround, everything vanishes into thin air, she's left on her own, like… a fly with the curse of eternity upon it. And so God in his mercy had finally chosen to call it a day. With the setting sun, on a quiet summer's evening, my old biddy departs this world. There is a moral here, of course. And it is this: that at the precise moment when a valedictory, sentimental tear would as it were have been called for, a young, desperate buck, an awful swankpot, both arms akimbo, sees her off the face of the earth with a torrent of choice Russian abuse on account of a godforsaken soup tureen! There is no doubting I was in the wrong, and though with the passage of years and the changes within myself, I've long been thinking about this episode in abstract terms, I can't help coming back to it. Nay, I repeat, I am astonished! I may really be guilty, but there must have been some mitigating circumstances – why should she have chosen to die at that precise moment? It stands to reason that if there were a justification, it ought to be based on psychological grounds. All the same, I couldn't rest until about fifteen years ago I adopted two chronically ill old grannies, maintaining them at my own expense at an almshouse in order to ease their remaining days on this earth with tender care. I'm thinking of perpetuating the arrangement when I come to make my will. Well, that's about all. I repeat, I may have committed many wrongs in my life, but, in all conscience, I consider this to be the worst one of the lot."

"But, instead of recounting your very worst deed," Ferdyshchenko observed, "Your Highness has recounted for us one of the best deeds of your life. Ferdyshchenko has been sorely cheated!"

"Really, General," Nastasya Filippovna spoke dismissively, "I had no idea you were so kind-hearted after all. Frankly, it's a pity."

"Pity? Why on earth?" the General asked, smiling cordially as he smugly took a sip of champagne from his glass.

But it was Afanasy Ivanovich's turn to speak now, and he too had been preparing his story. Everyone believed that, unlike Ivan Petrovich, he would not refuse, and his contribution was awaited with especial anticipation by all concerned for a variety of reasons. They now could not help casting furtive glances at Nastasya Filippovna.

Afanasy Ivanovich began one of his "genteel stories" with enormous dignity in soft, urbane tones that perfectly complemented his imposing bearing. (It should be said here that he cut a highly impressive figure; he was very tall and dignified, on the corpulent side, slightly balding with a touch of grey here and there; his soft, pinkish cheeks were inclined to droop a little, and he had artificial teeth. He always wore comfortable, elegant clothes as well as the finest underwear. His soft, white hands were a delight to the eye. On the index finger of his right hand he sported an expensive diamond ring.) In the entire course of the storytelling Nastasya Filippovna kept her eyes fixed firmly on the lace turn-up of her right sleeve as she picked at it with the fingers of her left hand; she never once looked up at the speaker.

"What eases my task most of all," Afanasy Ivanovich began, "is that I'm obliged to tell you the very worst thing I perpetrated in all my life. In such a case there can be no room for doubt. Memory and conscience will always come to the rescue. I will confess with an aching heart that amongst the innumerable, perhaps ill-judged and... frivolous acts in my life, there is one which troubles me enormously. This occurred about twenty years ago. I happened to be on a visit to Platon Ordyntsov in the country. He had been newly elected Marshal of the Nobility,* and had come with his young wife to celebrate the winter festival. His visit coincided with Anfisa Alexeyevna's birthday, and it was decided to organize two balls. At that time the splendid novel *La Dame aux camélias* by Dumas *fils* had just taken polite society by storm. In my opinion it is a work of art which will neither age nor go out of fashion. In the provinces all the ladies were in raptures over it, at least those that had read it. The appeal of the storyline, the refreshingly original portrayal of the principal character, that alluring world, depicted with such subtlety, and finally all the enchanting minutiae, scattered throughout the book (for instance the alternate choice of bouquets of white and pink camellias),* in a word, all those fascinating details, taken together, almost created an upheaval. Camellias became incredibly popular. Everyone demanded camellias, everyone had to have them. I ask you, how many camellias can one come by in a district when they are de rigueur at every ball even if these are not held particularly frequently? Poor Pyotr Vorkhovskoy was infatuated with Anfisa Alexeyevna. I don't know if there was anything between them, that is I don't know if he had the least hope, but the poor devil was desperate to procure camellias for Anfisa Alexeyevna by evening. Duchess Sotskaya of St Petersburg, specially invited by the Governor's Lady, and Sofya Bespalova, as it transpired later, were due to arrive, probably carrying a white bunch. Anfisa Alexeyevna thought she had to have a bunch of red for a special effect. Platon, poor soul, wasn't given a moment's peace – a husband's lot. He'd promised to procure a bouquet, but no luck! On the eve of the ball, they got hold of Mytishchev. Katerina Alexandrovna, Anfisa Alexeyevna's sworn enemy in every respect, was daggers drawn with her. Naturally, everyone was hysterical, people were fainting. Platon was nowhere to be found. Clearly, if only Pyotr could have got hold of a bunch at that vital moment, his prospects could have improved no end. A woman's gratitude in such cases is limitless. He tried every nook and cranny, but no luck! Out of the question! Suddenly, it was already gone eleven at night on the eve of the birthday party and the ball that I ran into him at Marya Petrovna Zubkova's, Ordyntsov's next-door neighbour. You should have seen him – happy as a sandboy! 'What's come over you?' 'I've found some! Eureka!' 'Well, my dear chap, that is a surprise! Where? How?' 'In Yekshaisk!' (A little town thereabouts, within twenty versts, across the boundary of the next district) 'There's a merchant there by name of Trepalov, bearded and rich as Croesus, lives with his wife, an old woman, and canaries in place of children. They've both a passion for flowers and he has camellias.' I said to him, 'Don't get carried away! Supposing he doesn't give you any?' 'I'll get down on my knees and roll over at his feet until he lets me have some. I shan't leave unless he does!' 'So when are you off?' 'Tomorrow at daybreak, at five.' 'Well, good luck!' And, you know, I was so happy for him. I got back to Ordyntsov's. It was already gone one o'clock, and I just couldn't rest. I was just on the point of falling asleep, when suddenly I was struck by a crazy idea! I crept down to the scullery, woke the coachman Savely, thrust fifteen roubles in his palm, 'Get my horses ready in half an hour!' In half an hour's time a carriage was ready and waiting for me at the gates. Anfisa Alexeyevna, I was told, had gone down with a migraine and was tossing and turning with a fever. I got in and we set off. Just after four we pulled into Yekshaisk and stopped at an inn. I waited till dawn, and was at Trepalov's gone six. 'I was told you've got camellias, is that right? Help me, for God's sake, it's a matter of life and death, help, I'll go down on my hands and knees.' I could see him standing there, a tall, erect, awesome greybeard. 'Never! Not on your life!' I fell at his feet, flat on my stomach! 'What's come over you?' he says. 'You can't do that!' he said in alarm. 'Truly, it's a matter of life and death!' I called out. 'In that case, help yourself, and Godspeed!' I'd never seen so many red camellias and I went to town on them! It was a miracle, a feast, a splendid little greenhouse, bursting with camellias. The old boy watched and sighed. I took out a hundred roubles. 'No, that won't be necessary, my friend, and I might even take offence.' 'In that case, venerable sir,' I said, 'please donate this hundred roubles to the local hospital for overall upkeep and food.' 'Now that's another matter altogether, my dear sir, it's good, gentlemanly and charitable of you. I'll be sure to donate it for the salvation of your soul.' You know, I took a real liking to that true Russian elder, a man of grit and substance, *de la vraie souche.** Pleased as anything, I immediately set off for home, taking side roads so as not to run into Pyotr. As soon as I got back, I sent the bunch to Anfisa Alexeyevna to gladden her on waking. You can imagine the excitement, the expressions of gratitude, the tears of thankfulness! Platon, who only yesterday was crushed and undone with grief – was shedding tears of joy on my breast. Alas! All husbands are like that since the institution of... lawful marriage! It goes without saying that poor Pyotr's prospects suffered a complete setback with this episode. At first I thought he'd kill me when he found out. I even took precautions, but things took a totally unexpected turn – he fainted, by evening he was raving and by morning had developed a fever with agonizing convulsions. A month later, when he was better, he enlisted for the Caucasus, in true romantic fashion! He ended up being killed in the Crimea. His brother, Boris Vorkhovskoy, commanded a regiment at the time, and distinguished himself in battle. I have to admit, I suffered pangs of conscience for many years after. Why, to what end had I brought him down? I suppose it would have made some sense if I had been in love myself! But it was just a prank, a rake's mean trick, no more. If I hadn't robbed him of the bouquet, who knows, the fellow would have lived to this day, would have been happy, successful, and it wouldn't have entered into his head to go and fight the Turk."

Afanasy Ivanovich paused in as demonstrably dignified a manner as when he began. It was noted that Nastasya Filippovna's eyes flared up unnaturally and even her lips twitched after Afanasy Ivanovich had spoken his closing words. People kept looking at one another.

"Ferdyshchenko's been swindled yet again! Well and truly!" Ferdyshchenko wailed tearfully, knowing full well that now he not only could, but was expected, to put in a word. "Swindled as never before!"

"It's your own fault for missing the point of the game!" Darya Alexeyevna (Totsky's tried and tested adherent) snapped back triumphantly. "You'll be wiser next time."

"You're quite right, Afanasy Ivanovich, this *petit jeu* is just too boring, let's do something else," Nastasya Filippovna said with ennui. "I'll tell my story, as promised, and then we can all have a game of cards."

"But your story first," the General piped up fervently.

"Prince," Nastasya Filippovna suddenly turned to him brusquely and unexpectedly, "my old friends, the General and Afanasy Ivanovich, are forever trying to marry me off. Tell me, what do you think, should I get married or not? I'll do exactly as you say."

Totsky went pale, the General was thunderstruck. Everyone stared and craned their necks. Ganya was rooted to the spot.

"To... to whom?" the Prince asked in a voice drained of emotion.

"To Gavrila Ardalionovich Ivolgin," Nastasya Filippovna continued as formerly in clipped, sharp and resonant tones.

There was a prolonged pause; the Prince was straining to speak but words failed him as though his chest was weighed down under a heavy load.

"N-no... don't get married!" he finally whispered and heaved a deep breath.

"So be it! Gavrila Ardalionovich!" she declared forcefully and exultantly. "Did you hear the Prince's decision? Therein is my reply. And let the matter now rest once and for all!"

"Nastasya Filippovna!" Afanasy Ivanovich spoke in an unsteady voice.

"Nastasya Filippovna!" the General pleaded in alarm.

Everyone shifted uneasily.

"What's the matter, ladies and gentlemen?" she continued, surveying the guests with a show of surprise. "Why are you so dismayed? And just look at your faces!"

"But... have you forgotten, Nastasya Filippovna!" Totsky stuttered, "You promised... quite voluntarily, this is most irregular... I don't know what to say and... of course it's most embarrassing, but... In a word, that you should now... end what is a serious matter of the heart and of honour in a *petit jeu*, in front of people... on which depends—"

"I am at a loss to understand you, Afanasy Ivanovich. You appear to be utterly confused. First, what do you mean 'in front of people'? First, is this not a friendly, intimate gathering? And why '*petit jeu*'? I really wanted to make my contribution, and *voilà*! Don't you like it? And why do you imagine I'm not serious? What's not serious about it? You heard me, I said to the Prince, 'I'll do exactly as you say.' Had he said 'Yes', I'd have given my consent immediately, but he said 'No', and I refused. My whole life hung on a thread. What could be more serious?"

"But the Prince, what has it got to do with the Prince? And who is this Prince anyway?" the General muttered, utterly unable to control his indignation that the Prince had been elevated to such a position of trust.

"For me the Prince happens to be the first person in my life in whom I recognized a truly loyal person. He believed in me from the first, and I believe in him."

"I must in all earnestness thank Nastasya Filippovna for the extraordinary sense of discretion with which... she has treated me," Ganya, his features drained of blood, replied at last in a quavering voice, his lips twitching, "it was only to be expected... But... the Prince... Is he—"

"Is he after the seventy-five thousand, is that what you mean?" Nastasya Filippovna suddenly interposed. "Is that what you wanted to ask? Don't deny, that is precisely what you meant! Afanasy Ivanovich, I quite forgot to add, you keep the seventy-five thousand roubles yourself in the knowledge that I'm letting you off for free. Enough! It's time you too had a rest! It's been nine years and three months! Tomorrow will be another day, but today it's my birthday and I'm my own mistress for the very first time in my life! General, here's your precious pearl too, why don't you give it to your wife? As from tomorrow I'm vacating this apartment. There'll be no more parties, ladies and gentlemen."

Having said this, she got up as if to leave.

"Nastasya Filippovna! Nastasya Filippovna!" voices resounded on all sides. Everyone was in turmoil, everyone had risen to their feet, everyone was crowding her, everyone was at pains to understand her disjointed, feverish, desperate words; everybody sensed something had gone wrong, but no one knew how to remedy the situation. At that moment there was a loud ringing of the doorbell, exactly as previously at Ganya's apartment.

"Aha! Here's the solution! At long last! Half-past eleven!" Nastasya Filippovna exclaimed. "Please be seated, ladies and gentlemen. The solution!"

With these words she sat down herself. A strange smile played about her lips. She sat quite still, her eyes fixed on the door in feverish expectation.

"Rogozhin with his hundred thousand roubles, that's for sure," Ptitsyn muttered to himself.

15

KATYA THE CHAMBERMAID entered the room, frightened.

"Goodness knows what's going on out there, Nastasya Filippovna. There's about ten of them, all pickled, asking to be let in, they say it's Rogozhin and that you know all about it."

"That's all right, Katya, let them all in straight away."

"What... all of them, Nastasya Filippovna? They're a right mob. They give me the jumps."

"Yes, all, let them all in, Katya, every single one of them or they'll make their way in anyway, don't be afraid. I can hear them from here, they haven't changed. My dear friends," she turned to her guests, "you may feel affronted that I am inviting in such company in your presence. I'm very sorry and I beg your pardon, but it's unavoidable, and I for one would be delighted to see you all stay behind as my witnesses, although of course it's up to you..."

The guests continued to express their amazement, to whisper and exchange glances, but it transpired that all this had been worked out and arranged in advance by Nastasya Filippovna, who though she had clearly lost her mind was not to be swayed from her decision. Everyone was dying of curiosity. Besides, there was no one there who would be easily frightened. There were only two ladies: Darya Alexeyevna, a lady who had seen life and who could not be easily upset, and the gorgeous, but silent, stranger. But the latter had little idea of what was going on anyway; she was a German visitor and didn't know a word of Russian; besides, she appeared to be as dumb as she was beautiful. She was quite a new arrival on the scene, but it had already become customary to invite her to certain soirées. Decked out in some dazzling outfit, her hair arranged with marvellous ingenuity, she was displayed as some magnificently decorative picture – precisely the way people do in fact borrow a painting, a vase, a statue or a screen from friends for just one night. As for the men, Ptitsyn for instance was Rogozhin's friend; Ferdyshchenko was clearly in his element; Ganya was still agitated but, however vaguely, felt an irrepressible compulsion to endure to the very end the ignominy of his situation; the old schoolmaster, who had scant understanding of what was going on around him and sensed an unusual excitation centred on Nastasya Filippovna, whom he adored as his own granddaughter, was close to tears and positively trembling with fright, but he would rather have expired on the spot than leave the gathering at that particular moment. As regards Afanasy Ivanovich, he of course could not afford to compromise himself in such adventures; but he was already too much involved in the proceedings in spite of them having taken such a bizarre turn; besides, Nastasya Filippovna had dropped one or two personal remarks in consequence of which it was quite impossible for him to leave without seeking a final clarification. He therefore decided to sit it out to the end merely as an observer without saying a single word, which of course accorded well with his dignity. That left only the General, whose gift had just been so unceremoniously and risibly returned to him. He may have had yet other and weightier excuses to feel offended, namely all the outlandish goings-on, not least the imminent appearance of Rogozhin; in any case, he had already conceded far too much by consenting to share the same space with Ptitsyn and Ferdyshchenko; but if his infatuation had so misled him, it could well be compensated by his sense of duty, his status and overall dignity, such that the presence of Rogozhin and his companions in the company of His Highness was quite unthinkable.

"Ah, General," Nastasya Filippovna interrupted his train of thought when he was just about to make his announcement to her, "I beg your pardon! Only rest assured I anticipated your possible objections. If you find it offensive, I shan't insist and will not detain you, although at this moment it is you of all people I'd have liked to have by my side. In any case I am extremely grateful for the pleasure of your acquaintanceship and for your flattering attention, but since you are afraid that—"

"My dear Nastasya Filippovna," the General exclaimed in an outburst of chivalrous sentiment, "who do you take me for? I shall stay by you solely out of my devotion to you and in case there should be any danger... Besides, I must admit, I'm consumed with curiosity. All I was worried about was that they're liable to ruin the carpet and will probably break something... If you ask me, I wouldn't have them in at all, Nastasya Filippovna!"

"Here comes Rogozhin!" Ferdyshchenko proclaimed.

"What say you, Afanasy Ivanovich," the General whispered furtively, "she hasn't gone mad, has she? I mean literally, clinically, eh?"

"I always told you she was inclined that way," Afanasy Ivanovich returned slyly. "And now her fever too..."

Rogozhin's company was more or less the same as in the morning; the only addition was a dissolute old fellow, an erstwhile editor of some disreputable scandal-mongering rag, of whom it was said that he'd once pawned his gold-mounted dentures to blow it all on drink; and an ex-army sub lieutenant, an opponent and rival by trade and calling to that morning's exponent of fisticuffs, but a stranger to the rest of Rogozhin's entourage, which he had contrived to join on the sunny side of Nevsky Prospect, busily accosting passers-by and in typical military vernacular, appealing for assistance under the cunning ruse that in his time he thought nothing of doling out a fifteen-rouble note to anyone who approached him. The two rivals took an immediate dislike to each other. The fisticuffs man, after the "supplicant" had been accepted into their midst, felt somehow aggrieved and, being by nature a man of few words, kept grunting in the manner of a bear as he eyed with deep contempt all the "supplicant's" skilful diplomatic attempts at pacifying and mollifying him. The sub lieutenant, when it came to it, tended to rely on speed and agility rather than brute force, and in any case he was rather shorter than the fisticuffs man. Discreetly, without engaging in an open quarrel, but in fulsome praises of his own self, he took the trouble to allude to the advantages of the English art of boxing, thereby betraying himself as an all-out disciple of the West. The word "boxing" provoked the fisticuffs man merely to smirk contemptuously and disparagingly and, not deigning to engage his rival in open debate, from time to time unexpectedly and wordlessly brought into view an item that truly qualified as a national emblem – to wit, a huge fist, sinewy, gnarled, covered in a species of reddish down, at the sight of which it became abundantly clear to all that, were this deeply national item to come into violent contact with its target, the latter would be reduced to pulp instantly.

Just as in the morning, hardly anyone of the company was actually blind drunk, largely due to the personal efforts of Rogozhin, whose only concern throughout was his visit to Nastasya Filippovna. He too also managed to sober up almost completely, but in consequence of all the emotional turmoil that he had endured in the course of that frenzied, totally unprecedented day in his life, he was on the brink of losing his own reason. All day long, every God-given minute and second, he nurtured only one aim in mind and heart. For the sake of this *one* aim he had spent all the available time – from five in the afternoon till eleven at night – in a state of endless tension and anxiety as he chased up the likes of Kinder and the Bishop, who too were nearly driven mad, hustling and bustling on his behalf. As a result, and against all odds, the hundred thousand roubles in ready cash, to which Nastasya Filippovna had mockingly and quite casually alluded in passing, had materialized, albeit at rates of interest which even the Bishop out of discretion dared not mention out loud but referred to in sotto voce when speaking to Kinder.

As on the previous occasion, Rogozhin was at the head; all the rest of the pack crowded behind him, pressing their advantage, but nonetheless visibly unsure of themselves. Interestingly, but goodness knows why, they were afraid of Nastasya Filippovna. Some even feared they were in imminent danger of being kicked down the stairs, one of these, incidentally, being the fop and heart-throb Zalyozhin. Others however – in the main, the fisticuffs gentleman – spoke of Nastasya Filippovna with the utmost contempt, bordering on hatred, not out loud but under their breath, and entered her premises as they would a fortress under siege. The exquisite elegance of the first two rooms – with objects quite beyond their ken and experience, rare pieces of furniture, paintings, a huge statue of Venus – all this inspired utter respect in them bordering on awe, which of course did not prevent them, with impudent inquisitiveness, from overcoming their inhibitions and squeezing, little by little, in the footsteps of Rogozhin into the drawing room. However, when the fisticuffs man, the "supplicant" and one or two others noticed General Yepanchin among the guests, they were initially so flustered that some of them even began slowly to retrace their steps. Lebedev was the only one who refused to be discouraged and strode forward almost level with Rogozhin, emboldened by the very idea of one million four hundred thousand roubles in prospect, of which a hundred thousand would be paid on the nail. It has to be owned though that they all, including even smart alec Lebedev, were somehow confused as to how far they could go and whether now they were indeed free to do anything they liked. At times Lebedev was ready to maintain that they were, but at other moments he was assailed by doubts and could not, just in case, help casting his mind back to certain sobering clauses in the Legal Statute Book.

Nastasya Filippovna's drawing room had an altogether different effect on Rogozhin himself. As soon as the door curtain was lifted and he caught sight of her, everything else ceased to exist for him as it had in the morning, only more so. He went pale and for a second stopped in his tracks; one could tell his heart was beating violently. For a few seconds he regarded Nastasya Filippovna in meek distress. Suddenly, as though totally bereft of reason, swaying from side to side, he reeled towards the table next to her; on the way he bumped into Ptitsyn's chair, and with his grimy boots trod on the delicate lacework round the bottom hem of the exquisite sky-blue gown belonging to the glamorous German; he neither noticed nor apologized for it. On coming level with the table, he deposited on it a rather curious object, which he had been holding in both hands when he entered the drawing room. It was a large bundle, a foot by a foot and a half, tightly wrapped in a copy of *The Stock Exchange News* and tied round and round its width and a couple of times lengthwise with string such as is commonly used for tying sugar loaves. There he remained standing, not saying a word, his hands at his sides as though awaiting his sentence. He was dressed just as before except for a new bright-green-and-red silk scarf round his neck with a huge diamond pin in the shape of a beetle and a massive diamond ring on a dirty finger of his right hand. As for Lebedev, he stopped about three paces before the table; the rest of Rogozhin's gang, as has been mentioned, wandered one by one into the drawing room. Nastasya Filippovna's chambermaids, Katya and Pasha, also came running into the room from behind the raised door curtain, fearful and amazed to see what was going on.

"What's this?" Nastasya Filippovna asked, her eyes coming to rest on the "object", after an intensive and puzzled look at Rogozhin.

"A hundred thousand!" he replied almost in a whisper.

"So you kept your word, fancy that! Sit down, please, here, take this chair. There's something I want to tell you later. Who's with you? The same old crowd? Well, let them all come in. There, on that sofa, here's another one. There are two more chairs over there... what's the matter with them, don't they want to, or what is it?"

Some of the party looked distinctly sheepish; they had slunk out into another room and sat down to wait; others accepted the invitation, but settled away from the table, occupying corner seats mostly so as not to be conspicuous. There the spirits of some of them revived rather more quickly than could have been expected. Rogozhin sat down on the chair that was offered to him, but not for long; he soon rose to his feet and did not sit down again. Little by little he began to distinguish and scrutinize the guests. Having spotted Ganya, he smiled wryly and whispered to himself, "Well I never!" He hardly accorded the General and Afanasy Ivanovich a second glance. But when he noticed the Prince right next to Nastasya Filippovna, he was unable to take his eyes off him for a long time in astonishment and as though struggling to make sense of his presence. At times Rogozhin gave the distinct impression of being in a trance. Besides all the commotion of the day, he had spent the whole of the previous night in the train and as a result had not slept a wink in the last forty-eight hours.

"Ladies and gentlemen, here is a hundred thousand," Nastasya Filippovna said, turning to everybody in a heightened state of feverish irritation, "in this filthy bundle. Earlier on he shouted like one demented that by nightfall he'd bring me a hundred thousand, and I kept waiting for him. He haggled over my price. He started with eighteen thousand, then suddenly increased it to forty, and finally he came up with this hundred thousand. I must say, he has kept his word! My, how pale he looks!... This all started at Ganya's. I went to pay his mother a visit, my future family home, and his sister confronted me and cried, 'Isn't there be anyone to chase this hussy away from here!' – and then she spat in the face of her brother, Ganya. She's got guts, that girl!"

"Nastasya Filippovna!" the General spoke reproachfully. He was beginning to put two and two together, after a fashion.

"What's wrong, General? Am I embarrassing you, or something? Let's be honest for once! Sitting in my box at the French Playhouse, holy and virtuous, unapproachable, swollen with pride of innocence, doing my level best to turn away all who were after me for those five years, can only be put down to my utter stupidity! And now, see for yourselves – the result of five years holier than thou – someone comes along and slaps down a hundred thousand on the table, no doubt with horses waiting outside to whisk me off. I say, he's priced me at a hundred thousand! Ganya, my love, I can see you're still angry with me! Would you really still have me in your family? Me, belonging to Rogozhin! Was that what the Prince said back then?"

"I never said you belonged to Rogozhin, and you don't!" the Prince said in a quavering voice.

"Nastasya Filippovna, that'll do, my darling, enough is enough, my angel," said Darya Alexeyevna, who could bear it no longer. "If you're so fed up with them, why bother! Could you really throw in your lot with someone like that even if it was for a hundred thousand! A hundred thousand roubles – yes, that's not to be sneezed at! Why don't you just take the money and send him packing, that's the only way to deal with his sort! Oh, if it were up to me, I'd kick the lot of them out... It's the only way!"

Darya Alexeyevna had got her hackles up. She was a kindly woman, and rather impressionable with it.

"Calm down, Darya Alexeyevna," Nastasya Filippovna remarked with a smile, "I didn't speak to Ganya in anger. Did I blame him for anything? I really can't understand how I could have been so wrong as to imagine I was joining a decent family. I saw his mother, and I kissed her hand. And if I took some liberties in your house, Ganya my pet, it was only to see for myself how far you'd go. I must say, you've astonished me. I could have imagined anything, but not this! Could you really have accepted me in the full knowledge that someone had given me a pearl virtually on the eve of the wedding day, and I had accepted it? And then there's Rogozhin! Didn't he haggle over me in your own house with your mother and sister present, and yet you've come here regardless to ask for my hand, and nearly brought your sister along! Is it really true what Rogozhin said, that for three roubles you'd crawl on all fours all the way to Vasilevsky Island?"

"He would," Rogozhin returned softly, but confidently.

"It would be one thing if you were dying of hunger, but they say you're getting a pretty good salary! And to cap it all, the ignominy apart, to bring a wife you detest into the house! Because, let's face it, you do detest me, don't you! Well, now I can see how someone like that could kill for money! They've all been so overcome by greed, they're so fixated on money, they've gone completely crazy. He's still wet behind the ears, but already wants to go into the moneylending business! Or else he'd wrap a razor in a piece of silk, creep up from behind and slash a friend to death as though he were no more than a grazing sheep, something I read recently. You ought to be ashamed of yourself! I'm bad, but you're worse. I don't even want to talk about that camellias man…"

"Can it, can it really be you, Nastasya Filippovna?" The General threw up his hands, genuinely pained: "You, who are so refined, with such sophisticated ideas, and then this! Such language! Such turns of phrase!"

"I'm in my cups now, General," Nastasya Filippovna laughed suddenly, "I want to enjoy myself! Today is my day, my red-letter day, my day to remember, I've been waiting for it a long time. Darya Alexeyevna, do you see that flower man, that *monsieur aux camélias*, there he is sitting and laughing at us…"

"I'm not laughing, Nastasya Filippovna, I'm merely listening with rapt attention," Totsky returned with dignity.

"Why ever did I torture him for five years and refuse to release him? Was he worth it? He cannot be other than what he is… He may yet shift the blame on me, after all he brought me up, I lived like a duchess, the money, the money he spent on me, he found a respectable man for me back then, and now dear old Ganya. And imagine, I didn't even live with him these five years, but I helped myself to his money and thought I was in the right! I'd got the wrong end of the stick altogether! So, you're telling me to take the hundred thousand and send him packing in sheer disgust. Yes, he's nothing short of disgusting… I could have got married long ago, and not just to sweet Ganya, but that wouldn't have been any less disgusting. And why did I squander a full five years of my life fretting for nothing! But, believe it or not, four years ago it had actually crossed my mind to marry my Afanasy Ivanovich! I thought of doing that out of sheer anger, the things that went through my mind then. I could have got my way with him! You mightn't believe it, but he was making advances! Of course he wasn't sincere, he was after one thing only, he'd lost all control over himself. But then I questioned myself, was he really worth all that anger on my part? And I felt so disgusted with him that even if he had actually asked for my hand himself, I'd have turned him down. And that's how I carried on giving myself airs and graces for five long years! No, I'd rather go and tramp the streets, where I really belong! Or should I go on a binge with Rogozhin, or start working as a laundry woman as from tomorrow! Because I've nothing of my own. I'll leave and throw everything back at him, down to the last rag, and with nothing to my name, who'd take me? Here, ask Ganya, would he take me! Not even Ferdyshchenko would!—"

"To be honest, Ferdyshchenko might not, Nastasya Filippovna, what's the use of denying," Ferdyshchenko interposed, "but the Prince would! There you are sitting there, feeling sorry for yourselves, but just take a look at the Prince! I've been watching him for some time now…"

Nastasya Filippovna turned to the Prince.

"Is that true?" she asked.

"It is," the Prince breathed out.

"You'd take me, poor as I am!"

"I would, Nastasya Filippovna—"

"That's all we needed!" the General muttered. "I suppose it was to be expected."

The Prince continued to regard Nastasya Filippovna with mournful, firm, penetrating eyes all the time that she kept looking at him.

"Listen to him!" she said suddenly, turning to Darya Alexeyevna again. "This has to be out of the goodness of his heart, I know it. There's a benefactor for you! Maybe it's right what they say about him, that… he's a bit?… What are you going to live on? You, a Prince, taking over Rogozhin's mistress!…"

"I take you for what you are, an honest woman, rather than Rogozhin's mistress," the Prince said.

"I, an honest woman?"

"Yes, you."

"Well... that's the stuff of novels! My gallant Prince, these are the ravings of yesteryear, people have got wiser nowadays, they won't be taken in by such nonsense! And can you really see yourself getting married? You need a nanny yourself to look after you!"

The Prince rose to his feet, and in a quavering, humble tone, but for all that with great conviction, said, "I know nothing, Nastasya Filippovna, I've seen nothing of the world, you're right, but... the honour would be mine, not yours. I am a nobody, but you have suffered in hell and have emerged unscathed, and that is no mean thing. You have nothing to be ashamed of and there's no reason for you to run off with Rogozhin! You are too excited... You gave Mr Totsky his seventy thousand back, and mentioned that you'd leave behind all that's here! No one here present would be capable of doing that. I... Nastasya Filippovna... I love you. I'd die for you, Nastasya Filippovna. I won't have anyone say a word against you, Nastasya Filippovna... If we are poor, I'm going to work, Nastasya Filippovna..."

These last words were accompanied by Ferdyshchenko's and Lebedev's suppressed sniggers, and even the General grunted to himself in great displeasure. Ptitsyn and Totsky could not suppress a smile, but managed to contain themselves. All the rest gaped open-mouthed in astonishment.

"But perhaps we may not be so poor after all, but very rich, Nastasya Filippovna," the Prince continued in the same humble tones. "I have to admit, I don't know for sure, and it's unfortunate that I've not had the opportunity to find out anything during the course of the day, but a letter from Moscow reached me in Switzerland from a certain Mr Salazkin, who informs me that I may be the beneficiary of a very large inheritance. Here is the letter..."

The Prince produced a letter from his pocket.

"Is he completely off his head?" the General muttered. "This is becoming a real madhouse!"

There followed a short pause.

"You did say, Prince, the letter is from Salazkin?" Ptitsyn asked. "He is a very highly regarded person in his circle, and if the communication is really from him, you can trust it with confidence. Fortunately, I know his hand, because I recently had business dealings with him. If you were to let me have a look, perhaps I could pass an opinion."

The Prince, without a word, held out the letter in a trembling hand.

"What's going on, what is this?" the General exclaimed, looking at everybody in turn in utter surprise.

All eyes were on Ptitsyn, who was reading the letter. The prevailing sense of curiosity had been given a new and extraordinary impetus. Ferdyshchenko was unable to keep still; Rogozhin looked lost as he glanced from Ptitsyn to the Prince, and back again. Darya Alexeyevna seemed all excited with expectation. Even Lebedev could resist it no longer; he had left his corner and, bending over awkwardly, was trying to read the letter over Ptitsyn's shoulder, giving the impression of one who at any moment was expecting to be kicked in the posterior.

16

"THIS IS BEYOND THE SHADOW OF A DOUBT," Ptitsyn announced at last, folding the letter and handing it back to the Prince. "Without any question you stand to receive a huge inheritance by virtue of your aunt's incontestable will and testament."

"I don't believe it!" the General exclaimed as though a gun had been discharged at his ear.

Ptitsyn, addressing predominantly Ivan Fyodorovich, explained that five months ago an aunt of the Prince's, his mother's elder sister, whom he'd never known in his life, had died; she was the daughter of one Papushin, a merchant belonging to the Third Guild of Merchants,* who had died a pauper and a bankrupt. But Papushin's elder brother, who'd also died recently, was a famously rich merchant. About a year previously his only two sons had died within the space of a month. This came as such a shock that soon afterwards the old man himself fell ill and died. He was a widower with no heirs except the Prince's aunt, Papushin's niece, an altogether poor woman, living in a house not belonging to her. At the time the inheritance was being made over to her, she was already at death's door, suffering from pleurisy, but she immediately made arrangements to look for the Prince, entrusting it to Salazkin and, just before she died, managed to draw up her will. It would appear that neither the Prince nor his Swiss doctor, with whom he resided, wished to await official confirmation or make enquiries about the demise, and the Prince, with Salazkin's letter in his pocket, decided to travel back to Russia.

"I can tell you only one thing," Ptitsyn concluded, turning to the Prince, "that everything should pass without a hitch, and that all that Salazkin tells you about the indisputability and legality of your case, is as good as money in your hand. I congratulate you, Prince! You may be entitled to about a million and a half, perhaps more. Papushin was a very rich man."

"That's what I call the last of the Myshkins!" Ferdyshchenko vociferated.

"Hurrah!" Lebedev intoned in a voice enfeebled by alcohol.

"And I stood him twenty-five roubles in the morning, the poor thing, ha-ha-ha! This is pure magic-lantern show!" the General proclaimed, quite beside himself with wonderment. "Well, congratulations, congratulations!" and, rising to his feet, he approached the Prince to embrace him. Others followed his example. Even those who had withdrawn to the other room began to make their way back. A vague hubbub ensued, there were exclamations, some voices demanded champagne; people moved about and jostled. For a brief moment everyone seemed to have neglected Nastasya Filippovna, forgetting that she was the hostess and the evening belonged to her. Somehow the conviction that the Prince had made her a proposal had gained universal currency. The proceedings threatened to get ever more curious and extraordinary. Totsky, deeply dismayed, merely kept shrugging his shoulders; he was almost the only one to remain seated, the rest were crowding in a disorderly fashion around the table. Subsequently everyone insisted that it was precisely at that moment that Nastasya Filippovna lost her reason. She remained seated and for a time surveyed everyone with startled eyes as though at pains to gather her thoughts. Then she turned to face the Prince; to look at him intently and sternly from beneath knitted brows, but only for a second. Perhaps it occurred to her that all that was going on around her was merely a joke, a tease; yet the look on the Prince's face dispelled that notion. She made an effort to think, then attempted to smile, distractedly...

"So, it's true, I'm going to be a princess!" she said softly to herself in mocking tones; then, looking up at Darya Alexeyevna, she burst out laughing. "Who could have thought... this... is totally unexpected... Why, ladies and gentlemen, are you standing, please be seated and wish the Prince and me well! I heard somebody call for champagne? Ferdyshchenko, go and see to it! Katya, Pasha!" she called out to her maids, whom she had noticed in the doorway. "Come here, I'm getting married, do you realize? To the Prince, he's got one and a half million, he is Prince Myshkin, and he's taking me to be his wife!"

"Blessings upon you, my dear, it's about time!" Darya Alexeyevna, deeply moved by the events, exclaimed. "Don't let such an opportunity slip by!"

"Why don't you come and sit next to me, Prince?" Nastasya Filippovna went on. "That's better, here comes the wine, drink to us, ladies and gentlemen!"

"Hurrah!" several voices rang out. A great number of people gravitated towards the wine, these nearly all from Rogozhin's party. But though they were readily disposed to give vent to their voices, many, amidst all the turmoil and confusion, could not help noticing that a change was in the air. Others stood around irresolute and looked on with mistrust. There were yet those who whispered that all was as it should be; that princes were free to marry anyone they chose, be it indeed a travelling gypsy girl. As for Rogozhin himself, he just stood and looked on, his features frozen in a smile of utter incomprehension.

"Prince, my dear fellow, think what you're doing!" the General whispered in horror as he came up alongside the Prince and tugged him by the sleeve.

Nastasya Filippovna noticed this and burst out laughing.

"Have a heart, General! Now I'm a princess myself, did you hear that? The Prince will see to it that I'm treated with respect! Afanasy Ivanovich, why don't you wish me well? Wouldn't you say a husband like that is an asset? A million and a half, a prince, and, they say, an idiot to boot, what could be better? This is when life really begins! You're too late, Rogozhin! Take your bundle away, I'm marrying the Prince and I've more money than you!"

Rogozhin now realized what was at stake. His face dropped under the weight of unutterable suffering. He threw up his hands and a groan from his chest rent the air.

"Back off!" he yelled to the Prince.

This exclamation was greeted with laughter on all sides.

"To back off for your sake, is that what you mean?" Darya Alexeyevna cut in, venting her indignation. "Just look at him, throwing his money about, the yokel! The Prince is offering his hand in marriage, and you're just a troublemaker!"

"I'm offering too! I am, this very minute! I'll give her everything..."

"A drunkard arrives here straight after a drinking bout, why doesn't someone just kick him out?" Darya Alexeyevna persisted in her obloquy.

There was more laughter.

"Do you see, Prince," Nastasya Filippovna said, turning to the Prince, "what a hard bargain this yokel of a merchant is driving over your bride-to-be?"

"He is drunk," the Prince said. "He loves you very much."

"How will you feel later when you'll think back that your bride nearly ran off with Rogozhin?"

"You were not well. You're not well now, you don't know what you're saying."

"And you won't be offended when later people will say that your wife had been Totsky's kept woman?"

"No, I won't... You did not stay with Totsky of your own accord."

"And you'll never hold it against me?"

"Never."

"Take care you don't promise too much, there's a lifetime ahead!"

"Nastasya Filippovna," the Prince said softly with feeling, "I told you before that I'd look upon your acceptance as an honour. You didn't want to take me seriously before, and I could see others thought it funny too. Perhaps it was the way I put it, and I sounded ridiculous, but I was pretty sure I... knew what I was talking about, and that I spoke the truth. You were on the verge of disaster just now, irretrievably, and you'd never have forgiven yourself for it later. You are guilty of nothing. Your life is far from ruined. So what if Rogozhin came to take you away, or that Gavrila Ardalionovich tried to take advantage of you? You shouldn't keep harking back to that! Few would have been capable of doing what you did, you heard me say that before, and if you wanted to throw your lot in with Rogozhin, it was your sick imagination speaking. You're far from well even as we speak, and you ought to be in bed. You'd run away to the end of the world after five minutes with him. You are very proud, Nastasya Filippovna, but perhaps you are so unhappy that you really think of yourself as the guilty party. You need to be looked after, Nastasya Filippovna. I shall look after you. When I saw your picture this morning, it was as though I'd seen you before. My feeling was that you were calling for me... I... I shall respect you all life long, Nastasya Filippovna," the Prince broke off with a start and blushed on realizing who his audience was.

Ptitsyn had lowered his head and was demurely staring at the ground. A thought passed through Totsky's mind, "An idiot who knows instinctively that flattery will get you everywhere." The Prince caught sight of Ganya, sitting in a far corner, darting looks that threatened to kill.

"Bless you, Prince!" Darya Alexeyevna said, moved by the Prince's speech.

"An educated man, but beyond all help!" the General muttered in a low voice.

Totsky had picked up his hat and was about to get up so as to slink off on the quiet. He exchanged glances with the General, motioning him to leave together.

"Thank you, Prince, no one has spoken to me like that before," Nastasya Filippovna said. "People haggled over me, but no upstanding man had ever offered to marry me. Did you hear that, Afanasy Ivanovich? What do you think of what the Prince has just said? It borders almost on the indecent... Rogozhin, don't go yet! Not that you would go anywhere, as I see it. I may yet take up your offer. Where were you going to take me?"

"To Ekaterinhof,"* Lebedev proclaimed from his corner of the room, which caused Rogozhin to shudder and stare ahead wide-eyed, incomprehensibly. He seemed bereft of reason as though stunned by a terrible blow to the head.

"What, what was that you said, my dearest!" Darya Alexeyevna protested in fear. "You really must be unwell, or totally out of your mind!"

"So, you really thought I was serious?" Nastasya Filippovna retorted, laughing out loud and springing to her feet from the sofa. "As if I really could bring myself to ruin the life of this innocent child! It's more in the line of Afanasy Ivanovich, fond as he is of minors! Let's go, Rogozhin! Where's that bundle of yours? Never mind your wanting to get married, let's have the money all the same. It doesn't yet mean I'll marry you. You thought if you got married, the bundle would stay with you. Wrong! You'll soon find out what I'm like! I've been Totsky's mistress... Prince, what you need now is Aglaya Yepanchina, not Nastasya Filippovna – or it may end with Ferdyshchenko poking

175

his finger at you! This may not worry you, but it does me, that I'd been the cause of your downfall and that you'd bear a grudge against me! As for your declaring that I'd be doing you an honour, you'd better ask Totsky about that. And Ganya, my pet, did you know that you've spoiled your chances with Aglaya Yepanchina for good? If you hadn't haggled with her, she'd definitely have married you! That's always the way with you men! There's a stark choice – you go either for the angels or the harlots! Or else you fall between two stools, that's for sure... Look at the General's mouth hanging wide open!..."

"This is real Sodom and no mistake!" the General remarked, shrugging his shoulders. He too had got up from the sofa; everyone was on their feet. Nastasya Filippovna was in a kind of an abandon.

"Can this really be true!" the Prince was heard to wail.

"And what did you think? Can I not have my pride, however dissolute I am? You said I was perfection itself! What's the good of such perfection if I'm ready to descend into the den of iniquity just to be able to say that I've trampled underfoot a million-rouble fortune and a princely title to boot! Just think, what sort of a wife would I make after that? Afanasy Ivanovich, you must agree, I flung a million roubles to the wind, did I not? So how could you imagine I'd jump for joy just to marry your precious Ganya and that seventy-five thousand roubles of yours? You keep the seventy-five thousand for yourself, Afanasy Ivanovich (couldn't quite make it a hundred, could you? Rogozhin beat you to it!) – as for dear old Ganya, he's in for a treat. I've just had an idea. But now I want to have fun, I'm a woman of the streets, didn't you know! I've spent ten years in jail, luck has now smiled upon me! What's the matter with you, Rogozin? Get ready, we're going!"

"We're going!" Rogozhin bellowed, wild with joy. "You there... wine all round! Whoopee!..."

"Make sure there's plenty of wine, I want to make merry. Will there be music?"

"There will, of course there will! Keep away!" Rogozhin yelled frenziedly when he saw Darya Alexeyevna draw near to Nastasya Filippovna. "She's mine! She's all mine! She's my queen! Damn it all!"

He was out of breath with elation; he was circling round Nastasya Filippovna and shouting at everyone, "Keep away!" By and by everybody had crowded into the drawing room. Some were drinking, others were shouting and roaring with laughter, the general atmosphere was one of the most uninhibited and boisterous conviviality. Ferdyshchenko was giving clear signs of wanting to join the Rogozhin faction. The General and Totsky made another surreptitious attempt to slip away. Ganya too was standing hat in hand, but he was silent and apparently unable to tear himself away from the scene unravelling before his eyes.

"Don't come near!" Rogozhin was bawling.

"Stop yelling, you!" Nastasya Filippovna threatened him, laughing out loud. "I'm in charge here, and I can still boot you out too if you're not careful. I haven't taken your money yet, there it still is. Give it to me, the whole lot! A hundred thousand in here, you say? Ugh, how disgusting! Have a heart, Darya Alexeyevna! Do you really want me to destroy him?" she pointed at the Prince. "How can he get married, he needs a nanny himself to look after him! The General would make a splendid nanny for him – look at the way he fawns over him! Look Prince, your bride-to-be has taken money because she's depraved, and you wanted to marry her! Stop snivelling! It's not the end of the world! Laugh and be merry, like me," Nastasya Filippovna went on as two large tears began to roll down her own cheeks. "Time will heal everything back to health! It's better to come to one's senses now, rather than when it's too late... But why are you all crying – there, there, Katya too. What's the matter, Katya, my dear? I'll leave plenty for you and Pasha, I've already made the arrangements, and now goodbye! I made you, honest girl that you are, wait on me, a fallen woman... It's better by far like this, Prince, really better, or you'd have detested me later, and we'd have been miserable. Don't say a word, I shan't believe you! And how silly it would have all been!... No, it's best we part in friendship, because I'm such a silly thing myself, nothing would have come of it! Do you think I didn't dream about you? You were so right, I dreamt about you way back in the country at his place, the five years I spent on my own. Dreams, dreams and more dreams – and it was always someone like you I'd conjure up, kind, honest, sensitive and silly just like you, who'd suddenly come to me and say, 'You're not guilty, Nastasya Filippovna, and I adore you!' I'd dream and dream to the point of despair... And then that one over there would creep up. He'd spend about a couple of months a year having his fill of disgracing, unsettling, rousing, corrupting me and be gone – the number of times I wanted to drown myself, but I was too much of a coward, I didn't have the guts, well, and now... Rogozhin, are you ready?"

"I am! Keep back!"

"We're all ready!" a number of voices rang out.

"And troikas with tinkling bells!"

Nastasya Filippovna grabbed hold of the bundle.

"Ganya, my dear fellow, I've had an idea! I want to recompense you, because it's unfair for you to end up empty-handed! Rogozhin, would he crawl for three roubles to Vasilevsky Island on all fours?"

"He would!"

"Well then, listen here, my dearest Ganya, I want to see your soul squirm for the last time. You well and truly plagued me for the last three months. It's my turn now. Do you see this bundle, there's a hundred thousand roubles in here! I'm now going to throw it into the fire, in the flames, here in front of everybody, in front of witnesses! As soon as the flames have enveloped it entirely – reach into the fire, no gloves mind, with bare hands and sleeves rolled up, pull the bundle out! If you manage to do it – it's all yours, the lot! You'll singe your fingers a little – but what's that for a hundred thousand roubles, think on it! Easily done! And I'll have the satisfaction of seeing you squirm, seeing you reach for my money into the fire. Everybody's a witness, the money will be yours to keep! And if you won't reach for it, it'll all burn to cinders. I shan't let anybody near. Back! Everybody get back! It's my money! It's mine in payment for one night with Rogozhin. It's true, the money's mine, Rogozhin, is it not?"

"Yours, my joy! Yours, my queen!"

"Well then, all stand well back, I'll do as I like! Nobody interfere! Ferdyshchenko, stoke up the fire!"

"Nastasya Filippovna, I haven't the strength!" Ferdyshchenko responded, utterly confounded.

"What a lot you are!" Nastasya Filippovna called out, grabbed the tongs, turned over a couple of smouldering logs and as soon as the tongues of flame began to lick them, threw the bundle into the fire.

People gasped with one voice; some crossed themselves.

"She's mad, she's gone mad!" was the general consensus.

"Shouldn't... shouldn't we just tie her up?" the General whispered to Ptitsyn, "or perhaps we should simply send for... Let's face it, she's gone mad, raving mad! She has!"

"N-no, this isn't just madness, there's more to it than that," Ptitsyn, white as a sheet, whispered in a quavering voice, unable to take his eyes off the smouldering packet.

"Mad, wouldn't you agree, totally mad?" the General continued to press his point home with Totsky.

"I told you she was an unusual personality," Afanasy Ivanovich muttered, his features also somewhat drained of colour.

"But we're talking about a hundred thousand!…"

"Lord, oh Lord!" the voices would not let up. Everybody clustered round the fireplace, everybody wanted to occupy a better vantage point, everybody vociferated… Some had even jumped on chairs to look over people's shoulders. Darya Alexeyevna had dashed into the other room and in a state of panic was conversing about something with the housemaids Katya and Pasha. The beautiful German was nowhere to be seen.

"Holy mother! Queen almighty!" Lebedev wailed, crawling on his knees in front of Nastasya Filippovna, his arms outstretched towards the fireplace. "A hundred thousand! A hundred thousand! I saw it with my own eyes being bundled! Have a heart, merciful mother! Command me to dive into the fireplace, and I'll go, grey head foremost, into the fire, all of me!… Crippled, invalid wife to care for, thirteen hungry mouths to feed – every one an orphan, lost my father the other week, he starved to death, Nastasya Filippovna!" and, having come to the end of his tale of woe, he moved towards the fireplace.

"Don't you dare!" Nastasya Filippovna exclaimed, pushing him away. "You there, make way! Ganya, don't just stand there! No need to be embarrassed! Go for it! This is your chance!"

But Ganya had suffered too much that day and night and was not prepared for this latest, unforeseen trial. The crowd parted down the middle and he found himself face to face with Nastasya Filippovna at three paces. She stood right by the hearth and waited, her eyes blazing with a penetrating intensity. Ganya stood before her in evening tailcoat, his hands crossed, clutching his hat and gloves, and gazing at the fire in silent resignation. A frantic smile played on his pallid cheeks. He truly could not take his eyes off the fire and the smouldering bundle; but, it seemed, a new emotion had stirred in his soul, as though he had resolved to endure the ordeal. He stood stock-still; a few seconds later it became patently clear to everyone that he would not reach out to pluck the packet from the fire, moreover that he had no wish to do so.

"The money will perish, and you'll be a laughing stock," Nastasya Filippovna called out to him. "I tell you, you'll hang yourself later, and I'm not joking!"

The fire, which had flared up between two smoking logs, appeared to go out initially under the weight of the bundle that fell on top of them. But a small blue flame continued to struggle up from under the end of one of the logs. Finally, a thin long yellow tongue shot up to give the bundle a tentative lick; the fire caught hold and ran along the paper edges up and over, and suddenly the whole thing flared up, and a bright flame surged upwards. Everyone gasped.

"Dearest lady!" Lebedev continued to plead, hurling himself forward again, but Rogozhin caught him and pushed him away once more.

Rogozhin himself appeared to have transformed his whole being into one intense, involuntarily stare, fixated on Nastasya Filippovna. He exulted. He was in the seventh heaven of delight.

"There's a real queen for you!" he kept repeating, addressing now one person, now another, all at random. "That's what I call a woman!" he called out repeatedly in a state of ecstasy. "Which one of you namby-pambies could do that, eh?"

The Prince looked on in dejected silence.

"I'll pull it out with my bare teeth for just one single thousand!" Ferdyshchenko made his offer.

"Same here, with my teeth!" the fisticuff gentleman responded, grinding his teeth in a fit of utter frustration. "Hell, this is too much! It's all going up!" he added, seeing the flames intensify.

"It'll burn, it'll all burn!" everybody shouted in one voice and practically everybody tried to jostle his way to the fireplace.

"Ganya, stop being awkward! I'm telling you for the last time!"

"Go for it!" Ferdyshchenko bawled, rushing at Ganya in desperation and tugging him by his sleeve. "Go for it, you fool! It's burning, damn you!"

Ganya gave him a hard push, turned on his heel and headed for the door; but he'd barely taken two steps, when he swayed and crashed to the ground.

"He's fainted!" voices resounded on all sides.

"My lady, it'll all go up in flames!" Lebedev wailed on.

"All for nothing!" the voices echoed.

"Katya, Pasha, some water, smelling salts!" Nastasya Filippovna commanded, grabbed the fire tongs and plucked the bundle out.

Nearly all the outer wrapping had burned and was smouldering, but it was immediately clear that the inner one was intact. There were three layers of newsprint altogether, and the money was safe. Everyone breathed a sigh of relief.

"Maybe just a thousand or so has got damaged, but the rest is all right," Lebedev announced, grinning with delight.

"It's all his! All the money goes to him! Do you hear me, ladies and gentlemen?" Nastasya Filippovna proclaimed, shifting the bundle towards Ganya. "So he didn't give in, he stood the test! I'm glad his pride's greater than his greed. Don't worry, he'll recover. Or who knows, he would have killed me... There, he's coming to. General, Ivan Petrovich, Darya Alexeyevna, Katya, Pasha, Rogozhin, did you hear me? The money is his, Ganya's. I'm letting him have it in full ownership, as a reward... or whatever else! Tell him that. Leave the bundle next to him... Let's go, Rogozhin! Goodbye, Prince, you're the first genuine man I've met! Goodbye, Afanasy Ivanovich, *merci*!"

Rogozhin's merry men, shouting, bawling and boisterous, all rushed through the rooms for the exit in the footsteps of their leader and Nastasya Filippovna. In the entrance hall the maids helped her on with her fur coat; the cook Marfa joined them from the kitchen. Nastasya Filippovna showered them all with kisses.

"Are you really leaving us for good, darling lady? Where will you be going?" the girls beset her with questions as they covered her hands with kisses, "On your birthday of all days!"

"Out on the street, Katya, you heard me, where I really belong, or else I'll become a washerwoman! I've had enough of Afanasy Ivanovich! Give him my regards, and bless you all..."

The Prince rushed headlong towards the forecourt where people were in the process of getting into four troikas, their harness bells tingling. The General caught up with him on the stairs.

"Prince, what are you doing, come to your senses!" he called out, grabbing him by the arm. "Let her be! Can't you see what she's like! I'm speaking to you as a father..."

The Prince looked at him, but without a word tore himself free and rushed down.

In the forecourt, where the last of the troikas had just pulled away, the General saw the Prince grab the first cab that came along and shout to the driver to follow the troikas to Ekaterinhof. A little later the General's own calash, drawn by a grey purebred, pulled up at the doorstep to convey him home as he mused along the way over new plans and schemes, and with the pearl necklace – which in spite of everything he did not neglect to take with him – safely in his possession. Once or twice in the middle of his musings Nastasya Filippovna's seductive image rose before him, and the General drew a deep breath.

"Pity! A real pity! Such a waste of a woman! Mad as a hatter!... But as for the Prince, Nastasya Filippovna is the last thing he needs now…"

Two of Nastasya Filippovna's other guests, who had decided to walk on foot, exchanged moral sentiments of a similar nature.

"Do you know, Afanasy Ivanovich, this reminds me of what happens in Japan," Ivan Petrovich Ptitsyn said. "They say the offended party goes to the offender and says, 'You've offended me, that's why I've come to slit my stomach open in front of you,' and with these words he really goes ahead and slits his stomach in front of the offender and, no doubt, experiences enormous satisfaction as though he'd really avenged himself. There's no end of weird characters in this world, Afanasy Ivanovich!"

"Do you suppose there was something of the kind in this case too?" Afanasy Ivanovich responded with a smile. "Hm! That's not bad actually… I like your parallel. But you could see for yourself, my dear Ivan Petrovich, that I did everything I could. After all, I couldn't do the impossible, could I? But you must agree also that this woman is possessed of enormous merit, of… some splendid qualities. I wanted to call out to her back then, if only I'd had the opportunity amid all that bedlam, that she herself is my best defence against all her accusations. Who could possibly resist being captivated by her, occasionally to the point of distraction or… more? Look, that yokel, Rogozhin, brought her a hundred thousand! Perhaps the scene we witnessed was wild, romantic, in poor taste, but, looked at another way, it was picaresque, it was unorthodox – you can't deny that! My God, with her beauty, with her personality, what couldn't she have achieved! And yet, despite my best efforts, even despite the upbringing I gave her – it was all in vain! A rough diamond – I said so many a time…"

And Afanasy Ivanovich heaved a heavy sigh.

Part Two

1

A BOUT TWO DAYS after the strange events at Nastasya Filippovna's soirée, with which we ended the first part of our story, Prince Myshkin hurried off to Moscow in order to make enquiries regarding his unexpected inheritance. It was rumoured at the time that there may have been other reasons for such a precipitate departure; however, on this, as on the Prince's adventures in Moscow generally during his absence from St Petersburg, we have precious little information. The Prince stayed away precisely six months, and even those who might have had certain motives for being interested in his comings and goings, could discover very little about his movements during that period. True enough, the odd snippet of news would, however occasionally, reach the ears of some people, but such items of news as there were, were for the most part very odd and practically always contradictory. The greatest interest of all in the Prince, of course, was to be found in the Yepanchin family, whom he did not even have time to visit before his departure. It must be said, the General did see him at the time, in fact, more than once, and they had serious discussions about something. However, the General took care not to inform his family of these meetings. On the whole, initially – that is, up to a month after the Prince's departure – all reference to the Prince was studiously avoided in the Yepanchin household. Only the General's Lady, Lizaveta Prokofyevna, observed at the very outset that she was "grievously wrong about the Prince"; and then two or three days later added, in general terms only, with no mention of the Prince this time, that her greatest failing throughout her life was her "constant inability to judge people correctly". And finally, ten days or so later, at the end of some contretemps with her daughters, she would always end up by saying, "Enough of mistakes! From now on there'll be no more!" One ought to mention here that for a considerable time the overall atmosphere in their house was not among the most benign. There was something oppressive in the air, something tense, inchoate, hostile; everyone went about with a long face. The General was busy day and night, snowed under with work; he had seldom been seen more preoccupied and engaged – in his official capacity, that is. His family hardly saw him. As for the Yepanchin girls, nothing was said explicitly by them of course. Perhaps even privately not nearly enough was said between themselves. They were a proud lot, a touch supercilious, but inclined to be shy amongst themselves; for the rest, they understood one another not just from the first word, but from the first glance, making verbal exchanges all the less necessary.

An outside observer, had there been one, might have come to only one conclusion: that, judging by all the aforementioned, admittedly sparse, information, the Prince had nevertheless managed to leave in the Yepanchin household a distinctly characteristic impression, and this despite the fact that he'd been there only once, and fleetingly at that. Maybe the impression was one of wonderment, based on the Prince's tales of the unusual and the adventurous? Be that as it may, the impression was not to be denied.

Little by little, the rumour that had swept the town too, began to subside. True, there was still talk of some silly princeling (no one could tell his name precisely), who'd come into a huge inheritance and had married a famous travelling French cancan dancer from Le Château des Fleurs in Paris. Others however said that it was a general who'd come into the inheritance, and that the bridegroom of the famous itinerant French dancer was a bluff young, fabulously rich Russian merchant, who on his wedding day, dead drunk, had out of sheer bravado burned seven hundred thousand roubles' worth of tickets for the current lottery draw in a candle flame. But, in the course of events, all these rumours soon petered out. For instance, the whole of Rogozhin's clique, many of whom could easily have thrown some light on the situation, had set out for Moscow en masse with their leader himself at the helm. This was almost exactly a week after a terrible orgy at Ekaterinhof, which Nastasya Filippovna also attended. Only a few of those who took an interest in the matter claimed to have heard that on the second day after the escapade at Ekaterinhof, Nastasya Filippovna had taken to her heels and vanished, though later it seems her whereabouts were traced to Moscow; Rogozhin's own subsequent departure for that city corroborated this information.

There was news too of Gavrila Ardalionovich Ivolgin, who continued to preoccupy the minds of those in his circle. But something happened to him too which soon diminished, and eventually completely dispelled, all unfavourable views of him: he fell very ill and was neither able to appear in society, nor to go to work. After a month he recovered but resigned from the company, and his position was taken by someone else. He also ceased to visit the Yepanchins and a new clerk took over as the General's secretary. His adversaries might have supposed he had been so traumatised by all that had happened to him that he dared not even show his face in the street; but it was all the result of his illness. He fell into a state of hypochondria, became absent-minded and irritable. That very winter Varvara Ardalionovna married Ptitsyn; all who knew them ascribed this marriage to the fact that Ganya did not wish to return to his duties and had not only ceased to maintain the family, but appeared himself to be in need of sustenance and care.

Let us note in parentheses that Gavrila Ardalionovich ceased to be mentioned at the Yepanchins – as though no one by that name had ever been to their house, or had even so much as existed. And yet they had all learnt (and with some dispatch) one rather curious detail about him. That fatal night, after experiencing the awful ordeal at Nastasya Filippovna's, Ganya, on his return home, instead of going to bed, had sat down to wait for the Prince in eager expectation. The Prince, who had set off for Ekaterinhof, arrived back after five in the morning. Ganya then entered his room and placed on the table in front of him the singed packet of money that Nastasya Filippovna had given him as he was lying unconscious. He earnestly begged the Prince to return the present to her at the first opportunity. On entering the room, Ganya had been in a hostile, almost desperate mood; but, apparently, after a few words had passed between them, Ganya had stayed on at the Prince's for two hours, crying bitterly all the while. They parted on friendly terms.

This piece of information that had reached the Yepanchins was indeed subsequently confirmed as being perfectly accurate. Of course, it was rather strange that information of this sort could travel so fast; for instance, all that had occurred at Nastasya Filippovna's was already common knowledge in the Yepanchin household almost the next day, and in some considerable detail at that. It is very likely that the information on Gavrila Ardalionovich was brought to the Yepanchins by Varvara Ardalionovna, who'd suddenly turned up in the company of the Yepanchin girls, it must be said, rather unexpectedly and, to

Lizaveta Prokofyevna's no small surprise, was very soon accepted by them on very intimate terms. However, even though Varvara Ardalionovna had for some reason found it necessary to establish such a close contact with the young Yepanchins, she was unlikely to have talked about her brother with them. She was a rather proud young lady, after her own fashion naturally, and this in spite of forming friendly ties with a household from which her brother had been well-nigh sent off with a flea in his ear. Although she had known the Yepanchin girls formerly, they had met infrequently. Even now she hardly ever ventured into the drawing room, and would access the house by the back stairs as if dropping in casually. Lizaveta Prokofyevna had never been fond of her, neither then nor now, although she greatly respected Nina Alexandrovna, Varvara Ardalionovna's mother. She affected surprise and annoyance, and ascribed her daughters' friendship with Varya to caprice and wilfulness, a desire "to hurt and upset their mother in every way possible"; all the same, Varvara Ardalionovna continued to pay her visits regardless, before and after her marriage.

Scarcely a month after the Prince's departure, the General's Lady, Madame Yepanchina, received a letter from the aged Princess Belokonskaya, who had two weeks previously left for Moscow to visit her oldest married daughter; the letter had a profound effect upon her. Despite the fact that she kept her daughters and her husband Ivan Fyodorovich in the dark about its contents, all concerned could not help but notice a certain restlessness bordering on vexation in her. She began to address her daughters in rather unusual tones, always with a peculiar choice of topics. She was evidently anxious to communicate something, but for some reason restrained herself. On the day she received the letter she overwhelmed everyone with kindness and even gave Aglaya and Adelaida a kiss, offering to make amends to them, only exactly what for remained unclear to them. Even Ivan Fyodorovich, who for up to a month had been held incommunicado by her, was restored to favour. It goes without saying that the very next day she was already consumed with anger for her previous day's frailty, and even before dinner was served had managed to have a row with everyone, though come the evening, the storm clouds were already beginning to disperse.

But, when at the end of the following week another letter arrived from Belokonskaya, the General's Lady decided to speak up. She solemnly announced that "old Belokonskaya" (she never referred to her indirectly as "Princess") had written to her about, well about that... "funny chap, you know, that Prince of ours!" The old woman had come across him in Moscow, and had made enquiries and found them very positive; in the end the Prince had called on her himself and left an impression that was almost extraordinary. "I understand she's invited him to call on her in the mornings, from one to two, and he ambles over to her every day and still hasn't bored her to death," the General's Lady concluded, adding that, thanks to the old woman, the Prince is now welcome in one or two respectable houses, "which is just as well, or he'd have stayed within his four walls, retiring simpleton that he is." The young ladies, for whose ears all this was meant, noted at once that their dear mama had somehow kept back a lot more from her letter. Perhaps they discovered this via Varvara Ardalionovna, who might have been expected to be privy, as indeed she was, to all that was known to Ptitsyn regarding the Prince's sojourn in Moscow. As for Ptitsyn, he was likely to know a great deal more than anyone. But he was a man who in matters of business kept his cards close to his chest, although this did not apply to Varya. The General's Lady immediately took exception to this, and her dislike of Varvara Ardalionovna at once increased even more.

Be that as it may, the ice had been broken, and it was now possible to speak freely of the Prince. Besides, that unusual impression and that truly excessive interest which the Prince had originally evoked in the Yepanchin household was revived yet again. The General's Lady, it must be said, was not a little surprised by her daughters' reaction to the news from Moscow. The daughters for their part were also not a little surprised at their mother who, having only recently declared for all to hear that her greatest failing throughout her life was her "constant inability to judge people correctly", should at the same time have drawn the Prince to the attention of the crotchety "high and mighty" Muscovite Belokonskaya, a stubborn old biddy, who at the best of times, could not, saving by superhuman effort, be cajoled and humoured into compliance.

But, as soon as the ice had been broken and there was a wind of change in the air, the General also piped up readily enough. It turned out that he too was burning with interest. However, he touched upon only one, strictly factual, aspect of the matter. It turned out that he had engaged, in the Prince's best interests, two highly trustworthy and influential gentlemen to keep the Prince, but more particularly his Moscow consultant Salazkin, under close surveillance. All that had been said relating to the inheritance, the factual side of it, was correct, except for the actual amount, which on enquiry turned out to be considerably less than had been first mooted. A good half of the estate was in a mess; there were debts outstanding, additional claimants surfaced, and the Prince, despite all the counselling he received, behaved in a highly unbusinesslike manner. "Of course, I wish him only the very best!" the General remarked now that the ice of silence had been broken, "from the bottom of my heart, because though the young fellow's clearly not all there, he's not a bad sort." It would appear, the Prince had behaved most unwisely. For instance, the deceased merchant's creditors had materialized with dubious, not to say worthless documents, while others, having found out more about the Prince, materialized with no documents whatsoever. And what did the Prince do? He accommodated nearly all of them, however hard his friends counselled him that all these claimants were completely bogus; and he had accommodated them simply because some of them had indeed sustained genuine losses.

To this the General's Lady responded that Belokonskaya had written to her in a similar vein, and that it was all, "Silly, very silly, an object lesson to an incorrigible fool," she added sharply, but by her face it was clear how proud she was that this "fool" had behaved precisely thus. In the end, the General made a mental note that, judging by his wife's concern in the matter, one would have thought the Prince was her own son; and that for some reason she had begun to lavish an unwonted tenderness upon Aglaya. Having established this, the General for some little time adopted a perfectly matter-of-fact, businesslike demeanour.

But yet again this benign atmosphere did not last long. Two weeks went by, and suddenly something changed yet again. The General's Lady put on a scowl, and the General, having shrugged his shoulders once or twice, reverted to the former, "glacial", silence. The reason was that a couple of weeks previously he had received a confidential letter – brief and hence not altogether explicit, but reliable nonetheless – informing him that Nastasya Filippovna, having initially gone missing in Moscow, had subsequently been tracked down by Rogozhin in Moscow, and, having disappeared once more and been tracked down by him for a second time, had finally given an almost inviolable promise to marry him. And, lo and behold, just two weeks later, His Excellency suddenly received a communication, informing him that Nastasya Filippovna had absconded for the third time – almost straight from the altar – and on this occasion had gone to ground somewhere in the provinces, and that Prince Myshkin, having left his affairs in the hands of Salazkin, had also vanished from Moscow. "Whether he had gone with her, or simply rushed after her – is a matter of conjecture, but the fact is undeniable," the General concluded. Lizaveta Prokofyevna for her part too received some rather unpleasant news. Be that as it may, two months after the Prince's departure all talk of him had almost ceased in St Petersburg, and in the Yepanchin household "the ice of silence" on the subject was back with a vengeance. All the same Varvara Ardalionovna's visits continued uninterrupted.

To put all this talk and rumour to rest, let us add that with the coming of spring the Yepanchins had to contend with a great many upheavals, such that it was not at all difficult to forget about the Prince, who possibly intentionally, gave no news about himself. In the winter they had little by little reached the decision to travel abroad for the summer, that is, Lizaveta Prokofyevna and her daughters; the General, it goes without saying, was not inclined to waste time on such "idle pursuits". The decision was taken at the particular behest of the girls, who were firmly convinced that the only reason they were not taken abroad was their parents' concern to find each of them a suitable match and to marry them off. Perhaps the parents too realized at long last that future husbands could be found abroad as well as at home, and that a tour lasting only one summer would not only not upset anything, but on the contrary could facilitate matters. Here it out ought to be mentioned in passing that Afanasy Ivanovich Totsky's proposal to the eldest of the Yepanchin sisters did not materialize and consequently neither did the marriage. It all came about somehow as a matter of course, with no undue discussions or family scenes. With the Prince's departure the matter simply fell into abeyance on both sides. Nevertheless it had been one of the reasons for the former oppressive atmosphere in the Yepanchin household, and at the time caused the General's Lady to exclaim that she was ready to fall on her knees and sing praise to the Lord. The General, being in his spouse's disfavour and aware that he himself was to blame, thought fit to put on a protracted show of ill-temper; he felt sorry for Afanasy Ivanovich; "so wealthy and so astute!" Before long the General learnt that Afanasy Ivanovich had fallen for the charms of a top-drawer French aristocrat, a marchioness and a legitimist, doing her foreign tour; that marriage was in the offing; that he'd subsequently be whisked off to Paris, and then somewhere to Brittany. "He's not going to last with a Frenchwoman though," the General postulated.

The Yepanchins were planning to set off by the beginning of summer. And suddenly an event occurred which again changed everything, and the trip was postponed, to the enormous delight of the General and his lady. St Petersburg saw the arrival from Moscow of Prince S., a famous and exceedingly well-regarded person. He was one of those men – or perhaps one should say latter-day activists – who are honest, decent, who conscientiously strive to do good and are distinguished by the fortunate quality of always being able to find employment for themselves. Without flaunting himself in any way, he shied away from conflicts and idle factional disputes, and when it came to it, was content to play second fiddle; however, he understood all too well the political climate of the day. At first he held a government post but subsequently also went into land-reform* administration. On top of that he was an active member of a number of Russian learned societies. Working in collaboration with an engineer friend of his, he researched and planned the optimum route for one of the most important railway lines then proposed. He was about thirty-five years of age. As well as belonging to the best society, he was also a man of property, "extensive, well-maintained and valuable" as the General had referred to it after he had had an occasion to meet and get to know him in connection with a highly important business deal being transacted in collaboration with the Duke, his immediate superior. The Prince, driven by a particular sense of curiosity, sought every opportunity to establish links with the Russian business community. In due course the Prince also got to know the General's family. Adelaida Ivanovna, the middle sister, made a fairly strong impression upon him. By springtime he'd already proposed to her. Adelaida liked him very much, and so did Lizaveta Prokofyevna. The General was over the moon. It was obvious that the trip abroad had to be put off. The wedding was set for spring.

Of course they could still have travelled in the middle or towards the very end of summer, if only for a couple of months or so, for

Lizaveta Prokofyevna and her two other daughters to take their minds off the sadness of losing their Adelaida. But something else intervened again. Towards the end of spring (the wedding had by then been postponed till mid-summer), Prince S. introduced into the Yepanchin household one of his distant relatives, one Yevgeny Pavlovich R., with whom incidentally he was on intimate terms. Yevgeny Pavlovich R. was an army aide-de-camp at the Imperial Court, a young man of about twenty-eight, incredibly handsome, well born, witty, a brilliant personality, broad-minded, extremely well educated and – of untold wealth. On this last point, the General was from the start a little dubious. He made enquiries, with the result that: "yes, there is indeed something there, but the matter calls for closer scrutiny." The reputation of this young aide-de-camp, whose future prospects were second to none, was enhanced enormously by the glowing reports the aged Muscovite Belokonskaya gave about him. There was, however, only one minor hitch – the number or relationships he had had and, as people insisted – "conquests", resulting in a trail of broken hearts. Having seen Aglaya, he became very attached to the Yepanchins. True, nothing was said on this score nor even suggested; all the same the parents realized that now was not the time for planning trips abroad. Aglaya herself might possibly have not been at one on this.

All this occurred almost immediately before the second appearance of our hero on the scene. By this time, to all outward appearances, Prince Myshkin had been almost totally forgotten in St Petersburg. Had he now turned up amongst the people who had known him, they'd have wondered and scratched their heads. All the same, we shall go on to report one more fact and that then will be the end of this introduction.

After the Prince's departure, Kolya Ivolgin carried on his life as before; that is, he attended high school, visited his friend Ippolit, looked after his father and helped Varya with the household chores – in other words he was her dogsbody. But the lodgers soon disappeared. Ferdyshchenko moved out three days after the events at Nastasya Filippovna's, and all talk of him ceased; some said he'd hit the bottle but no one could confirm it. With the Prince's departure for Moscow, they had lost their last lodger. After Varya got married, Nina Alexandrovna and Ganya moved in with Ptitsyn in the Izmailovsky Barracks.* As regards General Ivolgin, something quite untoward happened to him about this time: he was sent to a debtor's prison. The person responsible was his friend, the sub lieutenant's widow, after the promissory notes he'd issued her at various times to the value of about two thousand roubles proved worthless. All this came as a total surprise to him, and the poor General had literally "fallen victim" to his, as he termed it, "blind faith in the decency of the humankind", speaking in general terms, of course. Having adopted the easy and highly expedient habit of signing IOUs and promissory notes, he never allowed for the possibility that they might ever be cashed, and imagined that it was all just a formality. But it was not. "That's what comes of trusting people, of putting one's trust in them!" he would exclaim bitterly as he sat with his new friends in Tarasov's house* and over a bottle of wine regaled them with stories of the siege of Kars and of the soldier who'd been brought back to life from dead. All in all he had a better time of it there than anywhere else before. Ptitsyn and Varya thought that that was the best place for him; Ganya agreed entirely. It was only Nina Alexandrovna who continued to shed bitter tears in silence (the rest of the family couldn't quite understand this); and, perpetually ailing though she was, she never missed an opportunity to trudge her way to the Izmailovsky Barracks to visit her husband.

But ever since "the episode with father", as Kolya put it, and generally since his sister's marriage, he became quite a stranger in the family, so much so that lately he hardly ever came home even for the night. It was said he had formed many new friendships; and, what's more, become quite popular in the debtor's prison. Nina Alexandrovna would have been quite lost there without his help; when at home, he was left very much to his own devices. Varya, who had previously treated him so harshly, no longer required him to render any account of his wanderings; as for Ganya, despite his hypochondria, to everyone's immense surprise, he conversed and occasionally even associated with Kolya on perfectly friendly terms. This had never happened before, because at the time the twenty-seven-year-old had not been inclined to accord the slightest sign of empathy for his fifteen-year-old junior brother, whom he treated roughly, called upon other members of the family to be uncompromising and forever threatened to have the youngster by his short and curlies, which was calculated to bring Kolya to the limits of human endurance. Now, however, one could have been pardoned for thinking that Kolya had become indispensable to Ganya. The former was fairly bowled over by the fact that Ganya had returned the money; Kolya was ready to make many concessions to his brother for this.

About three months after Prince Myshkin's departure, the Ivolgins learnt that Kolya had got to know the Yepanchin family and was well received by the sisters. It was Varya who found this out; though it was not through her that he was introduced; he'd got to know them off his own bat. Little by little he became quite a favourite. The General's Lady was at first not best pleased with him, but he soon endeared himself to her, "for his candour and outspokenness". That Kolya was outspoken, was perfectly true; he managed to get on an equal and independent footing with them, though this did not prevent him from occasionally reading books and newspapers to the General's Lady – but then he was an obliging soul anyway. True, he had one or two flaming rows with her, declaring her to be a despot and promising never to set foot again in the house. The first row was over the "feminine question", and the second regarding the best time of the year for trapping siskins. However, incredible though it may seem, on the third day after the quarrel the General's Lady sent him a kind note with her servant asking that he should come back without fail; Kolya did not hesitate and returned at once. Only Aglaya was for some reason forever finding fault with him and treating him with disdain. And yet it was he who was destined to astonish her. One day – it was Eastertide – having caught her on her own, he handed her a note, saying only that it was to be passed to her alone. Aglaya looked "the self-opinionated lad" over sternly from head to foot, but Kolya did not stop to wait and left. She unfolded the note and read:

There was a time when you favoured me with your confidence. Perhaps you've now forgotten me altogether. How come that I'm writing to you? I've no idea; but I had an irrepressible urge to remind you of myself, you of all people. The number of times I yearned for all three of you, but of the three, I saw only you. I need you, I need you very much. I've nothing to write to you about myself, I've nothing to tell. Nor do I want to; I only wish one thing, that you should be happy. Are you? That's all I wanted to ask you.

Yours fraternally, Prince L. Myshkin

Having read this short, rather inept, note, Aglaya suddenly flushed and pondered. It would be difficult for us to follow her train of thoughts. Incidentally, she asked herself the question, "Should I show it to anyone?" She suddenly felt somehow embarrassed. In the end, however, she tossed the letter into her writing desk. The next day she withdrew it and placed it in a thick, hardbacked volume (she always treated her papers like that so as to find them more easily when the need arose). Only a week later did she discover what the book was – *Don Quixote of La Mancha*. Aglaya burst out laughing – it would seem without any rhyme or reason.

We have no knowledge of whether she showed the note to any of her sisters.

But when she was reading the letter, it occurred to her, could it really be that this conceited "whippersnapper" had been selected by the Prince as his go-between and that, shocking though it may be, he was his only contact here? Nevertheless, affecting an air of contempt, she took him to task. But the normally touchy "whippersnapper" on this occasion paid no attention whatsoever to Aglaya's dismissive attitude. In succinct and curt terms he explained that even though he had given his permanent address – just in case – to the Prince right before the latter's departure from St Petersburg and had at the same time offered his services, this was the first commission, as well as the very first note, which he had received; in support of this he produced a letter addressed to him personally. Aglaya read it without compunction.

Dear Kolya,
Be so kind as to pass the enclosed, sealed note to Aglaya Ivanovna.
With best wishes,
Yours affectionately, Prince L. Myshkin.

"Still, it's a bit much to confide in such a pipsqueak," Aglaya said derisively as she handed the note back to Kolya and walked past him pertly.

This was more than Kolya could bear – he'd specially persuaded Ganya to lend him his brand new green scarf for the occasion, without telling him the reason. Kolya was hurt to the quick.

2

I T WAS EARLY JUNE, and for a whole week the weather in St Petersburg was excellent. The Yepanchins kept a splendid dacha in Pavlovsk. Lizaveta Prokofyevna suddenly became restless and eager to get away; within two days they were up and gone.

On the second or third day after their arrival, Prince Lev Nikolayevich Myshkin too arrived by the morning train from Moscow. There was no one to meet him at the station; but as he was getting off the train, he fancied he felt a strange, blazing pair of eyes fastening on him from among the people thronging to meet the passengers. When he took a closer look, he could no longer make out anything. Of course, this must have been only an illusion; but the effect was unpleasant, and did nothing to relieve his inner gloom, absorbed as he was in his own thoughts and, it seemed, ill at ease about something.

A cab took him to a hotel not far from the Liteinaya. It was a shabby little place. The Prince took two small, dim, badly furnished rooms. He had a wash, and without ordering anything to eat hurried out as though he was short of time and afraid he'd miss someone.

If anyone who had come across him half a year ago on his first arrival in St Petersburg were to see him now, he'd probably have concluded the Prince had changed outwardly for the better. But this was hardly the case. Only his attire was completely different. He now wore a suit made in Moscow by a tailor who knew his job, and yet there was something about the suit itself that was not quite right; it was just a touch too modish – the typical handiwork of a well-meaning, but hardly talented craftsman, and, besides, made for a person who attached no importance to these things whatsoever. As a result, someone with sartorial sense might well have allowed himself a slight smile of disparagement at the sight of the Prince and his new outfit. But then who is immune from being disparaged?

The Prince took a cab and set off for Peski.* On one of the streets next to the Rozhdestvensky church he soon found a small timber house. To his surprise this house looked rather clean, pretty, well maintained and fronted by a flower garden. The windows, which gave out on the street, were open, and issuing from them was a sharp, unbroken voice, almost at shouting pitch, reading out loud or holding forth on some topic, punctuated from time to time by bursts of sonorous laughter.

The Prince entered the courtyard, climbed a flight of steps and asked for Lebedev.

"There he is," the woman who opened the door – evidently the cook – said, her sleeves rolled up to her elbows, pointing a finger at the sitting room.

In this room, hung with bluish wallpaper, everything was neat and tidy; it was furnished with some pretension to elegance, comprising a round table, a settee, a bronze clock under a glass dome, and in the gap between two windows a narrow wall mirror. Suspended from the ceiling on a bronze chain was a small, very quaint chandelier, festooned all over with glass reflectors. In the middle of the room, his back turned to the Prince, stood Mr Lebedev himself in a waistcoat – no frockcoat in the summer heat – pounding his chest and waxing lyrical on some subject. His listeners consisted of a lad of about fifteen, a young girl of about twenty in mourning weeds with a baby in her arms, a thirteen-year-old girl also in mourning, full of laughter, who stretched her mouth wide open in the act of expressing her mirth, and finally an extraordinarily strange fellow of about twenty, reclining on the settee, rather handsome, swarthy, with long, thick hair, large black eyes and just a suggestion of sideburns and beard. This member of the audience, it would seem, kept interrupting and contradicting the orator, thereby apparently provoking the guffaws of laughter.

"Lukyan Timofeyich, listen, Lukyan Timofeyich! I say, why don't you take a look here!... Very well, please yourself!..."

The cook, throwing up her hands and flushing with anger, left the room.

Lebedev looked round and, catching sight of the Prince, stood-stock still as though thunderstruck, then rushed forward with obsequious deference, but stopped on the way, rooted to the ground.

"M-m-most esteemed Prince!" he muttered.

But, as though still unable to compose himself, he suddenly and for no apparent reason turned reprovingly towards the young girl with the baby in her arms, causing her to shrink back with a start, then, equally suddenly, swung away from her and subjected the thirteen-year-old girl to a dose of tongue-lashing as she lingered in the doorway to the adjoining room with the remnants of her smile still playing about her lips. Unable to endure the onslaught, the girl dashed for safety into the kitchen; Lebedev even stamped his feet on the floor threateningly after her; but on meeting the Prince's eyes, who was looking on with dismay, said in self-vindication, "To... instil respect, he-he-he!"

"This is all quite unnecessary—" the Prince began.

"I'll be back, I will, I will... in two shakes of a lamb's tail!"

And Lebedev rushed out of the room. The Prince regarded the girl, the boy and the reclining figure on the settee with surprise; they were all laughing. The Prince joined in.

"He's gone to put his tailcoat on," the boy said.

"I'm terribly sorry about all this," the Prince hastened to offer his apologies, "I merely thought... tell me, is he—"

"Drunk, you mean?" the voice from the settee called out. "Sober as a judge! Well, perhaps three or four shots, five at the most, but what's that – that's normal."

The Prince was about to respond to the voice from the settee, but the young girl with the open expression on her comely face spoke first: "He hardly ever drinks in the morning, so if you're here on business, I suggest you speak to him now. It's the best time. By the evening, when he returns, he's bound to be tipsy. Lately he's been crying deep into the night and reading from the Scriptures to us, because our dear mother died five weeks ago."

"He's run away because he probably wasn't sure what to say to you," the young man on the settee observed with a laugh. "I'll bet anything in the world he's out to diddle you and is now turning over in his mind how best to do it."

"A mere five weeks! A mere five weeks!" Lebedev echoed, coming back in his tailcoat, blinking and pulling a handkerchief from his pocket to wipe his tears. "Orphans, my little orphans!"

"Why've you put the one with the holes on, daddy?" the girl asked. "There's a brand new coat hanging behind the door, haven't you seen it, or what?"

"What do you know, you chatterbox!" Lebedev turned on her. "None of your nonsense!" he said, stamping his feet to intimidate her; but she only burst out laughing.

"Why are you trying to frighten me, I'm not Tanya, I shan't run away. You'll only wake up baby Lyuba and bring on a fit*... stop shouting!"

"No, no, no! Don't say that, don't!..." Lebedev called out in a sudden outburst of panic and, rushing towards the infant sleeping in his daughter's arms, made the sign of the cross over it several times, his features transfixed with terror. "Lord, oh Lord, bless and protect her! She's my baby, my youngest daughter Lyubov," he said, turning towards the Prince, "born in legitimate wedlock to my recently deceased Yelena, my dear wife, who passed away in childbirth. And this ugly duckling is my daughter Vera in mourning... And this, this, oh this..."

"Why don't you say it?" the young man called out. "Go on, don't be embarrassed."

"Your Highness!" Lebedev suddenly called out effusively, "did you happen to follow the murder of the Zhemarin family in the papers?"*

"I did," the Prince said with some surprise.

"Well then, this is the true murderer of the Zhemarin family, the very man!"

"What do you mean?" the Prince said.

"That is, figuratively speaking, the future second murderer of the second Zhemarin family, if such a one should emerge. He's getting all ready for it..."

Everybody burst out laughing. It occurred to the Prince that Lebedev might really be clowning and prevaricating solely because, anticipating his questions, he didn't know what to reply and was merely playing for time.

"He agitates! He conspires!" Lebedev shouted as though he was no longer able to control himself. "I ask you, how can I, by what right should I nurture such a scandal-monger, such a, if I may put it to so, whoreson and monster as my very own nephew, as the only son of my sister Anisya, now deceased?"

"I wish you'd stop, you drunken man! Would you believe it, Prince, he's now started dabbling in legal matters and prowling around the courtrooms. He's dropped his conversational style, and will only talk hoity-toity with his children. Five days ago he pleaded before the justices of the peace. And in whose favour would you say? Not in the poor old woman's – she'd begged him, implored him after a crooked moneylender had robbed her of five hundred roubles, which was all she had – but in favour of that same moneylender, Seidler, a Jew, who'd promised him fifty roubles for his trouble..."

"If I won, but only five if I lost," Lebedev explained in an even tone as though he had never raised his voice.

"Of course, he fell flat on his face. He forgot it's not like in the old times, and they laughed him out of court. But that hasn't stopped him being very pleased with himself: 'Remember, honourable and impartial members of the bench, that an unfortunate old man, who has lost the use of his legs, plying an honest trade, is being deprived of his last morsel of bread. Think of the wise words of the Sovereign, "Let mercy thrive in Russia's halls of justice".'* And believe it or not, he repeats his speech to us every morning, word for word. It's the fifth time today. He did it just before you arrived – he's so fond of it, he drools over it. And he plans to do it all over again. Would you be Prince Myshkin? Kolya told me that he's never met anyone as clever in his life—"

"That's right! Absolutely right! There's no one as clever in the world!" Lebedev hastened to confirm.

"A likely story. The one speaks out of respect, the other out of flattery. As for me, I've no intention of flattering you, let that be well understood. You're a man of sense. Would you arbitrate between us? Well, do you want the Prince to arbitrate between us?" He turned towards his uncle. "I'm actually very glad you turned up, Prince."

"I do!" Lebedev returned determinedly with an involuntary glance at the listeners, who were again beginning to crowd round.

"What's going on between you?" the Prince asked and winced.

He really had a headache, besides he was beginning to get more and more certain that Lebedev was bent on fooling him and was doing his best to put him off his scent.

"To the facts of the matter! I am his nephew, in this he is right, though in every other particular he lies. I haven't finished my course of study, but I want to and shall make it because that's in my character. In the meantime, in order to keep body and soul together, I've found a job on the railways at twenty-five roubles. I have to be frank, he's already helped me out once or twice. I had twenty roubles from him, but I lost it. Can you believe me, Prince, I was so despicable, I'd sunk so low that I went and lost it at cards!"

"To a scoundrel, a scoundrel, who should never have been paid!" Lebedev cried.

"Yes a scoundrel, but I had to pay him," the young man went on. "I quite agree he is a scoundrel and not just because he gave you a drubbing. You see, Prince, this is a certain good-for-nothing army officer, an ex-lieutenant, one of Rogozhin's former gang, a boxing instructor to boot. They're all at a loose end, now that Rogozhin has sent them all packing. But the worst thing of all is that I knew what he was like, a nasty piece of work and a petty thief, and yet I sat down opposite him to play, and that when I was down on my last rouble (we were playing *palki*),* I remember thinking to myself, if I lose, I'll go to Uncle Lukyan, tell him the whole truth, and he won't let me down. Granted, that was mean, really mean of me! A premeditated dirty trick!"

"A premeditated dirty trick is right!" Lebedev repeated.

"Stop gloating, wait," his nephew retorted in offended tones, "it makes him happy. I came to him here, Prince, and made a clean breast of it. It was a gentlemanly thing to do, I didn't spare myself. I condemned myself out of hand in front of all these witnesses. To take that job on the railways I need some basic items of clothing, because I'm completely in rags. There, look at my boots! I can't turn up like that, and if I don't arrive at the appointed time, the position will be snatched up by someone else and I'll be in a pickle again with no way out. Now all I'm asking him for is fifteen roubles and I promise I'll never ask for anything again, and on top of that, in the course of the first three months I'll pay him back everything I owe to the last copeck. I'll keep my word. I can survive on bread and *kvas** for a month, because I'm a man of character. In three months I'll earn seventy-five roubles. If you add the two together, I'll owe him thirty-five, which I'll be able to manage with no trouble at all. Well, let him charge any interest he likes, to hell with it! As though he didn't know what I'm like! Ask him, Prince, when he helped me before, did I pay him back or not? Why won't he now? Is he mad at me because I paid this lieutenant? There's no other reason! That's the sort of man he is – dog in a manger!"

"And he won't budge!" Lebedev cried out. "He has installed himself on the settee, and won't budge."

"That's what I told you. I won't go away, unless you help me. I see you're smiling, Prince. Do you think I'm in the wrong?"

"I'm not smiling, but the way I look at it, you really are a little in the wrong," the Prince returned reluctantly.

"Why don't you say straight out that I'm completely in the wrong. No need to beat about the bush! Why 'a little'?"

"If you wish, yes – completely!"

"If I wish! That's ridiculous! Do you really suppose I don't know myself that it's improper of me? The money's his, he calls the shots and it looks like I'm extorting it from him. But you, Prince... have no idea of life. If you don't teach these people a lesson, they'll go on misbehaving. They have to be taught a lesson. My conscience is clear. It stands to reason he'll not be the loser, I'll pay interest. He's also had the moral satisfaction of seeing my discomfiture. What more does he need? What's the good of him if he won't help others? If only you knew what he gets up to! Ask him how he treats people, how he diddles them! How did he come by this house? I'll bet my life he's already hatched a plan to double-cross you! You don't believe me, you're smiling!"

"I don't think any of this has much to do with your problem," the Prince observed.

"I've been lying here nearly three days, and the things I've seen!" the young man cried, pursuing his own line. "Can you believe that he suspects this angel, this young girl, who is now motherless, my cousin, his own daughter, of having lovers every night! He sneaks in here and searches under my settee. He's gone crazy with mistrust. Everywhere he turns, he suspects the worst. He continually gets up in the middle of the night to check if the windows are shut properly, if the door is bolted, what's in the oven, he'll do this about seven times a night. He's given to standing up for felons in court, and three times a night he goes down on his knees to pray here in the room. You can hear him banging his head against the floor as he makes his obeisance, and the number of people he prays for, and the things he says in his drunken stupor, you can't imagine! He once prayed for the repose of the soul of the Countess du Barry!* I heard it with my own ears. Kolya did too. Mad, totally mad!"

"Do you see, do you hear, how he shows me up, Prince!" Lebedev protested loudly, flushed, in a genuine show of anger. "And what he doesn't know is that I, a drunkard and ne'er-do-well, a fiddler and a cheat, had only one care in the world, which was to see to this jackanapes when he was still an infant, wrapped in his swaddling clothes after I'd scrubbed him in a trough. He's my sister Anisya's only child, and she a widow and a pauper like myself. The nights I sat up at her place looking after the two of them in sickness, stole firewood from the caretaker downstairs, sang songs to him and clicked my fingers, on an empty stomach, and this is what I get for it. I'm being mocked! And what business is it of yours if I did really once make the sign of the cross over my pate for the repose of the soul of Countess du Barry?

Three days ago, Prince, I happened to read for the first time ever her life story in a gazette. And have you any idea who du Barry was? Speak up, do you or don't you?"

"Obviously you're the only one who does!" the young man retorted sarcastically, though for all that, reluctantly.

"This was a countess, who after a life of shame, ruled in place of the queen and whom a great empress in a personal letter referred to as *ma cousine*. The cardinal, the Pope's Nuncio, at the *lever du Roi*, if you know what a *lever du Roi* is, deemed it an honour to put her dainty silk stocking on her exposed legs with his own hands – august and saintly man that he was! Did you know that? I can see by your face that you didn't! Well, how did she die? Tell me if you know!"

"Stop pestering me. Go away!"

"She died, honoured and mighty that she had once been, when Samson the executioner, dragged her in all her innocence, frightened and confused, to the guillotine to the amusement of all the Paris fishwives. When she realized he was forcing her neck under the blade, kicking her not to resist – the others found it very funny – she yelled out, '*Encore un moment, monsieur le bourreau, encore un moment*!' Which means, 'Give me one more minute, Mr Executioner, just one more minute!' And it's for this 'one minute' that the Lord may perhaps pardon her, because it's hardly possible to imagine for the human soul a greater agony than that. Do you realize the real meaning of the word 'agony'? I tell you, that was real agony. Just reading about that cry, that plea for one more minute, made my blood curdle. And what is it to you, you maggot, if before I lay down for the night, I remembered her sinful soul in my prayers. Maybe I remembered her precisely because no one in the world had ever made, or thought of making, the sign of the cross over his pate for her sake. Who knows, she might light up with joy in the other world to feel there's a sinner, like she was, who has just said a prayer for her. What are you laughing at? You don't believe me, or what, you atheist? You think you're ever so clever! And if you've been eavesdropping on me, you've been in the wrong. I didn't just pray for Countess du Barry. What I said was, 'Oh Lord, peace be upon the soul of the great sinner, Countess du Barry and all those like her,' which is quite a bit different, you'll agree, because there are many such great sinners, victims of the wheel of Fortune, who have suffered and are still writhing and groaning and are held in limbo. And if you must know,

I prayed for you and the likes of you too, insolent beggars and nit-pickers that you all are. I did indeed, so before you start eavesdropping on me at my prayers—"

"All right, that'll do, you can pray for whom you like, to hell with you, stop shouting!" his nephew interrupted him with exasperation. "He's such a bookworm, he is. You didn't know that, Prince, did you?" he added with an awkward smile. "All he does is read books and memoirs."

"If you ask me, your uncle... is by no means an unkind man," the Prince observed with some reluctance. This young man was beginning to annoy him.

"You overestimate him! Look, he's already got his hand on his heart, he's licking his chops. He may not be unkind, but he's an awful cheat, that's his trouble. And on top of everything, he drinks. He's a complete wreck like any confirmed drinker, which is why he creaks in every joint. He loves his children – there's no denying that, he took care of my aunt too, may her soul rest in peace... He's even got a soft spot for me and, honest to God, I'm mentioned in his will—"

"No, you're not, I'm leaving you nothing!" Lebedev proclaimed furiously.

"Listen to me, Lebedev," the Prince said firmly, turning his back on the young man, "I know very well from experience that you're a man of business if you put your mind to it. At the moment I've very little time, and if you... Pardon me, what's your patronymic, I quite forgot?"

"Ti-Ti-Timofey."

"And?"

"Lukyanovich."

Everyone in the room again burst out laughing.

"It's a fib!" the nephew exclaimed. "Another of his lies! He's not at all Timofey Lukyanovich, Prince, but Lukyan Timofeyevich! Why on earth did you have to fib again? What difference does it make, Lukyan or Timofey, and what's it got to do with the Prince? I tell you, it's sheer force of habit with him!"

"Is this right?" the Prince asked irritably.

"Yes, I'm afraid, it's Lukyan Timofeyevich, really," Lebedev agreed in some embarrassment, humbly lowering his eyes and again laying his hand on his heart.

"My God, I never heard anything like it! Why?"

"Out of self-disparagement," Lebedev whispered, his head sinking lower and lower.

"Come now, what self-disparagement! All I wanted to find out was where Kolya is!" the Prince said and turned to go.

"I'll tell you where he is," the young man responded again.

"No, no, no!" Lebedev retorted, all of a dither.

"Kolya spent the night here, but the following morning he went to look for his father, the General, whom you, Prince, had bailed out of prison, goodness knows why. Yesterday the General had a mind to come and stay the night here, but didn't. He's probably booked himself into the Hotel Vesy, not far from here. Consequently, Kolya's either there, or with the Yepanchins at Pavlovsk. He had money and was planning to set out yesterday. And so, you'll find him either at the Vesy or in Pavlovsk."

"In Pavlovsk, in Pavlovsk!... In the meantime, let's retire to my little garden ... for a drop of coffee..."

And Lebedev led the Prince by the hand out of the room, across a yard and through a wicket gate. Here there was a neat little garden with all the trees in bloom thanks to the fine weather. Lebedev and the Prince settled down opposite each other on a green wooden bench at a table fixed in the ground. Shortly afterwards coffee was served. The Prince was glad to have some. Lebedev kept looking into his eyes with eager deference.

"I had no idea you ran such a household," the Prince said, in the manner of one whose thoughts were preoccupied with something quite different.

"We're a poor unfortunate lot..." Lebedev was about to launch forth, drawing in his shoulders, but stopped. The Prince looked absentmindedly ahead and was, of course, already quite oblivious of what he had just said. There was a pause of about a minute; Lebedev looked and waited.

"Well, where were we?" the Prince said. "Oh, yes! You know yourself, Lebedev, what the position is. I came in response to your letter. Speak."

Lebedev was at a loss; he wanted to say something, but could only manage a hiccup. The Prince waited a little with a heavy heart and smiled sadly.

"I think I understand you very well, Lukyan Timofeyevich. You probably didn't expect to see me. You didn't expect me to come all this way at your first beck and call, and you wrote merely to salve your conscience. But I did stir myself. Well, that'll do, stop prevaricating. It won't do to serve two masters. Rogozhin has been here three weeks already. I know everything. Have you managed to sell her to him like the last time, or not? Be truthful."

"The monster discovered where she was by himself."

"You needn't blame him. Of course, it's true, he was hard on you—"

"He beat me! He beat me!" Lebedev responded with unwonted vehemence. "And he set a dog on me in Moscow, the whole length of the street, a borzoi, a frightful wolfhound."

"Don't you take me for a fool, Lebedev. Tell me truthfully, has she really run away from him for good, here in Moscow, or not?"

"Honestly, honestly, and again from the altar steps, at the climax of the nuptials. Rogozhin was already counting the minutes, and she dashed back to St Petersburg and straight to my place: 'Save me, save me Lukyan, but not a word to the Prince!...' She's more scared of you, Prince, than of him – there's a conundrum for you!" And Lebedev raised a finger and winked slyly.

"And now you've brought them back together again?"

"My most illustrious Prince... how could I prevent it?"

"Well, that'll do, I'll find out myself. Tell me one thing though, where is she now? At his place?"

"Oh no, not at all! She's still very much on her own. She insists she's still free, and you know, Prince, she makes quite a point of it, 'I'm completely free!' she reckons. She's still in Peterburgskaya, at my sister-in-law's, just as when I wrote to you."

"Still there now?"

"Yes, unless she's gone to Pavlovsk, the weather being nice – to Darya Alexeyevna's dacha. 'I'm completely free!' she reckons. Only the other day she was on about her freedom to Nikolai Ardalionovich.* A bad sign that, sir!" And Lebedev pulled a face.

"Does Kolya visit her a lot?"

"A frivolous, inscrutable boy, and he can't keep a secret."

"Is it long since you've been there?"

"I'm there every day, every single day."

"So you were there yesterday too?"

207

"N-no, the day before the day before yesterday."

"What a pity you're in your cups, Lebedev! Otherwise I'd have asked you some questions."

"N-no, n-not a bit of it. Sober as a judge." Lebedev was suddenly all ears.

"Tell me, what was she like when you left her?"

"As if she were looking for..."

"Looking?"

"As if she were looking for something she'd lost. As regards the forthcoming marriage, she won't even hear of it, she objects to the very thought. And *him*? He's no more than the rind of an orange for her; moreover, she's in fear and awe of him, she won't even have him mentioned, and if they do meet, it's out of sheer necessity only... and he knows it all too well! She's going to get her comeuppance!... Restless, derisive, double-tongued, irritable—"

"Double-tongued and irritable?"

"Yes, quite, she nearly tore my hair out the other day over a conversation we had. I started lecturing her on the Apocalypse."

"What do you mean?" the Prince asked, thinking he had misheard.

"A reading of the Apocalypse. The lady has a very feverish imagination, he-he-he! And to cap it all, I concluded she's mighty partial to serious, be it ever so abstruse, topics. She simply devours them, nose held high. Yes, sir! Interpreting the Apocalypse happens to be my strong point. I've been doing it for the past fourteen years and more. She agreed with me we're at the third horse, the black one, and the horseman holding a pair of balances, since in our day and age everything is founded on weights, measures and concordance, and all folk seek to establish nothing save their rights and privileges, 'A measure of wheat for a penny, and three measures of barley for a penny'*... and they still mean to be free of spirit, pure of heart, healthy of body and in possession of sundry divine blessings! But the power of right will not suffice, and there will follow the pale horse and he, whose name is Death, and after him will come hell... We meet and ponder this, and it has a vast effect upon her."

"Do you believe it yourself?"

"I believe and interpret. For I am wretched and miserable,* and a mere atom in the whirlpool of humanity. But who will heed Lebedev? He is sport for the people, a plaything under their feet. In the matter of interpretation, however, I'm the equal of the greatest. It's all a matter of wit! A potentate has already quaked before me… in his chair of office. His Excellency, Neil Alexandrovich, two years back, before Eastertide, when he heard about me – he was my head of department – got Pyotr Zakharych to call me specially into his office, and asked me, looking me in the eyes, 'Is it true you're an authority on the Antichrist?' And I did not prevaricate. 'That, I am forsooth,' I replied, and I expounded and propounded, and put the fear of the Lord into him, and in my mind, having unfurled before him an allegorical charter, drew his attention to it and adduced figures. He affected to laugh at first, but when it came to figures and images, he began to quail and bade me shut the book and withdraw, promising me a reward for Eastertide, but come Whitsun he was dead."

"Lebedev, what are you on about?"

"That is what happened. He fell out of his carriage after a meal one afternoon… hit his head on a roadside stone, and like a child, like a babe, gave up his ghost on the instant. He was in his seventy-third year according to his service record. Such sweet, rosy cheeks topped with snow-white hair, all bathed in scent, and, I remember, he never ever stopped smiling, bless him! Pyotr Zakharych then pronounced: 'It was you that predicted this.'"

The Prince got up. Lebedev was surprised, even put out, that the Prince was about to leave.

"You have grown altogether rather indifferent, I note, he-he-he!" he ventured obsequiously.

"Quite so, I don't feel particularly well – I have a headache. It could well be the journey," the Prince replied with a frown.

"You ought to take a holiday," Lebedev remarked timidly.

The Prince thought a while.

"In about three days I myself and my whole family are moving to a dacha for the good of the newborn mite and to allow essential maintenance work to be carried out here in this house. And then we're also off to Pavlovsk."*

"You too are going to Pavlovsk?" the Prince suddenly enquired. "It seems everybody here is heading for Pavlovsk! And you say you have your own dacha there?"

"No, not everybody. You see, Ivan Petrovich Ptitsyn is giving me the loan of one of his dachas there, which he has come by on the cheap.

It's nice there, on high ground, plenty of greenery, affordable, good area, orchestras playing, that's why everybody likes to be in Pavlovsk. In truth, I'll only be occupying one wing, the rest of the building—"

"You've sub-let?"

"N-n-no. Not... quite exactly."

"Why don't you let it out to me?" the Prince suggested unexpectedly.

It would appear that this was precisely what Lebedev was angling for. This idea had flashed through his mind a few seconds earlier. In actual fact, however, he had no need of a tenant; someone had already been and expressed an interest. Lebedev knew there was no doubt about it – the man would definitely take it. But now he thought he could do better by offering it to the Prince on the grounds that the original enquirer had been insufficiently positive. "This is an unexpected coincidence and a completely new turn of events," he thought to himself. He was glad to accept the Prince's offer with the utmost delight, and when the Prince raised the question of the rent, he merely pooh-poohed the matter.

"Well, as you wish. I'll make enquiries. You won't lose out."

By now they were both coming out of the garden.

"And I could... I could well..." Lebedev chatted on, twisting and turning for joy as he walked beside the Prince, "if you were so minded, I could well communicate something rather interesting to you, my most esteemed Prince, appertaining to the selfsame subject."

The Prince halted.

"Darya Alexeyevna too has got a dacha in Pavlovsk."

"Well?"

"Aglaya Ivanovna—"

"That'll do, Lebedev!" the Prince interrupted him with a feeling of revulsion as soon as this painful subject was brought up. "You're mistaken... it's not like that at all. Why don't you tell me exactly when you're moving. As for me, the sooner the better, because I'm staying in a hotel..."

While talking, they left the garden and, without going back to the house, crossed the yard and approached the wicket gate.

"The best thing for you," Lebedev finally concluded, "is to move here straight from the hotel this very day, and the day after tomorrow we can all set out for Pavlovsk together."

"I'll think about that," the Prince said and went through the house gate.

Lebedev followed him with his eyes. He was taken aback by the Prince's unwonted absent-mindedness. On parting, he failed even to say goodbye; he didn't even motion with his head, which did not accord with the Prince's customary politeness and courtesy.

3

I T WAS GONE ELEVEN O'CLOCK. He knew that at the Yepanchins' in town he'd find, at best, only the General, detained by his business affairs. It occurred to him that the General might insist on immediately going to Pavlovsk with him, however he was still very anxious to make a call on someone before that. Risking being late at the Yepanchins' and having to postpone his trip to Pavlovsk till the next day, the Prince went in search of the house which he so wanted to visit.

This call to some extent filled him with anxiety. He thought and agonized over it. He knew that the house was in Gorokhovaya, not far from Sadovaya Street, and he decided to head in that direction hoping that on arrival he'd be able to pluck up the courage to make the final decision.

On drawing near the junction of Gorokhovaya and Sadovaya he was astonished at how agitated he was; he had no idea his heart would be pounding so violently. Probably because of its unusual façade, one house attracted his attention from a distance, and subsequently the Prince remembered saying to himself, "That's probably the one." He approached it, full of curiosity to see if he was right; he felt that if he was, he would for some reason find it particularly disagreeable. The house was large, bleak, three stories high, in no particular architectural style and painted a dirty green. It must be said that quite a few houses of this type, built at the end of the last century, have survived precisely in these streets of St Petersburg (where everything changes at breakneck speed) almost without change. They were built to last, with thick walls and very widely spaced windows; on the ground floor the windows are sometimes barred. There's usually a money-changing shop downstairs. The typical Skopets* running the shop lives over it. The appearance, both inside and outside, is somehow inhospitable and austere; there is a general air of secrecy and concealment about the place, and why this should be so just by looking at the façade – is difficult to determine.

The architectural lineaments of the structure undoubtedly create a mysterious ambience. These houses are almost exclusively occupied by business people. Standing at the gates and looking at the nameplate of this particular house, the Prince read "Honorary Hereditary Citizen Rogozhin".

Overcoming his indecision, he opened the glass door, which fell shut behind him with a clang, and began to ascend the main stairs to the first floor. The staircase was dark, of rough-hewn stone, and the walls were painted deep red. He knew that Rogozhin together with his mother and brother occupied the entire first floor. The manservant who opened the door for the Prince bade him follow without announcement; they crossed a banqueting room with walls in mock marble, oak parquet flooring and furnished in the style of the 1820s, clumsy and heavy; they also walked through a series of small anterooms, turning and zigzagging, up a few flights of steps and then down as many again, and finally knocked at a door. It was opened by Parfyon Semyonych himself; catching sight of the Prince, he went so pale and was so shocked that for a considerable period of time he looked like a stone statue: his face was transfixed by an immobile, terrified stare, his mouth twisted in a grotesque, senseless grin as though he could not accept the reality of the Prince's visit, regarding it as something inconceivable. Although the Prince expected a strong reaction, this came as a complete surprise.

"Parfyon, I may have come at the wrong time. I can go away," he said at last, embarrassed.

"Not at all! Not at all!" Parfyon came to at last. "Come right in!"

They had often had prolonged meetings in Moscow, and there were moments in those meetings which were memorably imprinted in both their hearts. This time, though, they hadn't seen each other for over three months.

The morbid pastiness of Rogozhin's face was augmented by a barely perceptible, tremulous ripple flickering over it. Even though he had invited the visitor in, he could not overcome the shock of seeing him. While he was showing the Prince to a seat at a table, the latter happened to glance back and catch a heavy, weird look in his host's eyes that fairly rooted him to the spot. It seemed to cut him to the quick and at the same time remind him of something recent, bitter and dismal. He remained standing motionless, staring straight back into Rogozhin's eyes, which momentarily flashed with unusual intensity. Finally Rogozhin forced himself to smile, but was still visibly nonplussed and distracted.

"Why are you staring at me like that?" he muttered. "Sit down!"

The Prince obeyed.

"Parfyon," he said, "tell me honestly, did you know I would come to St Petersburg today, or not?"

"That you'd come, I truly suspected and, as you can see, I wasn't mistaken," he added with a mordant smile, "but how could I tell that you'd turn up today?"

The note of brusqueness and irritation contained in the answer was, to the Prince's surprise, exacerbated in the question.

"But even if you knew that it would be precisely today, why get so upset?" the Prince said softly, deeply troubled.

"Why do you ask?"

"As I was getting out of the train a while back, I saw a pair of eyes just like yours when you turned just now."

"You don't say! Who was it then?" Rogozhin muttered. The Prince had a sense that Rogozhin started.

"I don't know. It was in a crowd. I think it was just something I imagined. I've noticed it a few times lately. You know, my friend Parfyon, I feel almost the same as I did five years ago, when I had my fits."

"Well, it could be just your imagination. I don't know..." Parfyon muttered.

He was affecting a benign smile, but it did not become him at that moment. It was as if it had got suppressed and Parfyon was vainly trying to restore it.

"Going abroad again, are you, or what?" he asked, and suddenly added, "and do you remember the two of us in the railway carriage, that autumn, on the way from Pskov – I was heading here, and you... in your cloak, remember, those gaiters of yours?"

And Rogozhin suddenly burst out laughing, on this occasion with unconcealed enmity as though delighted that he'd finally managed to find an outlet for it.

"Are you settled here for good?" the Prince asked, looking around the study.

"Yes, this is my place. Where else should I be?"

"It's been some time since we last met. I've heard such things about you, I could hardly credit it was you."

213

"I can't help the things people say," Parfyon observed drily.

"Still, you've dismissed your entourage, and here you are settled in your family house, well behaved. It's good, I must say. Is the house yours or the family's?"

"Mother's. Her quarters are at the end of the corridor."

"What about your brother?"

"My brother Semyon Semyonych lives next door."

"Is he a family man?"

"Widower. Why do you want to know?"

The Prince looked at him and did not reply; he was suddenly lost in thought and appeared not to have heard the question. Rogozhin did not repeat it and waited. There was a pause.

"As I was approaching I picked out your house at a hundred paces," the Prince said.

"How did you manage that?"

"I'm sure I don't know. This house bears the stamp of your whole family and the whole of the Rogozhin clan, but if you ask me what makes me say that – I can't explain. It's nonsense, I know. In fact it worries me that I'm taking it to heart so much. Formerly it would never have occurred to me that you live in such a house, but when I saw it, it hit me straight away, 'This is just the sort of house he would live in!'"

"You don't say!" Rogozhin said with a vague smirk, not quite able to follow the Prince's rather nebulous reasoning. "My grandfather built this house," he put in. "It was always Skoptsy who lived here, the Khludyakovs. Some still do, as tenants."

"It's so dismal here. You lead a dreary life," the Prince said, looking around the study.

It was a large, tall, rather dark room, cluttered with all kinds of furniture – for the most part with large work tables, writing desks, cupboards crammed with business ledgers and various papers. A wide red leather sofa probably doubled up as Rogozhin's bed. The Prince noticed two or three books on the table where Rogozhin bade him sit. One of them, Solovyev's *History** was open, exposing a bookmark. On the walls in dull gilt frames were several oil paintings, grown so dark with age it was difficult to make out what they depicted. One full-length portrait caught the Prince's attention. It showed a man of about fifty in a long-tailed frockcoat of European cut, sporting two medals round his neck and a sparse, greying stubbly beard on a creased yellowish doleful face, out of which looked a mistrustful, wary pair of eyes.

"I take it that's your father?" the Prince asked.

"That's him," Rogozhin replied with a nasty smirk as though waiting for an opportunity to launch into some joke about his father.

"He wasn't an Old Believer,* was he?"

"No, he attended Church, but he did say that the Old Faith came closer to truth. He held the Skoptsy in high regard. This room was his study. Why did you ask if he was of the Old Faith?"

"Are you going to hold the wedding here?"

"Y-yes," Rogozhin replied with a start at the unexpectedness of the question.

"Is it to be soon?"

"You know very well it's not up to me."

"Parfyon, I'm not your enemy and I've no intention of standing in your way. I'm repeating this now just as I once declared it formerly, almost in similar circumstances. When you were about to get married in Moscow, I did not interfere – you know that. The first time she herself rushed to me almost immediately before the wedding, and begged me to 'rescue' her from you. I'm quoting her very words. Subsequently, she ran away from me too, whereupon you found her, and again brought her to the altar and, they say, she ran away from you yet again. Lebedev informed me of this, and that's what made me return. As to your latest rapprochement, I heard of this for the first time only last night in the railway carriage from one of your former cronies, Zalyozhev, if you must know. I came here with one intention – to persuade her to go abroad for the sake of her health. She is in a bad way mentally and physically. As I see it, she needs peace of mind and a lot of care. I didn't want to go with her myself, but had a mind to arrange it without personal involvement. I'm telling you the honest truth. If, however, the two of you really have made it up between yourselves, I promise not to go to see her, nor will I ever come back to you. You know very well I'm not deceiving you, because I've always been honest with you. Nor have I ever concealed my thoughts from you on the matter – I've always maintained that with you, she'll be lost. And you wouldn't fare any better, perhaps worse. Were you to go your separate ways this time, I'd be very happy indeed but, of course, I wouldn't dream of driving a wedge between you two or try to estrange you. You can take my word for this and stop suspecting me. You know full well that I've never been a *real* rival of yours, even when she came running to me. You're laughing, and I know why. Yes, we lived there separately and in different towns, all of which you are well aware of. I've tried to explain to you before that it isn't love which binds her to me, but compassion. I think I've made it quite clear already. You said then that you understood my words, didn't you? Well, did you? There's so much hatred in your eyes! I came to put your mind at rest, because I care for you too. I care for you very much, Parfyon. I'm going now and shall never come back. Goodbye."

The Prince got up.

"Stay a while," Parfyon said softly, not stirring from his seat and resting his head in the palm of his right hand, "it's been some time since I saw you last."

The Prince resumed his seat. Neither spoke.

"Whenever you're away, I can't help hating you, Lev Nikolayevich. Every single minute these past three months I've been dead set against you, heaven knows. I'd have loved to poison you or something! Now, you've hardly been a quarter of an hour with me, and all my anger is passing and I want to be friends with you again. Stay a while with me…"

"When I'm with you, you trust me, but when I'm not, you immediately cease to trust me and start suspecting me again. You take after your father!" the Prince said with an amicable smile and in an attempt to conceal his true feelings.

"I trust your voice when I listen to you. You know fine well that I realize I can't hold a candle to you…"

"You shouldn't have said that! And now you've upset yourself again," the Prince said, looking quizzically at Rogozhin.

"No one asks us what we ought to be like," Rogozhin returned, "we are what we are. We've different ways of loving too, we're poles apart in everything," he continued softly after a pause. "You say you love her out of compassion. I've no compassion for her. Besides, she hates me more than anything in the world. Now I dream every night that she's mocking me with someone else. It's true, my friend. She follows me to the wedding altar, and won't even give me a second thought. I get tossed aside like a rag doll. You can believe me or not, I haven't seen her for five days, because I'm afraid to show my face there in case she asks, 'Why've you come?' I've had enough of her mockery…"

"She mocks you? That's awful!"

"As though you didn't know! Didn't she run away with you from the church before our very wedding? You said so yourself!"

"But surely you don't suppose that—"

"And as though she hadn't played fast and loose with me in Moscow with that officer, Zemtyuzhnikov? I know for sure she did, and this was even after she herself had named the wedding day."

"I don't believe it!" the Prince exclaimed.

"It's a fact, though," Rogozhin confirmed with conviction. "You didn't suppose she was like that, did you? My friend, you don't know the half of it! We're just wasting words. With you she won't carry on like that, and might even be shocked at the very idea, but with me, she will. That's just how it is. I'm nothing but dirt under her feet. I know for sure she teamed up with this army officer Keller, the boxing master, just to have a good laugh at me... You've no idea at all what she got up to in Moscow! And the money, the amount of money it cost me!..."

"So... how can you, after all that, contemplate marriage!... What's it going to be like later?" the Prince asked, horrified.

Rogozhin cast the Prince a tortured, woebegone look, and said nothing.

"I haven't been to see her for over four days," he continued after about a minute's pause. "I'm too scared she'll simply dump me. 'I'm still my own mistress. If I choose, I'll send you packing for good, and go abroad.'" ("She'd already mentioned going abroad to me," he observed as though in parentheses and looked meaningfully into the Prince's eyes.) "At other times she does it for sheer sport, to see me squirm. Though she can be dead serious too, frowning and glowering and not saying a word. That's when I fear her the most. I had an idea to stop turning up empty-handed. That only made her laugh. Even though she had lived in luxury, I brought her such a shawl as she had probably never seen in her life, and she only went and gave it to her serving maid Katya. As for marriage, it's not even to be hinted at. I'm supposed to be her bridegroom, and I daren't even show my face there! So here I am, and when it gets too much, I sneak past her house or hang around on the street corner, once – till daybreak. Something must have come over me then. And I know for a fact, she watched me out of her window on the sly. 'So what would you do if you caught me with someone?' she says. I could stand it no longer and said, 'You know what I'd do.'"

"What?"

"Why should I know?" Rogozhin said with a vicious laugh. "I couldn't catch her with anybody in Moscow at the time, and not for want of trying. I took her aside one day and told her, 'You promised to marry me and want to be part of a respectable family, and do you realize who you are after this?' And I told her!"

"You did?"

"Yes."

"Well?"

"'I probably wouldn't have you as a lackey in my house, let alone be your wife.' And I said to her, 'I'm not budging till I get a proper answer. This matter's got to end somehow!' 'And I,' she reckons, 'will get Keller to boot you out on the street.' This was when I went for her and beat her black and blue."

"You're making it up!" the Prince exclaimed.

"I told you, that's what happened," Rogozhin confirmed softly, but his eyes flashed dangerously. "I didn't sleep a wink, nor eat, nor drink for thirty-six hours as I knelt before her on the floor in her room. 'I'd rather die,' I said to her, 'than leave, unless you pardon me, and if you eject me by force – I'll go and drown myself. How can I go on living without you?' She was like a thing possessed all that day – she cried, she wanted to stab me with a knife, she called me all the names under the sun. She brought Zalyozhev, Keller, Zemtyuzhnikov – the whole lot of them to make fun at me. 'Let's go to the theatre, gentlemen,' she said, 'let him stay here if he doesn't want to leave. I'm not going to be restricted by the likes of him. They'll bring you tea, Parfyon Semyonych, in my absence, you must be famished today.' She came back on her own, 'A bunch of chicken-livered cowards,' she reckons, 'they're afraid of you and are trying to put me off too. They said, he won't leave of his own accord, and will probably end up knifing her. And what if I just walk into my bedroom and won't even lock the door behind me – that's how scared I am of you! So there! Have you had your tea?' – 'No,' I said, 'and I shan't.' – 'This is sheer posturing and ill becomes you.' And she was as good as her word, she never locked her room. In the morning she came out, laughing, 'You must be mad, or something! You'll starve to death!' – 'Forgive me,' I said. – 'I won't forgive you, and I shan't marry you, I tell you. Did you really sit up all night in this chair without sleeping?' – 'That's right, I did.' – 'Isn't that

clever of you! And aren't you having your tea again?' – 'I told you I'm
not. Forgive me first!' – 'If only you knew how ridiculous you look!
You won't frighten me, if that's what you're thinking of doing! See if I
care if you starve yourself to death! Go ahead!' – She lost her temper,
but not for long, and started teasing me again. And it hit me that she
wasn't really doing it in anger. And yet she is vindictive, very vindictive
with others! I then realized that she holds me in such low esteem she
won't even stoop to being vindictive towards me. And that's the truth.
– 'Do you know,' she turns to me, 'who the Pope is?' – 'I've heard of
him,' I said. – 'You, Parfyon Semyonych,' she reckons, 'haven't studied
your world history.' – 'I haven't studied anything,' I said to her. – 'In
that case you ought to read it. There was once a Pope who'd taken
umbrage at an emperor who then spent three days without eating or
drinking, barefoot before the Pope's palace, until the Pope pardoned
him. What do you think went through the emperor's head in those
three days while he knelt, what oaths did he swear?... Wait,' she says,
'I'll read it to you myself!' She jumped up and brought a book. 'This
is in verse,' she says, and she began to read in verse how this emperor
swore to avenge himself on the Pope.* 'Don't you find it interesting,
Parfyon Semyonych?' she asks. – 'What you've just read,' I said, 'makes
sense.' – 'There you are, you say it makes sense, that means you too
may be swearing, "Wait till she marries me, then I'll remind her of it
all, then I'll get my own back!"' – 'I don't know,' I replied, 'maybe I
do think that.' – 'What do you mean, you don't know?' – 'As I said,
I don't know, it's not what's uppermost in my mind now.' – 'What is
uppermost in your mind then?' – 'Every time you get up and walk past
me, that's all I can see. Every time I hear the swish of your dress, my
heart stops beating, and when you leave the room, I think of every word
you said, and all this night I thought of nothing, all I could do was to
listen out for you breathing in your sleep and how you turned over once
or twice...' – 'I wouldn't be surprised,' she said to me with a laugh,
'you don't even give a second thought to having beaten the daylights
out of me. You probably don't even remember any of it!' – 'Maybe I
do think about it,' I said, 'I don't know.' – 'And if I don't pardon you
and shan't marry you?' – 'I'll drown myself,' I said. – 'And kill me into
the bargain...' She said this and thought a while. Then she lost her
temper and left. An hour later back she comes, sad and gloomy. – 'I
will marry you,' she says to me, 'not because I'm afraid of you, Parfyon

Semyonych, but because we'll all have to perish in the end. What's the difference? There, take a seat,' she says, 'they'll bring you something to eat. And if I do marry you,' she added, 'I'll be a faithful wife, you don't have to doubt or worry yourself about this.' Then, after she paused a while, she said, 'No, you're no lackey, I was convinced though before, that you were a lackey through and through.' Here she named the day too, and a week later she ran off to Lebedev. After I followed her here, she said to me, 'I'm not giving you up completely, I just want to wait for as long as I choose, because I'm still my own mistress. If you want, you can wait too.' That's the way things stand with us now… What do you make of all this, Lev Nikolayevich?"

"And what about you, what do you make of it?" the Prince asked, looking at Rogozhin dejectedly.

"My mind's a blank," he snapped back. He appeared to want to add something else, but in the depths of despondency did not.

The Prince rose and was again on the point of leaving.

"You know, I don't want to be in your way, all the same," he said softly, lost in thought as though responding to his own very private arguments.

"Do you know what I'm going to say to you?" Rogozhin suddenly spoke, and his eyes lit up. "How it is you're letting me have her, is beyond me. Have you really stopped loving her altogether? Formerly you pined for her, I saw it. Why then have you rushed here in such haste? Out of compassion?" He screwed up his face in an evil grin. "He-he!"

"You think I'm deceiving you?"

"No, I believe you, only I can't understand anything. It looks as though your compassion is stronger than my love!" Something vicious was on the tip of his tongue, and his face flushed.

"Your love is indistinguishable from your hatred," the Prince said with a smile, "and if it were to pass, it'd be worse than ever. Mark my words, Parfyon…"

"You think I'll cut her throat?"

The Prince shuddered.

"You'll hate her for the very love you bear her now, for all the suffering you're putting up with. The most amazing thing for me is how she can keep on promising to marry you. When I heard about it yesterday, I could hardly credit it, and I felt so depressed. Let's face it, she has reneged on you and left you at the altar twice before, so she must have some sense of premonition!... What good are you to her? Do you think it's your money? Rubbish! No doubt you've squandered more than enough already! Could it be that she's just in need of a husband? Surely she could have picked anybody. Anybody but you would have been better, because you really will end up cutting her throat, and she knows that, she knows that already all too well. Or because you love her so much? Yes, that could be it... I believe there are women who yearn for just that kind of love... only..."

The Prince stopped and paused.

"Why've you smiled again at Father's picture?" Rogozhin asked, alert to every change, every fleeting movement in the Prince's features.

"Why I smiled? Because it struck me that if it hadn't been for this unfortunate love affair, you'd have turned into a spitting image of your father, and not before time. You'd have settled in this house morosely with your long-suffering wife, who'd be obedient to your every wish. Occasionally you'd have uttered a gruff word, mistrusting all and sundry, perfectly content in your isolation, hoarding money cheerlessly and secretively. Come old age you'd have taken to poring over old books and adopted the rites of the Old Believers..."

"Funny you should say that! She said exactly the same thing when she was looking at this portrait recently! It's marvellous how you both come up with the same thing now—"

"Has she been here already then?" the Prince enquired with surprise.

"Yes. She looked hard at the portrait and questioned me about the dead man. 'You'd have ended just like him,' was what she said in the end with a smile. 'You, Parfyon Semyonych, have these violent passions, enough to send you to the Siberian salt mines if you're not careful, but you've got your head screwed on, you've got your wits about you,' these were her very words, believe me! I had never heard anything the like from her before. 'Left to yourself, you'd have soon turned your back on all your present follies. And as you've no education to speak of, you'd have started hoarding money, stuck as you are in this your father's house with all the Skoptsy around you. In the end you'd probably have gone over to their faith and worked up such a liking for money, you'd have finished with not just two but ten million roubles, and would have given up the ghost from hunger stretched across your sacks of gold, because hoarding would have turned into a passion with you. You can't help working yourself into a passion about everything.' That's just how she spoke, almost word for word. That was the first time she ever spoke to me like that! For the most part she either talks nonsense to me or teases me. This time too she began by teasing, but then went deadly serious. She did a complete tour of the house, prying into every corner as though her life depended on it. I told her I'd change everything around, and if need be buy a new house as a wedding present. 'Not on your life,' she says, 'don't change a thing here. We'll manage just as it is. When I'm your wife, I want to live by the side of your mother.' I took her to Mother's. She was full of respect, like her own daughter. It's two years now Mother hasn't been quite all there – she's not at all well, and since Father's passing, she's been like a little child, not saying a word, just sitting there confined to her chair, nodding her head at whomever she sees. If you'd stopped feeding her, she wouldn't notice it for days. I took her right hand, arranged her fingers* and said, 'Bless her, my dear mother, she's going to be my wife.' She kissed Mother's hand with feeling and said, 'The poor lady's probably suffered enough in her time.' She happened to see this book lying around: 'What's this, you've started reading Russian history?' (She herself said to me back in Moscow once, 'Why don't you read Solovyev's *Russian History*. You haven't read a thing in your life.') 'That's what you ought to be doing,' she reckons, 'keep at it. I'll make a little list for you of what books you should read first and foremost. Would you like me to?' She'd never, ever, talked to me like that before. I could hardly believe my ears. It was such a weight off my chest."

"I'm very happy for you, Parfyon," the Prince said with genuine emotion, "very happy indeed. Who knows, God may grant you a life together."

"That'll never be!" Rogozhin exclaimed forcefully.

"Listen, Parfyon, if you love her so much, don't you want to earn her respect? And if you want to, aren't you hopeful that you'll succeed? All right, I did say just now that it's a mystery to me why she'd want to marry you. But even though I can't solve it, I've no doubt there must be a sufficient and convincing explanation. She's persuaded of your love, and she must be no less persuaded of some of your other qualities. Surely it can't be any other way! What you've said just now confirms this. You've said yourself she found a way of talking to you which was different from how she addressed and communicated with you previously. You're mistrustful and jealous, and that's why you exaggerate all the bad things about her. It's obvious she doesn't object to you half as much as you claim she does. Otherwise, it would look as though by marrying you, she'd have purposely been asking either to have her throat slit or be dumped in the river. Who'd do that? Who'd contemplate such a thing?"

Rogozhin listened to the Prince's impassioned appeal with a bitter smile. His mind appeared to be fully made up.

"If looks could kill, Parfyon!" the Prince observed with a heavy heart.

"Her throat slit or into the river!" Rogozhin said at last. "Ha! That's why she keeps coming back to me, because she fancies her throat slit! Do you really want me to believe you still don't realize what's really going on?"

"I don't know what you're talking about."

"Well, perhaps he really doesn't, he-he! They say you're… not quite… *all there*. She loves someone else – get that into your head! Just as much as I love her just now, she loves someone else. And do you know who this other man is? It's you! Don't tell me you didn't know!"

"Me!"

"Yes, you! She's been in love with you ever since that birthday party of hers. Only she thinks she can't marry you because she imagines she'd bring discredit upon you and ruin your whole life. 'Everybody knows who I am,' she reckons. She never stops going on about it, she confessed all this to my face. She wouldn't disgrace and ruin you, but to marry me is perfectly all right – that's how much she cares for me! Consider that!"

"So how could she have run from you to me, and then… from me—"

"And from you back to me! Ha! Who can tell what may enter her head! It's as if she's in some kind of fever. Didn't she shout out, 'Marriage to you is like death by drowning. Bring on the marriage!" It's all on, she's named the day, but when it starts drawing nearer – she gets cold feet, or she's changed her mind – God only knows! You saw for yourself – tears, laughter, violent attacks… Are you surprised she ran away from you? She ran away from you that time, because it suddenly hit her how much she was in love with you. She couldn't bear to be with you any longer. You said just now that I tracked her down in Moscow. Nothing of the sort – she came running to me herself to get away from you. 'Name the day,' she says to me, 'I'm ready! Champagne! Bring on the gypsies!...' Look, if it hadn't been for me, she'd have been at the bottom of the river long ago. And that's the truth. The only reason she hasn't jumped is that being with me is perhaps worse than death by drowning. It's her contrariness that drives her into my arms... If she does marry me, it'll be out of pure spite, let me tell you."

"So how can you... how can you possibly?..." the Prince cried out, unable to finish. He regarded Rogozhin with terror.

"Go on, finish," Rogozhin urged with a grin, "but if you wish, I can tell precisely what's going through your head just now, 'How can she marry someone like that? How can it be allowed to go ahead?' I know what's going through your head—"

"That's not what I came here for, Parfyon, I tell you, that's not what was on my mind—"

"It may well be it wasn't for that, and that that's not what was on your mind, but it is now, he-he! Well, that's enough! Why are you so upset? Did you really have no idea? You surprise me!"

"This is all jealousy, Parfyon, it's your illness, you're blowing it up out of all proportion..." the Prince muttered in extreme agitation. "What's come over you?"

"Don't," Rogozhin said and snatched the knife out of the hands of the Prince, who had picked it up from the table next to the book, putting it in its former place.

"I had a feeling when I was leaving for St Petersburg, I had a premonition..." the Prince went on. "I didn't want to come here! I wanted to forget all that had gone on here, to rip it out of my heart! Well, goodbye... What's the matter with you?"

While the Prince was speaking, he had again absent-mindedly picked up the same knife from the table, and again Rogozhin took it out of his hand and threw it on the table. It was quite an ordinary knife with a horn handle, not a folding one, with a blade about six inches long and of corresponding width.

On seeing that the Prince looked particularly put out at having the knife snatched out of his hand a second time, Rogozhin returned it in an irritated huff between the pages of the book and threw the lot across to another table.

"You cut pages with it or something?" the Prince asked abstractedly, still deeply absorbed in his own train of thought.

"Yes, pages—"

"But this is a gardening knife?"

"Yes, it is. What's wrong in using a gardening knife as a paper-knife?"

"But it's... brand new."

"So, what if it is? Why shouldn't I have bought a new knife?" Rogozhin snapped back with mounting annoyance.

The Prince shuddered and looked hard at Rogozhin.

"We're a right lot, we are!" he suddenly said with a laugh, snapping back into full consciousness. "Pardon me, my friend, I'm in such a state, my head, and then this illness of mine... I've become so absent-minded and ridiculous. I was going to ask you something else entirely... I forget what it was now. Goodbye..."

"Not that way," Rogozhin said.

"Sorry!"

"This way, come this way, follow me, I'll lead the way."

4

THEY WENT THROUGH THE SAME ROOMS that the Prince had already walked through. Rogozhin led the way. They entered a large hall. The walls were hung with a number of pictures, landscapes and portraits of churchmen, all faded and indistinct. Over the door into the next room hung an unusually proportioned picture over one and a half metres long and not more than a third of a metre high. It depicted the body of Christ shortly after the deposition. The Prince gave it a casual glance as though recalling something; however, he did not stop, but wanted to pass on through the door. But Rogozhin suddenly stopped in front of the picture.

"You see, all these pictures," he said, "were bought at auctions by my late father for a rouble or two each, he loved that sort of thing. One knowledgeable person looked at them all and declared they were all rubbish, except this one over the door, also bought for two roubles. There was someone way back who offered father three hundred and fifty roubles for it, and Savelyev, Ivan Dmitrych, a merchant with a passion for works of art, went as far as four hundred roubles, and last week was going to pay my brother Semyon Semyonych five hundred roubles. I turned it down."

"This is... this is a copy of a painting by Hans Holbein," the Prince said, having had a closer look at the picture. "I'm not much of a connoisseur, but it looks like an excellent copy. I saw this picture abroad and can't get it out of my mind. But... what's wrong?..."

Rogozhin had suddenly turned away from the picture and gone ahead. Of course, his absent-mindedness and the strangely volatile moodiness which had suddenly afflicted him could well have accounted for this brusqueness; all the same, the Prince was taken aback at the way the conversation, which he hadn't even initiated, was abruptly terminated.

"Tell me, Lev Nikolayevich, I've been meaning to ask you for a long time, do you believe in God or not?" Rogozhin suddenly spoke after they had taken a few steps.

"You've an odd way of asking, and... the way you look!..." the Prince remarked involuntarily.

"I like looking at that picture," Rogozhin muttered after a pause, apparently no longer aware he had asked a question.

"At that picture!" the Prince exclaimed, struck by a sudden thought. "Do you? Don't you realize that picture is enough to put a man from his faith?"

"Yes, I do," Rogozhin affirmed unexpectedly.

In the meantime they had reached the front door.

"Really?" the Prince said and stopped. "I'm surprised! I was merely joking, and you're taking it so seriously! Why did you ask me whether I believe in God?"

"No reason. But I did mean to ask you previously. Many people don't these days. You lived abroad though. I wonder if it's true – a drunk mentioned it once – that in Russia there are more non-believers than in all other countries put together? 'It's easier for us,' he said, 'than it is for them on account of us being more progressive...'"

Rogozhin flashed a caustic smile; having spoken, he suddenly opened the door and, with his hand on the handle, waited for the Prince to leave. The Prince was surprised, but went out. Rogozhin followed him on to the landing leading to the front steps and pulled the door half shut after him. They both stood facing each other, looking for all the world as though they had no idea where they were or what to do next.

"Goodbye then," the Prince said, putting out his hand.

"Goodbye," Rogozhin said, firmly but completely absent-mindedly shaking the hand that was offered him.

The Prince descended one step and turned around.

"Apropos faith," he began with a smile prompted by a sudden recollection (he did not want to leave Rogozhin without engaging him in a further discussion), "apropos faith, I had four different encounters in two days last week. In the morning I was travelling along a newly opened railway line and spent about four hours talking with a certain Mr S. We had never met before. I'd heard a lot about him previously and, incidentally, as an atheist. He really was very erudite, and I was jolly glad of an opportunity to talk to a man of genuine learning. Besides, he was exceptionally well brought up, so that he spoke to me as to a complete equal both as regards my fund of knowledge and intellectual capacity. He did not believe in God. There was only one thing which struck me. He always seemed to me to miss the point, the whole time that is, and it struck me precisely because no matter how many non-believers I had met and how many of their books I had read, it always seemed that what they said and wrote, was forever short of the mark, although on the face of it, it seemed to make sense. I put this point to him at the time, but I must have fudged it or been unable to express it, because he appeared not to understand me... In the evening I booked into a provincial hotel for the night, where a murder had been committed the previous night, and it was still on everybody's lips when I arrived. Two peasant friends, of advanced years, not at all drunk, who'd known each other well for quite some time, after drinking their fill of tea wanted to settle down in the same room for the night. But during the previous two days one of them noticed the other was sporting a silver watch that he hadn't seen before, on a string of yellow glass beads. He couldn't get the watch out of his mind, the temptation was too much for him. He took a knife, and when his friend had his back to him, stole up to him, took good aim, raised his eyes to heaven, crossed himself, and having said a fervent prayer to himself, 'Lord forgive me in the name of Christ!' he slit his friend's throat from ear to ear as though he was no more than a ram destined for the slaughter."

Rogozhin simply rolled with laughter. He laughed as though he was in a fit. It was in fact quite strange, especially after his recent attack of melancholy.

"I really like that! No, this takes the biscuit!" he kept calling out convulsively, almost choking himself. "One person may have no faith in God whatever, and another's is so strong, he knifes a person to death after a prayer... No, Prince, my friend, this is the best thing I've ever heard! Ha-ha-ha! No, this really takes the biscuit!..."

"In the morning I went out for a walk through the town," the Prince continued as soon as Rogozhin's laughter had abated somewhat, although his lips would still twitch involuntarily and spasmodically, "and ran into a drunken soldier, slouching along the wooden pavement in a totally ragged state. He came up to me, 'Will you buy this crucifix off me, sir, I'll let it go for twenty copecks, it's silver!' In his hands was a crucifix all right, which he must have taken off just then, on a fine well-worn sky blue ribbon, quite large, Byzantine, with a crosspiece – only it was tin, you could see it at first glance. I took out twenty copecks and gave it to him, and hung it round my neck straight away. You could see by his face how pleased he was to have diddled the gentleman, and I can guarantee he immediately headed for the nearest tavern to blow the money on booze. It's remarkable what a torrent of impressions gushed over me in Russia. Formerly I understood nothing, I was deaf and blind to it all, and in my five-year stay abroad my memories of Russia were nothing short of fantastic. So, there I was walking along, and I thought to myself, it would be too rash to condemn this hawker of Christ just yet. Surely God must know what goes on in the hearts of these drunken weaklings. An hour later I returned to my hotel, and ran into a peasant woman with an unweaned baby in her arms. The woman was still quite young and the infant about six weeks old. The child, as far as I could tell just by looking at her, had just smiled for the first time ever. And it was a sight for sore eyes to see her suddenly bless the little mite. 'What was that about, my dear?' I asked her. (I was full of questions at the time.) 'Well, you see, a mother's joy at seeing her child smile is the same as God's every time he looks down from heaven and beholds a sinner breaking into a heartfelt prayer.' These were almost the very words the woman spoke, and this deep, this subtle and truly religious thought is at the core of Christianity, which sees God as our father who rejoices at the sight of his children – it is the central point of Christ's teaching!* A simple peasant woman! Undeniably, a mother... and, who knows, perhaps the wife of that same soldier who sold me his crucifix. Listen, Parfyon, you asked me a question just now, here's my answer: the essence of a religious experience is not to be conveyed by any arguments, nor misdemeanours, nor crimes, nor atheist doctrines. There's something short of the mark there always, and will continue to be so till the end of time. There's something there that will for ever confound the atheists, and will for ever continue to be *short of the mark*. But the main thing is that it all manifests itself most clearly and most directly in the Russian heart, and that is the sum total of all my observations! It's one of my primary convictions, formed on this our Russian soil. There remains much to be accomplished, Parfyon! There remains much to be challenged in our Mother Russia, believe me! Think back to the short time we spent meeting together and conversing in Moscow... And I had no wish at all to return here now! Nor is this the kind of meeting I was planning on having with you, it really wasn't!... Still, let that pass!... Goodbye and so long! God be with you!"

He turned and went down the steps.

"Lev Nikolayevich!" Rogozhin called from above after the Prince had reached the bottom of the first flight, "that crucifix you bought from the soldier, have you still got it?"

"Yes, I'm wearing it."

And the Prince stopped once more.

"Show it to me!"

"What's this again?" the Prince wondered to himself. He thought a while, retraced his steps and showed the crucifix without taking it down from his neck.

"Let me have it!" Rogozhin said.

"What for? Do you really?..."

The Prince was reluctant to part with it.

"I'll wear it, and I'll give you mine."

"You want to exchange crucifixes? By all means, Parfyon, I'll be only too glad. This will make us brothers!"

The Prince took off his tin crucifix and Rogozhin held out his gold one, and they exchanged them. Rogozhin was silent. With a sinking heart the Prince noted that traces of the erstwhile mistrust were still evident on the face of his newly gained brother, and the same defiant, almost derisive smile still played fitfully about his lips. Without saying a word, Rogozhin finally took the Prince by his hand and after a few moments overcome by indecision, barely audibly whispered, "Come along!" and pulled him back into the house. They crossed the landing on the ground floor and rang at a door opposite the one they had come out of. It was opened without delay. A very old hunched woman in black, her hair tied in a kerchief, bowed low to Rogozhin; he said something fleetingly and, without waiting for an answer, led the Prince on through a series of rooms. They were dark, frigid in their tidiness; the pieces of old-fashioned furniture under their scrupulously clean white covers looked austere and forbidding. The room, much like a drawing room, that Rogozhin finally led the Prince into without any prior announcement, was smaller than the rest, divided by a polished mahogany screen, at one end of which was a double door, probably leading to the bedroom. In a corner, by the stove, sat a diminutive old lady, not particularly old, with fresh, round, rather pleasant features, but completely grey and in her second childhood, as was evident at the first glance. She was wearing a black woollen dress, a large black shawl round her neck and a clean white bonnet with black ribbons. Her feet rested on a small footstool. Next to her was another, tidily dressed, slightly older lady, also in mourning and also wearing a white bonnet, a poor relation of some sort, knitting a sock in total silence. The impression was that neither of them ever spoke. The first old lady, on catching sight of Rogozhin and the Prince, smiled and inclined her head several times as a sign of welcome and in evident pleasure at seeing them.

"Mother dear," Rogozhin said, having kissed her hand, "here is a great friend of mine, Prince Lev Nikolayevich Myshkin. We exchanged our crucifixes. He was like a brother to me at one time in Moscow, and he did a lot for me. Bless him, mother, as you would your own son. Wait, mother dear! That's better! Let me arrange your fingers..."

But, before Rogozhin reached out, the old lady raised her right hand in a three-finger benediction and made the sign of the cross three times over the Prince. After that she gave him another kind and gentle nod.

"Well, we had better be going, Lev Nikolayevich," Rogozhin said, "this is all I brought you here for..."

After they were on the front steps again, he added, "You know, she doesn't understand anything you say to her, and she had no idea what I said either, but still she managed to bless you. It shows she had a will to do it... Well, goodbye, we must both go our own ways." And he opened the door to his apartment.

"Let me at least embrace you in parting, you funny man!" the Prince exclaimed, looking at Rogozhin with kind-hearted reproof, and tried to embrace him. But no sooner had Rogozhin lifted his arms, when he dropped them again. He hesitated; he shuffled about and was disinclined to look at the Prince. He was reluctant to embrace him.

"Fear not! I may have taken your crucifix, but I'm not going to stab you for the sake of a watch!" he muttered indistinctly and suddenly burst into an odd laughter. But the expression on his face changed equally suddenly. He went deadly pale, his lips began to tremble, his eyes lit up. He raised his arms, gave the Prince a powerful hug and, choking over his words, said, "Take her then, if that's the way fate would have it! She's yours! I'm bowing out!… Your servant, Rogozhin!"

And, abandoning the Prince to his own devices, he hurried back to his apartment and shut the door behind him.

5

IT WAS ALREADY LATE, about half-past two, and the Prince did not catch General Yepanchin at home. Having left a visiting card, he decided to drop in at the Hotel Vesy, to ask for Kolya; and if he was not there, to leave him a note. In the Hotel Vesy he was told that Nikolai Ardalionovich had gone out in the morning, but had left a message that he'd perhaps be back by three, but if he were not back by half-past, it meant he had caught a train to Pavlovsk, to Madame Yepanchina's dacha, and would stay there for dinner. The Prince sat down to wait and, at the same time, ordered himself a meal.

By half-past three, coming on to four o'clock, there was no sign of Kolya. The Prince left and set off in a random direction. At the beginning of summer there are some wonderful days in St Petersburg – bright, hot and windless. This happened to be one of them. For some time the Prince wandered aimlessly. He did not know the city at all well. He would occasionally stop at a crossroads, in front of some houses, on squares, on bridges; once he went into a coffee house for a rest. Every now and again he would turn his attention to passers-by and study them with great interest; but for the most part he noticed neither passers-by, nor where he was going. He was in state of unbearable tension and anxiety, and at the same time yearned for solitude. He wanted to be on his own, to abandon himself to this agonizing tension passively, without seeking any kind of relief. He was positively disgusted at the prospect of attempting to resolve the problems that had burdened his heart and soul. "Am I to blame for what happened?" he would mutter to himself, hardly aware that he had asked the question.

By six o'clock he found himself at the Tsarskoye Selo Railway Station. His solitude now had become unbearable to him; a new longing had swept him off his feet, and for a moment the gloom which had been enveloping his heart was pierced by a shaft of bright light. He bought a ticket to Pavlovsk and could not wait to depart; but something was haunting him, not in the shape of a fantasy, which is how he might have been inclined to perceive it, but as a reality. He was on the point of boarding the train, when on an impulse he flung the newly purchased ticket on the ground and walked back to the main concourse of the station, confused and lost in thought. A little later, walking along the street, he suddenly seemed to recollect something, as though he'd stumbled on an unexpected resolution to a strange conundrum, which had been troubling him for some time past. He suddenly seemed to have caught himself, as it were, red-handed, pursuing an activity that had originated quite some time previously, but which he hadn't been fully aware of until that very moment. A good few hours earlier, at the Hotel Vesy, and it seemed even before that, he would suddenly cast around as though he was missing something. It'd pass eventually, for a considerable period of time, half an hour or so, but then he'd again look around in a panic, and start searching.

But as soon as he had noted this unwholesome but totally involuntary yet deeply compulsive urge, he had another recollection which brought him up short. He remembered that at the time when he realized he was looking for something, he was standing on the pavement in front of a shop, absorbed with the wares displayed in the window. He now wanted, come what may, to check whether he'd really been standing, it couldn't have been more than five minutes before, at this shop window, or whether it had been a figment of his imagination – or perhaps he had confused it with something else entirely. Was there ever such a shop with such wares? He really was in a peculiarly frail condition that day, almost identical to how he felt at the beginning of the attacks of his original illness. He knew that in these pre-attack stages, unless he made a conscious effort to concentrate his mind to the utmost, he would be abnormally absent-minded, to the extent of confusing objects and faces. But there was also an especial reason why he so badly wanted to verify whether he had stood in front of the shop. Amongst the wares on display was one particular object which he had been looking at and had even priced at sixty copecks in silver; he remembered that despite all his absent-mindedness and inner turmoil. If the shop existed, and this object was indeed displayed amongst the other items, then it must follow he had stopped expressly because of it. Moreover, it would mean that this item exercised such a strong interest in him that his attention was attracted to it even while he was in the throes of a most violent inner unrest when he had just left the precincts of the railway station. He began to retrace his steps, glancing to the right, and his heart was beating with impatient disquiet. But there was the shop, he had found it at last! He had been about five hundred paces away from it when he resolved to come back. And there was the sixty-copeck item. "Of course sixty copecks, not more," he reaffirmed with a laugh. But his laughter was hysterical; he became very depressed. He recollected clearly that it was while he had stood here in front of this window that he suddenly turned precisely as he had when, a little earlier, he had spotted Rogozhin looking at him. Having verified that he had not made a mistake (something he was fully confident of even before this verification), he turned from the shop and walked briskly away. All this had to be thought through without fail and delay; it was now evident that it was no hallucination at the station either, that he had had a tangible experience which was closely and necessarily linked to his former state of disquiet. But an irrepressible inner revulsion again overrode everything. He simply did not feel like thinking about anything, and nor did he; his mind homed in on something quite different.

Actually, he pondered that in an epileptic episode there was a stage, almost immediately preceding the attack (provided the attack came in the waking hours) when suddenly, amidst overbearing sadness, spiritual despondency and depression, there were moments when his brain seemed to blaze up and all his vital forces would be exerted in one extraordinary effort of will. His awareness of life and self-consciousness increased almost tenfold in rapid, lightning flashes. His mind and heart were illumined with an uncommon glow; all his anxieties, all his misgivings, all his uncertainties appeared to be resolved in an instant and transformed into some kind of a higher serenity, suffused with bright, harmonious joy and hope, replete with wisdom and the consciousness of an ultimate purpose. But these instants, these flashes, were mere precursors of that ultimate moment (never more than a moment), which precipitated the onset of the actual attack. This moment was, of course, pretty unbearable. Analyzing it subsequently in normal health, he would often say to himself that all the lightning flashes and revelations of a higher self-awareness and self-consciousness, and consequently of a "higher order of existence", were no more than an illness, a discontinuity of the normal state, and if so, then far from being of a higher order of existence – they ought on the contrary to be regarded as of the lowest. And all the same, in the end he reached a highly paradoxical conclusion, "So what if it is an illness? What does it matter if this tension is anomalous, provided that the end result itself, the very instant of perception as subsequently evoked and analyzed in a healthy state, is in the highest degree harmonious and beautiful, and offers a hitherto unprecedented, unimaginable sense of fulfilment, plenitude, propitiation and an exultant devotional experience of the highest synthesis of life?" These vague articulations appeared to him very understandable, though still very speculative. He did not admit any doubt, or the possibility of doubt, in perceiving these sensations other than as "things of beauty, divine prayer, the supreme synthesis of life". After all, it was not as if he had hallucinations at that moment – like those from hashish, opium or wine, which degrade the mind and warp the soul – abnormal and nonexistent! He could clearly vouch for this at the end of each episode of his illness. These moments of bliss – if one had to express them in so many words – were self-consciousness and at the same time self-awareness intensified to the absolute limit and perceived singularly and directly. If, in the very last instant of consciousness before the attack, he managed clearly and consciously to say to himself, "Yes, this is the moment to sacrifice one's life for!" then, clearly, this moment was worth his life. That said, he would not have insisted on the logic of his argument; torpor, depression, mental deterioration were all too palpable after-effects following those "higher moments of bliss". He would, of course, not enter into any kind of serious dispute about them. In his analysis, that is, in his evaluation of this instant, there was undoubtedly a flaw, nevertheless the reality of the perception caused him some unease. In the event, what was one to do with this reality? It did exist; he himself had had the time in that one brief second to say to himself that, by the immeasurable euphoria he himself had experienced, that instant could possibly be worth all his life. "At that moment," as he subsequently had occasion to relate to Rogozhin at one of their meetings in Moscow, "at that moment I could well understand the mystery of the written word that *there should be time no longer*.* It was probably," he had added with a smile, "that same instant in which Mohammed had managed to visit every corner of Allah's kingdom before a drop of water had spilled from his jug as it fell from the table." Yes, he and Rogozhin had met often in Moscow and talked of many other things besides. "Rogozhin said just now that I was his brother. That's the first time he's said that," the Prince thought to himself.

At the time, he was sitting on a bench under a tree in the Summer Gardens. It was about seven o'clock. There was no one around; something dark suddenly enveloped the setting sun. It felt close and muggy; somewhere far away a thunderstorm was brewing. He felt a peculiar pleasure in his present contemplative state. External objects surrounding him sank deep into his consciousness, and he enjoyed the experience; he constantly strove to forget something real and tangible, but on looking around he would again instantly be brought face to face with the nagging thought which he tried so hard to banish from his mind. He briefly recalled a conversation he had had with a waiter at an inn about a very strange murder that had attracted a lot of attention and was on everybody's lips. But no sooner had he thought of it than something extraordinary happened again.

He experienced an extraordinarily, irresistible longing, an indomitable temptation that took complete possession of his will. He got up from the bench and set off, leaving the gardens in the direction of the Peterburgskaya Storona. Earlier in the day he had asked a passerby on the quay to point out to him the Peterburgskaya Storona across the river, but at the time he had decided not to go there. He knew it would be a wasted journey to go there this time too. He'd had the address for a long time, and could easily have found the house of Lebedev's relative, but was almost convinced he would not find her in. "She's surely gone to Pavlovsk, otherwise Kolya would have left a message at the Hotel Vesy as agreed." And so if he was making his way there now, it was most certainly not in order to see her. A new, morbid and distressing sense of curiosity overwhelmed him. He was suddenly struck by a novel, unexpected thought...

But it was more than enough for him that he was at last on his way, and knew where he was heading; he pressed on, but from now on almost blindly. As he turned his "unexpected thought" over in his mind, he was all of a sudden overcome by an almost unbearable sense of revulsion. All he could do was, with painful effort, to force his attention on everything that met his gaze; he looked at the sky above, and at the river Neva. At one moment he stopped to talk to a small child. His epileptic condition was evidently getting more and more pronounced. There were distant claps of thunder. It was becoming very close...

For some reason, like an obtrusive tune, the image of Lebedev's nephew, whom he'd seen a few hours earlier, kept coming back to him again and again. The remarkable thing was that it was always in the guise of the murderer whom Lebedev had spoken of on introducing the nephew. Yes, he had read about this murderer quite recently. Since his arrival in Russia he'd had many opportunities to hear and read about such things; he followed them all up assiduously. It was precisely this Zhemarin family murder case that had excited his interest when talking to the waiter; he remembered, the latter regarded the incident in the same way as himself. He remembered too that the waiter was a sensible, even-tempered, decent fellow. On the other hand, this was just an impression. "It's not really easy to tell what people are like in a new country," the Prince said to himself. All the same, his faith in the Russian character was getting ever more passionate. Oh, what a great deal of what was new, unexpected and startling had come his way during these six months! But each man's soul is a closed book; especially the Russian soul, for many people anyway. Take Rogozhin, for instance, with whom he had a long and close, almost brotherly, association! But could he claim to know Rogozhin? In truth what a mess, what a shambles, what a mad place is a man's soul! And what a nasty, selfish little whippersnapper was this nephew of Lebedev's! "But what's the matter with me?" the Prince suddenly asked himself. "Surely he didn't murder those human beings, those six people! I'm getting confused... how odd! My head is spinning... What a sweet, pretty face Lebedev's eldest daughter has, the one with the child in her arms! What childishly innocent looks, and how winsome her laughter! Strange I should have forgotten her face till now! Lebedev, though he stamped

236

his feet, probably adores them all. But what is as plain as a pikestaff is that he thinks the world of his nephew too!

"But by what right is he judging them so peremptorily now – he, who only arrived today? By what right is he pronouncing such harsh judgements on them? Let's face it, Lebedev had set him a problem today! Had he expected anything of the kind from Lebedev? Lebedev and du Barry – my God! All the same, if Rogozhin does commit a murder, at least it won't be such a botch job. Not such carnage, please! A murder weapon, made to order from a drawing, and six people are killed in a moment of sheer madness!* Surely, Rogozhin hasn't got a weapon made to order!... All he has... but... who said he was going to kill anyway?" the Prince suddenly caught himself saying with a shudder. "Isn't it despicable, criminal even, for me to be making such cynically outrageous assumptions!" he exclaimed in shameful remorse. He was deeply shocked and stood there on the street, rooted to the ground. Recent memories came flooding back: the events at the Pavlovsk and the Nikolayevsky railway stations; the question he had put directly to Rogozhin about *the eyes*; Rogozhin's crucifix that he was wearing now; the blessing of Rogozhin's mother after Rogozhin himself took him to see her; their fitful embrace at the end; Rogozhin's final renunciation on the steps of the woman he loved; and after all that to have caught himself in the act of constantly snooping around for something! And that shop, and that object in the window... how mean and petty of him! And at the conclusion of it all to be now making his way forward with "his peculiar, his unexpected thought" in mind! Despair and suffering gripped his soul. He wanted to turn back to his hotel immediately, and had already taken a few steps, but stopped, thought a while, and pressed on again in the original direction.

And anyway, he had already reached the Peterburgskaya Storona and was close to that house; yet surely he was not going with the former idea in mind, not that "premeditated one"! That goes without saying! Yes, no doubt about it, he was having a relapse all right; perhaps his fit would come on today. The looming fit was surely the reason for his spiritual numbness, and – for that "thought" too! Now the numbness has eased, the demon has been driven off, all doubts have been laid to rest, his heart suffused with joy! And – it's been so long since he'd seen *her*, he had to see her, and... yes, he'd like to see Rogozhin now; he'd take him by the hand, and they'd go together... His heart was innocent.

He was no threat to Rogozhin! Tomorrow he'd go straight to Rogozhin and tell him he'd seen her. Hadn't he hurried here, as Rogozhin himself had observed, just in order to see her? Perhaps he would find her in, for it was by no means certain that she had gone to Pavlovsk.

Yes, everything must be spelled out clearly, everyone must be able to read one another's heart to avoid these miserable, passionate renunciations as Rogozhin had renounced the love of his life just then, and let it all come about easily and freely and... in an abundance of light. Surely Rogozhin was capable of seeing light! He said his love for her was different, that he had no compassion, no kind of pity for her. True, he had added later, "It looks as though your compassion is stronger than my love!" But he was being unfair to himself. Hm, Rogozhin reading a book! Was that not compassion, not the start of compassion? Was not the very presence of the book proof enough that he was quite aware of his relationship to *her*? And the story he recounted? No, this went deeper than mere passion. "And is it mere passion that her face inspires? Can there be talk of passion at the sight of her face now? It evokes suffering, it overwhelms the whole soul, it..." A searing, excruciating recollection suddenly stung the Prince to the quick.

Yes, it was painful! He remembered how he had suffered when he had begun to notice signs of mental instability in her for the first time. He had been on the brink of despair. And how could he have deserted her and let her run away from him to Rogozhin? He should have followed her rather than waiting for news of her. But... how was it that Rogozhin still hadn't noticed signs of madness in her? Hm... But he wouldn't, would he? With him it's always other reasons, fits of passion. And what unbridled jealousy! What did he mean by his offer just then? (The Prince suddenly blushed and his heart seemed to miss a beat.)

Still, why dwell on all this? There was mental aberration on both sides. As for him, the Prince, it was next to impossible to love the woman carnally, it would have been an act of cruelty, indeed of inhumanity. Yes, truly! "There's no doubt though, Rogozhin is doing himself an injustice. He has a generous heart, which is capable both of enduring suffering and of feeling pity. After he finds out the whole truth and discovers how pathetic this damaged, unhinged creature really is, is he not going to pardon her for all that had gone on before, all his former suffering? Is he not going to turn into her servant, her brother, her friend, her providence? Compassion will inspire him and put him on the right path. Compassion is the principal and perhaps the only law necessary for the survival of the whole of humankind." Oh, how badly, how unforgivably he had wronged Rogozhin! No, it's not the Russian soul that is a closed book, his own soul is a dark and dismal dungeon if he could come up with such dire thoughts. He only needed to utter a few fervent, heartfelt words in Moscow, and Rogozhin was ready to call him his brother, and he... No, this is sickness, stuff and nonsense! It will all come right in the end!... How hopeless Rogozhin sounded when he said he was losing his faith! This man must be going through hell. He said he liked looking at that picture; "liked" is not the word – he feels drawn to it. Rogozhin is not just a lustful soul; he is a fighter. He wants to restore his lost faith by force. He needs it now beyond measure... Yes! He needs to have faith in something! To have faith in someone! All the same, this picture by Holbein is so strange... Ah, there we are, that must be the house, number sixteen, owned by Mrs Filisova, wife of civil servant Mr Filisov. Good! The Prince rang the bell and asked for Nastasya Filippovna.

The lady in person informed him that Nastasya Filippovna had left for Pavlovsk in the morning to visit Darya Alexeyevna and it was possible she might not be back for a few days. Filisova was a diminutive, sharp-eyed, sharp-featured woman of about forty with shifty, penetrating eyes. When she asked him his name, she managed to imbue the question with an air of mystification; initially the Prince was reluctant to reveal it, and had already turned to go, but then changed his mind and made it quite clear that he wanted Nastasya Filippovna to know who it was that had called. Filisova heard him out with due deference and an enigmatic look, which presumably was calculated to assure him, "Don't you worry, I quite understand everything, sir." The Prince's name and title appeared to have a profound effect upon her. The Prince gave her an absent-minded glance and prepared to go back to his hotel. But he was no longer the same man who had just rung Filisova's doorbell. An instant and devastating change had come over him: he was yet again pale, weak, suffering and lacking confidence in himself; his knees were buckling, and a vague, sheepish smile played about his livid lips. His "unexpected thought" had been confirmed and proven right – his demon was back to plague him again!

But was it proven? Was it confirmed? Why was he shaking again? Whence the cold sweat, whence his hopelessness and despondency? Was it because he'd again seen those *eyes*? But he had left the Summer Gardens purposely in order to see them! Surely this was what his "unexpected thought" was all about. Come what may, he had been drawn to see those eyes again and to confirm absolutely that he'd see them precisely *there*, by that house. It was an irresistible compulsion with him, so now that he'd actually seen them, why was he so shattered and dejected about it? As though it had come to him as a surprise! Yes, these were *the same* eyes (no shadow of a doubt about it – they were *the same*) that had flashed at him in the morning, in the crowd as he was leaving the railway carriage at the Nikolayevsky Station; the same (precisely the same) that he felt boring into him from the back as he swung round to encounter them when he was in the act of taking a seat at Rogozhin's. Rogozhin wouldn't own up. He had asked with a wry, chilling smile, "So whose eyes were they?" And the Prince, getting into the carriage on the way to Aglaya's just recently at the Tsarskoselsky Station and suddenly seeing these eyes again for the third time that day, had an overwhelming urge to approach Rogozhin and tell *him* whose eyes they were! But he ran from the station forecourt and came to only after he had reached the cutler's shop and was looking at the object in the window with the horn handle which he'd priced at sixty copecks. A strange and terrifying demon had latched on to him resolutely and was unwilling to let go. This demon had whispered in his ear when he was sitting lost in thought under a lime tree in the Summer Gardens, that if Rogozhin was so determined to stalk him everywhere from the very morning, then, having learnt that he was not going to Pavlovsk (this of course was a fateful piece of information for Rogozhin), Rogozhin would be bound to go *there*, to stand outside that house in the Old Town, to watch the man who that same morning had given him his word of honour that he wouldn't attempt to see her, or that he had arrived in St Petersburg with that in mind. And so the Prince, agitated and unnerved, had made his way towards that house, and what of it, if he had actually run into Rogozhin there? All he saw was an unfortunate man, who was spiritually highly distressed, but this was perfectly understandable under the circumstances. This unfortunate man did not even attempt to conceal himself. Yes, back in the house Rogozhin had for some reason refused to own up and had lied, but at the station he had felt himself almost completely exposed. In truth, of the two, it was more likely to have been he, the Prince, who had been concealing himself, rather than Rogozhin. And now, at the house, Rogozhin stood on the other side of the street at about fifty paces diagonally across, his arms folded, and waited. Here he was in full view and, it would appear, deliberately so. He had stood there like an accuser and a judge, and quite unlike... Well, quite unlike what?

But why had not he, the Prince, approached him, instead turning away as though he hadn't noticed anything, even though their eyes had met. (Yes, their eyes had met! And they had looked at each other.) Surely he himself had wanted to take him by the hand for them to go *there* together! Surely he himself had wanted to go and tell him the next day that he had been to see her! Surely he had managed to shake off his demon when, halfway to the house, his heart had become suffused with joy! Or was there really something about Rogozhin, that is, in the overall make-up of the man on that day, in the sum of his pronouncements, his movements, his actions, his views, which could have justified the Prince's terrifying presentiments and the provocative whisperings of his demon? Something that is all too obvious to the eye but is difficult to analyse and relate, impossible to validate by reasoning, but which nonetheless, despite all difficulties and impossibilities, creates a cohesive impression which readily passes into an unshakable conviction?...

A conviction of what? (Oh, how the Prince was tortured by the monstrosity, the ignominy of this conviction, this unworthy presentiment, and how he berated himself for it!) "Speak, if you dare," he kept challenging and pointing an accusatory finger at himself. "What exactly are you convinced of! Why don't you formulate your ideas, why don't you dare say what you think, clearly, precisely, without beating about the bush? Oh, I'm such a coward" he would repeat again and again indignantly, his face flushing with shame. "How shall I be able to look this man in the face now! Oh, what a day this has been for me! Oh God, what a nightmare!"

There was a brief moment at the end of this arduous walk from the Peterburgskaya Storona when the Prince was nearly overcome by a desire to go back to Rogozhin, await his return, embrace him in shame with tears in his eyes and make a clean breast of it. But he was already at his hotel... In the morning he had taken an instant dislike to the place, the corridors, the whole building, his room; and several times that day shuddered at the thought of having to return there... "What's the matter with me, I'm like a hysterical woman, believing in all kinds of omens!" he reflected with an irritated smile, standing at the gates. A new, excruciating surge of shame, almost of despair, made him stop dead just as he was about to pass through the gates. He stood perfectly still for a moment. This sometimes happens: unexpected agonizing memories, especially if mingled with a sense of shame, will normally stop a man in his tracks, briefly. "Yes, I'm a man without a heart and a coward!" he repeated gloomily, and made a fitful attempt to move forward, but... stopped yet again.

The entrance at the gates, dark at the best of times, was even more so on that particular occasion; a passing storm cloud had obscured the remaining twilight, and just as the Prince was drawing near to the building, the cloud burst and the heavens opened. In the instant after his fitful move forward, following his brief stop, he was just outside the gateway fronting the street. And suddenly, at the far end of the gateway, in the semi-darkness, just inside the house entrance on the stairs, he caught sight of a figure of a man. The man appeared to be waiting, but did not linger and vanished. The Prince could not make out who the man was. Besides, any number of people could have been passing that spot; this was a hotel, and there was a continuous throng of people entering and leaving. But he was absolutely convinced that he recognized Rogozhin. In the following instant the Prince was on the stairs in hot pursuit. His heart was ready to burst. "All will be made clear in a moment!" he said to himself with singular conviction.

The stairs that the Prince reached led to the corridors of the first and second floors, along which were the individual rooms. As in all old houses, the staircase was built of stone; it was dark, narrow and wound round a wide stone column. On the first landing there was a niche-like cavity in the column, not more than a pace wide and half a pace deep, but large enough to accommodate one person. Dark as it was on the landing, the Prince nevertheless immediately realized that someone was hiding in the niche for some reason. His first instinct was to pass by and not look to the right. He had already taken one step beyond it when, unable to resist, he turned back.

Those eyes, that *very same* pair of eyes again met his gaze. The person hiding in the niche had also taken a step forward. For a second both men stood face to face. Suddenly the Prince grabbed him by the shoulders and turned him towards what light there was from the bottom of the stairs; he wanted a clearer view of the face.

Rogozhin's eyes glittered, and his features were convulsed with a fearsome grin. His right hand rose up in the air, and something flashed; the Prince made no attempt to stop it. All he remembered later was that he must have cried out at the time:

"Parfyon, I don't believe it!..."

Then suddenly something seemed to open up before him; an extraordinary *inner* light flooded his soul. This lasted for about half a second; however, he clearly and consciously recalled the beginning of a terrifying howl which involuntarily issued from his chest and which no force could have stopped. Then he lost consciousness and all was plunged into total darkness.

He had an epileptic fit, something that he had not suffered for a very long time. It is known that epileptic fits – "the falling sickness" – occur quite suddenly. At the instant when they commence, the facial features become terribly distorted, the eyes being particularly affected. Tremors and spasms spread over the whole body and face. A terrifying, unimaginable and inimitable cry issues from the breast; this cry is quite inhuman, and a listener would be hard put to imagine that it all comes from the same person. One almost gets the impression it's from another being, lodged inside the original one. In any case, that is how many people describe their impressions; on some, the sight of a person having an epileptic fit has a devastating and traumatic effect, bordering on the mystical. One can well imagine that the shock of this unexpected horror, combined with all the other terrible aspects of that moment, disabled Rogozhin on the spot and thereby saved the Prince from being inescapably stabbed with the knife that had already been raised over him. Then, not having had time to realize it was a fit and seeing the Prince tumble backwards down the stairs, hitting the back of his head with full force on one of the stone steps, Rogozhin himself dashed headlong down the stairs, side-stepped the body on the ground, and rushed out of the hotel in mindless panic.

Racked by convulsions, fits and starts, and shaking all over, the Prince's limp body slid down the steps – no more than fifteen – to the very bottom. Before five minutes had elapsed, he was spotted lying in a heap and a crowd had gathered. A large pool of blood around the head made people wonder if it was an accident or whether a crime had been committed. Before long, however, it was established that the cause was epilepsy, and a hotel waiter recognized the Prince as one of the recent arrivals. The whole unfortunate incident was finally resolved by a very lucky coincidence.

Kolya Ivolgin, who had promised to be at the Hotel Vesy by four o'clock but had gone to Pavlovsk instead, had left the General's Lady for some reason without staying for a meal and returned to St Petersburg to hurry off to the Vesy, where he arrived at about seven in the evening. Having read in the note left for him that the Prince was in town, he hastened to the address indicated. When he was informed that the Prince had gone out, Kolya went into the lounge and settled down to wait, drinking tea and listening to the mechanical barrel organ. When he heard about an accident he dashed off to investigate, urged on by a strong premonition, and recognized the Prince. All necessary measures were resorted to at once. The Prince was carried into his room; though he had come to, he was only partially conscious. A doctor who was called prescribed a poultice and stated that there was no danger whatever of concussion. When, after an hour, the Prince had more or less regained full consciousness, Kolya transported him in a carriage to Lebedev's. Lebedev welcomed the convalescent with open arms and deep bows. The trip to the dacha was expedited for his sake, and only three days later everyone was in Pavlovsk.

6

LEBEDEV'S DACHA WAS SMALL, but comfortable and even pretty. The section set aside for letting was especially attractively arranged. On the rather roomy terrace, at the entrance leading from the street to the interior, there was a collection of large, green wooden tubs with lemon and jasmine saplings, which were Lebedev's pride and joy. Some of these saplings came with the dacha, and he was so taken with the effect they produced on the terrace that he decided at the next convenient opportunity to buy a few more matching ones at an auction. On the day when all the tubs were finally delivered and arranged, Lebedev ran down the steps to the street many times in order to admire his property from a distance, each time mentally raising the rent he was going to charge his future tenants. As for the Prince, saddened, debilitated and physically affected as he was, the dacha was very welcome indeed. Incidentally, on the day of his departure for Pavlovsk – that is, three days after the attack – the Prince was almost completely recovered, to all outward appearances anyway, although inwardly he still felt unwell. He was glad to see all those who had been around him those three days: Kolya, who had hardly left him; the whole of Lebedev's family (not including the nephew, who had vanished somewhere); Lebedev himself. He was even delighted to see General Ivolgin, after the latter had called on him when they were still in town. Towards the end of the day of his arrival at Pavlovsk, quite a number of people had gathered around him on the terrace. First came Ganya, whom the Prince hardly recognized, such was the decline in his outer appearance in the intervening time. Then came Varya and Ptitsyn, also on holiday in Pavlovsk. As for General Ivolgin, he was almost a permanent fixture at Lebedev's townhouse, and in all probability came to the dacha along with the rest of the party. Lebedev kept a close eye on him and tried to keep him away from the Prince, but he treated him in a friendly enough manner and the two appeared to be long-standing acquaintances. The Prince noticed that during these three days they sometimes engaged in long conversations, occasionally raised their voices and apparently argued on learned topics, which must have given Lebedev a great deal of satisfaction. To look at them, one could easily have thought that Lebedev needed the General's company. But, ever since their move to the dacha, the same measures that Lebedev had adopted with the General regarding access to the Prince, he also put into practice with his own family. Under the pretext that the Prince ought not to be disturbed, he would not let anyone near him and stamped his feet. At the first suspicion that they were going out onto the terrace where the Prince was, he rushed around and stood in his daughters' way, making no exception for Vera and her child, and this despite all the Prince's pleas not to hold back anyone.

"First, there'll be a total loss of respect, if you let them have their way. And secondly it's not nice of them…" he explained in reply to the Prince's direct question.

"Why on earth not?" the Prince objected. "Really, all your care and solicitude just irritates me. I'm bored on my own, I've told you this several times, and all your waving of arms and tiptoeing about upsets me even more."

The Prince was implying that, although Lebedev was chasing away all and sundry under the pretext that they deprived the patient of his rest, he himself used every available opportunity during these three days to look in; first, he'd open the door, stick his head in, survey the room as if to assure himself that the Prince was still there, that he hadn't absconded, and then on tiptoe, slowly, stealthily approached the Prince's chair, such that at times he gave the occupant a fright. He would constantly enquire solicitously if there was anything he wanted, and when the Prince finally began to observe that he should be left in peace, Lebedev would quietly and obediently turn on his heel and make his way back to the door on tiptoe, at every step waving his arms about as though to show he had no ill purpose, that he would not utter another word, that he was already as good as gone and would not return – and yet, ten minutes later, quarter of an hour at the most, he'd be back again. Kolya, who had unimpeded access to the Prince, thereby earned Lebedev's displeasure, amounting to unmitigated resentment. Kolya had noticed that Lebedev was spending up to half an hour at a time skulking outside the door eavesdropping on their conversation, and of course he reported this to the Prince.

"You're keeping me under lock and key as though you've appropriated me," the Prince protested. "At least on holiday I'd like it to be different, and rest assured I shall see whomever I want and go wherever I want."

"Without the least shadow of a doubt," Lebedev returned, gesticulating lustily.

The Prince looked him over hard, from top to toe.

"Tell me, Lukyan Timofeyich, did you bring here with you that little cabinet that was fastened to the wall at the head of your bed?"

"No, I didn't."

"Are you telling me you left it there?"

"It couldn't be brought over, it's built into the wall... very solidly."

"Perhaps you've got a similar one here?"

"An even better one, yes sir, it came with the dacha."

"And who is it you didn't want to enter the room? An hour ago."

"That... would have been the General. Yes, I really didn't want him to see you, and he's no business to be here with you anyway. Prince, I respect the man deeply. He... is a remarkable man. You don't believe me? Well, there you are... all the same, my most esteemed Prince, it would be best if you didn't admit him into your presence."

"And why so, may I ask! And why, Lebedev, are you standing on tiptoe now? And why do you always approach me as though you wanted to whisper a secret in my ear?"

"My lowly nature, that's what it is, I feel it," Lebedev returned unexpectedly, and beat his breast demonstratively, "and I'm afraid the General's hospitality will be too much for you!"

"His hospitality too much for me! What are you on about?"

"He is too hospitable by half! First, he already wants to move in. That's as may be, but he is ever so enterprising and wants to be one of the family. We've been through it all several times in great detail and it turns out we are related. And yesterday he explained to me that you too are a distant cousin of his, twice removed on the maternal side. So, if you are a cousin of his, then you and I, most esteemed Prince, are kinsmen too. But we'll let that pass, it's a small detail, but just now he assured me that all his life, from the time he was a subaltern and right up to the eleventh of June last year, he never entertained fewer than two hundred guests at table. It had finally reached the point that people never left the table – they lunched, had tea and dined fifteen hours at a stretch for thirty years without let up, just a change of tablecloth and away they'd go again. One person gets up and goes, and another one comes to take his place. And on state commemorative days and royal jubilee occasions the numbers would reach three hundred. On Russia's Millennium celebrations* he counted seven hundred. That's simply awful! Such stories bode no good. One ought to think twice before inviting such hospitable gentlemen along. So I thought to myself he might be just too hospitable by half for the likes of you and me."

"But you two seem to be on very good terms, aren't you?"

"I look upon him as a brother and take it all as a joke. Why shouldn't we be kinsmen? It's no skin off my nose. Never mind the two hundred guests and Russia's Millennium celebrations, I know a great man when I see one. And that's the honest truth. You, Prince, mentioned secrets just now – how it's as though when I draw near I want to whisper a secret and, talking of secrets, we wouldn't be a million miles off target. It so happens, a certain person has let it be known that she'd very much like to have a secret meeting with you."

"Why a secret one? There's no need for secrecy. I'm going to call on her myself, today if necessary."

"Of course, there's no need for secrecy," Lebedev confirmed, waving his arms about. "And it's not what you think that's worrying her. Incidentally, the monster comes regularly every day to enquire after you, in case you didn't know."

"Funny, how you keep on calling him a monster all the time. It's very suspicious."

"There's no need for any suspicion, none whatsoever," Lebedev hastened to change the subject. "All I wanted to explain was that the person in question is afraid of something else – not him, but something else entirely."

"What then, hurry up and tell me!" the Prince insisted impatiently, observing Lebedev's mysterious antics.

"Therein lies the secret."

And Lebedev smirked.

"Whose secret?"

"Your secret. You yourself, most esteemed Prince, forbade me to speak in front of you…" Lebedev muttered and, taking great pleasure in the fact that he had brought his listener almost to exasperation, suddenly concluded, "She's afraid of Aglaya Ivanovna."

The Prince winced and hesitated for a while.

"Honestly, Lebedev, I'm going to pack my bags and leave this place," he said suddenly. "Where are Gavrila Ardalionovich and Ptitsyn? Here? You haven't stopped them too, have you?"

"They're coming, here they are. And the General is making up the rear. I'll fling open all the doors and call all my daughters, every single one, now, this minute," Lebedev mumbled softly in a fluster, dashing from door to door.

At this moment Kolya, having entered from the street, appeared on the terrace, and announced that he had visitors, Lizaveta Prokofyevna with her three daughters.

"To admit or not to admit in the Ptitsyns and Gavrila Ardalionovich? To admit or not to admit the General?" Lebedev hastened to enquire, all a-fluster at Kolya's announcement.

"Why on earth not?" the Prince asked with a laugh. "All who want to come are welcome! I assure you, Lebedev, you misunderstood my attitude to people badly from the very beginning. You seem to be labouring under some kind of a perpetual misapprehension. I've not the slightest reason to hide from or avoid anyone."

As they looked at each other, Lebedev too felt it incumbent upon him to burst out laughing. In spite of his excited state, he too seemed to be very pleased.

Kolya's announcement was quite accurate – he was just a few paces ahead of the Yepanchins, whom he had hurried along to announce. It happened then that visitors came in from two sides – the Yepanchins from the terrace, and Ptitsyn, Ganya and the General Ivolgin from the interior.

Just recently the Yepanchins had learnt from Kolya of the Prince's illness and that he was in Pavlovsk, whereas right up to then the General's Lady had been totally in the dark and felt much the worse for it. Only two days before, the General had handed his family members the Prince's visiting card; this card had the effect of assuring Lizaveta Prokofyevna beyond all shadow of a doubt that the Prince himself would hurry immediately to Pavlovsk to call on them. It was in vain that the young ladies tried to explain to her that a person who had not written for six months would perhaps not be so eager on this occasion and that he surely had enough to preoccupy him in St Petersburg to bother about them – his affairs were his own business! The General's Lady took such remarks decidedly in bad part and was ready to vouch that the Prince was bound to come the very next day, although even that would be late enough. When the following day came, she waited the whole morning; she expected the Prince for lunch, then for supper, and after it had already gone quite dark, Lizaveta Prokofyevna lost her self-possession completely and quarrelled with all and sundry – needless to say the Prince's name never came up once as being the root cause of her ill humour. There was not a word mentioned of him on the third day either. When Aglaya quite involuntarily remarked at dinner that *Maman* was in a temper because the Prince was staying away, to which the General immediately retorted that it had nothing to do with him, Lizaveta Prokofyevna got up and angrily left the table. Finally, by evening Kolya arrived bearing all the news with a full account of the Prince's misadventures as he knew them. As a result Lizaveta Prokofyevna was triumphant, but Kolya received a thorough dressing down: "He's been around for days, impossible to get rid of, but when it comes to it, he's nowhere to be seen. He could at least have sent us some news, never mind putting in a personal appearance!" Kolya was on the point of taking umbrage for the expression "impossible to get rid of", but decided to wait for another occasion, and had the reprimand been a little less offensive, he'd have thought nothing of it at all – such was his delight at Lizaveta Prokofyevna's solicitude for the Prince. She insisted on sending a courier immediately to St Petersburg to bring back by the first available train some eminent physician. But her daughters talked her out of it; all the same, they did not want to stay behind when their mother suddenly got ready and announced she was going to pay the patient a visit.

"There he is on his deathbed," Lizaveta Prokofyevna concluded in a state of unrest, "and we stand here on ceremony? Is he a family friend or not?"

"But it's hardly the done thing to foist ourselves upon him so either," Aglaya remarked under her breath.

"Well then, there's no need for you to come, you're welcome to stay behind, young lady. At least there'll be someone to see Yevgeny Pavlovich in, when he arrives."

After these words Aglaya immediately joined the others – which, of course, she had every intention of doing anyway. Prince S., who happened to be with Adelaida at the time, at her request readily agreed to accompany the ladies. He had quite early on, at the very start of his friendship with the Yepanchins, betrayed an intense interest when he heard about Prince Myshkin from them. It turned out he knew him, that they had met quite recently and spent a fortnight together in a little town somewhere. This had happened about three months previously. Prince S. had a great deal to say about his new friend and spoke of him very warmly, such that now he was genuinely pleased to have an opportunity to see him. General Ivan Fyodorovich was out at the time and Yevgeny Pavlovich had not yet arrived.

The Yepanchins' dacha was no more than three hundred paces away from Lebedev's. The first thing that thoroughly upset Lizaveta Prokofyevna was to find the Prince surrounded by a whole crowd of visitors, not to mention the fact that amongst them were two or three whom she hated with all her might; secondly, it was the shock of seeing a perfectly healthy, foppishly dressed and merrily laughing young man coming forward to great her, instead of beholding someone dying on his deathbed, which is what she had expected. She fairly froze in dismay, to Kolya's unspeakable delight, who of course could well have explained before they had even stirred from their dacha that no one was dying and that there was no deathbed; but he had not, mischievously and gleefully anticipating the General's Lady's anger when she, according to his surmises, would lose her temper on finding the Prince, her true darling, in rude health. Kolya was even indiscreet enough to voice his surmise out loud with the express intention of teasing Lizaveta Prokofyevna the more, as part of their mutual war of words, testifying incidentally to their deep friendship.

"Have a heart, my dear fellow, don't go too far," Lizaveta Prokofyevna parried as she took her seat in the chair offered by the Prince.

Lebedev, Ptitsyn and General Ivolgin rushed to offer seats to the young ladies. The General brought a chair for Aglaya. Lebedev picked one up for Prince S. too, contriving at the same time even in the arching of his back to convey an extra degree of deference. Varya, as usual, rushed straight over to the young ladies in a gush of excited whispering.

"It's true, my Prince, that I fully expected to find you laid up in bed, such was the extent of my exaggerated alarm and, I must be honest with you, your happy face irritated me no end just now, but I swear to you it was only for a second, while I was still gathering my wits about me. It's only when I've my wits about me that I act and talk sense, which I think would apply to you equally. But in truth, the recovery of my own son, if I had one, would not have brought me more joy than yours has, and if you refuse to believe me, it's your loss, not mine. But this spiteful boy thinks he can get away with far too much. I heard he's your protégé. So, let me warn you, one fine morning I may well decline myself the pleasure of having anything more to do with him."

"So what have I done?" Kolya protested. "However hard I'd have tried to assure you that the Prince was all right, you wouldn't have believed me, because to picture him on his deathbed is far more exciting."

"Have you come down here for long?" Lizaveta Prokofyevna asked the Prince.

"For the whole summer, and maybe even longer."

"You're on your own here, are you not? Not married, are you?"

"No, I'm not," the Prince returned, smiling at the naivety of her pointed question.

"No need to smile, anything can happen. I was thinking of the dacha. Why aren't you staying with us? We've a whole wing empty. Still, it's up to you. Are you renting it from him? That one?" she added in a low voice, motioning with her head towards Lebedev. "Why doesn't he keep still?"

At this moment Vera emerged on the terrace from the house with the infant in her arms, as was her wont. Lebedev, who was darting about between the chairs, totally at a loss what to do with himself, but wishing to be part of the action, went for Vera hammer and tongs, began to wave his arms about and, forgetting himself, even stamped his feet at her.

"Is he mad?" the General's Lady asked.

"No, he's—"

"Drunk, perhaps? I don't like the company you keep one little bit," she cut him off, taking in the rest of the group with her eyes. "Oh, but what a lovely young girl! Who is she?"

"This is Vera Lukyanovna, daughter to this same Lebedev."

"Really!... How sweet. I should like to get to know her."

But Lebedev, who had overheard Lizaveta Prokofyevna's praises, was already dragging his daughter behind him in order to introduce her.

"Poor, motherless mites!" he whined ingratiatingly. "And this babe in her arms is motherless too – she's her sister, Lyubov, born in the most legitimate wedlock of the newly deceased Yelena, my wife, who passed away six weeks ago, in childbirth, as pleased Almighty God... yes, ma'am... now she's taking the place of the mother, although she's just a sister and never more than a sister... never, never more—"

"And you, my dear sir, are never more than just a fool, pardon my saying so!" Lizaveta Prokofyevna suddenly cut him off in a burst of extraordinary indignation. "Well, that'll do, I'm sure you know what I mean."

"You are so right, ma'am!" Lebedev responded with the utmost deference and a low bow.

"I say, Mr Lebedev," Aglaya asked, "is it true what they say about you interpreting the Apocalypse?"

"True in every respect... I've been at it now nearly fifteen years."

"I've heard of you. There was something in the papers about you, if I'm not mistaken?"

"No, that was about a different interpreter, it was someone else," Lebedev spoke, beside himself with delight. "He died, and I took his place."

"Could you do me a favour as a neighbour and come and explain the Apocalypse to me? I can make nothing of it."

"I cannot help warning you, Aglaya Ivanovna, that this is complete humbug coming from him, believe me," General Ivolgin suddenly cut in. He had been on tenterhooks all this time, dying to take part in the conversation, seated as he was next to Aglaya Ivanovna. "Of course, this is in the spirit and tradition of holiday-making," he went on, "and having an awful impostor like him interpret the Apocalypse is, no doubt an idea like any other, extremely worthy in its concept, all the same I... It seems to me, I read dismay in your eyes the way you look at me! General Ivolgin, your humble servant. I held you in my arms when you were a child, Aglaya Ivanovna."

"I'm very glad to hear it," Aglaya muttered, trying with all her might not to burst out laughing. "I know Varvara Ardalionovna and Nina Alexandrovna."

Lizaveta Prokofyevna flared up. Something that had long been building up inside her suddenly required an outlet. She could not abide General Ivolgin, whom she had known at one time, but a very long way back.

"You're fibbing, my dear sir, as you are always in the habit of doing, you've never held her in your arms," she replied with indignation.

"You forget, *Maman*, honestly, he did – in Tver," Aglaya suddenly confirmed. "We lived in Tver at the time. I was about six then, I remember. He made me a bow and arrow, and taught me how to shoot, I killed a pigeon with it. Do you remember, we killed a pigeon together?"

"And I got a cardboard helmet and a wooden sword. I remember all that!" Adelaida exclaimed.

"I remember it too," Alexandra confirmed. "You quarrelled over the wounded pigeon, and as a punishment you all had to stand in separate corners of the room. Adelaida stood as she was in the helmet, sword in hand."

The General, in declaring that he had carried Aglaya in his arms, had said it without giving it any thought, merely because he always started a conversation with young people that way whenever he wanted to get to know them. But on this occasion, he happened to have hit upon a true event and as bad luck would have it, this truth had slipped his own memory. But when Aglaya brought up the incident with the pigeon, memories came flooding back, and he remembered everything in minute detail as elderly people are wont to when it comes to matters from the distant past. It is difficult to establish what it was precisely in this story that had so touched this wretched and by and large permanently inebriated old man, but all at once he was deeply affected.

"I remember, I remember it all!" he exclaimed. "I was a subaltern then. You were such a delightful poppet, a sight for sore eyes. Nina Alexandrovna… Ganya… I was welcome in your house. Ivan Fyodorovich—"

"And just look at yourself now!" the General's Lady cut him short. "I'm glad to say there's still some good left in you in spite of all your effort to drown it in drink! You've been the death of your wife. Instead of guiding your children, you've been locked up in a debtors' prison. Get along with you, my good man, and think of your days of innocence, the Lord may yet take pity on you. Go, get along with you, I'm being perfectly serious. Nothing redeems better than contrite memories."

But there was no need to say any more, her earnest words had struck home; the General, like all permanently inebriated men, was very sensitive and, having fallen upon hard times, like all habitual tipplers, he found happy memories from the past difficult to put up with. He rose from his seat and obediently headed for the door, which immediately evoked pity in Lizaveta Prokofyevna's heart.

"Ardalion Alexandrovich, my dear!" she called after him, "stay a while. None of us is free from sin. When you'll see that your conscience is bringing out a little of the good in you, be sure to come and see me for a chinwag about our dim and distant past. I myself may well be fifty times more culpable than you. Well, God be with you for now, keep going, there's nothing for you to do here now…" she suddenly added, afraid that he might change his mind and stay behind.

"I don't think it would be a good idea for you to follow him just yet," the Prince said to Kolya, who was about to run after his father. "Otherwise he may well have a change of mood, and turn on you."

"That's true, let him be. Perhaps in half an hour's time," Lizaveta Prokofyevna decided.

"What it is just once in your life to grasp the truth! It moved him to tears," Lebedev felt emboldened to remark.

"You're a right one to talk, my good man, if what I heard about you is remotely true," Lizaveta Prokofyevna immediately cut him to size.

The mutual relationships between the various visitors who had come to see the Prince were soon established. Naturally the Prince took pains to express to the General's Lady and her daughters the full extent of his appreciation of their solicitude for him and, of course, assure them sincerely that even prior to their arrival, he had fully intended to call on them, never mind his indisposition or the lateness of the hour. To which Lizaveta Prokofyevna, while surveying the visitors, replied that this could be acted upon even now. Ptitsyn, a man of superior manners and extremely easy temperament, very soon got up and headed for the outlying wing of the house, giving every indication that he wished Lebedev to follow him. The latter promised to come soon; Varya in the meantime fell into conversation with the young ladies and stayed behind. She and Ganya were rather glad to see the back of the General; Ganya himself soon went to join Ptitsyn. During those few minutes while he was on the terrace in the presence of the Yepanchins, he had maintained an unobtrusive, dignified presence and refused to be ruffled when Lizaveta Prokofyevna measured him sternly with her eyes twice from top to toe. Those who knew him from before could well have thought that he had changed a great deal. Aglaya found this most attractive.

"I say, wasn't that Gavrila Ardalionovich, who's just left the room?" she asked suddenly, as was her wont, loudly, sharply, cutting across other people's conversation and yet addressing no one in particular.

"Yes it was him," the Prince replied.

"I hardly recognized him. He has changed a great deal and... very much for the better," Aglaya said.

"I'm very glad for his sake," the Prince said.

"He was very ill," Varya added with joyful concern.

"How has he changed for the better?" Lizaveta Prokofyevna asked in angry consternation bordering on fear. "What makes you say that? There's nothing better about him. What precisely do you regard as being better?"

"There's nothing better than 'The Hapless Knight'!" Kolya, who had all this time been standing by Lizaveta Prokofyevna's chair, suddenly announced.

"I am of a like mind myself," Prince S. said and burst out laughing.

"And I too couldn't agree more," Adelaida pronounced solemnly.

"What 'Hapless Knight'?" the General's Lady asked, surveying all the speakers in baffled puzzlement; but, seeing that Aglaya's cheeks had flushed, she added resentfully, "Sheer nonsense, I'm sure! What 'Hapless Knight' are you on about?"

"It won't be the first time," Aglaya replied with haughty indignation, "that this stripling, your pet, has made a hash of other people's words."

Behind every one of Aglaya's angry outbursts (she was often given to angry outbursts), despite all her apparent seriousness and self-assurance, there lurked so much that was childish, girlishly excitable and spontaneous that, looking at her, it was impossible, to her great chagrin, not to laugh at her, the more so as she betrayed no understanding of why people laughed and was irritated that they should dare to do so. Her sisters started to laugh too, and so did Prince S.; even Lev Nikolayevich could not repress a smile. Kolya triumphed and was beside himself with laughter. Aglaya was simply incensed with anger and looked twice as pretty. Her embarrassment, augmented by her irritation with herself, became her very much.

"The number of times he's played fast and loose with your words," she added.

"I've got your own words to prove it!" Kolya called out. "A month ago you were going through *Don Quixote* and exclaimed that there's nothing better than 'The Hapless Knight'. I've no idea whom you had in mind then, Don Quixote or Yevgeny Pavlovich, or some other person, but there was someone, and you talked at length—"

"I see you, my dear, go too far with your surmises," Lizaveta Prokofyevna cut him short with a sad mien.

"As if I was the only one!" Kolya returned, refusing to be cowed. "It was common talk then, it still is. There, Prince S., and Adelaida Ivanovna, and the rest have declared they're for 'The Hapless Knight', it follows then that 'The Hapless Knight' does exist and, to my mind, if only it hadn't been for Adelaida Ivanovna, we'd all have known long ago who this 'Hapless Knight' really is."

"So what has it got to do with me?" Adelaida asked, laughing.

"You didn't want to paint the portrait – that's what it's got to do with you! Aglaya Ivanovna asked you to paint 'The Hapless Knight' and even described the whole subject to you, which she herself had devised, you remember the subject, don't you? But you didn't want—"

"But how could I have painted him, whom precisely? According to the tale:

The hapless knight
His steely visor never raised.

What face was I to paint? A steel grill? A mask?"

"This is all beyond me, what steely visor?" the General's Lady vented her irritation, and it slowly began to dawn on her who was meant (and probably long agreed upon) by 'The Hapless Knight'. But she was particularly incensed that Prince Lev Nikolayevich himself also appeared to be put out, like a ten-year-old. "Is there no end to this stupid prank? Will someone explain to me who is this 'Hapless Knight'? Is this some secret, some dreadful mystery, that cannot even be mentioned?"

But everyone just continued laughing.

"It's simply that there is a strange Russian poem," Prince S. suddenly intervened, by all appearances wishing to put an end to the matter and change the subject, "about a 'Hapless Knight', a fragment that has no beginning or end. After dinner about a month ago everybody laughed and mused, as we have been wont to do, what would be a good subject for Adelaida Ivanovna's future picture. You know well that it has long been a matter of family debate what subject for painting to suggest to Adelaida Ivanovna. It was thus that we stumbled upon 'The Hapless Knight'. I forget now who was the first to bring it up—"

"Aglaya Ivanovna!" Kolya exclaimed.

"Perhaps. I can't remember," Prince S. continued. "Some thought the idea hilarious, others held that nothing could be more elevated, but in order to depict 'The Hapless Knight', there had to be a face. We went through all the people we knew, but no one fitted, and the matter was laid to rest. That's all there is to it. I can't think why Nikolai Ardalionovich decided to bring the matter up again and make such a fuss. What was once amusing and witty, is now very much passé."

"Because some silly frolic is being planned anew, nasty and vicious," Lizaveta Prokofyevna parried.

"Nothing of the sort, except the deepest respect," Aglaya, who in the meantime had been able completely to overcome and suppress her former embarrassment, responded quite unexpectedly in a solemn and grave tone of voice. Indeed, judging by some indications, one could well form the impression that she was well pleased that the joke was gathering pace, and that the turnabout in her had happened precisely at the instant when the Prince's own mounting confusion had become all too evident and had reached its peak.

"First they split their sides laughing, and then it's suddenly deepest respect! This is madness! Why respect? Be so good as to tell me why, for no reason whatever, you're suddenly full of the deepest respect?"

"Deepest respect," Aglaya continued with the same gravity and solemnity in response to her mother's well-nigh inimical question, "because this poem clearly depicts a man capable of conviction and, secondly, having formed this conviction, able to put his trust in it, and having put his trust in it, blindly to devote his whole life to it. This rarely happens in our day and age. In the poem, to be sure, it is not made clear what was the nature of the Hapless Knight's conviction, but it is clear it was some beatific vision, 'vision of unbounded beauty', and the enamoured knight had twined a rosary instead of a kerchief round his neck. True, there is a puzzling, unexplained device, the letters A.N.B., which he had scrawled on his shield—"

"A.N.D.—" Kolya corrected.

"And I say A.N.B., and will not have it otherwise," Aglaya interrupted him in a temper. "Be that as it may, it is quite clear that it had become all one to this hapless knight, who this lady of his might have been or what she might have got up to. Suffice it to say that he had chosen her and put his faith in her 'untainted beauty', and had then gone on to bow down to her for ever more, his glory being that even if she were subsequently declared a felon, he would still have had to break a lance for her. The poet evidently strove to incorporate into one magnificent representation of some unblemished knight errant, the entire grandiose concept of chivalrous platonic love of the Middle Ages – needless to say, in terms of an ideal. In 'The Hapless Knight' this tendency reached its peak – asceticism. One cannot deny that the ability to harbour such a sentiment presupposes a truly sterling character, and this is by no means to draw too close a comparison with Don Quixote. On the other hand, 'The Hapless Knight' is a Don Quixote, but a serious, not a comical one. At first I failed to understand him and I sneered at him, but now I love the Hapless Knight and, most of all, I respect him for his chivalry and valour."

Aglaya stopped, and one would have been hard put to determine whether she was serious or not.

"He and his feats are pure poppycock, I tell you," the General's Lady decreed. "As for you, my child, you went well over the top, fancy reading us a whole lecture! It doesn't become you, if you want to know my opinion. And you oughtn't indulge yourself. What poem is it? Don't pretend you don't know! I insist you tell me. Couldn't stand poetry all my life, something about it. For goodness' sake, Prince, bear with me a little, it's our common lot, it would seem, to suffer," she concluded, turning to Prince Lev Nikolayevich. She was well and truly upset.

Prince Lev Nikolayevich wanted to say something, but in his embarrassment was unable to utter a single word. Only Aglaya, who had given herself such free rein in her "lecture", preserved her equanimity, even to the point of enjoyment. She got up at once, with the same serious and solemn demeanour as before, and looking as though she had been long preparing herself for this and was only waiting for the word, stepped out on to the terrace and stood facing the Prince, who was still sitting in his chair. Everyone regarded her with a measure of surprise, and they all, Prince S., her sisters and her mother, anticipated some kind of a newly hatched prank to cap all the rest. But it was clear that Aglaya enjoyed the sheer thrill of the build-up she had created for the opening of her rendition of the poem. Lizaveta Prokofyevna nearly shooed her back to her place, but just at the moment when Aglaya was about to begin declaiming the famous ballad, when two new visitors, talking loudly, entered the terrace from the street. It turned out to be General Ivan Fyodorovich Yepanchin, accompanied by a young man. A minor commotion ensued.

7

THE YOUNG MAN ACCOMPANYING THE GENERAL was about twenty-eight, tall, slim, with a handsome, intelligent face and a pair of large dark eyes, sparkling with vivacity and mischievous humour. Aglaya did not even look at him, but carried on declaiming the poem, looking at and addressing the Prince alone. The Prince realized that she was doing all this according to some deliberate, prearranged plan. It must be said, however, the new arrivals alleviated his awkward position somewhat. As soon as he saw them, he got up, nodded courteously at the General and indicated that the declamation was not to be interrupted; at the same time he positioned himself behind his chair and, with his elbow propped on the backrest, continued to listen to the ballad in greater comfort, and certainly feeling less exposed than he was when seated. For her part, Lizaveta Prokofyevna motioned twice to the visitors not to come any further.

The Prince was particularly interested in the new visitor; he immediately recognized him as Yevgeny Pavlovich Radomsky, of whom he had heard and thought about a great deal. He knew him to be a military man, and the civilian clothes he wore baffled the Prince a little. A derisive smile played about the visitor's lips as though he too had already heard something about 'The Hapless Knight'.

"Perhaps it was his idea in the first place, anyway," the Prince mused.

But in Aglaya there was a change. In place of the erstwhile affectation and pomposity with which she had stepped forward to declaim, she betrayed so much sincerity and so much insight and deep understanding of the spirit and sense of the poetic composition; she enunciated every word of the poem with such appreciation of its qualities, with such sublime simplicity, that at the conclusion of the performance she not only conquered everybody's hearts, but in conveying the uplifting tone of the ballad the way she did, somehow managed to make up for the exaggerated and forced gravity with which she so boldly strode out into the centre of the terrace in the first place. It was now her intuitive, and perhaps all too naive, awe in the face of what she had undertaken to convey, that was to the fore. Her eyes sparkled, and a slight, barely perceptible ripple of inspiration and exultation flitted across her wonderful features. She read:

Once there was a hapless knight,*
Taciturn, withdrawn,
Pale of visage, in behaviour stern,
Bold in spirit, generous in thought.

Lo, he had a vision
Fathomless and bold
Branding an impression,
Deep into his soul.

From that moment on, seared to the quick,
Women he abjured.
Not a word with any
Till his grave he vowed to speak.

Round his neck a string of beads
As a talisman he wound,
And behind a steely visor's grid
His face forever hid.

Brimming with unselfish love,
Faithful to a beatific vision
A.M.D.* in blood
On his shield he writ.

In the deserts of the East,
Scaling rocks and dunes surmounting,
Every Paladin into battle charged
His lady's name pronouncing:

Lumen cœli, sancta Rosa!
Was the hapless warrior's cry
And, like a thunderbolt from high,
Into battle he did fly.

On returning to his castle keep,
He survived in strict seclusion
Always silent, always stern,
Thus his lonely days drew to a mad conclusion.

When recollecting the whole of this episode subsequently, the Prince for the life of him could not get over one puzzling question, how it was that one could use such a truly wonderful sentiment as a vehicle for such a blatantly malicious joke. That it was malicious, there was not a shadow of a doubt: during the recitation, Aglaya had substituted the letters N.F.B. for A.M.D. He had not misheard it; there was no room for doubt, it was deliberate (this was actually proved later). At all events, Aglaya's little jape – meant as a joke, however vicious and thoughtless

NASTASYA

– was premeditated. 'The Hapless Knight' had been a standing joke on everyone's lips for over a month. And yet, try as hard as he could, the Prince, when he recalled the circumstances, could not but own that Aglaya had pronounced these letters not only without any attempt at irony or mockery, or even any undue stress such as to bring out their latent meaning all the more, but on the contrary had articulated them with such seriousness, such naive and innocent simplicity, that one could easily have believed these same letters were in the ballad and that that is how it was printed on the page. This realization struck the Prince with unbearably painful and unpleasant force. Lizaveta Prokofyevna, of course, noticed neither the difference in the letters, nor the implication thereof. General Ivan Fyodorovich saw nothing in it either beyond the mere fact that a recitation had taken place. Quite a number of the other listeners had understood and were astonished at the boldness and purposefulness of the joke, but had decided not to let on and remained silent. Yevgeny Pavlovich (the Prince would have been ready to vouch for this) was one of those who not only understood, but tried to indicate as much; his derisive smile was an all too evident giveaway.

"What a delight!" the General's Lady exulted as soon as the recitation came to an end. "Who's the author?"

"Pushkin, *Maman*, don't make us blush, this is most unfair!" Adelaida exclaimed.

"With you lot around who can possibly keep a sane head!" Lizaveta Prokofyevna returned bitterly. "For shame! As soon as we get back, I want you to show me this poem of Pushkin's!"

"I don't think we have any Pushkin in the house at all."

"It's been ages," Alexandra intervened, "but I do remember we had a couple of tatty old volumes lying about somewhere."

"Send someone into town at once to buy a copy, Fyodor or Alexei, by the next train – better Alexei. Aglaya, come here! Give me a kiss, you recited wonderfully well; but if it was sincerely spoken," she added almost in a whisper, "I pity you. If you did it to make fun of him, I don't approve of your sentiments, in fact in that case it would have been better not to have read it at all. Do you follow me? Go now, my dear, I shall speak to you about this later. It's high time we went."

In the meantime the Prince was saying hello to General Ivan Fyodorovich, who in turn was introducing Yevgeny Pavlovich Radomsky to him.

"I ran into him on the way from town, we were on the same train. When he found out that I was heading here and everyone else—"

"—including you were here," Yevgeny Pavlovich interrupted him, "and since it had always been my intention not only to get to know you, but seek your friendship, I decided on the spur of the moment not to lose an opportunity. You're not well? I only now discovered—"

"I couldn't be healthier and am delighted to meet you," Lev Nikolayevich replied, holding out his hand, "I heard lots about you and I even talked about you with Prince S."

After the exchange of mutual cordialities, they shook hands and looked hard into each other's eyes. In a trice everybody joined in the conversation. The Prince noticed (he was now in the habit of noticing everything everywhere, to the point of including things that perhaps did not even exist), that the civilian clothes worn by Yevgeny Pavlovich were causing a general and unusually intense surprise, so much so that everything else was for a time obscured and pushed into the background. One had the impression that in this change of apparel there was something unusually significant. Adelaida and Alexandra showered Yevgeny Pavlovich with questions. Prince S., who was a relation of his, spoke with extreme concern; the General was highly perturbed. Aglaya alone, after looking at him with a measure of curiosity as if to establish whether civilian clothes or uniform suited him best, turned her back on him and ignored him completely. Lizaveta Prokofyevna also did not wish to enquire about anything, even though she too may have been a little on edge. The Prince had the feeling that Yevgeny Pavlovich was in her bad books.

"I was surprised, I was astonished!" Ivan Fyodorovich kept on in reply to all the questions. "I didn't want to believe it when I ran into him back in St Petersburg. And why the rush, that's what I'm still asking myself? He's the first one, when you ask him, to caution against getting carried away..."

From the ensuing talk it transpired that Yevgeny Pavlovich had been announcing his resignation for a long time past; but on every occasion he had been so flippant that it was difficult to take him seriously. As a matter of fact, flippancy was his outstanding characteristic even when talking on the most serious topics, so that it was difficult to make out what he really meant, especially as the confusion he engendered was deliberate.

"It's temporary, I plan to spend only a few months, a year at the most, on leave," Radomsky observed with a laugh.

"But what need is there, at least from what I know of your affairs?" the General persisted.

"What about doing the rounds of all the property? On your advice, I hasten to add. And then I want to make a trip abroad..."

But the conversation soon changed. However, what struck the Prince, as the all too unusual and unceasing agitation continued to progress unabated well beyond the norm, was that there was probably something quite out of the ordinary behind all this.

"So 'The Hapless Knight' is centre stage again?" Yevgeny Pavlovich asked, approaching Aglaya.

To the Prince's amazement she measured him with a baffled and probing look as though to indicate that there could not even be a question of a discussion between the two of them about 'The Hapless Knight", and that she was utterly amazed he should so much as have raised the matter.

"It's too late to send to town for Pushkin, too late!" Kolya, at his wit's end, argued with Lizaveta Prokofyevna. "How many times do I have to tell you – too late!"

"Yes, I must say, it is too late to send to town," Yevgeny Pavlovich, anxious to get away from Aglaya, observed, sidling up to the two of them. "I think the shops must be shut in St Petersburg by now, it's gone eight," he confirmed, taking out his pocket watch.

"We've managed without Pushkin all this time, we could wait till tomorrow," Adelaida intervened.

"Besides, it's unseemly," Kolya added, "for well-placed people to show too great an interest in literature. Ask Yevgeny Pavlovich. A yellow charabanc with red wheels is far more up their street."

"You just can't help quoting from a book, Kolya," Adelaida remarked.

"He's turned it into a fine art," Yevgeny Pavlovich, quick off the mark, chipped in. "He will quote whole chunks from critical reviews at you. I've the pleasure of being familiar with Nikolai Ardalionovich's manner of speaking for some considerable time now. Nikolai Ardalionovich has made a direct reference to my yellow charabanc with the red wheels. The only trouble is, I've already exchanged it, you are a little too late."

The Prince listened carefully to what Radomsky had to say. He concluded that the latter's manners were impeccable – reserved, easy, and what particularly appealed to him was that Radomsky addressed the slightly provocative Kolya in all friendliness and quite as an equal.

"What is that, pray?" Lizaveta Prokofyevna turned to Vera, Lebedev's daughter, who was standing before her with several large format books in her hands, splendidly bound and almost brand new.

"Pushkin," Vera said. "Our Pushkin. Papa told me to present them to you."

"Well, I never! How am I meant to take it?" Lizaveta Prokofyevna asked in surprise.

"Not as a present, not as a present! I wouldn't have had the effrontery!" Lebedev exclaimed, popping up from behind his daughter's shoulder. "You may have it at cost price. This is our very own family copy of Pushkin, published by Annenkov, which is a rarity now – at cost price. I'm offering it for sale with the utmost respect so as to satisfy the worthy fervour of your worthiness's literary aspirations."

"If you're selling it, then thank you. I dare say, you won't be the loser. Only stop playing the fool, please, my good man. I've heard about you, they say you're uncommonly well read. We'll talk about it some time. Are you going to deliver them to me in person?"

"With deference and... respect!" Lebedev continued his tomfoolery, well pleased with the way things were going, and snatching the books out of his daughter's hands.

"Yes, but make sure you don't lose them along the way, respect or no respect. Only let it be clearly understood," she added, looking hard at him, "that I'll only let you as far as the door, because I've no intention of receiving you today. As for your daughter Vera, you may send her along any time, I'm very fond of her."

"Why won't you say anything about those people?" Vera addressed her father with impatience. "Else they might come in of their own accord. They've already started getting boisterous. Lev Nikolayevich," she turned to the Prince, who had already picked up his hat, "there are some people who've long been wanting to see you, four of them, they're waiting and making a fuss, but Daddy won't let them through."

"Who are they?" the Prince asked.

"They say they're on business, but they're the sort that if you don't see them now, they'll waylay you on the road. It's best you saw them now, Lev Nikolayevich, and have done with it. Gavrila Ardalionovich and Ptitsyn are trying to reason with them right now, but they won't hear of it."

"It's Pavlishchev's son! It's Pavlishchev's son! He's not worth it, he's not!" Lebedev vociferated, waving with his arms. "They're not worth listening to, and you shouldn't trouble yourself about them, my esteemed Prince. I assure you. They're just not worth it—"

"Pavlishchev's son! Good God!" the Prince exclaimed, utterly at a loss. "I know... but I... I had asked Gavrila Ardalionovich to deal with this matter. Gavrila Ardalionovich spoke to me just now..."

But Gavrila Ardalionovich had already stepped out on to the terrace; Ptitsyn followed him. From the adjoining room came General Ivolgin's stentorian voice, rising above the other voices and surrounding noise.

"This is highly interesting," Yevgeny Pavlovich remarked out loud.

"Here is one who knows what is afoot!" the Prince thought to himself.

"What Pavlishchev's son? And... where does Pavlishchev's son come into all this?" General Ivan Fyodorovich kept enquiring as he cast for clues in the surrounding faces and, to his surprise, was obliged to admit that he was the only person not au fait with this new development.

There was overall excitement and expectation. The Prince was truly surprised that such a completely personal matter of his could have attracted everybody's attention in this way.

"It would be altogether for the best if you yourself were to settle this matter here and now," Aglaya said, addressing the Prince in a particularly confidential tone of voice, "and allowed the rest of us to be your witnesses. There's an attempt to denigrate you, Prince. It's up to you to stand up for yourself vigorously, and I'm very pleased to support you in advance."

"I too wish that this sordid business were ended!" the General's Lady exclaimed. "Give them a piece of your mind, Prince! I've just about had enough on this score, and I've lost a lot of sleep over you. Besides, I'm dying with curiosity. Let them all come in, and we'll sit and watch. Aglaya's right. Have you heard anything of this, Prince?" she asked, turning to Prince S.

"Of course I have, at your house as a matter of fact," Prince S. replied. "I'm particularly keen to see what these young men are all about."

"They're nihilists, I take it?"

"No, not quite," Lebedev said, stepping forward, also bursting with excitement, "these are different, they're special, my nephew tells me, they've gone further than the nihilists. You're mistaken if you think you can cow them by your presence, Your Excellency. They're not to be cowed. The nihilists are sometimes a knowledgeable bunch, perhaps even learned, but this lot have gone further, because first and foremost they mean business. They're, so to speak, the second generation of nihilists, but not in the direct sense, rather in a roundabout way and by hearsay, and they won't choose to reveal themselves in some newspaper article or other, but directly in the field, so to speak. Nor will they go on about some absurdity in Pushkin or whoever, nor for instance the inevitability of the break up of Mother Russia into its constituent parts. No, this lot is about getting what they want, and nothing will stand in their way, even if it meant doing away with some eight people or so at a stroke. No, really, Prince, I'd think twice if I were you…"

But the Prince had already got up to open the door for the visitors.

"You're being unfair, Lebedev," he said with a smile, "you've been listening to your nephew too much. Pay no attention to him, Lizaveta Prokofyevna. I assure you, Gorsky and Danilov* are the exceptions, these are just… misguided individuals. The only thing is, I wouldn't like it all to come out here in front of everybody. With your permission, Lizaveta Prokofyevna, I'll let them come in so that you can have a look at them, and then I'll ask them to leave. This way, gentlemen, please!"

What worried him was another disturbing thought. He was troubled in case all this was stage-managed by someone and timed to take place precisely now in front of all these witnesses, in order to exhibit him in a bad light. But he was sick to death about what seemed to him was his monstrous and malicious alarmism. He thought he'd rather die than have anybody find out he ever harboured such thoughts, and as his new visitors were entering the room, he was genuinely ready to concede that his moral standing was the lowest of all those present in the room.

Five people entered, four of them new guests, with the rear made up by General Ivolgin; he was in a heightened emotional state and very effusive. "This one would never let me down!" the Prince mused with a smile. Kolya slipped through together with the rest. He was deeply immersed in conversation with Ippolit, who was one of the party. Ippolit listened and smiled.

The Prince saw to it that everyone was seated. They were all so young, hardly of age, that one inevitably wondered what all the fuss was about. Ivan Fyodorovich Yepanchin, for instance, who knew and understood nothing of what was going on as he surveyed all the youngsters, would probably have had some adverse comment to make if he had not been held back by the sight of his spouse's all too close concern for the Prince's private interests. It must be said that he had stayed behind partly out of curiosity and also out of a desire to lend a helping hand if necessary, or in any case to lend the weight of his authority to the proceedings, but General Ivolgin's bowing to him across the room again threw him into turmoil; he knitted his brows and decided on maintaining an obstinate silence.

Amongst the young foursome there was, however, one of about thirty, the retired staff captain from Rogozhin's former party, the pugilist, who could as easily as not pull out from his pocket fifteen roubles for the first beggar he encountered. By all indications he was accompanying the rest to lend them courage and, if need be, protection. The lead role undoubtedly belonged to him who was styled Pavlishchev's son, even though he answered to the name of Antip Burdovsky. He was a young man, poorly and slovenly dressed – in a frock coat that was incredibly greasy at the elbows and a grimy waistcoat buttoned up to the top with no evidence of a shirt underneath. He sported a dirty black silk scarf that more resembled a rope wound round his neck, had unwashed hands, fair hair, and if one may put it that way, displayed a naively arrogant look on his extremely blotchy face. He was not small in stature, wiry and about twenty-two years old. There was not a vestige of intellect or wit evident in his features; quite the contrary, they exuded a blind smugness and at the same time an ever-present sense of wounded dignity. His manner of speaking was agitated, hurried and uneven, words were left unfinished as though he suffered from a speech impediment, or was a foreigner, whereas he was in fact of pure Russian descent.

His two accomplices were Lebedev's nephew and Ippolit. Ippolit was the youngest, about seventeen, perhaps eighteen, with an intelligent, but permanently nerve-racked face on which illness had left terrible marks. He was as thin as a rake, with a pale yellowish complexion, his eyes shone, and his cheeks glowed with two red spots. He coughed incessantly; his every word, indeed his every breath, was followed by wheezing. This was consumption in its galloping stages. It would seem he had no more than about two or three weeks left to live. He was very tired and was the first to lower himself into a chair. The rest of the party on entering seemed a little lost almost to the point of being nonplussed. However, they managed to put on a show apparently for fear of loss of face that would have severely undermined their reputation as firebrands who had turned their backs on all social niceties, in fact on nearly everything in the world, except their own interests.

"Antip-p Bu-Burdovsky!" Pavlishchev's son introduced himself, somehow inappropriately quick off the mark, and tripping over his words awkwardly.

"Vladimir Doktorenko!" Lebedev's nephew pronounced distinctly and as though inordinately proud of being Doktorenko.

"Keller!" the retired staff captain muttered.

"Ippolit Terentyev!" resounded the thin voice of the consumptive, unexpectedly.

At last all were seated in a row facing the Prince. After their several introductions, all immediately knitted their brows and, as though by command, and to bolster their spirits, switched their caps from one knee to the other. Yet no one spoke, defiance written all over their features as though to say, "Easy does it, no one's going to put anything over us!" There was the distinct impression that if just one of them were to say the first word, they would all immediately start speaking, each interrupting and trying to outdo the other.

8

"Gentlemen, I hadn't expected to see any of you here," the Prince began, "I myself was ill until today, and I had entrusted your business" – so saying he turned to Antip Burdovsky – "to Gavrila Ardalionych Ivolgin about a month ago and duly informed you of it straight away. This does not mean I am avoiding a personal explanation, only you must agree, at such an hour... May I suggest you follow me into another room if it is not to be for long... I am now with my friends, and believe me—"

"Friends... are neither here nor there, only allow me," Lebedev's nephew suddenly interjected in a very peremptory, though as yet controlled, tone of voice, "allow me to point out that you could have treated us a good deal more cordially, instead of keeping us waiting in your servants' quarters—"

"And, of course... I too... this is princely high-handedness, no less! And you, a reasonable man! But don't think I'm your flunkey! I, I..." Antip Burdovsky suddenly exploded, his voice shaking petulantly as he spluttered in extreme agitation, unable to string two words together coherently.

"This was princely high-handedness!" Ippolit proclaimed in a high-pitched, off-key tone of voice.

"If it had been me instead of Burdovsky," the pugilist grunted, "that's to say, if it had concerned me directly as a respectable gentleman... I'd have—"

"Gentlemen, I learnt only about a minute ago that you were here, I assure you," the Prince repeated again.

"Prince, we're not afraid of your friends, whoever they may be, because we are within our rights," Lebedev's nephew asserted once more.

"Pray, explain," Ippolit screeched again, now thoroughly incensed, "by what right did you involve all your friends as arbiters in the Burdovsky case? What if we don't want to accept your friends' arbitration! It's all too obvious what arbitration by your friends may mean—"

"Look here, Mr Burdovsky," the Prince, extremely surprised at the turn things were taking at the outset, finally managed to interject, "if you don't wish to speak here, why don't we go to another room and, I repeat, I got to know about all of you just this very minute—"

"But you've no right, you've no right, you've no right!... Your friends... Look here!..." Burdovsky suddenly began to rattle on again, looking around wildly and warily with mounting agitation as his mistrust and ire increased, "you've no right!" He stopped abruptly as though he had run out of steam, his whole upper body thrust forward, and, rolling his myopic, bulging eyes criss-crossed with tiny red veins, gaped at the Prince inquisitively.

This time even the Prince was so taken aback that he too stopped talking, and looked back in silence, wide-eyed.

"Lev Nikolayevich," Lizaveta Prokofyevna suddenly intervened, "read this if you would, now, this very minute, it has a direct bearing on this matter."

She demonstratively held out a weekly paper of the satirical kind and pointed out an article. Just a minute before, as the visitors were trooping into the room, Lebedev had scurried up to Lizaveta Prokofyevna, whom he tried to please at every turn and, not saying a word, had produced this paper from his side pocket and held it right in front of her eyes, drawing her attention to an article, annotated specially. What Lizaveta Prokofyevna read, had astonished and shocked her dreadfully.

"Please though, better not out loud," the Prince muttered, highly embarrassed, "I'd rather read it on my own... later—"

"Well then, you read it, at once, go on, out loud!" Lizaveta Prokofyevna interrupted, addressing Kolya as she tore the paper out of the Prince's hands, which he'd hardly had time to look at properly. "Out loud for all to hear!"

Lizaveta Prokofyevna was a hot-tempered lady, easily carried away, such that very often – all anchors aweigh – she would cast off into the open sea without the least regard for the prevailing weather conditions. Ivan Fyodorovich shifted uneasily. But while everyone stood around in irresolute and helpless expectation, Kolya unfolded the paper and commenced from the place which Lebedev, who was at his side in a trice, indicated to him:

"Proletarians and their Progeny! A Case of Daylight (and Daily) Robbery! Progress! Reform! Justice!

"One comes across some strange goings-on in our so called Holy Russia, in this age of reform and market-economy initiatives, of nationalism and the migration of hundreds of millions of settlers abroad, of booming industry and the paralysis of the working population! And so on and so forth, the list can go on for ever, ladies and gentlemen, and therefore to business. A strange incident has occurred with one of the progeny of our defunct landed gentry (*de profundis!*), that progeny, whose grandfathers, incidentally, had lost all their wealth at roulette; whose fathers were obliged to serve as junior army officers and, not unusually, languish in custody for some trivial sum of government money remaining unaccounted for; and whose children, much like the hero of our tale, either moulder away their days as idiots, or are apprehended for illegal activities, for which, incidentally – to serve equity and justice – they are exonerated by juries; or, in the worst cases of all, give rise to one of those anecdotes that depress the public and further besmirch our singularly unpropitious times. Our brave hero, six months or so ago, caparisoned in a pair of gaiters as befits a true foreigner and shivering dreadfully in a threadbare mantle, arrived to a wintry Russia from Switzerland, where he sought to be freed from idiocy (*sic*!). It has to be said, Lady Luck favoured him, so that, his unusual illness apart, which he sought to cure in Switzerland (pray, what cure can there possibly be for idiocy, just think on it?!), he was fully able to justify the Russian adage, fortune favours the foolish! Judge for yourselves! As a suckling babe, after the death of his father (allegedly a staff captain), who'd died unexpectedly while in custody for the loss at cards of the whole of the regimental funds, or maybe for over-prescribing the birch to those under his command (you will recall, won't you, the good old days, gentlemen?), our baron was brought up by one of our kind-hearted and very wealthy Russian estate owners. In the good old days this Russian estate owner – let's call him P., say – was the owner of four thousand bonded souls (bonded souls! Do you understand such a concept, ladies and gentlemen? I don't! I need to consult a dictionary; 'though the tale be freshly told, we needs must take it with a pinch of salt'). This man was apparently one of those good-for-nothing layabouts, who spend their pointless existence abroad, in the summer months – taking waters in resorts and passing the winters in the Paris Château des Fleurs, where they are divested of enormous sums over the years. One can safely say that at least one third of the whole of the ground rent paid by the serf fraternity went into the pocket of the Paris proprietor of the Château des Fleurs (lucky fellow!) Be that as it may, the irresponsible P. managed to give the orphaned princeling a truly princely upbringing; he engaged governors and governesses (no doubt, pretty ones), whom he incidentally brought personally from Paris. But the last of the princely line turned out to be an idiot. The pretty governesses were of little help, and till the age of twenty our ward did not manage to learn to speak a single language, not even Russian. That in itself may, of course, be no great loss. One day the Russian serf-owner's mind was penetrated by a fantastic notion that the idiot might have sense drummed into him in Switzerland. There was some underlying logic in this, it has to be said: this capitalist, this parasite, naturally could imagine that for money one could purchase even sense on the open market, especially in Switzerland. There followed five years of medical care in Switzerland under the aegis of some famous professor, and heaps of money were expended. It goes without saying this was to little avail, since the idiot was none the wiser at the end of it all, though it must be admitted that he did end up with some basic human skills, however questionable. All of a sudden, P. dies unexpectedly. As was to be expected, there is no last will and testament of any kind; estate matters are in complete disarray; the number of avaricious claimants is legion, and these have not a care in the world for the last of the clan who, for all they knew, may have been receiving a course of treatment for idiocy out of charity in Switzerland. This remaining scion, though an idiot, was still able to bamboozle his professor and, it is said, spent two years receiving treatment and living off of him on full board without contributing a single penny, all the while concealing the demise of his benefactor. But the professor himself was a prize charlatan. Taking fright at the prospect of funds running dry, but more at the inordinate appetite of his twenty-five-year-old charge, he gave him a pair of his old gaiters, slung a tatty threadbare cloak over his shoulder and charitably put him in a third class carriage *nach Russland* – out of sight, out of mind. It would appear lady luck had finally turned her back on our hero. Nothing of the sort! Fate, which could starve to death province after province, suddenly bestowed all her favours upon the puny aristocrat, like a cloud that had raced across a parched field, only to burst over the ocean. Almost at the same moment that he returned from Switzerland to St Petersburg, a cousin of his mother, coming as she did from merchant stock, died in Moscow – an old, bearded, childless, crusty introvert, rich as Croesus, leaving several cool million behind, uncontested, in ready cash (think on it, reader, if it had been you or me!) and all this to our progeny, all this to our baron, who'd been treated for idiocy in Switzerland! Well, this was when things began to take off. Around our gaitered baron, who had taken a shine to an attractive fancy woman, a whole crowd of friends and comrades assembled. Even some relatives turned up, but the most persistent were the hordes of eligible young ladies, eager and anxious to tie the knot, and what could be better – an aristocrat, a millionaire and an idiot to boot, all qualities in one! Such husbands, to coin a phrase, do not grow on trees!…"

"This… this is too much for me!" Ivan Fyodorovich exclaimed, bursting with indignation.

"Stop it, Kolya!" the Prince pleaded. There were gasps all round.

"Read on! Read on, regardless!" Lizaveta Prokofyevna retorted. It was obvious she was barely able to contain herself. "Prince, if the reading stops, we shall quarrel."

There was nothing to be done. Kolya, agitated, flushed, continued his reading in a tremulous, unsteady voice.

"But while our newly baked millionaire was floating, as it were, in Elysium, something quite untoward occurred. One fine morning a visitor arrived on his doorstep, cool, calm and collected, politely spoken, dignified and businesslike, formally and soberly attired, with a palpably progressive turn of mind, and in a few well-chosen words explained the reason for his visit. He, an established lawyer, had his instructions from a young gentleman. This young gentleman is quite simply P.'s son, although he goes under a different name. The lascivious P., having in his youth seduced (no doubt taking advantage of the seigneurial rights of the by-now defunct feudal order) an honourable, decent young peasant girl, who, though poor had been brought up in the European ways, very quickly noticed the inevitable and imminent consequences of his liaison, whereupon he hurriedly married her off to an industrious, upstanding young man, with prospects of government employment, who had long been in love with the said young girl. Initially he helped the newlyweds, but very soon her husband's sense of honour would not allow him to accept assistance. Time passed. Little by little P. managed to forget both about the girl and the son he had sired by her and, as is subsequently known, he died intestate. In the meantime, his son, born in legitimate wedlock, but brought up under a different name and in the generosity of his heart completely adopted by the young girl's husband, who himself in time had passed away, was thus left with meagre means, having to care for his long-suffering, crippled mother, residing in one of the outlying provinces; he himself, however, staying on in the capital, continued to earn his keep by the sweat of daily labour as a tutor in merchants' families, thereby paying his own way first through high school, and then subscribing to a course of advanced lectures to pave the way to further advancement. But how much can one earn from a Russian merchant paying at the rate of ten copecks per lesson, with a sick, crippled mother, who finally even by her death in the far-flung province, was hardly able to alleviate his situation? The thought now arises, how in all fairness should our offspring have argued, 'All my life I have benefited at the hands of P.; tens of thousands went on my upbringing, on governesses and attempts to cure me of idiocy in Switzerland; now I am the owner of millions, while P.'s high-minded son, totally innocent of his undutiful, negligent father's peccadillo, has to slave away as a tutor. All that had been spent on me, should in fairness have been spent on him. The vast sums that have been expended on me, are actually not mine at all. It was merely fate acting blindly; they ought to belong to P.'s son. It is he, rather than I, who should profit by them, for even if they had been bequeathed to me, it was as a result of gross wilfulness, negligence and irresponsibility on the part of P. Had I been a true gentleman, discreet and fair-minded, I should have handed over to his son half of my whole inheritance; but as I am above all a calculating sort and know full well that there is no legal obligation for me to do so, I shall not share my fortune. All the same it would indeed be the height of vileness and infamy (the offspring forgot that it would also be a miscalculation) if I now don't return to his son the tens of thousands that have gone to pay for my – an idiot's – treatment at the asylum. This is nothing but a matter of conscience and fairness! For what would have become of me if P. had not taken charge of my upbringing, and had instead taken his own son under his wing?'

"But, have no fear, ladies and gentlemen! This is not how our offspring argued. Plead as the young man's lawyer did, who had taken the case on solely out of friendship and almost against his own will, nay being almost forced into it; plead as he did on grounds of honour, decency, fairness and even your common-or-garden self-interest – as far as our Swiss nursling was concerned, it all fell on deaf ears. And still all this was as nothing; what was clearly unforgivable and may not be excused by any fancy illness, was that this millionaire, who, hardly having discarded his mentor's gaiters, showed not the least understanding that it was not charity or beneficence that the young man in his dignity, wearing himself out as a tutor, was asking for, but rather his rightful due. Granted, this was not grounded in law, and he was not even so much pleading as appealing through the agency of his friends. Affecting a grandiose posture and intoxicated by his newly gained licence to oppress people with impunity using his millions, our offspring takes a fifty-rouble note and sends it to the high-minded young man as an act of disdainful kindness. You refuse to credit this, ladies and gentlemen? You are affronted, offended, you are bursting with indignation; nevertheless, that is precisely what he did! It goes without saying, the money was immediately returned to him, thrown back in his face, as it were. How then is the matter to be resolved? Not by recourse to law; there is but one way – publicity! Accordingly, we are making this story public, vouching for its authenticity. One of our most renowned humorists has penned a most charming epigram, worthy of gracing not only the provincial but also the national annals of our morals:

Leo,[1] cloaked in Schneider's[2] mantle,
Did a five-year stint.
He excelled in doing nil,
That was his great skill.

Coming back in narrow gaiters
A fortune he then grabs;
He offers up to God his prayers
And then the student robs."

After Kolya had finished, he quickly passed the paper to the Prince and, without a word, rushed into a corner, pressed himself right up against the wall and buried his face in his hands. He was dying of embarrassment, for his young soul, still unaccustomed to life's more sordid episodes, was outraged beyond measure. It seemed to him that something extraordinary had occurred, as a result of which everything had collapsed around his ears, and that he himself was somehow to blame for having read it out loud.

But others also experienced something similar.

The young ladies felt awkward and embarrassed. Lizaveta Prokofyevna was barely able to contain her anger and was also perhaps deeply sorry for having meddled in the affair; now she kept her silence. The Prince, like all self-effacing people in such circumstances, was so embarrassed at the effrontery of others, so taken aback by the conduct of his visitors, that for a time he could not even pluck up the courage to look at them. Ptitsyn, Varya, Ganya, even Lebedev, looked somewhat

---

1. The offspring's name.
2. The professor's name.

nonplussed. But the most astonishing thing was that even Ippolit and "Pavlishchev's son" appeared somehow put out; neither was Lebedev's nephew best pleased. Only the pugilist remained completely calm and collected, twirling his moustaches, eyes to the ground, but not in embarrassment – on the contrary, in dignified smugness and an all too apparent contentment. It was patently clear that the article was much to his liking.

"Hell and damnation!" Ivan Fyodorovich growled under his breath. "Fifty lackeys working as a team could not have come up with greater nonsense."

"I b-beg your pardon, my dear sir," Ippolit cut in, all a-flutter, "it is grossly insulting to cast such aspersions."

"That, that, that is quite out of order for a respectable gentleman... you must agree, General, that if one gentleman impugns the honour of another, it is insulting!" the pugilist growled, also betraying signs of unexpected agitation, twirling his moustaches all the harder, and hitching up his shoulders and the rest of his body.

"First, I will have no truck with your 'my dear sir', and secondly, I have no intention of giving you any kind of explanation," Ivan Fyodorovich retorted sharply, rose to his feet and without a word withdrew to the door opening onto the terrace, where he remained standing on the landing with his back to the rest of the company. He was fuming at Lizaveta Prokofyevna, who, despite everything, stood rooted to the spot.

"Gentlemen, gentlemen, allow me, gentlemen, to explain myself," the Prince pleaded in agony and desperation, "and let us try to come to some kind of an understanding. It's not the article as such, let that pass, only, gentlemen, none of what is written there is true. I'm saying this because you know it to be so yourselves. In the end it's quite disgraceful. I'll be frank, if anyone of you is responsible for writing this, it beggars belief."

"I knew nothing of this article right up till now," Ippolit declared. "I do not approve of it."

"Even though I knew it had been written," Lebedev's nephew remarked, "I... too wouldn't have wanted it to be published. It's been badly timed."

"I knew, but I am within my rights... I..." "Pavlishchev's son" muttered.

"I see! So it is you who wrote all this, is it not?" the Prince enquired, looking at Burdovsky full of astonishment. "This is beyond belief!"

"We would do well to deny you the right to pose such questions," Lebedev's nephew interposed.

"I was merely voicing my surprise that Mr Burdovsky had managed... but... what I meant was that since you had already published all this, why were you objecting when I raised it in front of my friends?"

"At last!" Lizaveta Prokofyevna observed in a temper.

"And, Prince, I shall even go on to say," the overwrought Lebedev, negotiating deftly between the chairs, interposed eagerly, "you failed to mention that it was only through your good will and excessive kind-heartedness that they were ever allowed access and permission to speak, and that they have no right whatsoever to make any demands, the more so since you'd already entrusted the matter to Gavrila Ardalionych, and that too on account of your boundless kindness. As for the present, my most esteemed Prince, being as you are amongst your chosen friends, you cannot sacrifice them for the sake of these, er, gentlemen, and could easily have them all, as it were, escorted down the steps, so much so that I as the owner of this house would be absolutely delighted to—"

"That is exactly right!" General Ivolgin suddenly thundered from the far end of the room.

"That'll do, Lebedev, that'll do, really..." the Prince was about to pour oil on troubled waters, but a veritable uproar drowned his words.

"No, I beg your pardon, Prince, I beg your pardon, this will no longer do!" Lebedev's nephew's voice rose above the others. "It's now time to clear up the matter once and for all, because evidently some people still haven't grasped it fully. Legal quibbles have cropped up and on their basis we've been threatened that we'll be kicked down the stairs! Now, do you really imagine, Prince, we're so stupid as to be incapable of understanding how weak our case is in law, and that were we to take it to court, we wouldn't get a penny? But that is the whole point, we maintain that while there is no legal right, there is a human, natural right, grounded in common sense and conscience, and though this right of ours may not have been recorded in any moth-eaten legal statute, an upright, decently minded person – which is tantamount to saying a sane person – would nevertheless be expected to maintain his dignity and probity even as regards those instances that have not been covered by statute. Then again, we came here without fear of being kicked down the stairs (as we have been threatened just now) only because we came not to ask, but to demand. As for the inappropriately late hour of our arrival – you must remember we arrived in good time, but you kept us hanging around in the antechamber – so, as I said, we came in all confidence, fully expecting to find in you a man of common sense, that is, a worthy gentleman. Yes, it is true, we did not enter in humility as obsequious fawners of yours, but with our heads held high as behoves people who are free; nor were we seeking favours, but with a bold, unapologetic demand on our lips (yes, not seeking favours, but a demand on our lips – put that in your pipe and smoke it!). We now put it to you fairly and squarely without beating about the bush: do you consider you are in the right or in the wrong in Burdovsky's case? Do you recognize Pavlishchev as your benefactor to whom you, perhaps, owe your very life? If you do (and it is after all a self-evident truth), then are you prepared – in other words, do you find it fair in all conscience – that for your part you should, having received millions, recompense the needy son of Pavlishchev, even though he may be going under the name of Burdovsky? Yes or no? If *yes*, that is, put another way, if you have that which in your tongue is called honour and conscience and which we more accurately describe as common sense, then satisfy our demand and that will be the end of the matter. Satisfy it without entreaties or indebtedness on our part – and do not expect these of us, because we seek not to reward ourselves, but to serve justice. Should you choose not to satisfy us – that is, to answer *no* – we shall leave forthwith, and the matter will be at an end. But we shall say to you in front of all these witnesses, that you're a man intellectually unrefined and of insufficient understanding, that henceforth you've forfeited once and for all your right to the title of a worthy gentleman, because you sought to acquire it at too low a price. I rest my case. I have made my point. You may now kick us down the stairs, if you dare. You can do it, you have the might. But remember this – we don't ask, we demand. We don't ask, we demand!…"

Lebedev's nephew, who had worked himself into a lather, fell silent.

"We don't ask, we demand, we demand, we demand!…" Burdovsky jabbered, going as red as a beetroot.

After Lebedev's nephew had spoken, there was a slight commotion, even murmur, although no one of the rest of the company wanted to get involved, the only exception being Lebedev, whose feverish excitement would not abate. (Strange to note – Lebedev, who to all intents and purposes appeared to be on the Prince's side, seemed to evince a certain family pride following his nephew's speech; be that as it may, he now surveyed the assembly with an all-round self-satisfied look.)

"As I see it," the Prince began in a rather low voice, "as I see it, Mr Doktorenko, all that you've just said, is full of half-truths – I might even go so far as to say, much more than half-truths, and I would have been ready to go along with you all the way, if you hadn't left something out. What it is you left out, I'm not in a position to reveal to you precisely, but most assuredly something was omitted from your words to make them ring true. But let us consider the matter in hand, gentlemen; tell me why did you publish this article? Every word in it is a slur, and I consider you are guilty, gentlemen, of acting disreputably."

"I beg your pardon!..."

"My dear sir!..."

"That... that... that..." several of the agitated visitors joined in at one and the same time.

"As regards the article," Ippolit's falsetto rang out, "as regards this article, I already said that I and the others do not approve of it! He's the one who wrote it" – he pointed at the pugilist sitting next to him. "He wrote it, I have to say, badly, crudely, like a trooper. He has no wit, a jack of all trades, take my word for it. I've been telling this to his face every single day, and yet in a way he is within his rights. To go public is everyone's inalienable right, including Burdovsky's. Any gaffe on his part is his own lookout. As to my protests on behalf of us all concerning the presence of your friends, I think it is necessary, ladies and gentlemen, to explain that I stood up merely in order to assert our rights, but that in essence we welcome the presence of witnesses, and in fact we four agreed as much before we even entered here. Whoever may be your witnesses, even if they are your friends, inasmuch as they cannot disagree with Burdosvky's right (a right as solid as the laws of mathematics); it's even preferable that the witnesses happen to be your friends. The truth will be that much more evident."

"It is true, we made that agreement," Lebedev's nephew confirmed.

"So what was all the shouting and noise about from the very start, if that's precisely what you wanted?" the Prince asked in surprise.

"Apropos the article, Prince," the pugilist interposed, raring to put his oar in and eagerly warming up to the occasion, (one could not escape the feeling that he was much influenced by the presence of ladies), "apropos the article, I have to admit that I am the author, even though my ailing friend, for whom I have a tender spot on account of his ailment, has taken me to task for it. But I composed and placed it in the journal of a true friend merely as a piece of polemic. As for the verses, they are indeed not my own but belong to the pen of a noted humorist. I managed to read only part of the article to Burdovsky, who immediately agreed for me to publish it, though it goes without saying I could have gone ahead on my own. To go into print is a universal, time-honoured, salutary right. I trust, Prince, you are enough of a liberal not to deny this—"

"I shall deny nothing, but you must agree that in your article—"

"I call a spade a spade, is that what you wanted to say? But, let's face it, it's in the public interest and, you must agree, an opportunity not to be missed. Too bad for the offending parties, the public good is what matters. As for certain inaccuracies, certain hyperbolae, so to speak, you must again agree, that it is the initiative which matters above all, the doing of it and the reason for it, first and foremost, as it were. It is about setting a good example, whereas the minutiae of the case may be considered at a later stage and, finally, it is a question of style! We are, so to speak, in the realm of humour – everyone writes like that, you can't deny that! Ha-ha!"

"But you're barking up the wrong tree! I assure you, gentlemen," the Prince exclaimed, "you published the article on the assumption that I would under no circumstances do anything for Mr Burdovsky, and consequently somehow to intimidate me and get your own back one way or another. But how did you know – perhaps I was fully committed to helping Mr Burdovsky, what then? Let me tell you now loud and clear, that I will—"

"At last, the sensible and correct response of a true gentleman!" the pugilist acknowledged.

"God almighty!" Lizaveta Prokofyevna gasped.

"This is perfectly intolerable!" the General muttered.

"Permit me, ladies and gentlemen, permit me, I will explain everything," the Prince pleaded. "About five weeks ago, Mr Burdovsky, your representative, Chebarov, called on me in Z. You, Mr Keller, painted a very flattering picture of him in your article," the Prince said, turning to the pugilist, "I did not like him at all. I'll be frank, it struck me from the first that this Chebarov himself was behind everything and that, taking full advantage of your inexperience, he may have put ideas into your head, Mr Burdovsky, to start all this sorry business in the first place."

"You've no right... I... I am not inexperienced... this is—" Burdovsky muttered all in a fluster.

"You have no right whatsoever to make such suppositions," Lebedev's nephew intervened gravely.

"This is quite out of order," Ippolit cried out in his falsetto. "Offensive, false and inept!"

"I beg your pardon, gentlemen, I beg your pardon," the Prince hurried to make amends, "please, don't hold it against me. It just seemed to me it would be so much better for us to be perfectly frank with one another. But it's up to you. I told Chebarov that since I was not in St Petersburg, I was immediately going to authorize a friend of mine to deal with the matter, and would keep you, Mr Burdovsky, fully informed. I'll be quite open with you, gentlemen, the whole undertaking struck me as highly fraudulent, purely because of Chebarov's involvement... Oh, don't be offended, gentlemen! For goodness' sake, don't be offended, gentlemen!" the Prince exclaimed anxiously, noticing Burdovsky's renewed agitation, and the disquiet and burgeoning opposition of his supporters. "This can in no way refer to you personally, if I say that the matter struck me as fraudulent! You must admit, I knew none of you personally at the time. Chebarov was all I had to go by. I'm speaking in general terms, because... if only you knew how badly I've been taken advantage of since I received the inheritance!"

"Prince, you are awfully naive," Lebedev's nephew remarked derisively.

"And a prince and millionaire to boot!" Ippolit pronounced. "With all your perhaps genuinely kind and artless character you cannot of course escape the censure of the common law."

"That may well be so, that may very well be so, gentlemen," the Prince acquiesced hurriedly, "though I am puzzled what common law you are talking about. But, to continue, please do not take offence needlessly. I swear, I've no intention of causing you offence. And really, gentlemen, why is it you take umbrage as soon as one attempts to speak one's mind. But, I was genuinely taken aback that there should be such a person as 'Pavlishchev's son' and, what's more, living in such dire circumstances as depicted by Chebarov. Pavlishchev was my benefactor and my father's friend. (Oh, Mr Keller, why did you have to write such an untruth about my father in your article? There was no misappropriation of regimental funds or violence perpetrated against the subordinates – of this I am firmly convinced. I just wonder how you could bring yourself to write such a lie?) And the things you wrote about Pavlishchev are perfectly disgusting. You accused this worthy gentleman of being lascivious and irresponsible with such aplomb as though you really knew the truth. Let me tell you, he was the most chaste man who ever walked the earth! He was remarkably erudite. He corresponded with some of the most eminent men of science and donated lot of money for the benefit of science. As regards his character, his charitable works, yes, you were right, I was a total fool at the time and understood nothing (though of course I was not deprived of speech and could follow some things). Now, however, I am in a position to reflect on all that I had heard and seen—"

"Look here," Ippolit would not desist, "this is too self-indulgent! We're not children. You wanted to get down to business, it's already after nine, don't forget!"

"But of course, but of course, gentlemen," the Prince hastened to agree, "after I'd got over the initial adverse impression, I really thought I could be wrong and Pavlishchev might indeed have had a son. But I was terribly astonished that this son could have so easily, that is to say, so publicly revealed the secret of his birth and, what's more important, denigrated his mother. You must remember Chebarov threatened to go public even at that stage—"

"This is too silly for words!" Lebedev's nephew exclaimed.

"You've no right... no right!" Burdovsky vociferated.

"A son is not answerable for the licentious behaviour of his father, and the mother is innocent," Ippolit screeched heatedly.

"All the more reason to spare her, it would seem—" the Prince put in tentatively.

"You are not only naive, you've gone considerably further," Lebedev's nephew remarked with a sneer.

"And by what right!..." Ippolit howled in an unnatural voice.

"None! None whatsoever!" the Prince hastened to reassure him. "You are quite right in this, I must admit, but I could not help thinking it at the time. However, I also immediately told myself that my personal feelings are neither here nor there, because if I consider myself duty bound to satisfy Mr Burdovsky's demands in the name of my feelings towards Pavlishchev, I have to do it whatever the case may be, that is regardless of whether I respect Mr Burdovsky, or not. I've only raised this subject, because I could not get over the feeling that it was unnatural for a son to reveal his mother's secret so publicly... In short, it was precisely this point which convinced me personally that Chebarov must be a crook, who had deliberately misled Mr Burdovsky to perpetrate such a fraud."

"But this is totally out of order!" his visitors protested, some jumping to their feet.

"Gentlemen! That's precisely why I concluded that Mr Burdovsky must be an artless, defenceless man who would easily fall under the spell of a crook, therefore it follows that I was all the more obligated to assist him, 'Pavlishchev's son', first – by standing up to Chebarov, and secondly by my devotion and comradeship, in order to guide him, and thirdly, I instructed that ten thousand roubles be paid to him, which is all that by my calculations Pavlishchev could have spent on me."

"What! Only ten thousand!" Ippolit exclaimed.

"Well, Prince, you are pretty weak in arithmetic, or if you're not, you're acting the fool!" Lebedev's nephew exclaimed.

"Ten thousand is not enough," Burdovsky said.

"Antip, take it!" the pugilist whispered hurriedly, leaning across the backrest of Ippolit's chair. "Take it! We'll talk later!"

"Look here, Mr Myshkin," Ippolit persisted, "don't take us for the imbeciles, vulgar fools, that your guests probably take us for – the ladies who keep smiling at us with such contempt, and especially that uppish gentleman (he indicated Yevgeny Pavlovich) whom I, of course, do not have the pleasure of being acquainted with, but have heard about—"

"Permit me, gentlemen, permit me, you've misunderstood me yet again!" the Prince again addressed them with feeling. "First, Mr Keller, you made a very inaccurate assessment of my fortune in your article. There was never any question of millions. I have perhaps only an eighth or a tenth of what you imagine. Secondly, it was nowhere near tens of thousands of roubles spent on me in Switzerland. Schneider used to get six hundred roubles per year, and only during the first three years at that. As for his going to Paris for pretty governesses, this is more slander. To my mind, far less than ten thousand was spent on me in all, but I set it at ten thousand and, you must agree, that in settling a debt, I could never have offered Mr Burdovsky more, even if he were ever so dear to me, out of discretion alone, for the simple reason that I was settling a debt rather than making a charitable donation. I am surprised, gentlemen, you seem incapable of understanding this! But I intended to cap all this later by offering the unfortunate Mr Burdovsky, who had been so cruelly deceived, my friendship, my unremitting solicitude, because it is impossible that he should have of his own accord, without being prompted, stooped so low as, for example, agreeing to publish in Mr Keller's article such details about his own mother... Look here, gentlemen, why are you getting upset again? This way we'll never reach an understanding! I've been proved right! I've now seen with my own eyes that my surmises were correct," the Prince continued to press his point home fervently in an attempt to quell the unrest, not realizing that he was only feeding it.

"What? What have you seen?" he was challenged furiously on all sides.

"Have a heart, gentlemen. First, I managed to have a good look at Mr Burdovsky, and I can see for myself what he's like... He is altogether guiltless, but is being deceived by everyone... which is why I should be compassionate to him. And secondly, Gavrila Ardalionych, who had been entrusted with the matter and from whom I had no news for some considerable while, being on the move and after that ill for three days in St Petersburg, had suddenly, about an hour ago, at our first meeting, informed me that he has seen through all Chebarov's intentions, for which he has concrete evidence, and that Chebarov is precisely what I had imagined him to be. I know very well, gentlemen, that many think I'm an idiot, and Chebarov, knowing by hearsay how readily I dole out money, thought it would be easy to dupe me, and relied on my feelings for Pavlishchev. But the main thing is that it turns out Mr Burdovsky is not Pavlishchev's son at all! Gavrila Ardalionych has just informed me of this, insisting that he has obtained incontrovertible evidence to that effect. Well, what do you say to that, the mind simply boggles after all that! And listen – incontrovertible evidence! I still haven't got used to it, I still don't believe it myself, I assure you. I'm still not quite sure, because Gavrila Ardalionych hasn't yet had time to give me all the details, but that Chebarov is a crook, there is not the least doubt! He has deceived both the unfortunate Mr Burdovsky and you all, gentlemen, who came in good faith to lend support to your friend (much needed support, I hasten to add), and embroiled you all in a fraudulent affair, for there is no other way to describe this matter!"

"Fraudulent affair!... Not 'Pavlishchev's son'?... We shan't stand for this!..." voices were heard on all sides. All Burdovsky's men were in an uproar.

"Yes, of course, a fraudulent affair! Don't you see if Mr Burdovsky now turns out not to be Pavlishchev's son, then his claim becomes an obvious fraud (assuming, naturally, that he is aware of the truth!). But the whole point is that he has been deceived, which is precisely why I insist that he should be exonerated. In his naivety, he deserves sympathy, and must not be left unaided, else he will be an accomplice. You see, I'm already convinced that he is ignorant of the whole affair! I've been in a similar position myself before my trip to Switzerland, I too mouthed incoherent words – I wanted to express myself, and couldn't... I can well understand the feeling. I can sympathize, because I myself am almost the same, that's why I have the right to speak! And, finally, in spite of the fact that there is no longer such a thing as Pavlishchev's son and that it is all a fabrication, I shall nonetheless not change my decision and am ready to donate the ten thousand in memory of Pavlishchev. Before Mr Burdovsky came on the scene, I had earmarked this money for a school in memory of Pavlishchev, now it'll be all be the same whether it goes to the school or to Mr Burdovsky, because Mr Burdovsky, even if he is not Pavlishchev's son, really seems like it, because he was so cruelly deceived that he sincerely believed himself Pavlishchev's son! After all, he sincerely believed he was Pavlishchev's son! Gentlemen, be so good as to hear what Gavrila Ardalionych has to say. That'll settle the matter, don't be cross, let's not get upset, please remain seated! Gavrila Ardalionych will explain everything forthwith, and I sincerely wish that you should be conversant with all the facts. He tells me that he even went to Pskov to see your mother, Mr Burdovsky, who, contrary to what it says in the article, is not dead at all... Do be seated, gentlemen, I beg you!"

The Prince sat down and managed to persuade Mr Burdovsky's friends, who were all on their feet, to do likewise. For the final ten or twenty minutes he spoke with fervent conviction, loudly, impulsively, as though attempting to out-talk and out-do everyone, and of course he subsequently came to bitterly regret some of the words and expressions that he gave vent to. Had he not been forced to justify himself and put on the defensive, he would have been more discreet and less precipitate in voicing his all-too-frank surmises. No sooner had he sat down than he was struck by a powerful feeling of remorse. Quite apart from the fact that he had offended Burdovsky by so openly accusing him of suffering from the same illness as himself, his offer of the ten thousand to Burdovsky, instead of going to the school, was referred to by him with such scant regard for personal feelings that it appeared to all like an act of charity. "I wish I had offered it to him privately and handed it to him some other day," the Prince repented almost immediately. "Now there's nothing for it! What an idiot, what a blithering idiot I am!" he concluded finally in an onrush of shame and utter disappointment with himself.

In the meantime, Gavrila Ardalionych, who up till now had kept himself to himself in complete silence, now stepped forward in response to the Prince's invitation and, standing next to him, began to put forward his case in measured and distinct tones. All other voices fell silent forthwith. Everyone listened with rapt curiosity, especially Burdovsky and his men.

9

"YOU WILL NOT GO ON TO DENY," Gavrila Ardalionovich began, addressing himself directly to Burdovsky who was all ears, his eyes dilated and thoroughly agitated, "you will not go on to deny, nor I hope will you want to with any degree of seriousness, that you were born precisely two years after the event of your beloved mother's legally solemnized wedding ceremony with the collegiate assessor Mr Burdovsky, your father. Your date of birth is all too well established, such that Mr Keller's highly disagreeable distortion of it in his article can only be accounted for by his all too lively imagination and his attempt to strengthen your claim and further your interests. Mr Keller indicated that he had read his article to you beforehand, though not in its entirety... most assuredly, he stopped short of this point—"

"Yes, I stopped short," the pugilist interrupted, "but all the facts come from a reliable source, and I—"

"Excuse me, Mr Keller," Gavrila Ardalionovich stopped him, "allow me to speak. I assure you I shall come to your article in the fullness of time, when you shall have the opportunity to put your point, but for now let's not jump the gun. Quite fortuitously, with the help of my sister Varvara Ardalionovna Ptitsyna, I obtained from a close friend of hers, one Vera Alexeyevna Zubkova, a widowed landowner, a letter written to her from abroad by the late Nikolai Andreyevich Pavlishchev some twenty-four years ago. Having got to know Vera Alexeyevna a little better, I followed her advice and approached ex-Colonel Timofey Fyodorovich Vyazovkin, Mr Pavlishchev's distant relative and intimate friend during the latter's lifetime. Mr Vyazovkin gave me two additional letters, also written by Nikolai Andreyevich while he was abroad. Going by these three letters, their dates and the facts mentioned in them, it is crystal clear, without any shadow of a doubt, that Nikolai Andreyevich went abroad (where he stayed a full three years) precisely a year and a half before your birth, Mr Burdovsky. Your mother, as you well know, had never left Russia... For the present I shall not read these letters. It is too late. I am merely stating a fact. However, should you be so inclined, Mr Burdovsky, you may see me as early as tomorrow morning in the presence of all your witnesses, however many, and handwriting experts, and I am perfectly convinced they will irrefutably prove the truth of what I have been saying. If so, this whole matter collapses of its own accord and there is no case to answer."

Again there was a general shuffling and deep restlessness. Burdovsky himself suddenly rose to his feet.

"If so, I've been deceived, indeed deceived, not by Chebarov, but long before him. I don't want experts. I don't want to see anyone. I believe you. I'm leaving... I don't want the ten thousand... Goodbye..."

He picked up his cap, and pushed the chair away to leave.

"I'd be most grateful, Mr Burdovsky," Gavrila Ardalionovich interposed in a soft, mellow tone, "if you could possibly bring yourself to stay for just five more minutes. There are also a few additional highly interesting and curious facts concerning you in particular which have come to light in this matter. To my mind, you cannot possibly remain in the dark about them, and it is quite likely you will feel much better yourself once the matter is finally cleared up…"

Burdovsky sat down again in silence, his head slightly bowed as though deep in thought. Lebedev's nephew, who had also got up to accompany him, followed suit; though he had not lost any of his outward self-assurance and aplomb, he was not a little rattled. Ippolit appeared sullen, gloomy and astonished. At that very moment he was overcome with such a bad bout of coughing that his handkerchief became covered in blood. The pugilist was in a state of near shock.

"Too bad, Antip!" he exclaimed bitterly. "Didn't I tell you… the other day that you might not be Pavlishchev's son after all?"

There was a suppressed guffaw all round, two or three voices rising above the others.

"What you just said, Mr Keller," Gavrila Ardalionovich was quick to pick him up on this, "is very valuable. All the same, with recourse to the most incontrovertible facts, I have every reason to believe that though Mr Burdovsky was well aware of the date of his birth, he was completely unaware of Pavlishchev's residence abroad, where Mr Pavlishchev spent most of his life, returning to Russia always for only short periods. Besides, the very fact of that particular departure some twenty years ago was so unremarkable in itself that even people close to him, let alone Mr Burdovsky, who wasn't even born at the time, could not recall it. Of course, difficult though it was to obtain the necessary information, it was not impossible. All the same, I must admit that everything that I learnt, came to me quite fortuitously, and could easily have eluded me. It follows therefore that for Mr Burdovsky, and even Chebarov, the facts really were next to inaccessible even if they had tried ever so hard to obtain them. But it is possible it might not even have entered their heads—"

"One moment, Mr Ivolgin," Ippolit suddenly interrupted him irritably, "why are you feeding us all this nonsense, pardon the expression? The matter has been resolved, we do not dispute the main point, so why drag out such unseemly and distasteful rubbish? Perhaps you intend to show off your investigative skills, or parade before the Prince and us as a talented detective, a gifted sleuth? Or perhaps you intend to justify and exonerate Burdovsky inasmuch as he got mixed up in this business through ignorance? But that is quite unbecoming, my dear sir!

289

Burdovsky has no need of your justifications and attempts to exonerate him, I'll have you know! He has been hurt, and feels awkward whatever you might say, and you ought to have realized and understood this—"

"Enough, Mr Terentyev, enough," Gavrila Ardalionovich at last succeeded in getting a word in, "calm down, don't upset yourself so. I heard you're very ill! I sympathize with you. In that case, if you wish, I have finished. In conclusion I'll only present you with a few brief facts, which, I'm convinced, would be of general interest," he added, noticing that there was again a stir of impatience. "I only wish, backed by evidence, to inform all concerned parties that your mother, Mr Burdovsky, was favoured and supported by Pavlishchev, solely because she was the sister of that peasant girl with whom Nikolai Andreyevich Pavlishchev had fallen in love in his very early youth and whom he was fully intending to marry but for her untimely death. I have proof that this family matter, accurate in every respect, is so little known that it has almost been forgotten. I have further evidence that your mother as a ten-year-old girl was taken by Mr Pavlishchev into his family for her upbringing, that she had been promised a considerable dowry, and that all this munificence had engendered much unsavoury talk amongst Pavlishchev's numerous relatives. Some even suspected that he'd marry his ward, but in the end at the age of twenty she married for love, for which I have the most unarguable proof, a clerk from the land survey department, one Mr Burdovsky. Here I can produce some incontrovertible facts to prove that this Mr Burdovsky, a highly impractical man, having come into fifteen thousand roubles of your mother's dowry, left his employment, launched a commercial enterprise, was swindled, lost his capital and his grip on himself, took to drink, fell ill as a result and, seven years into his marriage with your mother, died suddenly. Subsequently, on your mother's personal evidence, she was left destitute and would have perished totally but for Pavlishchev's generous assistance, who made her an allowance of up to six hundred roubles per annum. Then there is no end of evidence that he took you, as a child, deeply to his heart. According to this evidence, and the further corroboration of your mother, it transpired that his love for you stemmed in the main from the fact that since childhood you had the woebegone, pathetic aspect of a pitiable, underdeveloped child. Now, Pavlishchev, as I was able to establish incontrovertibly, all his life long displayed a peculiar tenderness to all who were oppressed and naturally discriminated against, especially children – to my mind this is significant and highly pertinent to the matter at hand. Finally, I am proud to reveal that my enquiries yielded a most incontestable detail of how this extraordinary attachment that Pavlishchev manifested for you (thanks to which you were able to enter a high school and continue your studies under special supervision) eventually gave rise to the suspicion in Pavlishchev's household and amongst his relatives, that you were his natural son and that your father was merely a cuckolded husband. But the important thing was that this suspicion turned into a cast-iron conviction only towards the latter days of Pavlishchev's life, when everyone became concerned as to his last will and testament and after the initial facts were forgotten, and enquiries became impossible. Doubtless, rumour of this suspicion reached you too, Mr Burdovsky, and captured your imagination. Your mother, whom I had the honour of getting to know personally and who, though she herself was aware of this rumour, has no idea even to this day (and I was not forthcoming on this point), that you too, her son, had fallen prey to this rumour. I met your highly esteemed mother, Mr Burdovsky, in Pskov, gravely ill and subsisting in the abject poverty which overtook her following Pavlishchev's death. She said with tears of gratitude that she owed her life to you and your assistance, and that she has high hopes in your future and believes with all her heart in your future fortune—"

"This really is intolerable!" Lebedev's nephew suddenly declared loudly and with a show of impatience. "Why do we need this long-drawn-out opera?"

"Frankly, it makes me sick!" Ippolit declared, shifting uneasily. But Burdovsky appeared not to notice anything and remained quite impassive.

"Why indeed?" Gavrila Ardalionovich returned, cunningly pressing home his arguments. "Yes, Mr Burdovsky may now be quite sure that Mr Pavlishchev loved him out of the fullness of his heart, rather than as his son. It was vital that Mr Burdovsky should know this fact above all else after he had confirmed and approved what Mr Keller had just read. I say this because I consider Mr Burdovsky to be a gentleman. Secondly, because here there was no fraud whatsoever, not least on the part of Chebarov. This is important even for me, because the Prince in the heat of the moment suggested that I too shared his views on fraud in this unfortunate affair. In this instance, however, everyone acted in good faith, and though Chebarov may in actual fact be an out-and-out rogue, in this case he has acted only as a professional lawyer presenting a case. He was hoping to make a good deal of money as an advocate, and his strategy was not only subtle and clever, but eminently sound. He took into account the ease with which the Prince parted with his money, and his nobly reverential attitude towards the late Pavlishchev. And lastly, he took note (and this is a key factor) of the Prince's chivalrous attitude towards the obligations of honour and conscience. As regards Mr Burdovsky specifically, one can safely say that in consequence of some of his views, he fell to such an extent under the sway of Chebarov and his entourage that he embarked upon the enterprise not at all out of self-interest, but almost as a tribute to the cause of truth, progress and humanity. Now, after the facts which have been presented, everyone, it would seem, realizes that Mr Burdovsky, despite all appearances, is a man of honour, and the Prince would be even more eager and willing than formerly to offer him both his friendly cooperation and that material assistance, which he mentioned previously, when he talked of schools and Pavlishchev."

"Stop, Gavrila Ardalionovich, stop!" the Prince called out in real fright, but it was too late.

"I said, I said three times already," Burdovsky shouted out irritably, "that I don't want any money! I will not accept it... what for... I won't take it... I'm going!..."

And he nearly ran from the terrace. But Lebedev's nephew grabbed him by the arm and whispered something. Burdovsky turned back sharply, took out a large unsealed envelope from his pocket and threw it on a side table next to the Prince.

"You had no right!... You had no right... no right!... Money!..."

"Two hundred and fifty roubles, which you had the nerve to send him via Chebarov as a favour!" Doktorenko explained.

"In the article it says fifty!" Kolya exclaimed.

"It's my fault!" the Prince said, approaching Burdovsky, "I've wronged you, Burdovsky, but it was not as a favour I sent the money, believe me. I'm being unfair to you even now... and I was wrong then." (The Prince was very upset, he looked tired and weak, and his speech was incoherent.) "I mentioned fraud... but I did not have you in mind, I made a mistake. I said that you... are just like me – ill. But you are not just like me, you... give lessons, you support your mother. I said that you had deserted your mother, but you love her, she has said so herself… I didn't know… Gavrila Ardalionovich hadn't fully put me in the picture… I beg your pardon. I dared to offer you ten thousand, but I beg your pardon, I should have gone about it differently, but now… it's no longer possible, because you detest me—"

"This is a veritable lunatic asylum!" Lizaveta Prokofyevna exclaimed.

"A lunatic asylum, you're so right!" Aglaya, unable to keep quiet, concurred sharply, but her words were lost in the general hubbub; everyone was already talking at the top of their voice – some argued for, others against, yet others laughed. Ivan Fyodorovich Yepanchin was absolutely bursting with indignation and, with affronted dignity, seemed to be waiting upon his spouse, Lizaveta Prokofyevna. Lebedev's nephew had the opportunity of squeezing in the last word.

"Yes, Prince, one has to give it to you, you really know how to make use of your… well, illness (to put it as politely as possible). The way you managed to offer your friendship and money, no decent person could accept either now. This is either too innocent or too clever by half… you must be the best judge."

"Just a minute, gentlemen," Gavrila Ardalionovich exclaimed, who had in the meantime opened the packet with the money, 'it's not two hundred and fifty roubles here at all, only a hundred. I'm pointing this out, Prince, to avoid any misunderstandings."

"Leave it, ignore it!" the Prince tried to silence him, motioning with his hands in protest.

"No, not at all!" Lebedev's nephew latched on immediately. "We take exception at your insistence to ignore it, Prince. We have nothing to hide, we admit openly, yes, here is only a hundred roubles rather than two fifty, but what difference does that make—"

"But, of course, it does," Gavrila Ardalionovich retorted with a look of naive consternation.

"Pray, do not interrupt me! We are not as stupid as you think, Mr Advocate, sir," Lebedev's nephew snapped back with peremptory irritation. "Of course, a hundred roubles are not the same as two hundred and fifty. But it's a principle that is at stake here, the initiative behind it, and the fact that we're a hundred and fifty roubles short, is a mere formality. What is important is that Burdovsky does not accept your favour, Your Highness, that he is throwing it back in your face, and in this sense it makes precious little difference whether it's a hundred or two hundred and fifty. Burdovsky did not accept ten thousand, you saw it. He wouldn't have brought along even a hundred, if he had not been a gentleman! That hundred and fifty roubles went to cover Chebarov's trip to see the Prince. You may laugh at our inexperience, at our inability to see a business transaction through. You've done your level best to turn us into a laughing stock, but don't you dare accuse us of being dishonourable. We shall, my dear sir, make a combined effort to return that hundred and fifty roubles to the Prince. If it comes to it, we will pay him back rouble by rouble and with interest. Burdovsky is poor, Burdovsky does not have a million at his disposal, moreover Chebarov has presented us with an invoice after his trip. We banked on winning... Who'd have acted differently?"

"How do you mean, who?" Prince S. exclaimed.

"I'm going out of my mind!" Lizaveta Prokofyevna intoned.

"This reminds me," Yevgeny Pavlovich, who had been a patient onlooker till then, observed with a laugh, "of a well-known speech by a defence counsel, who pleaded his client's poverty as an excuse for robbing and murdering six of his victims, on the lines that, 'My client's poverty drove him to murder six people, everybody else would have done the same!' That's the gist of it – charming, wouldn't you say?"

"Enough of this!" Lizaveta Prokofyevna pronounced, fairly shaking with anger. "Time to put an end to all this gibberish!..."

She was in a dreadful temper; she flung her head up portentously and, her eyes blazing, seemed to challenge the whole company with supercilious, passionate, uncompromising resolve, at that moment hardly able to distinguish friend from foe. She was at that point of long pent-up anger when the very next stage is war, an immediate urge to attack someone. Those who knew Lizaveta Prokofyevna realized at once that something extraordinary was about to happen to her. The very next day Ivan Fyodorovich was at pains to explain to Prince S. that such things happen to her, but never to the same extent as yesterday, that is, once in three years perhaps, but never more frequently. He particularly and assertively stressed the "never more".

"Enough, Ivan Fyodorovich! Let me be!" Lizaveta Prokofyevna fulminated. "Why do you keep thrusting your hand out towards me? You didn't have the good sense to conduct me out of the room earlier. You're a husband, the head of the family, had I not obeyed you to leave, you should have dragged me, a fool, screaming and kicking out of the room at once. For your daughters' sake if no one else's. Now we'll find our own way out, thank you very much, there'll be enough ignominy to last us a whole year... Wait, I still want to convey my thanks to the Prince!... Thank you, Prince, for the distraction! There I was, ready to lend my ears to the youth of the day... For shame, for shame! This is sheer bedlam, a shambles, the worst of nightmares! Are they really all like that these days?... Keep quiet, Aglaya! You too, Alexandra! It's none of your business!... Yevgeny Pavlovich, you keep getting in my way, please don't, I'm not amused!... So, bless you, you're going to ask these very people for their pardon, is that it?" she continued, turning to the Prince. "'It's all my fault I offered you money!...' And what do you find so funny, you gasbag?" she suddenly lashed out at Lebedev's nephew: "'We won't accept the money, we don't ask, we demand!' As though he didn't know that come the next day this idiot would again be knocking at their door offering his friendship and capital! You would go, wouldn't you?"

"Yes," the Prince said in a quiet, resigned voice.

"Did you all hear that? That's exactly what you're counting on, isn't it?" she turned to Doktorenko again. "I suppose the money is as good as in your pocket already, so you can go blustering about, pulling wool over our eyes... No, my dear sir, some fools may succumb to such ruses, but I can see right through you... I can see the whole of your game!"

"Lizaveta Prokofyevna!" the Prince exclaimed.

"Let's not stay here any longer, Lizaveta Prokofyevna," Prince S. said in a restrained voice, with a smile, "it's time we went and took the Prince with us too."

The young ladies stood somewhat apart, rather alarmed, the General was positively panicked; everybody was in a turmoil. Some, who stood furthest away, uttered a few half-stifled laughs and exchanged covert whispered comments. Lebedev's face was absolutely beaming with delight.

"Turmoil and chaos, my dear lady, are ubiquitous," Lebedev's nephew commented condescendingly, though visibly flustered.

"Nothing like this! Nothing like what I'm now witnessing, young man, nothing like it at all!" Lizaveta Prokofyevna remarked almost gloatingly with a note of hysteria in her voice. "Let me be, I say!" she shouted at those who tried to placate her. "Well, if you yourself,

Yevgeny Pavlovich, mentioned that a counsel for the defence in a court of law announced there was nothing more natural than on a plea of poverty to dispatch six people, then I must say the end of the world is upon us. I've not heard anything the like before. Now everything is crystal clear! Do you think this stutterer isn't capable of killing?" she said, pointing at Burdovsky, who was looking at her in extreme consternation. "I swear to God, he is! He may well in all conscience refuse your money, the ten thousand, that I grant you, but he'll come to you in the night to slit your throat from ear to ear and help himself to your money from your cash box – without so much as a twinge of conscience! This would be all in a night's work for him! This would be 'an act of noble desperation' for him, 'a rebellion' or some such rubbish... Bah! Everything's been turned inside out and upside down. You bring up a girl in your family, suddenly she will jump into a droshky on the road, 'Mother dear, I married Boris so-and-so or Ivan this-and-that the other day, goodbye!' And you would approve of such behaviour, wouldn't you? You'd consider it praiseworthy and natural, I suppose? Women's liberation movement? That boy there," she pointed at Kolya, "argued too the other day that it's a question of women's rights. But even if a mother has been foolish, you should still treat her with respect!... Why did you come here with your heads up in the air as if to say, 'Stay back, we're coming! Our might is right, and you lot pipe down! We'll rake in all the honours, no matter if we don't deserve them; as for you, we'll treat you like dirt!' They want to know the truth, they want to stand on their rights, but have themselves like a pack of infidels savaged the Prince in the article. 'We don't ask, we demand, and don't you expect any gratitude from us, because it's your own conscience you want to salve!' A fine set of morals! But don't you realize if there'll be no gratitude from you, the Prince can also turn around and say he feels no gratitude towards Pavlishchev, because Pavlishchev too did it to salve his own conscience. Whereas all you counted on was precisely this gratitude of his towards Pavlishchev. After all, the Prince didn't borrow the money from you, it's not you he's beholden to, so what precisely were you counting on if it wasn't gratitude? So how can you stand there and refuse it after all this? This is a madhouse! Society is being condemned for being inhuman and cruel for condemning a fallen girl. But if you admit that society is cruel, it follows that society is causing the girl pain. And if so, how can you yourself expose this girl in newspapers before this very society and expect her not to feel pain? You're mad, you people! You're overreaching yourselves! You've no faith in God, you've no faith in Christ! Arrogance and pride have possessed you to the extent that you'll end up devouring one another, that much I predict for you. Is this not sheer absurdity, bedlam, disarray? And after all that, this shameless fool is going to go crawling on all fours to beg their forgiveness! How many like you are there altogether? What's so funny? That I've lowered myself to your level? Well, I have, and it can't be helped now!... Wipe that grin off your face, you pipsqueak!" she suddenly turned on Ippolit. "You've hardly a breath left in your body and yet you're happy to waste it on spreading falsehood. You've corrupted this boy for me," she pointed at Kolya again. "All he does is to look up to you, while you teach him atheism! You don't believe in God, what you need is a good hiding, my dear sir, to hell with the lot of you!... So, you are going to go to them tomorrow, Prince Lev Nikolayevich, aren't you?" she concluded.

"Yes."

"I'll have nothing to do with you then!"

She turned sharply to go, but suddenly she halted.

"And are you going to see this atheist?" she asked, pointing at Ippolit. "Why are you grinning at me?" she exclaimed in an unnatural tone of voice and rushed up to Ippolit, unable to endure his caustic smile.

"Lizaveta Prokofyevna! Lizaveta Prokofyevna! Lizaveta Prokofyevna!" voices resounded on all sides at once.

"*Maman*, this is embarrassing!" Aglaya exclaimed loudly.

"Don't worry, Aglaya Ivanovna," Ippolit replied calmly. Lizaveta Prokofyevna, having rushed up to him, had grabbed him by his hand and was now for some reason holding it fast. She stood facing him, her crazed eyes boring into his, "Have no fear, your *maman* will soon learn that it's not the done thing to pounce upon a dying man... I'd be glad to explain why I was laughing... I'd be much obliged for the opportunity..."

Here he fell into a dreadful bout of coughing which lasted for a whole minute.

"The fellow's dying and still he wants to have his say!" Lizaveta Prokofyevna exclaimed and let go of his hand, observing Ippolit with horror as he wiped blood off his lips. "You've no business standing and spouting off here! You ought to be in bed..."

"Yes, of course," Ippolit replied in a soft, hoarse whisper, "as soon as I get back, I'll go to bed immediately... in two weeks, as I've been told, I shall dead... I had it from B.* personally last week... If you would allow me, I'd like to say a couple words to you in parting..."

"Are you out of your mind, or something? Rubbish! You need medical treatment, not speechifying! Be off with you, on the double, to bed!..." Lizaveta Prokofyevna commanded, full of concern.

"If I lie down, I shall never get up again," Ippolit said with a smile. "I had a good mind to take to my bed yesterday, and await the end, but decided to wait another couple of days, while my legs can still carry me... to join you here today... I'm completely exhausted though—"

"Here you are, sit down, sit down, you shouldn't be standing! Here's a chair for you," Lizaveta Prokofyevna livened up all of a sudden and brought a chair up to him herself.

"Thank you kindly," Ippolit said in a subdued voice, "and you sit opposite, and we'll talk... we must, Lizaveta Prokofyevna, this time I insist..." he said, smiling once again. "Just think, today I'm up and about, and amongst people, and in a fortnight I'll probably be pushing up daisies. So this is going to be a kind of farewell both to people and nature. Though I'm not particularly sentimental, you may all the same be surprised that I'm delighted it has all come about here in Pavlovsk, surrounded by trees in full leaf.

"That's enough of talking," Lizaveta Prokofyevna interposed, getting ever more concerned, "you're running a fever. After all that griping and posturing, you should settle down now and get your breath back!"

"I will. Why won't you grant me my last wish?... You know, Lizaveta Prokofyevna, I've long dreamt of getting to know you. I heard a lot about you... from Kolya. He's practically the only one who has stood by me... You're unusual, unconventional, I've seen it for myself... you know, I'm terribly fond of you."

"Goodness, and I nearly hit him."

"Aglaya Ivanovna held you back. I'm right, am I not? This is your daughter Aglaya Ivanovna, isn't it? She is so beautiful, that I knew her from first glance, even though I've never seen her in my life. Allow me at least to feast my eyes for the last time on true loveliness," Ippolit said with some kind of an awkward, wry smile. "My respects to the Prince, to your spouse and you all. But why do you deny me my last wish?"

"A chair!" Lizaveta Prokofyevna called out, but she grabbed one herself and sat down opposite Ippolit. "Kolya," she commanded, "you are to take him home immediately, and tomorrow I myself without fail—"

"With your permission, I'd like to ask the Prince for a cup of tea... I am very tired. You know what, Lizaveta Prokofyevna, I had the impression you wanted to take the Prince along with you to have tea together. Don't go, let's spend a while together, and I'm sure the Prince will treat us to some tea here. I hope you don't mind my talking things over... But I know you, you're very kind, so is the Prince... we are all laughably kind people..."

The Prince sat up, Lebedev rushed out of the room in all haste. Vera followed him.

"You're quite right," the General's Lady agreed emphatically. "Go on then, only don't raise your voice and don't get carried away. You've touched my heartstrings... Prince! You don't deserve that I should have tea with you. We'll let that pass, I'm staying, but I'm begging nobody's pardon! Nobody's! What nonsense!... To be sure, if I told you off, Prince, do forgive me – that's if you're so inclined. For the rest, I'm not detaining anyone," she suddenly turned with extreme fury on her husband and daughters as though it was precisely they who bore all the guilt. "I can very well find my own way home—"

But she was not allowed to finish. Everybody surrounded her, expressing utmost goodwill. The Prince immediately set to persuading everyone to stay and take tea, excusing himself at the same time for not thinking of this himself earlier. Even the General relented and mumbled something placatory and enquired politely of Lizaveta Prokofyevna if it was not too cool for her on the terrace. He was also on the point of enquiring of Ippolit how long he had been at the university, but thought better of it. Yevgeny Pavlovich and Prince S. were utterly charming and well pleased with themselves. Adelaida and Alexandra were both beaming with pleasure, when only shortly before their faces depicted puzzlement; in short, everybody was visibly glad that the crisis with Lizaveta Prokofyevna had been averted. Only Aglaya was sullen and she sat down a little apart. Everybody stayed put. No one wanted to leave; even General Ivolgin, in whose ear Lebedev managed to whisper something in passing, probably none too pleasant, merely retired into a distant corner. The Prince approached Burdovsky and his men, attending to each one. They muttered something with hangdog faces that they would wait for Ippolit, and immediately withdrew to the furthest part of the terrace, where they all sat down in a line. It looked as though tea had already long been made ready on Lebedev's instruction, because it was brought in without delay. The clock struck eleven.

10

IPPOLIT RAISED THE CUP OF TEA, passed to him by Vera Lebedeva, just enough to wet his lips, placed it on a little table beside him, and looked around timidly, overcome by a sudden onrush of confusion.

"Take a look at these china cups, Lizaveta Prokofyevna!" he said with some kind of strange urgency. "It's the very best china, I think. Lebedev always keeps them in a sideboard, locked away behind glass, never to be taken out... a family tradition, they came with his wife's dowry... they're all very particular about it... but now he's brought them out, in our honour, of course, he's so pleased..."

He wanted to add something, but stopped short.

"He's lost his thread, I was afraid of that!" Yevgeny Pavlovich whispered in the Prince's ear. "This is serious, wouldn't you say? A sure sign that in the offended state he is now in, you can expect any stupidity from him, which even Lizaveta Prokofyevna would probably not tolerate."

The Prince cast him a puzzled look.

"I take it you are not bothered by any stupidity, are you?" Yevgeny Pavlovich added. "I'm not, in fact, I'd welcome it. What I'd like most, is to see our delightful Lizaveta Prokofyevna have her comeuppance, tonight, as soon as possible. I'm not leaving before it happens. You look as though you've got the shakes."

"Later! Don't! Yes, I'm not well," the Prince responded absent-mindedly, even irritably. He had just heard his name mentioned; Ippolit was talking about him.

"You don't believe me?" Ippolit brought out with a nervous laugh. "I expected as much, but the Prince will believe me from the first, and won't be surprised at all."

"Did you hear that, Prince?" Lizaveta Prokofyevna asked, turning to face him. "Did you hear that?"

Everyone was laughing. Lebedev thrust himself forward, all agog with excitement, shifting restlessly right in front of Lizaveta Prokofyevna.

"He says that this buffoon, your host, mind… put the finishing touches to that man's article, which was just read out at your expense." *)L . P.*

The Prince regarded Lebedev with surprise.

"Why don't you say something?" Lizaveta Prokofyevna demanded, and even stamped her foot.

"What's to be done?" the Prince said, continuing to regard Lebedev. "I can see he has lent a helping hand."

"Is that true?" Lizaveta Prokofyevna turned abruptly to Lebedev.

"As true as you see me standing before you, Your Excellency!" Lebedev said firmly and resolutely with his hand on his heart.

"The man is proud of it!" she exclaimed with a start.

"I'm a knave, a veritable knave!" Lebedev mumbled, beating his breast and dropping his head more and more.

"What do I care if you're a knave! He thinks if he says he's a knave, that'll be the end of the matter. Aren't you ashamed of yourself, Prince, to have truck with such worthless people? Answer me! I'll never forgive you for this!"

"The Prince will!" Lebedev returned with sly conviction.

"It was out of a sense of honour," Keller suddenly announced in a loud voice, rushing up to Lizaveta Prokofyevna and addressing her directly, "purely out of a sense of honour, and so as not to betray and compromise a friend, that I did not let on about the emendations, my dear lady, even though he threatened to throw us down the stairs, which you heard. In the interest of truth I now declare that I did in fact approach him for a down payment of six roubles, as coming from a competent person to clarify some facts of which I was by and largely ignorant, but not regarding style. It was about the gaiters, about the Swiss professor's predilections, about the fifty rather than the two hundred and fifty roubles, in a word, all this six-roubles-worth of information stems from him, but he had no hand in the style."

"I must point out," Lebedev intervened somewhat tetchily and yet with an obsequious drawl amidst all round guffaws, "that I looked only at the first part of the article, and since when we reached the middle, we could not come to an understanding and even fell out over one point, I left the second half well alone, so that all the infelicities

301

contained there (and it is full of infelicities!) ought not to be ascribed to me—"

"So that's what he's concerned about!" Lizaveta Prokofyevna exclaimed.

"If I may ask," Yevgeny Pavlovich enquired, addressing Keller, "when was the article amended?"

"Yesterday morning," Keller replied, "when we met and gave mutually binding gentlemen's assurances to keep the matter strictly confidential."

"This at a time when he was crawling before you assuring you of his friendship! My word! You can keep your Pushkin, and don't let your daughter come near my house!"

Lizaveta Prokofyevna was about to stand up, but, breaking into sudden anger, she turned on Ippolit who was sniggering.

"What's so funny, my dear fellow, or is it me you're laughing at?"

"God forbid," Ippolit responded with a wry grimace, "but I must say I am taken by your very unconventional ways, Lizaveta Prokofyevna. I must admit though, I purposely brought Lebedev into all this, because I knew what effect it would have on you, and on you alone, seeing that the Prince would not bear any grudges against Lebedev, and may even have pardoned him altogether... for all I know he's already got an apology worked out, haven't you, Prince?"

He was short of breath and possessed by a strange disquiet, which was mounting with every passing minute.

"Well?..." Lizaveta Prokofyevna challenged him, surprised at his tone of voice. "Well?"

"I've heard a lot about you on these lines," Ippolit went on, "and... I am delighted... to assure you of my unbounded respect."

He was saying one thing, but it was as though these same words were meant to convey something quite different. There was a note of derision in his voice, but this was belied by his extreme agitation, his wary glances all round and the confused, faltering manner of his delivery, so that combined with his consumptive appearance, characterized by an intensely feverish glow in his eyes, he could not fail to be the centre of attraction.

"I am astonished – though of course, I do not pretend to know the ways of this world (I'm being perfectly frank here) – that not only did you yourself stay behind in such unbefitting company, but that you allowed these... young ladies too to hear out such a scandalous business, never mind that they had come across the like long ago in novels. Perhaps I'm not the one to speak... because my speech is confused, but all in all, who but you would have stayed... at the bidding of a mere juvenile (well yes, juvenile, I again admit freely) to spend an evening with him and delve into... all the ins and outs of the matter... to the extent... of being embarrassed the next morning (look, I know, I'm putting it badly), but I'm full of praise and deep admiration, even though I can tell just by looking at your spouse's – His Highness's – face, how utterly unpleasant all this is for him... He-he!" he ended with a giggle, completely at a loss what to say next, and suddenly fell to coughing, which lasted for a good two minutes, making it impossible for him to continue.

"That's all we needed!" Lizaveta Prokofyevna said coldly and sharply, observing him with stern interest. "But it's high time we put an end to all this talking, my young lad. Let's go!"

"Allow me too, my dear sir, to say for my part," Ivan Fyodorovich suddenly spoke up with irritation, his patience having been obviously sorely tried, "that my wife happens to be here at the invitation of Prince Lev Nikolayevich, our mutual friend and neighbour, and it does not behove you, young man, of all people, to remark on what Lizaveta Prokofyevna might or might not do, nor equally to comment out loud in my presence as to what you might read in my face. Is that understood? And if my wife has chosen to stay behind," he continued, his irritation mounting practically with every word, "it is more than likely, sir, to have been out of a sense of wonderment and well-justified curiosity at the sight of an outlandish bunch of latter day youths. I too have stayed behind, much as I sometimes stop in the street in order to observe something... something... something..."

"Something rare," Yevgeny Pavlovich came to the rescue.

"That's just the word I was looking for," His Highness responded joyfully, having run into some difficulties of articulation, "precisely, something rare. But what is particularly astonishing and aggravating for me is that you, young man, so to speak, have failed so much as to grasp that Lizaveta Prokofyevna has stayed behind simply because you are ill, and – as we are led to believe – dying; that is to say out of compassion, listening to your heart-rending words, sir, and that nothing whatsoever can besmirch her name, calling or her standing...

Lizaveta Prokofyevna," he concluded, growing red in the face, "if you wish to go, let's bid our kind Prince goodbye and—"

"Thank you for your lecture, General," Ippolit interrupted unexpectedly with a serious mien, looking at the General pensively.

"Shall we go, *Maman*? How much longer!..." Aglaya said impatiently, brimming with anger, and rose to her feet.

"Allow me two more minutes, my dear Ivan Fyodorovich, if you would," Lizaveta Prokofyevna said, turning with a dignified air towards her spouse. "I think he is in a state of fever, and is simply raving. I can see it in his eyes. He must not be left like this. Lev Nikolayevich, could he stay the night here to avoid him being escorted back to St Petersburg today? *Cher Prince*, are you bored?" she unexpectedly asked Prince S. "Come here, Alexandra – your hair, my child, let me see!"

She adjusted her daughter's hair, which needed no adjustment, and kissed her. That was all she called her over for.

"I supposed you progressive..." Ippolit resumed, coming out of his brown study. "Yes, that's what I wanted to say!" he called out, as though a bright idea had hit him suddenly. "There we have Burdovsky, who desperately wants to protect his mother, am I right? But it turns out he discredits her. The Prince wants to help Burdovsky, in the purity of his heart he fondly offers him his friendship and money and is perhaps the only one of you all who feels no aversion towards him, and yet it is these two who now stand opposed to each other as real foes... Ha-ha-ha! You detest Burdovsky because in your opinion he is uncouth and ungraceful in the treatment of his mother, isn't that so? Isn't it? Isn't it? What you all go for is prettiness and sleekness of form, that's all that matters for you, am I not right? (I long suspected as much!) Well then, let me tell you, there's perhaps no one amongst you who loves his mother as much as Burdovsky does! I know, Prince, you secretly sent some money with Ganya to Burdovsky's mother, and I'd bet... he-he-he!..." (he was seized by a hysterical fit of laughter) "I'd bet my last rouble that Burdovsky will now accuse you of disrespect towards his mother, I swear it, ha-ha-ha!"

At this point he again ran out of breath and began coughing.

"Well, is that all now? Have you had your say? Go to bed now, you've got a fever," Lizaveta Prokofyevna, who had been eyeing him anxiously all the time, interrupted him sharply. "My goodness! Will he never stop talking!"

"You're laughing, is that it?" Ippolit, vexed and irritated, suddenly turned on Yevgeny Pavlovich. The latter was indeed laughing. "Why are you all laughing at me? I noticed you're all laughing at me."

"I merely wanted to ask you, Mr... Ippolit... I'm sorry, I forgot your surname."

"Mr Terentyev," the Prince said.

"Yes, Terentyev, thank you, Prince, it was mentioned earlier, but it had escaped my... I wanted to ask you, Mr Terentyev, if it was true, as I heard, that you believe if you were to spend a quarter of an hour addressing people from your window, they'd agree with you on all points and would follow you immediately?"

"It's quite likely I may have said that..." Ippolit replied as though recalling something. "Come to think of it, I definitely did!" he added suddenly, perking up again, and giving Yevgeny Pavlovich a determined look. "But what of it?"

"Nothing whatever. Merely for information – to complete the picture."

Yevgeny Pavlovich stopped, but Ippolit still continued to regard him expectantly.

"Well, have you finished, or what?" Lizaveta Prokofyevna asked Yevgeny Pavlovich. "I wish you would, my good friend, it's high time he was in bed. Or have you got stuck?" She was in a foul mood.

"Frankly, I wouldn't mind at all adding," Yevgeny Pavlovich continued with a smile, "that all that I heard from your friends, Mr Terentyev, and all that you have just now so ably expounded, may, to my mind, be reduced first and foremost to the principle of Right is Might, over and above all else, that is, even to the exclusion of all else, nay even at the expense of establishing what would constitute Right proper. But I may be wrong."

"Of course, you are! I don't even know what you are talking about... but go on!"

There was some murmur at the far end of the terrace. Lebedev's nephew mumbled something under his breath.

"There's not much else left to say," Yevgeny Pavlovich continued, "all I wanted to point out was that as a consequence this may turn into Might is Right, that is into the Rule of the Jungle and of individual whim, as has incidentally often been the case in the world. Take Proudhon* for one, who became fixated on the idea of Might is Right!

305

In the American War of Independence many of the most progressive liberals declared themselves in favour of the colonists, on the grounds that negroes were negroes, inferior to the white race, who consequently had the right to dominate—"

"So?"

"Evidently you don't deny that Might is Right, do you?"

"I'm listening."

"You are consistent if nothing else. All I wanted to point out was that it is but a short step from Might is Right to the rule of the jungle and even Danilov and Gorsky."

"I wouldn't know. But go on."

Ippolit was barely listening to Yevgeny Pavlovich. "So?" and "But go on!" were merely standard, long established, responses used in conversation rather than expressions of curiosity or attentiveness.

"There's nothing more to say... I have finished."

"To be sure, I'm not angry with you," Ippolit concluded unexpectedly and, quite distractedly, put out his hand and even managed to smile. Yevgeny Pavlovich was a little surprised at first but was quite serious when he put out his own to make contact as though accepting pardon.

"I cannot help expressing," he said in the same ambiguously courteous tone of voice, "my gratitude for the consideration with which you allowed me to have my say, because according to my personal observation not a single one of our liberals would ever permit his opponent to hold a personal point of view and not challenge it other than by swearing or even something worse—"

"There you're quite right," General Ivan Fyodorovich observed, standing despondently in the doorway, his hands behind his back, unable to suppress a deep yawn.

"Look, say no more, my good friend," Lizaveta Prokofyevna suddenly observed to Yevgeny Pavlovich, "you bore me—"

"Time we went," Ippolit said apprehensively, almost in alarm, as he cast confused glances about him, "I've held you up. I meant to say everything to you... I thought you all... for the last time... it was silly of me..."

It was evident he came to life spasmodically, suddenly emerging for a few brief seconds from an out-and-out delirium to full consciousness to enunciate in snatches what he had, perhaps way back, pondered and agonized over in the course of lonely, interminably long sleepless hours of illness...

"Farewell then!" he suddenly said sharply. "You think it's easy for me to say farewell to you? Ha-ha!" He tried to make light of his own awkward question and, as though infuriated by his inability to express what had built up inside him, said in a loud, short-tempered voice, "Your Highness, may I cordially invite you to my funeral, if you would do me the honour and... the rest of you too, ladies and gentlemen, along with the General!..."

He laughed again, but it was the laugh of the insane. Lizaveta Prokofyevna rushed up to him in alarm and grabbed him by his hand. He regarded her closely; he was still laughing, but the laughter had congealed on his face and was not audible.

"Do you realize I came here to look at trees? Those over there..." he pointed at the trees in the park, "isn't it funny? Actually it isn't," he said to Lizaveta Prokofyevna, and fell back into his reverie; the next instant he raised his head and his eyes began to wander over the company in search of someone. He was searching for Yevgeny Pavlovich, who stood nearby, on the right, where he had stood previously, but Ippolit was no longer aware of this. "Ah, you're still here!" he said, after he had finally spotted him. "You were laughing just now that I wanted to speak from the window for a quarter of an hour... Do you realize I'm not even eighteen? I've spent so long lying on this pillow and staring out of the window, thinking of everybody... that... The dead are ageless, you know. I thought of it the other week when I awoke one night. And do you know what you're afraid of most of all? Though you may hate us, you're most of all afraid of our honesty! This also came to me on my pillow in the night... Did you think I wanted to mock you, Lizaveta Prokofyevna? No, I wasn't mocking you. I meant to pay tribute to you... Kolya said that the Prince called you a child... I like it... But now what... what else was I going to say?..."

He buried his face in his hands and thought.

"I know! When you were saying goodbye, I suddenly thought – here are all these people, and then there won't be any, ever! Same goes for the trees. All that will be left will be the red brick wall of Meyer's house... opposite my window... well, you try telling them about any of this... just try. Take a beautiful girl... you're a corpse, introduce yourself as a dead man, tell her there's nothing a dead man can't say, and who's to stop him, ha-ha!*... Why aren't you laughing?" he enquired, looking around warily. "Do you know, lying on my pillow, a lot of things crossed my mind... do you know, I came to realize that nature is very derisive... You said just now that I'm an atheist, but do you realize that this nature... Why are you laughing again? You're very cruel!" he suddenly observed, looking around with cheerless resentment. "I haven't been corrupting Kolya," he concluded in a much altered tone, firm and self-assured, as though calling something back to mind.

"No one, no one at all is making fun of you, calm down!" Lizaveta Prokofyevna took pains to reassure him. "A different doctor will come tomorrow, the first one was wrong. Do sit down, you shouldn't be up on your feet! You're raving... Oh, what is to be done with him?" she grieved, helping him into an armchair. A tear glistened on her cheek.

Ippolit stopped, quite overcome; he lifted his arm and put out his hand timidly to touch this tear. A childish smile flitted across his features.

"I... you," he began joyously, "you've no idea how I... he was so enthused whenever he talked about you, I mean Kolya, over there... I love his enthusiasm. I've not been corrupting him! He's the only one I shall miss... I know, I'll miss you all... but there's no one, no one, there's no one... I wanted to be a man of action, I had the right... Oh, the things I wanted! Now I want nothing, I want to want nothing, I promised myself, not to want anything. Let them seek truth and leave me out of it! Yes, Mother Nature is derisive! Why does she," he suddenly exclaimed with fervour, "why does she create the best of life forms just in order to deride them later? I ask you, did she not create the one life form, which everyone recognized as perfect... did she not in presenting Him to the people, call upon Him to say that which caused so much blood to be spilt that if it had been spilt all at once, people would probably have drowned in it? Oh, it's good that I'm dying! Or I too might have been led on by Mother Nature to come up with some terrible lie... I've not been corrupting anyone... I wanted to live in order to bring happiness to all people, in order to reveal and proclaim truth... I looked out on Meyer's wall out of my window and meant in a mere quarter of an hour to convince everyone, just everyone, and for once in my life I... found common ground with you, if not with people! And what happened? Nothing at all! What happened is that you have come to hate me! It follows, I'm surplus to requirement, it follows I'm a fool, it follows – my time has come! Nor have I been able to leave any kind of a memory after me! Not a sound, not a trace, not a single deed, nor have I introduced a single concept... Don't make fun of a fool! Forget! Forget everything!... Forget, please, don't be so cruel! Do you know, if it hadn't been for this consumption, I'd have killed myself anyway..."

It seemed there was much more he wanted to say, but could not; he flung himself into a chair, buried his face in his hands and burst out crying like a small child.

"Well, what now?" Lizaveta Prokofyevna exclaimed, and rushed up to him, flung her arms round his head and pressed it tight against her chest. He wept convulsively. "There, there now! Stop crying, look here, that'll do, you're a good boy, God will forgive you on account of your ignorance. That'll do, pull yourself together... You'll be sorry later—"

"I've a brother and sisters there," Ippolit said, trying to raise his head, "children, small, poor, innocent... *She* will corrupt them! You are a saint, you are... a child yourself – don't let them perish! Pull them away from this... she... disgrace... Please help them, help them, God will reward you a hundredfold, for God's sake, for Christ's sake—!"

"Say something at last, Ivan Fyodorovich, what's to be done now?" Lizaveta Prokofyevna appealed to her husband irritably. "Do me a favour, break your supercilious silence! Unless you come to a decision, I'm warning you, I shall stay here the night. You've tyrannized me enough under your arbitrariness!"

There was fire and resolution in Lizaveta Prokofyevna's demand, and she expected an immediate response. But in cases like that people in the main, even if there are many of them, usually respond with silence and passive curiosity, not wishing to commit themselves, and tend to air their views only much later. Amongst the company present there were such who were ready to remain seated there till the small hours if necessary and not utter a word; one such was Varvara Ardalionovna, who had been sitting silently all evening a little apart, taking in everything with the utmost curiosity, and perhaps for a very good reason.

"If you want to know what I think, my dear," the General said, seeing his opportunity to say his piece, "what is required here is a nurse, so to speak, rather than our sympathy, and, by all appearances, a reliable, clear-headed person for the night. At all events, we should ask the Prince and... immediately leave him in peace. Tomorrow we could again continue from where we left off."

"It is now twelve, and we're going. Is he staying here or coming with us?" Doktorenko addressed the Prince short-temperedly.

"If you wish, why don't you stay with him?" the Prince proposed, "there's no shortage of room."

"Your Highness," Mr Keller unexpectedly rushed up to the General, brimming with enthusiasm, "if a competent person is needed for the night, I'm ready to step in for my friend... he is such a man! I've long held him in the highest regard, Your Highness! Of course, I failed to keep up my education, but if he criticizes anything, each of his words is a pearl, he casts sheer pearls about him, Your Highness!..."

The General turned away in desperation.

"I'd be very glad if he stayed. The journey is bound to be very stressful for him," the Prince declared in response to Lizaveta Prokofyevna's petulant questions.

"And are you going to retire to bed yourself? If you prefer, my dear sir, I can take him with me! Good God, he can hardly stand up himself. Are you ill, what's wrong with you?"

Not finding the Prince on his deathbed and basing herself on outward indications, Lizaveta Prokofyevna had really severely overestimated his health and well-being. But his recent illness, the profound reminiscences that followed, the fatigue brought on by the turbulent evening, the incident with "the son of Pavlishchev", the more recent one just now with Ippolit – all this helped to raise his febrile imagination almost to fever pitch. Besides, he had something else on his mind which worried, nay inspired fear in him – it was Ippolit, whom he regarded with apprehension as though expecting some new turn from him.

Suddenly Ippolit rose to his feet, terribly pale, his features contorted by shame to the point of despair; this was evident predominantly in his eyes, which were ranging over the company with timid revulsion, and in his confused, cynical smirk, spread across his trembling lips. He immediately lowered his eyes and, shaking from side to side, staggered over to Burdovsky and Doktorenko, who stood at the door of the terrace; he was prepared to leave with them.

"Well, that's precisely what I was afraid of!" the Prince exclaimed. "This was bound to happen!"

Ippolit swung around towards him in utter fury, every muscle on his face in taut defiance.

"So that's what you were afraid of? 'This was bound to happen!' – you imagined it, didn't you? Well then, let me tell you, if there's anyone I detest here, and I detest the whole lot of you," he screeched hoarsely, wheezing and spluttering, "you, you mealy-mouthed Jesuit, idiot, millionaire do-gooder, I detest more than anything or anyone on earth! I had the measure of you and hated you a long time ago when I first heard of you, I hated you with every fibre of my body... It was you who brought me to this! It was you who have caused me to have this fit! You have caused a dying man to blush in shame, you, you, you are the cause of my base cowardice! Had I been allowed to live, I'd have killed you! I don't need your kindness, or anyone else's, did you hear that, I'll accept nothing from anyone! I was delirious, and you've no right to gloat!... Damn the lot of you for all time!"

Here he ran out of breath completely.

"He doesn't like to be seen crying!" Lebedev whispered to Lizaveta Prokofyevna. "'This was bound to happen!' What a man this Prince of ours! He read his innermost thoughts..."

But Lizaveta Prokofyevna did not deign to look at him. She stood proud, erect, her head held high, surveying "that lot" with supercilious disdain. After Ippolit stopped, the General squared his shoulders; but his wife looked him up and down angrily as though holding him to account for that movement, and immediately addressed the Prince.

"Thank you, Prince, our eccentric friend of the family, for the lovely evening you prepared for us. I do not doubt you are happy now for having dragged us down to your own level... Enough, our dear friend of the family, thank you for at least giving us the opportunity to see who you are!..."

She angrily began to adjust her mantilla, waiting for Burdovsky and his men to depart. At that moment a droshky pulled up outside, which Doktorenko had had sent for about a quarter of an hour previously by Lebedev's schoolboy son. The General followed his wife's example and put in his word.

"Really, Prince, this was the last thing I expected... after everything, after all our friendly relations... and, lastly, Lizaveta Prokofyevna—"

"How, how on earth is this possible!" Adelaida exclaimed, approached the Prince quickly and put out her hand.

The Prince smiled at her guiltily. Suddenly a fervent, hurried whisper seemed to scald his ear. It was Aglaya.

"If you don't get rid of all these despicable people immediately, I'll hate you all life long, especially you!" She seemed to be at her wits' end, but she turned away before the Prince had time to look at her. To be sure, there was no one left to be got rid of. In the meantime the ailing Ippolit was helped into the droshky and it drove off.

"So, how much longer is all this going to go on for, Ivan Fyodorovich? What do you think? How much more do I have to endure from these intolerable youngsters?"

"Yes, I, my dearest... I, naturally, am quite ready... so is the Prince..."

Ivan Fyodorovich put out his hand to the Prince but withdrew it before the Prince had time to react, and dashed after Lizaveta Prokofyevna, who was descending the terrace steps in a noisy show of anger. Adelaida, her bridegroom and Alexandra bid the Prince hearty farewells. They were joined by Yevgeny Pavlovich, who alone was in a jovial mood.

"It was all to be expected, only I'm sorry it turned out to be so painful for you, you poor thing," he whispered with the most benign smile. Aglaya left without saying goodbye.

But the evening had another surprise in store; Lizaveta Prokofyevna had to endure another rather unexpected encounter.

She had hardly time to descend the steps to the road, which skirted the park, when a splendid equipage, a calash, drawn by two white horses, suddenly sped towards the Prince's dacha. In the calash were two magnificently attired ladies. Ten paces further on it came to an abrupt halt. One of the ladies turned as though she had spotted some acquaintance she was longing to see.

"Yevgeny! Is that you?" a wonderful voice rang out, at which the Prince jumped, and he may not have been alone. "Look here, I'm so glad I've found you at long last! I sent a messenger, no – two! They've been looking for you all day!"

Yevgeny Pavlovich stood on the steps of the terrace, thunderstruck. Lizaveta Prokofyevna also stood stock-still, but there was no fear or consternation in her bearing as was the case with Yevgeny Pavlovich; she looked at the arrogant intruder just as haughtily and with an equal measure of cold disdain as when surveying "that lot" only five minutes previously, and she immediately transferred her eyes to Yevgeny Pavlovich.

"A piece of news for you, Yevgeny!" the ringing voice went on. "The Kupfer promissory notes are safe. Rogozhin bought them up for thirty thousand, I talked him into it. You can rest easy on that score for another three months if you wish. As for the Bishop and the rest of that misbegotten crowd, we'll deal with them in the family! Well, that'll be all – in a word, things are on the up. Be happy! See you tomorrow!"

The calash sped off.

"She's mad!" Yevgeny Pavlovich exclaimed at last, going red with indignation and at a complete loss, not knowing where to look. "I've no idea what she was talking about! What shares? Who the blazes is she?"

Lizaveta Prokofyevna continued to look at him for another second or two; then she turned on her heel and headed for her dacha, followed by everyone else. A minute later Yevgeny Pavlovich, highly agitated, returned to the terrace to see the Prince.

"Prince, in truth, have you any idea what all this is about?"

"I know nothing at all," the Prince replied, tense and fever-racked as he was.

"Really?"

"Really."

"Neither do I," Yevgeny Pavlovich suddenly burst out laughing. "I swear I've not dealt with any kind of shares, honestly!... I say, what's wrong? Are you going to faint?"

"No, not at all, I assure you..."

11

IT TOOK TWO MORE DAYS for the Yepanchins to relent completely. Even though the Prince as usual held himself responsible in many respects and awaited his punishment, yet from the start he was inwardly fully convinced that Lizaveta Prokofyevna could not bear a serious grudge against him, but that her displeasure was directed more against her own self. Thus it was that after such a protracted period of enmity he found himself towards the end of the third day in a very foul mood altogether. There were, of course, contributory circumstances, but one predominated. It grew steadily in his febrile imagination (lately the Prince accused himself of two extremes – a senseless gullibility, and along with it, a depressing, unworthy mistrustfulness). In a word, the impression created by the eccentric lady addressing Yevgeny Pavlovich from her equipage, took on rather frightening and mysterious proportions. The mystery element for the Prince was, apart from anything else, contained in the painful question: was he personally to blame for this new "outrage", or was it also the fault of... But he avoided mentioning who else it might be. As to the person with the initials N.F.B., to his mind hers was only an innocent prank, to boot a very childish prank, such that to bring it up would be unfair, and in some respects, even unworthy.

Be that as it may, the day after the scandalous soirée, in which he was so intimately involved, the Prince had the pleasure of a visit from Prince S. and Adelaida, who said they'd been out strolling and had popped in *principally* to enquire after his health. In the park Adelaida had noticed a tree, a wonderful old tree, sprawling, with long, misshapen boughs, all in verdant greenery, with a hollow and a split running the whole length of it. She was determined to paint it, and talked practically of nothing else during the whole half-hour of their visit. Prince S. was as usual cordial and gracious: he enquired about bygone days, reminisced about their first meeting, with the result that nothing much was said about the previous day's happenings. Finally, Adelaida admitted with a smile that they had dropped in without the knowledge of her parents; but that was as far as she went, although one could immediately deduce that her parents, predominantly Lizaveta Prokofyevna, were in a particularly unresponsive mood. Still, not a word was said about her, or about Aglaya or even about Ivan Fyodorovich either by Adelaida or Prince S. in the course of their entire visit. When they went out to continue their promenade, the Prince was not invited to join them. As for inviting him back to their place, this did not even crop up; in this connection Adelaida, incidentally, let drop a rather telling remark. Talking about one of her watercolours, she suddenly wanted the Prince to see it. "I wonder how best to arrange it? Let me see! I'll either send it to you with Kolya, if he comes, or I'll drop it in to you myself tomorrow when we go out walking again with Prince S." This seemed to her an admirable solution and she was well pleased to have resolved it so cleverly.

Finally, just before their adieus, Prince S. suddenly asked as though in passing, "Oh yes, what about that lady, my dear Lev Nikolayevich, who called out to our Yevgeny Pavlovich from her calash, who was she?"

"That was Nastasya Filippovna," the Prince said. "Did you really not know till now? But I've no idea who the other person was."

"I know, I heard!" Prince S. replied eagerly. "But what was it all about? I must say, I'm mystified... and so are others."

Prince S. affected total and manifest bafflement.

"She spoke of some kind of bills of exchange owned by Yevgeny Pavlovich," the Prince replied in all simplicity, "which Rogozhin had acquired at her request from a dealer, and that for Yevgeny Pavlovich's sake Rogozhin would delay redeeming them."

"That I heard, my dear Prince, but that's impossible! Yevgeny Pavlovich could never have had any bills of that kind! With his wealth... If truth be known however, formerly, in his wool-gathering days he did, and even I had to help him out... But with his wealth, to issue bills of exchange to a broker and to be concerned about them is quite impossible. Nor could he be on such intimate, first-name terms with Nastasya Filippovna, that's the crux of the matter. He swears he knows nothing about it, and I believe him. But the point is, my dear Prince, I meant to ask you in case there's something you know about this. That is, if by some remote chance you hadn't heard some sort of rumour?"

"No, I know nothing, and I assure you I had no part in this whatever."

"Really, Prince, what has come over you? I simply don't recognize you today. Could I possibly suspect that you were implicated in such a matter?... You must be out of sorts today."

He approached and hugged him.

"Implicated in such a matter? I see no 'such' matter."

"No doubt this person was bent somehow and in some way on compromising Yevgeny Pavlovich by imputing in the eyes of witnesses characteristics which he does not, and cannot, possess," Prince S. returned rather curtly.

Prince Lev Nikolayevich was taken aback, however, though he continued to regard Prince S. intently; the latter kept his silence.

"Perhaps it wasn't just simply a matter of bills of exchange? Perhaps it was really word for word as we heard it yesterday?" Prince Myshkin muttered finally, somewhat edgily.

"Look here now, this is elementary, what could there possibly be in common between Yevgeny Pavlovich and... her, not to mention Rogozhin? I repeat, he is fabulously wealthy, something I can vouch for. He's expecting another fortune from his uncle. Nastasya Filippovna simply..."

Prince S. fell silent again, presumably because he had no wish to pursue the subject of Nastasya Filippovna with Prince Myshkin.

"At all events, he knows her, does he not?" Prince Lev Nikolayevich asked suddenly after a short pause.

"It would appear so, gay dog that he is! But even if there was anything between them, it was some time ago – way back, two or three years at least. He even knew Totsky. Now, however, there could be nothing of the sort, and they could never have been on first-name terms! You know well that she was not here all this time, and no one knew where she was. Not many people know that she is back. I spotted her equipage about three days ago, not more."

"Yes, it's rather splendid, isn't it?" Adelaida said.

They both left, it has to be said, on the friendliest, if not the heartiest, of terms with Prince Lev Nikolayevich.

For our hero this visit spelt something quite remarkable. Of course, ever since the previous night (and perhaps before) he had had his own suspicions, but up to the time of their visit he dared not lend credence to them. Now, however, everything was beginning to become clear. Prince S.'s interpretation of the events was, of course, flawed; nevertheless, he was on the right track in that he suspected some kind of intrigue. ("This is not to say that he is not completely right in his own mind," the Prince reflected. "Maybe he just doesn't want to face up to things and therefore deliberately draws the wrong conclusions.") The significant fact however was that someone had come to see him (Prince S. in particular) in the hope of eliciting some explanations; if so, then he was obviously directly implicated in the intrigue. Besides, if things were indeed as they seemed and it was all so important, *she* must surely be hatching some dreadful plot! What plot though? The mind boggled! "How was she to be stopped? Once she has set her mind on something, there's nothing that can stop her!" The Prince knew this from experience. "Mad, mad woman!"

But there was a whole host of other unresolvable circumstances crowding in upon him at the same time that morning, which depressed him hugely. He was distracted a little by Vera Lebedeva, who brought little Lyuba in her arms with her, and told him a long-winded story, laughing all the while. She was followed by her sister, who had a tendency to gape, then by Lebedev's schoolboy son, who insisted that the star Wormwood of the Apocalypse,* which had fallen upon the fountains of the world's water, was, according to his father's interpretation, the network of railways that had spread across Europe. The Prince refused to believe that Lebedev had made such an interpretation; they resolved to ask him personally at the first convenient opportunity. From Vera Lebedeva the Prince learnt that Keller had been staying with them since the night before, and by all indications would not decamp for a long time yet, because he had fallen into good company and struck up a friendship with General Ivolgin; to be sure, he declared that he'd be staying with them solely in order to consolidate his education. All in all, as time passed the Prince grew to like Lebedev's children more and more. Kolya was away the whole of that day in St Petersburg. (Lebedev too had gone in the small hours to attend to some business matters of his own.) But it was Gavrila Ardalionovich whom the Prince awaited most eagerly and who was definitely due to call on him that day.

He arrived after six o'clock in the evening straight after dinner. Just by looking at him the Prince imagined that at least this gentleman would know straight off all the ins and outs of the matter – and small wonder, having such helpers to hand as Varvara Ardalionovna and her husband! But the Prince's relations with Ganya were somehow unusual. For instance, the Prince had entrusted him with managing the Burdovsky case and had urged him to accept it; but, despite this mark of confidence and what had passed between the two previously, there always remained some issues that both parties appeared to have agreed not to touch upon. Sometimes the Prince had the feeling that Ganya for his part perhaps wanted to be in a totally uninhibited friendship with him; even on this occasion, as soon as he came in, the Prince immediately thought that Ganya was perfectly convinced now was just the time to break the ice and come to an understanding on all points. (But Gavrila Ardalionovich made out he was pressed for time; his sister was expecting him at Lebedev's; there was some urgent matter to be settled.)

But if Ganya was really expecting a whole series of searching questions, involuntary admissions and friendly outpourings, he was of course much mistaken. During the whole of his twenty-minute visit the Prince appeared to be lost in thought, almost absent-minded. The expected questions – or rather, the one particular, crucial question which Ganya wished to hear – did not follow. Then Ganya too resolved to adopt a posture. He hardly stopped talking the whole twenty minutes he was there, he laughed, he bantered most harmlessly, but never touched upon what really mattered.

Incidentally, Ganya recounted that Nastasya Filippovna after merely four days in Pavlovsk was already attracting general attention. "She lives in one of the Matrosskaya Streets in Darya Alexeyevna's small incongruous-looking house, though her equipage is probably the best in Pavlovsk. A whole host of old and new aspiring admirers gather around her, and her calash is not infrequently accompanied by mounted riders. Nastasya Filippovna, as is her wont, is proving herself to be very selective, and only a chosen few are permitted to share her company. And yet a whole coterie of devotees, a veritable corps of bodyguards, manages to trail her constantly albeit at a distance. One young man, holidaying in Pavlovsk, is known to have already broken with his fiancée over her, while an aged general has been close to cursing his son on her account. On her outings she frequently takes with her an exquisitely beautiful young girl, just turned sixteen, distantly related to Darya Alexeyevna. The girl has a good voice, and the soirées that are frequently held in the house, have much enhanced the reputation of the place. Nastasya Filippovna, it must be said, deports herself with the utmost correctness, she dresses soberly but with utmost good taste, and all the ladies are envious of her for that, for her beauty and her equipage.

"Yesterday's incident," Ganya then let slip, "was of course unpremeditated, and must surely not be taken into consideration. To find fault with her, one would need to either spy on her or deliberately pin something on her, which, incidentally, will not be long in coming," Ganya concluded, expecting the Prince immediately to enquire why he took yesterday's incident to be unpremeditated, and why pinning something on her would not be long in coming. But the Prince did not ask this.

As regards Yevgeny Pavlovich, Ganya talked about him at length, of his own volition, without even being asked, which was very strange, especially as he had brought him in without any rhyme or reason.

Gavrila Ardalionovich was of the opinion that Yevgeny Pavlovich had not known Nastasya Filippovna before, and knew her only superficially even now, having met her just four days previously after an introduction on one of her outings, and was unlikely to have been to her house either. As for the bills of exchange, all was possible (Ganya even had some hard evidence on this). "Yevgeny Pavlovich's fortune is of course considerable, but in some respects his estate is in disarray." At this interesting juncture, Ganya suddenly had no more to say on the matter. As for Nastasya Filippovna's incident yesterday, he did not say any more than he had already said earlier in passing. Finally, Varvara Ardalionovna came to take Ganya away; she stayed a short while, and announced (also unprompted) that Yevgeny Pavlovich would stay in St Petersburg till the end of the day, and perhaps the following one too. Her husband (Ivan Petrovich Ptitsyn) would also be present in connection with Yevgeny Pavlovich's business. Something was clearly up. On parting, she added that Lizaveta Prokofyevna was in a foul mood, but the most remarkable thing was that Aglaya had managed to fall out with all the members of her family, not only with her father and mother, but with her sisters too, and that it was quite bad. Having casually let slip this (for the Prince vital) snippet of information *inter alia* as it were, brother and sister took their leave. Nor did Ganya mention "Pavlishchev's son"; perhaps due to false modesty, perhaps to spare the Prince's feelings. Still the Prince thanked him profusely for the trouble he had taken to settle the matter.

The Prince was very glad to be finally left alone; he descended from the terrace, crossed the road and entered the park; he needed to think things over and come to a decision. But this decision was not one to be pondered over, but to be taken without reflection: he simply wanted to leave everything behind and go back where he came from, far away from everyone, into complete solitude, now, without saying goodbye to anyone. He felt that if he were to stay there even just a few more days, he'd become sucked into this world irredeemably and his fate would be sealed for ever. But his mind was made up in less than ten minutes – to flee was impossible, it would be tantamount to cowardice; he was faced with problems which he had no right whatsoever to leave without at least attempting with all his powers to resolve. Turning this over in his mind, he was back in the house even before a quarter of an hour was up.

Lebedev was still not back, so that towards the evening Keller used this opportunity to barge into his room. He was not drunk but full of disclosures and avowals. He announced directly that he came to tell the Prince his life story, and that that was the sole reason for his staying behind in Pavlovsk. It would not have been possible to get rid of him under any circumstances. Keller made ready to launch upon what seemed a long and rambling discourse, but suddenly, after just a few words, he reached his conclusion and declared that he'd lost every trace of morality ("solely for lack of faith in the Almighty") to the extent that he had even stooped to thieving. "It just doesn't bear thinking about!"

"Listen, Keller, if I were you, I wouldn't go around admitting this," the Prince observed, "you may end up incriminating yourself."

"For your ears, for your ears only, and solely to advance my prospects! To no one else. When I die, I'll keep the secret with me under the shroud! But, Prince, if only, if only you knew, how difficult it is nowadays to raise money! Where the blazes is one meant to get it from, let me ask you, my good sir? They tell you: give us your gold and diamonds, and we'll help you, that is, they want precisely what I haven't got, can you imagine? I finally lost my temper, but what's the use? 'And would you accept emeralds?' – 'Emeralds would be just fine.' – 'Glad to hear it,' I said, put my hat on and left. To hell with the lot of you, scoundrels one and all! I swear!"

"Did you really have emeralds?"

"Emeralds, you must be joking! My dear Prince, I marvel at your innocent, as it were, bucolically simple outlook on life!"

The Prince was all at once overcome not so much by pity, as by a pang of conscience. It even flashed through his mind, "Could something not be done for this man in the way of good counsel?" To be sure, by virtue of some indications he regarded his own capacity to effect reform as totally ineffectual, not out of a sense of inferiority, as much as in consequence of certain other views on things. Little by little they fell to talking so that towards the end there was no parting them. Keller was simply unstoppable in recounting things that one could not possibly imagine anyone owning up to. Before getting down to relating each and every episode, he gave positive assurances that he was utterly contrite and inwardly "pouring tears", and yet he continued with his tales as though he was inordinately proud of his misdeeds, and at the same time with such touches of humour that he and the Prince were in the end killing themselves with laughter.

"I have to say there is some childish artlessness and extraordinary truthfulness about you," the Prince said at last. "Do you realize that that alone would redeem everything?"

"My thanks to you, the thanks of a gentleman!" Keller affirmed, beaming with delight. "Though, let me tell you, Prince, 'tis all in the mind and, as it were, in virtual valour, but in practice it never comes to anything! And why that should be so? Search me!"

"Don't lose courage! Now I can be sure that you told me all the innermost secrets. At least it seems to me there's nothing more that can be added to your story, is that not so?"

"Nothing?!" Keller exclaimed with a note of chagrin in his voice. "Really, Prince, what an, as it were, Swiss way you have of looking at mankind!"

"Is there really more?" the Prince enquired humbly. "I say, what were you expecting of me, Keller, tell me, please, and why did you come to me with your confession?"

"What I was expecting? Of you? First, it's such a pleasure to behold your frankness, to have a heart-to-heart chat with you. I, for one, know that I am looking at the most charitable of people, and secondly... secondly..."

He was lost for words.

"Perhaps you wanted to borrow some money from me?" the Prince ventured to suggest simply and directly, and yet discreetly.

Keller started. He darted a look of surprise straight into the Prince's eyes and brought his fist heavily upon the table.

"Bolts and shackles! Really, Prince, such innocence, such openness that no golden age could boast of, and at the same time such discernment, such arrow-like psychological penetration. Forgive me, Prince, but this requires explanation, because I... I'm simply floored! It goes without saying my end purpose was to borrow money, but the way you brought the subject up, it came across as though there was nothing untoward about it, as though it was just as it should be!"

"In your case, yes."

"And you are not offended?"

"Why should I be?"

"Look here, Prince, I stayed behind here since the night before, first out of my sincere devotion to the French Archbishop Bourdaloue* who was ever so fond of Bordeaux – ha-ha-ha (Lebedev and I were up till early in the morning sipping it slowly) – and secondly, and principally (cross my heart and hope to die!) I stayed behind, because I wanted by, as it were, imparting to you my all-embracing, my most heartfelt declaration of guilt, to minister to my personal development. Buoyed by this thought, I fell asleep, bathed in tears, when it was already gone three. Believe me as you would a true gentleman that as I was falling asleep, sincerely, so to speak, overflowing inwardly and outwardly with tears (because, dammit, I was weeping, I remember it clearly!) I was struck by a devilish thought, 'What about touching him for a rouble or two, now that I've made a clean breast of it?' So, with a spicy confession freshly improvised, I tearfully made a beeline to impose upon your generosity to remit me, say, one hundred and fifty roubles. Was that, in your opinion, a dastardly thing to do, or not?"

"That's all as may be, but perhaps it's merely one thing on top of another. Two ideas have merged into one, this happens frequently, with me – constantly. Of course, to my mind this is not good, and you know, Keller, I blame myself for this above all. It's as though you held up a mirror to me. I too happen to think sometimes," the Prince continued in all seriousness and with profound conviction, "that all people are like that, so much so that I started to exonerate myself, because it's extremely difficult to reconcile these *dual* ideas. I experienced all that. God only knows how these ideas germinate and take root. According to you this is a dastardly thing! From now on I too shall shun such thoughts. In any case I can't be your judge. Still, I wouldn't call it out-and-out dastardliness, what do you think? You tried to pull the wool over my eyes and resorted to tears to wheedle money out of me, but haven't you admitted that your confession had another, a more noble, intention, not merely one of monetary gain? As for money, you just want to have a binge, isn't that so? Which, coming after such a confession, is pretty spineless. But how to give up bingeing at the drop of a hat? It's impossible. So what is one to do? Best leave it to your own conscience, what do you think?"

The Prince regarded Keller with the utmost interest. It was obvious that the question of the duality of ideas had long been preoccupying him.

"But why do people call you an idiot after this, that's what I fail to understand!" Keller exclaimed.

The Prince blushed a little.

"Preacher Bourdaloue wouldn't have taken pity on a man like me, but you have and gave me the benefit of the doubt! To penalize myself and to show that I'm touched, I don't want the hundred and fifty roubles, give me just twenty-five, and that'll be the end of it! That's all I need to tide me over the coming fortnight. I'll not bother you for money at least for the next two weeks. I was minded to give Agatha a treat, but she's not worth it. Oh, my dear Prince, God's blessings upon you!"

At last Lebedev entered; he had just returned. Noticing the twenty-five rouble note in Keller's hands, he winced. But Keller, now that he had money, was in a hurry to slink off and was gone in a trice. Lebedev immediately began to castigate him.

"You're unfair," the Prince observed at last, "he really was contrite."

"What's the good of his contrition! Just like I was yesterday, 'I'm a knave, a veritable knave', but it was all just words!"

"So it was just words with you? And I thought—"

"All right, I'll reveal the truth to you, only to you, because you can penetrate right through to a man's soul. Words and deeds, truth and falsehood are all rolled into one for me, and this in perfect candour. You might as well know, truth and enactment are predicated on my genuine contrition, whereas words and falsehood are at the root of an infernal (and ever present) urge to wrong-foot a person and gain advantage even in the very act of shedding tears of contrition! That is the honest truth! I'd not have said this to anyone else, because anyone else would have jeered or told me to go to hell. But not you, Prince, you are full of understanding of mankind."

"Well, there you are, I heard precisely the same thing from him too!" the Prince exclaimed. "And you're both proud of it! I don't mind saying you surprise me, only he strikes me as the more sincere. You seem to have turned the whole thing into a fine art. Well, that'll do, stop making faces, Lebedev, and don't keep putting your hand on your heart. Have you something to say? You wouldn't have come here for nothing..."

Lebedev began to squirm and shuffle nervously.

"I've been waiting for you the whole day to ask you one question. Why don't you for once in your life give a straight answer right at the start? Did you, or did you not, have a hand in yesterday's incident with the calash?"

Lebedev continued to wriggle, he began to smirk, to rub his hands, in the end he even affected a bout of sneezing, but still he could not bring himself to say anything.

"I can see you did."

"But only indirectly, only very indirectly! God's own truth! I did no more than inform a certain person in good time that a particular group of people had gathered at my place and that one or two individuals were amongst them."

"I am informed you sent your son *there*. He told me himself. So what exactly is being plotted?" the Prince exclaimed.

"I'm not plotting anything, nothing at all," Lebedev said, accompanying his words with lively gestures of denial. "Other people are behind it, and what's all more likely, it's a figment of the imagination."

"Will you for God's sake explain what exactly is going on? Can you not understand it touches directly upon me? Yevgeny Pavlovich is being slandered, can't you see?"

"Prince! My most illustrious Prince!" Lebedev continued to play-act. "You yourself won't let me tell the whole truth. God knows I tried, but you stopped me every time..."

The Prince reflected a little in silence.

"All right, go ahead, tell the truth," he said with a heavy heart, after an inner struggle.

"Aglaya Ivanovna—" Lebedev began forthwith.

"Stop, stop!" the Prince shouted in a voice not his own, flushing with indignation or perhaps shame. "This is impossible, balderdash! You yourself are responsible for it, or the likes of you. Don't ever dare mention this to me again!"

Late that night, it was already gone ten, Kolya returned with a lot of news, half from St Petersburg and half from Pavlovsk. He first quickly recounted the main bits of the former (mostly about Ippolit and yesterday's incident) so as to return to them later, and hastened on with the Pavlovsk ones. He had arrived from St Petersburg three hours before and had gone straight to the Yepanchins. "It was sheer hell there!" The calash was of course the main topic of conversation, but there was evidently something else in the air that neither he nor the Prince could guess at. "Naturally, I didn't pry and had no wish to question anyone. I must say I was well received, much better than I expected, but not a word about you, Prince!" The funniest thing of all was that Aglaya had quarrelled with all the family over Ganya. He didn't know what it was all about, but over Ganya (imagine that!) and to quarrel fiercely, it couldn't have been a laughing matter. The General turned up late, in a foul mood. He brought Yevgeny Pavlovich with him, who was jovial and in excellent spirits, and everyone greeted him exceedingly well. The most stunning piece of news, however, was that Lizaveta Prokofyevna, without any ado, had summoned Varvara Ardalionovna, who had been sitting with the girls, and told her to leave the house for good, incidentally she did so in the most cordial terms. "Varya told me herself." But after Varya left Lizaveta Prokofyevna's room and had said goodbye to the girls, none of them knew that she'd been expelled from the house for ever or that she was saying goodbye for the last time.

"But Varvara Ardalionovna was here with me at seven o'clock?" the Prince asked in surprise.

"She was shown the door well after seven, perhaps at eight. I'm very sorry for Varya, sorry for Ganya... they're always bickering, that's just how they are, I can see it. And I can never make out what's on their minds, nor do I want to. But I assure you, my good, kind Prince, Ganya's heart is in the right place. Of course, in many respects he's an altogether hopeless case, yet on the other hand he's got qualities you'd be hard put to find in anyone else, and I'll never forgive myself for not understanding him before... I don't know if I should continue going to the Yepanchins after what's happened to Varya. True, right from the very start I took no sides whatsoever, still I'll have to think it over."

"You shouldn't worry about your brother so," the Prince remarked, "if it's reached that stage, it would seem Gavrila Ardalionovich is dangerous in Lizaveta Prokofyevna's eyes, and his hopes are coming to fruition."

"What – what hopes!" Kolya cried in surprise. "Are you perhaps imagining that Aglaya?... That's impossible!"

The Prince did not say anything.

"You're a terrible sceptic, Prince," Kolya observed after a long pause. "I notice you've turned into one lately. You're beginning to mistrust everyone and all you do is make suppositions... by the way, have I used the word 'sceptic' correctly, or not?"

"I think correctly, though, frankly, I'm not quite sure myself."

"But I take the word 'sceptic' back myself. I've found another explanation," Kolya exclaimed suddenly. "Not sceptic, you're simply jealous! You're unspeakably jealous of Ganya for the favours of a certain proud young lady!"

Having said this, Kolya jumped to his feet and burst into laughter as he had probably never done in his life before. On seeing that the Prince had blushed, Kolya laughed even more. He was thrilled at the thought that the Prince was jealous because of Aglaya, but he suddenly stopped when he saw that the former was genuinely hurt. They then spent the next hour or so in a serious, thoughtful discussion.

The next day the Prince spent the whole morning on an urgent matter in St Petersburg. On his way back to Pavlovsk – it was after four in the afternoon – he ran into Ivan Fyodorovich at the station. The latter grabbed him by the arm, looked around anxiously, and dragged the Prince into a first-class compartment in order to travel together.

"First, my dear Prince, don't be angry with me, and if you have anything against me, forget it. I had a good mind to call on you myself... last night but I wasn't too sure how Lizaveta Prokofyevna would take it... At home... it's sheer hell, a mythical beast has descended upon the house and I can't pretend to understand anything. As for you, the way I see it, you're the least culpable of us all, though in truth it's all come about on account of you, mostly. You see, my dear Prince, it's one thing to be a philanthropist, but there's a danger. I don't mind saying you've tasted the fruits thereof already. Of course I love and respect Lizaveta Prokofyevna for her kindness, but..."

The General spoke volubly in this vein for quite some time, but his manner was exceptionally rambling. It was clear that something highly unusual had astounded and perplexed him, and left him at a total loss.

"I have no doubt whatsoever that you are not involved in any of this," he observed at last, rather more sensibly, "but don't call on us for some time to come, I ask this of you as a friend, until the situation changes. As for Yevgeny Pavlovich," he exclaimed with extreme fervour, "it's all lies, lies and nothing but lies! It's a plot, character assassination, a wish to destroy and sow enmity between us. You see, Prince, between you, me and the doorpost, not a word has as yet been spoken between Yevgeny Pavlovich and ourselves, do you follow me?

We are not bound by anything, but this word may be spoken, and soon at that, and if comes to it, very soon indeed, I tell you! Simply for mischief's sake! For no other reason as far as I can tell! She's an astonishing woman, an eccentric woman, she inspires holy terror in me, and I lose sleep over her. The equipage she keeps, her white horses, it's all so magnificent, so chic as the French might say! Who's behind it all? Honest to goodness, I was absolutely mistaken the other day, I suspected Yevgeny Pavlovich! But it turns out this is unthinkable, and if it's unthinkable, why does she want to cause a rift? That's the conundrum! In order to retain Yevgeny Pavlovich at her side? But I repeat, he doesn't know her, cross my heart, he doesn't know her, and these bills of exchange are pure fiction! And the affront of calling him by his first name across the street! This is a conspiracy to end all conspiracies! It stands to reason it must not be countenanced and must be rejected with contempt, while Yevgeny Pavlovich must be accorded all manner of deference on our part. That's exactly how I put it to Lizaveta Prokofyevna too. And now I'll tell you my belief, between the two of us: I'm firmly convinced that she's doing all this out of personal vengeance, you remember, for what happened in the past, although I've never been guilty before her of anything. I blush at the thought alone. Now she's turned up yet again, and I thought she'd vanished for good. Where is that Rogozhin of hers, I'd like to know? I thought she was Mrs Rogozhin ages ago..."

In a word, the man was thoroughly perturbed. Practically during the whole journey he was the only one who talked, asking questions and supplying his own answers, he kept pressing the Prince's hand and at least convinced the Prince that he of all people bore him no suspicion. This was important. He eventually came to a halt with a story about an uncle of Yevgeny Pavlovich's, who headed some kind of administrative department in St Petersburg: "A man in the public eye, seventy years old, a lady-killer, gourmand and on the whole a jolly old fellow... Ha-ha! I knew he'd heard of Nastasya Filippovna and even lusted after her. I tried to call on him the other day, but he wouldn't receive me for health reasons, however he's wealthy, very, and influential and... may he thrive many a long year, though it'll all still revert to Yevgeny Pavlovich... Quite, quite... and all the same I'm fearful! What of, I don't pretend to understand, but I'm fearful... There seems to be something in the air, like a bat flapping about, disaster is looming, oh my, oh my!..."

And finally, as already indicated, it was only three days later that a formal reconciliation took place between the Yepanchins and Prince Lev Nikolayevich Myshkin.

12

I T WAS ALREADY three in the afternoon. The Prince was about to go to the park. Suddenly Lizaveta Prokofyevna, unaccompanied, entered the terrace to see him.

"*First*, don't so much as dare think," she began, "that I came to ask your pardon. Fiddlesticks! You're as guilty as they come."

The Prince did not respond.

"Are you, or are you not?"

"No more than you are. To be sure, on second thoughts, neither I nor you are guilty. The day before yesterday I considered myself guilty, but now I've thought about it, I no longer do."

"Well, well! All right then. Listen, and sit down, because I've no intention of standing."

They both sat down.

"Secondly, not a word about evil-minded youngsters. I shall stay and talk to you for ten minutes. I came to make an enquiry (you thought goodness what else?) and if you so much as say a word about arrogant juveniles, I shall get up and leave, and all will be off between us."

"All right," the Prince replied.

"Permit me to ask you, did you send Aglaya a letter about two and a half months ago, around Easter time?"

"I d-did."

"For what purpose, may I ask? What was in the letter? Let me see it!"

Lizaveta Prokofyevna's eyes were burning, she was shaking with impatience.

"I haven't got the letter," the Prince said in great surprise, visibly shaken, "if it has survived at all, Aglaya Ivanovna must have it."

"No excuses! What did you write about?"

"I'm not making any excuses and I've nothing to be afraid of. I see no reason why I shouldn't write—"

"Silence! You can speak later. What was in the letter? Why are you blushing?"

The Prince thought a while.

"I don't know what you're thinking, Lizaveta Prokofyevna. All I see is that the letter is not to your liking. You must own that I could refuse to answer such a question, but to demonstrate that I'm not afraid because of the letter and don't regret having written it, nor do I blush because of it," (the Prince went as red as a beetroot) "I'll recite this letter to you because, I think, I know it by heart."

Having said this, the Prince did in fact recite the letter almost word for word.

"Such balderdash! What can this claptrap mean in your opinion?" Lizaveta Prokofyevna asked sharply, having listened with rapt attention.

"I don't quite know myself. I know my feelings were genuine. I experienced moments of fulfilled life and of extraordinary expectations."

"What expectations?"

"It's hard to explain, only not such expectations as you are perhaps now thinking of. Expectations... well, in a word, expectations of the future and of joy that perhaps I'm not an alien in Russia, not a foreigner. I was suddenly very happy to be back on native soil. One sunny morning I took a pen and wrote her a letter. Why her – I don't know. Sometimes one wants to have a friend close by, and I probably felt the need for a friend..." the Prince added after a pause.

"Are you in love?"

"N-no. I... I wrote as to a sister. I signed – brother."

"Hm. Purposely. I understand."

"It is very difficult for me to answer your questions, Lizaveta Prokofyevna."

"I know it is difficult, but you see, I couldn't care less that it's difficult. Listen, I want the truth as before God, are you lying to me or not?"

"I'm not."

"Are you sure you're not in love?"

"I think, quite sure."

"There you are 'I think'! Was it that underage scamp who told you?"

"I asked Nikolai Ardalionovich—"

"A scamp! Juvenile scamp!" Lizaveta Prokofyevna interrupted him vigorously. "I don't know any Nikolai Ardalionovich! A juvenile scamp!"

"Nikolai Ardalionovich—"

"An juvenile scamp, I tell you!"

"No, not a juvenile scamp, but Nikolai Ardalionovich," the Prince returned firmly but rather softly.

"Well, have it your way, my dear friend, have it your way! I'll remind you of this some time."

During the pause that followed she tried to subdue her anxiety and compose herself.

"And what's a 'hapless knight'?"

"I've no idea, I'm sure. It has nothing to do with me. It must be some joke."

"It's a nice little surprise! Only could she really have taken an interest in you? Didn't she herself call you a little freak and a damn idiot?"

"There was no need to repeat that," the Prince said accusingly, almost in a whisper.

"Don't be angry. She's a wilful, crazy, spoilt filly – if she falls in love, the first thing she does is mock and poke fun in front of everybody. I was just like her. Only, please don't congratulate yourself, my dear, she's not for you. I won't have it, and that's the end of the matter! I'm saying this for you to take the necessary measures now. Listen, I want you to swear you're not already married to that *creature*."

"Lizaveta Prokofyevna, what on earth are you talking about?" the Prince asked, utterly shocked.

"But it wouldn't take much for you to marry her, would it?"

"No, I don't suppose it would," the Prince whispered and hung his head.

"So you love her after all if that's how it is? Have you now come here because of her?"

"I did not come here to get married."

"Do you hold anything sacred in this world?"

"I do."

"Swear to me it was not in order to marry *that one*!"

"I will swear by anything you wish."

"I believe you. Kiss me. Now I can breathe easily. But know this, Aglaya does not love you. Have no illusions, she'll not be your wife while I live! Did you hear me?"

"I did."

The Prince blushed so deeply, he could barely look at Lizaveta Prokofyevna.

"Well then, fix this firmly in your mind. I waited for you as I waited for Divine Providence. (You weren't worthy of it!) My pillow of a night was fairly soaked with tears – not for you, my good fellow, don't worry, I've my own, quite different, eternal, ongoing sorrow. But I waited for you with such impatience because I believe God himself has sent you as a friend and brother. I've no one to lean on, except Belokonskaya and she too has disappeared somewhere, and besides she's gone completely barmy in her old age. Now I want you to answer simply, yes or no! Do you know why that creature shouted out of her calash?"

"Honestly, I had no part in it and know nothing!"

"Say no more. I believe you. Now I've also changed my mind about this business, but even as late as yesterday morning I still blamed Yevgeny Pavlovich for everything. This mood persisted all day the day before yesterday and through to the morning of the next. Now I must agree with the rest, it's pretty obvious the hussy has for some unknown reason made him look a complete fool (very suspicious that, and highly irregular!). But Aglaya will never be his wife, that much I can tell you! He may be ever such a nice man, but I'll have it my way. I was in two minds earlier, but now my mind's firmly made up – over my dead body! After that, she can marry whomever she pleases. That's what I spelt out to Ivan Fyodorovich today. Can you see the sort of trust I'm putting in you, can you?"

"I can and I appreciate it."

Lizaveta Prokofyevna looked long and hard at the Prince; perhaps she was very keen to find out what effect news of Yevgeny Pavlych had on him.

"Do you know anything of Gavrila Ivolgin?"

"I know a lot about him… I suppose."

"Did you or did you not know that he's after Aglaya?"

"I had no idea," the Prince replied in astonishment, and even gave a start. "Are you saying Gavrila Ardalionovich is having a relationship with Aglaya Ivanovna? That's impossible!"

"Only started very recently. His sister has been doing her damnedest to encourage them for all winter."

"I don't believe it," the Prince repeated firmly after some reflection and heartache. "If it had been so, I'd have known all about it, I'm certain."

"No doubt he'd have come to you himself and owned up to everything in tears with his head on your chest! What a nincompoop you are! Everyone makes a fool of you, and how!... Aren't you ashamed of being so gullible? Can you really not see that he is running rings around you?"

"I know very well that he sometimes deceives me," the Prince said reluctantly in a hushed voice, "and he knows I know it..." he added without finishing the sentence.

"You know it, and yet you still trust him! That's all you need! But then again it was only to be expected of you. Why should I be so surprised! My God! Has there ever been anyone like you! Pah! But do you know that your Ganya, or was it that Varya, brought her and Nastasya Filippovna into contact?"

"Who?" the Prince exclaimed.

"Aglaya."

"I don't believe it! That's impossible! What for?"

He had jumped to his feet.

"I didn't believe it either, but there's evidence. The girl's as wilful as they come, and mad with it! She's a wicked one! I'll say it again and again – wicked! The whole lot are as bad as one another, even that brainless chicken Alexandra, but she's already as good as flown the nest. But even that I don't believe! Maybe because I don't want to," she added as an afterthought. "Why didn't you show up?" she suddenly again turned to the Prince. "For three days there was no sign of you, why?"

The Prince began to excuse himself, but she again interrupted.

"They all take you for a fool and deceive you! You went into town yesterday. I'll wager you kneeled before that scoundrel, asking him to accept the ten thousand roubles!"

"Nothing of the sort, it never entered my mind. I didn't even see him, and besides, he's no scoundrel. I've a letter from him."

"Let me see!"

The Prince produced a note from his briefcase and handed it to Lizaveta Prokofyevna. It read:

My Dear Sir,

It goes without saying I have no right in the eyes of the world to have any claim to self-esteem. I am considered to be too insignificant. But that is in the eyes of the world, not yours. I am led to believe that you, my dear sir, are perhaps better than others. I do not agree with Doktorenko, and our opinions diverge on this point. I shall never take a single copeck from you, but you have helped my mother, and for that reason I must be grateful to you, even though this may be a sign of weakness. Be that as it may, I regard you in a different light, and consider it only proper to inform you of this. In consequence I think there can be no further communication between the two of us.

Antip Burdovsky

PS: The sum needed to make up the two hundred roubles will in time be paid to you without fail.

"What twaddle!" Lizaveta Prokofyevna concluded, tossing the note aside. "Not worth reading. What's so funny?"

"You must agree, you also enjoyed reading it."

"What! This conceit-ridden piffle! Can you really not see that they're all out of their tiny minds with conceit and puffed-up pride?"

"Yes, but all the same he has eaten humble pie, he has broken with Doktorenko and, the prouder he is, the deeper it has hurt his pride. Oh, what a naive child you are, Lizaveta Prokofyevna!"

"Are you asking to have your face slapped?"

"No, not at all. But actually you welcome the note, and are bent on concealing it. Why are you ashamed to show what you feel? You're always like that."

"Don't you dare to come to my place ever again!" Lizaveta Prokofyevna shouted, jumping to her feet, pale with rage. "Get out and never darken my doorstep again!"

"And three days later you'll be back asking me to do just that... You ought to be ashamed of yourself! These are your best sentiments, why are you embarrassed by them? You only torture yourself unnecessarily."

"I'd rather die than ask you back! I'll delete your name from my memory! There, I've done it!!"

She dashed for the exit.

"You're not the only one who has forbidden me to come to see you!" the Prince called out after her.

"What? Who else has forbidden you?"

She wheeled around as though stung to the quick. The Prince hesitated. He realized that inadvertently he had let the cat out of the bag.

"Who has forbidden you?" Lizaveta Prokofyevna called out in a rage.

"Aglaya Ivanovna—"

"When? Don't just stand there, answer me!!!"

"She sent me a message the other day never to come to see her again."

Lizaveta Prokofyevna stood rooted to the ground; she was desperately trying to size up the situation.

"A message? How? Did she send a boy? By word of mouth?" she persisted loudly.

"I had a note from her," the Prince said.

"Where is it? Give it to me! Now!"

The Prince hesitated again, but produced a scrap of paper from his waistcoat pocket, on which was written:

Dear Prince Lev Nikolayevich,
If after all that has happened, you still have a mind to surprise me
by calling at our dacha, rest assured that I for one would not be best
pleased, Aglaya Yepanchina.

Lizaveta Prokofyevna reflected for a moment; she then rushed towards the Prince, grabbed him by the hand and began to pull him after her.

"Come! At once! Come now, this very minute!" she cried in a rare fit of perturbation and anxiety.

"But you're making me run the risk of—"

"I what? You innocent booby! Call yourself a man after that! Well, now I'll see all for myself, with my own eyes—"

"At least let me take my hat—"

"Here's your stupid wretched hat, come along! If you didn't even have the sense to find yourself anything better!... It was... it was after what happened this morning... in a moment of rashness," Lizaveta Prokofyevna kept muttering to herself as she dragged the Prince after her, not letting go of his hand for a moment. "I had spoken in your defence and had said out loud it was silly of you not to have called on us... If you had, she wouldn't have written such a silly note! Such an unbecoming note! Unbecoming for an upstanding, well brought-up, sensible, ever so sensible girl!... Hm," she continued, "of course, she was ruing the fact that you were staying away, only it didn't occur to her that that wasn't the way to write to an idiot, because he'd take it literally, which is exactly what happened. I shouldn't be saying this, you know!" she suddenly checked herself, realizing she had said too much. "She needs a buffoon like you. There's not been such a one around for ages, that's why she's so taken with you! And I'm glad, ever so glad she'll have you by the short and curlies! You've asked for it. Don't you underestimate her, please don't!..."

Part Three

1

THERE'S WIDESPREAD TALK of a dearth of practical people in our country; there's no shortage of politicians for example, plenty of generals too, various managers – more than enough; but practical people are in short supply. At least that's what one hears on all sides. They say that even some railways are short-staffed; some shipping corporations find it utterly impossible to find more or less competent personnel to run their offices. A report of a head-on crash or a bridge collapsing under a train may come in at any time from some newly opened railway; or again, a train might be snowed under in a field, a few hours' journey turning into a five-day-long wait in the snow. Or again, one may hear of hundreds of tons of produce rotting for up to three months in some siding waiting to be moved; and yet somewhere else (and this is almost too hard to credit), an official, that is a watchman, has administered a punch on the jaw to a merchant's clerk, who'd been pestering him about moving his consignment, and what's more, excused his administrative solution on the grounds that he'd been overhasty. The mind boggles at the number of organizations under government control; all the workforce is willing and able – so why then is it not possible, from such a large pool of human resources, to form a reasonably efficient shipping corporation?

The answer sometimes given is extremely simple – so simple, it is well-nigh impossible to take it seriously. True, it is said that everyone in our country is employed in the civil service, and this practice has been handed down from grandfather to grandson for the past two hundred odd years according to the very best practice inherited from the Germans – but, it had reached a point where, only until very recently, government servants, the least practical of all people, had amongst themselves regarded purely abstract knowledge and the lack of practical skills as the greatest asset and commendation. In truth, we did not mean to talk about civil servants, but rather about practical people only. Here there is not a shadow of doubt that self-effacement and complete absence of personal initiative have always been regarded

339

in our country as the principal and best signs of a practical turn of mind, even to this day. But why castigate only ourselves – if indeed we deserve to be castigated? Deficit of imagination has, throughout the whole world, from time immemorial always been considered a prime quality and the highest title of recommendation for men of action, business and accomplishment, such that at least ninety-nine percent ('at least' being a necessary qualification) of people have always clung to this conviction, with perhaps only one percent of people having a contrary opinion.

Inventors and geniuses have almost always at the start of their careers, and often at the end too, been regarded in society as no more than fools – this is on the whole such a routine observation that it has become a commonplace. If, for the sake of example, people had been hoarding their money for decades in savings banks and had accumulated billions at four percent interest, then it follows that the day these savings banks were to collapse and everyone was thrown back on his own initiative, the vast proportion of this money would be bound to be lost in the stock exchange upheaval or pocketed by crooks – a likely outcome in the prevailing moral and cultural atmosphere of the day. Above all it is a moral question; if risk aversion and deliberate lack of originality have up till now by common consent constituted in our country an inalienable characteristic of a businesslike and upright person, it would have been altogether improper, nay unseemly, suddenly to swing too much the other way. For instance, what loving mother would not take fright or worry herself to death if her son or daughter were to deviate, however slightly, from the beaten track? "No," every mother putting her child to bed would say, "I'd rather you live in happiness and contentment than aspire to originality." And one should listen to our nannies lulling their babies to sleep, "If you wish to bask in gold, / Aim to be a general bold!" And so, even in the eyes of our nannies the rank of general was taken to be the height of our Russian fortune, and in consequence was the most sought-after national exemplar of contentment and bliss. And truly, anyone who'd somehow managed to scrape through the entrance exams and had a thirty-five-year-long service record behind him, could without the least effort reach the rank of general, not to mention accruing a tidy little sum in a savings bank. Hence, it was open to any Russian, to reach almost without any effort, the calling of a successful and practical person. If the truth be known, the only person in our country who wouldn't be able to reach a high office would be a person with imagination and flair. There might of course be exceptions, though on the whole it is true, and our society is perfectly justified in depicting its ideal of a practical person in such a manner. All the same, we have said much that is not to the point; all we wanted was to make a few explanatory comments on the Yepanchin family, which we know so well. These people, or at least the more intelligent members of that family, constantly suffered from one, well-nigh common, family characteristic, precisely the reverse in nature to those described above. Without being fully aware of this situation, which was by no means easy to grasp, they nevertheless at times suspected that things were not as elsewhere. Other families functioned smoothly, whereas theirs was beset by hitches; other families proceeded on an even keel, whereas theirs was tossed hither and thither. They were different even in the matter of social conscience. In truth, Lizaveta Prokofyevna was perhaps the only one who agonized over it all. The girls were still too young, though they had their wits about them and were as sharp as needles. As for the General, even though he understood what's what (not without some effort, it must be said), at critical moments he always evaded the issue by a non-committal "Hm!" and in the event always devolved all responsibilities onto Lizaveta Prokofyevna, who shouldered them with resignation. And it was not as if this family stood out by being specifically enterprising or deviated from the norm as a result of a conscious striving for originality, which would have been altogether quite out of order. Not at all! In reality, there was nothing of the sort, that is, there was no consciously worked-out plan of procedure; all the same it turned out in the end that the Yepanchin family, though highly respectable, was not quite like all other respectable families were expected to be. Lately, Lizaveta Prokofyevna had begun to lay all the blame on herself and her "unfortunate" character, which only served to augment her anxiety. She constantly castigated herself as a "stupid, unseemly misfit"; she tormented herself for her apprehensiveness, and was always daunted and forever sorely tried by the most trivial problems, which amounted to turning molehills into mountains.

Right at the start of our story we mentioned that the Yepanchins enjoyed widespread and genuine respect. Even Ivan Fyodorovich himself, a man of obscure origins, was unquestionably welcomed with the utmost deference wherever he went. He well deserved it, first as a man of wealth and standing, and secondly because he was a thorough gentleman, though not one of the brightest. A certain intellectual obtuseness is in all probability almost de rigueur if not for every public figure, then at least for every serious moneymaker. Finally, the General had excellent manners: he was reserved, civil, he knew the golden value of silence, and would not let anyone take advantage of him, and this not just because of his rank, but by virtue of his being an upright, correct and proper gentleman. But his greatest strength lay in his powerful connections. As regards Lizaveta Prokofyevna, she was, in addition, as already indicated, very well born, though qualities of birth don't count for much with us if they are not coupled with strong connections. But in the end, it turned out that she had connections too; she came to be respected, indeed admired, by people of such standing, that after them everyone had to respect and welcome her. There is no doubt that her family worries were unfounded, the reason behind them being trivial and exaggerated out of all proportion; but if someone has a wart on his nose or forehead, one is forever imagining that people have nothing better to do than look and laugh at the wart and blame you for it, even though you might be one of the most progressive people in the world. There is no doubt that in society Lizaveta Prokofyevna was really regarded as an oddity, but she was respected nonetheless; however, Lizaveta Prokofyevna eventually ceased to believe she was respected, and that was the root of all her trouble. Every time she looked at her daughters, she was plagued by the suspicion that she was somehow damaging their prospects in life, that her character was ridiculous, unseemly and unbearable; for which she of course went on to blame the daughters themselves as well as Ivan Fyodorovich, spending days on end quarrelling with them, and at the same time loving them all almost to distraction.

Her principal concern was her suspicion that her daughters were turning as silly as she was, and that as such they would not, and could not, be accepted in society. "They're turning into a bunch of nihilists, that's all I can say!" she kept repeating to herself over and over again. In the course of the previous year, and especially the very recent past, this melancholy thought was gaining more and more ground in her mind. "To begin with, why are they not getting married?" she asked herself time and time again. "To cause grief to their mother – that's where they see the goal of their life, and this is of course so because of all the new-fangled ideas being mooted abroad – this confounded women's question!... Where did Aglaya get the idea of wanting to cut her gorgeous hair off six months ago? (Goodness, if only I had had such hair in my youth!) She already had scissors poised, it was all I could to dissuade her on my knees from such an act!... Well, it was all out of spite, that's for sure, to annoy her mother, because she's a spiteful, wilful, spoilt brat, but above all spiteful, spiteful, and I'll say it again – spiteful! And didn't this overfed Alexandra reach for the same scissors to shear her own curls off too, but not out of spite or caprice, but genuinely, fool that she is, having been persuaded by Aglaya that it'd be more comfortable for sleeping and she wouldn't have headaches with her hair off. And the number of proposals they've had in these past five years? To be sure, very good matches, some indeed excellent! What are they waiting for, why are they dithering? Just to displease their mother – there's no other reason! None! None whatsoever!"

At long last the sun smiled even on her maternal heart; at least one daughter, at least Adelaida would finally be taken care of. "At least one will be off my hands," Lizaveta Prokofyevna would say out loud (in her own mind she chose to express herself far more graciously). And in truth, it all turned out well and to everyone's advantage; even in the most select social circles the talk was of a successful match. The bridegroom was popular, titled, wealthy, and on top of everything, a man after her own heart; nothing, it would seem, could be better! Adelaida caused her fewer qualms than her other daughters, even though Adelaida's creative tendencies would not infrequently cause Lizaveta Prokofyevna's anxiety-ridden heart to flutter. "But then she's blessed with a cheerful disposition, and she's level-headed along with it – that girl will always land on her feet," she comforted herself in the end. Aglaya caused her the most headache. As for the eldest, Alexandra, Lizaveta Prokofyevna was at a loss whether to worry or not to worry about her. At times she was convinced the girl was beyond salvation. "Twenty-five! She'll be left on the shelf! All that beauty wasted!..." Of a night Lizaveta Prokofyevna was even liable to shed tears for her, whereas Alexandra Ivanovna slept the sleep of the just throughout. "I can't make out – is she really a nihilist or just a plain fool?" That she was no fool, Lizaveta Prokofyevna, of all people, had not the slightest doubt. She respected Alexandra Ivanovna's points of view enormously and liked to seek her counsel. But that she was a "wet lettuce" through and through, she had not the slightest doubt. "She's so unperturbed, nothing at all will stir her into action! To be sure, wet lettuces can be exceptionally unmanageable – pah! I'm talking nonsense – these daughters of mine will be the end of me!" Lizaveta Prokofyevna really had a soft spot for Alexandra Ivanovna, more so even than for her idol, Aglaya. But her caustic remarks (to be sure, the principal expressions of her maternal love and care), her fault-finding and such epithets as "wet lettuce", only made Alexandra laugh. It often happened that the most trivial things annoyed and exasperated Lizaveta Prokofyevna intensely. For instance, Alexandra was very fond of sleeping late and usually had copious dreams; but these were invariably distinguished by their utter vacuousness and naivety as might indicate the level of intelligence of a child under seven. This very naivety began to get on her mother's nerves. On one occasion Alexandra Ivanovna dreamt of a row of nine chickens, and this led to a full-blown row with her mother – why precisely? – there was no telling. Once, and only once, did she manage to have a more or less sensible dream. It was of a solitary monk in some dark room, which she was frightened to enter. The dream was immediately communicated to Lizaveta Prokofyevna by her two sisters, barely able to contain their laughter; but mother again flew into a temper and denounced all three as imbeciles. "Hm, imperturbable and as silly as they come, a silly goose to a tee, nothing will move her, all she knows is how to mope! What's wrong with her, what?" Sometimes she would address this question to Ivan Fyodorovich and, as was her wont, hysterically, in anger, requiring an immediate response. Ivan Fyodorovich would hem and haw, knit his eyebrows, shrug his shoulders, and spreading out his arms, conclude, "She needs a husband!"

"Only God forbid not such a one as you, Ivan Fyodorych," Lizaveta Prokofyevna answered in a flash, "not such a one who argues and reasons as you do, Ivan Fyodorych, not such a coarse bully as you, Ivan Fyodorych…"

Ivan Fyodorovich immediately sought sanctuary, while Lizaveta Prokofyevna calmed down after her outburst. It goes without saying, by evening of the same day she'd have regained her composure and equanimity, and reverted to being unusually kind and considerate towards Ivan Fyodorovich, towards her "coarse bully" Ivan Fyodorovich, towards her kind and loving, her adorable Ivan Fyodorovich, because all her life long she loved, indeed was in love with her Ivan Fyodorovich, which Ivan Fyodorovich himself was only too well aware of. He respected his Lizaveta Prokofyevna endlessly for it.

But her main and ongoing preoccupation was Aglaya.

"She's every, every bit like me, an exact copy," Lizaveta Prokofyevna was wont to repeat to herself, "a wilful, wayward mischief-maker! A born nihilist, a misfit, quite mad, spiteful, spiteful, spiteful! Oh, God, how unhappy she'll be!"

But, as we have already pointed out, the rising sun had lit up and mellowed everything for an instant. A whole month was vouchsafed in the life of Lizaveta Prokofyevna, during which she was able to escape from all her worries. In consequence of Adelaida's impending marriage, people began to talk of Aglaya too, and all this time Aglaya comported herself everywhere so agreeably, so demurely, intelligently, sanguinely, and a little loftily, but this only added to her charms! Wasn't she nice and ever so considerate towards her mother throughout a whole month! ("True, this Yevgeny Pavlovich must be investigated thoroughly, he must be unmasked, and it would seem Aglaya is no more disposed towards him either than she is towards others!") All the same, she has suddenly turned into such a wonderful girl! And how lovely she looks, goodness, how lovely, more and more so with every passing day! And lo and behold...

Lo and behold, the instant this paltry princeling, this miserable, inconsequential idiot made his appearance, everything went awry, topsy-turvy in the house!

So what exactly happened?

For some it would most probably have been nothing at all. But this is precisely where Lizaveta Prokofyevna differed from others, that in the turmoil and bustle of the most mundane events, by virtue of her inherently relentless apprehensiveness she always managed to spot something that inspired untold fear of the most abject kind in her. Imagine how she felt when suddenly in the welter of all the ridiculous and inconsequential commotion, something began to take shape that was genuinely vital, alarming and ominous.

"How could, how could anyone dare write this anonymous letter to me suggesting this *creature* has dealings with Aglaya?" Lizaveta

Prokofyevna fulminated inwardly while dragging the Prince after her, and continued in the same vein even after she had him seated at the round table where the whole family had assembled. "The very idea of it! I'd have died of shame if I'd given the slightest credence to it or shown it to Aglaya! That we, Yepanchins, should be exposed to such ridicule! And it's all through Ivan Fyodorych, all through you, Ivan Fyodorych! Oh, why didn't we move to Yelagin!* Didn't I say we should go to Yelagin Island? Come to think of it, perhaps it was that Varya who'd written the letter, or perhaps... But Ivan Fyodorych is to blame for everything, for everything! That *creature* played that joke on him in memory of former associations, making him a prize fool, just as she had laughed at him previously, fool that he is, and led him a merry dance while he was still lavishing his pearls on her... And still we are all implicated, your daughters are implicated, Ivan Fyodorych, gentlewomen, young ladies, young ladies of the best circles and brides-to-be. They were here, they stood right here and heard everything, and then again those youngsters – your daughters are implicated with that lot as well, you may be jolly glad to know, you were here and heard it all! This miserable princeling is not going to get away with it, I'll never forgive him! And why has Aglaya been hysterical for the past three days? Why has she quarrelled with both her sisters, even with Alexandra, whom she worships like her own mother? Why has she been posing riddles to everyone these past three days? Where does Gavrila Ivolgin fit into all this? Why did she attempt to praise Gavrila Ivolgin yesterday and today, and end up bursting into tears? Why is this confounded hapless knight mentioned in the anonymous letter, whereas not even her sisters got to see the Prince's letter? And why... why on earth did I have to run to him like a mad woman and drag him all the way here? Oh Lord, am I in my right mind, what have I done! To discuss a daughter's secrets with a young man, and in addition... in addition, secrets that might be of direct concern to him! Thank God, he's an idiot, and... and... a friend of the family! But has Aglaya really fallen for such a joker! Good God, what am I on about! Pah! We're such oddities... we should be exhibited behind glass, me above all, at ten copecks a go. I shan't forgive you this, Ivan Fyodorych, never in my life! And why isn't she taking him to task for it now? She promised she would, and she doesn't! There, there, she's looking at him now wide-eyed, won't leave, won't say a word, just sits there, and all this

346

after telling him not to come ever again... He's gone all pale. And this thrice-confounded chatterbox, Yevgeny Pavlovich, has taken over the conversation completely! There he is holding forth, no one else can get a word in edgeways. If only I could change the subject, I'd get to the bottom of it all..."

The Prince did indeed sit at the round table, quite pale, and he seemed extremely fearful of something, while at the same time he also experienced an inexplicable, breathtaking elation. He was so afraid to look in the direction, into that corner from where a pair of dark, familiar eyes regarded him intently, causing him almost to pass out with pleasure at the realization that he was again sitting there amongst them, listening to their dear voices, and after all she had written to him. "Lord, what on earth is she going to say now!" He himself hadn't said a single word yet, listening as he was with overwrought attention to Yevgeny Pavlovich's glib outpourings. He had seldom been in such an expansive mood as that particular evening. The Prince listened and for some time could not understand a single word. Everyone was there with the exception of Ivan Fyodorovich, who still hadn't returned from St Petersburg. Prince S. was also present... he and the others had planned to go to listen to a musical performance before tea was served. The conversation in progress at this time had by all indications been initiated before the Prince joined the party. Soon Kolya appeared on the terrace somewhat unexpectedly. "It seems he is welcome here as previously," the Prince thought.

The Yepanchin dacha was built in the style of a Swiss chalet, surrounded on all sides by luxuriant flowers and leafy plants. It was enclosed by a small, but splendid, flower garden. Everyone was out on the terrace, as they were previously at the Prince's; only the terrace was somewhat more spacious and more elegantly done out.

The subject of the conversation was not to everybody's liking. As far as one could tell it had arisen as a result of an inconsequential dispute and, naturally, everybody was dying to change the subject, but Yevgeny Pavlovich, it seemed, was all the more determined to press on, oblivious of the overall effect; the Prince's arrival appeared to give him new impetus. Lizaveta Prokofyevna was visibly irritated, not being able to follow everything that was said. Aglaya, who sat a little apart, ensconced in a corner, listened attentively, but maintained an obstinate silence.

"I beg your pardon," Yevgeny Pavlovich insisted fervently, "I never said anything against liberalism. Liberalism is not a crime. It's an essential constituent of a whole, which without it would disintegrate or atrophy. Liberalism has the same right to existence as the most benign conservatism. But I attack Russian liberalism, and repeat once more that I attack it precisely because a Russian liberal is not a *Russian* liberal, but a *non-Russian* liberal. Give me a Russian liberal, and I shall immediately kiss him in your presence."

"That's if he agrees to be kissed by you," Alexandra Ivanovna said, seething with excitement. Even her cheeks flushed unusually.

"What about that!" Lizaveta Prokofyevna thought to herself. "Most of the time she just eats and sleeps and shows no sign of life, and then about once a year she'll get up and say something that'll leave everyone speechless."

The Prince noticed briefly that Alexandra Ivanovna seemed irritated by Yevgeny Pavlovich's mock-serious tone of speaking.

"I was saying just now, shortly before your arrival, Prince," Yevgeny Pavlovich continued, "that up to now Russian liberals came from only two classes – the former landowning (now defunct) and the educated. And since both have turned into distinct castes, into something alien to our nation, becoming more and more entrenched with every passing generation, it follows that everything they did, or now do, has lost all national—"

"What? You mean all that has been accomplished is not Russian?" Prince S. interposed.

"Not national. It may be Russian, but it isn't national. Neither our liberals, nor our conservatives are Russian, everything... And rest assured that the nation will not accept anything that has been accomplished either by the landowners or the educated classes, not now, not later—"

"I like that! How can you!" Prince S. countered with feeling. "How can you maintain such a paradox, that is, if you're at all serious? I cannot allow such attacks on the Russian landowner. You're a Russian landowner yourself, are you not?"

"But I'm not talking about the Russian landowner in the sense that you understand it. The class is undoubtedly venerable, if only because I belong to it, especially now that it has ceased to exist—"

"And was there really nothing national in literature too?" Alexandra Ivanovna interrupted.

"I'm no expert in literature, but to my mind Russian literature too, except for Lomonosov, Pushkin and Gogol, is not essentially Russian."

"First, that in itself is saying quite a great deal, and secondly one was of the people, and the other two were landowners," Aglaya observed with a laugh.

"Exactly so, but please bear with me. Since of all the Russian writers so far only this trio have managed to say something of their *own*, something truly distinctive, not borrowed from anywhere else, by virtue of which they immediately become national. The minute a Russian says, writes or accomplishes something of his own, something inalienably his *own* and not borrowed from someone else, he inevitably becomes national, even if his Russian was not up to scratch. This is axiomatic. But we didn't start by talking about literature, we started by talking about socialists, and one thing led to another. Well, I maintain that we haven't got a single Russian socialist in the country, never had one, because all our socialists come either from the landowners or the educated class. All our diehard, proclaimed socialists, whether they reside here or abroad, are no more than liberals of the landed gentry going back to the feudal times. Why are you laughing? Give me their books, give me their teachings, their memoirs, and I, not claiming to be a literary critic, undertake to write a most convincing literary disquisition in which I shall prove as two times two is four that every single page of their books, their pamphlets, their memoirs has been first and foremost written by a former Russian landowner. Their invective, resentment and wit are patrician, going back to the pre-Famusov* days. Their triumphs and their tears are real, perhaps even genuine, but they're those of landowners! Of landowners or the clergy... You're laughing again – and you too, Prince? You don't agree, do you?"

It was true, everybody had started to laugh, and the Prince joined in.

"I can't quite say outright if I agree, or not," the Prince returned with a shudder, ceasing to smile abruptly and looking for all the world like a trapped animal, "but I can assure you I'm listening to you with the greatest of pleasure..."

As he spoke, he gasped for air and even felt beads of cold sweat appear on his forehead. These were the first words that he had spoken since his arrival. He wanted to look around, but dared not; Yevgeny Pavlovich spotted this and smiled.

"Gentlemen, I will tell you a fact," he said in his former tone, which gave the impression of being unusually involved and animated and yet at the same time sardonic and as though making light of his own words, "a fact, the identification, indeed the discovery, of which, I take the honour of attributing to myself and only to myself – at least there has never yet been anything said or written about it anywhere. This fact encapsulates the whole essence of that Russian liberalism which I have been talking about. First, what is liberalism, talking of course in general terms, if not an attack (rational or irrational, that is another matter) on the established order of things? Is that not so? Well, in fact I have revealed that liberalism is not merely an attack on the established order of things, it is an attack on the very essence of our being, on the being itself, on Russia proper. My liberal has reached a stage when he is in denial of Russia itself, that is he detests and chastises his own mother. He well-nigh gloats over every unfortunate and abortive Russian fact. He detests national customs, Russian history, the lot. If there is a justification for him, it is perhaps that he knows not what he is doing, and regards his detestation of Russia as the most fertile liberalism (yes, you will often come across a liberal who is lauded by others and who is perhaps in essence the most inept, the most obtuse and dangerous conservative, without ever realizing this himself!) Not so many years ago some of our liberals regarded this hatred of Russia almost as a veritable expression of love of the fatherland, and boasted that they were better placed than others to comprehend what this love should entail. But now they've become a shade more open, and abhor the very idea of 'love of one's motherland', they've even done away with the very concept as pernicious and worthless. What I say is true and I stand by it and... it is about time someone spoke the whole truth, simply and honestly. And yet at the same time there has never been since the beginning of time anywhere, in any other nation, another example where liberalism has taken such a shape and form, hence it is a chance occurrence, and may be transient, I must agree. Only there can never anywhere else be a liberal with a hatred of his own fatherland. So how can it be explained in our country? By the same fact as previously – that a Russian liberal, is not yet a Russian liberal. There's no other way as I see it."

"I assume everything you said is a joke, Yevgeny Pavlovich," Prince S. observed in all seriousness.

"I can't claim to have seen all the liberals there are, and cannot judge," Alexandra Ivanovna said, "but what you have just said, makes my blood boil. You took a particular case and elevated it to a generalization, which is a travesty."

"A particular case? A-ha! The word has been spoken," Yevgeny Pavlovich was quick to respond. "Prince, what would you say, is it a particular case or not?"

"I too have to admit I've met only a few... liberals and have had little truck with them, but it seems to me you may be right to an extent, and that the Russian liberal you had in mind, may really be particularly inclined to abhor Russia proper, and not merely the prevailing order of things. Of course, only in part... of course, it can never be true of all..."

He began to fumble for words and did not finish. In spite of his emotional unrest, he evinced a great deal of interest in the discussion. The Prince had one peculiar characteristic, comprising an extraordinary naivety with which he not only invariably listened to everything that was of interest to him, but also replied to questions directed at him. His features as well as his whole body seemed to reflect this naivety, this trust, which made no allowances for the least signs of irony or sarcasm. But though Yevgeny Pavlovich had never addressed him except with a measure of a rather peculiar brand of derision, now however, on hearing his reply, he looked at him in all seriousness, not knowing quite what to make of the reply.

"So... well, I never!" he said. "Are you really serious, Prince?"

"Yes I am, if you were," the Prince returned with some surprise.

There was a general burst of laughter.

"Believe him if you wish!" Adelaida said. "Yevgeny Pavlovich never misses an opportunity to make a fool of everyone! You should sometimes hear him talk seriously!"

"Look, this conversation is getting me down," Alexandra observed sharply, "I wish it had never been started. I thought we wanted to go for a walk?"

"Yes, let's, it's such a wonderful evening!" Yevgeny Pavlovich exclaimed. "But to prove to you that on this occasion I'm perfectly serious, and most important of all, to prove this to the Prince (incidentally, Prince, you've intrigued me no end, and – however frivolous I may be deep down – I swear, basically I'm not as frivolous as you might necessarily imagine!), with this in mind, ladies and gentlemen, I'll ask the Prince one final question, purely out of personal curiosity, and then that'll be the end of the matter. This question as it happens occurred to me about two hours ago (you see, Prince, I too, occasionally ponder over serious matters). I've resolved it, but let's see what the Prince has to say. We've just heard the phrase 'a particular case' brought up. It's very significant, and gets bandied about a lot. Recently there was a lot said and written apropos this terrible murder of six people by this... young man and about the rather strange speech of the defence counsel, who indicated that in view of the poverty of the accused, it was *natural* for him to have thought of murdering those six people. I haven't got the exact words, but that was more or less the gist of it. To my mind, the counsel, in voicing such an unusual opinion, must have been perfectly convinced it was the most liberal, the most humane, the most progressive idea one could ever come up with in our times. So what would your opinion be then? Would this distortion of common sense and rationality, this perverse and bizarre way of thinking, represent an isolated phenomenon or a general trend?"

Everyone burst out laughing.

"Isolated, no doubt about it – isolated!" Alexandra and Adelaida exclaimed, laughing.

"Nevertheless, allow me to remind you, Yevgeny Pavlovich," Prince S. added, "your joke has worn pretty thin."

"What do you think, Prince?" Yevgeny Pavlovich, who appeared to have missed the last remark, asked, noticing Prince Lev Nikolayevich's serious and inquisitive gaze fixed on him, "is this an isolated instance or not? I have to admit it was with you in mind that I thought of the question in the first place."

"No, not isolated," the Prince replied softly but firmly.

"Bless my soul, Lev Nikolayevich," Prince S. remonstrated, "can't you see, he's trying to catch you out. He's being completely disingenuous and wants to play fast and loose with you of all people."

"I thought Yevgeny Pavlovich was serious," the Prince said, blushing, and lowered his eyes.

"My dear Prince," Prince S. went on, "think what the two of us talked about three months or so ago. Didn't we agree that in our recent, newly constituted courts of law one could point out any number of excellent, talented defence counsels? And what of the number of truly wonderful verdicts reached by our jurors? How happy you were on this score, and how I was too to see you so happy... it gave us both a sense of pride... As regards this clumsy defence, this odd way of arguing, it is surely an isolated case, one among many thousands."

Prince Lev Nikolayevich thought awhile but then spoke with the utmost conviction, though in a mild, almost diffident tone of voice. "I merely wished to point out that distortion of ideas and concepts (to quote Yevgeny Pavlovich) occurs very frequently and constitutes by and large a widespread phenomenon rather than an isolated case, unfortunately. To the extent that if this distortion was not so common, there might not have been such unheard-of crimes committed as these—"

"Unheard-of crimes? But I assure you precisely such crimes, perhaps even more dreadful ones, occurred before, and they never stopped – and not just in Russia, but everywhere – and I dare say will continue to be committed for a long time yet. The only difference being that previously they were given less publicity, but now people talk and even write about them openly, that's why it only seems as though these criminals appeared only now. That's where your mistake lies, Prince, I assure you," Prince S. concluded with a smile.

"I know perfectly well there were many crimes before too. I have quite recently visited prisons, and have got to know some convicted criminals and those awaiting trial. There are still criminals even more dreadful than the one in question, who'd killed dozens of people without any compunction. But this is what I discovered, that the most hardened and unrepentant murderer is nevertheless aware that he is a *criminal*, that is, his conscience tells him he has done wrong, even though he remains unrepentant. And this true of them all. But the ones that Yevgeny Pavlovich mentioned, do not even want to consider themselves criminals and they think they have the right... indeed, that they did well, or something of the sort. That's where in my opinion the dreadful difference lies. And note this, it is predominantly young people, at an age at which it is easiest of all to fall prey to perverted ideas."

Prince S. was no longer laughing, and listened in disbelief. Alexandra Ivanovna, who had for some time been trying to say something, seemed to change her mind abruptly as though struck by a novel thought. As for Yevgeny Pavlovich, he regarded the Prince in undisguised wonder, and this time without a trace of mockery.

"I don't know why you're so surprised, my dear sir," Lizaveta Prokofyevna intervened unexpectedly, "did you imagine he was not as smart as you just because he had a different point of view?"

"No, that's not what I meant," Yevgeny Pavlovich said, "only how is it, Prince (pardon my asking), if you observe everything so well, how is it (pardon me again) when it came to that strange situation... the other day... with that Burdovsky, was it?... how is it you didn't notice precisely the same perversion of ideas and moral values? I mean exactly the same, in every respect! I had an idea that at the time it all went over your head."

"Look here, my friend," Lizaveta Prokofyevna persisted with ever greater animation, "we all noticed something, sitting here as we do full of ourselves, but he had a letter from one of them today, their leader, the blotchy one, you remember, Alexandra, don't you? He's asking for pardon in his own peculiar way, and announces that he's parted with that friend of his who had been egging him on all along – you remember, Alexandra, don't you? – and that now he trusts the Prince more. Well, we've not had any such letters, have we, whatever airs we might give ourselves in front of him?"

"And Ippolit too has come to join us!" Kolya called out.

"What! Already?" the Prince responded in alarm.

"I would wager," Lizaveta Prokofyevna flared up suddenly, forgetting that only a second ago she had been praising the Prince, "I'd wager he went to him last night in his attic and begged pardon on his knees to persuade that nasty sourpuss to grace us with his presence. Did you go last night? You said as much at the time. Did you or didn't you? Did you kneel before him or not?"

"He didn't do any such thing," Kolya exclaimed, "quite the opposite. Ippolit grabbed the Prince by his hand last night and kissed it twice, I saw it myself, and that was that, except that the Prince simply said it'd be better if he joined him at the dacha, and Ippolit agreed at once, as soon as he felt better."

"You shouldn't have, Kolya..." the Prince muttered, rising and picking up his hat, "why did you need to tell all this? I—"

"Where are you off to?" Lizaveta Prokofyevna asked, stopping him.

"You needn't worry, Prince," Kolya said with enthusiasm. "You should leave him alone and not disturb him. He's fallen asleep after the journey. He's very happy. And you know, Prince, it'd be better if you didn't see him today. Leave it till tomorrow, otherwise it'll embarrass him. The other morning he said he hadn't felt so well and strong these past six months. He's even stopped coughing so much."

The Prince noticed that Aglaya suddenly left her seat and approached the table. He dared not look at her, but he was aware with every fibre of his body that she was staring at him, and perhaps with anger, that her dark eyes were without doubt full of indignation and her face was flushed.

"It seems to me," Yevgeny Pavlovich remarked, "you needn't have bothered bringing him here, Nikolai Ardalionovich, if it's that same consumptive youngster who burst into tears and invited us all to his funeral. He talked so eloquently about his neighbour's brick wall, he'll be sure to miss it here, you can take it from me."

"True enough. He'll pick a quarrel with you, start a fight and leave. End of story."

Having spoken, Lizaveta Prokofyevna, pulled her handiwork basket towards her, forgetting that everybody else was getting up to go for a walk.

"I recall he was very fond of that wall of his," Yevgeny Pavlovich resumed again. "Without that wall he won't be able to die in style, and all he wants is to die in style."

"Well all right then," the Prince muttered, "if you don't wish to forgive him, he'll die without your forgiveness. Now he's come here for the trees."

"Oh, I'm ready to forgive him everything. You can tell him so."

"That's not what this is all about," the Prince observed softly and hesitantly, his eyes fixed on one particular spot on the floor. "It would have been far better if you too had agreed to accept his pardon."

"What have I got to do with this? What wrong have I done him?"

"If you don't understand, I shan't insist... but you do understand, don't you? He wanted to... bless us all and receive your blessing in return, that's all..."

My dear Lev Nikolayevich," Prince S. hurried to interpose tactfully, exchanging knowing glances with one or two members of the present company, "Paradise doesn't come easily on this earth, and as I see it, you have set your sights on Paradise. Paradise is a difficult matter, Prince, much more difficult than your cheery heart can possibly imagine. Let's leave it for now, or we'll upset one another again, and then—"

"Let's go and listen to the music," Lizaveta Prokofyevna proclaimed sharply, rising to her feet angrily.

Everyone followed her example.

2

THE PRINCE suddenly approached Yevgeny Pavlovich.

"Yevgeny Pavlych," he said with unusual warmth, "rest assured I consider you, despite everything, to be an exceptionally kind and honourable man. There must be no room for doubt in your mind…"

Yevgeny Pavlych was so surprised, he took a step back. For a second he was on the brink of an irresistible fit of laughter; but, having taken a closer look, he noticed the Prince appeared not to be his usual self: at the very least he was in an odd state.

"I will wager a bet, Prince" he exclaimed, "you meant to say something quite different, and, very possibly not to me at all… But what's wrong? Are you feeling well?"

"You may be right, absolutely right, and it was good of you to notice I may have meant to address someone else."

Having said this, he gave a strange, almost comical, smile, but in a sudden fit of agitation, he exclaimed, "Do not remind me of what happened three days ago! I've been very ashamed these past three days… I know I'm to blame…"

"But… but what have you done that's so terrible?"

"I can see, Yevgeny Pavlych, you may be more embarrassed than anyone on my account. You are blushing, that is a sign of a wonderful heart. I'm leaving directly, rest assured."

"What's the matter with him? Is that how his fits come upon him?" Lizaveta Prokofyevna turned in fright to Kolya for explanation.

"Take no notice, Lizaveta Prokofyevna, I'm not about to have a fit. I'm leaving directly. I know I've had… an unfair deal from nature. I've been a sick man these past twenty-four years, to be sure till the twenty-fourth year since the day of my birth. So put my present state down to my sickness too. I'm leaving directly, now, rest assured. I'm not blushing, because, let's face it, it would have been odd to blush under the circumstances, don't you think? But I'm not fit for society... This has nothing to do with my self-esteem... I've thought long and hard these past three days, and have decided that I must in all honesty and fairness make a clean breast of it all to you. There are such matters, such lofty matters, that I must not venture to talk about or I'll make everyone laugh. Prince S. brought this to my attention just now... I haven't the knack of propriety, I don't know when to stop, my words are out of step with my thoughts, and this does not do justice to my thoughts. And therefore I've no right... besides, I'm mistrustful, I... I'm convinced no one would offend me in this house and everyone loves me more than I deserve, but I know (I know without a shadow of doubt) that after being ill for twenty-four years, I must surely have been affected in some way. This makes it impossible not to laugh at me... sometimes... I am right, am I not?"

He looked around, seemingly in expectation of an answer and a verdict. Everyone stood, deeply and awkwardly perplexed at this unexpected, manic, and it would seem at all events, unprovoked outburst. But this outburst led to a strange incident.

"Why are you saying all this?" Aglaya suddenly exclaimed. "Why are you saying all this to *them*? To them! To them of all people!"

She seemed to be incensed beyond all measure; her eyes flashed. The Prince stood before her completely dumbstruck, his cheeks drained of blood.

"There's no one here who'd deserve such words!" Aglaya gave vent to her pent-up emotions. "No one here is worthy of wiping the dust off your feet! You are worthier and nobler than any of them, you are better, kinder and wiser! There are those here who are unworthy to pick up your handkerchief if you were to drop one... Why then are you demeaning yourself and running yourself down? Why have you warped and twisted everything inside you, where is your pride?"

"God, who would have thought?" Lizaveta Prokofyevna threw up her hands in resignation.

"The hapless knight! Hurrah!" Kolya exclaimed, beside himself with elation.

"Shut up!... How dare anyone insult me in your house!" Aglaya suddenly turned on her mother. She was in that state when one ceases to heed any restrictions and oversteps all limits. "Why is every single one of you torturing me! Why have they all, Prince, been plaguing me because of you these past three days? I shall never under any circumstances marry you! Get that into your head, never, under any circumstances! Get it firmly into your head! How can anyone possibly marry someone as ridiculous as you? Just look at yourself in the mirror, the way you're standing now!... Why, oh why are they mocking me that I'm going to marry him? You must tell me! Unless you're in league with them yourself!"

"No one ever mocked you!" Adelaida said in a fright.

"It hadn't been in anyone's wildest dreams. Not a word has passed our lips!" Alexandra Ivanovna exclaimed.

"Who is it who mocked her? When did anyone mock her? Who could have told her such a thing? Is she in her right mind?" Lizaveta Prokofyevna, shaking with anger, turned to everyone in turn for an explanation.

"Everybody did, they all did, three days in a row! I shall never, never marry him!"

Having shouted this out, Aglaya dissolved in bitter tears, buried her face in her hands and collapsed in a chair.

"And as yet he hasn't even ask—"

"I haven't asked you, Aglaya Ivanovna," the Prince suddenly blurted out.

"W-what?" Lizaveta Prokofyevna intoned – surprised, dismayed, horrified. She was unable to believe her ears.

"I meant to tell you... I meant to tell you," the Prince fumbled for words, "I merely meant to explain to Aglaya Ivanovna... to have had the honour of explaining that I had no intention at all... of having the honour of asking for her hand... not at any time... It has nothing to do with me, honest to God, nothing at all, Aglaya Ivanovna! I never wanted, it had never occurred to me, nor will it ever, you'll see for yourself, rest assured! Surely some evil person must have spread this rumour! Don't get upset!"

Saying this he drew near to Aglaya. She removed her handkerchief from her eyes, glanced at him, at the whole of his fear-ridden figure, took in his words and suddenly burst out laughing straight in his face – joyous, uncontrollable, provocative and infectious laughter to the extent that Adelaida, unable to resist, especially after glancing at the

Prince, was the first to rush to her sister, hug her and burst into the same paroxysm of uncontrollable, girlishly joyous laughter. Looking at them both the Prince also began to smile, his face beaming with joy and happiness. "Well, God bless, God bless!"

Alexandra could not resist either at this stage and joined in the merriment with all her heart. It seemed the threesome could not have their fill of laughter.

"They've gone mad!" Lizaveta Prokofyevna muttered to herself. "One moment they scare the wits out of you, the next..."

But by then Prince S. too was laughing, and so was Yevgeny Pavlovich; Kolya was simply doubling up, and as the Prince looked on, he too succumbed to the general merriment.

"Let's go out, let's go out for a walk!" Adelaida called out. "We must all go together and the Prince must definitely come with us. You've no right to leave, you dear man! What a darling of a man he is, Aglaya! Wouldn't you agree, Mama? Besides, I must, I simply must kiss and hug him for... for what he said to Aglaya just now. Mama, darling, would you allow me to kiss the Prince? Aglaya! May I kiss *your* Prince!" the mischievous creature exclaimed and did in fact bounce up to the Prince and kiss him on the forehead. The Prince caught her hands, squeezing them so tightly Alexandra nearly cried out with pain; he glanced at her with infinite tenderness, and then suddenly brought her hands up to his lips and kissed them three times.

"Let's go then!" Aglaya said. "Prince, you will escort me. Is that all right, *Maman*? The man who has turned me down? You have turned me down for all time, Prince, haven't you? No, that's not the way to offer a lady your arm, don't you know how to do it? That's better, let's go, we shall go ahead. Do you want us to go ahead of everybody, tête-à-tête?"

She was talking incessantly, still laughing spasmodically.

"Thank God! Thank God!" Lizaveta Prokofyevna kept on repeating, not at all conscious of what it was she was grateful for.

"Very odd, these people!" Prince S. thought to himself, perhaps for the hundredth time since he had joined them, but... he found these odd people rather likeable. As regards Prince Myshkin, he wasn't at all sure, but he didn't strike him as being particularly so; Prince S. kept frowning and was lost in thought as they all emerged from the house to take their walk.

Yevgeny Pavlovich, it seemed, was in the best of moods and kept making Alexandra and Adelaida laugh all the way to the station, both of whom seemed to respond to his jokes all too readily, to the extent that he began momentarily to suspect they might not even be listening. When this thought hit him, he could not help bursting out into the most heartfelt laughter (such was his character!). The two sisters, who were incidentally in the most cheerful mood, kept casting intermittent glances at Aglaya and the Prince, walking just ahead; it was apparent that their youngest sister had given them something very serious to think about. Prince S. made several attempts to engage Lizaveta Prokofyevna in a conversation on extraneous matters, perhaps to distract her, but succeeded only in annoying her intensely. She appeared to be quite distraught, answered incoherently, and sometimes not at all. But Aglaya Ivanovna's mystery game did not end there that evening. She had one more trick up her sleeve, this time for the benefit of the Prince alone. After they had gone about a hundred paces away from the dacha, Aglaya spoke hurriedly in a subdued voice to her escort, who continued to maintain a stubborn silence. "Look to your right."

The Prince obeyed.

"Look closely. Do you see that park bench by the three large trees... the green one?"

The Prince replied that he did.

"Do you like the setting? Sometimes early, at about seven in the morning when everyone's fast asleep, I come and sit there on my own."

The Prince muttered that the setting was wonderful.

"And now leave me, I don't want to walk arm in arm with you any more. Or, better still, let me hold on to you as we are, but don't say a word. I need to think in silence..."

The behest was altogether unnecessary: even without it the Prince would probably not have spoken a single word all through their promenade. His heart began to pound frantically when he heard the bench mentioned. A second later he had gathered his thoughts and dismissed a silly thought that had momentarily occurred to him.

On weekdays the public at the Pavlovsk Voksal* is on the whole more select, or so it is alleged, than on Sundays and feast days when "all sorts of people" flock from town. The long-stay holidaymakers may not necessarily be dressed sumptuously, but certainly elegantly. To come to listen to music is a pleasure. The orchestra, probably the best among those that perform in our public spaces, plays a contemporary repertoire. Politeness and decorum are de rigueur, which does not, however, preclude the holiday atmosphere from being warm and family friendly. Everyone comes to see and to be seen. For some it is a source of great pleasure and the sole object of the exercise; but there are those who come for the music alone. Public spats, though extremely rare, do happen – inevitably.

The evening was exquisite and the attendance was good. All the places by the orchestra were taken. Our company took up seats well away from the centre at the extreme left entrance to the venue. The crowd and the music raised Lizaveta Prokofyevna's spirits somewhat and distracted the minds of the young ladies, who managed to exchange glances with one or two acquaintances and once or twice incline their heads politely in mutual recognition, taking in at a glance the dresses that were worn, noting any odd feature here and there, and picking it to bits immediately with gently mocking smiles playing about their lips. Yevgeny Pavlovich also bowed very frequently. Aglaya and the Prince, who still kept together, had already managed to attract a few looks. Soon mother and daughters were approached by a number of young men; two or three engaged in polite conversation; all were from Yevgeny Pavlovich's circle. Amongst them was a young, very handsome officer – in high spirits and very voluble; he hastened to engage Aglaya in conversation and did his level best to hold her attention. Aglaya treated him highly considerately but quite ironically. Yevgeny Pavlovich asked the Prince if he could introduce him to this friend of his; the Prince hardly understood what was wanted, but they exchanged mutual cordialities – bowed and shook hands. Yevgeny Pavlovich's friend asked a question, but it seemed the Prince did not reply to it or muttered something quite unintelligible under his breath such that the officer looked at him very quizzically, then back at Yevgeny Pavlovich, and immediately understood the reason for the introduction. He frowned slightly and again turned towards Aglaya. Yevgeny Pavlovich was the only one who noticed Aglaya blush.

The Prince was not only almost totally unaware that there were some who sought to engage Aglaya in a conversation and to pay her compliments, but at times he was even oblivious of the fact that he himself was sitting next to her. Occasionally he had the urge simply to get up and go away, leave the venue altogether. He would even prefer some gloomy, desolate place just in order to be on his own, alone with his thoughts, and that no one should know where he was. Or at the very least to be at home, on the terrace, but so that there was no one else present, neither Lebedev, nor the children; to collapse on the sofa, bury his face in a cushion and stay that way a whole day, a night and a day more. He had momentary visions of the Swiss mountains, especially one particular spot, which he always liked to think back to and to which he liked to return again and again when he was still living there; to look down upon the village, upon the faintly glistening ribbon of the waterfall down below, on the white clouds and the ruins of the old castle. Oh, how he longed to be there now and think of one thing only – one thought in a lifetime – it would have sufficed him for a thousand years! Would that all memory of him vanished here. Oh, that was in fact what he wished, or better still, that he'd never been known to exist, and all this had been a mere vision in a dream. And in the end, what was the difference – dream or reality? Every now and again he would suddenly stare at Aglaya for up to five minutes at a time, unable to tear his eyes away from her face, but oddly enough, he seemed to be looking at her as at an object miles away, or as at a portrait rather than a living being.

"Why are you looking at me like that, Prince?" she asked suddenly, turning away from an amusing conversation which was in progress. "You frighten me. I get the impression you want to put out your hand and touch my face with your finger all the time. Wouldn't you agree, Yevgeny Pavlovich, the way he keeps looking?"

The Prince listened with surprise, astonished, it seemed, that anyone should have addressed him, pondered on it, though perhaps still not quite aware of what was going on; gave no reply, but seeing that she and everyone else was laughing, suddenly opened his mouth and burst out into laughter himself. The laughter intensified all round; the officer, a mirthful person at the best of times, simply exploded with laughter. Aglaya suddenly whispered to herself in anger, "Idiot!"

"Good Lord! Is she really going for such a one... is she really going to go out of her own mind completely in the end?" Lizaveta Prokofyevna hissed through clenched teeth.

"It's a joke. The same as 'the hapless knight' previously," Alexandra whispered in her ear forcefully, "and nothing more! I think she's making fun of him again. Only the joke has gone too far. This must be stopped, *Maman*! All her previous histrionics only frightened us—"

"It's lucky she happened upon such an idiot," Lizaveta Prokofyevna whispered back. Nevertheless, her daughter's observation had a calming effect upon her.

The Prince, however, heard himself being called an idiot and shuddered, but not because of "idiot". The "idiot" he forgot at once. But in the crowd, not far from where he was sitting, out of nowhere (he'd never have been able to specify precisely the exact spot) he glimpsed a face, a pale face, dark curly hair, a familiar – all too familiar – smile and features. It was there one minute and gone the next. It could well be he'd only imagined it; all that was left for him of the vision was a wry smile, a pair of eyes and a bright green, foppish scarf, worn by the gentleman he had glimpsed. Whether he vanished in the crowd or dashed away, the Prince also could not be certain.

But a second later the Prince began to cast around quick, anxious glances. This first vision could well presage or pave the way for the next. This was inevitable. Could he really have failed to foresee such an encounter when he was setting off for the Voksal? True, on his way there, he hardly knew where he was going – such was the state he was in. Had he been more attentive, he'd have noticed a good quarter of an hour earlier that Aglaya too had been looking around anxiously and intermittently as though searching for someone in the crowd. As his own disquiet grew and became all too evident, so did Aglaya's, and each time he swung round to look, so did she. The reason for their unease soon became evident.

Through the same entrance, near which sat the Prince and the Yepanchin company, a whole crowd suddenly streamed in, at least ten people in all. At the head were three women, two of whom were unusually beautiful, and there was nothing surprising that they were followed by a great many admirers. But there was something about the admirers as well as the women that immediately set them apart, something that distinguished them radically from the run-of-the-mill audience, which had gathered for the musical performance. They immediately attracted attention to themselves, but for the most part people pretended not to notice them, only a few of the younger members of the public smiled furtively, exchanging amongst themselves snippets of observations in hushed tones. But it was impossible not to notice them. They flaunted themselves, conversing in loud voices and laughing. No doubt some were tipsy, but even among these, some were well enough, and some even elegantly turned out; but there were others who looked positively strange, in outlandish outfits and with markedly bloated faces. Finally there were some military officers, and even a few who could no longer qualify as young. Most were in comfortable, well-cut suits, displaying expensive rings and cufflinks; some wore excellently fitting jet-black wigs and sported bushy sideburns, lending their faces a sedate, though scornful, aspect, which in normal society is calculated to make people avoid them like the plague. There are of course in our suburban communities those who stand proudly on their imposing demeanour and exceptional respectability. However, it is the case that even the most circumspect person cannot every minute of his life protect himself from a stray brick or tile that may fall on him from a nearby building. Such a brick was about to descend on the respectable public who had gathered to enjoy a musical performance.

In order to cross from the Voksal concourse to the orchestra podium, the visitor has to descend three steps. The new arrivals stopped at these steps and hesitated; but one of the ladies went ahead; only two members of her entourage dared follow her. One was a fairly unassuming middle-aged man, quite proper in every respect, but with something about his appearance that immediately marked him out as an odd fish, that is one who neither knows or wants to know anyone. The other was a complete and utter vagrant. No one else followed her, but as she descended the steps, she did not even bother to look back, unconcerned if anybody followed her or not. She laughed and talked loudly as before; she was dressed expensively and in extreme good taste, though with a touch more showiness than was proper. She moved past the podium, on the far side of which stood someone's horse-drawn calash.

The Prince had not seen *her* for over three months. Every day since his return to St Petersburg he had been planning to call on her; but perhaps some mysterious presentiment was stopping him. At least he was totally unable to anticipate the effect a meeting with her would have on him, but he sometimes tried to picture it to himself with dread. He was clear about one thing – the encounter would not be easy. During all these six months he recalled on a number of occasions that first impression which the woman's face had had on him when he first glimpsed her portrait; but even the memory of the portrait alone was difficult enough. That month in the country, when he saw her practically every day, left a terrible mark on him, to the extent that he shrank from the very memory of those all too recent days. For the Prince there was always something painful in the very features of the woman; talking to Rogozhin, he attributed this sensation of pain to one of infinite pity, and this was true. The sight of her face even on the portrait evoked a torrent of pity in his heart. This feeling of pity, indeed of compassion for this creature, never waned in his heart, nor did it on this occasion. Oh no, it was even stronger. But what he had said to Rogozhin left the Prince dissatisfied. Only now, at the moment of her unexpected appearance, did he by direct association, as it were, realize what it was that was missing from his words to Rogozhin. It was words to convey the full horror of her condition. Yes, horror! For that was precisely what he felt on this particular occasion. He was convinced, indeed from his private knowledge of her – fully convinced that she was mad. If, while loving a woman more than anything else in the world, or anticipating the possibility of such a love, one were to see her on a chain, behind iron bars, surveyed by a guard wielding a stick – that would be something of what the Prince felt on that occasion.

"What's wrong?" Aglaya whispered hurriedly, glancing over at him and involuntarily tugging at his sleeve.

He turned his head, looked at her, glanced with surprise into her dark, strangely scintillating eyes, made an effort to smile, but suddenly, as though dismissing her from his mind, looked to his right again, attracted by the vision which appeared to mesmerize him. Nastasya Filippovna had at that instant come level with where the young ladies were seated. Yevgeny Pavlovich was in the act of recounting to Alexandra Ivanovna with passion and conviction something highly amusing and interesting – he was in full flow. The Prince recalled that at this stage Aglaya suddenly exclaimed in a half-whisper, "Ah! What a... "

She did not finish and her words were left hanging in the air; she had checked herself instantly and said nothing else, but the damage had been done. Nastasya Filippovna, who while walking past appeared not to recognize anyone in particular, suddenly turned as though she'd noticed Yevgeny Pavlovich for the very first time.

"B-bah! So that's where he is!" she called out, stopping dead. "You can search for him far and wide and, lo and behold, all the while he's been sitting in the most unlikely of places... I thought you were back there... at your uncle's!"

Yevgeny Pavlovich flushed, cast Nastasya Filippovna a furious glance, and quickly turned away.

"What? Do you mean you don't know? I like that, he still doesn't know! He's shot himself! Your uncle shot himself this morning! I heard about it at two, the whole town knows about it by now. Three hundred and fifty thousand roubles of government money is missing, some say, five! And there I was hoping he'd leave you a fortune. He's blown the lot, dirty old man that he was!... Well, goodbye then, *bonne chance*! So you're really not going over to have a look for yourself? I can see now why you handed in your resignation in such a hurry, you slyboots! Nonsense, you knew, you knew all along. Perhaps you knew it since yesterday!..."

Although the impudence with which he was accosted, no less than the flagrant inference of a non-existing association and intimate relationship, had an ulterior motive, which could no longer be doubted, still Yevgeny Pavlovich hoped against hope to get away unscathed, and in any case to avoid embroiling himself with his tormentress any further. But Nastasya Filippovna's words cut him to the quick. When he heard the news of his uncle's death, he went as white as a sheet and turned towards the bearer of the news. At this moment Lizaveta Prokofyevna quickly left her seat, urged everyone to follow suit and almost ran for the exit. Only Lev Nikolayevich stayed behind briefly, seemingly undecided, as did Yevgeny Pavlovich, who was still standing, utterly bewildered. But the Yepanchins had not gone twenty paces when all hell broke loose.

The officer talking to Aglaya, who was a close friend of Yevgeny Pavlovich's, flared up indignantly.

"One should take a horse whip to her, there's no other way to deal with someone like that!" he said in a fairly distinct voice. (He had for some time past been Yevgeny Pavlovich's confidant.)

Nastasya Filippovna turned to face him instantly. Her eyes flashed. She rushed towards a young man, a complete stranger, standing not two paces from her, holding a slender wicker cane, tore it out of his hands and lashed her offender with all her strength across the face. All this was over in a split second... The officer, wild with rage, rushed towards her; Nastasya Filippovna was by now quite exposed, there was no one of her entourage close to her. The respectable middle-aged gentleman had by then managed to disappear without a trace, while the inebriated one stood at a distance and was laughing his head off. A minute later the police would of course have arrived, but in the meantime Nastasya Filippovna might have fared very badly indeed, were it not that unexpected help was at hand. The Prince, who was hovering close by, managed to grab the officer's hand from behind. While extricating his hands, the officer dealt the Prince a hard blow in the chest; the latter staggered backwards about three paces and collapsed into a chair. But help for Nastasya Filippovna was at hand from another quarter. Facing the attacking officer stood the pugilist Keller, whom the reader will remember as the author of the newspaper article and active member of Rogozhin's erstwhile troupe.

"Keller! Ex-sub lieutenant at your service," he rattled off in an affected style. "If it's with bare fists, guv, to protect the weaker sex, I'm always ready to oblige. Queensberry rules is my speciality. No shoving now, guv, you have my full sympathy for the bloody offence you sustained, but I can't allow anyone to raise a hand against a lady in public. If, however, being a gentleman, you'd prefer some other form of settlement, then of course, you must understand, guv—"

But the officer, having in the meantime gathered his wits, was no longer listening. At this moment Rogozhin emerged from the crowd, grabbed Nastasya Filippovna by the arm, and the two hurried away. For his part, Rogozhin seemed badly shaken, he was pale and trembling all over. As he led Nastasya Filippovna away, he laughed angrily into the officer's face and called out with gloating malevolence, "Bah! You had it coming! Blood all over your face! Bah!"

The officer, covering his face with a handkerchief and having got a grip on himself, as well as realizing whom he was dealing with, turned with all courtesy to the Prince who was by now up on his feet. "Prince Myshkin, I presume, to whom I had the pleasure of being introduced?"

"She's not in her right mind! She's mad! I assure you!" the Prince replied in a shaking voice, for some reason proffering him both his trembling hands.

"It goes without saying I'm not privileged to have any such information, but I just wanted to make sure I knew your name." He saluted with a nod and withdrew.

The police turned up exactly five seconds after the last of the people involved in the unpleasant incident had disappeared. To be sure the action lasted no more than a couple of minutes from start to finish. Some members of the audience got up and left, others merely exchanged places; yet others enjoyed the fracas, and there were those who laughed and talked about it a great deal. In a word, the affair drew to a close in a most mundane fashion. The orchestra struck up again. The Prince followed the Yepanchins. If only it had occurred to him or if he had had time to look to his left when he was still slumped in his chair, he'd have noticed Aglaya, who had stopped not twenty paces away from him, in contemplation of the confrontation, not heeding her mother's and sisters' exhortations from a distance to follow them. Prince S. came running up to her, and managed at last to persuade her to move on swiftly. Lizaveta Prokofyevna noticed that Aglaya, after she joined them, was so shaken she had probably been unaware that they had called to her. But a couple of minutes later, just as they were filing into the park, Aglaya was heard to say in her customarily indifferent, slightly capricious tone of voice, "I only wanted to see how the comedy would end."

3

THE INCIDENT AT THE VOKSAL had a shattering effect on both mother and daughters. Lizaveta Prokofyevna, alarmed and perturbed, well-nigh ran with her daughters all the way home. As she saw and understood the situation, much too much had happened and come to light to give her mind, confused and fearful as it was, food for serious thought. But others too saw that something extraordinary had occurred, and that perhaps, luckily, some deep mystery was being unravelled. In spite of all Prince S.'s former explanations and assurances, Yevgeny Pavlovich was now "brought out into the open", exposed, laid bare and "formally unmasked in his dealings with this creature". That was how Lizaveta Prokofyevna and even her two elder daughters argued. All they managed to gain from such talk was the propagation of yet more riddles. Much though the young ladies re-sented their mother's panic and such an obvious retreat from the scene, they dared not question her, at least not until some of the dust had settled. Apart from this, it seemed to them for some reason that their sister, Aglaya Ivanovna, perhaps knew more of what was going on than all three of them put together. Prince S. too was in the dumps and lost in thought. Lizaveta Prokofyevna did not exchange a single word with him all the way and it seemed he did not even notice this. Adelaida tried asking him, "What was all that about an uncle, and what ex-actly happened in St Petersburg?" But, putting on a most sour mien, he muttered something vague about certain ongoing enquiries but that in short people of course had got the wrong end of the stick altogether in the matter. "Assuredly so!" Adelaida replied, and had no further ques-tions to put. Aglaya, on the other hand, showed no emotion whatever, and merely remarked that they should perhaps slow down. Once she looked back and saw the Prince, who was following them. Realizing that he was intent on catching up with them, she smiled derisively and made no more attempts to look back.

At last, when they were already within reach of the dacha, they met Ivan Fyodorovich, who'd just then returned from St Petersburg, coming the other way. His first question, immediately, was to enquire after Yevgeny Pavlovich. But his spouse marched past him angrily, without replying and with not so much as a glance at him. By what he could glimpse in her and his daughters' eyes, he immediately realized there was a storm brewing in the house. But this apart, his own features too portrayed some strange unrest. He immediately took Prince S. by the arm, stopped at the entrance to the house, and in subdued tones exchanged a few confidential words with him. Judging by the agitation on their faces, after they had mounted the steps to the terrace and headed to see Lizaveta Prokofyevna, one would have thought they had become privy to some extraordinary piece of news. One by one everybody assembled at Lizaveta Prokofyevna's upstairs, while on the terrace the Prince was finally left behind alone. He sat in a corner as though in wait for something, but in fact he had no clear idea of what he was about; even though the atmosphere in the house was tense, it did not even occur to him to get up and leave; it seemed he was oblivious to everything in the world and was prepared not to stir from wherever he was seated for years and years. Agitated voices reached him from time to time from above. He had no idea how long he sat. It was getting late, and the light was fading completely. Suddenly Aglaya came out on to the terrace; she was visibly calm, though somewhat pale. On seeing the Prince, whom she clearly did not expect to find seated on a chair, in a corner, she smiled somewhat awkwardly.

"What are you doing here?" she asked, approaching him.

The Prince muttered something in reply but stopped in embarrassment, and jumped to his feet; but Aglaya sat down by him at once, and he too resumed his seat. She looked him over hurriedly, then darted a glance through the window as though with nothing on her mind, then back at him again. "Perhaps she wants to make fun of me?" the thought crossed his mind. "No, it doesn't look like it."

"Would you like a glass of tea?" she asked after a pause. "I'll ask for some to be brought."

"N-no... I don't know..."

"How can one not know such a thing? Oh yes, supposing someone were to challenge you to a duel, what would you do? I meant to ask you this before."

"Really... who?... No one's going to challenge me to a duel."

"But if you were to challenge someone? Would you be very frightened?"

"I think, I would be very... frightened."

"Seriously? So you're a coward?"

"N-no. Perhaps I'm not," the Prince said with a smile after reflecting. "A coward is one who takes fright and runs away. But one who takes fright and doesn't run away, may still not be a coward."

"And you wouldn't run away?"

"Perhaps I wouldn't," the Prince replied, no longer able to resist bursting out in laughter at her questions.

"Even though I am a woman, I myself would never run away," she returned with a note of reproof in her voice. "No matter, I can see you're not being serious with me and as usual are turning it all into a selfish joke. Tell me, they normally shoot at twelve paces? Some at ten, don't they? That would be certain death or injury, would it not?"

"They shoot wide at duels, mostly."

"Mostly, really? Pushkin was killed though."

"That may have been by accident."

"Not at all. It was a duel to the death, and he was killed."

"The bullet came so low, it would suggest d'Anthès aimed much higher, at the chest or the head. But the way the bullet passed shows it went wide, hence it's almost certain Pushkin was hit by chance, wide of the mark. I discussed this with experts."

"But a soldier once told me that in battle they must, according to the book, aim for the midriff. It says clearly to go for the midriff. Not the chest, or the head, but they have to shoot at the midriff. I later asked an officer and he said that was exactly right."

"Yes, that's because they shoot at long range."

"Do you know how to shoot?"

"I've never shot."

"Don't you even know how to load a gun?"

"I don't. That is, I know how it's done, but I have never done it myself."

"Well, that means you don't, because you need plenty of practice! Listen carefully: first, you must buy some good gunpowder, I was told it must be absolutely dry, not damp. It's got to be fine too, I believe – you'll need to ask. The type they use in cannons won't do. As for bullets, people cast their own, I'm told. Have you got pistols?"

"No, and I don't need any," the Prince said with a laugh.

"Oh, you are silly! You must buy a good one, of French or English make, they say they're the best. Then you take about a thimbleful of powder, perhaps two, and shake it into the barrel. More would be better. Then ram it in with hemp (for some reason hemp's essential) – you can easily get it from somewhere, a mattress or something, or it's sometimes used round door frames as a draught excluder. Then after you've stuffed in the hemp, you roll the bullet in – did you hear me, first the powder, then the bullet, otherwise it won't work. Why are you laughing? I want you to practice shooting every day several times and always to hit the target. Would you do it?"

The Prince laughed; Aglaya stamped her foot in annoyance. The serious tone of her voice, bearing in mind the subject, came as somewhat of a surprise to the Prince. He couldn't help feeling he needed to find out something, ask about something – about something that was a little more serious than loading guns. But all this went clean out of his head; all he knew was that she sat before him, and he was looking at her, and what it was they were talking about, made no difference for him whatsoever.

Finally Ivan Fyodorovich came down on to the terrace from upstairs; he was bound for somewhere, frowning, absorbed and in a state of vexation.

"Ah, Lev Nikolayevich, it's you?... Where are you off to?" he asked in spite of the fact that Lev Nikolayevich had no intention of going anywhere. "Come with me, I've something to tell you."

"Goodbye," Aglaya said and put out her hand to the Prince.

It was already quite dark on the terrace, and the Prince would not have been able to see clearly the expression on Aglaya's face. A minute later, when the General and he were going out, he suddenly blushed terribly and clenched his right fist tightly.

It turned out that Ivan Fyodorovich was going the same way; in spite of the late hour he was on his way to meet someone. In the interim he struck up a conversation with the Prince; he spoke quickly, fitfully and fairly incoherently, often mentioning Lizaveta Prokofyevna. Had the Prince been just a little more attentive, he'd have perceived that Ivan Fyodorovich was, amongst other things, anxious to pump him for something or, to be more precise, ask him something outright, but held back, unable to bring himself to go to the heart of the matter. To his shame the Prince was so distraught that from the very start he hardly listened, and when the General came to a dead halt, facing him with some important question, he had to admit he hadn't the slightest idea.

The General shrugged his shoulders.

"You've all gone very funny, you lot," he resumed. "I'm telling you, I've no idea what it is Lizaveta Prokofyevna is so worried or preoccupied about. She's hysterical, claiming we've been slurred and maligned. By whom? How? On account of what? When and why? There's no denying, it's my fault, *mea culpa*. I'm greatly at fault, but I'm afraid the antics of this... unruly woman, who makes no effort to hold herself in check, have to be brought to an end, by the police if necessary, and I've a mind to see someone about it today. Everything can be arranged quietly, smoothly, even amicably without any fuss. I'd also be the first to agree that the future is fraught and that much is still shrouded in mystery. There's some intrigue afoot, but when nobody knows a thing here, and nobody is any the wiser there – if I heard nothing, you heard nothing, the whole world, every Tom, Dick and Harry has heard nothing, then who the dickens has been listening, I ask you? How is it all to be explained, sir, except that half the trouble is we've a mirage on our hands, it's all hocus-pocus through and through, it simply doesn't exist, like the light from the moon… or other such make-believe."

"*She* is mad," the Prince muttered, suddenly recalling painfully all that had passed.

"I couldn't agree more, if we're talking about the same person. It also occurred to me many a time, and then I was able to sleep in peace. But now I can see there's more to it than meets the eye, and I no longer believe in her madness. She's a heady type, but far from being mad, her head's screwed on perfectly all right. Her outburst with Kapiton Alexeyevich is a case in point. She's got some devilish, Jesuitical trick up her sleeve."

"What Kapiton Alexeyevich?"

"Heavens, Lev Nikolayevich, you've not been listening at all. Kapiton Alexeyevich was the first thing I mentioned to you. I was so shocked my hands and feet are still shaking. That was the only reason I was held up in town today. Kapiton Alexeyevich Radomsky was Yevgeny Pavlovich's uncle—"

"Well!" the Prince exclaimed.

"He shot himself this morning, at dawn, at seven o'clock. A venerable old chap, seventy years of age, but a dreadful womanizer – and it was just as she said, state money missing, a considerable sum!"

"But, how on earth did—"

"She knows? Ha ha ha! Well, no sooner did she turn up than she was surrounded by a whole council of war. Have you any idea the kind of people who now call upon her and seek her acquaintanceship? She could easily have heard something from her visitors, because all St Petersburg knows now and half of Pavlovsk too, or should I say the whole of Pavlovsk. And wasn't it clever of her to bring in the resignation, as I was told later! That is, that Yevgeny Pavlovich managed to resign his commission in time! A hell of a slur, that! No, this doesn't suggest madness. Of course, I refuse to believe that Yevgeny Pavlovich could have known anything in advance about the tragedy – that is, that it occurred on such-and-such a date, at seven o'clock in the morning, and so on. But he could at least have had a hunch about all this. And there was I, there we all were, including Prince S., thinking that the old boy would leave him an inheritance! Awful! How awful! You must understand, however, I'm not accusing Yevgeny Pavlovich of anything,

I can't overemphasize that, but all the same, that said, it is suspicious. Prince S. is simply stunned. It all came about so unexpectedly."

"But what is suspicious in Yevgeny Pavlovich's behaviour?"

"Nothing! He acted like a true gentleman. I made no aspersions against him. His personal fortune is, I think, safe. Lizaveta Prokofyevna, of course, won't hear of it... But what's so awful is all these family tragedies, or to be more precise, squabbles – words fail me in fact... You, Lev Nikolayevich, are a true friend of the family, and imagine – it now turns out, though it may well all be inaccurate, that Yevgeny Pavlovich had, it appears, proposed to Aglaya over a month ago, and allegedly received a formal refusal from her!"

"That's impossible!" the Prince exclaimed with passion.

"Are you perhaps privy to anything? You see, my dearest Prince..." the General said, surprised and startled, stopping as though rooted to the spot, "perhaps I've been rash and careless enough to say more than I ought to have done, but that's because you're... because you're... one can safely say, an extraordinary man. Perhaps you know something special?"

"I know nothing... about Yevgeny Pavlovich," the Prince muttered.

"That makes two of us! They literally want to bury... me... bury me alive, six feet under and no one cares what it'll do to me. What a scene there was just now, it was simply awful! I speak to you as to a son. And the main thing is, Aglaya keeps poking fun at her mother. That she apparently turned down Yevgeny Pavlovich's offer of marriage about a month ago and that there was a rather formal exchange of views between them, was reported by the sisters in the form of a surmise... to be sure, a firm surmise. But then the girl is such a wilful and fanciful thing, it beggars description! Such dignity, such depth of sentiment and mind – all of which she has perhaps in abundance, and along with it this capriciousness, this urge for mischief-making, in a word – a veritable fiend and full of fancies to boot. She just laughed at her mother, and her sisters and Prince S. too. As for me, it doesn't bear talking about, there's never been a time she hasn't laughed at me, but what am I, I love her, you know, I love her even for laughing at me – and, I suspect, the little prankster loves me just for that especially, that is, more than all the others, it seems to me. I wouldn't mind betting she's had a go at you too. I came upon you two after the row upstairs, and she was sat next to you as though she didn't have a care in the world."

The Prince blushed terribly and clenched his right fist, but did not say a word.

"My good, kind Lev Nikolayevich!" the General suddenly said with feeling and warmth. "I myself... and even Lizaveta Prokofyevna (who incidentally has recently taken to censuring you again, and along with that me too because of you – only I can't quite make out why) – we love you all the same though, we love you dearly and respect you despite everything, that is, despite all the indications. But you must, you must agree, my dear boy, what a conundrum and what a shame it was to hear this little she-devil (because she was confronting her mother with the utmost contempt because of all our questioning, mine especially, because I, dammit, put my foot in it, I tried to read the riot act to her, being the head of the family – well, a total disaster!). So this little she-devil suddenly declares with a smirk – cool as a cucumber, mind you, that this demented one (as she called her, and I can't get over it that you and she are at one on this, 'How is it you haven't,' she reckons, 'cottoned on to that so far?') that this crazy woman, 'has taken it into her head, come what may, to marry me off to Prince Lev Nikolayevich, and to bring this about is doing her utmost to oust Yevgeny Pavlovich from this house...' That's all she said, laughed out loud, while we just stood there, mouths open, then banged the door and left. Then someone told me about what had passed between you and her... and... and... listen to me, Prince, my dear chap, you won't take offence, will you, and you're a very sensible man, I've noticed that about you, so don't be cross, but honestly – she's laughing at you. It's a childish laughter, and that's why you're taking it so well, but the fact remains. Just don't think about it – she's merely having fun at your and others' expense, for lack of something better to do. Well, goodbye! You know our feelings, don't you? Our genuine feelings towards you! They are as steady as a rock, always have been, always will be... but... I'm going this way, so long! I've rarely felt so out of sorts as now... Some holiday!"

When he was left alone at the crossroads, the Prince looked around, went over to the other side of the road and drew near the light from a dacha window, where he unfolded the little note he was holding tightly in his right hand all the while he had been speaking to Ivan Fyodorovich, and read it, holding it up to catch the dim rays of light:

I'll be waiting for you at the green bench in the park tomorrow at seven. I've resolved to speak to you on an extraordinarily important matter, which concerns you directly.

    PS: I hope you won't show this note to anyone. Though I feel embarrassed giving you such instructions, to my mind it was unavoidable, and I went ahead – blushing in shame at your funny character.

    PPS: It's that same green bench which I pointed out to you. For shame! This too I felt I had to add.

The note was written in haste and folded just anyhow, most probably just before Aglaya had come out on the terrace. In extraordinary fear, bordering on panic, the Prince again clutched the piece of paper in his hand and recoiled from the window and out of the light, like a frightened thief; but in so doing, bumped into a man who stood right behind him.

"I've been keeping an eye on you, Prince," the man said.

"Is that you, Keller?" the Prince said in astonishment.

"I've been looking for you, Prince. I waited for you at the Yepanchins' dacha – naturally I didn't dare enter. Then I followed you as you walked with the General. At your service, Prince – Keller's at your disposal. I'm ready to sacrifice myself, and even to die, if necessary."

"But… what for?"

"Well, you're bound to be challenged to a duel.* I know this Lieutenant Molovtsov – not personally, that is… he won't tolerate any insult. He's bound to look upon the likes of me and Rogozhin as the scum of the earth, and perhaps rightly so – but in that case, the responsibility falls squarely upon your shoulders. You'll be held to account, Prince. He has made enquiries about you, I heard, and you can rest assured a friend of his will call on you tomorrow, he may in fact be waiting for you right now. If you'd do me the honour of choosing me as your second, I'd be ready for anything. I looked for you especially to tell you just that, Prince."

"So you're on about the duel too!" the Prince said and, to Keller's immense surprise, suddenly burst out laughing. It was a deep, raucous laugh. Keller, in his earnestness to impart to the Prince the seriousness of his situation, nearly took offence.

"You see, Prince, you grabbed him by his arms. A gentleman can hardly be expected to live that down, especially in public."

"And he pushed me in the chest!" the Prince went on, laughing. "Why on earth should we fight! I'll ask his pardon, and that'll be the end of the matter. But if it should come to a fight, I don't mind! Let him shoot. I'd welcome it. Ha ha! I know how to load a gun now! Do you realize, I've just been taught to do it? Do you know how to load a gun, Keller? First you have to buy some gunpowder, dry pistol gunpowder, not the coarse stuff for blasting out of a cannon. You pour the powder in first, stuff some hemp in from the gaps of door frames, and only then roll the bullet in – not bullet first and then powder, that wouldn't do. Did you hear that, Keller, that wouldn't do at all. Ha ha ha! Isn't that capital, Keller, my friend! Do you realize, Keller, I want to hug you for this. Ha ha ha! The way you suddenly materialized in front of me then! Come and see me sometime soon to crack a bottle of champagne. We'll all get drunk! Do you realize I've a dozen bottles of the stuff in Lebedev's cellar? Lebedev sold them to me the day after I moved in, at a bargain price. I bought the lot! I'll get the whole crowd to come over! Will you be sleeping soundly tonight?"

"Yes, as ever, Prince."

"Well, sweet dreams then! Ha ha ha!"

The Prince crossed the road and disappeared into the park, leaving Keller standing rather perplexed. He had never before observed the Prince in such a strange mood, nor could he have imagined him thus.

"He's got a fever," Keller mused. "Maybe it's his nerves, and all the rest of it coming to a head together, but he's not going to funk it. Such people never do, bless them! Hm, champagne! Very interesting. A dozen bottles, twelve that is! A proper little line-up! I bet my life someone pawned them to Lebedev. Well, well… a nice fellow, this Prince, all in all. I really love people like that – they're the salt of the earth. But, time's precious, and… if it's a matter of champagne, now's just the right time…"

That the Prince was in a fever, was quite correct.

He spent a long time walking through the shadowy park, and suddenly found himself wandering up and down a certain alley. Deep in his consciousness he had memories of having already walked along this alley, starting from a bench and finishing by a certain old tree, huge and prominent, a distance of about hundred paces, repeated thirty or forty times up and down. To recall what went on in his mind during that hour or more in the park, would have been next to impossible for him at the best of times. But one thing struck him forcibly, however, and it made him roll with laughter, though in truth there was nothing funny; all the same he couldn't help laughing. It struck him that the possibility of a duel could have occurred to one other person besides Keller and that the talk of loading a gun could well not have been fortuitous... "Well, well, well!" he suddenly exclaimed, coming to a halt abruptly, as something else dawned upon him. "When she came down onto the terrace and found me sitting in a corner, she was most surprised to find me there, and she smiled... she then went on about tea. But she must already have had this slip of paper in her hand, therefore it follows she definitely knew I was sitting on the terrace, so why was she surprised? Ha ha ha!"

He snatched the note out of his pocket and kissed it, but then immediately paused and became lost in thought.

"How strange! How strange this all is!" he brought out after a while with some sadness. In moments of extreme happiness he would always, inexplicably, be overcome with sadness. He glanced around and was surprised to have wandered upon this place. He walked over to the bench and sat down, very tired. All around there was an extraordinary silence. The music at the Voksal was over. The park was probably completely empty; the time was already after half-past eleven. The night was still, warm and light – a St Petersburg night in early June – but in the dense, shadowy park, in the alley where he was, it was all but dark.

If someone had suggested at that moment that he was in love, deeply and passionately in love, he'd have rejected the suggestion with surprise, perhaps with indignation. And were that someone to add that Aglaya's note was a love letter, a call to a rendezvous, he'd have died of shame and perhaps challenged him to a duel. He was perfectly sincere in this, and would admit of no equivocation in the possibility of this girl's love for him and, for that matter, of his love for her. The notion that she might have fallen in love with "a man like him" filled him with dread. He imagined it was simply a prank on her part, at most; but the idea of a prank left him pretty unconcerned on the whole and he appeared to take it all in his stride; deep down, however, he was preoccupied with something else entirely. The remark the General had let slip, that Aglaya was holding up everybody, and him especially, to ridicule, he took at face value. In so doing, he did not feel the least bit offended; it was as it should be, in his opinion. All he cared for was that early tomorrow he'd be sitting next to her on the green bench, listening to instructions on how to load a gun, and gazing at her. That was all he wanted. True, the question of what it was she actually intended to communicate to him that was so important and of direct concern for him did flash through his mind once or twice. Besides, he never once doubted that such an important matter actually did exist; but as for delving into it deeper, he felt no inclination whatever.

The soft sound of steps in the sand of the alley made him raise his head. A person, whose face it was difficult to make out in the darkness, approached the bench and sat down beside him. The Prince moved quickly towards him, almost right up, and recognized Rogozhin's pale features.

"Something told me you were wandering somewhere hereabouts," Rogozhin muttered through his teeth. "Didn't take long to find you."

This was their first meeting since their encounter on the tavern stairs. Rogozhin's unexpected appearance fairly bowled the Prince over, and the agonizing feeling welled up in him yet again. Rogozhin clearly realized the effect he had produced; but though at first he gave the impression of being put out and talked haltingly at first, giving the impression of forced familiarity, the Prince soon concluded that in reality he was quite composed and at ease with himself; any inhibition that may have been detected in his gestures and manner of speaking was superficial to say the least. Deep down this man was incapable of change.

"How did you... find me here?" the Prince asked, merely for something to say.

"Keller told me (I dropped by at your place). He said to me, 'He went into the park.' Well, I thought to myself, that must be that."

"What do you mean 'that must be that'?" the Prince enquired in alarm, picking on the words which had slipped out inadvertently.

Rogozhin smirked, but offered no explanation.

"I got your letter, Lev Nikolayevich. You've got the wrong sow by the ears... what are you hoping to get out of it all?... And now I've got a message to you from *her*. She must see you badly. She's got something to say to you. It's got to be today."

"I'll go tomorrow. Now I'm going home. Are you... coming with me?"

"What for? I've told you everything. So long."

"So you're not going to drop in?" the Prince asked softly.

"You're a funny man, Lev Nikolayevich, I sometimes wonder."
Rogozhin smirked wryly.

"Why? Why do you detest me so?" the Prince returned with sadness
in his voice. "Surely you realize that all your former surmises were
wrong. To tell you the truth, I very much suspected that your hatred
of me isn't spent to this day, and do you know the reason? Because you
made an attempt on my life, that's why you still hate me. I'm saying to
you, I remember only one Parfyon Rogozhin, the brother I exchanged
crucifixes with that day. I wrote about this to you in my letter yesterday,
so that you'd put all this nonsense right out of your head and never
even mention it to me again. Why are you avoiding me? Why do you
keep hiding that hand? I'm telling you, all that occurred then was just
a bad dream as far as I'm concerned. I now know exactly what went
on in your mind that day as though it were in my own. The thing you
imagined never did nor could have happened. So why should we carry
on hating each other?"

"Who cares for your hatred!" Rogozhin retorted with a dismissive
laugh at the Prince's impassioned and ardent plea. He had in fact backed
off about a couple of paces and was keeping his hands out of sight.

"It wouldn't be right for me to come to your place now, Lev
Nikolayevich," he added slowly and gravely in conclusion.

"You really hate me that much, do you?"

"I don't like you, Lev Nikolayevich, so why should I go to see you?
Really, Prince, you're just like a small child who's after a toy, 'Give it
to me, give it to me!' and yet you've not the faintest idea of what the
toy is all about. What you said just now, you explained perfectly in
your letter, and do you suppose I don't believe you? I believe everything
you say, and I know that you never deceived me, nor ever would.
And all the same I don't like you. You say in your letter that you've
put everything behind you and you've only time for Rogozhin, your
brother, with whom you exchanged crucifixes rather than the Rogozhin
who threatened you with a knife. Anyway, how do you know what I
feel?" (Rogozhin smirked again.) "Perhaps I never regretted from the
very start what I'd done, and there you are sending me your fraternal
absolution. Perhaps that very evening my mind was already on other
things, and that business—"

"Had been put right out of your mind!" the Prince said on his behalf. "How else! I'd wager my last rouble that you immediately caught the train to Pavlovsk to stalk her here just like you stalked and snooped around today. I can see it all! If you hadn't then been in a state in which you could only think of one thing, you wouldn't have raised the knife against me. I had a premonition about you that very morning, looking at you. Have you any idea what you looked like? Perhaps it was precisely when we were exchanging crucifixes that the idea was born in me. Why did you take me to the old woman if not to stay your own hand? And I don't believe you thought it all through to the end, it was just a feeling you had, same as I... We were both thinking of the same thing at the time. If you hadn't raised your hand against me then (God stopped it), how would you feel about me now? I had my suspicions about you all along – we're in it together, you and I! (No need to pull faces! And stop laughing, will you?) You never felt sorry! Well, even if you'd wanted to, you wouldn't have been able to, because on top of everything, you don't like me. Even if I had been as innocent as an angel before you, you still wouldn't be able to stand me, at least while you thought she loved me rather than you. That then is true jealousy. This alone has occupied my thoughts this week, Parfyon. Listen carefully! Do you realize that right now she loves you perhaps more than anyone, to the extent that the more she plagues you, the more she loves you. She'll never say this in so many words, you have to see it for yourself. If one thought about it, why the deuce is she marrying you? One day she'll tell you all. Some women enjoy that kind of love, and she is just that kind of woman! What with your character and your love for her, you must have had a huge effect on her! Do you realize a woman is capable of torturing a man to death with her cruelty and gibes and not feeling the slightest pang of conscience, because all the while, she'd say to herself, 'Now I'll make his life as miserable as sin, but then I'll make up for it with my love...'"

Rogozhin burst out laughing.

"I say, Prince, you haven't fallen for someone like that yourself, have you? I heard one or two things about you, is it true?"

"What, what have you heard?" the Prince enquired with a shudder, and stopped in utter confusion.

Rogozhin carried on laughing. He had listened to the Prince with interest and perhaps pleasure; the Prince's buoyant and ardent enthusiasm had a surprisingly uplifting effect upon him.

"Not only have I heard, I can see for myself that it's all true," he added. "When have you said anything like that before? It all sounds as though it was someone else speaking. If I hadn't heard something about you, I wouldn't have come here, into the park of all places, at midnight."

"I can't understand you at all, Parfyon Semyonych."

"She took the trouble to tell me all about you some time ago, and then I had a chance to see for myself the way you sat up close to the other one during the music-making. She swore to me it was the truth, she swore yesterday and again today that you're head over heels in love with Aglaya Yepanchina. It's all the same to me, Prince, nor is it any of my business, but if you've fallen out of love with her, she hasn't with you. Surely you know she wants to marry you off to the other one, and has given her word on it, he-he! She said to me, 'It's either-or: if they go to the altar, so will we, otherwise forget it.' I've really no idea what's going on, and never had. She either loves you beyond all reason, or… if she loves you, how is it she wants you to marry someone else? She says to me, 'I want to see him happy,' which means she must love you."

"I told you and I wrote to you that she… is not quite all there," the Prince said, having heard out with a pained heart what Rogozhin had to say.

"Lord knows! Perhaps you're mistaken… by the way, she named the day for me today as soon as I brought her back home. She said, in three weeks, perhaps before, she said, I'll marry you. She took the icon down from the wall and kissed it. So, it all depends on you now, Prince, he-he!"

"This is complete nonsense! What you're saying about me will never, never come about! I will come and see you both tomorrow—"

"How can she be mad?" Rogozhin asked. "How is it she's in her right mind as far as everybody else is concerned, but you alone regard her as mad? If she was mad, that lot would have been able to tell it by her letters."

"What letters?" the Prince asked in alarm.

"She keeps writing to the other one, who is only too glad to read them. Didn't you know? Well, you will. I'm sure she'll show them to you herself."

"I don't believe any of this!" the Prince exclaimed.

"My, oh my! You, Lev Nikolayevich, are still pretty green in all this, you've still a lot of catching up to do, if you ask me. Wait until you've your own sleuths to keep a lookout day and night and know every step the opposition takes, unless—"

"Stop that, I never want to hear about it again!" the Prince exclaimed. "Listen, Parfyon, I was walking here before you turned up and all of a sudden burst out laughing; why – I've no idea. The only reason might have been that tomorrow, I remembered, happens to be my birthday. It's close on twelve now. Let's go and see the day in! I've some wine in the house. We'll drink and you can wish me things I haven't thought of myself, I want it to come from you of all people, and I'll wish you all the luck in the world too. Otherwise give me my crucifix back! Let's face it, you didn't send it back to me the day after! I bet you're wearing it still, aren't you?"

"I am," Rogozhin said.

"Let's go then. I don't want to enter upon my new life without you, because my new life has begun! You didn't suspect, Parfyon, did you, that today marks the beginning of a new life for me?"

"Now I can see for myself it has. I'll be sure to tell *her* just that. You're not at all your usual self, Lev Nikolayevich!"

4

As THE PRINCE, followed by Rogozhin, approached his dacha, he was fairly bowled over with astonishment when he saw a numerous and noisy crowd gathered on the brightly lit terrace. The convivial assembly was laughing and talking loudly; some were even arguing at the top of their voices; the impression was that everyone was having a good time. On mounting the steps of the terrace, the Prince noticed that everyone was drinking champagne no less, and it appeared they had been at it for some considerable time, to such an extent that quite a few of the merry-makers were already three sheets to the wind. The guests were all acquaintances of the Prince, but the surprising thing was that they had all assembled as though by invitation, whereas the Prince hadn't invited anyone. As regards his birthday, he himself had remembered it only quite by chance.

"You must have told someone there was champagne going and they all came running," Rogozhin muttered, following the Prince up the terrace steps. "I know this lot. You only have to whistle…" he added almost with anger, no doubt reflecting on his own recent exploits.

The Prince was met with exclamations and good wishes, and was surrounded on all sides. Some were boisterously noisy, others more subdued, but they were all falling over one another in an attempt to wish him many happy returns, and each awaited his turn. The presence of some people was rather intriguing, for instance that of Burdovsky; but the most astonishing thing of all was to see Yevgeny Pavlovich in their midst; the Prince could hardly believe his eyes, and was almost shocked to see him.

In the meantime Lebedev, already fairly well-oiled – flushed and in high spirits – ran up to him offering his explanations. From his chatter it transpired that everyone had arrived quite spontaneously, as though by chance. The first to arrive early in the evening was Ippolit and, feeling much better, he offered to wait for the Prince on the terrace. He had made himself comfortable on the settee; then he was joined by Lebedev, followed by the whole of his family, that is, his daughters, and General Ivolgin. Burdovsky had arrived together with Ippolit as his help and support. By all indications Ganya and Ptitsyn had called in quite recently as they were walking past (their arrival coincided with the incident at the Voksal); then came Keller. It was he who announced there was going to be a birthday party and he called for champagne. Yevgeny Pavlovich had dropped in just half an hour previously. Kolya was amongst those who clamoured for champagne to mark the occasion. Lebedev was only too happy to oblige.

"It's on me, the champagne's on me!" he prattled on for the Prince's benefit. "At my own expense to mark and celebrate your birthday, and the comestibles, the snacks will follow. My daughter's seeing to it right now. And if only you knew, Prince what topics are being discussed! Do you remember in *Hamlet*, 'To be or not to be?' How topical, how very topical! It's questions and answers… And Mr Terentyev is also in excellent form… not at all inclined to sleep! He's only had a mere sip of champagne, just a mouthful, it won't harm him… Come a little closer, Prince, and be our judge! Everybody's been waiting for you, to benefit from your superior wit…"

The Prince caught the mild, caressing gaze of Vera Lebedeva who was struggling to get to him through the crowd. He stretched out his hand to her ahead of all the other guests; she blushed with joy and wished him all happiness from this day on. Then she dashed off to the kitchen where she was preparing the snacks; but even before the Prince's arrival, whenever she could spare a moment from her work, she'd come out on to the terrace to listen eagerly to the inebriated guests' ongoing and heated debates on the most abstruse and unlikely subjects. Her younger sister, who for a while had been attending the proceedings open-mouthed, had curled up on a chest in the neighbouring room and was fast asleep, but her little brother had positioned himself next to Kolya and Ippolit and, judging by the intense concentration on his face, was ready to remain rooted to the spot for hours and hours to come.

"I looked forward to seeing you and I'm glad you're so happy," Ippolit said after the Prince had approached to shake his hand immediately following his exchange with Vera.

"What makes you think I'm happy?"

"I can see it in your face. After you've done the rounds, come and sit with us here. I was waiting for you especially," he added, laying particular stress on the fact of having waited. In response to the Prince's observation that it might be bad for him to be up so late, he replied that he wondered himself how was it that only three days ago he expected to die, whereas this evening he had never felt better in his life.

Burdovsky leapt to his feet and muttered that he'd just... all by pure chance, that he was with Ippolit really, looking after him, but that he too was glad; that what he'd said in his letter was all rubbish, but now he was delighted simply... Without finishing, he shook the Prince's hand firmly and slumped back in his chair.

Last of all the Prince approached Yevgeny Pavlovich, who immediately took him by the arm.

"Just a couple of words in your ear," he whispered, "something terribly important, let's go over there for a minute."

"Just a couple of words," another voice whispered in the Prince's other ear and another hand took him by the arm from the other side. The Prince was surprised to see a figure with a terribly tousled head of hair over a flushed, winking, grinning face by which he immediately recognized Ferdyshchenko, who had suddenly popped up from goodness only knows where.

"Do you remember Ferdyshchenko?" he asked.

"Where did you come from?" the Prince exclaimed.

"He wants to say he's sorry!" Keller explained, popping up beside him. "He's been hiding himself in that corner over there and wouldn't come out to join us. He's ever so sorry, Prince, he feels guilty."

"But what for, what on earth for?"

"I bumped into him, Prince, I bumped into him just now and brought him over. He's unlike any of my friends, but he feels sorry."

"I'm delighted, gentlemen! Go and sit down over there with the rest, and I'll join you in a moment," the Prince at last managed to fob them off as he hurried back to Yevgeny Pavlovich.

"Everyone's having a good time here," Yevgeny Pavlovich remarked. "I enjoyed the half hour I was waiting for you. Look here, my kind Lev Nikolayevich, I've settled everything with Kurmyshev and came to put your mind at rest. You've nothing to worry about; he was very, very sensible about the whole thing, the more so since to my mind the fault was largely his."

"What Kurmyshev?"

"The one whom you grabbed by the arms earlier… He was in such a rage, he was going to demand satisfaction from you in the morning."

"With respect, that's nonsense!"

"I couldn't agree more, and it would all have probably ended quite harmlessly, but there are people in Russia who—"

"Perhaps there was something else you came to tell me, Yevgeny Pavlovich?"

"Oh, yes of course, there was indeed something else," he returned with a laugh. "Tomorrow, my dear Prince, at first light I'm going to St Petersburg on this unfortunate business (well, I mean what happened to my uncle). Imagine, it's all true and everyone knows about it, except me. It all came as such a surprise that I didn't even have time to drop in (at the Yepanchins'), and I shan't have a chance to do so tomorrow either, because I'll be in St Petersburg, do you follow me? I may be away about three days, in a word – my affairs are in a bad way. Though the matter is not absolutely vital, nevertheless, I argued, I'd need to make a clean breast of something to you without losing any time, that is to say before my departure. If you don't mind, I'll sit and wait here till the people have dispersed; besides I'm in such a state, I couldn't possibly go to sleep now. Finally, however unseemly it may be to pester a man so, let me be perfectly honest with you – I came to seek your friendship, my dear Prince. You're quite an extraordinary man, that is, you don't tell lies at every step and turn, and perhaps never, and it so happens I badly need a friend and counsellor in a certain matter, because right now I really am in a spot of bad luck..."

He laughed again.

"The problem is," the Prince said after a pause, "you offered to wait till everyone has dispersed, but God only knows how long that will be. Wouldn't it be better if we went to the park now? They can wait. I'll explain to them later."

"Not on your life, I have my reasons for not wanting us to be suspected in engaging in a conspiratorial conversation. There are people here who are very interested in our goings-on – you're not aware of this, Prince, are you? It would be far better if they saw that we're on the best of terms and completely out in the open – if you know what I mean? They'll all be gone in a couple of hours, and I shan't take more than twenty minutes of your time, well – half an hour at the most—"

"Be my guest, I'd be delighted, no need to explain yourself. As for your kind words about us being on the best of terms, I thank you profoundly. But you must excuse my absent-mindedness today. I just can't seem to concentrate right now."

"I understand, I quite understand," Yevgeny Pavlovich muttered with a slight smile. One way or another he was given to smiling quite a lot that evening.

"What is it you understand?" the Prince asked in alarm.

"Didn't it occur to you, my dear Prince," Yevgeny Pavlovich went on, the smile still playing about his features, and without replying to the Prince's question directly, "didn't it occur to you, that I came simply to lead you up the garden path and pump you for something while I was about it, how about that?"

"That you turned up here to pry into something, there can be no doubt," the Prince also responded with a laugh at last, "and perhaps even to make me look a little foolish. Well, what of it, I'm not afraid of you. Besides, I care for just about nothing right now, believe me! And... and... and, above all, since I am convinced that you're nevertheless an upstanding person, we should in truth end up being friends. I like you a lot, Yevgeny Pavlovich. You... are a thoroughly decent man as I see it!"

"Well, at all events, it's a pleasure to have dealings with you, no matter what kind," Yevgeny Pavlovich concluded. "Come with me,

I'll drink your health. I'm terribly glad I managed to get hold of you. Ah!" he exclaimed abruptly. "Has Mr Ippolit moved in with you for good?"

"Yes."

"He's not going to die just yet, is he?"

"How do you mean?"

"Nothing really. I spent half an hour in his company..."

All this time Ippolit was waiting for the Prince and kept a close eye on him and Yevgeny Pavlovich while they conversed close by. He came feverishly to life when the two of them approached the table. He was worried and agitated; beads of sweat stood out on his brow. His gleaming eyes, apart from looking lost and permanently inconsolable, cast around in abstracted impatience, flitting from object to object and from face to face. Even though up to this point he made strenuous efforts to participate in the general conversation, his energy derived from his fever. On the whole he was quite inattentive to what was being said; his arguments were inconsequential, derisive and exasperatingly offhand; he was liable to break off in mid-flow on any topic, regardless of the fact that he may have brought it up with frantic enthusiasm in the first place. The Prince learnt with surprise and sorrow that he'd been allowed to drink two full glasses of champagne and that the one he held in his hand, and which he had already begun, was his third. But this the Prince discovered only later; at the given moment he was not particularly observant.

"Do you know, I'm terribly pleased it's your birthday, today of all days!" Ippolit shouted out.

"Why is that?"

"You'll soon see. Come, sit down quickly! First, well because of all these... people of yours, gathered here. I thought there would be people here. It's the first time in my life I happened to be right! Pity though I didn't know about your birthday, or I'd have brought a present... Ha ha! Maybe I have! How long is it to daybreak?"

"It's less than two hours to daybreak," Ptitsyn observed with a glance at his watch.

"Who needs daybreak if it's light enough to read a paper outdoors anyway?" someone remarked.

"Because I want to have just one tiny glimpse of the sun. Can one drink the sun's health, Prince, what do you say?"

Ippolit addressed the whole assembly in a sharp, superior tone of voice as though on a parade ground, but he seemed quite unaware of this.

"Yes, let's drink to it, if you promise to calm down. What do you say, Ippolit?"

"All you can think of is sleep. You, Prince, are my nanny! As soon as the sun looks out and... 'intones' in heaven... (Who was it who said in verse, 'The sun intones in heaven'?* Doesn't make sense, but it's altogether brilliant!) And all you know is sleep! Lebedev! Isn't the sun the font of life? What is the font of life in the Apocalypse? Have you heard of the star Wormwood, Prince?"

"I've heard, Lebedev sees the star Wormwood as the railway network that has spread throughout Europe."

"No, I beg your pardon, that won't do!" Lebedev shouted, jumping to his feet and waving his arms about as though wishing to put a stop to the general laughter which was about to burst out. "I beg your pardon! With these gentlemen... all these gentlemen," he suddenly turned to the Prince, "you know, in some respects, it is..." and without further ado, he rapped the table twice with his knuckles, which only caused the laughter to increase.

Though Lebedev carried on as was his wont every evening, on this occasion – precipitated by the preceding lengthy and "learned" debate – he was even more on edge and volatile, and consequently treated his interlocutors with an all too obvious disdain.

"That's not right, gentlemen! Half an hour ago, Prince, we came to an agreement not to interrupt one another, not to laugh while someone was speaking in order to give him freedom to express himself, after which let even the atheists make their objections if that's what they want. We've put General Ivolgin in the chair, so there! How else, I say? Otherwise anyone who was developing an elevated and profound idea could be tripped up—"

"Go ahead, for goodness' sake, go ahead and speak, no one's trying to trip you up!" several voices called out.

"Speak and let speak."

"What is the star Wormwood?" someone enquired.

"Haven't got a clue!" General Ivolgin replied, settling down with all seriousness to his recently appointed role of chairman.

"It's the deuce of a pleasure to hear all these things, all these arguments and dissensions, Prince, on learned topics, it goes without saying,"

Keller muttered *inter alia*, savouring the occasion as he shifted in his chair in eager anticipation, "learned and political," he added, turning unexpectedly to Yevgeny Pavlovich, who was sitting almost right next to him. "You know, I adore reading in the papers about the English Parliament, that is to say, not what they actually debate there (I'm no politician as you know), but how they address one another, what they get up to, their statesmanlike ways, so to speak: 'My Lord opposite', 'My honourable member of the opposition who has astounded the whole of Europe with his proposal' – that is, all these fiendish turns of phrase, all this cant of a free parliamentary democracy – all of this is so beguiling to the likes of us! I revel in it, Prince. I've always been an artist at heart, I swear to you, Yevgeny Pavlovich!"

"So what follows then," Ganya called out from where he sat in a far corner, "does it follow that railways are doomed, that they are a curse unto mankind, that they are a plague that has come down on earth in order to destroy the founts of life?"

Gavrila Ardalionovich was in a particularly excited mood that night, happy to boot, well-nigh triumphant as the Prince could not but fail to note. He was of course pulling Lebedev's leg, provoking him, but soon he got into the spirit himself.

"Not railways, no!" Lebedev protested, at once exasperated and savouring the moment to the limit. "In themselves railways are not going to pollute the fonts of life.* It's the combination of all these damned things that is accursed – all the damned trends of the past ages, with all their scientific and practical goals in their totality – that are perhaps well and truly accursed."

"Accursed for certain, or merely just – perhaps?" Yevgeny Pavlovich desired to know. "Surely this is important for our purposes."

"Accursed, accursed, accursed for certain!" Lebedev confirmed passionately.

"Steady on now, Lebedev," Ptitsyn remarked, smiling, "you are far less virulent of a morning."

"But more honest in the evenings! In the evenings I'm kindlier at heart and more sincere!" Lebedev declared with fervour, turning to face him. "I'm more open and sensible, more fair-minded and deferential, and though you may take advantage of this, I don't care. I challenge the lot of you, all you atheists: how are you going to save the world and lead the way to a better life – you, men of science, industry, trade associations, working wages and all the rest of it? How? By way of supplying credit? What is credit? Where will credit lead you?"

"If you ask me, you want to know too much!" Yevgeny Pavlovich remarked.

"My answer to that is, whoever ignores such questions is a stuck-up oaf!"

"Credit can at least bring about universal solidarity and a balance of interests," Ptitsyn observed.

"And that is all, all it can do! Its only moral basis is the satisfaction of personal egoism and material need. Universal freedom, universal happiness – out of necessity! Do I, if I may be so bold as to ask, understand you correctly, my kind sir?"

"But surely the universal need to live, eat and drink in the face of a firm scientific conviction that it will not be satisfied other than by universal solidarity and balance of interests is, to my mind, a sufficiently powerful argument to serve as a point of departure and a source of life for future generations," Ganya declared with passionate conviction.

"Need to eat and drink, in other words, merely instinct of self-preservation—"

"Well, isn't instinct of self-preservation by itself not enough? Surely instinct of self-preservation is a fundamental law of nature—"

"Who told you that?" Yevgeny Pavlovich suddenly called out. "Law – that's true enough, but fundamental only in as much as the law of destruction, or say, self-destruction is fundamental. Do you really imagine that the basic law of nature is founded on self-preservation alone?"

"There's a thought!" Ippolit exclaimed, turning abruptly to face Yevgeny Pavlovich and to study him with intense curiosity; but, seeing that Yevgeny Pavlovich had burst out laughing, he burst out laughing too, and poked Kolya, who was standing next to him, in the ribs, asking him again what the time was, even reaching for Kolya's silver watch to verify eagerly for himself. Then, as though oblivious to everything, he stretched himself out on the settee, put his hands under his head and fixed his eyes on the ceiling. Half a minute later though, he was already sitting erect at the table, listening closely to Lebedev's unstoppably voluble chatter.

"The idea is damnably intriguing, provocative and tricky," Lebedev responded readily to Yevgeny Pavlovich's paradox, "calculated to trigger a struggle between the opposing parties, but it is justified! Because, sceptic as you are in your capacity of a man of the world and a cavalry officer (albeit not without talent!), you may be unaware of the profundity, indeed the correctness, of your observation! Quite right, sir! The instinct of self-preservation and the urge to self-destruction are equally strong in man! The Devil has as equal a sway over humanity as God until a time still unknown to us. You laugh! You don't believe in the Devil? Refusal to believe in the Devil is a French idea, a frivolous one. Have you any idea who the Devil is? Do you know what his name is? And without even knowing his name, you laugh at his image like Voltaire did, at his hooves, his tail and his horns, which are of your own invention. For the Prince of Darkness is a mighty awesome spirit, devoid of horns and hooves which you yourselves have attributed to him. But he's beside the point for the present!..."

"How do you know he is nothing to the point now?" Ippolit exclaimed suddenly and burst out into a fit of nervous laughter.

"That's a smart and intriguing notion!" Lebedev commended. "But again that's beside the point, whereas what we're talking about is whether or not 'the founts of life' have weakened with the development—"

"Of the railways?" Kolya exclaimed.

"Not of railways, you young, unruly hothead, but of all that movement of which the railways may serve merely as an illustration, a creative manifestation as it were. They hurry, they clatter, they chug and speed along in pursuit of happiness, for the good of man, they say! 'Man's life is getting much too industrial and noisy, there's not enough spiritual harmony left,' one departing philosopher remarks. 'No matter, but the clatter of cartwheels bringing bread to the starving mankind is perhaps one degree better than spiritual harmony,' another philosopher, journeying extensively, replies triumphantly as he turns away from his fellow thinker with disdain. I, obnoxious Lebedev, do not believe in horse carts delivering bread to mankind! For carts that bring bread to the whole of mankind may, if they lack spiritual purpose, perfectly cold-bloodedly deprive a significant part of mankind of that very sustenance, which has already been known to—"

"You mean to say carts can cold-bloodedly deprive?" someone enquired.

"It has been known to happen," Lebedev confirmed, ignoring the question, "we've already had Malthus,* that friend of mankind. But a friend of mankind unsure of the moral ground he's standing on is as bad as a cannibal, not to mention his puffed-up pride. For you only have to puncture the pride of one of these countless friends of mankind, and he'll be ready to set fire to the world at all four corners out of petty revenge – to be sure, just like every one of us would, if the truth be known, me, the most abject of them all, included, for I may indeed be the very first to fetch some firewood and then take to my heels. But that again is not the point!"

"What is then?"

"What a bore!"

"The point is in the following story from times gone by, because I feel obliged to tell you a story from times gone by. In our times, in our country, which I hope you love as much as I do, ladies and gentlemen, because I for my part would even be ready to spill all my blood for my—"

"Get on with it! Get on with it!"

"Our country, as well as the rest of Europe, is visited by a total, widespread famine not more – as far as it can be calculated and my memory serves me – than once every quarter of a century, in other words, once every twenty-five years. I shall not insist on the exact figure, but this is relatively rarely."

"Relative to what?"

"Relative to the twelfth century, and the one which preceded and followed it. For in those days, as told and maintained by authors, total famines visited mankind once every two or at least three years, such that under that state of affairs, man resorted even to cannibalism, though in strict privacy. One particular felon, with the approach of old age, acknowledged of his own accord and without coercion of any kind, that in the course of his long and miserable existence, he had slain and eaten personally, and in conditions of complete secrecy, sixty monks and a number of – maybe six – infants, but no more, that is to say, unusually few in comparison with the number from the religious fraternity. As regards adult lay people, it transpired, he would abstain altogether, that is, in the eating of them."

"That is impossible!" the chairman, General Ivolgin, exclaimed, in a voice that was not quite like his own. "I often have occasion to dispute and argue with him, ladies and gentlemen, and it's all about suchlike matters. But for the most part he comes up with such drivel, enough to make you sick, not an ounce of truth in it."

"General! Remember the siege of Kars, and you, ladies and gentlemen, will see that my story is the gospel truth. Let me add for my part that practically every actual occurrence, even though it may be governed by immutable laws, is almost always unlikely and improbable. And the more actual, the more improbable at times."

"Surely, no one can eat sixty monks!" people protested, laughing out loud.

"He wouldn't have eaten them in one sitting, that stands to reason, but if you spread it over fifteen or twenty years, it becomes completely normal and natural—"

"Natural?"

"Yes, and natural!" Lebedev fought back stubbornly. "Apart from anything else, a Catholic monk is by nature gregarious and inquisitive, and can all too easily be enticed into a forest or some other isolated place and then dealt with accordingly. All the same I wouldn't deny that the number of persons consumed turned out to be extraordinary, even to the point of gluttony."

"Perhaps it may all be quite true, ladies and gentlemen," the Prince suddenly observed.

Till then he had listened to the arguments in silence and had not participated in the discussion; if others burst out laughing, he readily joined in with all his heart. It was clear, he was very happy that the general atmosphere was so cheerful and boisterous; he even liked to see people drink so much. Perhaps he had never intended to say a single word throughout the whole evening, but suddenly he was moved by an urge to speak. He began on a note of extraordinary seriousness, which made everyone suddenly turn to him with curiosity.

"All I wanted to say, ladies and gentlemen, that in those dark days terrible famines took place. I heard about that, even though history is not my strong point. But, I don't think it could possibly have been otherwise. When I found myself in Switzerland, I was terribly surprised by all the ruins of old feudal castles, built along mountainsides, on sheer cliffs, up to half a mile high (which meant several miles along steep paths to reach them). The castle is, as you know, a huge heap of stones. The work must have been mind-boggling, quite unimaginable.

And it was of course all performed by the poor, the vassals. Apart from everything else, they had to pay all kinds of tithes to maintain the clergy. How could they till their land and feed themselves under such circumstances? They were not numerous then, and in all probability lots of them died of hunger, for they probably had literally nothing to eat. I often wondered how was it that the people didn't perish altogether, or something terrible didn't happen to them, and that they managed to hold out and survive? I'm sure Lebedev is quite right there were cannibals about. Only I'm not sure, why he brought monks into it, and what exactly he had in mind."

"Probably because in the twelfth century only monks were edible for they alone had any fat on them," Gavrila Ardalionovich suggested.

"A well-founded and brilliant thought!" Lebedev responded. "The fellow never touched a single layperson. Not a single layperson for every sixty of the clergy, and that's an awesome fact, a historical fact, a statistical fact, and in the end it is on the basis of such facts that the intelligent man builds his history of the world, because he can prove with numerical exactitude that the clergy were at least sixty times better off and freer than the whole of the rest of the population in those days—"

"Not true, you exaggerate, Lebedev!" people remarked on all sides with laughter.

"I agree it's a historical fact, but what are you driving at?" the Prince continued his line of questioning. (He spoke with such earnestness and such absence of irony towards Lebedev, whom everyone was laughing at, that his tone cut right across the prevailing one and was itself beginning to sound comical and on the point of being laughed at, except that he remained unaware of it.)

"Can't you see, Prince, that this man is mad?" Yevgeny Pavlovich said, leaning across to him. "I was told recently that he has the crazy notion of becoming a lawyer and acting as a defence counsel at court. He's all set to take an exam. I'm expecting something quite amusing now."

"I'm leading up to a momentous deduction," Lebedev thundered forth in the meantime. "But let us first examine the psychological and legal state of the accused. We shall see that the accused or, so to speak, my client, in the course of his rather curious career, despite the whole impossibility of procuring any foodstuffs, had manifested a wish to repent and had shied away from people of the cloth. We only have to look at the facts. He did consume five, or was it six, infants – comparatively speaking an insignificant number, but rather telling in another respect. It is apparent that, tortured by terrible pangs of conscience (my client was a religious and conscientious man, which I shall prove) and, to reduce his sin had, by way of experiment, changed his diet six times from monastic to secular. That it was an experiment, is also apparent, inasmuch as had it been for purely gastronomic variation, the number six would have been far too paltry, for why only six times, and not thirty? (I take half and half.) But if it was only an experiment, prompted by fear of sacrilege and giving offence to the church, the number six becomes only too understandable, inasmuch as six attempts at salving one's conscience is more than sufficient, since the experiments could not after all have been successful. And, first of all, as I see it, an infant is much too small, that is diminutive, such that in the given time one would have needed three, nay five times the number of lay infants as compared to men of the cloth, so that the sin of it, even though it might have been diminished in one respect, would have been augmented in another, not qualitatively, but quantitatively. Arguing thus, ladies and gentlemen, I of course do so by stepping into the shoes of a felon of the twelfth century. As regards me personally, that is, a man of the nineteenth century, I would perhaps have argued differently, whereof I give you due notice, ladies and gentlemen, consequently you have no grounds for looking daggers at me; for you, General, it is especially unbecoming. Secondly, if you want to know my personal opinion, an infant is not nearly nourishing enough, perhaps even much too sweet and rich; so far from satisfying physical needs, it only brings on pangs of conscience. And now for the conclusion, my summing-up, ladies and gentlemen, which will contain the clue to one of the main problems of the past as well as the future! The accused ends up by making a clean breast of it to the clergy and surrendering himself to the authorities. Let us now imagine what agony awaited the accused according to the laws and customs of those times – what racks, what stakes, what fires? Who compelled him to denounce himself? Why not simply stop at the figure sixty and retain the dread secret till one's last breath? Why not give up the diet of monks and live in the desert as a repentant hermit? Why indeed did he not take the tonsure himself? Herein lies the answer! Evidently there was something stronger than stakes and fires and even the habit of twenty long years! Evidently there was a consideration which outweighed all the disasters, harvest failures, ordeals, pestilences, leprosy and all that hell which mankind would never have survived were it not for that force by which all hearts are bonded and guided and the founts of life rejuvenated! Show me something to approach such a force in our age of vice and railways... that is, I should have said in our age of steamships and railways, but I said, in our age of vice and railways, because I'm drunk, but fair! Show me a force that bonds present mankind even half as strongly as it did in those centuries. And, finally, I dare you to assert that the founts have not weakened and not been polluted under this 'star', under this network in which people have become enmeshed. And do not attempt to put me off with talk of your well-being, your wealth, the infrequency of famines and the speed of transport! Wealth has increased, but our strength has diminished. The bonding force has vanished. Everything has gone slack, all and sundry have become enfeebled!... But enough, and it's not what we need to concern ourselves with at the moment, but rather whether you shouldn't, my most excellent Prince, see about providing some food for your guests?"

Lebedev, who had brought some of his listeners to the brink of exasperation (it must be noted that the corks in the bottles continued to be popped all the while), managed with this unexpected closure of his speech to placate all his opponents. He himself called it "a deft lawyerly manoeuvre". General laughter resumed, the guests perked up; everyone rose from the table to stretch their legs on the terrace. Keller alone was not content with what Lebedev had to say, and was thoroughly disgruntled.

"All he did was to attack enlightenment, extol the injustices of the twelfth century, clown around, and hypocritically at that," he went around saying out loud to one and all. "Let me ask you if I may, by what means did he come by his own house?"

"I happened to know a real expounder of the Apocalypse," General Ivolgin held forth to another circle of listeners, more particularly to Ptitsyn, whom he had button-holed in a corner, "the late Grigory Semyonovich Burmistrov, who as it were was a past master at inflaming people's hearts. He'd begin by putting on his spectacles, then he'd open a huge ancient tome bound in black hide, well, and what with his grey beard and two medals for charitable works!... His opening words were always stern and strict. Generals kowtowed to him, ladies fainted at the sound of his voice, well – and all one can do is to finish by calling for snacks! I give up!"

Ptitsyn, as he listened, kept smiling and appeared from time to time to be reaching for his hat, but desisted after each attempt, or seemed to be distracted from his purpose. Ganya, while everyone was still sitting at the table, suddenly stopped drinking and pushed the glass away from him; some dark shadow seemed to glide across his features. After everyone had stood up, he approached Rogozhin and sat down next to him. One could have thought that they were the best of friends. Rogozhin, who at first had also made several half-hearted attempts to slink off, now sat motionless, his head on his chest. Throughout the evening he had had not a drop to drink, and was lost in thought; very occasionally he would raise his eyes and look intently at everyone in turn. He now gave the impression of deliberately waiting for something to happen and seemed determined not to leave before it did.

The Prince had no more than just two or three glasses, and was merely in a good mood. As he rose from the table, he met Yevgeny Pavlovich's gaze, and smiled cordially. Yevgeny Pavlovich nodded back and suddenly pointed at Ippolit, whom he happened to be looking at intently at that particular instant. Ippolit was asleep, stretched out on the settee.

"Tell me, what is this youngster doing here, Prince?" he enquired suddenly, but with such force, bordering on anger, that it caused the Prince to start. "I'd wager he's up to no good!"

"It strikes me," the Prince said, "perhaps I'm wrong, but you, Yevgeny Pavlovich, seem to be particularly interested in him tonight. Am I right?"

"You might have added that my personal circumstances being as they are, I'd have enough on my plate not to keep staring at that ugly mug all night!"

"There's nothing wrong with his face—"

"There, look, look there!" Yevgeny Pavlovich called out, catching the Prince by his arm, "there!..."

The Prince once again glanced at Yevgeny Pavlovich with astonishment.

5

Ippolit, who towards the end of Lebedev's discourse had suddenly fallen asleep, now awoke with a start as though someone had poked him in his ribs. He shuddered, raised his head and looked around, his face drained of blood. There was terror in his features as he appeared to gather his thoughts.

"What, is everybody going?" he asked the Prince in alarm, grabbing him by the arm. "Is that the end? The end of everything? Is the sun up? What time is it? For God's sake – the time! I've overslept. How long have I been asleep?" he added with a look of despair as though he had really overslept something on which his whole fate depended.

"You slept for seven or eight minutes," Yevgeny Pavlovich replied.

Ippolit glanced at him eagerly and thought for a few seconds.

"Ah... is that all! That means, I..."

And he exhaled a deep, satisfying breath of air as though shedding an extraordinarily heavy load. He finally realized that nothing was "all over", that it was not light yet, that the company had got up merely to have a bite to eat, and that the only thing that had come to an end was Lebedev's chatter. He smiled and two bright spots, the sure marks of consumption, appeared on his cheeks.

"So you've been counting the minutes while I slept, Yevgeny Pavlovich," he remarked sarcastically, "you've been keeping an eye on me the whole time tonight, I saw it... Ah! There's Rogozhin! I dreamt of him just now," he whispered to the Prince with a frown, motioning with his head at Rogozhin, sitting at the table. "Oh yes, where's the orator," he suddenly switched themes, "where's Lebedev? Has he finished talking then? What was he on about? Is it true, Prince, you once said that 'beauty' would save the world? Ladies and gentlemen," he called out loudly to everyone, "the Prince insists that beauty will save the world! But I'd say that he gets such fancy notions because he's now in love. Ladies and gentlemen, the Prince is in love. The minute he walked in, I was convinced of it. Don't blush, Prince, or I'll start feeling sorry for you. What beauty will save the world? I heard it all from Kolya... You're a diehard Christian, aren't you? Kolya says you call yourself a Christian."

The Prince studied him closely but did not say anything.

"You are not answering me! Perhaps you imagine I like you very much?" Ippolit added abruptly.

"No, I don't imagine anything. I know you don't like me."

"Really, even after what happened yesterday? Was I not perfectly frank with you yesterday?"

"I knew yesterday that you didn't like me."

"You mean because I'm jealous of you, jealous? You always thought that, you're thinking that now, but... why am I telling you all this? I want to have some more champagne. Pour me a glass, Keller."

"You mustn't drink any more, Ippolit, I'm not going to let you..."

And the Prince moved the glass away from him.

"Very well!..." he agreed at once and sank into a kind of reverie. "Otherwise people might talk... but who the hell cares what they might say! Isn't that right? Well, isn't it? Let them say whatever they want afterwards, wouldn't you agree, Prince? What business is it of ours what will happen *afterwards*!... To be sure, I'm still half asleep. What a horrible dream I had. It's only now coming back to me... I wouldn't wish such a dream on you, Prince, even though I probably really don't like you. If you don't like a person, that's no reason for wishing him bad though, is it, Prince? Why do I keep on asking questions? I keep asking on and on! Give me your hand! I want to shake it hard, that's better... You see, you gave it to me after all, didn't you? So you knew it was sincerely meant on my part?... Look here, I'm not going to drink any more. What's the time? No, don't bother, I know what the time is. The hour has come. Now's the best time. What, are they putting out food over there in the corner? That means this table is free? Jolly good! Ladies and gentlemen, I... however, none of these ladies and gentlemen want to listen... I propose to read an article, Prince. Eating is, of course, more fun, but..."

Suddenly, completely unexpectedly, he pulled out of his top inside pocket a large foolscap envelope bearing a red seal. He placed it in front of him on the table.

This unexpected move produced a great effect upon the whole company, which though it was expecting something, it was not this. Yevgeny Pavlovich fairly leapt into the air on his chair; Ganya quickly moved up closer to the table; Rogozhin likewise, but with some kind of a resentful mien as though he knew what it was all about; Lebedev, happening to be close by, sidled up too, his eyes full of curiosity fixed on the envelope, trying to work out what was inside.

"What have you there?" the Prince asked anxiously.

"With the first glimpse of the sun, I'll settle down, Prince, as I said, honestly. I gave my word, you'll see!" Ippolit insisted loudly. But… but… do you really think I'm not capable of breaking the seal of this envelope?" he added, surveying all the occupants to indicate he meant to address them all without distinction. The Prince noticed he was shaking all over.

"It never occurred to anyone to think that," the Prince replied on behalf of everyone, "anyway why do you imagine anyone should, and why… why do you feel this strange compulsion to read? What's the matter with you, Ippolit?"

"What's going on? What's wrong with him again?" people enquired on all sides. Some moved up, a few were still eating; the envelope with the red seal attracted them, like a magnet.

"I wrote it myself yesterday, immediately after I gave my word to move in with you, Prince. I spent the whole of yesterday writing, then the following night and finished this morning. Just before sunrise I had a dream—"

"Why don't you wait till tomorrow?" the Prince interrupted him gently.

"Tomorrow 'there should be time no longer'!"* Ippolit rejoined hysterically with an awkward grin. "But, don't worry, the reading will take forty minutes, well – an hour at the most… See, how interested everybody is! You're all here? Everyone's fascinated by the seal, and if I hadn't applied it to the envelope containing my article, the effect would have been lost! Ha ha! That's why it pays to keep one's cards close to one's chest! Shall I break the seal, ladies and gentlemen, or not?" he called out, laughing weirdly with a strange lustre in his eyes. "Mystery! Mystery! Incidentally, Prince, do you know who it was that said, 'there should be time no longer'? It was the great and mighty Angel of the Apocalypse."

"It'd be better if you didn't read!" Yevgeny Pavlovich suddenly pronounced, but with such unexpected expression of alarm on his face that it took some fairly by surprise.

"Do not read!" the Prince too exclaimed, laying the flat of his hand on the envelope.

"This is no time to read! Food is served," someone rejoined.

"An article? Is it meant for a journal, or what?" enquired another.

"Perhaps it's going to be a bore?" someone else asked.

"Look here, what's going on?" the rest of the people wanted to know. But an irresolute gesture of anxiety, which the Prince could not help making, made even Ippolit stop and think.

"So... you'd rather I didn't read?" he whispered hesitantly, his livid lips twisted out of shape in a vain effort to smile. "You don't want me to?" he muttered, his gaze roaming over the assemblage, taking time to look closely at every face, into every pair of eyes, as though seeking approval of his former, aggressive bonhomie. "You're... frightened, aren't you?" he turned to the Prince again.

"Why should I be?" he responded, looking ever more concerned.

"Has anyone got a twenty copeck piece?" Ippolit called out, suddenly leaping to his feet as though catapulted from his chair. "Any coin?"

"Here!" Lebedev was immediately ready to oblige. The thought flashed through his mind that the ailing Ippolit had gone mad.

"Vera Lukyanovna!" Ippolit addressed her hurriedly. "Take and toss it on the table – heads or tails? If it's heads, I'll read!"

Vera glanced in terror at the coin, at Ippolit, then at her father, and with an ungainly movement, her head thrown back as though convinced that she herself must keep her eyes off the coin, tossed it on to the table. It came up heads.

"I must read!" Ippolit muttered as though crushed by what fate had decreed for him; he could not have been paler if the death sentence itself had been pronounced on him. "Funny this," he said with a shudder after a half a minute's pause or so, "what's happening? Have I really been casting lots?" He surveyed everyone again with the same relentless frankness as before; then, addressing the Prince, he suddenly exclaimed in genuine surprise, "But this is an astonishing psychological phenomenon! It is... it is an unfathomable phenomenon, I assure you, Prince!" he confirmed, his spirits rising and seeming to pull himself together. "You must write this down and remember it well, Prince. You are, aren't you, looking for material on the death penalty?... That's what I've been told anyway, ha ha! Oh my God, how absurd all this is!" He sat down on the settee, propped both his elbows on the table and buried his head in his hands. "This is in fact embarrassing!... But what the Devil if it is?" he cursed and raised his head almost immediately. "Ladies and gentlemen, your attention please, I'm opening the envelope!" he announced with unexpected resolve. "Naturally, you're not obliged to listen!..."

He opened the envelope with shaking hands, took out a few sheets of notepaper covered in dense writing, placed them in front of him, and began to smooth them out.

"What's all this? What's going on? What is he going to read?" a hubbub of irritated voices resounded. Other guests kept their silence, but everyone sat down and looked on with curiosity. Perhaps they really expected something out of the ordinary. Vera held on tightly to her father's chair and was near tears with fright; Kolya appeared to be equally frightened. Lebedev, who was already seated, suddenly rose, grabbed a branched candelabra and brought it near Ippolit, to provide him with more light.

"Ladies and gentlemen, you'll... you'll soon see what this is all about," Ippolit remarked inconsequentially and suddenly started to read: 'A Necessary Explanation!' The epigraph: '*Après moi le déluge*'... Ugh! Hell!" he exclaimed as though he'd scalded himself. "Did I really choose such a stupid epigraph?... Listen, ladies and gentlemen!... I assure you all this may really in the end perhaps turn out to be utter nonsense! Only a few thoughts here belong to me... If you think there's... something mysterious here or... proscribed... in a word—"

"I wish you'd read without any preambles," Ganya interrupted.

"He's dodging!" someone remarked.

"Too much talk," Rogozhin, who had kept his silence till then, now added.

Ippolit suddenly glanced at him, and when their eyes met, Rogozhin grinned a bitter, bilious grin and slowly came out with some strange words, "That's not the way to go about your business, young fellow, no..."

What it was Rogozhin wanted to say, no one understood, but his words produced a rather strange effect on everybody who felt the wing tip of a shared idea float through the air. As for Ippolit, the reaction was overwhelming. He began to shake so violently that the Prince put out his hand to steady him, and he would surely have yelled out if his voice had not given up suddenly. He struggled for a whole minute to utter a word and continued to fight for breath, not taking his eyes off Rogozhin for a second. Finally, choking, and with extraordinary effort, he brought out:

"So, it was you... it was... you!"

"What was I? What?" Rogozhin responded, baffled, but Ippolit flared up and in a state of frenzy, shouted at the top of his voice:

"*You* came to me last week in the night, gone one o'clock, the same day I went to see you in the morning, it was *you*!! Own up, it was you, wasn't it?"

"Last week in the night? Are you out of your mind, lad?"

The "lad" paused again for about a minute with his forefinger pressed against his head as though in thought; but something mischievous, nay triumphant, suddenly began to play about his pallid, fear-ridden features, distorted by a feeble smile.

"It was you!" he finally repeated almost in a whisper but with extraordinary conviction. "You came to see me and sat in silence on a chair by the window for a whole hour; longer, between twelve and two o'clock in the night. After two, you got up and left... It was you, you! Why you came to frighten me, why you came to torture me, I cannot understand, but it was you!"

And although he still continued to shake with fear, there was now a glint of irrepressible hatred in his eyes.

"You'll soon find out everything, ladies and gentlemen. I... I... listen..."

In dreadful haste he again reached for his pieces of paper, which needed some more sorting out and rearranging; they shook in his unsteady fingers, and it took a while before he was done with it.

"He's either gone mad, or it's his fever!" Rogozhin muttered, barely audibly.

Finally the reading was under way. At the very beginning, the first five minutes or so, the author of the unexpected article kept running out of breath and his delivery was discordant and uneven; but gradually his voice grew firmer and began to match the content of the text. Every now and again he was interrupted by bouts of coughing, and halfway through his voice grew hoarse. But his gusto increased as the reading progressed, and towards the end was at its peak, as was the impression his illness made amongst the listeners. Here is the whole of his piece.

My Necessary Explanation
Après moi le déluge

"Yesterday morning the Prince came to see me; incidentally, he persuaded me to move to his dacha. I definitely knew he'd insist on it, and was convinced he'd blurt out something to the effect that it's easier to die surrounded by people and by trees. Today he did not use the word *die*, but said 'it would be easier to live', which, in truth, amounts to one and the same thing for me in my condition anyway. I asked him what he meant by 'trees', which he kept on mentioning and why was he foisting them on me – and to my surprise, learnt from him that apparently I myself had said the other evening that I had come to Pavlovsk to have a last look at the trees. When I pointed out to him that it made no difference whether one died in the shade of trees or staring through the window at a pile of bricks, and that it was hardly worth going to all that trouble merely for the sake of two weeks, he immediately agreed. But greenery and pure air would in his opinion definitely produce some kind of a physical change in me, and my inner strife and *my dreams* would change and perhaps trouble me less. I once more pointed out that he spoke like a materialist. He replied with a smile that he always was a materialist. As he never lies, these words were rather significant. His smile is pleasant. I took the trouble of taking a good look at him. I still don't know if I like him or not, but now that there's so little time left, I can't be bothered with this. My five-month-long hatred of him had, in the last month, been steadily abating. Who knows, maybe I came to Pavlovsk in the main to see him. But... why did I then leave my room? Whoever has been condemned to death, must not stir from his cranny. And if I hadn't now taken my final decision but, on the contrary, had decided simply to await my final hour, then of course I wouldn't have left my room and surely under no circumstances would have accepted his offer to move in with him to die in Pavlovsk.

"I must hurry up and, come what may, finish this declaration by tomorrow. Clearly I shan't have the time to reread it and make corrections; I'll look over it again tomorrow before I read it to the Prince and two or three listeners, whom I hope to find there. Because there won't be a single mendacious word here, only the bare truth – final and uncompromising – it'd be fascinating to know myself what effect it will have on me in the moment when I actually come to read it. To be sure, I ought not to have written 'the bare truth, final and uncompromising'. It's not worth the trouble of lying for the sake of just a fortnight; come to that, it's not worth living a fortnight – this alone would be the best guarantee that I shall write only the honest truth. (NB: Not to forget to check how sane I am at that moment, that is – from moment to moment. I've been reliably informed that consumptives in their terminal stages sometimes go insane, from time to time. To verify this tomorrow by listeners' reaction during the reading. This matter to be resolved in full, else there's no way forward.)

"It strikes me I've written an awful lot of rubbish; but, as I said, I've no time to revise any of it; besides, I've promised myself deliberately not to amend a single line in this manuscript, even if I notice that I'm contradicting myself every other line. I particularly want to establish at tomorrow's reading whether my train of thought was logically sound; whether I spot any flaws, and, in the final analysis, how well that which I've been turning over in my mind in this room of mine these past six months will stand up to scrutiny, or if it was just the ravings of a disturbed brain.

"If only two months ago I'd been obliged, as now, to leave my room for good and say goodbye to Meyer's brick wall, I would have been sad. Now, however, I don't feel a thing, and yet tomorrow I shall part from the room and the wall – *for ever*! Hence, the belief that it's not worth feeling sorry for myself, or falling prey to any kind of sentiments, for the sake of a fortnight, has taken full control of my faculties and is now capable of regulating all my feelings. But is it really so? Is it true that I have now completely mastered my nature? If I were subjected to torture now, I would probably yell out and would hardly say that it's not worth yelling and feeling pain merely because I've only a fortnight left to live.

"But is it true that I've only a fortnight left to live, and not more? I told a lie in Pavlovsk; B***n didn't say anything to me and he never saw me, but about a week ago they brought Kislorodov to me. He is a materialist, atheist and nihilist, that's really why I asked him to come. I wanted a man who'd tell me the truth at last without embellishing it and being mealy-mouthed about it. And that's what he did, and not just readily and without being mealy-mouthed, but even with undisguised pleasure (I took it to be unwarranted). He blurted straight out that I had only a month left; perhaps a little more if the conditions were good; but, it could be I'd die much sooner. According to him I could die unexpectedly, perhaps even the next day. Such cases were not unknown, and not more than three days ago a young lady, suffering from consumption and in a condition similar to my own, in Kolomna, was just about to go to the marketplace to buy some groceries, but had suddenly felt ill, lain down on a settee and died. Kislorodov told me all this with a certain cavalier callousness and frivolity as though he was doing me the honour of taking me for as rabid a denier of all higher powers as he was himself, and who could die, as it were, at the drop of a hat. Be that as it may, the fact remained – a month, and not more! That he was not wrong – of that I'm fully convinced.

"I was surprised no end how it was the Prince knew that I was having bad dreams. He literally said that in Pavlovsk 'my inner strife and my dreams' would affect me less. Why dreams? He is either a physician, or really a man possessed of exceptional intelligence who can foresee a great deal. (But that he is, when all's said and done, an idiot, of that there can be no doubt whatever.) As it happens, just before he arrived, I had a pretty little dream (incidentally, such as I now have by the hundred). I fell asleep – I think an hour before he arrived – and I dreamt I was in a room (not mine). The room was larger and the ceiling higher than mine, better furnished, bright; a cupboard, a chest of drawers, a sofa and my bed, large and wide, with a quilted green silk counterpane. But in this room I noticed a terrible creature, some kind of a monster. It was like a scorpion, but not quite, more repugnant and terrifying, and this was perhaps by virtue of the fact that there were no such creatures in nature, and that it had turned up purposely in my room and was all bound up with some kind of a mystery. I managed to have a good look at it. It was a brown reptile about a foot long with a scaly shell, its head was about two fingers wide, and it was tapering towards its tail, so that its tip was no more than a fraction of an inch thick. About two fingers' width from the head, at an angle of forty-five degrees, two paws protruded one either side from the body, each about half a foot in length, such that the animal, if seen from above, would have the shape of a trident. I did not have a chance to see the head, all I saw were two whiskers, not long, like two stiff needles, also brown. There were similar whiskers on the tip of the tail and at the end of each paw – all in all, eight whiskers. The creature, supported on its paws and tail, was scurrying about the room very fast, and as it ran, it wriggled about with enormous speed despite its scales, like a snake, which was horrible to behold. I was terrified that it would sting me; I was told it was poisonous, but what worried me most of all was who might have let it into my room, what was the idea and the mystery behind it. It ran under the cupboard, under the chest of drawers, crept into corners. I got on to a chair and tucked my feet under me. It darted across the room and disappeared somewhere near my chair. I kept looking around in terror, but as I sat with my feet under me, I was hoping it wouldn't get up on my chair. Suddenly I heard behind me, close to my head, some kind of swish and rustle; I swung around and saw that the creature was clambering up a wall and was now almost level with my head and was even touching my hair with its tail, which was coiling and twisting with enormous rapidity. I leapt to my feet, and the animal vanished. I was afraid to go back to bed, in case it crept under my pillow. My mother and an acquaintance of hers then came into the room. They began to look for the creature, and were quite calm about it, not even afraid. But they knew nothing about it. Suddenly it reappeared; this time it slithered very slowly as though with some intent, which made it even more repugnant, again diagonally across the room, towards the doorway. At this point my mother opened the door and called Norma, our dog – a huge shaggy Newfoundland; she's been dead these five years. The bitch rushed into the room and stopped dead over the creature, which too stopped running, but continued to thrash about on the floor with the extremities of its paws and tail. If I'm not mistaken, animals are incapable of experiencing mystical fear; but at that moment it seemed that there was something very unusual in Norma's fear, something almost supernatural, and that she sensed, like I did, that there was something inscrutable and fated about the creature. She began to retreat slowly from it, as it advanced on her slowly and menacingly; it suddenly appeared to be ready to pounce and sting. But despite her fear, Norma stared back angrily, though she shook in every limb. Suddenly she slowly bared her awesome teeth, opened her huge red mouth, set to, ducked, took heart and suddenly grabbed the creature in her jaws. It began to flail around, desperately trying to free itself, so that Norma had to catch it once more, this time in mid-air, then secure her hold by releasing it briefly and bouncing it further between her jaws as though to swallow it. The scales cracked between her teeth; the creature's tail and paws, protruding from between her jaws, beat about furiously. Suddenly Norma yelped piteously – somehow the creature succeeded in stinging her in the tongue. Whining and howling with pain, she opened her jaws, and I saw that the crushed monster still continued to move in her mouth, releasing from its mangled body on to the dog's tongue a quantity of whitish fluid that looked like the innards of a black squashed cockroach... Here I woke up and the Prince came in."

"Ladies and gentlemen," Ippolit said, suddenly interrupting his reading and even looking quite sheepish, "I've never reread it, but it seems to me I've written a great deal of unnecessary stuff. This dream—"

"Go on—" Ganya could not help butting in.

"This dream contains much that is personal, I agree, that is, it revolves around me…"

Ippolit wore a fatigued and disturbed expression; he frequently dabbed the sweat on his forehead with his handkerchief.

"Truly, too much navel gazing," Lebedev murmured disapprovingly.

"Ladies and gentlemen, I hasten to add, I'm not compelling anyone. Those who don't wish to listen, may leave."

"It's not even his own house… for him to decide," Rogozhin muttered, barely audibly.

"Well, and what if we were all to stand up and walk out in single file?" Ferdyshchenko, who up till then had not dared to open his mouth, suddenly spoke up.

Ippolit suddenly lowered his eyes and grabbed his manuscript; but almost immediately raised his head again and, his eyes glinting, and with the two red spots glowing on his cheeks, said, looking Ferdyshchenko squarely in the eyes:

"You don't like me at all, do you?"

There was a burst of laughter; true, the majority did not laugh. Ippolit flushed terribly.

"Ippolit," the Prince said, "why don't you shut your manuscript and give it to me, then you can go to sleep here in my room. The two of us will have a little chat before you fall asleep, and we can continue our conversation in the morning, but on one condition only: that you should never open these pages again. Would you like that?"

"Is that really possible?" Ippolit said, looking at him resolutely. "Ladies and gentlemen!" he shouted out again with feverish buoyancy. "That was a silly interlude on my part. I shan't interrupt my reading again. Whoever wants to listen, is welcome…"

He took a quick gulp of water, hastily rested his elbows on the table, and with obstinate determination resumed his reading. His embarrassment, it must be said, was soon gone…

"The idea," he went on, "that it's not worth living an extra couple of weeks, began to haunt me seriously, I think, about a month previously when I still had four weeks to live, but it came to dominate me completely only three days ago, as I was returning from Pavlosk after that soirée. The initial instance of complete and direct surrender to the idea took place on the Prince's terrace, precisely at the same moment that I decided to make my final attempt at living, of wanting to see people and trees (very well, have it your way, I did say it), of getting worked up, insisting on Burdovsky's rights – my fellow creature's – and I was dreaming that they'd all suddenly open up their arms to me and would beg my pardon for something, and I'd beg for theirs; in a word, I ended up a prize fool. And it was precisely in those solitary hours that my 'final conviction' was born in me. I am astonished how it was I was able to survive six months without this 'conviction'! I knew without a shadow of a doubt that I have consumption, incurable consumption; I did not delude myself and knew very well what was in store for me. But the more the truth sank into me, the greater the desperation with which I wanted to cling to life; I clung to life and wanted to live, come what may. Of course, I could very well have been angry at my blind, random lot which had determined that I should be swatted like a fly, without knowing why. But why did I not stop at being merely angry? Why did I really want to live again, have another bite at the cherry, knowing full well that it was ruled out in my case? I reached for it, knowing full well I could never reach it. In my state I couldn't even finish reading a book, and I gave up reading. Why read, why find out anything for six months? And I'd invariably cast the book aside.

"Yes indeed, Meyer's brick wall really could tell a story! The things I wrote on it in my mind's eye! I knew it like the back of my hand. Damn you, wall! And yet it's dearer to me than all the trees in Pavlovsk – at least should have been dearer, if it weren't that everything now is all the same to me.

"I recall now what avid interest I then began to take in other people's lives; previously I had no such interest. I would sometimes fret impatiently, waiting for Kolya to arrive, when I myself was too ill to leave the room. Nothing was too trivial for me to enquire into, to the extent that in the end I turned into a kind of gossip-monger. It was beyond me, for instance, to understand how it was that these people, who had such long lives at their disposal, failed to become fabulously wealthy (incidentally, I still can't understand it). For instance, I knew a pauper, of whom it was later said that he died of hunger and, I recall, this annoyed me intensely. If the man could have been brought to life, I think I'd have executed him. At times I felt better for weeks on end and I could go out on the street; but there came a time when I began to detest the street so much that I would deliberately shut myself up indoors for days. I could not abide these scurrying, shuffling, constantly disgruntled, cheerless, troubled multitudes which hurried past me on the pavements. What was the point of their perpetual misery, their perpetual anxiety and commotion, their perpetual dismal anger (because they were angry, they were, they most certainly were). Whose fault was it they were unhappy and had no idea how to live, though they had up to sixty years of life to look forward to? And each and every one pointed to his ragged clothes, his calloused hands, and fumed with anger, crying, 'We work like slaves, we toil, we're hungry like dogs and we're poor! Others do nothing and they are rich!' (That was their constant refrain all right!). And close by there'd be some poor devil, an erstwhile aristocrat, who'd be up and about at all hours, with never a minute's rest, I mean our Ivan Fomich Surikov – lives just above us, in our house – always down at heel, buttons missing, running errands for various people, a general dogsbody. If you had stopped to talk to him, he would have said, 'I'm poor, needy and destitute, my wife has died, there's no money to buy medicine, and with winter upon us, my little'n has perished of cold. My eldest daughter is a kept woman...' Always whining, always whingeing! Oh, I never had and never will have a single ounce of pity for those fools – and I mean it! Why is he not a Rothschild? Whose fault is it that he is not a millionaire like Rothschild, that he has no mountains of gold like Rothschild? If he's alive, everything is in his power! Whose fault is it he can't get hold of it?

"Well, now it's all the same to me, the time has passed for me to feel angry, but previously, previously, I tell you, I gnawed at my pillow of a night, I tore my blanket with rage. Oh, how I prayed at the time, how I wished, how I yearned that I, an eighteen-year-old, barely clothed, barely clad, should be driven out on to the street and left completely alone, without a place to live, without employment, without a crust of bread, without loved ones, without a single person to turn to in a huge city, hungry, downtrodden (so much the better!), but healthy, and that's when I'd have shown...

"Shown what?

411

"Oh, do you really imagine I don't realize how I've discredited myself with this 'Explanation' of mine! Everyone will look upon me as a silly youngster who knows nothing of life, and will forget that I'm not even eighteen, and that six months for me are easily the equal of many long years into ripe, grey-haired old age! But let people laugh and say that it's all childish fairytales. I resorted to telling myself fairytales too. I filled my long nights with fairytales; I remember every one of them.

"Am I to recount them now, now that my time for fairytales is up? And to whom? They kept me amused when it was obvious that I was even prohibited from studying Greek grammar, and it was then that I realized I'd be six feet under by the time I reached the syntax. I thought about it and threw the book under my table. It's still there. I told Matryona not to touch it.

"Let him who comes across my 'Confession', and can muster sufficient patience to read it, take me for a madman, or even a schoolboy, but better still, for one condemned to death, who naturally has begun to imagine that all people, himself excepted, place insufficient value on life, have got into the habit of wasting it too profligately, are too slipshod and inconsiderate in their attitude to it, and as a consequence are one and all undeserving of it! And then what? I will point out that the reader is wrong and that my conclusion is quite independent of my death sentence. Do but ask people what they understand by happiness. Oh, it can be taken for granted that Columbus was at his happiest not when he discovered America, but just before; you can be assured that his happiness was at its peak perhaps three days before he came across the New World, when in desperation his mutinous crew nearly turned the ship round back to Europe! The New World was neither here nor there, it could go hang! Columbus died having hardly glimpsed it and, in effect, unaware of what he had discovered. What counts is life, and life alone, the perpetual and eternal discovery of it, the arriving, not the arrival! But enough of verbiage! I suspect that everything I've put down so far is so obvious that I'd be taken for a lower-form schoolboy who'd been set an essay to write, say, 'on sunrise'. Alternatively, people may remark that yes, he strove to say something, but with the best will in the world couldn't... bring it off. But I will add, however, that in any idea worth its salt, or if it bears the stamp of novelty, or even if it's just the considered end product of a contemplative mind, there'll always be something about it that will never be communicable to other people, were you to write volumes or spend thirty-five years explaining it; something will always refuse to leave your brain and will stay put there for ever more. You may easily die and take the most important part of your idea with you to your grave without ever having passed it on to anyone else. But if I too had been unable to pass on all that preoccupied me these past six months, people will at least see that, having reached my present 'final conviction', I have perhaps paid an inordinately high price for the privilege. It is this which, for certain reasons of my own, I consider I need to expound in my 'Explanation'.

"But, to continue."

6

" I DON'T WANT TO TELL A LIE. Reality constantly set subtle traps for me these past six months to the extent that I often forgot about the sentence hanging over me or, more accurately, refused to think about it and even found things to distract me. Incidentally, a word about my circumstances. When about eight months ago I became very ill, I broke off all my relationships and abandoned all my friends. As I was always fairly morose by nature, my friends easily forgot me; of course, I dare say they would have forgotten me anyway. At home too, that is in the family, I led a solitary life. About five months ago I locked my room from inside and shut myself off once and for all from the rest of my family. Everyone acquiesced in this, and no one dared enter my room except at certain times to tidy up and bring me my food. My mother cowered before me and did not so much as utter a plaintive sound on the rare occasions when I used to let her come in. She constantly used to chastise the children to stop them making a noise and disturbing me; I often complained of their shouting. I can imagine just how popular I am with them now! 'Faithful Kolya', as I used to call him, also had a lot to put up with me, I think. Towards the end, he too enjoyed needling me. All this was as it should be; people are born to make one another suffer. But I noted that he endured my irritability in such a way as though he had promised himself in advance to spare the patient. Naturally, I found this irritating; but I think he fancied he'd copy the Prince's 'Christian humility', which was of course faintly ridiculous. The boy is young and eager and, naturally, is given to emulating his elders; but it seems to me it's high time he started being his own man. I like him a lot. I tormented Surikov too, the one who lived a floor above us and was constantly running errands for various people, from dawn till dusk; I kept telling him it was his own fault he was so poor. In the end he took fright and stopped coming to see me. He is a very humble man, exceptionally humble! (NB: They say humility is an awesome power; I must ask the Prince about this, it's what he himself said.) But when in March I went up to have a look how it was they'd managed, as he put it, 'to freeze' their child to death, and inadvertently smiled at the sight of the infant's corpse, because I'd again started demonstrating to Surikov that he alone was to blame, the misery guts' lips began to tremble suddenly. He put one hand on my shoulder and, pointing to the door with the other, said softly, that is, in a barely audible whisper, 'Out please!' I left, highly delighted; I felt this delight even as he was ushering me out, but for a long time afterwards, every time I recalled his words, they evoked in me a peculiarly nasty kind of sympathy for him, which I resented. Even at the instant of giving the offence (I know I offended him, even though it was not my intention), even at such a moment this man could not bring himself to be angry! It was not at all due to anger that his lips began to tremble, I swear to it; he grabbed me by the arm and pronounced his splendid, 'Out please!' without the least trace of anger. There was a lot of dignity, too much, even a touch unbecoming for him (such that, truth be told, it verged on the comical), but there was no anger. Maybe he just suddenly began to despise me. From that time on, the couple of times I met him on the stairs, he would all of a sudden raise his hat, something he had never done previously, but he wouldn't stop as he had always used to, but ran past in embarrassment. Even if he did despise me, he did so according to his own lights. He despised me *humbly*. There again he may have raised his hat to me simply out of fear as to his creditor's son, because he forever owed my mother money and could never get out of debt. And this is probably the most likely explanation. I had a mind to come clean with him, and I know for certain that within a matter of minutes he'd have begged my pardon; but I thought better of it.

"Just at that time, that is, roughly when Surikov had 'let' his child freeze to death, round about the middle of March, I began for some reason to feel considerably better, and this went on for two weeks. I started going out for walks, mostly towards dusk. I loved the March evenings, when the frost set in and the streetlights were being lit; I sometimes ventured out quite far. Once, walking in the Shestilavochnaya Street, I was overtaken in the dark by an unmistakably gentlemanly figure. I couldn't make out anything more about him. He was carrying something wrapped up in brown paper, wearing a shortish, ungainly looking coat, much too light for the time of year. When he came level with a lamp-post about ten paces ahead of me, I noticed something fall out of his pocket. I hurried to pick it up – and not before time, because a man in a long caftan was about to do the same, but on seeing the object already in my hands, did not stop to argue, took a quick glance at it and walked on. This object was a large, rather old-fashioned leather wallet, stuffed full of something; but for some reason I knew from the first glance that whatever it was, it wasn't money. The man who had dropped it was already about forty paces ahead of me and would soon have been lost amongst the pedestrians. I ran after him and called out, but as all that occurred to me was 'Hey!' – he didn't even turn around. Suddenly he turned left and disappeared in the gateway of a large house. When I reached and entered it myself, where it was very dark, there was no one there. It was a huge building, one of those monstrosities that smart operators build to split into small apartments, up to a hundred in some instances. After I had run through the gates, I had the impression that in the far corner of the vast courtyard to the right, a figure was moving, though I could hardly distinguish it in the dark. When I reached the spot, I saw a stairway before me; it was narrow, full of rubbish and there were no lights; but there was someone ascending the steps hurriedly up above, and I dashed in pursuit, reckoning that before someone managed to open a door for him, I'd have caught up with him. I was right. The flights were very short, but their number endless, so that I became dreadfully short of breath; a door was opened and shut on the fourth floor; I guessed this while I was still on the first one. While I was running up, stopping to catch my breath on the landing and looking for the doorbell, a good few minutes must have gone by. An old hag opened the door for me. She had just left a tiny kitchen where she'd been trying to light a samovar. She listened to me without saying a word, clearly understanding none of my questions, and still without a word spoken, opened the door to the next room which was also small, terribly low, with some basic bits of furniture and an enormously wide bed under a canopy. Stretched out on the bed lay 'Terentych' (or so the old hag addressed him), whom I surmised to be drunk. On the table an overnight candle, now a mere stump, was sputtering its last in an iron holder and next to it was a bottle of spirits, drained almost to the end. Terentych muttered something under his breath and pointed to another door, whereupon the woman left, so that I had no alternative but to open that door. This I did, and went through.

"The adjoining room was if anything even narrower and more cramped, such that on entering I was hardly able to turn. A narrow single bed in a corner occupied an awful lot of space; the rest of the furniture was made up of just three ordinary chairs, heaped with all kinds of odds and ends of clothing, and the most ordinary kitchen table, standing up against an old, oilcloth-covered settee with hardly enough room to squeeze past between the two. On the table burned an iron nightlight similar to the one in the other room, while on the bed a tiny infant was screaming, not more than three weeks old, judging by the pitch. A pale, sickly-looking woman in a loose negligee, still young it would seem, and apparently just able to be up and about, was changing the baby's napkins, but the tiny tot refused to calm down and reached for its mother's empty breasts. A second child lay asleep on the settee, a three-year-old girl, covered by what looked like a tailcoat. By the table stood a man in a very tattered frock coat (he'd already taken off his overcoat, and it lay on the bed) unwrapping the blue paper which yielded a two-pound loaf of white bread and two small cured sausages. A teapot stood on the table and a few slices of rye bread were scattered around. From under the bed protruded an unfastened suitcase and a couple of bundles of assorted rags.

"In a word, the place was a mess. It struck me from the first that both the lady and the gentleman were respectable people, but brought by indigence to that pitch of degradation in which disorder, with its tendency to gather pace daily, finally overcomes every attempt to combat it, till eventually people have no alternative but to succumb to a perverse and resentful kind of satisfaction derived from that very disorder.

"When I entered, the gentleman who'd come in just before me and was in the process of unwrapping his provisions, was absorbed in a deep and rapid conversation with his wife. The latter, while still attending to her baby, was already whining away; evidently the news she was hearing was, as usual, none too comforting. The man, who by the looks of it was about twenty-eight with a lean and swarthy face, framed by dark sideboards, the rest being scrupulously clean shaven, struck me as upright and even genteel; his dejected, careworn aspect was nevertheless sustained by a streak of pent-up feverish defiance. My entrance gave rise to a curious scene.

"There are those who derive enormous satisfaction from their irascibility, especially when it reaches its peak (which happens all too readily); at such moments, it would seem, they rather enjoy their sense of degradation. These irascible souls are afterwards always abjectly contrite, that is if they've got their heads screwed on of course, and have enough savvy to realize that they've been at least ten times more irascible than they ought to have been. The gentleman in question regarded me for a good few moments with enormous astonishment, and his wife with fear, as though it were an unprecedented occurrence that someone should have entered their abode; but suddenly he challenged me with the utmost fury; I had not yet time to open my mouth when – especially on seeing that I was dressed respectably – he thought fit to demonstrate his sense of grievance that I had dared to intrude so unceremoniously upon his privacy and witness the shocking circumstances in which he lived and which irked him so much. Of course he welcomed the opportunity to have someone on whom to vent his anger at all his series of mishaps. For a moment I thought he'd attack me physically; he grew pale as a woman having a hysterical fit, and gave his spouse a terrible fright.

"'How dare you barge in like that? Out!' he yelled, shaking all over and hardly able to articulate his words. But suddenly he saw his wallet in my hands.

"'You must have dropped it,' I said as calmly and drily as possible. (Which, of course, was the best way.)

"The man stood before me utterly defeated and for some time appeared to be at a complete loss; then he abruptly reached for his side pocket, his face dropped and he brought the flat of his hand to his brow.

"'My God! Where did you find it? How did it happen?'

"I explained in as few words as possible, and perhaps in an even drier tone than before, how I came to pick up the wallet, how I ran after him and called to attract his attention and how, finally, more by guesswork than anything else, I literally had to feel my way up the stairs to their door.

"'Oh God!' he exclaimed, turning to his wife. 'All our documents are here... all my instruments, the lot... Oh my dear sir, do you realize what you've done for me? I'd have perished!'

"In the meantime I reached for the door handle so as to make myself scarce without replying; but I myself was out of breath, and suddenly my agitation brought on such a fit of coughing that I was barely able to stand on my feet. I noticed the man cast around in all directions for an empty chair, that he finally swept the rags off one them onto the floor and, in utmost haste, brought it up to me, taking great care that I sat down comfortably. But my coughing would not abate and continued for about three more minutes. After I had recovered, he was already sitting opposite me in another chair, which too he had probably cleared from bits and pieces of clothing, and was looking at me intently.

"You appear to be... in a bad way?" he said in the tone which doctors usually adopt when talking to their patients. 'I'm... a physician,' (he did not say doctor) and, having spoken, he swept his arm round the room for some reason as though in protest at his present circumstances, 'I can see you are—'

"'I have consumption,' I said as curtly as possible and stood up.

"He too leapt to his feet.

"'Perhaps you exaggerate and... if you were to take the appropriate treatment—'

"He was very nonplussed and appeared unable to recover; he was still clutching the wallet in his left hand.

"'Oh, don't worry,' I interrupted him and again reached for the door handle, 'I was examined by B***n last week (there – B***n yet again!), and my fate is sealed. Excuse me—'

"I was about to open the door again and leave my embarrassed, noble-minded and utterly crushed physician to his own devices, but the confounded coughing started up again. Here the doctor made me sit down and rest once more; he turned to his wife who, standing as she was, said a few kind words of gratitude to me. In doing so, her sallow, fallen cheeks reddened bashfully. I remained seated, but preserved an aspect which clearly went to show that I dreaded the thought of embarrassing them (which was only right and proper). My kind doctor's remorse had at last got the better of him, this much was clear to me.

"'If I...' he began, stuttering and faltering, 'I'm so grateful to you and feel so guilty... I... you can see for yourself...' he indicated the room again, 'I'm in such circumstances right now—'

"'Oh,' I said, 'that's nothing at all. It happens all the time. I'd say you must have lost your position, and have come here to clear the matter up and seek a new post, is that not so?'

"'How... did you know?' he asked in amazement.

"'It's pretty obvious,' I replied in an involuntarily mocking tone of voice. 'Lots of people full of hope flock to the capital from the provinces, scrabble about and somehow or other eke out a living.'

"He suddenly began to speak with passion. His lips trembling, he began to pour his heart out, to confide in me and, I have to admit, swept me along; I stayed there almost an hour. He recounted his story, which incidentally was pretty uninspiring. He was a doctor from the country, where he had an official position, but had fallen victim to some intrigues in which even his wife was implicated. He had stood on his pride, had lost his composure; there had been a change in the local administration in favour of his adversaries; people had delved into his records, complaints were lodged; he had lost his position, and, down to his last copeck, had come to St Petersburg to clear his name. In St Petersburg, as was to be expected, his appeal took an inordinately long time to be heard, then it was heard, then it was turned down, then it was reviewed with some promises thrown in, then he was reprimanded, then he was ordered to put something in writing, then his written submission was thrown out, then he was ordered to lodge a petition – in short, he'd already been battling for five months, his money had run out; the last of his wife's belongings had been pawned, and then the baby arrived, and, and... 'today has come the final rejection of my appeal, and I've nearly run out of bread, I have nothing, my wife has given birth. I, I...'

"He jumped to his feet and turned away. His wife was weeping in one corner, the baby began to scream. I took out my notebook and began to take notes. After I had finished, he stood before me and regarded me with apprehensive curiosity.

"'I wrote down your name,' I said to him, 'well, and all the rest of it: your place of work, the name of your District Governor, dates, months. I've a friend, we were at school together – Bakhmutov – and his uncle is Pyotr Matveyevich Bakhmutov, acting State Councillor and current Head of Department—'

"'Pyotr Matveyevich Bakhmutov!' my medical practitioner exclaimed, all atremble. 'But he is the man who practically has the final say!'

"The upshot was that my medical practitioner's case, in which I so fortuitously played a role, was resolved and settled in every particular, as though the whole thing had been purposely arranged, just like in a novel. I told those poor people not to build any hopes on me, that I myself was a poor high-school student (I deliberately played down my part; it was already some time since I'd finished my course of studies and left school) and that there was no need for them to know my name, but that I'd now go straight to Vasilevsky Island to see my friend Bakhmutov, and since I know for certain that his uncle, the acting State Councillor, a childless bachelor, thinks the world of him and loves him to distraction as the last of his line, it is therefore 'quite possible that my friend may be able to do something for you and for me – through his uncle, it goes without saying—'

"'If only I were allowed to put my case to His Excellency! If only I were granted the honour to explain everything verbally!' he cried, trembling as though in a fever, his eyes burning. Those were his very words, '*If only I were granted the honour.*' Having repeated once more that the matter would probably come to nothing and end in failure, I added that if I didn't come to see them tomorrow morning, it meant there was no hope, and they need not expect anything. They saw me out with deep bows, and appeared to be barely able to contain themselves. I shall never forget the expression on their faces. I took a cab and made a beeline for Vasilevsky Island.

As far as this Bakhmutov was concerned I had been on pretty bad terms with him for a number of years running at the high school. He was looked upon as an aristocrat, at least that's how I styled him. He had an excellent dress sense, he always pulled up at the school gates in his own equipage, but was no snob, indeed an exceptional friend – always extremely cheerful and occasionally even witty, though he never had the reputation of being particularly bright, and yet he always came first in class, a distinction I never managed to enjoy myself. Everyone liked him; I was the only one who did not. In those years he made several approaches to me; but I rejected him bad-temperedly every time. At the present time he was at the university and I hadn't seen him for about a year. When – it was gone eight o'clock – I turned up at his place (it was a bit of a to-do – a butler announced me), he was taken aback at first and was far from welcoming, but cheered up almost immediately and, looking at me, suddenly burst out laughing.

"'So what brings you here, Terentyev?' he exclaimed with his customary bonhomie, at times tongue-in-cheek, but never offensive, for which I always admired and hated him in equal measure. 'But look here!' he exclaimed. 'You look so ill!'

"I fell to coughing again. I slumped into a chair and could hardly get my breath back.

"'Don't worry, it's my consumption,' I said, 'I've come to ask for something.'

"He sat down full of surprise, and I immediately recounted the doctor's story and explained that, seeing the extraordinary influence he wielded over his uncle, he could possibly be of assistance.

"'I'll do my best, rest assured, my level best, and I'll get hold of my uncle tomorrow. It'll be my pleasure, and you described it all so vividly... Still, Terentyev, how is it you decided to turn to me?'

"'So much depends on your uncle and, besides, Bakhmutov, we've always been enemies, and since you're a gentleman, I thought you wouldn't refuse a favour to an enemy,' I rejoined with irony.

"'Like Napoleon turned to England!'* he exclaimed, bursting out laughing. 'But of course, I'll do it! In fact I'll go straight away, if he'll see me,' he added in some hurry, noticing that I was getting up from my chair with a serious and determined expression on my face.

"And lo and behold, the matter was indeed settled in the most unexpected manner and on the best possible terms. Within a month and a half our medical practitioner received a posting in another district, his moving expenses were covered, and he even received a subsidy. I suspect that Bakhmutov, who since then became a frequent visitor at the couple's house (by contrast I deliberately avoided them, and when the doctor did drop by, I received him almost drily) – Bakhmutov, as I suspect, had even persuaded the doctor to accept a personal loan. Personally I saw Bakhmutov about twice in those six weeks, the third time was when we were seeing the doctor off. Bakhmutov threw a champagne dinner party for the occasion; the doctor's wife came too, but as it happened, she soon left to look after her child. This was at the beginning of May. The huge disk of the sun was slowly sinking into the Gulf.* Bakhmutov came along to see me home; we were walking over the Nikolayevsky Bridge; we were both under the influence. Bakhmutov spoke of his delight that the matter had ended so satisfactorily, he kept thanking me for something, kept going on about how pleased he was after a good deed well done, insisted that the credit was all mine and that it was a shame that so many people were now in the habit of preaching and teaching that isolated good deeds were of no value. I too had an overwhelming urge to talk.

"'Whoever makes sport of individual acts of charity,' I began, 'makes sport of man's better nature and offends his human dignity. Moreover, the institution of public charity and the question of individual freedom are two distinct, though not mutually exclusive issues. Good deeds on the part of individuals will never cease, because they are the vital urges of mankind, the urge of one personality to exercise an influence over another. There was once an elderly gentleman* in Moscow, a general, with a German name, a State Councillor. All his life he went round prisons and visited convicts; every batch of prisoners consigned for deportation to Siberia knew in advance that the little old general would come to see them on the Sparrow Hills. He went about his business in a dedicated, God-fearing way; he would arrive, walk along the files of convicts who crowded around him, stopped in front of each, enquired of each about his needs, was hardly ever known to moralize, referred to them all as 'my poor devils'. He distributed money, everyday articles – puttees, sheets; sometimes it included spiritual books, which he gave to those who could read, fully convinced that they'd read them on the way to those who couldn't read. He very seldom questioned them about their crimes; at most he would hear them out if they themselves volunteered to speak. All the convicts were on an equal footing for him – he made no distinction between them. He spoke with them as with brothers, but towards the end they themselves came to regard him as their father. If he noticed a woman convict with a child in her arms, he'd go up to fondle it and snap his fingers to make it laugh. He carried on like this for many years, right up to the days of his death; eventually it reached a stage where he was known throughout Russia, throughout Siberia – that is, amongst the convict population. One former Siberian convict told me himself that he heard the most diehard criminals recall the general with affection, never mind that when he walked amongst them, he could seldom afford to give more than twenty copecks each. And it's not as though they attached much importance to their recollections or were particularly serious about them. One or other of such 'unfortunates', who may have had up to a dozen lives on his conscience, who may have stabbed up to six children to death purely for the hell of it (there were such too, they say), could very well have turned around and, quite out of the blue and maybe just once in all his twenty-odd years of confinement, have said with a sigh, 'You know that old boy, the general, I wonder if he's still around?' He might even have smiled into the bargain – and that'd be that. But who knows what seed may have been implanted in his soul by the old general, whom he had not forgotten in twenty long years? How could you know, Bakhmutov, what effect this communion of one soul with another may have on the fate of his associates?... Aren't we dealing here with human life in the round and a countless number of latent ramifications? The best chess player, the sharpest of them all can calculate only so many moves ahead; one French player, who could manage ten, was spoken of as a genius. So how many moves do we make blindly? When you sow your seed, when you perform your beneficence, your act of charity, in whatever shape or form, you surrender some part of your personality and absorb a part of another; you commune with another being. There need be only some other, some further token of your consideration for you to be rewarded with knowledge, with the most unexpected revelation. You'll inevitably begin to regard your good deeds as a science, which will take over your life and lend it purpose. Furthermore, all your ideas, all the seeds you have implanted, no doubt long forgotten by your good self, will germinate and grow. Whoever benefited from you, will pass the benefit on to others. And how can you tell what your part will be in the future resolution of men's destinies? If, however, knowledge and a lifetime's effort will eventually elevate you to that state where you'll be capable of sowing some huge seed, bequeath the world some unique idea, then... And so forth. I said a good deal more on the subject at the time.

"'And to think that, given all this, you of all people should be denied life!' Bakhmutov exclaimed ardently, as though reproaching someone.

"We were standing on the bridge at that moment, leaning on the handrail, looking down at the Neva.

"'And do you know what has passed through my head?' I asked, and leant further over the handrail.

"'Surely not to throw yourself into the water?' Bakhmutov exclaimed in terror. Perhaps he had read my mind.

"'No, for now it's mere speculation, namely – here I am with two or three months left to live, four at the outside. But say, once I had a total of two months left, with a violent urge to do some good deed which would require considerable effort, involving enquiries, arrangements, something like what our general did, then I'd surely have to cry off by dint of not having sufficient time at my disposal, and be obliged look for some other 'good deed', a less ambitious one which would be within my *means* (to be brutally blunt about it). You must agree, it's a fiendishly amusing thought, is it not?'

"Poor Bakhmutov, bless him, was very shaken; he saw me right up to my door and was discreet enough not even to attempt to comfort me, and practically didn't say a single word. At parting, he shook my hand warmly and asked to be allowed to come and see me. I replied that if he were to visit me as a 'comforter' (because even if he didn't say a word, he'd still be comforting me – I took pains to explain this to him), his presence would be a constant reminder of my impending death. He shrugged his shoulders, but did not argue. We parted quite cordially, which I must say I hadn't expected.

"But that evening, that very night, the first germ of my 'inevitable conclusion' was implanted. I clutched at this *new* idea eagerly, I eagerly investigated it in all its ramifications, in all its guises (I spent a sleepless night), and the more I delved into it, the more I absorbed it, the more frightened I became. Finally I was overcome with a simply devastating terror, which persisted for days to come. Sometimes, while contemplating this persistent terror which had gripped me, I was quickly plunged into yet deeper panic. It told me that the 'inevitable conclusion' was all too firmly embedded in me, and would inevitably push me to the final resolution. But for the final resolution I lacked personal courage. Three weeks later all was over, and I had the necessary courage, but under rather curious circumstances.

"Here, in my attempt to explain things, I'm giving all the facts and figures. It will, of course, make precious little difference to me, but now (and perhaps for the duration of this single moment only) I wish that whoever sits in judgement upon what I'm about to do can clearly follow the train of logical arguments which brought me to my inevitable decision. I indicated above that the necessary resolve which I lacked in order to carry out my inevitable decision, came to me I believe not as a result of a logical train of thought, but in consequence of a strange shock, a strange occurrence, which was perhaps totally unrelated to the events at hand. About ten days ago Rogozhin called on me on a personal matter, which I'm not going to go into now. I'd never seen Rogozhin before, but had heard about him a great deal. I gave him all the required information, and he soon left, and as all he wanted was information, that would have been the end of the matter between the two of us. But he intrigued me too much, and the whole of that day I was beset by the most outlandish thoughts, so that in the end I decided to go and see him myself, to repay the visit. Rogozhin, it seemed, was not best pleased to see me, and even 'discreetly' gave me to understand that there was no point in continuing our acquaintanceship; nonetheless, I spent a very exhilarating hour or so with him, as probably he did too. There was such a contrast between us that it could not but amaze us both, especially me. I was a person whose days were clearly numbered, whereas he, one who lived life to the full, burned the candle at both ends, without a moment's thought for any 'final' conclusions, or concern for figures or whatever... that is... without a care in the world for anything, for anything... well... for anything except that one thing which was driving him out of his mind. I hope Mr Rogozhin will pardon me my choice of words as one who is a poor wordsmith and incapable of expressing his thoughts at all well. In spite of his boorishness, I saw that he was intelligent and perceptive, but one who took little interest in what was going on around him. I made no mention of my 'ultimate conviction', but for some reason I had a feeling that while listening to me, he read my mind. But he said nothing; he is a man of very few words. At parting I mentioned that in spite of all the difference between us and all the contradictory tendencies – *les extrémités se touchent** (I explained it to him in Russian), and my impression was that he himself was closer to my 'ultimate conviction' than might have been supposed. In answer he screwed his face into a very sour and disagreeable mien, stood up, fetched me my cap as though affirming that it had been my idea to leave, and simply escorted me out of his dismal house, pretending he was seeing me to the door out of courtesy. His house gave me the shivers; it was as cheerful as a graveyard, but he seemed to like it, which did not surprise me – if one considers how full and intense his way of life is, what need of externals?

"This visit to Rogozhin's took a lot out of me. Besides, I didn't feel too well from the morning on; by evening I was very weak and I lay down in bed, in between times I felt the fever coming on, and was delirious for short periods. Kolya stayed with me till eleven o'clock. However, I can remember all that he said and all we discussed. Occasionally when my eyes fell shut, I imagined I saw Ivan Fomich Surikov, who'd become a millionaire. He was constantly in a state as to where to put his money, agonized over it, shook with fear that it'd be stolen, and finally appeared to want to bury it in the ground. I talked him out of it, saying it'd be a shame to bury such a heap of gold in the ground and that instead he should melt it down and cast it into a little coffin for his 'frozen' infant who ought to be exhumed. Surikov appeared to be over the moon at the idea and immediately got down to work. I simply turned on my heel and left him to it. After I'd fully come to my senses, Kolya assured me that I hadn't slept a wink but had talked to him about Surikov all the while. There were moments I felt down in the dumps and was intolerably restless, so that Kolya eventually stood up and left, helpless and looking worried. When I got up to shut the door after him, I suddenly remembered the picture I saw at Rogozhin's, in one of the gloomiest of his rooms, over the doorway. He pointed it out himself to me as we were passing; I remember I spent about five minutes in front of it. There was nothing to recommend it from the artistic point of view, but it had a terribly disturbing effect on me.

"The picture depicts Christ just taken down from the cross. I think artists usually depict Christ, on or off the cross, with vestiges of unusual beauty in his face; they strive to retain this beauty in spite of his extreme agony. In Rogozhin's painting there's not even a trace of beauty; it is in every respect the corpse of man who'd undergone insufferable pain even before his crucifixion – wounds, traumas, beatings at the hands of the guards and the crowd when he was still carrying the cross and had fallen under its weight and, finally, the excruciating pain he endured in the course of six hours (that's, at least, how I see it all). True, this is a face of a man only *just* taken down from the cross, still retaining many traces of life; rigor mortis had not yet set in, such that there's still ongoing suffering in his features (the artist has captured this to a nicety); but neither has the face been spared anything; this is nature in the raw, and truly that's how the corpse of a man, whoever he may be, should look after undergoing such mortal agony. I know that the

Christian Church had laid it down as a dogma in the very first centuries that Christ's suffering was real, not symbolic,* and that consequently his body on the cross was subject completely and utterly to the laws of nature. In the picture the face is terribly battered, bloated, with dreadful, puffed-up bruises, the vacant eyes are wide open, the pupils stare aimlessly, the inert, distended, whites have a murky, glassy sheen to them. But curiously enough, when one regards the corpse of this ravaged man, one can't avoid asking a startling question. If all his pupils – the principal future disciples of his; if all the women who had followed him and stood by the cross; if all who believed in him and adored him – beheld such a corpse (and such it must necessarily have been), how could they possibly, looking at such a corpse, believe that this martyr would rise from the dead?

Here one cannot help but wonder that if death is so terrible and the laws of nature so powerful, how may they be overcome? How may they be overcome now if they hadn't been overcome even by him who during his lifetime had commanded nature and it had obeyed him, who had said, '*Talitha cumi*'* – and straightway the damsel arose, 'Lazarus, come forth'* – and he that was dead came forth, alive? At the sight of this picture nature appears as a huge, implacable and mute monster, or, more accurately, much more accurately, and strange as it may sound, as some enormous machine of the very latest construction, which had grabbed, crushed and devoured – mindlessly and brutally – an exquisite and priceless Being, a Being which of itself was worth the whole of nature and all its laws put together, and of the whole world, which had probably been created for naught other than the advent of this Being! This picture appears to represent the idea of that dark, menacing, mindlessly timeless force which holds sway over everything and pervades us insidiously. Those people* who had surrounded the dead man, and none of whom are shown in the picture, must have experienced an enormous sense of sadness and loss that evening, all their hope and even faith having been shattered at a stroke. They must have dispersed in fear and trepidation, even though each and every one of them was sustained by a prodigious Idea which would not abandon them for ever more. And if the Lord and Master had chanced to see this image of his prior to his execution, would he have been crucified and died in quite the same way as he did? This question also comes to mind involuntarily when one contemplates the picture.

"After Kolya's departure all these thoughts coursed through my mind pell-mell, interspersed with bouts of delirium for an hour and a half; some even in visual form. Can something be perceived visually which essentially has no visual form? But at times I thought I actually saw this boundless force, this undiscerning, dismal and insentient being manifestly in some strange, inconceivable form. I remember as though someone, holding a candle, led me by the hand to show me a huge and revolting tarantula, assuring me that that was in fact that selfsame dismal, insentient and all-powerful being, and he laughed over my show of indignation. In my room there's always a nightlight by the icon, dim and feeble – all the same one can make out everything by it, and close up it's even possible to read. It must have just gone midnight; I was wide awake and lay with my eyes open; suddenly the door opened and Rogozhin walked into my room.

"He entered, shut the door, looked at me without saying a word and went softly over into the corner where there's a table almost directly beneath the icon. I was rather surprised and waited to see what would happen next. Rogozhin put his elbows on the table and began to stare at me. This went on for about two or three minutes, and I recall his silence offended me and made me feel uncomfortable. Why doesn't he want to speak, I wondered? The fact that he came so late did, of course strike me as odd, but as I remember, it wasn't actually that which surprised me most. Quite the contrary! Even though I hadn't explained my idea to him that morning in so many words, I knew that he'd understood it. Now this idea implied that it wouldn't have been at all surprising if one came back to enquire about it some more, be it ever so late. I was pretty sure therefore he came precisely with that in mind. Our parting in the morning was not particularly amicable and, thinking back, I even remember he looked at me derisively once or twice. It was precisely this derision which I read in his eyes that offended me. As for it being Rogozhin himself, rather than an apparition, a figment of a diseased brain, I had at first no doubt whatsoever. It didn't even enter my mind.

"Meanwhile he sat quite still and continued to regard me with that same derisive look in his eyes. I shifted in my bed angrily, dug my elbows into the pillow and was determined not to speak either, however long it took. For some reason or other I longed for him to begin first. I think about twenty minutes elapsed. Suddenly it occurred to me, what if it wasn't Rogozhin at all, only his shadow?

"Neither during the course of my illness, nor before, had I ever experienced an apparition; but I've also believed since my early childhood, and even now, that is until quite recently, that were I to see an apparition, I'd die on the spot, no matter that really I don't believe in apparitions of any kind. But when it occurred to me that it wasn't Rogozhin but only an apparition, I wasn't a bit frightened, as I remember. On the contrary, I felt my hackles rise. What was also strange was that I wasn't, as might have been expected, so much interested or bothered whether it was Rogozhin himself or only his shadow; I think my mind was on something else altogether. I was, for instance, far more concerned why it was that Rogozhin, who in the morning had a dressing gown and slippers on, was now wearing a tailcoat, white tie and a white waistcoat. The thought also kept flashing through my mind: if it was an apparition and I wasn't frightened, why did I not get up, approach him and verify for myself? Maybe I was frightened after all, and just couldn't pluck up the courage. But as soon as I realized I might be frightened, cold shivers ran down my spine, and my knees began to buckle. At that very instant, as though he'd realized I was terrified, Rogozhin let drop the arm he was leaning on, straightened up and began to open his mouth as though preparing to burst out laughing. He was looking straight into my eyes. I was so mad, I positively wanted to attack him, but since I'd resolved not to be the first to speak, I stayed in my bed, the more so since I still wasn't sure if it was Rogozhin or not.

"I can't quite remember how long it all went on for; nor do I remember properly whether or not I lost consciousness at any time. Finally Rogozhin got up, looked me over slowly and carefully again, like he'd done when he came in, but he didn't smirk any more, just tiptoed without a sound over to the door, opened and shut it carefully behind him. I didn't get out of bed; I can't recall how long I lay there with my eyes open and kept thinking – God only knows what about; my mind was a blank afterwards. I was woken up next morning by loud knocking on the door; it was gone nine. It was as I'd instructed – if I wasn't up till gone nine and hadn't called for my cup of tea, Matryona was to knock on the door herself. As soon as I opened the door, the first thing that came to my mind was, how the blazes could he have entered, if the door had been locked shut all the time? I checked again, and concluded that it was impossible for the real Rogozhin to have entered, since all our doors are locked at night.

"It was this particular incident, which I described in such detail, that led to my taking my 'decision' – finally. Hence the end decision was precipitated not by logic, much less by logical conjecture, but rather by a sense of revulsion. One can't put up with a life which plays such unbecoming tricks on you. This apparition thoroughly demeaned me. I refuse to submit to a force of darkness which takes on the shape and form of a tarantula. And it was only when at daybreak I finally perceived in me the moment of inexorable resolve that I experienced a sense of relief. But that was only the first moment; I went to Pavlovsk to experience the second, but I've dealt with that at sufficient length already."

7

" I HAD IN MY POSSESSION a little pocket pistol. I'd acquired it when I was still a child, at that peculiar age when one suddenly begins to be fascinated by stories of duels, of derring-do and robbers, of being challenged to a duel and of standing like a true gentleman, staring into the barrel of a gun. I had checked it a month previously and ensured it was in full working order. With it in the box were two bullets, and enough powder in the powder horn for three shots. The piece was completely useless, you couldn't aim accurately with it and its reach was only about fifteen paces; but if you held it right up against your head, it would split your skull open with no trouble.

"I made up my mind to die at sunrise down in the park in Pavlovsk so as not to disturb anyone at the dacha. My 'Explanation' would suffice to explain everything to the police. Those with a penchant for psychology are free to make anything they like of this. All the same, I wouldn't like this manuscript to become public. I'd like the Prince to keep one copy for himself and give the other to Aglaya Ivanovna Yepanchina. That is my will. I'd like to bequeath my body to the Medical Institute in the interests of science.

"I do not recognize anyone's right to sit in judgement over me and I know that I'm now outside the jurisdiction of any law. I was amused the other day at the thought that if I'd suddenly taken it upon myself to kill anyone, say a dozen people, or perpetrate the most heinous crime ever, what a quandary I'd have put the judiciary into with only two or three weeks left in me, and all in the absence of torture chambers and other like means of punishment? I'd have died in all comfort in one of their hospitals, in the warmth with an attentive doctor by me, and perhaps in greater comfort and warmth than at home. I can't imagine why people in a position such as mine don't really come to similar conclusions, if only for the hell of it? Perhaps they do; there's surely no shortage of fun-loving people hereabouts.

"But even if I don't recognize anyone's right to sit in judgement over me, I know people will judge me after I'm mute and voiceless. I refuse to depart without having had my say – freely and under no compulsion, not to justify myself – not at all! I've no one and nothing to ask pardon for, but simply because that's what I'd like to do anyway.

"Now, for a start, here's a curious thought. Who, and in the name of what law, on the basis of what principle, would want to contest my right to spend these two or three weeks left to me as I wish? What business is it of any authority? Who would want to see that I'm not only sentenced, but that I dutifully complete my sentence to the last letter? Why would anyone want to take the trouble? For the sake of morality? I could just about understand it if I'd made an attempt on my life in the full bloom and vigour of my health. While my life could still be of benefit to my fellow man, customary morality could just about condemn me by tradition, as it were, for disposing of my life without sanction, or for whatever else it might fancy. But surely not now, not now that my sentence has already been spelled out to me! What kind of morality would call not just for your life but also for your croaky exhalations as the last vestiges of vitality drained out of you listening to the Prince's accompanying blandishments, to his Christian arguments, inevitably ending with the blithe conclusion that in essence it's clearly just as well that you're about to die? (Christians like him always come to such a conclusion – they can't help themselves.) And what do these people want with their ridiculous 'Pavlovsk trees'? To sweeten the last days of my life? Do they really not understand that the more I shall forget myself, the more I shall succumb to this last chimera of life and love, behind which they want to hide my Meyer's wall and all I've written on it with such care and honesty – the more miserable they'll make me? What use to me is your nature, your green parks, your sunsets and your sunrises, your blue skies and all your happy faces if at this grand performance that is without end, I'm the only one who'd

431

been blackballed right from the start? What good is this beauty to me if at every step and turn I'm constantly being reminded that even this tiny mosquito, which buzzes around me in the sun's ray, is enjoying his share of feasting and revelling to the full, knows its place and is happy with it, whereas I alone am an outcast, too spineless to have admitted it till now! Oh, I know only too well how happy the Prince and all the rest would be to see that instead of all this 'mean and subversive' talk, I'd have recited in praise of universal morality Millevoye's* famous and classical lines:

> Ô, puissent voir votre beauté sacrée
> Tant d'amis sourds à mes adieux!
> Qu'ils meurent pleins de jours, que leur mort soit pleurée,
> Qu'un ami leur ferme les yeux!

"But take my word, please take my word, you simple-hearted people, that in these well-meaning lines, in this academic paean to the world in French verse, there is so much latent bile, so much irreconcilable, self-perpetuating poetic loathing that perhaps the poet has himself come a cropper in having mistaken this loathing for tears of blithe compliance, and so departed this world. RIP! Take my word: there's a limit to man's mortification at the thought of his own worthlessness and helplessness beyond which he cannot go and after which his very disrepute becomes a source of enormous pleasure for him… Well, humility, of course, becomes a very potent force in this case, I will allow this – although not in the same sense in which religion takes humility to be a force for good.

"Ah, yes! Religion! That there may be life hereafter, that I will allow, and perhaps have always done. Let's assume my consciousness had been begotten by a higher power, let's assume this power had looked about and said, 'Let him be!' – and let this newly created being be subsequently required by the will of this higher power to cease to exist – no reason or explanation given, it simply must go out of existence, and that's that – I'll readily allow all that too, but then we still can't get away from the accursed question, what is my humility for in all this? Couldn't I simply be devoured, without having to sing praises to him who had devoured me? Will someone out there really take offence because I didn't want to tarry an extra fortnight? I don't believe it!

It's much more likely to be the case that my worthless life, the life of an insignificant atom, had found an application for the restoration of some kind of global harmony – a plus here, a minus there, a shade more contrast, a shade less contrast and so on and so forth – just as there's a daily need to sacrifice the lives of a whole host of creatures, whose death the rest of the world needs simply in order to keep going round (though it must be noted that this is not a particularly honourable notion per se) But never mind! I agree that 'dog eat dog' is the order of the world and it could not possibly have been arranged in any other way; I'd even agree to admit that I haven't got the faintest clue what this arrangement is all about; but if there's one thing I do know for certain, it is this: Once I'd been given to understand that 'I am', what concern is it of mine that there are mistakes in the way the world has been arranged, and that there's no other way in which it can be kept going? Who will sit in judgement over me after that and for what? Please yourselves, but all this is hard to understand and unfair.

"That said, I have never – and this despite my best endeavours – been able to imagine that there's no future life and no providence. The likelihood is that both exist, but that we simply haven't got a clue what future life is all about or what the laws are that govern it. Now, if this is so difficult and goes way beyond all understanding, how can I possibly be held responsible for not having grasped the incomprehensible? True, they will say – and of course the Prince amongst them – that that's precisely where humility comes in, that I must submit without questioning, out of piety alone, and that I shall be rewarded in heaven for my submissiveness. We do providence an injustice when, frustrated at our inability to comprehend it, we ascribe to it our own responses. But there again, if it is beyond comprehension, then, I repeat, it is difficult to feel any responsibility for that which is not given man to understand. And if that is so, how can I be judged for my inability to comprehend the will and the laws of providence? No, let's just leave religion out of it.

"And really that's enough! When I have reached these lines, the sun will surely be up – triumphant and resplendent – and a mighty, immeasurable force will have engulfed everything in its path. So be it! I shall die looking straight at the source of power and of life, and reject this life! Had it been within my power not to have been born, I'd surely not have accepted existence on such ludicrous terms. But it is still within my power to die, albeit I'm surrendering that which has already been written off. Not much of a power, not much of a rebellion!

"My final declaration: I choose to die not at all because I cannot bear the thought of these three weeks. I'd have easily found sufficient strength, and if I so wished, I'd have been sustained sufficiently by the mere thought of the offence inflicted upon me; but I'm not a French poet, and I've no need of such comforts. Finally, there's a temptation here. Nature, in giving me only three weeks to live, has so severely limited my freedom of action that suicide may perhaps be the only mission which I may still have time to initiate and bring to a conclusion of my own accord. Well, perhaps that's all I ever wanted to do – to make use of my last opportunity to accomplish something active. A protest is sometimes no mean feat..."

The reading of the "Explanation" was at last over.

There is in extreme cases that degree of final, cynical absence of inhibition when a nervous person, irritated and wound up, is not afraid of anything and is ready for any confrontation, and even welcomes the opportunity for such; he will challenge people, nurturing at the same time a vague, but firm intention to throw himself a minute later from a bell tower and thereby solve at a stroke all misunderstandings if such were to arise. A symptom of such a condition may be an increasing exhaustion of physical strength. The extraordinary, almost unnatural, state of stress, which had hitherto kept Ippolit going, had reached this critical stage. On the face of it, this eighteen-year-old young man, wracked by illness, seemed as weak as a solitary leaf fluttering in the wind; but the moment he had swept his eyes over the listeners – the first time in the whole of the preceding hour – the most haughty, the most disdainful and affronted loathing became evident in the shape of his lips as he smiled and the look in his eyes. He pressed ahead with his challenge. But the listeners too were thoroughly incensed. Everybody was getting up noisily from their chairs around the table. Fatigue, the effect of wine and the built-up tension added to the general disorderliness and awkwardness hanging in the air.

Suddenly Ippolit jumped quickly to his feet as though propelled from below.

"The sun's up!" he exclaimed, as he looked at the sun-bright treetops and, turning towards the Prince, pointed at them as though it were a miracle. "The sun's up!"

"So what?" Ferdyshchenko responded.

"Another blazing hot day in store," Ganya muttered in bad-tempered ennui, holding his hat in one hand, stretching himself and yawning. "This drought is set for the rest of the month!... Are you coming or not, Ptitsyn?"

Ippolit listened with rapidly mounting astonishment. Suddenly he went terribly pale and began to shake all over.

"You have a very heavy-handed way of expressing your couldn't-care-less attitude at my expense," he said, looking Ganya straight in the eye. "You're a scoundrel, sir!"

"Well, this just about takes the biscuit. Fancy anyone getting so carried away!" Ferdyshchenko bellowed. "You should pull yourself together!"

"Simply a fool, if you ask me," Ganya observed.

Ippolit stiffened visibly.

"I can well see, gentlemen," he began, stumbling over every word and shaking as previously, "that you may have something personal against me, and... I'm sorry I've bored you to death with this rubbish." (He pointed at his manuscript.) "On second thoughts, it's a pity I haven't bored you to death..." (he smiled sheepishly) "or have I, Yevgeny Pavlovich?" he suddenly turned on Yevgeny Pavlovich. "Have I, or haven't? Answer me!"

"A bit on the long side, but then again—"

"Come out with it! Tell the truth for once in your life!" Ippolit commanded, shaking in every limb.

"Look, I'm not interested! Do me a favour, leave me alone," Yevgeny Pavlovich said with an expression of disgust, and turned his back on Ippolit.

"Good night, Prince," Ptitsyn said, approaching the Prince.

"He's going to shoot himself in a minute, do something! Look at him!" Vera exclaimed, rushing towards Ippolit in extreme terror and grabbing him by his arms. "Didn't he say he'd shoot himself at dawn, help him!"

"He won't!" a number of people, including Ganya, sneered under their breath.

"Gentlemen, take care!" Kolya called out, also having grabbed hold of Ippolit's hand. "Just take a look at him! Prince! Prince, don't just stand there!"

Vera, Kolya, Keller and Burdovsky surrounded Ippolit in a tight circle; all four of them were holding on to him.

"He has every right, he has!..." Burdovsky muttered, though with singular lack of confidence in his voice.

"Excuse me, Prince, but what would your instructions be?" Lebedev asked the Prince with drunken, bad-tempered arrogance.

"What instructions?"

"No, excuse me, my dear sir, I'm the host here, though with no disrespect to you... I will concede you are a host too, of course, but I've no wish that under my own roof... So there!"

"He's not going to shoot himself. The lad's just fooling around!" General Ivolgin unexpectedly declared with indignant aplomb.

"Hear, hear!" Ferdyshchenko voiced his agreement.

"I know he won't shoot himself, General, my highly esteemed General, I meant, all the same... as I am the host here."

"I say, Mr Terentyev," Ptitsyn suddenly said after he had taken his leave of the Prince and was extending his hand to Ippolit, "I thought I heard you mention in your notebook a skeleton which you're leaving to the Academy? Did you mean your own skeleton, really your own, that is, you're bequeathing your bones?"

"Yes, my bones..."

"Just wanted to be sure. Mistakes have been known. They say there was a similar case already."

"Why are you making fun of him?" the Prince suddenly exclaimed.

"He's on the point of tears," Ferdyshchenko observed.

But Ippolit was not crying at all. He made an attempt to move forward, but the foursome, who surrounded him, held him back. There was a burst of laughter.

"That was the whole idea, that people should hold him by his hands. He read his notebook with just that in mind," Rogozhin said. "So long, Prince. I need to stretch myself after all this sitting around. My bones are killing me."

"If you really had a mind to shoot yourself, Terentyev," Yevgeny Pavlovich said, laughing, "after all the compliments that have been paid to you, I really wouldn't do it if I were you, now of all times, if only to have a good laugh at them all."

"They're dying to see me shoot myself!" Ippolit retorted. He spoke in an aggressively belligerent tone of voice. "They're afraid they won't get to see it happen."

"Do you think they won't?"

"I'm not egging you on, quite the contrary, I think it's very likely you will shoot yourself. The main thing is to keep your temper..." Yevgeny Pavlovich drawled, patronizingly savouring his words.

"It's only now that I can see I made a dreadful mistake reading them my notes!" Ippolit said, looking at Yevgeny Pavlovich with such an unexpectedly confiding expression on his face as though asking a dear friend for advice.

"The situation is rather comical, and... I really am not sure how I can help you," Yevgeny Pavlovich replied, smiling.

Ippolit regarded him intently and did not say a word. It looked as though his mind was wandering from time to time.

"No, have a heart, gentlemen, it's the arrogance of it all," Lebedev said, "'I'll shoot myself in the park,' he reckons, 'not to cause any disturbance!' He imagines that just by going three steps down into the park he's not going to cause any disturbance!"

"Gentlemen—" the Prince began.

"No, my dear Prince," Lebedev cut in with uncontrolled anger, "since you yourself realize that this is no laughing matter, and since a good half of your guests are of like opinion and are convinced that after what has been said, he has no alternative but to shoot himself, for honour's sake if nothing else, I – the active host here – invite you before all these witnesses to be cooperative."

"What is it you want to be done, Lebedev? How can I cooperate?"

"For a start, why doesn't he immediately surrender the pistol he has been bragging about with all its accessories? If he does, I'd be willing to let him stay the night in this house on account of his ill health, under my surveillance of course. But tomorrow he must be on his way. Sorry about that, Prince! If he does not surrender the weapon, I shall immediately take him by one hand, the General by the other, and I will call the police at once, who can then deal with him accordingly. Mr Ferdyshchenko, as a friend of the house, will oblige us by going to report."

There was a minor uproar: Lebedev refused to calm down, and his state of excitement was getting out of hand; Ferdyshchenko got ready to go to the police; Ganya kept on insisting angrily that there would be no shooting. Yevgeny Pavlovich said nothing.

"Prince, have you ever attempted to jump off a bell tower?" Ippolit suddenly asked in a whisper.

"N-no—" the Prince replied in all innocence.

"Do you really imagine I didn't foresee all this hatred?" Ippolit whispered again, his eyes blazing and looking at the Prince as though truly expecting him to come up with an answer. "That'll do!" he suddenly shouted for all to hear. "I'm to blame... more than anyone! Lebedev, here's the key," (he took out a wallet and a steel ring with three or four small keys on it) "this one... Kolya will show you... Kolya! Where's Kolya?" he called out, looking at Kolya and unable to recognize him. "Yes, he'll show you, we packed the suitcase together. Take him to it, Kolya! You'll find... in the Prince's study under the table... my case... with this key, at the bottom, in a box... my pistol and a powder horn. He packed them himself, Mr Lebedev, he'll show you. But only provided if, when I go back to St Petersburg early tomorrow morning, you'll give me the pistol back. Do you hear me? I'm doing it for the Prince, not you."

"That's better!" Lebedev said, smiling gleefully, grabbing the key and dashing into the adjoining room.

Kolya hesitated and was about to say something, but Lebedev dragged the boy out of the room with him.

Ippolit stared at the laughing faces of the guests. The Prince noticed his teeth were chattering as though in a bad fever.

"What a vile lot!" he whispered again in a state of despondency. When he spoke to the Prince, he always leant across to him and spoke in a whisper.

"Leave them, you are very weak—"

"Yes, yes... I'll go soon."

Suddenly he flung his arms around the Prince.

"Perhaps you think I'm mad?" he asked, looking at the Prince and laughing oddly.

"No, but you—"

"There, there, don't say anything, not a word. Don't move... I want to look into your eyes... Stand just like that, let me look. I want to bid farewell to a true human being."

He stood stock-still and looked at the Prince for about ten seconds, very pale. Beads of sweat were running down his temples, and he grabbed with one hand at the Prince oddly as though afraid to let go of him.

"Ippolit, Ippolit, what's the matter with you?" the Prince exclaimed.

"All right… that'll do… I'm going to lie down. I want to drink to the health of the sun, a quick one… I must, I must, let me go!"

He quickly picked up a glass from the table, rushed forward and the next moment was already at the top of the terrace steps. The Prince rushed after him, but it so happened that just at that same moment Yevgeny Pavlovich put out his hand to him in parting. There was a momentary confusion, and suddenly people on the terrace cried out in one voice, followed by a general commotion.

This is what happened. After Ippolit had reached the edge of the landing, leading from the terrace, he stopped; in his left hand he still held the glass of wine, while his right hand rested in the right pocket of his coat. Subsequently Keller insisted that Ippolit had been holding this hand in the right hand pocket for quite some time, that is, while he was still talking to the Prince and was reaching with his left hand for the Prince's shoulder and collar, and that it was precisely this right hand in his pocket, Keller alleged, which had roused his, Keller's, first suspicion. Be that as it may, but a certain disquiet caused him too to run after Ippolit. But he too was too late. All he saw was that something flashed in Ippolit's right hand and that at the same instant a small pocket pistol was pressed tight up against his right temple. Keller tried to grab his hand, but Ippolit had already managed to squeeze the trigger. There was a short sharp click, but the gun did not fire. After Keller had clutched Ippolit in his arms, the latter sank into a limp, almost lifeless heap, no doubt imagining that he was already dead. The pistol was instantly in Keller's possession. Others rushed to support Ippolit, a chair was brought up, he slumped into it as everyone crowded around, shouting and asking questions. They all heard the click and the man before them was alive, without even a scratch. Ippolit sat, unable to understand what was going on around him; his eyes wandered aimlessly from person to person. Lebedev and Kolya rushed back into the room.

"A misfire?" people wanted to know.

"Perhaps it wasn't even loaded?" others surmised.

"It was!" Keller announced, inspecting the pistol, "but—"

"So it had misfired?"

"There's no primer," Keller said.

It is difficult to describe the pathetic scene that followed. The initial and all-pervading sense of shock was quickly replaced by laughter; some even held their sides, such was their glee at another man's predicament.

Ippolit sobbed as though hysterical; he wrung his hands, rushed up to everyone, even Ferdyshchenko, grabbed hold of him with both hands and swore that he'd forgotten, "forgotten, quite by accident, not at all intentionally, here they are, in my waistcoat pocket, about a dozen of them" (he held them up for all to see); that he hadn't inserted them earlier for fear the pistol might go off accidentally in his pocket; that he'd counted on being able to do it any time, whenever necessary, and at the last he suddenly forgot. He appealed to the Prince, to Yevgeny Pavlovich, he implored Keller to give him the pistol back to allow him to prove on the spot that "...it's my honour, my honour..." and that he was now "disgraced for ever!..."

Finally he collapsed unconscious. He was carried into the Prince's study, and Lebedev, who had by then sobered up completely, sent for the doctor post-haste, after which he, his daughter, his son, Burdovsky and General Ivolgin stayed behind at the patient's bedside. After the unconscious Ippolit had been carried out, Keller stood up in the middle of the room and declared for all to hear in an inspired, resolute voice, enunciating and stressing every syllable, "If any of you gentlemen should at any time in my presence cast aspersions or doubt that the percussion cap had been left out deliberately, and should insist that the unfortunate young man was only play-acting – he will have to deal directly with me."

No one replied. At length all the guests dispersed hurriedly in a crowd. Ptitsyn, Ganya and Rogozhin set off together.

The Prince was rather surprised that Yevgeny Pavlovich had changed his mind and was leaving without having had the planned tête-à-tête.

"I thought you wanted to speak to me after everyone was gone?" He asked.

"You're perfectly right," Yevgeny Pavlovich said, suddenly sitting down in a chair and inviting the Prince to do likewise, "but I've changed my mind temporarily. I must admit I feel a little awkward, as you must too. My thoughts have gone a little haywire. Besides, what I want to thrash out with you is a matter of cardinal importance for me, as for you too. You see, Prince, for once in my life I'd like to do something perfectly honourable, that is, without any ulterior motive, well, and I think that just at this moment I'm not quite capable of a perfectly honourable deed, and you too, perhaps, also... so... well... in short, let's have it out some other time. Perhaps the matter itself will clear up a little for both of us in the course of the next three days which I intend to spend in St Petersburg."

Here he again rose from his chair, which made it all the more puzzling why he had sat down in the first place. The Prince could not help noticing that Yevgeny Pavlovich was not best pleased about something; he was irritated and there was something hostile in his looks, which had not been the case previously.

"Incidentally, are you going to see the patient now?"

"Yes... it worries me that—"

"No need to worry about anything. He's probably good for another six weeks, and who knows, may even recover here. But the best thing for you to do would be to kick him out tomorrow."

"Perhaps I really provoked him... I should have said something. Perhaps in the end he thought I didn't believe he was going to shoot himself. What do you think, Yevgeny Pavlovich?"

"Not at all. You're much too kind, you shouldn't worry about him so. I have heard people say, though I never witnessed it myself, that a man can deliberately shoot himself merely in order to be commended for it, or out of frustration that no such commendation would be forthcoming. What I can say is that I'd never have thought that such frank admission of lack of willpower was at all possible! All the same you should kick him out tomorrow."

"Do you think he will make a second attempt at his own life?"

"No, he won't. But be very careful of these Russian Lacenaires* of ours! I'll say it again, crime is a very convenient refuge for this obtuse, irascible nonentity, consumed by greed."

"Do you see a Lacenaire in him?"

"In essence yes, though the setting is different. You'll see if this gentleman isn't capable of massacring ten people in cold blood just for a 'joke' as he described it in his "Explanation". These words won't let me sleep in peace now."

"Perhaps you take it all too seriously."

"I sometimes wonder at you, Prince! Do you really not think that *now* he's capable of killing a dozen people?"

"I hesitate to answer this. It is all rather strange, but—"

"Well, please yourself, please yourself!" Yevgeny Pavlovich returned irritably to cut the conversation short. "Besides, you being so brave, take care you don't find yourself one of the dozen."

"It's unlikely he'll kill anyone," the Prince said, looking at Yevgeny Pavlovich thoughtfully.

Yevgeny Pavlovich guffawed violently.

"Goodbye, time I hit the road! Did you notice though that he bequeathed a copy of his confessions to Aglaya Ivanovna?"

"Yes, I did and… I'm thinking about it."

"So you should, especially if it comes to that dozen," Yevgeny Pavlovich said, laughed again, and left.

An hour later – it was by then gone three – the Prince went into the park. He tried to have a nap at home, but unsuccessfully because of strong palpitations of the heart. In the house everything had been brought under control and to an extent settled; the patient had fallen asleep, and the doctor, who had arrived on the scene, had declared that there was nothing particular to worry about. Lebedev, Kolya and Burdovsky went to sleep in the patient's room to keep watch in turn; consequently there were no grounds for anxiety.

But the Prince's disquiet rose by the minute. He roamed through the park, glancing around absent-mindedly, and stopped in surprise when he reached the square in front of the Voksal and saw the rows of empty seats and the raised orchestra platform before him. He stared, and for some reason the place struck him as awfully incongruous. He turned back and took the direct route he and the Yepanchins had followed to the Voksal yesterday; coming upon the green bench, where the rendezvous was to take place, he sat down and burst into a sudden loud fit of laughter, but he checked himself immediately with extreme indignation. His irritation persisted; he wanted to withdraw somewhere… He knew not where. In the tree overhead a small bird was singing, and he began to search for it in the foliage; suddenly the bird fluttered into the air and at that precise moment he remembered for some reason that mosquito in the warm ray of the sun, of which Ippolit wrote that it too knew its place and was a participant in the overall scheme of things, whereas he alone was an outcast. This thought, which had also astounded him earlier, returned to haunt him again. One long-forgotten memory suddenly stirred in him and came back to mind with exceptional clarity.

It was in Switzerland, in the first year of his course of treatment, indeed in the first months. At that time he was still plainly an idiot, he even had difficulty in speaking, and often could not understand what was expected of him. One bright, sunny day he strayed into the mountains, and wandered about for a long time, torn by a gnawing thought that eluded all his efforts to give it a specific form and shape. The sky was brilliant, down below was a lake, all around a horizon, luminous and endless. He watched it all for a long time and his suffering would not abate. He recalled now how he had stretched forth his arms into this bright, infinite vault of heaven and wept. He was tortured by the realization that he was a stranger to all this. What kind of a feast, what kind of an eternal magnificent celebration was that, a celebration he had been drawn to for a long time, always, since childhood, and in which he could never participate? Every morning the same bright sun rises; every morning there is a rainbow over the waterfall; every evening the snowy peak of the highest mountain there in the distance on heaven's very edge is bathed in purple iridescence; every tiny mosquito, which buzzes around him in the warm ray of the sun, is part of the glorious ensemble, knows its place, is sure of it and is unspeakably happy; every blade of grass grows and is happy. And all things have their appointed path, and all things can find their way along that path, they go with a song and they come with a song; he alone knows nought, understands nought, neither people, nor sounds; a stranger to all, an alien, a reject. Oh, of course, he could not have said these words then or given voice to his question; he had borne his suffering in mute silence at the time; but now it seemed to him that he had said all this back then after all, and in so many words, and the bit about the mosquito Ippolit had actually taken straight out of his mouth, tears and all. He was sure of that, and his heart for some reason beat all the faster at the thought.

He dropped off to sleep on the bench, but even as he dozed his alarm did not relinquish its hold. Just before sleep overcame him, he remembered that Ippolit would kill a dozen people, and he smiled at the absurdity of the thought. Everything around him was steeped in glorious, translucent silence, broken only by the rustle of the foliage, which appeared only to intensify the stillness and seclusion of the surroundings. He had a multitude of dreams, all of them disturbing, which caused him to shudder every time. Finally he was joined by a woman. He knew her to the point of suffering; he knew her by name, he could always identify her, but – curiously – her face now was unlike the one he'd always known, and he desperately did not want to admit it was the same woman. In this face there was so much anguish and terror that it seemed she was a vicious criminal who had just committed an atrocious crime. A tear was glistening on her pallid cheek; she beckoned him with her hand and put her finger to her lips as though bidding him to follow her in silence. His heart stood still; he would under no circumstances admit she had committed a crime, but he felt that something appalling was about to happen that would blight his whole life. She seemed to want to show him something – near by, in the park. He stood up to follow her, and suddenly right next to him he heard a peal of fresh, bright laughter; someone's hand found itself in his; he clutched it, squeezed it firmly and woke up. Aglaya was standing before him, laughing out loud.

8

S HE LAUGHED, but she was furious too.
   "He's fallen asleep! You were sleeping!" she exclaimed with indignant surprise.

"Is that you!" the Prince, who'd not yet come to, muttered as he recognized with surprise who it was. "Ah, yes! The rendezvous... I fell asleep here."

"I know."

"Did anyone try to wake me up? Was there no one else here apart from you? I thought there was... another woman here."

"Another woman here?!"

At last he came to completely.

"It was merely a dream," he said, thoughtfully. "Strange though, a dream like that at such a moment... Take a seat."

He took her by the hand and bade her sit down on the bench; he sat down next to her and was absorbed in his thoughts. Aglaya did not speak, but looked at him with intense concentration. He too kept glancing at her, but sometimes in a way which suggested he was not aware of her presence. She began to blush.

"Ah, yes!" the Prince said with a shudder. "Ippolit tried to shoot himself."

"When? At your place?" Aglaya asked, but with no great surprise. "Last night I seem to remember he was still alive? I wonder you could sleep after that!" she exclaimed, coming suddenly to life.

"But he's not dead, the pistol didn't go off."

At Aglaya's behest the Prince had to recount immediately, and in great detail, all that happened the night before. She could not wait to hear the whole story, and kept interrupting at every step and opportunity with questions, mostly irrelevant ones. Incidentally, she paid great attention to what Yevgeny Pavlovich had said, and even asked for it to be repeated a number of times.

"Well, that'll do, we must hurry," she concluded, after she had heard everything. "We've only an hour left here, till eight, because at eight I must definitely be back at the house before they realize I was here, and I've something important to discuss. I've lots to tell you. Only I've lost the thread because of you. As for Ippolit, I think it's typical of him that the pistol didn't go off, it goes with his character. But are you quite sure he wanted to commit suicide, and that it wasn't just play-acting?"

"Yes, quite sure."

"I suppose that is the likeliest explanation. So he actually wrote that you should bring me his 'Explanation'? Why haven't you then?"

"But he's not dead. I'll ask him."

"Make sure you do, and there's no need to ask. I'm sure he'll be pleased, because it's very likely he wanted to kill himself just so that I read his 'Explanation' afterwards. Please don't laugh, if you would be so kind, Lev Nikolayevich, because it may very well be the case."

"I'm not laughing, because I myself am quite sure that in part this may indeed be so."

"You are quite sure? Do you really think so?" Aglaya could hardly contain her surprise.

Her questions came thick and fast, but sometimes she appeared to lose the thread and her words would be left hanging in the air inconclusively. She was forever in a hurry to issue forewarnings; on the whole she was in a heightened state of elation, and though she looked about resolutely and almost defiantly, there was something vulnerable in her too. She wore a plain, completely unpretentious frock, which nevertheless became her extremely well. She sat on the edge of the bench, her face flushed frequently and every now and again she shifted about uneasily. She was most surprised when the Prince confirmed that Ippolit may have wanted to kill himself merely so she would read his 'Explanation'.

"Of course," the Prince went on, "he wanted not only that you but we all should congratulate him—"

"Congratulate?"

"Well... how shall I put it? It's not easy to explain. But he probably wanted everyone to surround him and tell him that they liked and respected him, and beg him to stay alive. It's possible you were uppermost in his mind, or he wouldn't have mentioned you at such a moment... though he may not have been aware that you were in his mind."

"You have lost me: to have something in mind and not be aware of it! But on second thoughts, you may have something there. Would you believe it, but I tried, maybe thirty times ever since I was thirteen, to poison myself, and write all about it in a letter to my parents, and I kept imagining myself lying in a coffin and everyone in tears around me, reproaching themselves for having been so cruel to me... You're smiling again," she added quickly, knitting her eyebrows. "So what do you think about when you're alone with your thoughts? Maybe you fancy yourself a field marshal who's just beaten Napoleon?"

"How did you guess? That's exactly it, especially before I fall asleep," the Prince returned with a laugh. "Only it's not Napoleon I battle with, it's the Austrians every time."

"I'm in no mood for jokes with you, Lev Nikolayevich. I shall see Ippolit myself. Would you kindly notify him of this. As for you, I'm rather disappointed, because it's not very nice to pry into the soul of another person as you're doing in the case of Ippolit. You lack finesse. All you care for is the truth – and that is hardly fair."

The Prince thought before he answered.

"I think you're being unfair," he said, "you must remember I don't find anything wrong in what he thought, because everyone is inclined to think that way. Besides, it may not even have been a question of thinking, but merely of wanting... he wanted to commune with people for the last time ever, he craved their love and respect. Surely that is very praiseworthy, only it all went awry. There was his illness and something else too! Moreover, some people have a knack of getting everything right, others haven't—"

"You are talking about yourself?" Aglaya cut in.

"Yes, I am," the Prince replied, betraying no awareness of the implicit sarcasm.

"Only I'd never have been able to fall asleep the way you did. You seem to do it at the drop of a hat – that's hardly gentlemanly."

"I hadn't slept the whole night last night, after which I wandered about and ended up at the concert stand—"

"What concert stand?"

"Where the orchestra was playing yesterday, after which I came here, sat down, started thinking and fell asleep."

"Aha, so that's how it was? This changes things in your favour, does it? And why did you have to go to the concert stand?"

"I've no idea, I just did—"

"All right, all right, later. You keep interrupting me, as though I cared where you went? What woman did you dream of?"

"It was... of... you saw her—"

"I understand, I understand very well. Are you very much in... In what shape did she come to you in your dream? No, don't, I'd rather not know," she declared in resolute ill humour. "Don't interrupt me..."

She paused for a little while as though to pluck up her courage or maybe to overcome her vexation.

"This is what I want and why I asked you to come. I want to propose that you be my friend. Why are you staring at me like that all of a sudden?" she added, almost with fury.

The Prince really was in fact eyeing her with great intensity, having noticed that she was again beginning to blush to the roots of her hair. The more she blushed, the more she seemed to be irritated with herself – all of which found its due reflection in her blazing eyes; she'd soon be ready to pick an argument. Being only too well aware of her own defensiveness and shyness, she was normally reluctant to enter into conversations and was more taciturn than her sisters, sometimes too much so. When, on the other hand, there was a need for her to speak up, especially if the matter was at all delicate, as now, she would begin on a very arrogant, not to say provocative, note. She could always tell in advance if she was going to blush.

"Perhaps you don't want to go along with my proposal," she said with a haughty look at the Prince.

"Oh no, but I do, only it was not at all necessary... that is, I wouldn't have thought it was necessary to make such a proposal," the Prince returned, in some embarrassment.

"And what did you imagine? Why would I have invited you here? What's on your mind? But I wouldn't be surprised if you took me for a little fool, like the rest of my family do!"

"I didn't know that! I... I don't think you're a fool."

"You don't? That's very clever of you. And I appreciate you saying so."

"The way I see it, you are actually very clever at times," the Prince continued. "Indeed you unexpectedly said a very clever thing just now. You said about my opinion of Ippolit, 'All you care for is the truth – and that is hardly fair.' I shall remember that and give it a thought."

Aglaya suddenly flushed with pleasure. All these changes occurred in her spontaneously and with great rapidity. The Prince was also immensely pleased and even burst out laughing as he looked at her.

"Listen carefully then," she began once more, "I waited for you for a long time to tell you everything, I waited ever since you wrote to me that time, and even earlier... You already heard one half from me. I regard you as the most honest and truthful man, the most honest and truthful man there ever was, and if people say that your mind... I mean that you're sometimes sick in the mind, then that is grossly unfair. I've held this opinion and have argued for it, because even though you are truly sick in the mind (please don't take this the wrong way, I'm speaking in terms of higher things now), your higher intelligence is better than anyone else's there, in fact it's altogether beyond their imagining, because let's face it, there are two kinds of intelligence – the higher and the lower. Well? Isn't that so?"

"Perhaps it is," the Prince said barely audibly; his heart was pounding at an enormous rate.

"I knew you'd understand me," she continued self-assuredly. "Prince S. and Yevgeny Pavlovich haven't got a clue about these two types of intelligence; neither does Alexandra, but imagine, *Maman* does."

"You've a lot in common with Lizaveta Prokofyevna."

"Are you sure? Really?" Aglaya said in surprise.

"Honestly, you have."

"Thank you," she said after a pause. "I'm very glad I've taken after *Maman*. I can see you have a high opinion of her, have you not?" she added, blissfully unaware of the naivety of her remark.

"Indeed I do, I do, and I'm ever so glad you interpreted it so directly."

"And I'm glad too, because I've noticed how people sometimes... laugh at her. But listen to the main thing I have to say. I thought a great deal about it and have at last settled on you. I don't want people to laugh at me at home, I don't want to be looked upon as a little fool. I don't want to be teased... I realized all this from the very start and turned down Yevgeny Pavlovich's offer flat, because I don't want constantly to be offered up in marriage! I want... I want to... well, I want to run away from home, and have chosen you to assist me."

"To run away from home!" the Prince exclaimed.

"Yes, yes, yes, to run away from home!" she exclaimed suddenly, flaring up in a real temper. "I don't want, I really don't want that people should constantly make me blush. I don't want to endure it in front of them, or in front of Prince S., or Yevgeny Pavlovich, or anybody at all, and that's why I've chosen you. I want to talk of everything, absolutely everything with you, even of what touches me most, when I'm ready for it. And you mustn't hide anything from me either. I want to have at least one person I can talk to about everything as I do with myself. They suddenly started going on about my pining for you and being in love. This was still before you arrived, and I didn't show them the letters. Everybody's talking about it now. I want to be brave and not be afraid of anything. I don't want to attend their parties, I want to do some good. I've long been planning to leave. I've been cooped up in the house with them these twenty years, and still they keep trying to marry me off. I was quite silly at fourteen, but I'd already been thinking of absconding. Now I have worked everything out and was just waiting for you to ask you what it's like abroad. I haven't seen a single Gothic cathedral, I want to go to Rome, I want to see all the scientific collections, I want to study in Paris. I've spent the whole of last year preparing myself and studying, and I've read a great many books. I read all the forbidden books. Alexandra and Adelaida can read any book they want, they're allowed to, but I'm not, I'm under surveillance. I don't want to quarrel with my sisters, but I have told my mother and father that I really want to change my social status. I've made up my mind to go into education, and I was counting on you because you said you loved children. Could we not both go in for education together, maybe not straight away, later say? The two of us could be a force for good. I don't want to be the privileged daughter of a general... Tell me, are you a very learned man?"

"Oh, not at all."

"That's a shame. I thought that... I wonder why I thought you were? Still, you must be prepared to guide me, because I have chosen you for it."

"It's absurd, Aglaya Ivanovna."

"I want to, I really want to run away from home!" she cried, and her eyes began to blaze yet again. "If you will refuse, I shall marry Gavrila Ardalionovich. I don't want people in the house to take me for a wayward woman and accuse me of goodness knows what."

"Are you in your right mind?" the Prince exclaimed and fairly leapt into the air. "Who accuses you? Of what?"

"Everyone, at home, Mother, sisters, Father, Prince S., even your horrid Kolya! And if they don't come out with it openly, it's what they're thinking about. I told them so to their faces, to Mother and to Father. *Maman* was ill all day. And the next day Alexandra and Papa told me that I don't know what I'm talking about, or the words I'm using. And I cut them short by saying that I know precisely what I'm talking about, to the last word, that I'm no longer a little girl, that I've already made a point of reading two of Paul de Kock's* novels two years ago to find out about everything. After *Maman* heard this, she nearly fainted."

The Prince was suddenly struck by a strange thought. He looked at Aglaya intently and smiled.

He could hardly believe that facing him was that same haughty girl who had once read out to him with such pride Gavrila Ardalionovich's letter. He could not understand how a touchy, fine beauty could at the same time be such a child, who even *now* was perhaps unaware of the true meaning of her words.

"Have you always lived at home, Aglaya Ivanovna?" he asked. "I mean, have you attended a school or an institute?"

"I've never attended anything. I've always stayed at home, cooped up as in a cage, and out of the cage straight into wedlock. Why are you smiling again? I can't help noticing that you too appear to be laughing at me and are taking their side," she added, knitting her eyebrows ominously. "Don't upset me... it's bad enough for me as it is... I'm convinced you came here in the full knowledge that I'm in love with you and have asked for a meeting."

"Yesterday I really was afraid that might be the case," the Prince let slip in all innocence (he was dying of embarrassment), "but this morning I'm convinced that you—"

"What!" Aglaya exclaimed and her lower lip suddenly began to tremble. "You were afraid that I... you had the effrontery to think that I... My God! You very likely suspected that I invited you here to entrap you, for us to be discovered and you to be made to marry me—"

"Aglaya Ivanovna, you should be ashamed of yourself! How could such a vile idea have entered your pure, innocent heart? I swear you don't believe a word you say and... and you haven't got a clue what you're saying."

Aglaya sat quite still, stubbornly staring into the ground as though frightened at what she had just said.

"I'm not ashamed one bit," she muttered. "How do you know my heart is innocent? How dare you write me a love letter then?"

"A love letter? My letter – a love letter? That letter was the most respectful one ever. It poured out of my heart at the most difficult period in my life! I thought of you then as a figure of light... I—"

"Well, all right, all right," she suddenly interrupted him in a totally altered tone of voice, this time repentant, almost fearful as she leant across to him, avoiding looking straight into his eyes, with a tentative attempt at touching his shoulder in order to further emphasize her plea to stop him being angry. "All right," she added, deeply embarrassed, "I know I said a very silly thing. It was merely... to put you to the test. Pretend I never said it. If I gave you offence, forgive me. Don't look me in the eyes. Please, turn away. You said it was a very vile idea. I said it deliberately to hurt you. Sometimes I myself am frightened at the things I want to say, and then I say them just the same. You said just now you'd written the letter at the most difficult period in your life... I know the period you have in mind," she said softly, looking at the ground again.

"Oh, if only you could know everything!"

"I know everything!" she exclaimed, full of a new anxiety. "You lived a whole month in the same lodgings with that despicable woman with whom you ran away..."

She no longer blushed, but grew pale as she spoke; at one time she suddenly leapt to her feet distractedly, but recovering herself almost immediately, she sat down again; her lip continued to tremble a while yet. Neither of them spoke for about a minute. The Prince was astonished at the force of her reaction and was at a loss what to attribute it to.

"I don't love you one little bit," she suddenly said cuttingly.

The Prince did not reply, and again a minute passed in silence.

"I love Gavrila Ardalionovich..." she rattled off, but barely audibly and inclining her head even more.

"That is not true," the Prince said, also practically in a whisper.

"You mean I'm lying? It is true. I gave him my word the day before yesterday, here on this bench."

The Prince was shocked and for a second did not know what to say.

"That is not true," he repeated decisively, "you've made it all up."

"That's not a very nice thing to say. If you must know, he has changed. He loves me more than life itself. He burned his hand in front of me just to prove he loves me more than life itself."

"He burned his hand?"

"Yes, his hand. I don't care if you don't believe me."

The Prince again said nothing. Aglaya was not joking; she was angry.

"Did he bring a candle along if it all happened here? Otherwise the mind boggles—"

"Yes... a candle. What's wrong with that?"

"A whole candle or a stump in a candlestick?"

"Well yes... no... half of one... a stump... a whole candle. What difference does it make, leave me alone!... If you want, he brought matches. He lit the candle and for half an hour he held his hand over the flame. Is that so hard to credit?"

"I saw him yesterday. There's nothing wrong with his fingers."

"Do you want to know why I lied just now?" she suddenly asked, turning towards the Prince in the most childlike manner and unable to control the laughter on her lips. "Because when one lies, and then inserts something out of the ordinary, something eccentric, well, something that occurs only seldom or even never, the lie then becomes much more plausible. I observed this. Only I bungled it, because I'm not good at it..."

Suddenly she frowned again as though she had thought of something.

"If I had," she said again, looking at him in all seriousness, even with a tinge of sadness, "if I had read about 'The Hapless Knight' to you, it was not only to... commend you, but at the same time to penalize you for your behaviour, and to show you that I know it all..."

"You're being very unfair towards me and towards that unfortunate woman on whom you were so hard just now, Aglaya."

"Because I know everything, everything, that's why I said what I said! I know that six months ago you publicly offered to marry her. Don't interrupt me, you can see I'm sticking to the point. After that she ran off with Rogozhin. Some time later you lived together in a village, or was it a town, and she left you for someone." (Aglaya blushed crimson.) "Then she again came back to Rogozhin, who loves her like... one possessed. After that, clever man that you are, you galloped here in all haste as soon as you discovered that she'd come back to St Petersburg. Last night you rushed to her defence, and just now you saw her in your dreams... You see, I know everything. You returned here for her sake, didn't you?"

"Yes, for hers," the Prince replied softly, his head inclined in calm and pensive reflection, unaware what a fiery glance Aglaya shot at him, "for hers, merely to find out... I don't believe in her happiness with Rogozhin, although... in a word, I don't know what I could have done for her or how I could have helped her, but I came."

He shuddered and looked at Aglaya who listened seething with hatred.

"If you came without knowing why, it means you love her very much," she said at last.

"No," the Prince replied, "no, I don't love her. Oh, if only you knew with what horror I recall the time I spent with her!"

His whole body shuddered at these words.

"Tell me everything," Aglaya said.

"There's nothing in this that wouldn't be fit for your ears. Why I particularly wanted to tell it all to you, and to you alone – I don't know. Perhaps because I really loved you very much. This unfortunate woman is deeply convinced that she's the most irredeemable, the most aberrant creature in all the world. Oh, don't shame her, don't cast stones at her. She has tortured herself enough by the thought of her own undeserved ignominy! And what is her fault? Oh my God! Oh, she shouts desolately at every convenient opportunity that she admits of no guilt, that she is the prey of other people, the prey of an evil debauchee. But whatever else she may say, rest assured she's the first who doesn't believe a word of it and believes with all her soul that she alone... is to blame. When I tried to dispel this fog, she'd reach such levels of suffering that my heart will never heal while I continue to recall that awful time. It was as though I had been stabbed through the heart. Do you know why she ran from me? Just so as to prove to me that she is so – fallen. But the worst of it is that she herself was perhaps unaware that it was only to me that she wanted to prove this, whereas she ran because she was inwardly compelled to commit a foul deed, so as to be able to say there and then, 'There I've committed a new outrage, therefore I'm a low-down creature!' Oh, perhaps you may not be able to understand this, Aglaya! Do you realize that in this continual awareness of ignominy, there lies some kind of terrible, unnatural enjoyment like an act of vengeance against someone. Sometimes I succeeded in making her believe that she was again surrounded by light, but she would immediately recant and heap bitter blame upon me that I was exalting myself over her (whereas it never entered my head to do so), and in the end when I proposed to her, she announced that she required no one's self-righteous sympathy, nor help, nor that anyone should 'elevate her to his own level'. You saw her last night – do you really believe that she is happy in that company, that it is her kind of society? You've no idea how intelligent and bright she is! I couldn't believe it myself sometimes!"

"So you read her such... sermons there too?"

"Oh no," the Prince continued deep in thought, not noticing the tone of the question. "I did not say anything for the most part. I often wanted to speak, but I really did not know what to say. Do you know, in some cases it's best not to say anything. Oh, I loved her. Oh, I loved her very much... but afterwards... afterwards... afterwards she guessed everything."

"What did she guess?"

"That I merely pitied her, and that I... no longer loved her."

"How do you know, maybe she really fell in love with that... landowner, she ran away with?"

"No, I know, she merely made fun of him."

"And she never made fun of you?"

"N-no. She mocked me out of sheer anger. Oh, she accused me of awful things at the time, in anger – and suffered as a result! But... later... oh, don't remind me of it!"

He buried his face in his hands.

"But do you realize she writes letters to me nearly every day?"

"So it is true!" the Prince exclaimed in alarm. "I heard that but still did not want to believe it."

"Who did you hear it from?" Aglaya asked and stiffened with fear.

"Rogozhin told me yesterday, only he was very vague about it."

"Yesterday? Yesterday morning? Yesterday when? Before or after the concert?"

"After. In the evening, gone eleven."

"Ah, well, if it was Rogozhin... But do you know what she writes about in her letters?"

"Nothing would surprise me. She is mad."

"Here are her letters." (Aglaya produced three letters from her pocket and threw them before the Prince.) "It's a whole week now since she's been entreating, imploring, trying to tempt me to marry you. She is... well yes, clever, even though she is out of her mind, and you are quite right she is much cleverer than me... she says she likes me, that every day she waits for an opportunity to see me, if only at a distance. She says you love me, that she knows it, and has done so for a long time, and that you have discussed all this with her. She wants you to be happy. She's confident I will make you happy... she gets so carried away... it's strange... I haven't shown the letters to anyone, I was waiting for you. Do you realize what all this means? Can you not guess?"

"It's her madness. A proof of her insanity," the Prince said, and his lips began to tremble.

"You're not going to cry, are you?"

"No, Aglaya, I'm not going to cry," the Prince said, and looked at her.

"What am I to do? What would you advise? Surely, I can't go on receiving such letters!"

"Oh, let her be, I implore you!" the Prince exclaimed. "Turn your back on this quagmire. I shall do everything in my power to stop her writing to you."

"If that's so, you're a man with no heart!" Aglaya exclaimed. "Can you really not see it's not me she's in love with, but you – she loves you and you alone! How is it you've been able to understand everything about her, but have failed to note this? Do you know... do you realize what these letters are about? It's jealousy! It's more than jealousy! She..."

do you really suppose she will marry Rogozhin, which is what she says in these letters? If we married, she'd kill herself the next day!"

The Prince shuddered; his heart froze. But he regarded Aglaya with surprise; he found it difficult to come to terms with the fact that she was no longer a child, but a mature woman.

"As God is my witness, Aglaya, I'd have sacrificed my life to give her peace of mind and make her happy, but... I cannot love her any more, and she knows it!"

"Then go ahead and sacrifice yourself, that would be just up your street! You, the grand philanthropist! And don't be so familiar with me! You did it once before!... You must, you're simply duty bound to give her a new lease of life, you must again take her away somewhere to soothe and mollify her heart. On top of which you love her!"

"I cannot sacrifice myself to such an extent, even though I had a mind to once and... may wish to still even now. But I know *for certain* that with me she is bound to perish, which is why I shall stay away from her. I'm supposed to see her today at seven. I don't think I'll go now. In her pride she'll never come to terms with my love for her – and we shall both perish! This is unnatural, but then everything is unnatural in this sorry business. You say she loves me, but is this really love? Can there still be any room for love after everything I've already had to endure? No, there's something else here, not love!"

"You have gone so pale!" Aglaya exclaimed, frightened.

"It's nothing. I've had little sleep. I feel weak, I... we really did speak about you then, Aglaya..."

"So it's true? You really could bring yourself to speak to her about me and... and how could you fall in love with me after seeing me only once?"

"I don't know how. In the state I was in then I dreamt, I fantasized perhaps of a new dawn. I have no idea how you came into my thoughts first. When I wrote to you at the time that I didn't know, that was the honest truth. It was merely a daydream brought on by the horrors of the occasion... I then found myself something to keep me busy. I wouldn't have come back here for ages—"

"But you came back for her, did you not?"

There was slight tremor in Aglaya's voice.

"Yes, for her."

There followed two minutes of gloomy silence. Aglaya got up.

"If you are telling me," she began in a faltering voice, "if you are telling me yourself that this... woman of yours... is insane, I have nothing to do with her insane fantasies... I am asking you, Lev Nikolayevich, to take these three letters and throw them at her from me! And should she," Aglaya suddenly raised her voice, "should she dare to write me another line, tell her I shall complain to father and she'll be taken to a house of correction..."

The Prince leapt to his feet, terrified at Aglaya's sudden rage; a kind of fog seemed to descend before his eyes.

"You can't feel that way... it is not true!" he muttered.

"But it is! It's the truth!" Aglaya cried, quite beside herself.

"What truth? What is true?" a frightened voice resounded near by.

Before them stood Lizaveta Prokofyevna.

"That I am getting married to Gavrila Ardalionovich! That I'm madly in love with Gavrila Ardalionovich and am eloping with him tomorrow!" Aglaya went into attack. "Have I made myself clear? Is your curiosity satisfied? Is this what you wanted to hear?"

And she ran off.

"No, my dear sir, I wouldn't go away now if I were you," Lizaveta Prokofyevna stopped the Prince in his tracks. "Be so kind as to come with me into the house and explain what this is all about... Another fine mess after a sleepless night..."

The Prince followed her into the house.

9

Lizaveta Prokofyevna stopped in the first room she entered; she could not proceed any further and slumped into a sofa totally exhausted, forgetting even to offer the Prince a seat. The room was rather spacious with a round table in the middle, a fireplace, lots of flowers on shelves by the windows and, opposite, a french window leading into the garden. Adelaida and Alexandra entered almost immediately, casting quizzical and puzzled glances at the Prince and their mother.

Usually the girls got up at about nine. Aglaya alone in the past two or three days fell into the habit of getting up somewhat earlier and of going into the garden for a stroll, but never at seven – rather at eight or even later. Lizaveta Prokofyevna, who really had had a sleepless night on account of various worries, got up at about eight, intending to meet Aglaya in the garden, but did not find her either there or in her bedroom. At this point her anxiety got the better of her and she woke her other daughters. The maidservant informed her that Aglaya Ivanovna had gone into the park shortly after six. The young ladies smiled at the novel prankishness of their romantically inclined younger sibling, and took the trouble to remind their mother that Aglaya might not take it in good part if she were to go looking for her in the park, and that in all probability she was already sitting book in hand on the green bench, which she had been talking about three days previously and over which she nearly fell out with Prince S., because the latter found nothing noteworthy in its precise location. On coming across the trysting couple and hearing her daughter's strange exclamations, Lizaveta Prokofyevna was for various reasons overcome with fear; but, having now brought the Prince into the house, she began to lose heart for having got involved. "Why on earth shouldn't Aglaya have met and talked to the Prince in the park, even if it had all been prearranged?" she asked herself.

"Don't imagine, my kind Prince," she finally resolved to break the ice, "that I brought you here for an inquisition... After what happened last night, my dear, I might not have been inclined even to see you in too much of a hurry..."

She hesitated briefly.

"All the same you'd be very interested to know how it was Aglaya Ivanovna and I ended up in the park together, wouldn't you?" the Prince completed her thought with equanimity.

"Well, even if I were, what of it?" Lizaveta Prokofyevna stood her ground defiantly. "I'm not afraid to call a spade a spade. I've no mind to offend anyone and never had—"

"With the deepest respect, there can be no question of offence. Your need to know is natural – you are her mother. Aglaya Ivanovna and I met at the green bench this morning at seven sharp as a result of an invitation of hers yesterday. She informed me in a note last night that she needed to speak to me on an important matter. We met and talked a whole hour of things concerning herself only. That's all."

"Of course, that's all, my dear sir, there can be no doubt, that's all," Lizaveta Prokofyevna retorted with dignity.

"Well done, Prince!" Aglaya said, coming into the room suddenly. "I thank you with all my heart for realizing that I'd be incapable of stooping to tell a lie. That's quite enough, *Maman*, or would you like to continue your interrogation?"

"You know well that so far I've had nothing to be ashamed of until now... though perhaps you might have been glad if I had," Lizaveta Prokofyevna replied reproachfully. "Good day, Prince, forgive me for troubling you. And I hope you will remain in no doubt as to my undying respect for you."

The Prince immediately bowed to mother and daughters and withdrew without saying a word. Alexandra and Adelaida smiled and exchanged whispers. Lizaveta Prokofyevna looked at them sternly.

"We just thought it was funny," Adelaida said, laughing, "the way the Prince bowed out. Normally he's like a sack of potatoes, and now he was quite the equal of... Yevgeny Pavlovich."

"Dignity and grace comes from the heart, not the dancing instructor," Lizaveta Prokofyevna remarked sententiously, and sailed past on her way upstairs without even a glance at Aglaya.

When the Prince reached his house he found Vera Lukyanovna and a maid on the terrace. They were sweeping and tidying up after the previous night's gathering.

"Thank God, we managed to finish before you returned!" Vera said, joyfully.

"Good morning. My head is spinning a little, I've not slept well. I wouldn't mind having a nap."

"Here on the terrace, like yesterday? Very well. I'll tell everybody not to disturb you. Father has gone out somewhere."

The maid left. Vera was about to follow her, but turned back and approached the Prince with an anxious air.

"Prince, take pity on this... on this poor soul, don't turn him out today!"

"Under no circumstances! He can stay as long as he likes."

"He's not going to do anything now, and... don't be too hard on him."

"Quite, why should I?"

"And... don't make fun of him! That's the most important thing of all."

"Not on your life!"

"It's silly of me, I know, to say this to a man like you," Vera said, blushing. "But even though you're tired," she added with a laugh, half-turning and heading for the exit, "you've such lovely eyes this minute... full of happiness."

"Happiness, are you sure?" the Prince asked, much encouraged and burst out laughing, joyfully.

But Vera, simple-hearted and artless, like a young boy, suddenly became very shy, blushed even deeper and, still laughing, left the room.

"What a... sweet girl..." the Prince thought to himself briefly and forgot about her immediately. He went to a corner of the terrace, where there was a chaise longue with a table before it, covered his face with his hands and sat for about ten minutes; suddenly he thrust his hand in his side pocket and produced three letters.

But the door opened again and Kolya entered. The Prince was very glad to have to put the letters back in his pocket and to have postponed reading them.

"Well, never a dull moment!" Kolya said, sitting down on the chaise longue and coming straight to the point as was his wont. "What do you think of Ippolit now? Has he come down in your estimation?"

"Why should he have... but, Kolya, I'm tired... Besides, it would be too painful to go all over it again... But how is he, anyway?"

"He's sleeping and will sleep for another couple of hours. I quite understand. You haven't slept at home, but have been wandering in the park... and what with all your worries... small wonder!"

"How do you know I was wandering in the park and hadn't been sleeping at home?"

"Vera told me just now. She tried to stop me, but I couldn't resist popping in just for a minute. I've been at his bedside these past two hours. Now it's Kostya Lebedev's turn. Burdovsky has gone. Go on then, go to sleep, Prince. Good night – or should I say, good day. Only, you know, I'm astonished!"

"Of course... all this—"

"No, Prince, no! I'm astonished by his 'Explanation'. Especially the bit where he talks about providence and the life to come. He makes a gi-gan-tic revelation there!"

The Prince looked at Kolya kindly, who of course had popped in raring to discuss the gi-gan-tic revelation.

"But the point is not just in the discovery, but in the circumstances under which it was made! Had it come from Voltaire, Rousseau, Proudhon, I'd have read it, but it wouldn't have astonished me quite to that extent. But, coming from a person who knows he's only got ten minutes left to live – it is magnificent! Surely it is the highest manifestation of the independence of personal dignity, it's equivalent to openly challenging... Yes, it's a gigantic feat of willpower! And after that to insist that he deliberately did not insert a cap – is undignified and absurd! But, you know, he told a lie yesterday, the cunning fox. I never helped him to pack any bag and didn't see any pistol. He did his own packing, and I was absolutely stunned when he suddenly brought me into it. Vera says you're letting him stay here. I swear he poses no danger, especially since we're all keeping an eye on him round the clock."

"And which one of you was there in the night?"

"I myself, Kostya Lebedev and Burdovsky. Keller stayed a while, but then went to sleep in Lebedev's room, because there was nowhere to lie down in our room. Ferdyshchenko also stayed with Lebedev, and left at seven. My father's always with Lebedev, but he has gone off too now... Lebedev may drop in to see you any time now. He was looking for you, I don't know why, and asked after you twice. Shall I let him in or not, if you're asleep? I'm off to sleep myself. Oh yes, there was another thing I wanted to tell you about. My old man really surprised me. Burdovsky woke me up shortly after six to begin my watch, or was it at six? I went out for just a minute, and suddenly I bumped into my old man, who was so drunk, he couldn't recognize me, he just stood there in front of me like a lamp-post. Then he suddenly went on the attack: 'How's the patient? I was on my way to visit the patient...' I put him in the picture, well with this, that and the other. 'That's all well and good,' he reckons, 'but I was on my way, and got up specially to warn you that one must be careful not to say everything in front of Mr Ferdyshchenko and... it behoves one to be circumspect.' Do you follow me, Prince?"

"Really? But then... what has it got to do with us?"

"Yes, no doubt precious little, we're no conspirators, which is why I was so surprised he was coming deliberately to wake me up in the night for this."

"Did you say Ferdyshchenko has left?"

"At seven o'clock. He popped in on his way while I was on my watch. He said he was going to spend the rest of the night at Wilkin's. There's an alcoholic hereabouts – goes by the name of Wilkin. Well, I'm off. Ah, if it isn't Lukyan Timofeyich?... The Prince wants to sleep, Lukyan Timofeyich. Some other time!"

"I'll only be a minute, my inestimable Prince, on a significant, to my way of looking, matter," Lebedev interposed in a strained, emotionally charged, muffled voice as he advanced into the room and delivered a low obeisance. He had only just returned, still holding his hat in his hands, and had not even called at home yet. His face wore a preoccupied aspect with an extraordinary awareness of his personal dignity. The Prince bade him take a seat.

"I believe you enquired twice after me, did you not? Perhaps you are still concerned by what happened yesterday—"

"You mean the upheaval caused by the youngster? Not at all, sir! Yesterday my thoughts were confused... but today I no longer propose to *contrecarrer* your instructions in any way whatsoever."

"*Contreca*... what did you say?"

"I said – *contrecarrer*. It's a French word, as are many that have entered the Russian language. But I shan't insist on it."

"What's the matter with you today, Lebedev?" the Prince asked with a smile. "Why are you so pompous and full of yourself, and talk as though you're reading from a sheet?"

"Nikolai Ardalionovich, do you mind!" Lebedev said in a pleading voice, turning to Kolya. "I've a communication to make to the Prince, which relates only..."

"Yes, of course, of course, it's none of my business! So long, Prince!" Kolya said and immediately left.

"I love the child for being so quick on the uptake," Lebedev said, following him with his eyes. "A nippy lad, even though he can be a bit of a handful. I've endured a terrible misfortune, my worthy Prince, last night or today at dawn... I'm still uncertain as to the exact time."

"What happened?"

"The loss of four hundred roubles from my side pocket, my worthy Prince. A pretty state of affairs!" Lebedev added with a wry smile.

"You lost four hundred roubles? That's a pity."

"Especially for a poor man who lives honestly by the sweat of his brow."

"Yes of course, of course. But how did it happen?"

"It was the demon wine. I turn to you as to providence, my worthy Prince. I collected a sum of four hundred roubles from a creditor last night at five o'clock and caught a train back here. I had my wallet in my pocket. After I took my uniform off and put my frockcoat on, I transferred the money to have it on me as I knew I'd have to pay it out later that same evening, which I'd promised I would... I was expecting an agent to call on me."

"By the way, Lukyan Timofeyich, is it true you advertise in papers that you lend out money against gold and silver articles?"

"Through an agent. My name appears nowhere, nor does my address. With only a meagre capital at my disposal and having an increasing family to support, you must agree that an honest profit margin..."

"Well yes, yes. I merely wanted to know for the sake of information. Pardon me, you were saying..."

"The agent failed to turn up. In the meantime the poor devil was brought in. I was already a little on the merry side, in a true postprandial condition. Then these visitors arrived, we all had a drink... of tea, and... to my undoing, my spirits rose. After which (it was already getting late) Keller arrived to announce your birthday and what had been decided apropos the serving of champagne, whereupon I, my dear and worthy Prince, in my kind-heartedness (with which, as you may have had occasion to observe, I have been richly endowed), in my kind-heartedness – I would not go so far as to say munificence, but, you must allow, gentlemanliness too – I decided to exchange my out-at-elbows domestic item of clothing for the official vestment which I'd doffed on arrival, and having duly carried this out, you, Prince would no doubt would have observed that I was in uniform throughout the evening. In swapping the items of clothing, I forgot the wallet in the frockcoat... Truly it has been said, when the gods want to punish, they deprive you of your sanity. And only this morning, it was already half-past seven, on waking up, I leapt out of bed like a madman, and the first thing I did was to reach for the coat – the pocket was empty! The wallet was gone."

"Oh, that is unfortunate!"

"Yes, really unfortunate. And it is right tactful of you to have chosen the most appropriate word for it," Lebedev observed not without mischievousness.

"Still, I have to say, this is a serious matter—" the Prince remarked, perturbed and with a thoughtful mien.

"Serious indeed! And that's another aptly chosen word on your part, Prince, to describe—"

"Oh, that'll do, Lukyan Timofeyich, what's there to choose? We shouldn't dwell on words... Have you considered that in your inebriated state you might have dropped it from the pocket?"

"I might. Everything is possible in an inebriated state as you correctly observe, my esteemed Prince! But please note, if I'd dropped the wallet while exchanging one article of clothing for another, the said object should have been lying there on the floor. Where is it though?"

"Perhaps you put it in a drawer somewhere?"

"I looked everywhere, I turned everything upside down, the more so since I never hid it anywhere nor did I pull any drawers out; I remember it very distinctly."

"Have you looked in that little cabinet of yours?"

"That's the first thing I did, and several times at that... And anyway, why should I have put it in the little cabinet, my inestimable Prince?"

"I have to admit, Lebedev, this worries me. It stands to reason, someone must have found it on the floor!"

"Or purloined it from the pocket! Two alternatives."

"I'm seriously worried about this, because who could have done it?... That is the question!"

"Without a shadow of a doubt that is the question. You have a surprising knack of choosing the right words and drawing the right conclusions, my most illustrious Prince."

"Really, Lukyan Timofeyich, enough of your sarcasms, what—"

"Sarcasms!" Lebedev exploded, throwing up his hands.

"Steady now, steady, I'm not blaming you. There's something else behind all this... I fear for people. Whom do you suspect?"

"That is a very difficult and... complicated question! I cannot suspect the maidservant, she had been in the kitchen all the time. My children neither..."

"That goes without saying."

"Which only leaves one of the visitors."

"But is that likely?"

"That is totally and absolutely unlikely, and yet it cannot inevitably be otherwise. I would agree though, nay I'm convinced that if it were

cf Sherlock Holmes' saying

464

a question of theft, it couldn't have been perpetrated in the evening, when everybody was present, but during the night or even nearer the morning by one of those who were staying overnight."

"Oh my God!"

"Burdovsky and Nikolai Ardalionovich are out, naturally. Neither entered my room."

"That's clear, but even if they had entered! Who stayed overnight?"

"If you count me, there were four of us, in two adjoining rooms – I, the General, Keller and Mr Ferdyshchenko. Thus it must have been one of us four!"

"One of three! But which one?"

"I included myself for fairness's sake and to maintain a sense of proportion. But you must agree, Prince, I could not have stolen from myself, although such things have been known to happen in this world—"

"Lebedev, this is getting boring!" the Prince exclaimed impatiently. "Come to the point, and don't go on about it!"

"We are left with three in that case. First, there was Mr Keller, a highly versatile individual, fond of the bottle and in some respects a liberal, that is with regard to out-of-pocket matters. For the rest, he is more of the chivalrous, knightly than the liberal turn of mind. At first he stayed in the patient's room, and moved into ours only in the night under the pretext it was too hard sleeping on the bare floor."

"Do you suspect him?"

"I did. After I had woken up with a start in the morning gone seven and had slapped my forehead with the flat of my hand, I roused the General immediately, who was sleeping the sleep of the innocent. Having noted Ferdyshchenko's strange disappearance, which in itself roused our suspicions, we both decided to search Keller who was lying there like… like… almost like a log. We searched him all over. There wasn't a copeck in his pockets, nor a single pocket without a hole in it. The other items included a blue check cotton handkerchief, of which the less said the better; a love letter from a housemaid demanding money with threats, and scraps of the notorious article. The General pronounced him innocent. For total assurance we woke him up in person, which was no easy matter. It took him some time to realize what was going on. He stared at us open-mouthed, bleary-eyed, uncomprehending, innocent-looking, not to say stupid. No, it wasn't him!"

"I'm so glad!" the Prince breathed a sigh of relief. "I really was afraid for him!"

"You were afraid? That means you already had grounds for it?" Lebedev said, narrowing his eyes.

"Oh, not at all," the Prince returned, flinching. "It was very stupid of me to say that I was afraid. Do me a favour, Lebedev, don't tell anyone—"

"Prince, Prince! Your words are locked in my heart... in the depths of my heart! Entombed!..." Lebedev said with elation, pressing his hat to his heart.

"All right, all right!... That means, it was Ferdyshchenko! I mean to say, you suspect Ferdyshchenko, is that right?"

"Who else?" Lebedev said softly, looking hard at the Prince.

"Quite, quite... who else?... But then again, what is the evidence?"

"There is evidence. First, his disappearance at seven or just gone seven in the morning."

"I know, Kolya told me that he had popped into his room to say he was going to spend the rest of the night at... I forget his name, at his friend's."

"The name is Wilkin. So, Nikolai Ardalionovich mentioned it to you already?"

"He did not say anything about the theft."

"He knows nothing of it, because so far I've kept the matter secret. And so, he sets off for Wilkin's. What's so unusual about that – one drunk going off to see another, even if it be in the small hours and for no apparent reason? But this is where we start picking up clues. Before he goes, he leaves an address... Now tell me, Prince, why would he deliberately go to Nikolai Ardalionovich, making a detour, and tell him, 'I'm going to Wilkin's to spend the rest of the night there.' Who'd need to know that he was leaving, to go to see Wilkin of all people? Why announce it? No, this is a ruse, a thief's ruse! It means, 'There you are, folks, I'm deliberately not hiding any clues, what sort of a thief am I after that? Would a thief have announced where he was going?' This is a careful attempt to divert suspicion, to rub out the traces in the sand, as it were... Do you follow me, my highly esteemed Prince?"

"I do, indeed I do, but you realize, don't you, that is not enough?"

"The second piece of evidence is that the clue was false, the address was incorrect. An hour later, that is at eight o'clock, I was already

knocking at Wilkin's door. He lives on Pyataya Street, and I happen
to know him. No sign whatever of Ferdyshchenko. Even though I
managed to extract from the housemaid – deaf as a doornail – that
someone really had been knocking at the door, and rather violently
at that, such that the doorbell cord had snapped. But the maid hadn't
opened, unwilling to disturb Mr Wilkin, or perhaps not wishing to get
out of bed herself. These things happen."

"Is that all the evidence you have? It's not enough."

"Prince, but whom else to suspect? Think!" Lebedev finished on a
pleading note, and a faintly mocking smile flitted across his features.

"You know you should check all your rooms and drawers once
again!" the Prince said after a pause, full of concern.

"Indeed I already have!" Lebedev said with an even greater emotional
emphasis.

"Hm!... And why on earth did you have to take that frockcoat of
yours off?" the Prince exclaimed, bringing his hand down upon the
table in annoyance.

"This is a question fit for a music-hall comedy. But my most high-
minded Prince! You seem to take my misfortune all too much to heart!
I'm not worthy of it. That is, I on my own am not worthy, because
you are commiserating for the felon too... for the unworthy Mr
Ferdyshchenko, are you not?"

"Well, yes, yes, you really have caused me a headache," the Prince
interjected abstractedly and moodily. "And so, what do you propose to
do... if you are so sure it was Ferdyshchenko?"

"Prince, my most esteemed Prince, who else could it have been?"
Lebedev pressed his point home with mounting weak-kneed emotional
emphasis. "The very absence, nay the impossibility of naming any
other suspect, saving Mr Ferdyshchenko, is in itself, so to speak,
incriminating testimony against Mr Ferdyshchenko, who thus stands
condemned on three counts! I repeat, who else? Surely, you wouldn't
expect me to point an accusatory finger at Burdovsky, he-he-he?"

"You're talking nonsense!"

"Or the General, if you please, he-he-he?"

"What rubbish!" the Prince said in a temper, shifting uneasily in his
seat.

"You can say that again! He-he-he! Funny man, I mean that General
of ours! There we were, the two of us in hot pursuit heading for Wilkin's

place... and please note, the General was awfully astonished when he
realized I'd gone to wake him first on noticing the loss, to the extent that
everything about him changed, including his looks, which went from
pale one second to bright red the next, and finally he simply burst out
with indignation, righteous and violent, that came as quite a surprise
to me. A gentleman through and through! His tendency to tell untruths
is legendary – he suffers from that weakness, true, but he is a man of
the finest sentiments with a wealth of spiritual accomplishments, who
exudes total trust by virtue of his innocence. I've already had occasion
to draw your attention, my inestimable Prince, to the fact that I not only
have a weak spot for him, but that I hold him very dear indeed. And the
way he suddenly turned to me in the middle of the street, unbuttoned
his frockcoat, uncovered his upper body – 'Search me!' he says, 'you
frisked Keller, why don't you frisk me? It's only fair that you should!' His
hands and feet shook, his cheeks were drained of colour, stony faced.
I laughed and said, 'Look here, General,' I said to him, 'if anyone else
had said that to me about you, I'd have decapitated myself on the spot
and with these same hands have placed my head on a salver and offered
it to all the doubting Thomases, "Behold this head," I'd have said. "It
is with this head of mine that I vouch for him, and not just head alone,
but I'd leap into the fire too." That is the sort of undertaking I'm ready
to perform for you!' Here he hugged me, right there in the middle of the
street, tears stood out in his eyes, he held me so tight, I nearly coughed
to death when he let go. 'You,' he reckons, 'are my one and only friend,
surrounded as I am by my misfortunes!' A soulful person if ever there
was one! Well, in passing he recounted an amusing story from early
youth when he was supposed to have been suspected of having stolen
five hundred thousand roubles, but that the very next day he had rushed
into the flames of a burning house and had brought out the Count who
had raised the suspicions against him as well as Nina Alexandrovna,
then not yet espoused to him, and that a day later the money box with
the missing sum was found in the burned-out ruins. It was a metal job
made in England with a cleverly concealed locking mechanism that had
fallen in between the cracks in the floor, and had only come to light in
consequence of the fire. A complete pack of lies, if you ask me. But
when he mentioned Nina Alexandrovna, he truly began to whimper. A
lady of the highest integrity is the long-suffering Nina Alexandrovna,
though I am in her bad books."

"Are you not acquainted?"

"Hardly at all, but I wish from the bottom of my heart that I were, if only to exonerate myself before her. Nina Alexandrovna has it in for me, that I'm allegedly corrupting her spouse with alcohol. But not only do I not corrupt him but I keep him on the straight and narrow. I may well have kept him from falling into the worst company possible. Besides, he is my friend and, you might as well know, henceforth I shall not quit his side however briefly – where he goes, I go, because it is only by kindness he can be won over. He's stopped seeing his lady friend altogether now, although deep down he still pines for her, sometimes to the point of groaning – especially of a morning while he's getting up and pulling his boots on. Why then of all times, I wouldn't know. His trouble is he has no money, and to show up at her place without money is quite out of the question. He hasn't been asking for money from you, my most esteemed Prince, has he?"

"No, he hasn't."

"Too embarrassed. He had a mind to, you know, he even said as much to me: he wanted to trouble you, but he can't bring himself to do so, especially as you had helped him out recently, and on top of everything he knows you won't. He poured his heart out to me as to a friend."

"And do you give him money?"

"Prince! My most esteemed Prince! Not just money, but for this man I'm even ready to lay down... no, in all honesty, I mustn't exaggerate – not life, but, I'd gladly as it were put up with a fever, a nasty boil or, if it came to it, a bad cough, that is provided he was right up against it of course, for I tell you this, I regard him as a great, but fallen man! So, it's not just a question of money!"

"I take it then you do give him money, is that right?"

"N-no, I gave him no money, and he knows perfectly well I shan't, but this is only in order to sustain and reform him. Now he's raring to go to St Petersburg with me. As you know, I'm going to St Petersburg merely to get hold of Mr Ferdyshchenko while the trail is still hot, because I know for sure he's there already. My General just can't keep still, but I suspect that once in St Petersburg he'll immediately slope off to his lady friend. Actually, I've a mind to let him go free deliberately as we had already agreed between us to split up immediately on arrival to make it easier to catch out Mr Ferdyshchenko. I shall accordingly let him go, and then suddenly descend on him out of the blue at his lady friend's, putting him to shame, family man that he is, come to that – man that he is."

"Only don't cause any trouble, Lebedev, for goodness' sake, don't," the Prince said in a low but highly charged voice.

"Have no fear, it will only be to shame him and to see his face – for a great deal may be deduced from a person's face, my much esteemed Prince, especially in someone like him! Oh, Prince! Great though my own misfortune is, but I cannot even at this stage not think of reforming him morally. I have an enormous favour to ask of you, my esteemed Prince, and I confess it is for this reason that I have in truth come to see you. You are already acquainted with that house and have even resided there, so if you would, most noble Prince, agree to assist me solely for the General's sake and for his happiness..."

Lebedev even folded his hands as though in supplication.

"What do you mean? How can I possibly help you? Rest assured that I am very anxious to put myself in your position, Lebedev."

"It is for this reason alone that I have come to you! There may be a way of influencing him through Nina Alexandrovna, by keeping, as it were, a constant eye on His Excellency from within the bosom of his own family. Unfortunately I myself am not acquainted... besides, we have Nikolai Ardalionovich with us, who admires you so, as it were, from the bottom of his youthful heart, who could very possibly be of assistance—"

"N-no... To involve Nina Alexandrovna in matter!... God forbid! And Kolya too... On top of that, perhaps I'm still not at all sure I understand what you are driving at, Lebedev."

"Well, it's all pretty straightforward really!" Lebedev remarked, fairly bouncing into the air off his chair. "Tenderness and compassion – that is the only fit medicine for our patient. You will allow me, Prince, to refer to him as patient, won't you?"

"That actually shows your discretion and intelligence."

"For clarity, I shall illustrate by way of an example taken from real life. You see, this is the sort of man he is – he has a weakness for this widow, whom he cannot call upon unless he brings some money with him, and at whose place I intend to surprise him for his own good. But let's suppose it was not just the Captain's widow, let's suppose he were to commit a real crime, well, some unspeakable offence or other (that he is quite incapable of, really); even then, I tell you, there's nothing one couldn't get him to do by treating him with kindness, for he is the most sensitive soul ever! Believe you me, before five days had passed, he'd have made a clean breast of it, he'd have collapsed in tears and confessed to everything – especially if one were to tackle the matter smartly and discreetly under the family's and your own supervision by keeping track of all his comings and goings, so to speak... Oh most noble Prince!" Lebedev called out, jumping to his feet almost in a state of exultation. "Don't get me wrong, I'm not insisting that it was him, definitely... I'd be willing to shed all my blood for him if need be now, on the spot, inasmuch as you must agree that intemperance, and drunkenness, and the Captain's widow, and all that sort of thing taken together can have the most devastating consequences."

"Of course I am always ready to lend support to such aspirations," the Prince said, getting up, "only I have to admit, Lebedev, this business has upset me terribly. Tell me, do you still... in a word, you said yourself you suspected Mr Ferdyshchenko, did you not?"

"Who else is there? Who else, my most sincere Prince?" Lebedev entreated, again folding his hands pleadingly and smiling uneasily.

The Prince frowned.

"You see, Lukyan Timofeyich, a mistake here could have the most devastating consequences. This Ferdyshchenko... I would not like to speak ill of him... but this Ferdyshchenko... in a sense, who knows, perhaps it was him!... What I meant to say was that perhaps he really was more capable of such a thing than... someone else."

Lebedev narrowed his eyes and pricked up his ears.

"You see," the Prince went on, knitting his brows ever more and becoming less and less fluent as he paced up and down the room terrace, trying to avoid eye contact with Lebedev, "I was given to understand... I was told that Mr Ferdyshchenko, on top of everything else, is a man one has to be wary of and that one ought to be careful what one says... in his presence, do you understand? My point is that perhaps he really was more likely than someone else... I hope I have made myself clear? That's where the root of the problem lies, do you understand?"

"And who told you this about Mr Ferdyshchenko?" Lebedev demanded to know eagerly.

"I heard it whispered. Personally, I do not give it much credence, I have to say... I'm dreadfully sorry I had to mention it. I assure you I personally do not believe it… it's bound to be just idle talk… Ugh, how silly of me!"

"You see, Prince," Lebedev said, twitching all over, "it is important, it is most important to be precise, not as regards Mr Ferdyshchenko, but the manner by which the information reached you." (Lebedev kept running up and down after the Prince as he spoke, trying to keep in step with him.) "Listen, Prince, to what I have to say now. When the General and I were making our way to Wilkin's, which was after he had told his story about the fire, and was of course bursting with indignation, he began to make the same insinuations regarding Mr Ferdyshchenko, but so ineptly and clumsily, that I just couldn't help asking him some questions, and as a result it became perfectly clear to me that the whole thing was nothing more than a figment of His Excellency's own imagination… testifying in the event to the generosity of his nature. For even if he tells a lie, it is out of the kindness of his heart. But now tell me this – if he had told a lie, and I'm sure he had, so how did you too hear of it? Try to understand, Prince, it was but a momentary flight of fancy for him – so who then could have communicated it to you? This is important, this is… very important and… as it were—"

"It was Kolya who told me just now and he in turn heard it from his father who had got up to go somewhere, and the two met in the hall at six, or just after."

And the Prince recounted to him everything in detail.

"Well, that's what I call a clue," Lebedev said, rubbing his hands and smiling inwardly, "that's exactly what I thought! It means His Excellency interrupted his sleep of innocence purposefully after five in the morning to awaken his favourite son and warn him of the grave danger of Mr Ferdyshchenko's proximity! What danger is there then in Mr Ferdyshchenko after this, and how remarkable is His Excellency's parental concern, he-he-he!…"

"Listen, Lebedev," the Prince said, highly embarrassed, "listen, don't do anything rash! Don't cause any trouble! I ask you, Lebedev, I implore you… In which case I shall cooperate, but no one must know, no one!"

"Rest assured, my most magnanimous, my most open-hearted, my most noble Prince," Lebedev exclaimed enthusiastically, "rest assured it will all die a death in this well-intentioned heart of mine! Let us proceed softly then, hand in hand! I'd gladly lay down my life… Look

472

here, illustrious Prince, I'm a low creature in spirit and soul, but ask any scoundrel you wish, never mind some villain, whom is it better to do business with – such a villain as he, or the noblest of men, such as you are, my ever-honest Prince? He will reply – with the noblest of men. And therein will virtue's triumph lie! Goodbye, my most esteemed Prince! Let us therefore proceed... softly, and... in unison."

10

A T LAST THE PRINCE REALIZED why a chill ran down his spine every time he touched those three letters, and why he put off reading them till the very evening. In the morning, when, still lacking the courage to open any of the envelopes, he had nodded off in his chaise longue, he was again visited by his former "criminal" in another disturbing dream. She again regarded him through glistening tears on her long eyelashes, she again beckoned him to follow her, and again he woke, as previously, trying desperately hard to recall her features. He'd have liked to have gone over to *her* immediately, but he could not; at last, almost in desperation, he grabbed the letters and began to read.

These letters also resembled a dream. Sometimes there are strange, impossible and unnatural dreams. On waking, you recollect them in all clarity, marvelling at a strange fact. First, you remember that your powers of reason had never left you during the whole of the dream sequence. You will even recall that in the interminably long period when, surrounded by felons who had tried to outwit you, outsmart you and treated you as a friend – while at the same time keeping their weapons at the ready and merely waiting for some sign – you had dealt with all contingencies extremely cleverly and logically. You will finally recollect how craftily you had deceived them and hid from them; then it would hit you that they'd known of your ruse all along, that it had been only a pretence on their part, and that they'd known where you had been hiding too; but later you had outwitted and outsmarted them again, all of which you would remember distinctly. But why could your mind have simultaneously tolerated such obvious absurdities and incongruities? Your dream was, incidentally, filled to capacity with these. One of your killers had, for instance, turned before your very eyes into a woman, and the woman, into a sly, hideous dwarf – and you had accepted it all as an incontrovertible fact, without even the slightest attempt at questioning, and this particularly at a time when, by contrast, your mind was at the peak of alertness and power, and functioned with extraordinary, cunning, perception and logic. Why too, having shaken off your sleep completely and finding yourself squarely back in reality, do you feel nearly every time, sometimes with an uncommon intensity of perception, that in coming out of your slumber, there's a nagging sense of leaving behind something that's deeply unresolved for you personally? You smile at the ineptness of your dream and you sense at the same time that in the intertwining of these ineptitudes there is something there after all, something meaningful which is firmly rooted in reality, and which is part and parcel of your daily life, something which has existed and will continue to exist for ever in the depths of your heart. Your dream appears to have communicated something new to you, something prophetic, something you've been waiting for. You are in awe at the experience, perceiving it as either joyful or arduous, but having no clue as to what it entails or what you are meant to have learnt by it – it all being as much beyond your powers of comprehension as capacity for recollection.

It was very nearly so after the perusal of the letters. But even before he unfolded them, he felt that their existence, indeed the very possibility of their existence, was akin to a nightmare. How could she have dared to write to Aglaya? he kept asking himself as he wandered alone in the evening (sometimes without any clear idea of where he was going). How could she have broached *this matter*, and how could such a crazy idea have been born in her mind? But this idea had already been brought into execution, and the most surprising thing of all was that while he read the letters, he himself was partly convinced of the feasibility of the idea, indeed, of its justification. Yes, of course, it was a dream, a nightmare and an absurdity; but at the same time there was something painfully real there and agonizingly fair, which validated the dream as well as the nightmare and the attendant absurdities. For several hours at a stretch he appeared to be obsessed with what he had read; time and again he kept repeating isolated excerpts, dwelt on them, pondered on them. Sometimes he even wanted to say to himself that he'd anticipated and predicted it all beforehand; he even fancied he'd read it all before, sometime long ago, and everything he had longed for since then, everything that had caused him anguish, that had tormented him and inspired fear in him – all that was contained in these letters.

"After you've unfolded this letter," thus began her first missive, "you will first glance at the signature. The signature will tell you all and clarify all, consequently there is no need for me to justify myself or offer explanations. Were I in any way your equal, you might have had a cause to be offended by such effrontery; but who am I and who are you? We two are polar opposites, and I'm so much your inferior that I can't possibly offend you, even if I wished to."

In another place she went on to say:

"Do not look upon my words as the feverish outpourings of a diseased brain, but for me you are – perfection! I saw you, I see you every day. I am not judging you; it is not by reasoning I've come to believe that you are perfection; it is simply an act of faith. But I am also guilty of a sin – I love you. You see, one cannot love perfection; perfection may only be regarded as perfection, is that not so? All the same, I am in love with you. It is true that love makes people equal, but do not worry, I am not putting myself on the same level as you, even in my wildest dreams. I have written 'do not worry', as though you would... If it were possible, I'd have kissed the ground you stand on. Oh, I do not aspire to be your equal... Look at the signature, quick, look at the signature!"

"I notice, however," she wrote in another letter, "that I am bringing him and you together without ever having asked you whether you love him. He has fallen in love with you at first sight. He used to talk of you as of 'radiance' – I am quoting him, I heard it myself. But quite apart from words, it has always been patently clear to me that you represent radiance for him. I lived a whole month next to him, and in the event it became clear to me that you too love him; you and he are one to me."

"What am I to make of it?" she wrote in another part of the same letter. "I walked by you yesterday, and you seemed to blush. That's impossible, I must have imagined it. If one were to take you into the vilest den of iniquity and show you vice at its most blatant, you still ought not blush; you ought not under any circumstances take offence at a transgression. You may detest all who are mean and low, but not out of personal resentment – only for the hurt they cause others. As for you, no one can hurt you. You know, I think, you ought even to love me. You are for me, what I am for him: a radiant spirit; an angel is incapable of hating, is incapable of not loving. Can one love all, all people, all one's fellow creatures? – I often ask myself this question. Of course not! It would in fact be unnatural. Abstract love for mankind almost always boils down to love of one's self. But this is not given to us, whereas you are different: how could you not love at least someone when you cannot compare yourself to anyone and when you are above all offence, above all personal resentment? You alone are capable of love without egoism, you alone can love not for your own sake, but for the sake of him whom you love. Oh, what a bitter pill it would be if I found that you felt embarrassed or angry because of me! That would be fatal for you. You'd immediately become my equal...

"Yesterday, having met you, I came home and thought of a picture. Artists always paint Christ according to biblical traditions. I'd have done it differently. I'd have depicted Him on his own – let's face it, His disciples sometimes did leave Him to His own devices. I'd have left only a small child with Him. The child would have been playing next to Him; perhaps would have told Him something in his childlike manner. Christ would have listened, but then paused to think, His hand involuntarily, absent-mindedly resting on the child's fair head. He is looking into the distance, at the horizon; a monumental thought, encompassing the whole world, is writ in His gaze; his face is sad. The child has fallen silent; his elbows are propped up on his knees, his cheek resting on the flat of his hand, looking up at Him, pensively as children are wont to. The sun is setting... That's my picture! You are innocent, and in your innocence is the whole of your perfection. Oh, do remember this, if nothing else! Why should you concern yourself with my passion for you? You are mine already, I shall be with you all my life... I shall soon die."

In her last letter she wrote:

"For God's sake, do not think anything of me: do not imagine either that I am demeaning myself writing to you like this, or that I am one of those people who find it pleasant to debase themselves, be it even out of a sense of pride. No, I have remedies of my own, but it would be difficult for me to explain this to you. I find it difficult to admit this fully even to myself, and this despite its being a source of anguish to me. But I know I cannot demean myself even in a fit of arrogance. And self-abasement out of the purity of the heart is not my way. Hence, I am in no way abasing myself.

"Why do I want to bring you two together – for your or my sake? Of course for mine; for me it would be the perfect solution as I told myself long ago... I heard your sister Adelaida say about my portrait that with such beauty one could turn the world upside down. But I have turned away from the world. You may find this funny coming from me whom you are used to seeing adorned with diamonds and lace in the company of drunkards and scoundrels! Pay no attention to this, I've almost ceased to exist, and I know it; God only knows what is left in me now that my real self is gone. I read this every day in a pair of fearsome eyes which never let me out of their sight even when they are away from me. These eyes are now *inscrutable* (they are always inscrutable), but I know their secret. His house is bleak and dreary, and it harbours a secret. I am convinced he has a razor wound with a silk cord hidden in one of his drawers, like that Moscow murderer,* who also lived with his mother in the same house and had tied a silk cord round the handle the easier to slit someone's throat. All the time when I was in their house it seemed to me that somewhere under the floorboards there was a corpse, since his father's time perhaps, covered with an oilcloth, like the one in Moscow, dotted round with jars of Zhdanov's solution.* I could even show you in which corner. He never says a word; but I know he loves me so much that he can no longer help hating me. Your wedding and our wedding are to take place together. That's what the two of us have decided. I have no secrets from him. I could kill him out of fear... But he's going to kill me first... He burst out laughing when he saw me writing and said I was out of my mind; he knew I was writing to you."

And there was much else in the same mad vein in the letters. One of them, the second, was on two sheets of large-size paper, covered in close writing.

At last the Prince left the dark park where, like yesterday, he spent a long time wandering about. The bright, translucent night struck him as being brighter than usual. "Is it really that early?" he thought to himself. (He had forgotten to take his watch with him.) He fancied he heard strains of music in the distance. "In the Voksal no doubt," he thought to himself again. "Of course they stayed away from it today." As he reflected on this, he realized he was standing right in front of their dacha; somehow he knew he'd end up there, and with bated breath ascended the steps to the terrace. No one greeted him, the terrace was empty. He paused a while and then opened the door into the sitting room. "This door has always stood open before," the recollection flashed through his mind, but the sitting room was empty too; it was almost dark. He stood in the middle of the room, undecided. Suddenly the door opened and Alexandra walked in holding a candle. On catching sight of the Prince, she stopped in astonishment and regarded him quizzically. Evidently she was merely passing from one room to another, not expecting to find anyone there.

"How do you come to be here?" she asked finally.

"I... dropped in—"

"*Maman* is not quite well, neither is Aglaya. Adelaida is about to go to bed and I too. We have been at home on our own the whole evening. Papa and Prince S. have gone to St Petersburg."

"I came... I came to see you all... now—"

"Do you realize what the time is?"

"N-no—"

"Half-past twelve. We always go to bed at one."

"Oh, I thought it was... half-past nine."

"Never mind!" she said, and burst out laughing. "But why didn't you come earlier? We may have been expecting you, you never know."

"I... I thought—" he mumbled as he withdrew.

"Goodbye! I'm going to make everybody laugh tomorrow."

He took the road skirting the park to his dacha. His heart was pounding, his thoughts were confused, and everything around him was as in a dream. And suddenly, just as previously when he woke up twice seeing the same vision, this same vision appeared once more. That woman came out of the park and stood before him as though she had been expecting him. She shuddered and stopped; she grabbed his hand and squeezed it hard. "No, this is no vision!"

And so she stood face to face with him for the first time after their parting; she was saying something to him, but he looked at her without uttering a word; his heart overflowed, and was gripped with pain. Oh, afterwards he could never forget that meeting with her, and his heart seemed to die within him every time he remembered it. She dropped to her knees before him, right there on the street, as though in delirium; he shrank back in fear; she tried to grab his hand to kiss it as before in his dream, tears were glistening on her long eyelashes.

"Get up, get up!" he exhorted her in a terrified whisper, trying to bring her to her feet. "Get up, quickly!"

"Are you happy? Are you?" she kept asking. "Just one word from you, are you happy now? Today, at this moment? Have you been with her? What did she say?"

She would not get up; she refused to listen to him. She kept firing questions and spoke very fast as though she was on the run from someone and was afraid of being caught.

"I'm going away tomorrow as you have ordered me to. I won't... I'm seeing you for the last time, the last! Now it is for the very last time!"

"Calm down, get up!" he spoke in desperation.

She looked at him avidly, refusing to let go of his hands.

"Farewell!" she said at last, got up, and went off quickly. She almost ran. The Prince saw that Rogozhin suddenly appeared at her side, took her under her arm and led her off.

"Wait a little, Prince!" Rogozhin shouted. "I'll be back in five minutes for a short while."

Five minutes later he really was back; the Prince had waited for him on the same spot.

"I've put her in a calash," he said. "It's been waiting round the corner since ten. She knew you'd be with that young girl all evening long. What you had written to me earlier, I passed on to her word for word. She won't write to her again. She promised. And she won't stay here any longer either, which is what you wanted. She just wished to take a last look at you, even though you didn't want her to. She'd been waiting for you at this spot to catch you on your way back, on that bench over there."

"Did she ask you to go with her?"

"What do you think?" Rogozhin responded with a sneer. "I didn't see anything I didn't know before. Don't tell me you haven't read the letters?"

"And what about you, have you really read them too?" the Prince asked, startled at the thought.

"How else? She showed me every one of them. You remember the bit about the razor, he-he!"

"She's out of her mind!" the Prince exclaimed, wringing his hands.

"Who can tell? Perhaps not," Rogozhin said softly, as though to himself.

The Prince did not reply.

"So long then," Rogozhin said. "I'll also be going away tomorrow. No hard feelings! So, which was it then, my friend," he asked, turning around abruptly, "you didn't answer her question? Are you happy or not?"

"No, no, I'm not!" the Prince exclaimed in unutterable grief.

"As though you could possibly have said yes!" Rogozhin returned with a malicious laugh, and strode on without another look back.

Part Four

1

A BOUT A WEEK PASSED since the rendezvous on the green bench between the two characters in our story. One fine morning at about half-past ten Varvara Ardalionovna Ptitsyna, who had popped out to visit one of her acquaintances, was returning home deeply mortified and lost in thought.

There are those people of whom it is difficult to say something that would describe them fully, in a nutshell, with all their characteristics and foibles. It is usually people who are conventionally referred to as "plain" – "the majority" that is – and who in actual fact comprise the best part of any community. Authors in their novels and stories normally try to pick out such characters from society and depict them vividly and artistically in a way in which they very seldom appear in real life. Podkolesin* in his typical state may perhaps be an exaggeration, but never an impossibility. Having discovered about Podkolesin from Gogol, a huge number of clever people immediately began to realize that dozens upon dozens of their good acquaintances and friends are terribly like him. They knew even before Gogol came along that these friends of theirs are like Podkolesin, only they didn't have a name for it. In real life very few bridegrooms indeed jump *à la* Podkolesin out of windows on the eve of their wedding days – if only, apart from anything else, because it is rather an awkward act to perform. All the same, the number of bridegrooms, in themselves worthy and intelligent people who on the eve of their wedding had considered themselves in their heart of hearts very much in the Podkolesin mould, is legion! It is also by no means all husbands who on every occasion cry, "*Tu l'as voulu, George Dandin!*"* But, my God, how many millions upon billions of times have husbands the world over repeated this *cri de cœur* after their honeymoon, and perhaps even the very next morning after their wedding day!

And so without labouring the point, we shall merely point out that in real life the most typical characteristics of persons are as it were watered down, and though all these George Dandins and Podkolesins do exist, and scurry round about us on a daily basis, they do so in a somewhat restricted form. Finally, in the name of truth, and having made the reservation that even a George Dandin in all his glory, as created by Molière, may, however seldom, be encountered in real life, we shall thereby put an end to our discourse, which is beginning to resemble an article in a literary monthly. Nevertheless we are faced with the dilemma – what is a novelist to do with ordinary people, people who are completely featureless, and how to make them the least bit interesting to readers? One cannot possibly avoid them altogether in a story, because ordinary people form an essential and vital link in the chain of life's events; were we to miss them out, this would be at the expense of verisimilitude. To pack novels with types alone or even simply for interest's sake with strange and unusual people, would be to violate reality, and, come to that, would be uninteresting. To our mind, one ought to identify interesting and instructive types even amongst colourless people. However, when for instance the very essence of some ordinary people is contained in their very constant and immutable ordinariness, or, what is even better, when despite the extraordinary effort of these personages to break out of the rut of ordinariness and routine, they nevertheless end up being inevitably and necessarily the archetypes of routine, such people then even acquire some kind of typicality, exemplifying an ordinariness, which under no circumstances wishes to remain what it is, and, come what may, strives to become original and independent without having the least grounds for this.

To this category of plain, ordinary people necessarily belong some personages of our tale, who (I freely admit) have so far been inadequately explained to the reader. Such, first and foremost, are Varvara Ardalionovna Ptitsyna, her husband Ptitsyn and Gavrila Ardalionovich, her brother.

Truly, there is nothing sadder than to be wealthy for instance, to hail from a decent background, be of presentable appearance, have a reasonable education, a reasonable level of intelligence, even be reasonably benign, and at the same time to be bereft of any talent, come to it of any individuality, any idiosyncrasy, not to have a single idea of one's own to boast of and to be to all intents and purposes "just like the rest". Wealth there is, but not on the Rothschild scale; family background – without blemish, but nothing distinguished about it; outer appearance – fine, but bland; education – sufficient, but of no practical application; intelligence – not to be gainsaid, but without ideas of its own; a good heart – but no magnanimity, and so on and so forth in all categories. There's no end of such people in the world, and their numbers are far greater than one might imagine. Like all people they fall into two main groups: "the dullards" and "the slightly brighter lot". The first are the more happy. A run-of-the-mill dullard would, for instance, find it the easiest thing in the world to imagine he was an extraordinary and original person and derive pleasure therefrom without a moment's hesitation. Some of our young ladies have only to cut off their hair, put on blue-tinted spectacles and style themselves nihilists, to convince themselves immediately that having put on blue-tinted spectacles, they immediately acquired convictions of their own. Someone need only sense in his heart the least glimmer of something positive and humane, immediately to assert that no one else is capable of such sensitivity and that he is in the vanguard of all spiritual development. Someone only has to accept on trust an idea or two, or peruse a page of something that has no beginning and no end, in order to proclaim immediately that these ideas are his very own and originated directly in his own brain. The arrogance of naivety, if one can put it that way, is quite astonishing in such cases; this behaviour seems highly improbable, but in reality occurs time and time again. This arrogance of naivety, this confidence of the foolish man in himself and his own talent, has been brilliantly illustrated by Gogol in the person of his sub-lieutenant Pirogov.* Pirogov has not the least doubt that he is a genius, even more than a genius; his lack of misgiving is such that it does not even occur to him to question the matter; to be sure, the very notion of such a misgiving is completely alien to him. In the end the great author simply has to have Pirogov flogged to satisfy the offended finer feelings of his reader, but on seeing that the man of genius only picks himself up, dusts himself down and, to bolster his strength after the punishment, consumes a piece of puff pastry, Gogol washes his hands of him in resignation and leaves his readers none the wiser. I've always rued the fact that Gogol had accorded the illustrious Pirogov such a lowly rank, because Pirogov is so full of himself that he'd have had no difficulty in believing himself to be an outstanding leader of men on the grounds of his imaginary epaulettes getting wider and thicker in the course of his career. Did I say "believing"? No, there'd be no room for doubt in the matter. If he were promoted to a general, there'd be no stopping him! The number of such people who subsequently suffered complete rout on the field of battle! And the number of Pirogovs that our literature, our science, our public institutions have all produced! Did I say "have"? They still do...

Our personage, Gavrila Ardalionych Ivolgin, belonged to the second category; he belonged to "the slightly brighter lot", although the whole of him, from top to toe, was infected with the desire for originality. But this category, as we have already said above, is much less happy than the first. The crux of the matter being that an *intelligent* "ordinary" man, even if he had fleetingly (or, come to that, throughout the entire course of his life) imagined himself to be a genius of supreme originality, would nevertheless have retained in his heart of hearts a niggling worm of doubt, which in the end would have caused him to fall into utter despair; and, even if he had renounced his delusions entirely, he'd still have remained for ever poisoned by the sense of repressed vanity within him. To be sure, we have in any case taken an extreme example. In the vast majority of cases in this *intelligent* category of people the outcome is not at all so tragic; they may in the end sustain some damage to the liver, but that's about all. Just the same, long before laying down their arms and submitting – from early youth right up to the age of their submission – these people like to have their fill of clowning, and all out of an urge for originality. Some cases are truly weird and wonderful. For the sake of originality some perfectly honest individual may easily stoop low; it may easily happen that one of these unfortunates is not only honest but even kind-hearted – the mainstay of his family, the long-suffering protector and provider not only of his own kith and kin, but of people at large – but he may suddenly flip – something he'd been desperate to do all his life! He is not at all comforted or satisfied by the thought that he had perfectly adequately fulfilled his obligations as a human being; quite the contrary, it is the root cause of his frustration. "This is," he reckons, "what the best years of my life have been wasted on, this is what has bound me hand and foot, this is what has stopped me from going down in history! But for it, I might well have invented something, or made a discovery along the lines of gunpowder or America – I don't yet know quite exactly what, but I'm confident I could have invented or discovered something or other!" The trouble with these gentlemen is that they really are unable to tell all their life long what it is precisely they are about to invent or discover: is it to come up with gunpowder or stumble upon America? But it is certain that in their pioneering zest and ambition they would have rivalled a Columbus or a Galileo.

Gavrila Ardalionovich was beginning to set out along this path – the operative word being "beginning". His clowning days would not be over for a good while to come. A deep and enduring awareness of his own lack of talent, coupled with an indomitable urge to ascertain that he was a man with an independent turn of mind, had had a most adverse effect upon his heart almost since his youth. He was a young man with spiteful and erratic inclinations, and appears to have had a nervous predisposition from the day of his birth. He had mistaken the fitfulness of his desires for their strength. In his passionate desire to distinguish himself, he was sometimes ready to perform the most reckless act; but the minute it came to making the decisive leap, our hero always turned out to be too wise by half to take the plunge. This frustrated him. Perhaps, if the occasion were right, and if only it could have somehow brought him a little nearer his goal, he might well have plucked up the courage to do some extremely dastardly deed; but, as ill luck would have it, as soon as it came to it, he was invariably prevented from doing anything nasty by his innate sense of decency. (Incidentally, he was always ready and willing to perform some petty unkindness.) He regarded his family's poverty and decline with revulsion and hatred. He even treated his mother haughtily and with disdain, and this in spite of the fact that he himself was well aware that as things stood, his mother's reputation and character formed the mainstay of his own career. Having entered Yepanchin's service, he immediately said to himself, "If I'm going to act deviously, let it not be by halves as long as it gets me what I want," and in the event, whenever he acted deviously, it was always by halves. The question arises: why was it he imagined he would necessarily have to be devious? At the moment of crisis with Aglaya, he took fright all right, but did not turn his back on the relationship, dragging it out – just in case, even though he never seriously believed she would condescend to him. Later, in his affair with Nastasya Filippovna, he suddenly imagined that it was *all* a matter of money. "If it's a question of stooping, let's go the whole hog," he would repeat to himself every day smugly, but not without some trepidation. "What's the good of debasing oneself by halves, best to go all the way," was how he encouraged himself time and time again. "A mediocrity would lose heart on such occasions – not I!" Having failed with Aglaya and finding himself undone by circumstances, he was utterly crestfallen and really did take the money to the Prince – money that a mad woman had flung at him and which in turn was brought to her by one no less mad. Subsequently he sorely regretted having returned the money, though this did not prevent him from constantly bragging about it. He really did weep the three days that the Prince had stayed in St Petersburg, but in those three days he also managed to develop a hatred for the Prince because the latter looked upon him much too solicitously, whereas the fact that he'd returned the money "was not something that just anyone would have been capable of". But his gracious admission that the whole of his grief was just one long-drawn-out process of trampling underfoot his personal vanity, worried him immensely. It was only much later that he saw and understood what a dangerous turn his relationship with such an innocent and strange creature as Aglaya might have taken. Remorse gnawed at him. He left his employment and fell into misery and depression. He, his mother and father included, lived with Ptitsyn at the latter's expense. He detested Ptitsyn openly even though at the same time he listened to his advice and was sufficiently astute to go out of his way to seek it whenever occasion demanded it. Amongst other things Gavrila Ardalionych was annoyed with Ptitsyn for not trying or aspiring to be a Rothschild. "Once a moneylender, why not go to the limit, why not squeeze the people, extort money from them, establish a reputation, do as the Jews?" Ptitsyn was discreet and reserved; he merely smiled, but on one occasion he found it necessary to explain himself to Ganya and he carried it out with some dignity. He proved to Ganya that he did nothing disreputable and resented being called a Jew; that it was not his fault money was so valuable; that he was above board and honest in all his dealings, and that in fact he was only "an agent" in these matters; and that finally, thanks to his scrupulousness in business matters, he was already looked upon by the best of people in a very positive light, and his business was expanding. "I shall not be a Rothschild, and see no sense in aiming to be one," he remarked with a laugh, "but to possess a house on the Liteiny Prospect is another matter – perhaps two, and that will be that." "Well, who knows, I might stretch it to three!" he mused to himself, but he never revealed the whole extent of his aspirations. Nature loves and favours such people. It will reward

Ptitsyn with not just three, but probably four houses, and this precisely because from his very childhood he knew full well that he'd never get to be a Rothschild. But to more than four houses nature will never go, and that'll be the end of Ptitsyn's hour of glory.

Gavrila Ardalionych's sister was altogether quite different. She was also motivated by strong desires – persistent rather than sporadic. She had a lot of common sense when it came to the crux of the matter, and even beforehand. True enough, she too belonged to the "ordinary" category of people who dream of originality, but to her credit she soon came to realize that she did not have an iota of true originality in her and did not grieve over it too much – who knows, perhaps out of a peculiar kind of pride. She betrayed enormous resolve in the first practical step she took, which was to marry Mr Ptitsyn; but in the process it did not even occur to her to say to herself, "If it's a question of stooping, let me go the whole hog as long as I get what I want," which is what no doubt Gavrila Ardalionych would surely have said (and he nearly did, in her presence what's more, when he was commenting – positively – on her decision in the capacity of her elder brother). Quite the contrary – Varvara Ardalionovna married after she had fully ascertained that her future husband was an unpretentious, pleasant, reasonably well-educated man who would never in his life stoop to any major misdemeanour. As regards minor misdemeanours, Varvara Ardalionovna made no attempt to enquire, dismissing them as trivia; let's face it, the world is full of trivia! After all, she couldn't be expected to chase after an ideal, could she now? Besides, she knew that in getting married, she was providing shelter for her mother, father and brothers. On seeing that her brother was in trouble, she decided to help him, in spite of all previous family misunderstandings. Ptitsyn from time to time insisted in the nicest possible way that Ganya should seek employment. "I can see you hate all generals and the whole set up," he would remark sometimes in a mock serious manner, "but all of 'those' who see it through will one day end up as generals in their turn – just wait and see." "Why on earth do they imagine I hate generals and all they stand for?" Ganya wondered to himself resentfully. In order to help her brother, Varvara Ardalionovna decided to widen her circle of activity. She inveigled herself into the Yepanchins' household, which was greatly assisted by childhood recollections; both she and her brother had played with the Yepanchin children in the past. Let us make it quite clear at the outset that had Varvara Ardalionovna been chasing some wild hope in frequenting the Yepanchin family, she would thereby perhaps have immediately excluded herself from that category of people to which she had assigned herself; but it was no wild hope that she was chasing – she had a specific, calculated aim in mind, and she was counting on her knowledge of the type of family she had to deal with. She had long been busy studying Aglaya's character. She had set herself the goal of bringing her brother and Aglaya together again. Perhaps she actually managed to achieve something along those lines; perhaps she kept falling into the error of relying, for instance, too much on her brother to deliver something he was never in his life capable of delivering. Be that as it may, her tactics at the Yepanchins' were quite smart. For weeks on end she refrained from mentioning her brother, was always very truthful and candid, and conducted herself self-effacingly, but with dignity. As far as her innermost feelings were concerned, she was not afraid to delve into them, and felt perfectly at ease with herself. It is this which actually lent her strength. Only occasionally she caught herself sliding into anger, standing on her pride too much and even berating herself for a sense of suppressed vanity; this welled up in her with particular force virtually every time she came back after a visit to the Yepanchins.

And there she was on her way from them and, as we already had occasion to remark, beset by gloomy thoughts. In her state of dejection there was a bitterly comical element evident too. Ptitsyn resided in Pavlovsk in a nondescript but spacious timber house, situated in a dusty side street, which was soon to come into his possession completely, so that he in his turn was already trying to sell it on to someone else. As she ascended the steps of the porch, Varvara Ardalionovna suddenly became aware of an extraordinarily loud commotion coming from the top of the house and she distinguished her father's and brother's voices shouting at each other. On entering the front room, she caught sight of Ganya running up and down, pale with rage and almost tearing his hair. She winced and slumped down on the sofa in exhaustion, still keeping her little hat on. Well aware that he would surely fly into a rage unless she broke the silence and asked her brother the reason for his agitation before another minute was up, she finally managed to formulate her question:

"Is it still the same old story?"

"You must be joking!" Ganya exploded. "The same! No, the Devil only knows what's going on now, never mind – the same! The old man has gone totally berserk... mother is crying her eyes out. Honest to God, Varya, you can say what you like, I'm either going to throw him out of the house or... leave myself," he added as an afterthought, probably because it dawned on him that the house was not his for him to throw people out of.

"One must be tolerant," Varya muttered.

"Why tolerant? Of whom?" Ganya objected. "Tolerant of his depravity? No, please yourself, but that's impossible! Impossible, impossible, impossible! And the effrontery of it all – he's guilty up to his neck, but he won't hear of it! He's like a bull in a china shop!... What's wrong with you? Have you seen your face?"

"There's nothing wrong with my face," Varya muttered resentfully.

Ganya looked at her dubiously.

"Did you go there?" he asked suddenly.

"Yes."

"Listen, he's bawling again! How embarrassing, especially at a time like this!"

"What has the time got to do with it? There's nothing special about the present time."

Ganya looked at her even more dubiously.

"Did you find out anything?" he asked.

"No, at least nothing unexpected. I discovered that all our suppositions were true. My husband knew better than either of us. What he predicted from the very start has all come to pass. Where is he?"

"Out. So what happened?"

"The Prince is the formal bridegroom, it's a done deal. The two elder ones told me. Aglaya has agreed. Everything is out in the open now. (Remember, until recently there was such an air of mystery about it all.) Adelaida's wedding is going to be put off again to celebrate the two together, on the same day – how romantic! A real fairytale occasion! You'd do better to commemorate the happy event in rhymed verse instead of rushing around the room to no avail. Belokonskaya is coming to see them tonight. She has timed her arrival well. There'll be lots of guests. He'll be introduced to Belokonskaya even though he knows her already. I suppose the engagement will be made public.

The only thing they're afraid of is that he's going to drop or break something when he makes his entry with all the guests about, or fall flat on his face, you can never be sure with him."

Ganya heard her out patiently, but to her surprise this astonishing news appeared to leave him singularly unimpressed.

"Well, it was obvious from the start it couldn't be helped," he said after a short reflection, "so that's the end," he added with an enigmatic smile, looking furtively at Varya and still pacing up and down the room, but somehow less vigorously.

"I'm glad you're able to take it all so philosophically," Varya said.

"One thing less to worry about – for you at least."

"I think I stood by you loyally without arguing or nagging you. I didn't enquire what kind of happiness you were after with Aglaya."

"Do you suppose it was happiness... I was after with Aglaya?"

"Philosophizing doesn't become you! Of course I know how things stand between you two. It's all over, we've done our bit and have ended up with egg on our faces. I have to be frank with you, I never expected anything to come from this venture. As far as I was concerned, it was just a shot in the dark. I was counting on the funny side of the girl's character, but my main objective was to please you. The odds were, nothing would come of it. To this day I still don't know what it was you were after exactly."

"You and your husband will now be pestering me to take up my post again, preaching to me about diligence and willpower, not to despise small things and so on, I know it all by heart," Ganya said, and burst out laughing.

"He's hatched some new plan, I'm sure," Varya thought to herself.

"So how is it over there now? Are the parents happy, or what?" Ganya enquired suddenly.

"I d-don't think so. But you can draw your own conclusions. Ivan Fyodorovich is pleased. His wife is apprehensive. In the past she always dreaded the very thought of him as a husband. Everyone knows it."

"I didn't mean that. Of course it's absurd and ridiculous to think of him as the future husband, that much is clear. I'm asking about how things stand now – what's it like there now? Has she given her formal consent?"

"So far she hasn't said 'no' – but that's all, and it couldn't be any other way where she is concerned. You know how impossibly shy and bashful she is. As a child she used to lock herself up in a wardrobe and sit there for two, three hours just so as not to show her face to the visitors. She's a big girl now, but she hasn't really changed a bit. You know, for some reason I think there's something quite serious going on there, even on her part. They say she makes fun of the Prince mercilessly from morning till night, but that's just for show. On the quiet no doubt she whispers all sorts of sweet nothings to him, because he seems up in the clouds all the time, as pleased as Punch, goes around beaming… They say he's awfully funny. Incidentally, they themselves told me so. It struck me too that they were laughing at me, to my face, the two elder ones."

Ganya started to pull faces at last – perhaps Varya was purposely prying into this matter to find out what was really on his mind. But there was a renewed outburst of shouting from upstairs.

"That's it, he's got to go!" Ganya yelled as though glad of an opportunity to vent his anger.

"And then he'll go around putting us to shame again everywhere, like he did yesterday."

"What – like yesterday? What do you mean – like he did yesterday? You don't mean—" Ganya asked in unfeigned terror.

"Oh my God, didn't you know?" Varya asked in shock.

"I don't believe it… is it really true he'd been there?" Ganya yelled, going red in a fit of shame and rage. "My God, you're just back from their place! What have you found out? Has the old man been there or not? Has he or has he not?"

And Ganya rushed for the door. Varya ran after him and grabbed him with both hands.

"What's the matter with you? Where are you off to?" she kept asking. "If you let him go now, he'll go around causing even more trouble!"

"So what's he done already? What has he said?"

"They had no clear idea themselves, least of all were they able to explain anything. He scandalized everybody. First he went to Ivan Fyodorovich – he wasn't in. He demanded to see Lizaveta Prokofyevna. First, he asked her for a post, to be given employment, and then started complaining about us – about me, about my husband, and about you most of all… the list was as long as your arm."

"Couldn't you find out what he said?" Ganya asked, shaking as though in fever.

"How could I! I doubt if he realized what he was saying himself, and it's just as likely they kept something back from me."

Ganya clasped his head in his hands and rushed towards a window; Varya settled down at another.

"Funny girl, this Aglaya," she suddenly remarked. "I was just about to leave when she stopped me and said, "'Give my kindest, personal regards to your parents. I trust I shall soon have an occasion to see your father.' And it was said in all seriousness. I was speechless—"

"She wasn't sarcastic, or was she – was she?"

"That's the point, she wasn't. That's what's so surprising."

"Does she know what the old man did, or not? What do you think?"

"I'm pretty sure most of the family have no idea, but it's a thought – perhaps Aglaya does know after all. She alone and no one else, because her sisters were also surprised when she sent her regards to Father so graciously. And why especially to him? If she knows – it must be the Prince who told her!"

"It won't be difficult to find out who told her! A thief! That's all we needed. A thief in our own family, 'the head of the family'!"

"That's rubbish!" Varya shouted back, getting seriously angry. "Drunkards' talk, nothing more. I'd like to know who started it? Lebedev, the Prince... what a pair! Clever shins! I don't care a fig for any of it!"

"The old man's a thief and a drunkard," Ganya continued maliciously, "I'm a pauper, my brother-in-law – a moneylender! What more could Aglaya ask for? A fine family to join, I must say!"

"This brother-in-law, the moneylender, is the one who—"

"Feeds me, is that it? You don't have to mince words, please."

"What's wrong with you?" Varya retorted. "You don't understand anything, you talk like a schoolboy. You think all this could have brought you down in Aglaya's eyes? You've no idea what she's like. She'd gladly turn her back on the most eligible suitor in the world and run off with some student to starve to death in a garret with him – that's her dream! You've no idea how you would have risen in her eyes had you but known how to put up with our situation steadfastly and proudly. That's precisely how the Prince made his mark. First, because he never made an effort to chase after her, and secondly, because everyone knows him for an idiot. To see her family squirm and squall is all she wants now. My God, how little you understand!"

"It still remains to be seen if I understand or not," Ganya replied enigmatically, "only I wouldn't like it at all if she were to find out about the old man. I'm sure the Prince will keep himself in check and not say anything. He had managed to exercise control over Lebedev. He didn't even want to tell me everything, when I tackled him—"

"So you see – never mind him, it's all common knowledge anyway. Why do you keep on fretting? What else are you hoping for? And even if there had been some remote prospect left for you, it would only have lent you a long-suffering martyr's aspect in her eyes."

"Don't worry, in spite of her romanticism, she'd have shied away from a scandal. So far and no further, that applies to everything and everybody – you're all like that."

"Aglaya would shy away? You make me laugh!" Varya objected with a dismissive look at her brother. "You're pathetic! What a worthless bunch you all are! She may be funny and ridiculous, but then she's got more guts than all of us put together."

"Well, all right, all right, don't upset yourself," Ganya muttered again, smugly.

"It's Mother I'm sorry for." Varya continued. "The thought of Father's escapade reaching her frightens me, it really does!"

"And it surely has already," Ganya observed.

Varya had already got up to go to Nina Alexandrovna upstairs, but she stopped and looked hard at her brother.

"Who on earth could have told her?"

"Ippolit, probably. I think as soon as he moved in with us, he took great pleasure in reporting it all to Mother."

"But why would he know about it? Tell me, please! The Prince and Lebedev weren't going to tell anyone. And Kolya doesn't know anything about it anyway."

"Ippolit, you mean? He found out himself. You've no idea what a cunning fox he is, what a gossip-monger, what a nose he has for all that's mean and scandalous. You can think what you like but I'm sure he has managed to take Aglaya in hand! And if he hasn't yet, he will shortly. Rogozhin too has teamed up with him. I wonder the Prince sees nothing! He's dying to do me a nasty turn now! I'm his personal enemy, I realized it way back, only where it all comes from, what he hopes to gain by it, with one foot in the grave – I can't understand it! But I'm going to trick him. You'll see, it won't be I, but he, who will squirm."

"Why did you lure him over then, if you dislike him that much? And is he worth all the trouble?"

"It was you who advised me to lure him over."

"I thought he would come in useful. Do you know he has fallen in love with Aglaya himself and has written to her? I was asked about this... I'm not sure it wasn't Lizaveta Prokofyevna herself he wrote to."

"In this regard he doesn't pose a threat!" Ganya said with a vicious laugh. "There may actually be something else behind all this. That he has fallen in love is not surprising – it's a schoolboy's infatuation! But... he wouldn't write anonymous letters to the old woman. He's just a vindictive, worthless, self-satisfied mediocrity!... I'm convinced, I know for certain that he told her I'm a troublemaker – that was his opening gambit. I must admit I was foolish enough to confide in him at first. I thought he'd come over to my side out of his vendetta for the Prince alone. He's such a nasty piece of work! Oh, I've cracked him completely now. As for this theft, he heard about it from his mother, the Captain's widow. The old man took the risk only for her sake. Suddenly the youngster turns to me and says quite out of the blue that the General had promised his mother four hundred roubles, and this quite unexpectedly, without any rhyme or reason. I realized immediately what was happening. He has this way of looking into your eyes, oozing with delight. I'm sure it was for the pleasure of seeing Mother's heart break that he told her everything. And why doesn't he hurry up and die, please tell me? Didn't he promise to die in three weeks' time; instead he's put on weight here! His cough has eased as well. Yesterday he said himself he's not coughing up blood any more."

"Get rid of him!"

"It's not that I hate him – I scorn him," Ganya said proudly. "All right, all right, I hate him too, I really do!" he suddenly shouted in uncontrollable rage. "I'll tell him that to his face, even when he's lying there dying on his deathbed! If only you had read his 'Explanation' – God, what naive arrogance! It's all the clowns of literature rolled into one – a pipsqueak above all! Oh, how I'd liked to have given him a good hiding then, just to see his astonished face. Now he's blaming others for him bungling his suicide attempt... But what's going on? That noise again! This is really too much! I'm not going to stand for

496

any of this! Ptitsyn!" he yelled just as Ptitsyn came through the door. "What's all this about, where will it all end? This is… this is…"

But the noise came nearer and nearer fast. The door suddenly flew open and Ivolgin, beside himself with rage, red in the face and shaking all over, launched himself at Ptitsyn. The old man was followed by Nina Alexandrovna, Kolya and last of all by Ippolit.

2

F IVE DAYS HAD PASSED since Ippolit had moved in with the Ptitsyns. This happened quite spontaneously, without any bad blood being created between him and the Prince; not only did they not quarrel, but to all intents and purposes they appeared to part as friends. Gavrila Ardalionovich, who had been so badly disposed towards Ippolit that memorable evening, came to visit him of his own accord on the third day after the event, probably on a sudden impulse. For some reason even Rogozhin began to visit the patient. Initially the Prince considered that it really would be in the "poor lad's" interests if he moved out of his house. But even in the process of moving, Ippolit was stressing that he was moving in with Ptitsyn, "who'd been good enough to give him a roof over his head", and never once did he mention that he was moving in with Ganya, even though it was Ganya himself who had insisted that he be admitted to the house. Ganya noticed this immediately and he buried a deep grudge in his heart.

He was right when he said to his sister that the patient had improved. There was no doubt, Ippolit was beginning to feel somewhat better, and this was clear just by looking at him. Ippolit entered the room unhurriedly, making up the rear, with a derisive, malicious grin on his face. Nina Alexandrovna looked very frightened. (She had changed perceptibly in these past six months, had become frailer. After marrying off her daughter and having moved in with her, she had to all intents and purposes almost completely stopped engaging herself in her children's affairs.) Kolya appeared troubled and somewhat at a loss. There was a great deal in the General's "manic behaviour", as he himself called it, that he could not make head or tail of, largely because he was ignorant of the causes of the latest commotion in the family. But it was quite clear to him that his father was getting so unruly, frequently and ubiquitously, and had undergone such a change of personality that he no longer appeared to be the same man as previously. He was concerned also that in the last three days he had totally abstained from drink. He knew that he had parted company, and even quarrelled, with Lebedev and the Prince. Kolya had just come home with a small bottle of vodka, which he had bought with his own money.

"Really, mother," he had tried to assure Nina Alexandrovna while they were still upstairs, "it really would be better for him to have a drink. It's three days since he's had a drop. Something's wrong with him. I tell you, it would be better. I used to take him some when he was in the debtors' clink…"

The General threw the door wide open and stopped in the doorway, shaking with indignation.

"My dear sir!" he yelled in a stentorian voice to his son-in-law Ptitsyn. "If you really have decided to sacrifice to this whippersnapper and atheist a venerable old man, your father – father-in-law, I should say – distinguished in the service of his Tsar, then let me shake the dust of this house off my feet. Make your choice, sir, make it immediately – either I, or this… screw! Yes, screw! It was a slip of the tongue, but I stand by it – screw! Because he bores like a screw into my soul, with total lack of respect… in the manner of a screw!"

"A corkscrew, perhaps?" Ippolit suggested.

"No, not a corkscrew, because I stand before you a general and not a bottle. I have medals, decorations for distinguished service… and you have nothing! It's either him or me! Decide now, on the spot, sir!" he yelled again, at the end of his tether. Kolya in the meantime brought up a chair for him, and he slumped into it in exhaustion.

"I really think it would be better if you had… a nap," Ptitsyn muttered, utterly dismayed.

"He has the effrontery to utter threats!" Ganya said to his sister in a hushed voice.

"A nap!" the General yelled. "I'm not drunk, my dear sir, and you should not insult me. I can see," he continued, getting up again, "I can see everything here is against me, everything and everybody. Enough! I'm leaving… But know you, my dear sir, know you…"

He was not allowed to finish and persuaded to take his seat. The others implored him to calm down. Ganya, beside himself with rage, withdrew into a corner. Nina Alexandrovna was trembling all over and crying.

"What have I done to him? What is he complaining about?" Ippolit exclaimed, baring his teeth.

"You're asking what you have done to him?" Nina Alexandrovna suddenly intervened. "You ought to be especially ashamed and… it's cruel to torture an old man… especially in your position."

"First, what precisely do you mean 'my position', my lady? I respect you very much, you in particular, personally, but—"

"He's a screw!" the General yelled. "He is boring into my soul, into my heart! He wants me to believe in atheism! Remember, you milksop, you weren't even born when I was already heaped with honours. And you're just a wretched worm, cut in half, coughing your heart out… dying of hatred and atheism… And why in God's name did Ganya bring you here in the first place? Everyone's against me – not only strangers but my own flesh and blood."

"I wish you'd stop play-acting!" Ganya exclaimed. "You shouldn't go around the town bringing your family into disrepute. That's the least you could do!"

"I bring my family into disrepute, you milksop? You of all people! I'm giving you an opportunity to bask in my glory, not damage your reputation!"

He jumped to his feet and appeared to have lost all self-control. But so apparently had Gavrila Ardalionovich.

"You can talk of reputation!" he snapped angrily.

"What did you say?" the General roared, taking a step towards him.

"I only need to say a word for you to…" Ganya cried suddenly, and did not bring the sentence to an end. Both stood eyeball to eyeball. He appeared to be the first ready to blink.

"Ganya, for God's sake!" Nina Alexandrovna exclaimed, rushing forward to restrain her son.

"This is too bad of all of you!" Varya cut in, bursting with indignation. "That'll do, Mother!" she said, clinging to her mother.

"It's only out of respect for Mother I'm letting you get away with it," Ganya said with a tragic overtone.

"Go ahead, say it!" the General yelled at the end of his tether. "Say it under pains of being cursed by your father… say it!"

"As though I was afraid of your curse! Whose fault is it you've been acting like a fool these past eight days? Eight days, you see, I know the exact dates… Watch your step, don't push me too far!… Why did you have to go to the Yepanchins' yesterday, I ask you? You who call yourself a venerable old gentleman, grey-haired, head of the family! For shame!"

"Shut up, Ganya!" Kolya yelled. "Shut up, you fool!"

"I really, I really don't know how I could have offended him!" Ippolit insisted, but still in the same derisive tone of voice. "Why is he calling me a screw as you all heard? Why won't he leave me alone? As soon as he saw me today he started going on about some Captain Yeropegov. I never sought your company, General. I always avoided it as you well know. Why should I be concerned about Captain Yeropegov, have a heart? I haven't moved here because of Captain Yeropegov. I merely voiced my opinion that perhaps there never was such a person as Captain Yeropegov. That's where he went berserk."

"Of course there never was!" Ganya butted in.

But the General was flabbergasted and looked around in consternation. His son's contribution stunned him by its stark unambiguity. For a moment or so he was speechless. And only after Ippolit had burst out laughing and called out, "There you are, your own son has said there never was a Captain Yeropegov," the old man muttered:

"Kapiton Yeropegov, not Captain... Kapiton... Ex-Lieutenant Colonel Yeropegov... Kapiton."

"And there was no Kapiton either!" Ganya insisted angrily.

"W-why not?" the General muttered, and his face coloured red.

"Don't get upset!" Ptitsyn and Varya said, trying to calm him down.

"Will you shut up, Ganya!" Kolya yelled again.

But the General appeared to take heart at these interventions.

"What do you mean there was no Kapiton either? Why shouldn't there have been?" he challenged his son menacingly.

"Because there wasn't! There simply wasn't and that's all there is to it. He didn't exist, end of story, I tell you! Stop it! I don't want to hear any more about it!"

"And this is... this is my own son talking, whom I... Oh my God! No Yeropegov, Yeroshka Yeropegov – you didn't exist!"

"There you are, now it's Yeroshka, now it's Kapitoshka!" Ippolit jeered.

"Kapitoshka, sir, Kapitoshka, not Yeroshka! Kapiton, Captain Alexeyevich, I mean Kapiton... Lieutenant Colonel... retired... married Marya... Marya Petrovna Su... Su... he was my friend and comrade-at-arms... his wife was a Sutugova – he married her when he was still a subaltern. I shed my blood for him... I shielded him with my body... he was killed. There was no Kapitoshka Yeropegov! You didn't exist, old chum!"

Ivolgin got carried away and the gravity of his voice was at variance with the triviality of the subject. True, some other time he would easily have borne something much more unpalatable than the non-existence of Kapiton Yeropegov; he'd have blustered about for a while, made a scene, let off some steam, and in the end would have crept upstairs and slept it off. But at this particular instant, due to the perversity of human nature, it so happened that an offence such as doubt regarding the existence of Kapiton Yeropegov was the straw that broke the camel's back. The old man went scarlet and yelled:

"That's enough! My curse... I am leaving this house! Nikolai, bring me my travelling bag... I'm leaving!"

He hurried out of the room in a rage. Nina Alexandrovna, Kolya and Ptitsyn rushed after him.

"Look what you've done now!" Varya said to her brother. "He's sure to go there again now. How awful, how simply awful!"

"He shouldn't have been thieving!" Ganya cried, choking with anger. Suddenly his eyes met Ippolit's. He fairly shook with fury. "And you, my dear sir," he shouted, "should have remembered that you don't happen to be in your own home but... are enjoying somebody else's hospitality where you've no right to goad an old man, whose mind is obviously clouded..."

Ippolit also seemed to reel somewhat under the onslaught, but he quickly regained his equanimity.

"I beg to disagree with you that your father's mind is clouded," he returned calmly, "I think quite the reverse, he has gained in intelligence recently, honestly! You don't believe me? He has become very cautious, wary, inquisitive, weighing up every word he says... You know, he had a reason for bringing up this Kapitoshka fellow. Believe it or not, he wished to imply that—"

"What the hell do I care what he wished to imply! I ask you not to beat about the bush, or take me for a fool, sir!" Ganya screeched. "If you are aware of the true cause why the old man is in such a state (and you've been so busy snooping around at my place these past five days surely you must be aware), you ought not to have needled... the poor man and tormented my mother by your exaggerations of the matter, because all this is sheer nonsense, nothing but a stupid lie with no basis in truth, and I don't believe any of it... But you are bent on mischief and you can't resist snooping, because you... you are a—"

"A screw," Ippolit sneered.

"Because you're a nasty piece of work. You've been tormenting people for half an hour with your threats to kill yourself with that unloaded pistol of yours which you brandished about so ignominiously in your failed suicide attempt, you clot of oozed bile... on two legs. I took you in in all good faith, you've grown fatter, you stopped coughing, and this is how you repay—"

"Just two words, if I may. I'm staying here courtesy of Varvara Ardalionovna, not you. You have offered me no hospitality and, as I see it, you are enjoying Mr Ptitsyn's hospitality yourself. Four days ago I asked my mother to find lodgings for both of us in Pavlovsk, because I do indeed find it more congenial here, but I've not put on weight and I still continue to cough. Last night my mother informed me that the lodgings were ready, and for my part I hasten to inform you that, having thanked my mother and your sister, I shall this very day move to my new address, a decision I arrived at last night. I apologise for interrupting you. No doubt you've plenty more to say."

"Oh, if that's so—" Ganya returned, shaking with agitation.

"Well, if that's so, may I please sit down," Ippolit added, calmly settling himself in a chair, which had formerly been occupied by the General. "I've not yet fully recovered. Well, now I'm ready to listen, the more so since this is our last conversation and, possibly, our last meeting."

Ganya suddenly felt a pang of shame.

"Oh, rest assured I'm not going to stoop to settling scores with you," he said, "and if you—"

"There's no need to put on airs," Ippolit interrupted him, "I for my part, the very day I moved here, I promised myself in all honesty not to deny myself the pleasure of giving you an earful of what I thought of you when we came to part. I intend to do it right now – after you, of course."

"And I'm asking you to leave this room."

"I think you had better have your say, or you'll never stop regretting it."

"That'll do, Ippolit. All this is so undignified. Do me a favour, and don't go on."

"Well, if only to please the lady," Ippolit said, laughing and rising to his feet. "For your sake, Varvara Ardalionovna, I'm ready to curtail, but only to curtail this dispute, because some exchange between myself and your brother has become quite unavoidable, and I shall never agree to forgo this opportunity to clear the air."

"You're just a simple gossip-monger," Ganya exclaimed. "That's why you won't leave, unless you satisfy your craving."

"There you are," Ippolit remarked coolly, "here's the proof of the pudding. Really, you will live to regret not having had your say. I'm giving you the floor once again. I can wait."

Gavrila Ardalionovich kept his silence, disdainfully.

"You don't wish to. You want to prove a point. Please yourself. For my part, I shall be brief, circumstances permitting. Two or three times today I was rebuked for having enjoyed your hospitality. That is unfair. By inviting me to stay with you, you were laying a trap for me. You counted on my desire to get my own back on the Prince. Besides, you heard that Aglaya Ivanovna had expressed sympathy for me and had read my 'Explanation'. Expecting for some reason that I'd embrace your interests, you were hoping that I'd perhaps support your cause. I shall refrain from a more detailed explanation! Nor do I expect from you either admission or confirmation. It is enough that I leave you with your conscience and that we now understand each other perfectly."

"But you are making a mountain out of a molehill!" Varya exclaimed.

"I told you – a gossip-monger and a schoolboy," Ganya said.

"Permit me, Varvara Ardalionovna, I shall continue. It goes without saying, I can neither like nor respect the Prince. But he is decidedly a good man, though at the same time… a little comical. However, I've no reason whatsoever to hate him. I did not let on in the least that I knew your brother was setting me up against the Prince. I merely wanted to have a good laugh when it all came to a head. I knew your brother would give the game away and put his foot in it in a big way. And that's exactly what's happened… I'm now ready to spare him, but solely out of respect for you, Varvara Ardalionovna. But, having explained to you that it's not so easy to catch me out, let me also explain why it is I so desperately wanted your brother to see for himself what a fool he is.

You might as well know I'm doing it out of hatred, I freely confess. As I die (because die I will, no matter that I've grown fatter, as you have observed), as I die, I shall enter paradise that much more contentedly for having managed to make a fool of at least one representative of that countless category of people which has plagued me all my life long, which I have detested all my life long, and of which that much esteemed brother of yours is a prime example. I detest you, Gavrila Ardalionovich, *solely because* – it may, perhaps, strike you as odd – solely because you are the very incarnation, the embodiment and the height of the most smug, the most self-satisfied, the most banal and nasty middle-of-the-road mediocrity! You are a mediocrity to end all mediocrity! You are pompous with it and unquestioning, and your complacency is truly monumental. Not a single original thought is destined to pass either through your mind or your heart ever. But your envy knows no limits. You are firmly convinced you are a supreme genius, though you too have your moments of doubt, and then anger and envy take over. These, paradoxically, are the dark spots on your otherwise bright horizon. They'll disappear after you'll have lost what remains of your reason, which will not be long in coming. All the same, you have a long and varied journey ahead of you, I wouldn't say a happy one, which gives me much joy. First, I predict you will not win the hand of a certain lady—"

"This is quite intolerable!" Varya exclaimed. "Will you never stop, you obnoxious whelp?"

Ganya went pale. He was shaking and not saying a word. Ippolit stopped talking. He measured Ganya with an intent look, savouring his discomfiture, turned his eyes on Varya, smiled, made a bow, and left without adding another word.

Gavrila Ardalionovich had every cause to feel hurt and hard done by. For some considerable time Varya did not dare to speak or even look at him as he walked past her, up and down, with a heavy, uneasy tread. At last he stopped at a window with his back to her. The expression "two sides of the same coin" came to Varya's mind. Some more noise reached them from upstairs.

"Are you off?" Ganya asked, turning to her suddenly when he heard she was getting up. "Wait. Take a look at this."

He approached and threw a small piece of folded paper on the chair beside her.

"Good Lord!" Varya exclaimed and threw up her hands in surprise.

The note consisted of just seven lines. "Gavrila Ardalionovich, as a result of your friendly attitude towards me, I have resolved to seek your advice regarding what I consider to be a very important matter for me. I would like to see you tomorrow morning at seven sharp at the green bench. This is quite close to our dacha. Varvara Ardalionovna, who must accompany you without fail, knows the spot very well. A.Y."

"I give up trying to understand her!" Varvara Ardalionovna said, spreading out her hands in resignation.

However little disposed Ganya was at that moment to sound his own trumpet, he was unable to conceal his triumph, especially after Ippolit's unflattering predictions. A confident, self-satisfied smile spread over his features. Varya too beamed with joy.

"And this on the very day when they're planning to announce their betrothal! Who can make anything of her after that?"

"Have you any idea what it is she wants to talk about tomorrow?" Ganya asked.

"It doesn't matter, the main thing is she wants to see you for the first time in six months. Listen to me, Ganya – whatever it is, and no matter what turn things may take, you must remember this meeting is important for you! Very important! Don't get on your high horse again, don't funk it again, but don't be reticent either! All right? Could she possibly have guessed why I kept visiting them these past six months? And imagine, she didn't breathe a word today, she didn't let on a thing. I popped in to see them on the quiet. The old girl had no idea I was there, or she'd have probably thrown me out. I took a risk going there, I had to find out one way or—"

There was more noise from upstairs. Some people were coming down the stairs.

"This must never be allowed to happen now!" Varya exclaimed, out of breath and frightened. "There must not be even a suggestion of a scandal! Go on, ask him to pardon you!"

But the head of the family was already out on the street. Kolya was dragging his travelling case after him. Nina Alexandrovna stood on the steps and wept. She wanted to follow him, but Ptitsyn held her back.

"You would only encourage him," he said to her. "He's got nowhere to go. Before half an hour is up, he'll be back. I already had a word with Kolya. Let him get over it."

"Don't be so silly! Where are you going to go?" Ganya shouted out of the window. "You've nowhere to go!"

"Father, come back!" Varya shouted. "The neighbours are getting curious."

The General stopped, turned, raised his hands and exclaimed:

"My curse upon this house!"

"Ever the showman!" Ganya muttered, slamming the window shut.

The neighbours were indeed peeping out. Varya ran out of the room.

After Varya had left, Ganya picked up the note from the table, kissed it, clicked his tongue and performed a little entrechat.

3

A T ANY OTHER TIME the spat with the General would have just petered out of its own accord. There had been similar occasions in the past when he had flared up unreasonably, though this was infrequently, because on the whole he was a very docile and harmless person. He had perhaps tried hundreds of times to shake off the sense of disorder which had possessed him in recent years. He would suddenly recall that he was the paterfamilias, and he would rush to make peace with his spouse and shed tears of innocence. He adored Nina Alexandrovna to distraction, because she always forgave him his foibles and loved him however much he clowned and made a fool of himself. But his high-minded intolerance of chaos never lasted long; the General was also highly impulsive, in his own way of course. By and large, he could not abide the ineffective and idle life he was obliged to lead and would habitually rebel; next, he would not infrequently fly into a temper, though perhaps almost immediately rebuke himself for it, but all to no avail. He would pick quarrels, talk sententiously and convolutedly, demand excessive, almost impossible respect for himself, and would finally abscond from the house, sometimes for very protracted periods of time. In the past two years he had only scant, hearsay knowledge about his family, refusing to involve himself in its day-to-day problems, for which he could summon no personal interest whatsoever.

But on this occasion the spat was marked by something quite extraordinary: there was something in the air that everyone was aware of and yet afraid to talk about. The General had "officially" returned to the family fold – that is, to Nina Alexandrovna – only three days previously, not in a penitent, submissive mood as was the case on previous occasions, but on the contrary – in a highly irritable frame of mind. He was garrulous, restless, he would buttonhole anybody he'd meet and aggressively involve the person in a heated debate, invariably appertaining to the most varied and outlandish subjects such that it was quite impossible to ascertain what it was precisely that preoccupied him. Although he experienced moments of elation, most times he was meditative, quite unaccountably so even to himself. He was apt to break into stories now about the Yepanchins, now about the Prince, now about Lebedev, but was just as likely to break off equally abruptly, and respond to all further questions with a sheepish smile, unconscious both of having been asked questions or of himself smiling back. The night in question he had spent moaning and groaning, driving Nina Alexandrovna almost to distraction. She had spent the whole night preparing for some reason hot poultices for him. Towards the morning he fell asleep for four hours and awoke in a state of the most acute and disturbing hypochondria, which culminated in his quarrel with Ippolit and his "curse upon this house". Let us also point out that throughout these three days he was constantly liable to get on his high horse and as a result proved to be terribly touchy. Kolya assured his mother that all this stemmed from his craving for the hard stuff or maybe because he missed Lebedev, with whom he had lately become great friends. But three days previously he had fallen out with Lebedev and parted with him in utter rage; there was even some kind of a contretemps with the Prince. Kolya had asked the Prince for an explanation and in the end came away with the feeling that the latter too appeared to be reluctant to divulge something. Even if, as Ganya was firmly convinced, some extraordinary conversation had taken place between Ippolit and Nina Alexandrovna, it was nevertheless strange that this nasty young man, whom Ganya so unceremoniously referred to as a gossip-monger, had not thought fit to impart the same information to Kolya too. It could well be that he was not that sinister "youngster" whom Ganya portrayed in his conversation with his sister, but sinister in an altogether different way. As far as Nina Alexandrovna was concerned it was extremely doubtful that he had communicated to her some observation or other of his for the sole purpose of wounding her heart. Let us not forget that people's motivations at a particular time are usually infinitely more complex and varied than we are subsequently able to explain, and seldom do they manifest themselves with any degree of clarity. It is always better for the narrator to limit himself to a straightforward exposition of the events. This is precisely what we intend to do in analysing the present catastrophe with General Ivolgin.

The events in question took place roughly in the following sequence:

When Lebedev, after his trip to St Petersburg in search of Ferdyshchenko, returned the same day in the company of Ivolgin, he had nothing unusual to report to the Prince. Had the latter not been distracted by and deeply preoccupied with highly important personal matters, he would have noticed that in the course of the next two days also Lebedev did not only not offer any explanations, but appeared to be fighting shy of meeting him. When the Prince eventually became conscious of this, he noticed that every time they did happen to run into each other, Lebedev was invariably in the best of moods, and almost always together with the General. The two friends were inseparable. From time to time the Prince heard coming from upstairs loud and persistent voices – light-hearted banter, interspersed with laughter. On one occasion, late at night, to his surprise and bewilderment, he heard a soldiers' drinking song, and he immediately recognized the General's hoarse bass voice. But the singing was very short lived. For the next hour or so there was a lively but by all indications drunken dispute in progress. It was a fair surmise that the friends carousing upstairs had fallen to hugging each other and one of them had finally burst into tears. Then all of a sudden came a stormy quarrel, but it was over almost as soon as it had begun.

All this time Kolya had been in a particularly preoccupied state of mind. The Prince was out for the most part and would sometimes return when it was already quite late; he would invariably be informed that Kolya had been asking after him and looking for him all day. But when they met, Kolya had nothing concrete to say, except that he was very annoyed with the General and his present behaviour. "They wander around together and end up drinking in the tavern not far from here, hugging each other, quarrelling in the street, egging each other on and unable to go their separate ways." When the Prince pointed out to him that this was how it had always been, Kolya was totally at a loss to say anything and unable to account for his present anxiety.

The morning after the singing of the song and the drunken quarrel, when the Prince was going out at about eleven, he suddenly bumped into the General, who was very upset, almost distraught.

"I've long been seeking the honour and opportunity of meeting you, my most esteemed Lev Nikolayevich, long, yes, very long," he muttered, clasping and shaking the Prince's hand to the point of pain, "long, long indeed."

The Prince asked him to take a seat.

"No, I shan't, besides I'm holding you up. Another time. I believe this calls for congratulations on the... fulfilment... of your heart's desires."

"What heart's desires?"

The Prince was embarrassed. Like many another man in his position, he wanted to pretend that no one at all had seen, surmised or understood anything.

"Rest assured, rest perfectly assured! I shall not intrude upon your sensitivities. I've been through it all myself and know how it is when another person... as it were, pokes his nose in... as the saying goes... where he's not wanted. I go through it every morning. I came on another matter, a very important one. A very important matter indeed, Prince."

The Prince bade him once more to sit down, and took a seat himself.

"Well, if it's only for a second... I have come for advice. I, of course, am a man with no practical purpose in life, but, with due regard to my own and, let it be said, the Russian people's business acumen in general, in which it is so singularly deficient... I'd like to provide for my wife, my children and myself... in a word, Prince, I need your advice."

The Prince congratulated him warmly on his good intentions.

"As a matter of fact all this is of no importance," the General interrupted him abruptly. "I've something else in mind altogether, something more important still. I have resolved to take you, Lev Nikolayevich, into my confidence, as a man of whose probity and sincerity I am more than convinced, as... as... Are you surprised, Prince?"

If it was not in extreme surprise, it was surely with the utmost attention that the Prince listened to his visitor. The old man was a little pale in the face, his lips twitched from time to time and his hands moved about restlessly. He had been sitting only a few minutes and even in that short while had managed to leave his chair a couple of times and sit back down again, apparently quite oblivious of what he was doing. There were some books on the table; he picked up one, flipped it open, glanced at the pages in mid-conversation, closed it and immediately put it back, then he picked up another, which he did not open, but continued to hold in his right hand, waving it about for the rest of the time.

"That's enough!" he exclaimed suddenly. "I can see I've been an awful nuisance."

"Not at all, don't mention it, nothing of the sort, quite the contrary – I have been listening hard, doing my best trying to work out—"

"Prince! I want to put myself in a position of regard and respect... Indeed I want to respect my own self and... with all due regard for my rights."

"A person with such aspirations deserves all manner of respect for that alone, if for nothing else."

The Prince made this observation, which might have come from a book of homilies, in the firm conviction that it would have a benign effect. He instinctively realized that some such vacuous but well-timed soothing sentiment could do wonders in pacifying and calming such a man as the General, especially in the state he was in. In any case, he felt it behoved him to humour his visitor before sending him on his way.

It worked. The General was touched and pleased. He suddenly became maudlin, his tone of voice changed immediately and he launched into long and rapturous explanations. But no matter how hard the Prince tried, how hard he listened, he could not make head or tail of what was said. The General spoke for about ten minutes, fervently, as though straining to articulate all the thoughts which pressed on his mind; tears even stood out in his eyes, but still these were just phrases without beginning or end, random words and random thoughts, delivered rapidly and in confusion.

"That'll do! You have understood me, Prince, and I am much relieved," he suddenly concluded, getting up. "A heart like yours cannot but understand a troubled soul. Prince, you are a gentleman to your fingertips! How can anyone else hold a candle to you? But you are young, and I give you my blessing. To be quite honest, I came to ask you to fix the hour for a very important conversation, therein rests my principal hope. All I seek is friendship and heartfelt understanding, Prince. I've never been able to come to terms with the pressing exigencies of my heart."

"But why not now? I am ready to listen—"

"No, Prince, no!" the General interrupted him fervently. "Not now! Now is but the stuff of dreams! It is all too important, much too important! That hour of parley will be the hour when destinies are settled. That hour will be *mine*, and I would hate it if at that sacred moment we were to be disturbed by the very first chance intruder, the first scoundrel who happened to come along, and not infrequently it is just such a scoundrel," he suddenly dropped his voice to a low, mysterious, almost terrified whisper as he conspiratorially leant across to the Prince, "such a scoundrel, who is not worth so much as the heel... of your shoe, my beloved Prince! Mark, I did not say of my shoe! Mark it well, I made no mention of my shoe, for I have too much self-respect to come out with it just like that without any further ado. But it is given to you alone to understand that in rejecting my heel in like manner, I am perhaps giving utterance to an extraordinary expression of pride... of dignity. Between you, me and the gatepost no one else will be any the wiser, but *he* will preside over the rest. *He* is clueless, Prince. Totally and utterly incapable of putting two and two together! To put two and two together you must have your heart in the right place!"

At the end of this speech the Prince nearly took fright and made an appointment with the General for the following day at the same hour. The latter went out at a brisk pace well comforted and almost at peace with himself. In the evening, after seven, the Prince sent for Lebedev to come and see him briefly.

Lebedev turned up with great alacrity. "I find it an extraordinary honour..." he immediately announced before he had even entered the room. There was not a trace of that apprehensiveness which three days ago made him studiously avoid the Prince. He perched himself on the edge of a chair, pulling faces, smiling, his eyes sparkling and darting about, rubbing his hands gleefully in the most naive expectation of hearing some momentous, long-awaited, generally anticipated piece of news. The Prince shuddered yet again; it became immediately clear to him that all who surrounded him had begun to mill around as though in wait of an opportunity to congratulate him on something or other, making copious subtle hints, and nodding and winking in the process. Keller for his part had contrived to pop in about three times – merely for a minute – clearly intending to wish him all the best. On each occasion the well-wisher had begun to speak enthusiastically but incoherently, and not finishing what he had come to say, had promptly sloped off. (In the last few days he had taken to the bottle in a bad way and was said to be making a thorough nuisance of himself in the local billiard room.) Even Kolya, despite the problems which beset him, had made one or two half-hearted attempts to strike up a conversation with the Prince.

The Prince then turned directly and somewhat irritably to Lebedev for his thoughts on the General's present behaviour and moodiness. He described in a few brief words the scene that had taken place.

"Each to his own troubles, Prince... especially in our unusual and unsettled times," Lebedev replied somewhat drily and stopped in a sullen bad temper, giving the impression of someone bitterly deceived in his expectations.

"More of your philosophy!" the Prince returned with a smile.

"Philosophy is necessary, it ought to be very necessary in our day and age in its practical application, but people are in the habit of neglecting it; that's what is so bad. Speaking for myself, my highly esteemed Prince, even though I was deeply honoured by your confidence in me as regards a certain matter, but it was only as far as it went and not a jot beyond the circumstances relating to that particular matter... I understand all full well and am taking everything in good part."

"Lebedev, I have a feeling you're upset about something, is that right?"

"Not a bit of it, not in the least, my highly esteemed and many-splendoured Prince, not in the very least!" Lebedev exclaimed excitedly, pressing his hand to his heart. "Quite the reverse. I particularly and immediately perceive that it is neither by virtue of my position in society, or of my spiritual or intellectual attainments, or of my hard-earned material wealth, or my former behaviour, much less of my erudition that I am in the least deserving of your highly esteemed confidence, which far exceeds my wildest expectations. And that if I can be of service to you, it is only as a slave and mercenary, and in no other capacity... I am not angry, I am sad, sir!"

"Lukyan Timofeyich, have a heart!"

"I stand by what I say. No less now, in this particular instance. I stand before you here, alert in body and mind, reminding myself constantly that I deserve nothing personal in the way of information, but in my capacity as landlord, perhaps I could, with the eventful day in the offing, be vouchsafed as appropriate with an indication, as it were, a communication of the forthcoming and anticipated changes to come, so to speak…"

In declaring this Lebedev's gimlet-like eyes bored into the Prince, who stared back at him in disbelief. Lebedev was forever hopeful of satisfying his curiosity.

"I really have not the foggiest idea what you're talking about," the Prince exclaimed, barely able to contain his temper. "And… and you're a dreadful mischief-maker!" he added, and suddenly burst into a fit of the most wholesome laughter.

Lebedev immediately followed suit, and his radiant face testified to the fact that his prayers had been answered.

"And do you know what I'm going to tell you, Lukyan Timofeyich? Only please don't be angry with me, for I'm surprised at your naivety, and as a matter of fact, not just yours alone! You are so eager to hear something from me, now, this very moment that frankly I feel embarrassed and awkward that I've nothing to communicate to you. I swear to you that I've nothing at all to tell you!"

The Prince again burst out laughing.

Lebedev assumed a dignified pose. It is quite true that he was sometimes all too naive and obstinate in his inquisitiveness. But he was at the same time quite astute and worldly-wise, at times even too much so, bordering on the covertly perfidious. In consequence of the continuous rebuffs he was meting out to Lebedev, the Prince had almost earned himself an enemy. But the Prince rebuffed him not because he hated him, but because the subject of Lebedev's curiosity was so personal. Even a few days previously the Prince himself looked on certain aspects of his expectations as criminal, whereas Lukyan Timofeyich interpreted the Prince's rebuffs as purely personal expressions of revulsion and mistrust, felt he had been wronged and wounded to the quick and was jealous not only of Kolya and Keller, but even of his daughter Vera in vying for the Prince's goodwill. Even at that very moment he'd have been only too glad to communicate a highly desirable piece of news to the Prince, but he peevishly clammed up and did not say a word.

"So how could I possibly be of service to you, my most esteemed Prince, seeing as it was you who in effect... called for me?" he said at last after a considerable pause.

"Yes, well, I really meant to ask you about the General," the Prince, who had briefly fallen into a brown study, responded with a start, "and... that stuff of yours that you mentioned had gone missing—"

"What precisely was that?"

"Now look here, don't tell me now you don't know what I mean! Goodness, Lukyan Timofeyich, stop pretending! Money, the money, the four hundred roubles, which you lost – from your wallet – and which you came here to tell me about, that morning when you were setting out for St Petersburg. Now do you remember?"

"Ah, that four hundred roubles!" Lebedev drawled as though the penny had just dropped. "Thank you, Prince, for your genuine solicitude. I'm very touched, I'm sure, but... I did find it, quite a while ago."

"You have! Ah, thank God!"

"Your exclamation is apt and highly appreciated, because four hundred roubles is no mean sum for a poor, hard-working man having a large family of motherless—"

"That goes without saying! Of course, I'm jolly glad you found it," the Prince hastened to add. "But... how exactly did you find it?"

"Couldn't be simpler, under the chair on which my coat had been hanging. Evidently the object had slid from the pocket straight under the chair."

"What do you mean under the chair? I don't believe it, because you yourself told me you'd searched high and low. How could you have overlooked it, and in the most obvious place of all?"

"That's what I find fiendishly difficult to account for myself! I remember looking there, I remember it all much too well! I crawled on all fours, I touched the place with my hands, I moved the chair, I didn't want to trust my own eyes, but I could see there was nothing there, a bare and perfectly smooth patch of floor space, like the flat of my hand. And still I continued to run my hand over it. Such faint-heartedness is all too common in man when seeking to make good... some significant and distressing loss. You can see there's nothing there, nix, and yet you can't help being drawn to look it over and over again."

"Yes, quite. Only, I'm still puzzled!... I still cannot for the life of me understand," the Prince muttered, utterly confused, "formerly you said there was nothing there, and you had inspected the place, and lo and behold, it's suddenly there!"

"And lo and behold, it's suddenly there!"

The Prince cast Lebedev a curious glance.

"And what about the General?" the Prince asked suddenly.

"So what about the General?" Lebedev again returned, uncomprehending.

"Oh my God! I'm asking, what did the General have to say after you had found the wallet under the chair? You had been looking for it together, hadn't you?"

"At first together. But on this occasion, I must admit, I said nothing and resolved not to explain to him that I'd already found the wallet myself."

"W-why on earth not? And was the money all there?"

"I looked into the wallet. The money was all there – not a single note missing."

"I wish you had come and told me," the Prince said thoughtfully.

"I was afraid to trouble you, Prince, bearing in mind your personal, and perhaps, extraordinary, so to speak, expectations. Besides, I myself pretended I hadn't seen anything. I opened the wallet, went through it, then I shut it and placed it back under the chair."

"What for?"

"N-no reason. Just curious what would happen next," Lebedev suddenly snickered, rubbing his hands.

"So it's still there since the day before yesterday?"

"No, not really. It was there just for a day and a night. You see, I was partly anxious that the General should find it too. Because, let's face it, if I had found it, why shouldn't the General have noticed the object, which hit you in the eye as it were, lying as it did under the chair. I lifted the chair several times and moved it, so that the wallet was completely out in the open, but the General still didn't want to know, and so it went on till the next day. He's been so absent-minded lately, it isn't true. He can be talking to you one moment, telling stories, laughing and the like, and suddenly he'll fly at you for no reason at all. At long last we started moving towards the door, which I'd kept open deliberately. He appeared to hesitate, wanted to say something, more than likely worried about the wallet with all that money in it, but suddenly flew into a rage and said nothing. We only walked a couple of paces along the street when he suddenly swung around and went off in the opposite direction. It was evening when we ran into each other again in a tavern."

"But I trust in the end you removed the wallet from under the chair, did you not?"

"No! It disappeared from under the chair that same night."

"So where is it now?"

"Here," Lebedev returned, laughing as he rose to his full height from his chair and fixed the Prince with a cordial regard, "it suddenly turned up here, in the folds of my frock coat. Here, be so kind as to feel for yourself."

True enough, in the front left hand side of his frock coat, in full view, one could see a kind of a sack with a prominent bulge, which when touched proved unmistakably to be that leather wallet which had slid down through a hole in the pocket.

"I took it out and checked to see everything was there. I let it drop back down again and have been carrying it like this since yesterday morning behind the lining. It fairly knocks against my shins."

"Which you hardly notice?"

"Which I hardly notice, he-he! And imagine, my worthy Prince – even though the object is not worth your august attention – my pockets have never had holes in them, and here surprise, surprise – one has sprung such a hole in the space of a single night! I had a more careful look – the impression was that someone had had a go with a penknife. Simply marvellous, isn't it?"

"And... the General?"

"He was in a huff all day, and yesterday too. He is very displeased. One moment he is as jolly as anything and full of kind words, the next he's sentimental to the point of tears, and the next he will fly into a temper that makes me quail, honest to goodness. You see, Prince, I've no military skills. Yesterday in the tavern the flap of my coat as though inadvertently came into full view, the bulge was just unmistakable. He stared at it out of the corner of his eye, getting angrier and angrier. He's been avoiding looking me straight in the eye for ages now, except when very much under the influence or maudlin. But he shot me a couple of glances yesterday that sent shivers down my spine. Come tomorrow I intend to find the wallet, but in the meantime I want to have my fill of fun with him."

"Why on earth are you torturing him like that?"

"I'm not torturing him, I'm not, Prince," Lebedev responded with fervour. "I genuinely love and... respect him. Believe it or not, but now he's dearer than ever to me! I've never had more regard for him!"

Lebedev said all this with such seriousness and sincerity that it infuriated the Prince.

"You love him, and yet you torture him! The very fact that he left the missing object in such a conspicuous place under the chair and later slipped it into your frockcoat shows that he wants to be above-board with you and is seeking your pardon in all simplicity. Do you understand? He is seeking your pardon! He is relying on your discretion, which gives him hope. It means he believes in your friendship. Whereas all you do is mire him in disrepute... the worthiest of men!"

"The worthiest, Prince, the worthiest, I'll say it again!" Lebedev returned with sparkling eyes. "And, it goes without saying, you alone, the noblest of Princes, could make such a deserving observation! It is for this reason that I'm devoted to you to the point of adoration, rotten that I am to the core! It will be done! I've found the wallet now rather than that I shall find it tomorrow. Here, I'm taking it out in front of your eyes. Here it is! And here's the money too, the lot! Here, take it, my most noble Prince, take it and keep it till tomorrow. I'll come for it tomorrow or the day after. You know, Prince, apparently it had been lying somewhere under a stone in my garden since the night it went missing, wouldn't you say?"

"Make sure you don't just tell him to his face that it has been found. Let him simply see that there's nothing more behind the lining, and he'll understand."

"Are you sure? Wouldn't it be best to say I'd found it, and pretend I'd not even missed it?"

"N-no," the Prince said after a short reflection, "n-no, it's too late for that, it's too dangerous. Actually, it would be better if you didn't say anything! Just be kind to him. But... don't make it too obvious, and... and... you know——"

"I know, Prince, I know, I mean, I know I probably shall not be able to bring it off, because you need a heart like yours for that. And on top of everything, I myself am irritable and touchy – he's been too high-handed by half with me lately. One minute he's snivelling and hanging round your neck, the next, he's running you down and berating you contemptuously. Well, at that stage I might just be a devil and show him

517

the coat flap, he-he! Goodbye, Prince, because I'm obviously detaining and preventing you from enjoying your blithe thoughts—"

"But for God's sake, keep it all to yourself as before!"

"All in good time, all in good time!"

But though the matter was now settled, the Prince nevertheless remained more uneasy than ever. He was looking forward impatiently to the next day's meeting with the General.

4

THE TIME OF THE MEETING was fixed for twelve, but quite involuntarily the Prince was late. On arriving home, he found the General was already waiting for him. At first glance he noticed that his visitor was out of sorts, perhaps precisely because he had been obliged to wait a little. After making his apologies the Prince hastened to sit down, but somehow circumspectly and with unusual care as though the General were made of china and might shatter into pieces at any moment. Formerly he felt very comfortable in the General's presence and it had never occurred to him to stand on ceremony. Soon the Prince realized that the person facing him was quite different from what he had been the day before. In place of confusion and embarrassment there was extraordinary self-discipline in evidence; one could easily conclude that the man had irreversibly resolved on something. To be sure, his self-composure was more superficial than genuine. On the whole the visitor was courteously expansive, though not unwilling to stand on his dignity; at first he was even prone to treat the Prince with some condescension, volubly betraying the wounded dignity of the unjustly offended. His tone of voice was temperate though not without a suggestion of bitterness in it.

"There's the journal I borrowed from you lately," he said, motioning with his head at a journal lying on the table. "Thank you."

"Oh yes! Have you read the article, General? What did you think of it? It is intriguing, is it not?" the Prince replied, glad that a conversation on an unrelated topic had started.

"Intriguing, I will concede, but it's crude and, of course, exasperating. Maybe it's all lies from beginning to end."

The General spoke with aplomb, even contriving a perceptible drawl.

"Oh, the story is so innocuous – the story of an old trooper and eyewitness of the French occupation of Moscow. Some passages are simply wonderful. Besides, any eyewitness records, wherever they come from, are precious. Isn't that so?"

"Had I been the editor, I wouldn't have published it. As regards records of eyewitnesses in general, people would much rather believe an out-and-out liar with a sense of humour, than a respectable, worthy storyteller. I could tell a story or two from the 1812 campaign, which... I have made a decision, Prince, to leave this house – Mr Lebedev's residence."

The General looked at the Prince meaningfully.

"You are staying here in Pavlovsk, at... at your daughter's..." the Prince said, at a loss what to answer. He recollected that the General had called on him to seek advice on an important matter on which his whole fate depended.

"At my wife's place. In other words, in my own and my daughter's home."

"You must excuse me, I—"

"I'm leaving Lebedev's residence, my dear Prince, because I have nothing more to do with that man. I broke with him last night, more's the pity I hadn't done so earlier. I demand respect, Prince, and expect it even from those whom I take to my heart. Prince, I frequently take people to my heart and am nearly always bitterly deceived. That man was unworthy of my trust."

"He can be very irritating," the Prince remarked discreetly, "and he has traits which... but along with all that, his heart is in the right place, and sometimes he is undeniably witty and humorous."

The Prince's way of putting it and his respectful tone of voice flattered the General, though every now and again he still looked about with mistrust. But the Prince's manner was so natural and convincing that it was impossible to question his sincerity.

"That he is not devoid of positive qualities," the General replied, "I was the first to acknowledge by my readiness to offer him the gift of my friendship. Surely, having a family of my own, I have no need of his house or hospitality. I do not excuse my faults. I am unruly. I drank wine with him and perhaps rue the fact now. But it was not merely the drinking (pardon, Prince, the directness with which I, the offended party, speak), it was not merely for the sake of drinking that I entered into association with him! I was particularly attracted, as you put it, by his qualities. But everything has its limits, even qualities. And if he suddenly, to my face, had the temerity to declare that when he was still a child in 1812, he lost his left leg and buried it in the Vagankovo Cemetery in Moscow, that is what I call going right over the top – it shows disrespect, demonstrates a species of arrogance—"

"Perhaps it was merely a great joke to raise a laugh."

"I could well understand that. A harmless lie for comical effect, even if it is crude to the core, cannot offend a man's sensibilities. One can well lie through one's teeth for the sake of friendship and to humour the listener. But if behind it all there is a smidgen of disrespect, if this disrespect is perhaps a signal that the relationship is burdensome, an honourable man has no alternative but to turn around and break this relationship, if only to teach the offender a lesson."

The General turned deep red as he spoke.

"To be sure it was impossible for Lebedev to have been in Moscow in 1812. He is too young. It's too funny for words."

"First, that's as may be. But let's for the sake of argument assume that he may have been born then, how dare he in the same breath maintain that a French artilleryman had trained his cannon on him, had shot off his leg, so to speak, for fun, that he had picked up this leg, taken it home and subsequently buried it in the Vagankovo Cemetery, where he'd later erected a memorial with an inscription, 'Here lies buried the leg of Councillor Lebedev' on one side and on the other, 'RIP beloved dust till the joyous morn of resurrection',* and, to cap it all, has a requiem mass sung for it annually (which is a sacrilege) and he visits Moscow for that purpose each year. To prove his point he invites people to Moscow to show them not only the grave, but even that selfsame French cannon in the Kremlin that had been captured from the French. He maintains it's the eleventh one from the gates, a French piece of ordnance of the old design."

"And yet both his legs are very much his own, if one is to believe the testimony of one's eyes," the Prince remarked, laughing. "I assure you it's a harmless joke. Don't get upset over it!"

"But let me put my own interpretation upon the facts as I see them, which may not be as fanciful as it might appear. He maintains it's a Chernosvitov leg—"*

"Oh yes, they say you can dance with a Chernosvitov leg."

"Quite. After Chernosvitov invented his artificial leg, the first thing he did was to pop in to show it to me. But the Chernosvitov leg was invented a good deal later... And besides, he maintains that his late wife throughout their whole marriage never knew that he, her husband, had a wooden leg. 'If you,' he said to me after I had explained to him the full absurdity of his assertion, 'if you had been a chamber page at Napoleon's court in 1812, you must allow that I had my leg buried in the Vagankovo Cemetery.'"

"Were you then?..." the Prince began and stopped, embarrassed.

The General looked at the Prince condescendingly, almost derisively.

"Go on, say it, Prince," he said with alacrity, "don't hesitate. I am not oversensitive, have your say. Have the goodness to admit that you laugh at the very idea of facing a man in truly reduced circumstances, a man who has... come down in the world... and at the same time to learn that he had personally witnessed... momentous historical events. Has *he* been... talking about any of this to you yet?"

"No, Lebedev has not said anything... if it's Lebedev you have in mind—"

"Hm, I expected he had. You see, it was that... odd article in *The Archive** that started it all. I pointed out the incongruities in it, and since I'd been an eyewitness... You are smiling, Prince, you are looking at me!"

"N-no, I—"

"I look young for my years," the General said with deliberation, "but I am actually somewhat older in years than I seem. In 1812 I was about ten or eleven. I can't be quite sure of my exact age. It's been reduced in my service record. I myself always had a tendency to decrease it."

"I assure you, General, I find nothing unusual in your having been in Moscow in 1812 and... of course, you have stories to tell like many another who lived through those events. One of our countrymen* starts his autobiography precisely by saying that in 1812 when he was an infant, French soldiers gave him bread to eat."

"There you are!" the General exclaimed triumphantly. "My case is of course well out of the ordinary, but it entails nothing far-fetched. Truth very often appears implausible. Chamber page! Sounds strange, I know. But the adventures of a ten-year-old may perhaps be explained precisely by his tender age. A fifteen-year-old would have fared far differently, I assure you, because at the age of fifteen I would not have run away from home, that timber house where we lived on Old Basmannaya Street, the day Napoleon entered Moscow, as I did from my mother who, poor woman, had not managed to leave in time and had stayed behind, shaking with fear. At fifteen I'd have been dead scared, but at ten I was not frightened of anything and made my way through the crowd right up to the steps of the Palace as Napoleon was dismounting from his horse."

"No doubt at all, you are perfectly right that at ten you could well have had far more courage…" the Prince affirmed, concerned that he would not be able to keep a straight face.

"No doubt about it, and everything happened so simply and naturally as can occur only in real life. Had a novelist got hold of the story, he'd have blown it out of all proportion, I'm sure."

"Oh, you are so right!" the Prince exclaimed. "I was just thinking about it. I know of an actual murder perpetrated over a watch, it's in all the papers now. Had an author imagined the crime, social pundits and critics would immediately have been up in arms saying it's not true to life. But once you've read about it in the papers, you accept it as a fact and you feel that it is precisely on the basis of such facts that one learns what life in Russia is all about. It was a splendid observation on your part, General!" the Prince concluded with enthusiasm, terribly glad that he had avoided betraying himself.

"Precisely! Precisely!" the General exclaimed and his eyes lit up with delight. "A boy, a mere child, oblivious of the danger, makes his way through the crowd to view the glitter, the uniforms, the entourage and finally, the great man himself of whom he'd heard so much. Because for several years running at the time he alone was on everybody's lips. The world was besotted with his name. I had, as it were, imbibed it with my mother's milk. Napoleon, passing by a short distance from me, fortuitously caught my eye. I had a noble bearing, my parents dressed me well. I stood out in that crowd, you must agree—"

"Surely! This must have impressed him and proved to him that not everyone had left the city, and that even some nobility with their children had chosen to stay behind."

"Too true, too true! He wanted to win over the hearts and minds of the boyars!* When he cast his hawk eye on me, my eyes must have glinted in response. '*Voilà un garçon bien éveillé! Qui est ton père?*'* I immediately replied, almost choking with fear, 'A general, who has fallen on the field for his fatherland.' – '*Le fils d'un boyard et d'un brave par-dessus le marché! J'aime les boyards. M'aimes-tu, petit?*'* To this instant question, I gave an instant reply, 'A Russian deep in his heart can recognize a great man!' Actually, to be perfectly frank, I don't recall if that was word for word what I said… I was too young… but that was the gist of it! Napoleon was astonished. He thought awhile and said to his suite. 'I admire this boy's pride! But if all Russians think like this lad, then…' He did not finish and entered the Palace. I immediately mingled with his suite and ran after him. Members of his entourage parted to make way for me and treated me as their favourite. But all this was over in a flash… I merely remember that on entering the first hall, the Emperor stopped suddenly before a portrait of Empress Catherine, looked at it for a long time, lost in thought, and at last pronounced, 'A grand lady indeed!' and passed on. Two days later everyone knew me in the Palace and Kremlin and called me '*le petit boyard*'.* I used to go home only at night. At home people nearly went wild. In another two days Napoleon's chamber page Baron de Bazancourt died without making it through the campaign. Napoleon remembered me. I was summoned, brought in without a word of explanation, told to put on the uniform of the deceased, a lad of about twelve and, after I was brought before the Emperor in my new outfit and he had given me a nod, was told I had been specially favoured and elevated to His Majesty's chamber page. I was delighted. I really felt a strong attraction for him from the start… well, and on top of that there was the splendid uniform which meant so much to a young lad… I wore a dark green tailcoat with long, narrow flaps, gold buttons, red cuffs, stitched with gold thread, a high, stiff, open, gold-embroidered collar, the flaps being similarly decorated, tight-fitting, white, chamois leather pantaloons, a white silk vest, silk stockings, shoes with buckles… and when the Emperor went out riding, and I was included in his suite, I wore a pair of high riding boots. Although the general situation was not brilliant to say the least and there was the whiff of enormous disaster in the air, etiquette was observed whenever possible and the more punctiliously, the closer disaster loomed."

"Surely… " the Prince muttered, quite at a loss, "your memoirs would be… quite fascinating."

The General of course was merely repeating what he had already communicated to Lebedev the day before, and consequently was in excellent flow. But suddenly he stopped and regarded the Prince with suspicion.

"My memoirs," he echoed with redoubled satisfaction, "write my memoirs? I have no inclination to do that, Prince! If you wish, my memoirs have already been written, but... they are lying in my bottom drawer. When I am dead and buried, let them be published and without a shadow of a doubt translated into other languages, not for their literary merit, not at all, but for the significance of the momentous historical events to which I bore personal witness, albeit as a child. And therein is contained their especial value – as a child I had access, so to speak, to the most intimate bedchamber of the great man! Of a night I heard the groans of this 'giant in adversity'.* He gave full vent to his tears and groans in front of a child, although I understood well that the reason for his suffering was Emperor Alexander's* silence."

"But he wrote letters... with offers of peace—" the Prince acquiesced hesitantly.

"To be sure we have no idea what the precise nature of his offers was, but he wrote every day, every hour, letter after letter! He was terribly upset. Once in the night, when it was just the two of us, I rushed to him with tears (oh, I loved him!) – 'Ask, do ask Emperor Alexander for pardon!' I shouted. That is, I ought to have said, 'Make peace with Emperor Alexander!' but, being a child, I put it all too naively. 'Oh my child!' he replied – he was walking up and down the room – 'oh my child!' He appeared not to heed that I was ten years old, in fact, he loved talking to me. 'Oh my child, I'd be ready to kiss Emperor Alexander's feet, but as for the King of Prussia, as for the Emperor of Austria, everlasting hatred on them both, and... come to think of it... you understand nothing of politics!' He appeared to realize suddenly whom he was talking to, and fell silent, but his eyes glinted furiously for a long while yet. Well, let's suppose I commit all these facts to paper – and I witnessed some momentous facts – let's suppose I publish them, then will follow all these critics, all this literary backbiting, all these disgruntled sensibilities, factions and... no thank you, that's not my cup of tea!"

"As regards factions, you are of course quite right, and I agree with you," the Prince replied softly after a pause. "I also quite recently read Charras's book on Waterloo.* The book is clearly very serious and experts assure us that it has been written with a deep knowledge of the subject, but on every page there's a hint of gloating over Napoleon's humiliation, and if even any hint of his genius could have been disputed on the basis of other campaigns, Charras, it would seem, would have been extremely pleased. And this is not good for such a serious composition. It smacks of factionalism. Were you kept very busy when you were in the service of... the Emperor?"

The General was over the moon. The Prince's observations, serious and uncontrived, dispelled any vestige of doubt in the General's mind.

"Charras! Oh, I myself was seething with indignation. I wrote to him there and then, but... I... it has to be owned, cannot recall right now... You asked if I was kept busy at the Emperor's. Not at all! I was styled chamber page, but even at the time I didn't take it seriously. Besides, Napoleon very soon lost any hope of winning the Russians over, and would of course have forgotten all about me too, whom he had befriended out of political considerations, had he not... had he not grown to like me personally so much. I can say this now without the least hesitation. I was drawn to him body and soul. The service was not demanding. I had to make the odd appearance at the Palace and... accompany the Emperor on horseback during his outings, that was all. I was a tolerably good horseman. He was used to setting out in the mornings. His suite usually included Davout,* myself, the Mameluke Roustan—"*

"Constant,"* the Prince interposed involuntarily.

"No, Constant was not there. He was taking a letter to... the Empress Josephine at the time. His place was taken by a couple of ordnance officers, some Polish uhlans... well, that was about it, apart from the generals, you understand, and marshals, whom Napoleon used to take with him to survey the lie of the land, the disposition of the troops, to take counsel... Of them all Davout was most frequently in attendance. I remember him well. Huge, corpulent, a dispassionate man in glasses, with hawkish eyes. The Emperor sought his counsel most of all. He had a high regard for him. I remember they held counsel for several days in a row. Davout used to come both in the morning and in the evening, often they didn't see eye to eye with each other. In the end Napoleon would give the impression he agreed. It was just the two of them in the office, apart from me, who remained unnoticed. Suddenly, Napoleon's eyes fell on me, a strange thought flashed in them. 'My child!' he said unexpectedly. 'What think you, if I were to embrace the Orthodox faith and free your slaves, would the Russians follow me, or not?' – 'Never!' I exclaimed with indignation. Napoleon was astonished. 'In this child's eyes, resplendent with patriotism,' he said, 'I have read the mind of the whole Russian people. Enough, Davout! All this is sheer fantasy! Come to your other project.'"

"Yes, but this project was grandiose!" the Prince said with awakened interest. "So you ascribe the project to Davout, do you?"

"All I can say is they discussed it between them. Of course the initial idea belonged to Napoleon, a thought of truly leonine power, but the other project was no less impressive... It was that selfsame *'conseil du lion'*, as Napoleon himself famously referred to Davout's proposal. It envisaged stationing the whole army within the Kremlin walls, building barracks, erecting fortifications, positioning cannon strategically, slaughtering a maximum number of horses and salting the meat, and looting as much corn as possible from the surrounding countryside all in order to last out till spring. And come spring, to break through the Russian lines. This project had a great fascination for Napoleon. Every day we rode along the Kremlin walls and he indicated where to breach, where to build – a lunette here, a ravelin there, a line of blockhouses in another place – all at a glance, authoritatively, without hesitation! Finally, everything was concluded. They went into secret counsel again, I was the third one there. Again Napoleon paced up and down the room, his arms folded on his chest. I could not tear my eyes from his face, my heart was pounding. 'I'm off,' Davout said. 'Where to?' Napoleon asked. 'To salt the horses,' Davout said. Napoleon shuddered. His fate was in the balance. 'My child!' he suddenly said, turning to me. 'What think you of our intention?' Of course the manner in which he asked was that of a man of enormous intellect calling out 'heads or tails' as a last resort. Instead of turning to Napoleon, I turned to Davout and said to him, as though inspired from above, 'Why don't you clear off back to where you came from, General?' The project was off. Davout shrugged his shoulders and, on leaving the room, whispered, *'Bah! Il devient superstitieux!'* The next day orders were given for the retreat from Moscow.

"This is all extremely interesting, I'm sure," the Prince said very softly, "if that's what really happened... that is, I meant to say..." the Prince made an effort to correct himself.

"Oh Prince!" the General exclaimed, enraptured by his own story to the extent that he would not have been able to stop even in the face of the grossest slip-up on the Prince's part. "You said, 'If that's what really happened!' But what happened was more, immeasurably more! All this has been merely the bare, political facts. But I repeat, I was witness to the nocturnal tears and groans of this great man. And that was something no one but me ever bore witness to! Towards the end, it is true, he no longer wept, his eyes had run dry, he only groaned from time to time, but his face grew ever darker. It was as though he had been touched by the hand of eternity. Sometimes we would pass a night completely on our own. Mameluke Roustan would be snoring in the adjacent room – it's unbelievable how soundly the man slept. 'But set against that, he is loyal to me and my dynasty,' Napoleon would remark. One day I felt really down in the dumps, and suddenly he noticed tears in my eyes. He looked at me kindly: 'You are sorry for me!' he exclaimed. 'You are still a child, but another child may yet take pity on me, my own son, *le roi de Rome*,* everyone else, everyone, hates me, and my brothers will be the first to betray me in my adversity!' I rushed up to him in tears. We opened our hearts to each other, and our tears mingled. 'You should, you should write to Empress Josephine!' I urged him, amidst tears. Napoleon shuddered, paused and said, 'You have reminded me of the third heart which loves me. I thank you, my friend!' He sat down and immediately dashed off a letter to Josephine, which was dispatched with Constant the next day."

"You did the right thing," the Prince said. "Overwhelmed as he was by gloomy thoughts, you evoked a tender feeling in him."

"Precisely, Prince, and how well it chimes with the sentiments of your own heart!" the General cried enthusiastically as, strangely, genuine tears shone in his eyes. "Truly, Prince, truly, that was a sight to behold! And would you believe it, I nearly left with him for Paris and, naturally, would have shared his fate 'on the sweltering prison isle',* but alas, our destinies parted! We went our separate ways. He ended up on the sweltering island where he may in a moment of extreme anguish have recalled the tears of his poor lad, who had hung about his neck at parting in Moscow. Whereas I was sent to the cadet corps, subjected to constant military drills, bullying and... alas, everything went down the drain! 'I don't want to take you away from your mother, I'm not taking you with me!' he said to me on the day of the retreat. 'But

I'd like to do something for you.' He was about to mount his horse. 'Write something in my sister's album as a remembrance,' I said with trepidation, because he was very upset and out of sorts. He turned back, asked for a quill and took the album. 'How old is your sister?' he asked, quill at the ready. – 'She is three,' I replied. – '*Petite fille alors.*' And he dashed off:

> *Ne mentez jamais*
> *Napoléon, votre ami sincère.*

Such counsel and at such a time, you must admit, Prince!"

"Yes, that is noteworthy."

"This sheet of paper, in a gilt frame, under glass, occupied the pride of place on the wall of my sister's drawing room all her life till her death – she died in childbirth. Where it is now, I've no idea... but... oh, my God! It's already two o'clock! I must have detained you awfully, Prince! This is unforgivable."

The General got up from his chair.

"Oh, think nothing of it!" the Prince muttered. "It was such a pleasure and... I must say... it was so interesting. I am most grateful!"

"Prince!" the General said, again shaking the Prince's hand with painful force, and looking at him hard with glinting eyes as though something had just dawned on him and he was trying to come to grips with some unexpected thought. "Prince, you are so kind, so charming that I can't help feeling sorry for you sometimes. You are a sight for sore eyes! May God bless you! May your life begin anew and... prosper in love. Mine is at an end! Forgive me, forgive me!"

He left the room quickly, his face buried in his hands. The Prince could not doubt the sincerity of his anguish. He knew also that the old man had left exulting at his own success; all the same he sensed that the General belonged to that category of fibbers who, though they may get carried away and lie through their teeth to the point of abandonment, inwardly suspect that no one really believes them, indeed cannot believe them. In the present case, it was touch and go that the old man might have come to his senses, been overwhelmed with embarrassment, accused the Prince of excessive sympathy towards him and taken offence. "Perhaps I ought not to have allowed him to reach such a peak of exultation?" the Prince reflected ruefully and suddenly could bear it no longer, and burst out laughing; he well understood at the same time that there was no cause for him to reproach himself as he held the General in the highest regard and pitied him immensely.

His premonitions came true. In the evening he received a note which was brief and unambiguous. The General made it known to him that he was parting from him for good; that he respected him and was grateful to him, but that he would not accept "tokens of sympathy that undermined the dignity of someone who was already down on his luck." After the Prince learnt that the old man had locked himself in with Nina Alexandrovna, his anxiety for him abated. But we have already seen that the General had also caused a fracas at Lizaveta Prokofyevna's. Though we cannot go into the details here, we shall merely mention in passing that the upshot of his meeting with her was to frighten her, and his bitter allusions to Ganya had exasperated her completely. He was ignominiously shown the door. That explains why he had spent such a miserable night and the following morning, had lost his composure entirely and rushed out on to the street almost totally demented.

Kolya still had no clear idea what was going on and he hoped to bring his father to his senses by threat and stricture.

"So where do you think you're off to now?" he shouted. "You don't want to go to the Prince, you've fallen out with Lebedev, you've no money, and neither have I – as always, so there you are – out on the road and without a bean!"

"I've always been... without a bean!" the General muttered. "Back in eighteen... hundred and... forty I made the officers roar with laughter when I said that, yes sir!... I don't remember... Oh, remind me not, remind me not! 'Where is my youth, where my prime of life!' Did someone exclaim that... who exclaimed that, Kolya?"

"It comes up in Gogol's *Dead Souls*, father," Kolya said, and looked apprehensively at his father.

"*Dead Souls*! Oh yes, dead! After you have buried me, write on the tombstone, 'Here lies a dead soul!' – 'Disgrace is ever at my heels!' Who said that, Kolya?"

"I don't know, Father."

"Yeropegov wasn't there, you say! Yeroshka Yeropegov!..." he cried out in exasperation, coming to a halt in the street. "And this from my own son, my very own! Yeropegov, who was like a brother to me for eighteen months, a man for whom I fought a duel... Prince Vygoretsky, our captain, turned to him and said over a bottle, 'Listen, Grisha my lad, how did you come by your St Anne's Cross,* tell me that?' — 'In defence of my country, on the battlefield, that's how!' — 'Bravo, Grisha!' I called out. Well, that led to a duel, and then he married... Marya Petrovna Su... Sutugina and was killed on the battlefield... The bullet ricocheted from a medal on my chest and hit him square in the head. 'I'll never forget this!' he cried and fell stone dead. I... I served my country with honour, Kolya, but disgrace, 'disgrace is ever at my heels!' You and Nina will come to my grave... 'Poor Nina!' I called her that formerly, Kolya, long ago that was, early on, and she liked it so much... Nina, Nina! What have I done with your life! Why should you love me, longsuffering soul that you are? Your mother has the soul of an angel, Kolya! Do you hear me? The soul of an angel!"

"I know, Father. Father dear, let's go back home, to Mother! She ran after us! Why are you standing there? As if you didn't understand... Look, why are you crying?"

Kolya was in tears himself and was kissing his father's hands.

"You are kissing my hands, mine?"

"Yes, yours, yours. What's so surprising about that? Look, stop crying here in the street, and you call yourself a general, a soldier! Come, let's go!"

"God bless you, my dear boy, for being considerate to one fallen from grace – yes, to a miserable dotard, your father... may you have a son like that too... *le roi de Rome*... Oh, my curse upon this house!"

"But really, what is all this?" Kolya suddenly expostulated. "What has come over you? Why don't you want to go back home now? Why are you behaving like a madman?"

"I shall explain, I shall explain everything... I'll tell you everything. Don't shout... *le roi de Rome*... Oh, I'm so upset, I'm so miserable! 'Nanny dear, where is thy grave?' – Who was it who said that,* Kolya?"

"I don't know, I've no idea who said that! Let's go home now, immediately! I'll beat Ganya black and blue if you want... where are you off to now?"

The General was dragging him towards a nearby house.

"What's wrong with you? This is not our house!"

The General sat down on the porch and kept pulling Kolya towards him.

"Lean over, lean over!" he muttered. "I'll tell you everything... disgrace... lean over... your ear, your ear. I'll whisper it in your ear..."

"Stop it!" Kolya exclaimed, taking fright, but he leant over in spite of himself.

"*Le roi de Rome*..." the General whispered, shaking in every limb.

"What?... What on earth do you mean, '*le roi de Rome*'?... What are you on about?"

"I... I..." the General went on wheezing, clinging ever tighter to his son's shoulder, "I... want... I'll... tell you everything, Marya, Marya... Petrovna Su... Su-Su-Su..."

Kolya wrenched himself free, grabbed his father by the shoulders and stared at him wildly. The old man went deep red, his lips turned blue, a light shudder flitted across his face. Suddenly he leant forward and collapsed in his son's arms.

"A stroke!" Kolya exclaimed at the top of his voice, at last realizing what was happening.

5

TRUTH TO TELL, Varvara Ardalionovna, in her conversation with her brother, somewhat exaggerated the accuracy of her information regarding the Prince's betrothal to Aglaya Yepanchina. Maybe, being an astute woman, she had anticipated what was to occur in the near future; maybe, in her disappointment at seeing her scheme (in which, in all honesty, she had no faith) go up in smoke, she could not deny herself the all too human pleasure of magnifying the disaster by pouring some more poison into the heart of her brother, for whom she yet bore a sincere and compassionate love. Be that as it may, she could not glean from her friends, the Yepanchin sisters, any clear-cut information; there were only hints, half-spoken words, pregnant silences and riddles. It could also be that Aglaya's sisters had intentionally let slip some untruths in order perhaps to fish something for themselves from Varvara Ardalionovna; finally, it could well be that they too could not deny themselves the female pleasure of teasing their childhood friend. Surely in all that time they could not have failed to detect some vague trace of the web that she was spinning.

On the other hand, the Prince, though he was perfectly right in assuring Lebedev that he had nothing to communicate to him and that nothing significant had occurred in his life, may also have been labouring under a false impression. In actual fact something most unusual had happened to all of them. On the one hand it was nothing, and at the same time – quite a great deal. It is the latter which Varvara Ardalionovna with her unerring feminine instinct had divined.

However, it would be difficult to render an orderly account of how it came about that everyone in the Yepanchin family had simultaneously come to the same conclusion that something momentous had occurred with Aglaya and that her fate was in the balance. Still, no sooner had this thought struck all and sundry at one and the same time than everyone began to be wise after the event and claim to have seen it coming long ago, it had all been evident from the time of the 'Hapless Knight', indeed earlier, only the idea had seemed too absurd to contemplate. That was what the sisters maintained. Of course, Lizaveta Prokofyevna too had been the very first to foresee and find out everything, and her heart had long ago been aching; but whether it had been long ago or not, the thought of the Prince now was not at all to her liking, if only because it robbed her of all piece of mind. There was a question to be resolved without delay; but not only could it not be resolved, but poor Lizaveta Prokofyevna, try as she might, could not even formulate it properly. The matter was a delicate one. Was the Prince a good match or not? Was the very idea sound or not? If not (which was beyond dispute), why not, precisely? But if, by chance, it was sound (which was also possible), then also why, precisely? The head of the household, Ivan Fyodorovich, was initially surprised, but then suddenly made an admission that, by Jove, he too had been suspecting something of the kind all along, on and off, so to speak! But one stern look from his spouse and he desisted; he desisted in the morning, whereas in the evening, in the privacy of the bedchamber when he felt obliged to broach the subject again, he suddenly with unwonted keenness let slip a few unexpected observations. "In effect, what is the problem?..." (A pause.) "Of course, it's all a bit unusual, if it is indeed true, and one has to concede, but..." (Another pause.) "But looked at in another way, at the heart of the matter, the Prince, dammit, is a thoroughly upstanding fellow, and no mistake, and... and, and – well, there's his name, our family roots, all this will go to enrich the family line, which is on the wane in the eyes of society, that is, because... of course, society... society is society. And then again the Prince is not without means, even if his fortune is not exactly great. He has... and... and... and..." (A pregnant pause, after which he dried up completely.) Having heard out her husband to the end, Lizaveta Prokofyevna was utterly beside herself.

In her opinion, all that had taken place was "just an inexcusable and even culpable nonsense, a stupid, grotesque travesty, pure and simple!" To begin with, who was this Prince but an ailing idiot, and secondly – a fool, with neither knowledge of the world, nor of his place in it! To whom could one present him, and what use was he? A half-baked democrat of sorts, with no rank and nothing to show for himself, and... and... what would Belokonskaya say? Was it such a husband we had sought for Aglaya?" Naturally this was the strongest argument of all. The mother's heart sunk at the very thought, she felt it would break and bleed to death, although at the same time something rankled deep down within her, "And what was actually so wrong with the Prince?" Well, it was in fact this very argument, coming from her own heart, that caused Lizaveta Prokofyevna the greatest anxiety.

Aglaya's sisters for some reason liked the idea of the Prince; they did not even see anything odd in it. In a word, they could easily have been totally on his side. But they had decided to remain silent. It was noted once and for all in the family that the more obstinate and resolute were Lizaveta Prokofyevna's objections on any general or particular point at issue within the family, the more likely it was that she had already agreed to the idea. Curiously, Alexandra Ivanovna could not maintain total silence on the subject. Having for some considerable time past chosen Alexandra as her confidante, Lizaveta Prokofyevna now kept on appealing to her and pressing her for an opinion at every step and turn; but in the main, she sought her daughter's help in jogging her memory. "How could all this have happened? Why had no one seen it coming? Why had no one spoken up? What was that confounded 'Hapless Knight' all about? Why was she, Lizaveta Prokofyevna, condemned to sort out the matter all by herself, keep an eye on everything and anticipate everything – while everyone else around her just gaped and gawked, and so on and so forth? Alexandra Ivanovna initially maintained a cautious stance and merely remarked that she shared her father's view that in the eyes of the world it might seem rather sensible that the Yepanchins had chosen Prince Myshkin as a husband for one of their daughters. Gradually warming to the idea, she even added that the Prince was far from being a simpleton, indeed never had been one, and as for his standing in society – who could tell what would determine an upright man's standing in Russia in years to come: whether it would be advancements in the civil service or something quite different. Her mother's response was swift and furious. Alexandra was just a libertarian and it was the wretched "woman question" which was at the bottom of it all. Half an hour later she was already on her way to the town and from there to the Kamenny Island to see Belokonskaya, who quite by chance happened to be in St Petersburg at the time, but was intending to depart fairly imminently. Belokonskaya was Aglaya's godmother.

The old lady listened to Lizaveta Prokofyevna's desperate and frantic outpourings, and was not in the least moved by the maternal woes and tears of her distressed visitor. In truth, she dismissed them as ridiculous. She was a formidable despot. She scoffed at the very notion of equality with her friends of however long standing, and she still regarded Lizaveta Prokofyevna as her protégée going back thirty years, never able to come to terms with the latter's abrupt and wilful character. Belokonskaya remarked in passing that the way she saw it they'd all been far too hasty and, as usual, were making a mountain out of a molehill; that listening now, she could not for the life of her credit that anything serious had occurred; that it would surely be better to wait until further developments; that the Prince in her opinion was a perfectly decent young man, though unfortunately ailing in health, odd, and quite inconsequential. The worst of it was that he openly kept a mistress. Lizaveta Prokofyevna realized full well that Belokonskaya was still a little annoyed with her for the setback suffered by Yevgeny Pavlovich, whom she had recommended. Lizaveta Prokofyevna returned to Pavlovsk even more irritated than when she had left, and immediately began to chastise everyone. "People have gone out of their tiny minds! No one mismanages their affairs like we do! What's the hurry? Has anything happened? For the life of me I just cannot see that anything significant has! Wait until it does! Who cares what Ivan Fyodorovich might have imagined! It won't do to make mountains out of molehills!" and so on and so on.

Her message now was that they should all calm down, stay cool and wait. But alas, the calm state of affairs did not last more than ten minutes. The first blow to the prescribed coolness was dealt by the news of what had happened while she was away on Kamenny Island. (Lizaveta Prokofyevna had departed on the morning after the Prince arrived – after twelve instead of at nine.) The sisters answered their mother's persistent questions in great detail and assured her that nothing had in fact happened in her absence. The Prince had come; Aglaya had kept him waiting for about half an hour, and when she finally did appear, she immediately suggested to the Prince they should have a game of chess; the Prince was absolutely hopeless at chess and Aglaya thrashed him; this had cheered her up immensely and she had teased and laughed at the Prince cruelly for playing badly, reducing him to a sorry sight. She had then suggested a game of cards, fools. But now the tables were turned on her. The Prince proved himself a past master at this game; he played like... like a professional. Aglaya had resorted to all kinds of trickery, had cheated and stolen his tricks before his very eyes, and still he beat her every time; about five in a row. Aglaya had flown into a passion, forgetting herself completely; had mocked and taunted him so much so that the poor man had stopped laughing altogether, and had gone completely pale especially after she had said she'd never stay a minute longer in the room while he was sitting there, and that he had the cheek to turn up at their place in the middle of the night of all times – gone midnight – and this *after all that had happened*. She had then slammed the door and left. The Prince too, in spite of all attempts to comfort him, had slunk off with a hangdog countenance. Suddenly, a quarter of an hour after the Prince left, Aglaya dashed down from upstairs on to the terrace, and so quickly that she hadn't even had time to dry her tear-sodden eyes before she ran out. The reason why she had come running down was that Kolya had brought a hedgehog. They had all started looking at the hedgehog. Kolya had explained that the hedgehog wasn't his, but that a friend had bought it, another schoolboy, Kostya Lebedev, who had stayed behind on the street, too embarrassed to come in because he was carrying an axe. They had bought both the hedgehog and the axe just now from a passing peasant. The peasant had sold the hedgehog for fifty copecks, and they had then persuaded him to sell the axe, which was just right for them, and it was a pretty good axe. At this point Aglaya had begun to plead with Kolya for all she was worth to sell her the hedgehog at once, she even went so far as to call Kolya "my dear". For a long time Kolya resisted giving in, but finally could stand it no longer and called for Kostya Lebedev, who came in with the axe and became very embarrassed. And suddenly it had transpired that the hedgehog didn't belong to either of them, but to a third boy, Petrov, who had given them both some money to buy Schlosser's* *History*, from yet another boy, which that boy, being in need of money, was selling at a bargain price; that they had gone fully intending to buy Schlosser's *History*, but hadn't been able to resist temptation and had bought the hedgehog instead, therefore it was plain that the axe and the hedgehog now belonged to that third boy and they were now taking them to him instead of Schlosser's *History*. But Aglaya would not take no for an answer, so in the end they had given in and sold her the hedgehog. As soon as she had acquired the hedgehog, she at once with Kolya's help put it in a wicker basket, covered it with a piece of cloth and began to plead with Kolya to take it to the Prince in her name as a token of her boundless respect. Kolya had gladly agreed and had given his word he'd deliver it, but had immediately demanded to know what the hedgehog signified and what sort of a present was that. Aglaya had told him to mind his own business. He'd replied that he was certain there was some kind of symbolism behind it. Aglaya had lost her temper and told him he was just a boy and nothing else, to which Kolya had immediately retorted that if it hadn't been for the fact that he respected her as a woman, and moreover held his own principles high, he'd have immediately proved to her that he knew how to respond to such an insult. Be that as it may, he was in the event delighted to carry out the commission and went off to the Prince's with the hedgehog, followed by Kostya Lebedev running at his heels. Aglaya, seeing that Kolya was swinging the basket too much, was unable to resist and called after him from the terrace, "Please, Kolya, my dear, don't drop the hedgehog!" as though she had never spoken a harsh word to him. Kolya stopped and also called out as though he had never quarrelled with her either. "No, I shan't drop it, Aglaya Ivanovna. Have no fear whatever!" and ran off at full pelt. Aglaya followed this with a hearty laugh and ran off to her room laughing. She remained in excellent spirits for the rest of the day.

These reports totally stunned Lizaveta Prokofyevna. One couldn't help but wonder why. But such apparently was her mood at the time.

Her state of disquiet was extreme, and then, to make matters worse, there was the hedgehog. "What was the hedgehog all about? Was it a plot? What was behind it? What was one to make of it? Was it some kind of a coded message?" Lizaveta Prokofyevna kept asking. Besides, poor Ivan Fyodorovich, who had happened to be around at the time of the interrogation, really put his foot in it with his observation. In his opinion there was no coded message of any kind, and as for the hedgehog, "It was simply a hedgehog – nothing more, apart from perhaps a token of friendship, an indication that all was forgiven and forgotten, in a word, it was just a prank, in all events innocent and harmless!"

In parentheses let us remark that he hit the nail on the head. The Prince, on returning home, disgraced and ridiculed, sat for over half an hour licking his wounds in utter despair. When suddenly Kolya appeared, bearing the hedgehog, the clouds lifted immediately; the Prince appeared to rise from the dead. He questioned Kolya; he hung on his every word, asked him to repeat things up to a dozen times, laughed like a child and kept on shaking the hands of both boys as they looked at him and laughed their heads off. It was clear then that Aglaya had forgiven him and the Prince could go to see her again that same night, and for him that was not only the most important thing, for him that was in fact everything.

"What children we are, Kolya! And... and... how good it is that we are children!" he finally exclaimed, joyfully.

"There are no two ways about, she is in love with you, Prince, and that's all there is to it!" Kolya returned with a sense of gravity and conviction.

The Prince coloured, but on this occasion he did not say a word, whereas Kolya was simply killing himself with laughter and clapping his hands; a minute later the Prince also burst out laughing, and after that kept looking every five minutes to see how long it was before he could go to see her.

As for Lizaveta Prokofyevna, it was all too much for her; she could stand it no longer and was on the brink of a nervous breakdown. Disregarding all the admonitions of her husband and daughters, she sent for Aglaya forthwith in order to ask her the final question and to elicit from her the most clear-cut and definitive response. "This has to be settled once and for all," she declared. "We must rid ourselves of this burden and never bring it up again! Otherwise I shall die before the day is out!" It was only at this moment that everyone realized how far things had gone. But apart from some sham expressions of surprise, bursts of laughter, mockery and asides directed at the Prince and those who questioned Aglaya, nothing else could be drawn from her. Lizaveta Prokofyevna took to her bed and reappeared only at teatime, the expected time for the arrival of the Prince too. The Prince was awaited with anxiety, and when he arrived, she nearly had a nervous attack.

He walked in gingerly, almost feeling his way along, smiling strangely, looking people in the eyes as though questioning them; Aglaya was again not in the room, which alarmed him. That evening it was just the family present. Prince S. was still in St Petersburg on a matter to do with Yevgeny Pavlovich's uncle. "I wish he had been here, he'd have said something useful, I'm sure," Lizaveta Prokofyevna could not help thinking to herself with regret. Ivan Fyodorovich sat very much immersed in his thoughts; the two sisters were straight-faced and kept quiet as though they had taken a vow of silence. Lizaveta Prokofyevna did not know how to start the conversation. Suddenly she launched into an attack on the railways and turned her eyes on the Prince defiantly.

Unfortunately Aglaya still did not make her appearance and the Prince's heart sank. Fumbling for words, he tried to pass an opinion to the effect that it would have been highly desirable if the system had been kept in a better state of repair, but Adelaida suddenly burst out laughing. It was at this instant that Aglaya entered, calm and collected. She ceremoniously acknowledged the Prince's bow and solemnly took the most prominent place at the round table. She cast the Prince an enquiring look. Everyone realized that the moment had come when all unanswered questions would be resolved.

"Did you get my hedgehog?" she asked firmly, almost crossly.

"Yes, I did," the Prince replied, blushing and wishing to vanish on the spot.

"Kindly explain without delay what you think about it! Mother and the rest of our family will not rest until you do."

"Listen, Aglaya—" the General suddenly attempted to intervene timidly.

"This, this is quite out of order!" Lizaveta Prokofyevna suddenly interposed in alarm.

"It is not a question of order, *Maman*," Aglaya cut her off firmly. "Today I sent the Prince a hedgehog and I wish to know his opinion. Well, Prince?"

"Opinion about what, Aglaya Ivanovna?"

"About the hedgehog."

"That is... I think, Aglaya Ivanovna, you wish to find out, my attitude to... the hedgehog... in which case, I presume that... in a word..."

He ran out of breath and stopped dead.

"I expected to hear more," Aglaya said after pausing for a few seconds. "Very well, I'm willing to let the hedgehog rest. But I'm glad I'll finally be able to resolve all the disturbing rumours that are going about. Would you mind telling me yourself now if you intend to ask me to marry you, or not?"

"Oh, my God!" Lizaveta Prokofyevna exclaimed.

The Prince shuddered and recoiled. Ivan Fyodorovich was thunderstruck. The sisters frowned.

"Tell me the truth, Prince! Because of you I've been subjected to all manner of enquiries. Are they at all justified, or not? Well!"

"I have not asked to be engaged to you, Aglaya Ivanovna," the Prince said, suddenly coming to life, "but... you know yourself how much I love you and believe in you... even now—"

"My question was if you intend to ask me to marry you, or not!"

"I do," the Prince said softly.

There followed a considerable commotion on all sides.

"This is all highly irregular, my dear friend," Ivan Fyodorovich said, unable to conceal his agitation, "it... is almost unheard of, Aglaya!... I beg your pardon, Prince, I beg your pardon, my dear Prince!... Lizaveta Prokofyevna!" he turned to his wife for help: "This needs... looking into—"

"I refuse, I simply refuse!" Lizaveta Prokofyevna exclaimed, waving her arms in protest.

"Permit me to put my word in, *Maman*, after all I think I too have a part to play in this matter. My whole future is to be decided in an instant," (these were Aglaya's exact words) "therefore I want to be clear about this myself and, besides, I'm glad you are all here... So, let me ask you, Prince, if you 'nourish such honourable intentions' towards me, how precisely do you propose to make me happy!"

"I don't really know, Aglaya Ivanovna, how to answer that. What... what is there to say? And... is it necessary?"

"I can see you are embarrassed and out of breath, are you not? Have a little rest and pull yourself together! Have a glass of water, or someone will fetch you a cup of tea."

"I love you, Aglaya Ivanovna, I love you very much. You are the only one I love and... do not make light of it, I beg you. I love you very much."

"All the same, this is an important matter. We are not children, and we must be practical... Would you have the goodness to inform me now what means have you at your disposal?"

"I say, look here, Aglaya! What's come over you? This is highly improper, my word!..." Ivan Fyodorovich muttered under his breath.

"A disgrace!" Lizaveta Prokofyevna whispered for all to hear.

"She's gone out of her mind!" Alexandra remarked in a similar tone of voice.

"Means... you mean, money?" the Prince enquired in surprise.

"Precisely."

"I... I have a hundred and thirty-five thousand," the Prince said, going red.

"Is that all?" Aglaya enquired in a ringing voice, innocently and without batting an eyelid. "Well, that'll do, especially if we're frugal... Do you intend to seek employment?"

"I wanted to take an examination to become a private tutor—"

"An excellent idea! Of course this would make a difference for us. You weren't contemplating taking a position as a butler?"

"A butler? It never crossed my mind, but..."

But her sisters could resist it no longer and doubled up with laughter. Adelaida had for some time been aware that Aglaya was about to break into uncontrollable laughter which she had been holding back with immense effort. Aglaya wanted to cast a stern look at her sisters, but the very next second was unable to contain herself and exploded into a veritable paroxysm of mad, almost insane, hilarity in the middle of which she leapt to her feet and dashed out of the room.

"I knew all along it was no more than just a big joke!" Adelaida exclaimed. "It all goes back to the hedgehog."

"No, I can stand this no longer, I really cannot stand this any longer!" Lizaveta Prokofyevna burst out and quickly followed Aglaya out of the room. The two sisters ran after her at once. Only the Prince and the father of the household were left behind.

"This, this is... could you ever imagine such a turn of events, Lev Nikolaych?" the General exclaimed sharply, clearly unable to think of anything better to say. "No, seriously, you have to admit!"

"I can see that Aglaya Ivanovna was merely making fun of me," the Prince replied sadly.

"Wait, my boy, I'll go myself, but you stay here... because... but why don't you, Lev Nikolaych, perhaps try to explain to me how it all came about and what it all means, everything, as it were, the long and the short of it! You must agree yourself, my boy, I am her father. A father, true enough, and yet I'm damned if I can understand anything of it all. Why don't you at least try to make sense of it to me!"

"I love Aglaya Ivanovna. She knows it and... and, I know she has known it a long time."

The General shrugged his shoulders.

"Strange, very strange... and do you love her very much?"

"Yes, very much."

"Strange, all this is very strange to me. It's such a surprise, like a bolt from the blue, so to speak... You see, my boy, it's not your means (though frankly I did expect you to have more), but... it's my daughter's happiness... What worries me is... would you be able, as it were, to provide... that happiness? And... and... was it a joke on her part, or was she serious? I'm not talking about you, I mean on her part."

Alexandra Ivanovna's voice resounded from the adjoining room, calling her father.

"Wait here, my boy, wait here! Wait and think it over, I'll be back directly..." he said hurriedly and disappeared out of the room in response to Alexandra's summons, looking rather frightened.

He found mother and daughter in each other's embrace, tears streaming down their faces. They were tears of joy, of tenderness and of reconciliation. Aglaya was covering her mother with kisses, her hands, her cheeks, her lips; they both clung to each other.

"Here, take a good look at her now, Ivan Fyodorych! Here you have her real self!" Lizaveta Prokofyevna said.

Aglaya lifted her happy, tear-sodden face from her mother's chest, glanced at her father, burst into a loud peal of laughter, darted over to him, clung to him tightly and kissed him several times. Then she rushed back to her mother again and completely buried her face in her chest to be completely invisible, and burst out crying again. Lizaveta Prokofyevna covered her with the end of her shawl.

"So, what... what are you doing to us after all this, you cruel girl!" she said, but joyfully, taking a deep breath of relief.

"Cruel! Yes, cruel!" Aglaya suddenly seconded. "Nasty! Spoilt! Tell that to Father. Oh, silly me, he's here. Daddy, are you here? Did you hear me?" she asked, laughing through her tears.

"My dearest girl, my idol!" the General exclaimed, beaming with joy and covering her hands, which she did not withdraw, with kisses. "So, I take it you love this... young man?..."

"No, no, not at all! I can't stand... this young man of yours, I can't stand him!" Aglaya suddenly cried and raised her head. "And if you ever, Daddy, dare... I'm being serious, do you hear me, I'm being very serious!"

And she really was speaking seriously; her face was flushed and her eyes were glinting. Her father fell silent and took fright, but Lizaveta Prokofyevna gave him a sign behind Aglaya's back, to stop asking questions.

"If that's so, my angel, it's up to you, you decide, my dear, he's waiting there on his own. Wouldn't it be best to mention to him discreetly to go away?"

The General in his turn winked at Lizaveta Prokofyevna.

"No, no, that wouldn't be nice at all, especially if 'discreetly'. You go out to him, I'll come later, in a minute. I want to ask this... young man for pardon, because I have offended him."

"Indeed you have, very gravely," Ivan Fyodorovich confirmed sternly.

"In that case... you all stay here, and I'll go on my own first, you come after me, a second later! That'll be best!"

She was already at the door, but suddenly turned back.

"I won't be able to keep a straight face! I'll die of laughter!" she observed wistfully.

But the next second she swung around and ran off to the Prince.

"What's going on? What do you think?" Ivan Fyodorovich asked in haste.

"I can hardly bring myself to say it," Lizaveta Prokofyevna returned equally hurriedly, "but I think it's pretty obvious."

"I agree, it's obvious. It's as clear as day. She loves him."

"She doesn't just love, she's head over heels in love with him!" Alexandra Ivanovna observed. "Only what a choice!"

"God bless her, if that's what she wants!" Lizaveta Prokofyevna remarked, crossing herself piously.

"It seems that is her fate," the General affirmed, "and who can escape one's fate?"

And everyone moved into the sitting room, where another surprise awaited them.

Aglaya not only did not burst out laughing as she feared she would when she approached the Prince, but spoke to him in all meekness.

"Forgive a silly, nasty, spoilt girl," (she took him by the hand) "and be assured that we all respect you beyond measure. And if I had the audacity to poke fun at your wonderful... your kind ingenuousness, please forgive it as you would a childish prank. Forgive me for insisting on an absurdity, which, of course, cannot possibly have any repercussions..."

The last words Aglaya pronounced with especial emphasis.

Father, mother and sisters hurried into the sitting room to see and hear it all, and everyone was surprised by the "absurdity, which, of course, cannot possibly have any repercussions", and even more so by Aglaya's serious mood when she spoke of this absurdity. Everyone exchanged puzzled glances; but the Prince, it seemed, failed to understand her words and was in a transport of joy.

"Why do you say this?" he muttered. "Why do you... ask... for pardon?..."

He even wanted to add that he was unworthy of being asked for pardon. Who knows, perhaps he did not even take in the significance of the words "absurdity, which, of course, cannot possibly have any repercussions", and, odd man that he was, he may even have been glad of them. Doubtless, for him it was the height of bliss to know that henceforth he would be able to come unhindered to see Aglaya, that he would be allowed to talk to her, sit next to her, take walks with her, and who knows, be content in this alone all his life long! (It is probable that it was precisely this contentment which Lizaveta Prokofyevna was afraid of in her heart; she anticipated it; she anticipated much that inspired fear in her, most of which she could not even articulate.)

It is difficult to describe how the Prince cheered up and how happy he was the rest of that night. He was so cheerful that just by looking at him one could not help but be happy oneself, as Aglaya's sisters later observed. He became extremely talkative, which had not happened since that morning six months back when he first got to know the Yepanchins. On his return to St Petersburg he had been noticeably and intentionally reserved, and had in the very recent past admitted to Prince S. in front of others that he should keep a hold on himself and say as little as possible, or his deficient manner of delivery would distort the thought. That evening he was practically the only one who talked. He told a great many stories and answered all questions with alacrity and in great detail. But there was nothing in his speech to suggest a man in love. He stuck to serious, at times involved, themes. He even expounded a few of his pet views, his most closely guarded personal observations, which would have appeared ridiculous had they not been so "skilfully articulated", as all the listeners subsequently wholeheartedly agreed. Now, though the General was fond of weighty conversational themes, it must be said that both he and Lizaveta Prokofyevna found the Prince a little too clever by half so that by the end of the evening they felt thoroughly disenchanted. All the same, the Prince had got so much into the spirit of things that he ended up by telling a number of rather funny anecdotes at which he himself laughed the loudest, so much so that his hearty laughter provoked more amusement in his listeners than the stories themselves. As for Aglaya, she hardly spoke the whole evening; instead, she listened spellbound to Lev Nikolayevich or, more accurately, she just looked at him rather than listened.

"Did you see, she never took her eyes off him? She hung on his every word. Nothing escaped her, nothing," Lizaveta Prokofyevna confided to her husband later. "And if you'd dared say she was in love, she'd have bitten your head off!"

"Can't be helped – that's fate!" the General concluded, shrugging his shoulders and using his favourite word for the umpteenth time. Let us add that for a man of affairs, such as he was, there was a great deal about the whole thing that was not at all to his liking; in the main it was the overall lack of clarity in the matter. But he chose to let time take its course and say nothing, putting all his reliance on... Lizaveta Prokofyevna.

The happy family atmosphere was short lived. The very next day Aglaya again quarrelled with the Prince, and this was repeated continually for the next few days. She persisted in mocking the Prince for hours and made a veritable laughing stock of him. True, they also spent sometimes as much as two hours at a stretch in the summer house in their garden, where it was noticed the Prince almost invariably read a paper or some kind of book to her.

"Do you realize," Aglaya once said to him, interrupting his reading of the paper, "it strikes me you're terribly uneducated. You don't know anything in depth. If one turned to you for something, you wouldn't for instance have a clue as to who, or what, or in what year, or by what statute. You're absolutely pathetic."

"I told you before that I'm not at all erudite," the Prince replied.

"So what are you about then? How can I possibly have any respect for you after that? Carry on reading! On second thoughts – don't! I don't want you to read any more!"

And that same evening she again contrived to astonish everyone. This coincided with the arrival of Prince S. Aglaya was very nice to him and asked him a great deal about Yevgeny Pavlovich. (Prince Lev Nikolayevich had not yet arrived.) Suddenly Prince S. let drop something to the effect that there were likely to be some intimate and significant new changes in the family. As a matter of fact he said this as an aside to Lizaveta Prokofyevna's inadvertent suggestion that it may be necessary to postpone Adelaida's wedding yet again so as to hold both ceremonies together. It is impossible to describe the violence of Aglaya's reaction to "all these silly suppositions!" Incidentally, she was heard to remark that she was not at all prepared to take the place of anyone's mistress.

These words left everyone speechless, especially the parents. Lizaveta Prokofyevna insisted on a private conference with her spouse in order to decide how best to draw the Prince on his relationship with Nastasya Filippovna.

Ivan Fyodorovich swore that it was all merely "a prank", at the root of which lay Aglaya's "bashfulness"; that if Prince S. had not mentioned the wedding, she would not have felt the need to go on the defensive, because Aglaya knew full well that it was all the unadulterated gossip of idle tongues and that Nastasya Filippovna was getting married to Rogozhin; that none of it had anything to do with the Prince, least of all of his being involved in any kind of relationships in which, if the bare truth be known, he never had been implicated.

As to the Prince himself, he appeared to be blissfully unaware of anything and continued to be as happy as a sandboy. Of course, there were occasions when he too detected some dark shades of irritation in

Aglaya's eyes; but he chose not to dwell on the fact and expected the gloom to vanish of its own accord. Having come to this conclusion, he would not allow himself to be swayed from it. Perhaps he was altogether too tranquil about it; this at any rate was how it appeared to Ippolit, who once ran into him in the park by chance.

"Well, wasn't I right when I told you then that you were in love?" he began, approaching the Prince and blocking his way. The Prince put out his hand and congratulated him on how well he looked. The patient's spirits seemed indeed to have revived considerably, which is not uncommon with consumptives.

His sole purpose for approaching the Prince was to say something caustic apropos the latter's blissful appearance, but he tripped mid-sentence and began to talk about himself. He began to moan, and went on and on, and not altogether coherently at that.

"You won't believe it," he concluded, "how irritable everyone is there, how petty, selfish, vain and common. You know, the only reason they asked me to move in with them was to see me die as soon as possible, and now they're all furious that I'm not only not dead, but, contrary to their expectations, am feeling better. This is pure vaudeville! I bet you don't believe a word I say!"

The Prince was not inclined to argue.

"Sometimes I'm even thinking of moving back in with you," Ippolit added casually. "So you don't suppose they're capable of offering accommodation to someone they expect to die imminently and as soon as possible, do you?"

"I thought you had been invited for quite some other reason."

"Aha! You're not at as naive as people make you out to be! This is not the time, otherwise I would have revealed to you a thing or two about this Ganya and his high hopes. They're trying to take advantage of you, Prince, mercilessly so, and I'm quite... sorry for you. All the same, it's a great pity you are so calm about it. But, alas, you cannot do otherwise!"

"Really, is that why you're sorry for me?" the Prince asked, laughing. "Would I have been any happier if I had not been so calm? Is that what you are trying to say?"

"It's better to be unhappy, and *to know* the reason why, than live in a fool's paradise. You appear not to be aware in the least that you've a rival... in the other camp!"

"What you say about rivalry is a little cynical, Ippolit. I am sorry I can't reply to you. As regards Gavrila Ardalionovich, if only you had the least idea of his circumstances and the loss he has suffered, you'd realize it would be next to impossible for him to stay calm. I'm sure that is the best way to look at things. There's still plenty of time for him to change. He has a long life ahead of him, and life is a very splendid thing... however, on second thoughts... on second thoughts..." the Prince appeared to lose his thread, "what you said about taking advantage of... I don't even know what you were talking about. Let's just drop the subject, Ippolit, shall we?"

"Yes, let's, for the time being. You can't possibly do otherwise than proclaim what a gentleman you are. Yes, Prince, you're not going to believe, unless you touch it with your own finger, ha ha! Tell me, do you hate me a lot now?"

"What for? Because you suffered more than us and are still suffering, is that why?"

"No, because I'm not worthy of my suffering."

"Whoever has suffered more, it follows, was worthy of suffering more. After Aglaya Ivanovna had read your 'Explanation', she wanted to see you, but—"

"She's putting it off... she mustn't, I understand, I understand..." Ippolit interrupted him as though in a hurry to change the subject. "Incidentally, I heard you read all that nonsense to her yourself. It really was conceived and... written in a delirium. I simply don't understand how – I shan't say cruel (that would be insulting), but childishly vain and vindictive one must be to reproach me for this 'Explanation' and use it as a weapon against me! Don't worry, I'm not talking about you—"

"But it's a pity you want to disown that piece of writing, Ippolit, because it's so full of sincerity. And believe me, even the most ridiculous bits, and there are many," (Ippolit winced at this) "are redeemed by suffering, because to own up in them was to suffer too and... badly at that. The idea which gave you the initial impetus was a thoroughly noble one, I'm sure. I'm not sitting in judgement upon you, I'm merely giving voice to my own thoughts, and I'm sorry I didn't speak up at the time..."

Ippolit flushed. He had an idea the Prince was just dissembling and trying to trap him; but looking him in the face closer, he did not doubt his sincerity.

"And still I must die!" he said (nearly adding, "A man like me!"), "And imagine what a pain this Ganya of yours is. He has suggested that of those who listened to me then, three or four would die before me! What do you say to that! He imagines it's a consolation, ha ha! First, none have yet died, and even if they had, what comfort would there be in that, tell me! He measures by his own yardstick. In truth, he has gone even further. He just keeps swearing and insisting that an honourable man would in the event have simply died in silence, whereas the way I presented it, it reeked of selfishness! What do you say to that! What I mean is, what selfishness on his part! What finesse, or to put it better, how impenetrably thick-skinned of him not to be aware of his own egoism!... Have you ever read the story of the death of one Stepan Glebov* in the eighteenth century? I came across it by chance—"

"What Stepan Glebov?"

"He was impaled in Peter's time."

"Oh, my God, I know whom you mean! He spent fifteen hours impaled on a stake, in the freezing cold, under a fur coat, and died extraordinarily bravely. Yes, of course, I too read about him... what about him?"

"Some people are granted such a death by God, but not the likes of me! Do you suppose I wouldn't be capable of dying a death like Glebov's?"

"Oh, not at all," the Prince said, caught off his guard, "I merely meant that you... not that you are unlike Glebov but... that you... are more—"

"I know what you wanted to say: 'more like an Osterman* than a Glebov.' That's what you wanted to say, wasn't it?"

"Who was Osterman?" the Prince asked in surprise.

"Osterman was a diplomat in the reign of Peter the Great," Ippolit muttered, suddenly losing concentration. There was an awkward pause.

"Oh n-n-o! I meant something else," the Prince drawled, "I don't think... you could ever be like Osterman..."

Ippolit furrowed his brow.

"The reason why I am convinced of this," the Prince went on suddenly in an obvious attempt to prevent a misunderstanding, "is because people of former times (I swear this was a always a source of never-ending wonderment to me) were quite different to what they are now, another breed to what we have nowadays, really, almost a different species... People then appeared to be possessed by a single idea, now they're much more nervous, sophisticated, sensitive, capable of handling two or three tasks at one and the same time... modern man is more wide-ranging, and – I assure you, that is what is stopping him being as single-minded as people were in the distant past... I... I'm only saying this because—"

"I follow you. In order to make up for your naivety and for disagreeing with me, you're now hell bent on comforting me, ha ha! You're such a child, Prince. Besides, I notice you still treat me like... a piece of china... All right, all right, I'm not angry. In any case, our conversation has taken a rather amusing turn. You're a complete child sometimes, Prince. Remember, though, I may perhaps have wished to be something rather better than a mere Osterman. It would hardly be worth one's while coming back from the dead in the shape of an Osterman... Still, I'm convinced I must hurry up and die, otherwise I myself... Leave me alone. Goodbye! Well, go on then, tell me, how would you have me die?... That is, to make it as virtuous as possible! Well, tell me!"

"Be on your way and forgive us our good fortune!" the Prince said softly.

"Ha ha ha! That's just what I expected! I was convinced you'd come up with something like that! All the same, you're... you're a real case... My oh my! How some people always have a slick phrase at the ready! Goodbye, goodbye!"

6

WHAT VARVARA ARDALIONOVNA had to say to her brother about the forthcoming evening reception at the Yepanchins' dacha, which Belokonskaya was expected to attend, also turned out to be perfectly accurate – the guests were due that very same day in the evening; nevertheless the manner in which she spoke of this lacked a certain discretion. True, all the arrangements were put in place in somewhat of a hurry and with what seemed completely unnecessary anxiety, and this precisely because "in this household nothing ever happens normally". Everything was to be explained by Lizaveta Prokofyevna's impatience, refusal "to entertain any more doubts", and the ardent concern with which the two parental hearts were beating for the happiness of their favourite daughter. Besides, Belokonskaya was indeed expected to leave the town soon; and, since her patronage really counted for much in society and it was hoped she would treat the Prince favourably, the parents calculated that the bridegroom would have the advantage of entering society directly under the sponsorship of the all-powerful lioness. Even if there were any eyebrows raised in the process, her august patronage would ensure that all would not appear too outlandish.

The whole crux of the matter was that the parents could not make up their own minds if there really was anything outlandish about the whole arrangement. A friendly, sincere counsel from competent, authoritative people would have been worth its weight in gold at that moment of crisis, at which, thanks to Aglaya, nothing had yet been decided finally. Come what may, sooner or later the Prince would have to be introduced into a society of which he had not the slightest concept. In short, he would have to be "presented". The proposed soirée was to be quite informal; only a small number of close family friends was expected to attend. Besides Belokonskaya, one other lady had been invited, the wife of a high-ranking official and dignitary. Of the younger people, all hope appeared to be centred on Yevgeny Pavlovich, who was to be Belokonskaya's escort.

The Prince had known that Belokonskaya was due three days before her arrival; as to the soirée itself, he found out about it only the night before. He could also not help but notice the anxious looks of the members of the family and, judging by some indications and tellingly apprehensive exchanges, realized that people were concerned about the impression he would create. But the Yepanchins, every single one of them, were convinced that in his simplicity he would never himself be able to realize that he was a source of anxiety. In consequence, everyone regarded him with doleful looks. In truth, he really did not attach much importance to the forthcoming event. He was preoccupied with something altogether different. Aglaya was with every passing hour becoming more and more capricious and dejected – this pained him very much. After he found out that Yevgeny Pavlovich too was expected, he cheered up enormously and said he had been wanting to see him for a long time. For some reason this remark did not go down well at all. Aglaya left the room in umbrage and only late that night, coming on for twelve, when the Prince was about to take his leave, seized an opportunity to say a few words to him in private on parting.

"I'd prefer if you stayed away all day tomorrow, and came only in the evening after... the guests have already assembled. I take it you know we're having guests?"

She spoke in an edgy, peevish tone of voice. This was the first occasion that she had alluded to the soirée. She too found the idea of this reception almost intolerable; this had not gone unnoticed. Perhaps she was desperately anxious to make an issue of this with her parents, only her pride and sense of mortification would not allow her to broach the subject. The Prince realized immediately that she was also anxious because of him (and did not want to admit it), and suddenly he himself lost heart.

"Yes, I have been invited," he replied.

She was apparently unsure how to continue.

"Can one ever speak seriously about anything with you? If only once in a lifetime?" she blurted out suddenly in high dudgeon, unaccountably unable to control herself.

"Of course you can, and I am listening. In fact, I'm delighted," the Prince muttered.

Aglaya paused for a while and then spoke, but with evident aversion.

"I didn't want to argue with them about this. There are occasions when they're impervious to reason. I've always been put off by some of Mother's attitudes. I'm not talking about Father – what can you expect of him? Of course, I look up to *Maman* enormously. She has a very aristocratic personality. Try to suggest to her something unworthy, and you'll see for yourself. And yet she kowtows before this... wretch. I don't mean just Belokonskaya. She's a nasty piece of work and a loathsome character, but she's got her head screwed on and knows how to hold everyone in check – which is good in a way. How awful! And it makes me laugh. We've always been middle-class people, the most bourgeois you can possibly imagine. So why try to aspire above our station? My sisters are just as bad. It's Prince S. who's to blame. Why were you so glad that Yevgeny Pavlovich is coming?"

"Listen, Aglaya," the Prince said, "I have the feeling you're very worried about me, that I might come a cropper tomorrow night in front of... those people!"

"About you? I – worried?" Aglaya exclaimed, indignantly. "Why should I be worried about you, were you... were you to come a cropper completely? What's it got to do with me? And how dare you say such a thing? What does it mean 'a cropper'? It's a horrible expression! I don't like it!"

"It's... schoolboyish."

"Yes, schoolboyish! I hate it! I assume it will form part of your vocabulary tomorrow too, won't it? You should have a closer look in your lexicon for some more phrases like that. The effect will be shattering. More's the pity, I understand you know how to make an entrance into a salon. Where, I wonder, have you learnt that? Would you be able to accept and drink a cup of tea properly with everyone staring at you?"

"I think I would."

"Shame, or I would have had a good laugh. Why don't you at least break the china vase in the sitting room? It's expensive. Please, break it. It's a present, and mother will go berserk and burst into tears in full view of everyone – it's so precious to her. Gesticulate grandly like you always do, knock it over and break it."

"On the contrary, I'll try to sit as far as possible. Thank you for warning me."

"So, it means you know in advance you'll be making sweeping gestures. I bet you won't be able to stop yourself launching forth on some 'topic', about something serious, learned, elevated! It will be so... proper!"

"I would say, silly... at best inappropriate."

"Listen, once and for all," Aglaya said in utter exasperation, "if you touch upon something like the death penalty, or the economic situation in Russia, or that the world will be saved by beauty, I shall, of course be... delighted and laugh my heart out, but... let me warn you in advance, don't ever dare to show your face to me after that! Did you hear that, I'm being perfectly serious!"

She did indeed enunciate her threat in a perfectly serious tone of voice which was even reflected in the look in her eyes, so much so that it took the Prince completely by surprise, and told him it was certainly no joke.

"Well, you'll be glad to know that now I'm a bag of nerves and bound to launch on some topic or other and shall even... probably...

break the vase too. Earlier I was not afraid of anything, now I'm afraid of everything. I shall definitely come a cropper."

"In that case, don't say a word. Sit still and keep your mouth shut."

"That won't be possible. I'm sure I'll start speaking out of fear and break the vase out of fear too. Perhaps I'll trip up, or something like that will happen to me, because it already has once or twice. I shall be dreaming about it all night. Why did you have to mention it?"

Aglaya looked at him despondently.

"Do you know what, I'd better not come at all tomorrow! Let me pronounce myself dyspeptic, and that'll be the end of it!" he decided.

Aglaya stamped her foot and went pale with rage.

"My God! Whoever heard the like! He won't come, when the whole thing has been arranged expressly… my God! Isn't it a pleasure to have to deal with a duffer like you!"

"All right, I'll come, I will!" the Prince hastened to assure her. "And I give you my word of honour I shall sit all evening and not say a word. I promise."

"I'm glad, I'm sure. You said just now, 'I'll pronounce myself dyspeptic'. Really, where do you get such expressions from? Why do you insist on talking to me in such a turn of phrase? Are you making fun of me, or what?"

"I beg your pardon. It's also a schoolboyish expression. I'm sorry. I can see quite plainly that you… mistrust me… go on, don't get upset about it, I'm overjoyed. You've no idea how frightened I am, and yet how glad I am to hear what you've said! But my fear, I swear to you, is unimportant and insignificant. Honestly, Aglaya! However, my joy is no passing matter. I'm so glad you're such a child, such a charming, gorgeous child! Really, you can be so wonderful, Aglaya!"

Aglaya was about to flare up with anger, but suddenly an unexpected sentiment overwhelmed her momentarily.

"Will you not reproach me for these rude words of mine… one day… later?" she suddenly asked.

"Not on your life! And why have you blushed again? There, you're looking daggers at me again! There's sometimes too much severity in your eyes, Aglaya, where there was none before. I know why this is—"

"Don't, don't say that!"

"I think we should talk about it. I've been meaning to for a long time. I had already mentioned it earlier, but... it was not enough, because you did not believe me. There is someone between us—"

"No, no, don't say it, don't say it!" Aglaya suddenly interrupted him, grabbing his hand firmly and staring at him in terror. At that moment someone called her. Relieved by the distraction, she let go of his hand and ran off.

The Prince spent the whole of that night in a fever. Strangely, he had been feverish several nights in succession. On this occasion, however, semi-delirious though he was, he suddenly asked himself, what if he had a fit in front of everybody tomorrow? After all, hadn't he had fits before when he was fully awake? He broke out in a cold sweat at the thought. All night long he imagined himself in the company of some amazing, exquisite people, quite unlike anyone he had met before. The main thing was that he tried to strike up a conversation. He knew he ought not to speak, yet he did all the time. He tried to persuade them of something. Yevgeny Pavlovich and Ippolit were also amongst the guests, and they seemed to be on unusually good terms with each other.

He woke after eight with a splitting headache, an inability to gather his thoughts and beset by strange emotions. For some reason he felt a strong urge to go and see Rogozhin; to see him and talk to him at length –about what, he had no idea. Later on, he had resolved for some reason to go to Ippolit. He felt a vague unease in his heart, so much so that, however strong an impression the events of the morning had on him, he experienced a sense of their inadequacy. One of these events was Lebedev's visit.

Lebedev turned up quite early, just after nine, very much under the influence. Even though the Prince was not particularly observant lately, he could not help but notice that in the last three days since General Ivolgin's departure, Lebedev's behaviour had deteriorated markedly. He had all of a sudden become very slovenly and untidy. His necktie was pulled over to one side, and the collar of his frockcoat had a tear in it. In his own quarters, he even threw tantrums and this could be heard across the little yard. Once Vera came in tears and complained about something. On turning up now, he launched into a strange tirade, pounded his chest and reproached himself for something...

"I've had my comeuppance for my treachery and my malice... I got slapped in the face!" he concluded at last in a tragic tone of voice.

"A slap in the face! From whom?... At this time of the morning?"

"At this time of the morning?" Lebedev retorted, smiling deviously. "The time of morning is neither here nor there... even if it had been a question of physical assault... but I received a moral... a moral slap in the face, I tell you, not a physical one!"

He suddenly sat down unceremoniously and began to speak. His story was very disjointed. The Prince winced and wanted to leave him to it, but suddenly he heard a few words which made him sit up. He was thunderstruck... Mr Lebedev told a strange story.

It began with some kind of a letter; Aglaya Ivanovna was mentioned. Then Lebedev took to reproaching the Prince; one could have been forgiven for thinking that the Prince had offended him. At first the Prince had allegedly drawn him into his confidence as regards the affairs of a certain personage (Nastasya Filippovna); but had subsequently broken with him and chased him away ignominiously, and this was all the more hurtful as it came hard on the heels of a callous refusal "to satisfy even an innocent enquiry regarding some forthcoming changes in the household". Maudlin tears streaming down his face, Lebedev declared that after this "he could hold out no longer, the more so because he was privy... privy to a great many things as revealed... by Rogozhin, and Nastasya Filippovna, and Nastasya Filippovna's friend, and Varvara Ardalionovna... herself... and... and even personally by Aglaya Ivanovna, can you imagine, through the good offices of Vera, my beloved daughter, my one and only... yes, quite... correction, no, not one and only, I've three. And who was it who kept Lizaveta Prokofyevna in the know by letters in conditions of the utmost secrecy, he he he? Who kept her abreast of all the relationships and... movements of a certain personage, namely Nastasya Filippovna, he he he? Who could have been this mysterious individual, I ask you, sir?"

"It wasn't you by any chance, was it?" the Prince exclaimed.

"Indeed it was," the drunk replied with a show of dignity, "and today at half-past eight, which was half an hour... correction, there-quarters of an hour ago, I promptly informed the worthy mother that I am in a position to pass on to her details of an incident... to boot a significant one. I did it by means of a folded note that I slipped to the maidservant at the back entrance. She received me."

"You have been to see Lizaveta Prokofyevna just now, have you?" the Prince asked, hardly believing his ears.

"I saw her just now and she slapped my face... morally that is. She returned the letter, you may say she threw it back in my face... unopened... and sent me packing with a flea in my ear... a figurative flea that is, not a real one... come to think of it, though, it was as good as a real one, it was that close!"

"What unopened letter did she throw at you?"

"Didn't I?... He he he! Well, I never, I could've sworn I'd told you already. So I haven't, have I?... There only was one to be delivered—"

"From whom? To whom?"

But it was difficult to follow or make anything of some of Lebedev's "explanations". All the same, the Prince managed as best he could to establish that the letter had reached Vera Lebedeva via a maidservant early in the morning for delivery to the addressee... "just like the previous time... just like the previous time – a letter from the same lady to a certain personage, sir... (for I designate one of them a lady and the other a personage in order to lower the one and to differentiate between the two; for there is a world of difference between the virginal innocence and virtue of a General's daughter and... a woman of the world) and so, to continue, the letter was from a lady whose name begins with *A*—"

"How can that be possible? To Nastasya Filippovna? Rubbish!" the Prince cried.

"And yet, and yet, one can't get away from it. If it wasn't to her, it was to Rogozhin, which comes to the same thing... and there had even been a letter to Mr Terentyev to be passed on, originating with a lady whose name begins with *A*," Lebedev said, winking and smiling.

Because he frequently kept jumping from one thing to another and lost track himself every time he began to speak, the Prince paused to let him finish. It was still very unclear whether the letters had passed through his or Vera's hands. If he himself maintained that to Rogozhin and to Nastasya Filippovna came to the same thing, it would suggest it wasn't through his hands that the letters passed, that is provided there had been such letters in the first place. How he had come by one such letter now, was a total mystery. The likeliest explanation was that he had simply filched it from Vera... and had for some reason best known to himself delivered it to Lizaveta Prokofyevna. That, as far as the Prince was concerned, was the likeliest interpretation.

"You are out of your mind!" he exclaimed, utterly bewildered.

"Not quite, my highly esteemed Prince," Lebedev returned, not without a note of malice in his voice. "To be honest, I had a mind to hand it to you personally, straight into your own fair hands, all in the line of duty and service... but I thought better of it and directed my good offices elsewhere to put the most admirable mother into the picture... seeing as I had already kept her au fait on a previous occasion by way of an anonymous letter. And the note I sent her asking for an audience at eight twenty, I also signed, 'Your servant and secret correspondent". Imagine, I was admitted forthwith, truly expeditiously, by the back entrance... into the presence of the worthiest of mothers."

"Well, go on!..."

"Well, the rest is history, she nearly killed me. That is it came as near to it as makes no difference, so that you might as well take it that she did. Only she threw the letter back at me. Mind you, I'm sure she'd have liked to have kept it – I could see it, I could tell – but she changed her mind, and threw it at me. 'If such a one as you has been charged with delivering it, then go ahead and deliver it...' You should have seen how angry she was! If she did not scruple to speak like that in front of me, she must have been well and truly offended. A fiery lady if ever there was one!"

"So who's got the letter now?"

"I have. Here it is."

And he gave the Prince Aglaya's note to Gavrila Ardalionovich, which the latter, just two hours later that same morning, showed his sister in triumph.

"This letter must not remain in your hands."

"It's yours, it's all yours," Lebedev acquiesced fervently. "Now I'm again unremittingly yours, at your service, body and soul, your servant, following a fleeting bout of betrayal, sir! Execute the heart, spare the beard, as Thomas More said*... in England and Great Britain. *Mea culpa, mea culpa*, so says Papa Roma... I know he's the Pope of Rome, but to me he's Papa Roma."

"This letter must be forwarded immediately," the Prince insisted. "I shall do it."

"Wouldn't it be better though, I wonder, my scrupulously minded gentleman Prince... if... you know what I mean!"

Lebedev pulled a strange, obsequious grimace; he began to shift about weirdly as though he'd been pricked with a needle and, winking slyly, began to execute contortions with his hands in an attempt to convey something or other.

"What's the matter with you?" the Prince demanded sternly.

"Shouldn't we open it first?" he brought out softly and conspiratorially.

The Prince leapt to his feet with such fury that Lebedev took to his heels. But on reaching the door, he paused, expecting the Prince to relent.

"Oh, Lebedev, how could you stoop so low?" the Prince vented his frustration. Lebedev's features relaxed.

"Lowest of the low!" he sighed, approaching the Prince, pounding his chest and with tears in his eyes.

"It's just so mean!"

"Yes, mean! There's no other word for it!"

"And where do you get these... strange urges from? You're nothing short of a common spy after this! What made you write anonymous notes and disturb... such a respectable and kind lady? Why, in the end, can Aglaya Ivanovna not write to whom she pleases? Did you go to lodge some kind of a complaint today? What was it you were after? What made you go and cause trouble?"

"Solely a benign and overwhelming sense of curiosity and... a desire to be of service as becomes my better nature, yes sir!" Lebedev mumbled. "Now I'm wholly yours, your obedient servant! You may hang me, if you wish!"

"Is this how you presented yourself to Lizaveta Prokofyevna?" the Prince asked him with repugnance.

"No... my complexion was fresher and... more becoming. What you see before you now, is after the humbling... not how I looked before."

"Well, all right, leave me now."

In the event, it took several more repetitions before the visitor finally departed. He had already been in the doorway, but turned back, walked to the middle of the room on tiptoe and again began to make gestures mimicking the opening of letters; however, he did not dare to articulate his suggestion; eventually he withdrew with a soft benign smile playing about his lips.

The Prince found it very difficult to listen to all this. The result of all this was one important extraordinary fact, that Aglaya was for some reason ("because of jealousy," the Prince whispered to himself) deeply troubled, undecided and pained. It was also evident that some malicious people were out to confound her, and the surprising thing was how trusting she was towards them. Of course, in that inexperienced, pretty little head of hers, some rather peculiar plans were being hatched that could well prove disastrous... and were certainly most unconventional. The Prince was very uneasy about this and in his state of quandary did not know where to turn to. Something definitely had to be forestalled, that much he felt certain of. He cast another glance at the address on the sealed letter. Oh, he had no qualms whatsoever as far as he himself was concerned – his faith would sustain him: it was Gavrila Ardalionovich he mistrusted. In spite of that, he was resolved to hand it to him personally and was already on his way to do so, but before he reached his destination, he changed his mind. Right in front of Ptitsyn's house, quite by chance, he bumped into Kolya, and the Prince asked him to pass the letter to his brother as though it came directly from Aglaya. Kolya did not bother to enquire and carried out his errand, so that Ganya had no idea through how many stages the letter had passed. After he returned to his place, he called for Vera Lukyanovna, put her in the picture and calmed her down, because up to that time she had been looking for the missing letter and crying. She was shocked when she learnt that her father had taken it. (The Prince learnt from her subsequently that she had on several occasions run errands for Rogozhin and Aglaya Ivanovna in their secret correspondence. It had never in her life occurred to her that there may have been something harmful for the Prince in that...)

Finally, the Prince had managed to work himself up into such a state that when, two hours later, a messenger arrived from Kolya with news of his father's illness, he could not for a minute or so get a grip on himself. But this same incident had the effect of settling him, because it took his mind away from his own troubles. He stayed with Nina Alexandrovna, to whom naturally the sick man was brought, and stayed almost till evening time. There was nothing much he could do, all the same there are people whose presence is sometimes most welcome at time of stress. Kolya was in a bad way. Tears were running down his cheeks, all the same he was constantly on the move, now fetching the doctor – he managed to track down three – now running to the chemist's, now to the barber's. The General was revived, but he remained unconscious. The doctors declared that the patient was by no means out of danger. Varya and Nina Alexandrovna never left his bedside. Ganya was in a state of shock and confusion, and would not go upstairs, seemingly afraid to face the ailing General. He wrung his hands, and in an incoherent conversation with the Prince, kept reiterating, "What a disaster – and, to make matters worse, at a time like this!" The Prince more or less surmised what was meant by "at a time like this". Ippolit had already gone by the time the Prince arrived at Ptitsyn's. Just as it was getting dark, Lebedev turned up in a hurry. After his exchanges in the morning, he had been sleeping it off, and had only now woken up. He was almost completely sober and was shedding genuinely bitter tears over the sick man as though he were his own brother. He accused himself out loud of something without offering any explanation of what he may have done wrong, and persisted in assuring Nina Alexandrovna that it was he, he alone, who was behind it all, and no one else, save he... that it was purely out of benign curiosity... and that the "deceased" (that was how for some reason he insisted on referring to the General who was still very much alive) was in truth a man of genius! He was particularly keen to stress the word genius as though some vital benefit was liable to accrue as a result. Nina Alexandrovna, at the sight of his tears of penitence, finally said soothingly, without the least tone of reproach in her voice, "There, come along now, don't cry, God will be merciful!" Lebedev was so astonished to hear these words and the way they were spoken that he would not leave Nina Alexandrovna for the rest of that evening. And all the rest of the time, till the day the General died, he spent almost exclusively with the family. In the course of the day a messenger from Lizaveta Prokofyevna called on Nina Alexandrovna to enquire after the patient's state of health. When at nine o'clock that evening the Prince entered the Yepanchins' drawing room, which was already filled with guests, Lizaveta Prokofyevna immediately began to question him about the General in detail and with concern, and rendered Belokonskaya a dignified and detailed account in reply to her question, "Who is this sick man and who is Nina Alexandrovna?" The Prince was very gratified to hear this. When conversing with Lizaveta Prokofyevna, he comported himself "beautifully", as Aglaya's sisters subsequently testified: "He was reserved and calm, spoke to the point without waving his arms about, and was dignified and excellently dressed". Not only did he not "trip up on level ground" as he feared he would the day before, but by all indications he managed to create a favourable impression on everyone.

Having had time to settle down and look around, he concluded that the whole of this gathering was not at all as terrifying as Aglaya had painted it, or as frightening as were his own nightmares the night before. For the first time in his life he had a glimpse of what is ominously referred to as "society". In consequence of some private inclinations, beliefs and tendencies, he had long striven to make his way into this magic circle and was therefore dead keen to know what his first impression would be. This first impression turned out in fact to be very gratifying. Somehow it immediately struck him that all these people were in fact born to be together; that the Yepanchins were not having any kind of a special soirée or that there were any select guests, but that everyone was on intimate terms with one another and that he himself was a long-standing loyal friend of theirs, fully sympathetic with their views, who'd only just been reunited with them after a recent separation. The allure of good manners, lack of inhibition and apparent goodwill were almost intoxicating. It never even entered his head that all these charming good manners and this graciousness, these clever remarks and the dignified, self-possessed bearing, were merely a well-rehearsed front. Looked at more closely, the majority of the guests were, never mind their imposing exterior, rather vacuous people, who in their self-delusion did not realize that much of what was positive about them was a mere veneer which they had inherited unconsciously, by proxy. It is this that the Prince, under the charming delusion of his first impression, refused even to countenance. He was bowled over, for instance, by the fact that that old man, that venerable dignitary, who in years could well have passed for his grandfather, was ready to stop in mid-flow merely to hear him out, young and inexperienced as he was, and not merely to hear him out, but to give due weight to his opinion, to respond to him warmly, with such sincere concern, never mind that they were total strangers and had met for the very first time. Perhaps it was precisely this refined cordiality which had such a radical effect on the Prince's sensitive nature. Perhaps he was already too much predisposed towards, indeed beguiled into, forming a favourable impression.

And yet all these people, though they were of course "friends of the family" and friends amongst themselves, were in reality neither such good friends of the family nor amongst themselves as the Prince took them to be immediately he was introduced to them. There were some who would never have accepted the Yepanchins even remotely as equals. There were those who simply detested one another: the old duchess Belokonskaya had all her life despised the wife of the venerable dignitary, who in turn could not abide Lizaveta Prokofyevna. This dignitary, who for some reason had favoured the Yepanchins from their very young days, and who was now presiding at the party, was such a significant personage in the eyes of Ivan Fyodorovich that the latter could experience nothing but veneration and fear in his presence, and would have hated himself for the rest of his days were he to imagine himself even for a minute to be his equal or the dignitary anyone other than an Olympian deity. There were those also who had not seen one another for years and cared not a jot what had happened to them, indifference being superseded only by revulsion, but on coming together now made out as though they'd always been in daily contact and on the best of terms at that. The gathering, it must be said, was not numerous. Besides Belokonskaya and the old dignitary, who really was influential, and his wife, it included a very highly regarded general, a baron or count, bearing a German name, a man of very few words, with a reputation for an astonishing knowledge of governmental affairs, and almost the same in the sciences. He was one of those Olympian administrators who, it must be said, know everything, "except perhaps Russia itself"; a man who, having promulgated in the course of five years one single, "mind-bending" idea, had seen it gain acceptance in the highest echelons; one of those executive bureaucrats who, after an extremely, almost unbelievably, long service career, finally dies, showered with honours, in splendour and in wealth, though in fact with meagre accomplishments to boast of, indeed being deep down somewhat hostile towards them. This general was Ivan Fyodorovich's immediate superior, whom Ivan Fyodorovich in the ardour of his heart and perhaps even out of a kind of self-esteem, regarded as his benefactor, but who in his turn did not regard himself as Ivan Fyodorovich's benefactor and treated him with indifference, although was always happy to take advantage of his numerous services. Had an opportunity arisen, he'd surely have replaced him with someone else at the drop of a hat even if the motivation for such a move had not been of the highest. Also present was an elderly, very imposing gentleman, supposedly a relative of Lizaveta Prokofyevna, although this was manifestly not so. He was a man of rank and calling, wealthy and well-born. Physically he was brawny and in good health; personality-wise – very garrulous and even with the reputation of being hard to please (although in the most agreeable sense only)... bilious too, to an extent (but even this worked to his advantage). He affected the mannerisms of an English aristocrat and an Englishman's tastes (for instance as regards rare roast beef, riding accoutrements, butlers and so on). He was a great friend of the venerable dignitary, whom he liked to humour. Moreover, Lizaveta Prokofyevna for some reason cherished the bizarre hope that this elderly gentleman (no getting away from it, intellectually shallow and an opportunistic womanizer) would, without much ado, make Alexandra happy by asking for her hand in marriage on the spur of the moment. Beyond this – the highest and the most respectable category of guests – followed a lesser one, comprising a younger, though still brilliant contingent of invitees. Prince S. and Yevgeny Pavlovich apart, to this contingent belonged the renowned and admirable Prince N., an erstwhile seducer and lady-killer renowned throughout the whole of Europe, now a man of about forty-five, still wonderfully well preserved, a brilliant raconteur, a man of means, true, now somewhat depleted, and through force of habit residing mostly abroad. Finally, there were those who appeared to comprise as it were a third, rather odd, tier and who did not belong to the "golden circle" of society, but who – like the Yepanchins – could often be encountered within this "golden circle". By dint of a certain convention, which had become habitual, the Yepanchins liked, on the rare occasions when they organized grand receptions, to mix members of the high society with those ranking well below them and representatives of the middle strata of society. They even came in for a quite a lot of praise on this score and it was held that they were people who knew their role and were tactful to a fault, and this could not but be a source of pride for them. One of the representatives of this middle tier of people that evening was a military engineer, a colonel – a man of a decidedly serious disposition, a close friend of Prince S., who in fact had introduced him into the Yepanchin household. He avoided small talk. On his right index finger he wore a large and prominent ring, no doubt a gift from the Imperial Court. Finally, there was even a German-born Russian writer and poet, who it must be said was perfectly respectable, and could without embarrassment be taken into good society. He had a happy-go-lucky countenance, which for some reason was rather off-putting; his age was about thirty-eight, he dressed immaculately, maintained his German roots, bourgeois in the extreme but for all that highly respectable. He had a sure eye for the main chance in that he always managed to find himself on the right side of wealthy patrons and clung to that position regardless. At some time past he had translated from the German some important composition in verse of some important German poet, had dedicated it to advantage, had made a felicitous reference of friendship with a famous but deceased Russian poet (there is a whole host of writers who enjoy claiming in print to have been friends with famous but deceased writers) and had been only recently introduced to the Yepanchins by the wife of the venerable dignitary. This lady had the reputation of being a benefactress of men of letters and scientists and had in fact managed to obtain a pension for one or two writers through the good offices of some prominent people with whom she curried favour. And curry favour she did! She was a lady of about forty-five (it goes without saying, very young for an old husband such as hers), a former beauty, who liked even now, in consequence of an unfortunate craze to which many a forty-five-year-old succumbs, to dress ostentatiously. Her intelligence was limited and her knowledge of literature dubious. Her patronage of literature was as much of a craze as her desire to dress ostentatiously. But authors and translators kept dedicating many works to her; two or three of them, with her permission, published some of their letters to her, touching on some extremely important topics... All these people the Prince took completely at face value without questioning their motives in any way. It must be said that on that evening they all were as though by prior arrangement in the best of moods and were well pleased with themselves. Every single one of them knew that by turning up at the Yepanchins, they were doing them an immense honour. Alas, however, the Prince did not even suspect such subtleties. For instance, he did not suspect that the Yepanchins, having such an important mission as the marriage of their daughter in mind, could possibly have failed to introduce him, Lev Nikolayevich, to the aged dignitary, the acknowledged patron of their family. As for the dignitary himself, he would quite readily have ignored any calamity that might have befallen the Yepanchins, but would most assuredly have taken offence had they promised to give away their daughter without seeking his advice and, as it were, approval. Prince N., this amiable, undeniably witty, exceedingly good-natured man, was absolutely convinced that he was the knight in shining armour, who had graced the Yepanchins' drawing room with his presence that night. He looked down upon them with infinite condescension, and it was precisely this simple-hearted, disarmingly vainglorious attitude which caused him to be so easygoing and affable towards them. He knew full well that he had to recount something that evening to charm the assembled company, and he was raring to live up to this challenge. After Prince Lev Nikolayevich had listened to Prince N.'s story, he later had to own that he had never before heard anything the like. The brilliant humour, the extraordinary jollity and ingenuousness, coming from the lips of such a Don Juan as Prince N., had something touching about it and swept the Prince off his feet. And yet if only he had known how old and hackneyed that story was; how rehearsed, oft-repeated and done to death it was in all salons, and that it was only at the naive Yepanchins' that it was again received as a fresh, unexpected, earnest and fascinating reminiscence of an outstanding and brilliant young man! Even the miserable Germanic poetaster, however unpretentious and reserved his manner was, appeared to want to indicate that his presence too was bestowing a mark of special honour upon the house. But the Prince was blind to all this and perceived none of the undercurrent of feelings among the guests. It was this unfortunate contingency which Aglaya had not foreseen. She herself was remarkably lovely that night. All the three young ladies were turned out very beautifully, though without undue showiness; their coiffures alone were quite remarkable. Aglaya sat next to Yevgeny Pavlovich and was engaged in an unusually friendly and amusing conversation with him. Yevgeny Pavlovich himself appeared to be somehow more restrained than at other times, perhaps out of homage to the august assembly. To be sure, he had already established himself in society and, in spite of his young years, was accepted on an equal footing by all. That evening he had turned up with a crape round his hat, which had earned him a word of praise from Belokonskaya: some other nephew she could mention would not have mourned for such an uncle in similar circumstances. Lizaveta Prokofyevna also approved of it, but on the whole she gave the impression of not being at her ease. The Prince noticed that Aglaya had looked at him attentively a couple of times, and appeared to be well pleased with him. Little by little he felt his heart begin to glow with happiness. Recollections of his former apprehensions and "fantasies" (following his conversation with Lebedev), which kept assailing him unexpectedly with ever greater frequency, he now dismissed as a far-fetched, implausible and even ludicrous dream! (All that day his primary, albeit unconscious, wish and longing had been to put himself in a frame of mind that would prevent him from taking that dream seriously!) He spoke little, and only when spoken to, and finally he went completely quiet, just sat and listened, apparently savouring every minute of it. Little by little he felt his spirits rise, akin to euphoria, ready to peak at the first opportunity... It was pure chance that he began to speak; he happened to be responding to some questions, and it seemed had nothing particular in mind...

7

WHILE HE KEPT LOOKING ADMIRINGLY AT AGLAYA, who was absorbed in an entertaining conversation with Prince N. and Yevgeny Pavlovich, the elderly Anglophile gentleman, who had been enthusiastically plying the aged dignitary with some interesting stories in another corner of the salon, suddenly mentioned the name Nikolai Andreyevich Pavlishchev. The Prince quickly swung around to face them and began to listen.

The conversation centred on the new land reforms and the consequent teething troubles which left some land owners in the province of ***sky badly out of pocket. The Anglophile's story must have been rather amusing, because in the end the venerable sage responded with lively laughter to the caustic humour of the storyteller. The latter recounted with an easy, condescending lilt, accentuating his vowels with affectation, how specifically under the new regulations he himself had been obliged to sell a perfectly viable estate of his for half its market value although experiencing no pressing need for the money. And at the same time he had retained a completely rundown one, which was operating at a loss, had dues to pay on it, and was subject to legal constraint. "To avoid an additional lawsuit over some stretches of land claimed by Pavlishchev, I took to my heels completely. Another one or two such inheritances and I'd be a ruined man. As a matter of fact, I was done out of five thousand acres of prime land out there!"

*YEPANCHIN

"There you are... Ivan Petrovich happens to be a relative of the late Nikolai Andreyevich Pavlishchev... You were looking for relatives, were you not?" Ivan Fyodorovich said to the Prince in a low voice. He had made a beeline for the Prince, who, he had noticed, was taking a lively interest in the conversation. Up till then Ivan Fyodorovich had been entertaining his superior, but out of the corner of his eye had for some time been aware of the Prince's unusual reticence, which made him feel uneasy. He had an idea of involving the Prince in a conversation and thereby showing him off for the second time to the distinguished company.

"Lev Nikolayevich, after the death of his parents, was brought up by Nikolai Andreyevich Pavlishchev," he hastened to announce, seeing Ivan Petrovich's gaze rest on him.

"I'm delighted, I'm sure," he replied. "I remember you well. When Ivan Fyodorovich was introducing us just now, I recognized you at once. I knew your face. To be sure, you haven't changed much to look at even though I knew you only as a child. You were about ten or eleven. There's something about your features that is quite unforgettable..."

"You knew me as a child?" the Prince enquired with surprise.

"Oh, that was a long time ago," Ivan Petrovich continued, "in Zlatoverkhovo, where you were staying with my cousins. I used to come over to Zlatoverkhovo rather a lot. I don't suppose you remember me, do you? No, perhaps you don't... You had at the time... you had some kind of an illness, so much so that it fairly took me aback on one occasion..."

"I cannot remember a thing!" the Prince affirmed with emphasis.

A few more words of explanation, decidedly calm on the part of Ivan Petrovich and highly agitated on the part of the Prince, and it was established that a certain two ladies, both elderly spinsters, relatives of the late Pavlishchev, who were resident on his estate in Zlatoverkhovo and had been charged with the Prince's upbringing, were in turn Ivan Petrovich's cousins. Ivan Petrovich, like everybody else, could give no coherent explanation as to why Pavlishchev should have been so exercised in his care for the little Prince, his adopted charge. "I myself neglected to ask him about it at the time," he said. It turned out, however, that he had an excellent memory, because he even went on to recall how strict the elder cousin, Marfa Nikitishna, was with the young child. "I even had words with her because of the regime she was imposing upon you. Thrashing and still more thrashing of a sickly child… that… you must agree yourself…" And how gentle, on the other hand, had been the younger cousin, Natalia Nikitishna, towards the poor boy… "The last I heard, they both lived in the country," he explained, "only I'm not sure if they're still alive. They inherited a nice little estate from Pavlishchev. There was talk of Marfa Nikitishna wanting to go into a nunnery, though I can't be sure. Maybe it was someone else… Yes, I've mixed her up with the wife of a doctor I heard about the other day…"

The Prince listened to him with eyes full of admiration and excitement. For his part he announced with unusual fervour that he could never forgive himself for not finding occasion to visit his two former teachers in the six months that he had spent travelling to the remotest interior provinces. He had in fact been any number of times on the point of going to look them up but had always been distracted by other things… now though he was giving his word of honour… come what may to make an effort… "So, you really know Natalia Nikitishna? What a splendid, what an angelic woman! But Marfa Nikitishna too… sorry, but I think you are wrong about Marfa Nikitishna! She was strict, but… one couldn't help losing one's patience… with such an idiot as I was then (he he!). Let's face it, I was a total idiot then, you will hardly credit it (ha ha!). So… you say you saw me then, did you? And… it's awfully strange how I remember nothing of you! So you are… oh, my God, you really are a relative of Nikolai Andreyevich Pavlishchev?"

"I most cer-tain-ly am," Ivan Petrovich said, looking the Prince up and down with a smile.

"Oh, I did not mean to imply… I have any… doubts… and, let's face it, how could one possibly have any doubts on this score (he he)?… I mean, the least possible doubts! (He he!) All I meant was that the late Nikolai Andreyevich Pavlishchev was such an outstanding man! A real gentleman, I can assure you!"

To say that the Prince was short of breath would be an understatement. "He was gulping, blithe of heart that he was," as Adelaida put it the next morning in conversation with her fiancé, Prince S.

"Well, I never!" Ivan Petrovich returned with a laugh. "Why ever should I not be a relative even of a gent-le-man?"

"Goodness me!" the Prince exclaimed, getting ever more embarrassed, flustered and animated. "I… I said the wrong thing again, and… that's how it was surely, because I... I... I've got the wrong end of the stick yet again! And what merit, pray tell me, is there for me in the face of such aspirations... such high aspirations! And compared to such an exceptional man, because, honest to God, he was pretty exceptional, was he not? Pray tell me!"

The Prince was shivering from top to toe. Why had he become so excited, why had he reached such a mawkish state for no apparent reason – and, it would seem, quite out of keeping with the general tenor of the conversation – it would be impossible to determine. Suffice it to say that at that particular moment he was in a mood and an emotional state in which he could not help but experience the warmest feelings for and the most heartfelt gratitude to all and sundry, perhaps even Ivan Petrovich. His feeling of exhilaration had clearly got the better of him. Ivan Petrovich began to regard him with decided wariness; the elderly dignitary likewise. Belokonskaya fixed him with a menacing stare and tightened her lips. Prince N., Yevgeny Pavlovich, Prince S. and the young ladies, all stopped talking and pricked up their ears. It seemed Aglaya was frightened; as for Lizaveta Prokofyevna, her courage failed her completely. The behaviour of the Yepanchin distaff side was strange indeed, both of mother and daughters. It was they who had proposed that it were better for the Prince not to say anything throughout the whole evening; but no sooner had they caught sight of him sitting in a corner, totally withdrawn and perfectly content with his condition, than they began to feel uneasy. Alexandra had even intended to go over to him and carefully take him across the room to make him join Prince N.'s company, which had gathered around Belokonskaya. But, lo and behold, as soon as the Prince had opened his mouth of his own volition, their unease grew even stronger.

"That he was a splendid man, you are perfectly right," Ivan Petrovich affirmed this time without a hint of a smile. "Yes, yes... he was a wonderful man! Wonderful and worthy," he added after a pause. "Quite worthy even, so to speak, of every mark of respect," he added still more weightily after the third pause, "and... and it is indeed heartening to see that you for your part—"

"Wasn't this same Pavlishchev mixed up in some... scandal... with... an *abbé*... yes, an *abbé*... ?" the dignitary interposed as though straining to remember something. "The name escapes me, only there was no end of talk about it at the time."

"Abbé Gouraud, a Jesuit," Ivan Petrovich confirmed. "Well, yes, that's our most splendid and worthy people for you! Because you must remember, the man came from ancient stock, he was wealthy, he was a member of the Chamberlain's office, and had he... continued in the service... And suddenly he turns his back on his career and prospects merely to convert to Catholicism and become a Jesuit, and openly at that, with a passion. Frankly, he died just at the right moment... yes, quite. Everyone said so at the time..."

The Prince was beside himself.

"Pavlishchev... Pavlishchev converting to Catholicism? That's impossible!" he exclaimed, horrified.

"Why 'impossible'?" Ivan Petrovich muttered, standing on his dignity. "But you are quite wrong there, my dear Prince, you must agree... Still, you have such a high opinion of Pavlishchev... True enough, he was the kindest of men, which as a matter of fact accounts in general terms for that rogue *abbé*'s success. But you should ask me... me... how much trouble and bother I had afterwards in consequence of this business... in particular with this same Gouraud! Just imagine," he suddenly turned to the old man, "they even wanted to question his will, and I was obliged to take recourse to some very drastic measures... to save the day... because when it comes to it they are past masters at it! Amazing! Thank goodness it all took place in Moscow so that I could immediately make a beeline for the Count and together... we made them see... reason—"

"You have no idea how shocked and surprised I am!" the Prince exclaimed again.

"I'm sorry, I'm sure. But, come to think of it, it's all very unimportant, and as such would have been destined for oblivion, as always, take my word. Only, last summer," he turned to the little old man again, "they say Countess K. also ended up by joining some Catholic convent abroad. We Russians always cave in once we fall in with these... knaves... especially abroad."

"It all comes because of our, I think... lassitude," the little old man asserted authoritatively. "Well, and it's their manner of preaching... the elegance of it... and they can put holy fear into you. I say this because back in eighteen thirty-two they had a go at me too, in Vienna. I was frightened to death, I assure you. Only, I stood my ground and gave them the slip, ha ha!"

"What I heard was that you, my dear sir, fled with that beautiful Countess Livitskaya from Vienna to Paris," Belokonskaya suddenly intervened, "and you resigned because of her and not because of some Jesuit."

"Still, the fact remains there was a Jesuit involved," the little old man returned, bursting into a good-natured fit of laughter at the memory of it all. "You strike me as being very religious, which is a rarity now amongst the younger generation," he turned benignly to Prince Lev Nikolayevich, who was still listening open-mouthed and bewildered. For reasons of his own, the old fellow obviously wanted to get to know the Prince closer.

"Pavlishchev was a man of vision and a Christian, a true Christian," the Prince suddenly declared, "so how could he convert to an... unchristian faith?... Because Catholicism is a through-and-through unchristian faith!" he added suddenly, his eyes glinting and staring straight ahead as he took in the whole room with a broad sweep of his head.

"Well, that's a bit much," the little old man muttered and looked at Ivan Fyodorovich in surprise.

"What do you mean, Catholicism is an unchristian faith?" Ivan Petrovich enquired, swinging around in his chair. "What kind of a faith is it then?"

"Unchristian, that's one!" the Prince again began in extreme agitation and inappropriately stridently. "That's one. Two, Roman Catholicism is even worse than atheism, that's my opinion anyway! Yes, my opinion! Atheism merely propounds naught, but Catholicism goes further. It presents a distorted Christ, whom it has itself traduced and denigrated, an Antichrist! Catholicism propounds an Antichrist, I swear to you, I guarantee! That is my personal and long-standing conviction, and it has cost me no end of suffering... Roman Catholicism believes that without a worldwide temporal power, the Church will not survive on this earth, and it proclaims, '*Non possumus*!'* To my mind Roman Catholicism is not even a faith, but simply the continuation of the Western Roman Empire, and everything about Catholicism, including faith itself, is subordinate to this idea. The Pope has appropriated a piece of land, mounted a temporal throne and taken up the sword. Since then everything has been developing as expected, only that to the sword has been added falsehood, prevarication, treachery, bigotry, superstition and evildoing. The churchmen have played fast and loose with the most sacred, virtuous, decent and impassioned feelings of the populace... everything but everything has been exchanged for pieces of silver, for worthless temporal power. And is that not in the spirit of Antichrist?! Did it not pave the way to atheism? Atheism originated there and then, in direct line of descent from Roman Catholicism. Catholicism begat atheism. It is nothing saving a selfish belief in one's own self! It is an expression of rebellion. It is the spawn of their untruth and spiritual impotence! Atheism! In our country, as Yevgeny Pavlovich correctly observed, only isolated strata of society profess it, those who have lost their roots. Whereas over in Europe countless masses from amongst the thick of the people are beginning to lose their faith – it was an account of ignorance and deception to begin with, but now bigotry is at the bottom of it along with hatred of the Church and of Christianity!"

The Prince stopped to draw his breath. He spoke with extraordinary rapidity. He was pale and was gasping for air. Everybody exchanged glances; finally the little old man burst into a fit of good-natured laughter. Prince N. took out his lorgnette and fixed it point-blank on the Prince. The German poetaster crept out into the open and shifted nearer the table, grinning provocatively.

"You exa-gge-ra-te too much," Ivan Petrovich said, stressing each syllable with a degree of ennui and discomfiture. "The Roman Church is not without its worthy and charitable votaries—"

"I did not mean to talk about individual representatives of the Church. I spoke of Roman Catholicism as a whole, I spoke of Rome. Surely no church can ever disappear entirely! I never meant to suggest that!"

"Quite, but all this is common knowledge and hardly needs to be repeated and... it belongs to the realms of theology—"

"No, not at all! Not just theology, I can assure you, not at all! It concerns us much more than you may imagine. Our mistake lies precisely in our inability to see that it is not merely a question of theology! Remember, socialism too is a by-product of Catholicism and manifestly goes to the very root of it! Like its twin brother atheism, it too has emerged out of desperation, as counterbalance to Catholicism in the moral sense, as a substitute for the vanished moral authority of religion, purposing to quench the spiritual thirst of the yearning mankind and to save it

– not in Christ, but also by way of brute force! This too is liberty by way of brute force; harmony by way of the sword and of blood! 'Do not presume to put your faith in God, do not presume to acquire property, do not presume to have a mind of your own, *fraternité ou la mort** at the cost of two million heads!' It is said, you will know them by their ways and their doings!* And do not think you will come out of it all safe and sound. We must put up a fight, soonest, soonest! In defiance of the West, our Christ must shine forth, whom we have safeguarded and whom they never even knew! We must not fall slavishly into the Jesuit trap but hold up our Russian civilization to them, we must take a defiant stand, and stop all talk of their message being elegantly delivered as someone had remarked just now—"

"With respect though, I beg your pardon," Ivan Petrovich interposed, looking around in alarm, "all your observations are of course commendable and nothing but patriotic, but it is all so wildly exaggerated and... best left well alone—"

"No, not exaggerated at all, quite the reverse, understated. Yes – understated, because words fail me, but—"

"I beg your pardon!"

The Prince fell silent. He sat very erect, motionless, his eyes blazing.

"I have a feeling you were much affected by the events concerning your benefactor," the little old man, brimming with kindness, observed with perfect equanimity. "You are much too excited... perhaps on account of your solitary mode of life. Had you mixed with people more, and in society I dare say you'd have been very welcome, an upstanding young man like you no doubt would have found an outlet for your passions and realized that all this is far simpler... and besides, the way I look at it, such rare eventualities are in my opinion partly the result of our complacency, and partly of... tedium—"

"Exactly, exactly so," the Prince exclaimed, "a brilliant idea! It is because of tedium, because of our tedium, rather than complacency! You are wrong here! Far from being complacent, we are dying of thirst, of feverish thirst! And... and don't imagine it is all such small beer that we can simply laugh it off. Pardon my saying so, but one must have a sense of foreboding! When my fellow Russians feel they've reached terra firma, when they know their feet are on terra firma, they will be overcome with joy, they will press on to the bitter end! I wonder why? Pavlishchev amazes you. You put everything down either to his insanity or his goodness, but you are wrong! And it is not just we, but the whole of Europe, when it comes to it, is astonished by the passion that we Russians generate in such cases. If a Russian converts to Catholicism, he must needs become a Jesuit, and of the most subversive kind at that. If he turns to atheism, he will definitely insist on destroying faith in God root and branch, with the sword if necessary! Why should that be so, why such frenzy all of a sudden? I'll tell you why! Because he had found a new promised land that he'd overlooked, and this had brought him joy. He fetched up on firm land, solid ground, and he took to kissing it! And not merely out of vanity. It is not just vanity, or mere ignoble conceit that drives Russians to become Jesuits and atheists. They are born of spiritual torment, of spiritual longing, of desperately reaching out for higher goals, for firmer shores; they are born of wanting to retrieve a land they'd lost faith in because they had never been able to fathom it! A Russian can turn into an atheist at the drop of a hat, easier than anyone else in the world! And atheism for the Russians is a matter of faith, of a new religion, and it never occurs to them that it is grounded on nothing. That is the extent of our thirsting! 'Whoever has no firm ground to stand on is Godless.' It is not I who said it. It was said by an Old Believer, whom I met during my journeys. Actually his words were, 'Whosoever has spurned his native land, has spurned his God.' Imagine, the most educated of our Russians indulged in self-flagellation*... And why should self-flagellation in this regard be any worse than nihilism, Jesuitry or atheism? It may in fact be a good deal more profound! But that is what spiritual desolation leads to!... Show the hungering, frantic followers of Columbus the shores of the New World, show the Russians Russia as she really is, let him discover this gold, this treasure that is hidden underground! Show him how in times to come the rejuvenation and rebirth of all mankind will be accomplished solely and exclusively on the strength of the Russian way of thinking, the Russian God and Christ, and you will see what a mighty giant, truthful, wise and meek, will materialize before the startled world, startled and astonished, because people had expected only the sword from us, the sword and brute force, since, in judging us by their own yardstick, they could not see us other than as barbarians. Thus it has been to this day, and the longer it goes on, the more of the same there will be! And..."

But at this point something happened, and the orator's speech was interrupted in the most unexpected manner.

574

The whole of this untamed tirade, the whole of this torrent of obsessive, troubled words and tumultuous ideas whirring in wild disorder, indicated something dangerous, something unusual that had welled up apparently without rhyme or reason in the young man's mental disposition. All those present in the salon who knew the Prince were overcome with fear (not unmixed with embarrassment) at his outburst, which was so out of keeping with his wonted, even self-effacing reticence, with his refined sense of propriety and instinctive decorum. No one could understand what might have precipitated it; surely not what he had heard about Pavlishchev! The ladies, huddled in a corner of the room, regarded him as though he were a lunatic, and Belokonskaya subsequently admitted that had it gone on a minute longer, she would have ran for dear life. The little old man was initially so overcome with astonishment that he lost all power of speech; Ivan Fyodorovich's superior regarded the scene from his chair with stern disapproval. The military engineer sat quite motionless. The German had gone pale in the face, yet he continued to force himself to smile as he looked around slyly to see how the others would react. It has to be said that nothing untoward would have happened and the whole rumpus could easily have been prevented almost there and then in the most natural and trouble-free manner. Ivan Fyodorovich, having got over his initial shock of surprise, was also the first to spring into action and had signalled several times to the Prince to stop, but without success; he was now wending his way towards him, firmly resolved to put an end to the matter. He had nearly made it, his intention being if necessary simply to usher the Prince out politely under the pretext of his illness, which Ivan Fyodorovich truly believed was the cause of his distemper... But this was not to be.

When the Prince had first entered the salon, he had taken a seat as far away as possible from the Chinese vase, of which, thanks to Aglaya, he was in such awe. It was hardly surprising that after listening to Aglaya, he should have been possessed by a weird, obsessive presentiment that no matter how hard he tried to avoid disaster, come the next day, he would definitely break the vase. In the course of the evening, other, blithe impressions began to crowd in on him; but we have already spoken of this. Gradually he forgot his presentiment. After he had heard about Pavlishchev and after Ivan Fyodorovich had taken him across to Ivan Petrovich for the second time, he had changed his seat closer to the table and ended up in the immediate vicinity of the huge, magnificent Chinese vase, standing on a pedestal, now almost right up against his elbow.

Having spoken his concluding words, he suddenly got up, swung his arm awkwardly, raised his shoulder, and... there followed an explosive gasp all round! The vase swayed, at first as though unable to make up its mind whether or not to come down on the head of one of the elderly guests, but it suddenly tilted over in the opposite direction towards the German, who just managed to jump out of the way in terror, before it crashed to the floor. The loud noise, the exclamations, the splintering of the precious object into shards scattered across the carpet were accompanied by shrill cries of disbelief and alarm. The effect it had on the Prince beggared all description! But it is worth mentioning one strange feeling, which had fairly astonished him at that very instant, cutting right through a whole host of other vague feelings: it was not the embarrassment, not the breakage, not the fear, not the suddenness which had astonished him as that the presentiment itself had come true! What was so fascinating about it, he could never have explained adequately even to himself; all he felt was that he was shaken to the very core, and could do no more than just stand there overcome with fright that bordered on the mystical. A moment passed, and the world appeared to open up before him. Instead of terror, light and joy, a feeling of exultation. His chest began to tighten, and... but the moment passed. Thank God, it was not what he had feared most! He drew a breath of relief and looked around.

For some considerable time he appeared not to comprehend the commotion which was going on around him, that is to say he understood and saw everything, but he perceived himself like one divorced from reality, like a fly on the wall, fascinated by the people milling beneath him. He saw the shards being swept up, heard hurried snatches of conversation, saw Aglaya – pale, regarding him most curiously. There was no hatred in her eyes, much less anger; she looked at him with frightened compassion, but at the others with a hard glint in her eyes... his heart suddenly melted pleasurably. At long last he saw with extreme amazement that people had resumed their seats and were even laughing as though nothing had happened! Another minute passed, and the laughter grew. People were laughing, looking straight at him now, at his stupefaction; but their laughter was benign, full of hilarity;

many spoke, with genuine compassion, above all Lizaveta Prokofyevna. She was saying something, unable to contain her laughter, and it was something very kind. Suddenly he felt Ivan Fyodorovich slapping him affably on the back; Ivan Petrovich too was laughing. But it was the little old man who outdid everyone else in his kindliness and good humour. He took the Prince's hand, and shaking it slightly, patted it with the flat of his other hand in an effort to console him as one would a frightened little child, which appealed to the Prince enormously. Finally, he made the Prince sit right next to him. The Prince looked into his face full of admiration but was still unable to utter a word. He was out of breath. The old man's face was a sight for sore eyes.

"I don't believe it," he muttered at last, "is it true you are letting it pass? You too... Lizaveta Prokofyevna?"

The laughter intensified. Tears stood in the Prince's eyes. He could not believe his luck.

"Of course the vase was superb. I remember it standing here about fifteen years... yes, fifteen—" Ivan Fyodorovich said.

"It's not the end of the world! All life comes to an end, so why cry over a clay pot?" Lizaveta Prokofyevna said loudly. "Did it really frighten you that much, Lev Nikolayevich?" she added apprehensively. "Well, enough of that, I say. You really are beginning to frighten me, my dear sir."

"And you are prepared to think nothing of it? To forgive me *everything*, not just the vase?" the Prince said, rising to his feet, but the little old man again pulled him down. He would not let go of him.

"*C'est très curieux et c'est très sérieux*,"* he whispered across the table to Ivan Petrovich, loud enough for the Prince perhaps to have heard it.

"Are you sure I haven't offended anyone here? You will not believe how glad this makes me! But that is only fair! Surely, you all know I did not mean to offend anyone? The very idea of it would be an offence too."

"Calm down, my friend, you – exaggerate. And there's no need for you to thank anyone. Your sentiments are wonderful, but out of proportion."

"I am not thanking you, I'm merely... admiring you. It makes me so happy just to look at you. Perhaps I'm talking nonsense, but... I must have my say, I have to explain... even if only out of respect for myself."

Everything about him was spasmodic, indeterminate and agitated. Very likely he frequently chose the wrong words and he knew it. With his eyes he questioned people if it would be all right for him to speak. His gaze fell on Belokonskaya.

"Pay no attention, dear boy, get on with it, get on with it, only don't run out of breath," she observed. "You got off to a bad start just then, and look at you now. But don't hesitate, have your say. These people here are no shrinking violets, nothing will come to them as a surprise, I can tell you. And you're not as smart as you may think, only breaking that vase was altogether a bad idea, if you ask me."

The Prince kept smiling all the time he listened to her.

"It was you, was it not," he suddenly addressed the little old man, "who three months ago saved the student Podkumov and the clerk Shvabrin from exile?"

The man's cheeks flushed at this, and he muttered something to the effect that there was no need to make a fuss.

"I'm sure I heard," he said, turning to Ivan Petrovich next, "that you released a quantity of building timber for free to some of your peasants after a fire in their village even though they were no longer bonded and had been causing you a good deal of trouble!"

"Well, that is an exa-gge-ration," Ivan Petrovich muttered, though he could not help easing himself into a posture of dignified gratification; but on this occasion he was perfectly correct that this was an exaggeration. The Prince's information was indeed inaccurate.

"And was it not you, Princess Belokonskaya," he suddenly turned with a bright smile to Belokonskaya, "who welcomed me six months ago in Moscow as though I were your own son on a letter of recommendation from Lizaveta Prokofyevna, and gave me truly motherly advice, which I shall never forget? Do you remember?"

"What's got into you?" Belokonskaya said irritably. "You're a nice enough chap, but you are funny. I gave you a couple of copecks and you're making out as though someone had saved your life. You may think you're doing the right thing, but this sort of thing can put people off, you know!"

She was close to being seriously annoyed, but suddenly she burst out laughing, and this perfectly good-naturedly. Lizaveta Prokofyevna's face also brightened up, as did Ivan Fyodorovich's.

"I always said Lev Nikolayevich is a man… a man… in a word, if only he didn't run out of breath, as Princess Belokonskaya has just observed…" the General muttered in an access of joy as he echoed Belokonskaya's words, which had so struck him.

Aglaya alone remained gloomy; but her face was still glowing, perhaps with indignation.

"I say, he really is a nice chap," the little old man muttered again, addressing Ivan Petrovich.

"I came here with an aching heart," the Prince continued with mounting anxiety, ever faster, ever more ill at ease, but energetically, "I was fearful of you, I was fearful of myself. Most of all of myself. On my way back to St Petersburg, I definitely promised myself to meet our foremost people, families of ancient stock, the salt of the earth, of whom I am myself one, who are my kith and kin. For surely it is with princes, like myself, that I am now rubbing shoulders, am I not right? I wanted to get to know you, and it was necessary I should – very, very necessary!… I always heard much more bad than good about you, about your small-mindedness, your exclusiveness, your outmoded ways, the shallowness of your education, your ridiculous lifestyle – oh, the things one hears and reads about you! I came here today brimming with curiosity, full of anxiety. I needed to ascertain personally if the whole of this upper-crust Russian society really was worthless, had outlived its time, had exhausted its vital sources and was only fit to perish while still waging a petty, grudging struggle with the people… of the future, blocking their way and not realizing that its days are numbered. I had never been one to share such a belief wholly, because in truth we never had what may be called a true aristocracy, apart from some select courtiers who paraded in uniforms or who owe their fortune to… a blind stroke of fate, and are now totally extinct. Is that not so, am I not right?"

"Come, come, it's nothing of the sort," Ivan Petrovich observed with a caustic smile.

"He's at it again!" Belokonskaya burst out.

"*Laissez-le dire,** he's shaking all over," the little old man said thoughtfully in a low voice.

The Prince was decidedly not himself.

"And what do I find? I find elegant people, simple-hearted and intelligent. I find a sage who listens and is full of kindness to an

inexperienced young man. I find people who are capable of understanding and forgiving, Russian people, people full of the milk of
human kindness, almost as kind and warm-hearted as the ones I had
occasion to come across there, every bit as good – almost. You can
judge for yourselves how pleasantly surprised I was! Oh, do let me make
this perfectly clear! I've heard it said a lot, and I myself was perfectly
ready to believe that in society everything is mere show, empty form,
and that the core itself was rotten. But I can now see for myself that
this can never be the case here – anywhere else, but not here. Or is it
that you are all Jesuits and dissemblers? I heard Prince N. speak just
now. Was that not a species of honest, inspired humour, was that not
a manifestation of true goodwill? Could such words have issued from
the mouth of a... corpse, dead of heart and brainless, I ask you? Could
cadavers have treated me as you have? Is that not food for... future
thought, for hope? Can such people be accused of being reactionary
and lacking in understanding?"

"I beg you once more, calm down, my dear," the dignitary observed
with a smile, "we can talk about this some other time, and I shall be
only too happy..."

Ivan Petrovich cleared his throat and shifted uneasily in his chair; Ivan
Fyodorovich was thoroughly nonplussed; his superior, the General,
was engrossed in a conversation with the wife of the dignitary and was
not paying the slightest attention to the Prince; the wife on the other
hand was all ears and looked frequently over at the Prince.

"No, I think I'd better continue!" the Prince resumed with a fresh
access of feverish vigour, addressing the little old man with a peculiar
show of confidentiality and even condescension. "Last night Aglaya
Ivanovna forbade me to speak and even named the topics that I must
not touch upon. She knows I make a pig's ear of them! I am twenty-six
years old and I realize how immature I am. I've no right to voice my
ideas, I've known it all along. It was only with Rogozhin in Moscow
that I was perfectly frank... We read Pushkin together, nearly the whole
of it. He was completely ignorant, he didn't even know who Pushkin
was... I'm always afraid my ridiculous looks get in the way of my
theory and *main idea*. I lack the grand gesture. My attempts at it have
always ended in failure, and this has led to ridicule and debased the
idea. I don't know when to stop either, and that is important, vitally
important in fact... I realize it were better for me to sit still and not say

a word. When I knuckle under and hold my peace, I know I cut a very sensible figure indeed, and I adopt a reflective mood. But now it were best I continue to speak. I've taken to speaking because you've such a nice way of looking at me. You look so charming! Yesterday I promised Aglaya Ivanovna not to say a word."

"*Vraiment!*"* the little old man said with a smile.

"Every now and again it strikes me I may be wrong in thinking as I do. Sincerity is surely worth cutting a dash for, if I'm not mistaken! Tell me if I am!"

"It all depends."

"I want to explain everything, everything, absolutely everything! I say, you think I'm a daydreamer, do you not? An ideologue perhaps? Not a bit of it, honestly, I hold such simple thoughts... You don't believe me, do you? You smile! You know, sometimes I am given to deceitfulness, because I'm not strong of faith. When I was coming here, I thought to myself, 'How should I address them? What should I say to make myself just the least bit comprehensible?' You've no idea how apprehensive I was, but mostly on your behalf, dreadfully, dreadfully apprehensive! And along with that, what right had I to be apprehensive, shouldn't I have been ashamed of being apprehensive? What matter if for every trailblazer there is a whole host of retrogrades and bad apples? But my enduring joy lies in my conviction that it is by no means a host of moribund nonentities, but a bunch of thoroughly lively folk! Nor do we need to feel abashed at being ridiculous, am I not right? Because that is the honest truth, we are ridiculous, thoughtless, we have bad habits, we are prone to be bored, we are undiscerning, we are uncomprehending, that is what we're all like, all, you and I and the world and his wife! I take it you are not offended at my telling you to your faces that you are ridiculous? And if that is so, are you in consequence not the stuff of humanity? You know, the way I look at it, it is sometimes quite good to be a touch ridiculous, it is all for the better – we are more likely to forgive one another and to make friends. One mustn't ever strive to comprehend everything in one go, or claim perfection as the point of departure! In order to reach perfection, one must first learn to plead ignorance! If we make too much haste to understand everything, our understanding will turn out to be flawed. I am saying this to you, you who have already managed to understand so much and... to misunderstand! I am no longer fearful for you.

I am sure you do not take it amiss that someone as immature as I say such things to you! You are laughing, Ivan Petrovich. You think I am a democrat, a champion of egalitarianism, that I stand here before you as their defender and quake in my shoes for them, is that it?" he said, bursting finally into a prolonged hysterical fit of laughter, his speech being interspersed throughout with short, nervous chuckling. "I am apprehensive about you, about all of you and all of us taken together. You must remember I myself am of princely stock and feel the equal of all of you here. I speak that I may save you all, that our kin should not vanish for nothing, in obscurity, in ignorance of what has befallen it, reviling everything and totally bankrupt. Why disappear off the face of the earth and make way for others if it is perfectly feasible to remain in the vanguard and in a position of seniority? If we stay in the vanguard, we shall maintain our seniority. Good servants make good masters."

He made several attempts to rise to his feet, but the little old man stopped him every time, as he kept looking at him with steadily mounting concern.

"Listen to me! I know it is not good to speak, best of all is to set an example and make a start... I've already done so... and – and can one really be unhappy? Oh, what does my grief and my misfortune matter, if I can bring myself to feel happy? You know, it is beyond me that one can walk past a tree and not feel happy seeing it? How can one talk to a man and not feel happy for loving him? Oh, I wish I knew how to put it better... there are so many wonderful things at every step and turn that even the most disoriented person would find wonderful! Observe a child, observe the rising sun, observe the grass, the way it grows, look into the eyes that look back at you and love you..."

As he was saying this, he had already been up on his feet for quite some time. The little old man was looking at him in terror. Lizaveta Prokofyevna, who was the first to realize what was happening, threw up her hands in a state of shock and cried, "Oh, my God!" Aglaya, pained and frightened, ran up to him quickly just in time to catch him in her arms with the vicious shrieks of "the spirit that rent him sore" still ringing in her ears. He was lying stretched out on the carpet. Someone had put a cushion under his head.

This was the very last thing anyone had expected. A quarter of an hour later Prince N., Yevgeny Pavlovich and the little old man made an attempt to revive the soirée, but another half-hour passed and all the guests were already taking their leave. Many words of sympathy and sorrow were spoken with the occasional piece of advice thrown in. Ivan Petrovich opined amongst other things that the young man was a "Sla-vo-phile or something of the kind, but it really is nothing to worry about". The little old man said nothing at all. True, a day or two later there were some harsh words exchanged between the people concerned. Ivan Petrovich was even offended to an extent, but he chose not to make an issue of it. Ivan Fyodorovich's immediate boss, the general, made a point of keeping his subordinate at arm's length for a time. The Yepanchin family's benefactor, the aged dignitary, also mumbled something moralizing into Ivan Fyodorovich's ear, capping it with highly gratifying assurances that he would continue to be very, very interested in Aglaya's fate. He really could lay some claims to being a good man; but amongst the reasons for his interest in the Prince throughout the soirée was the Prince's involvement with Nastasya Filippovna; he had got wind of this story and was dying to find out more – curiosity was slowly getting the better of him.

Belokonskaya said to Lizaveta Prokofyevna at parting, "What can I say, he's good and bad. But if you want my honest opinion, I'd say – mainly bad. You can see for yourself what sort he is, he's pretty sick!"

Lizaveta Prokofyevna came to a final decision that the match was impossible, and in the night she promised herself that while she was alive, the Prince was not going to be Aglaya's husband. On waking up in the morning she was as firm in her resolve as ever. But later, over lunch, just after twelve, she was plunged into an amazingly contradictory state of mind.

The reply that Aglaya gave to a very harmless question put to her by her sisters was cold, provocative and dismissive: "I never promised him anything. Never in my life have I regarded him as my bridegroom. He is no closer to me than the next man."

Lizaveta Prokofyevna exploded.

"I did not expect this from you," she said with bitterness. "He is not fit to be a husband, that I know, and thank God it has all ended this way. But I did not expect you to say what you did! I imagined you'd come up with something else. If I had had my way, I'd have thrown out all who were here last night, but him I'd have kept back, because that's the sort of man he is..."

She stopped suddenly, realizing what she had just said. But if only she knew how unfair she was to her daughter at that instant! Aglaya had already made up her mind. All she was waiting for was for the hour to strike, which would resolve everything, and every reference, every reminder, every careless remark on the subject was like a stab in the heart for her.

8

FOR THE PRINCE ALSO, the morning started under a heavy cloud; this could be explained by his feverish state. But he could not put his finger on what actually troubled him, and this was hardest of all for him to bear. True, the facts that confronted him were unambiguous enough, but his sorrow went further than anything he could fathom or recollect; he knew he would not be able to find peace of mind on his own. Little by little he was overcome by an expectation of something significant and irrevocable happening this very day. The attack which he had suffered the previous night was on the mild side. Apart from a bout of depression, a certain heaviness in his head and some aches and pains in his extremities, he experienced no other physical discomfort. His mind was quite alert, but his soul ached. He woke up quite late, and immediately recalled the events of the previous night. He even recalled, however indistinctly, being brought home half an hour after the attack. He learnt that a messenger had already been sent by the Yepanchins to enquire after his health. At half-past eleven came another one; he found it very gratifying. Vera Lebedeva was amongst the first to visit him and attend to him. When she first saw him, she burst into tears, but after the Prince had quickly managed to calm her down, she began to laugh. He was much taken by the sense of concern this young girl expressed for him; he reached for her hand and kissed it. Vera flushed.

"Really, goodness!" she exclaimed, much flustered and quickly snatched her hand away.

She soon left in a peculiar state of anxiety. But before that, she managed to inform him that shortly before dawn her father had dashed off to the "departed", as he referred to the General, to establish if he had died in the night, seeing it was rumoured he would soon do so. A little after eleven Lebedev himself turned up to enquire "for a brief moment only as to the health of our most cherished" and so on, and in addition to look into his little "cabinet". For the most part it was just moans and groans on his part, so that the Prince was soon happy to see the back of him; all the same he managed to throw in a few questions about the previous day's seizure, although it was quite plain that he already knew all the details. Kolya was the next one to drop in, also briefly. He was in a genuine hurry and a state of utter panic. He started off by openly and earnestly challenging the Prince to render an account of all that had hitherto been concealed from him, adding incidentally that for the most part he had already got to the bottom of nearly everything the day before. He was in a profoundly agitated frame of mind.

The Prince confided in him with all the compassion he could muster of how matters stood exactly. This shook the troubled youngster to the very core. He could not bring himself to say a single word and merely burst into tears. The Prince sensed that the boy was experiencing one of those indelible life-changing mental upheavals, which stay with one for ever. He hastened to put his own interpretation on the matter, adding that in his opinion, perhaps the old man's impending death too was precipitated in the main by that heartfelt terror following his misdemeanour, which spoke of a sensitivity to which few people could lay claim. Kolya's eyes sparkled when he heard this:

"I hate Ganya, Varya and Ptitsyn! I shan't pick a quarrel with them, but from now on we go our separate ways! Really, Prince, there are so many things I see in a totally different light since yesterday. It has been such a lesson for me! I already regard myself as wholly responsible for my mother's welfare, even though she is well provided for at Varya's, but there's more to this…"

He jumped to his feet when he remembered people were expecting him, enquired in haste after the Prince's health and, having heard him out, suddenly asked quickly, "Maybe there's more to it than meets the eye? I heard it said yesterday… but, on second thoughts, I've no right… However, should you ever need unstinted help, I'm at your service. It strikes me neither of us two is particularly happy, is that not so? But, I'm not prying, don't worry…"

He left, and the Prince was plunged into even deeper thought: everyone was full of foreboding, everyone had reached a conclusion, everyone appeared to be privy to something, except himself. Lebedev had been asking around, Kolya had hinted at something directly, Vera had been crying. Finally, he threw up his hands in desperation. "Confound this feverish sense of doom and gloom of mine!" he thought. His face lit up when shortly after one o'clock he saw the Yepanchins arrive ("Just popping in for a minute!") at his place. It was literally just for a minute. Lizaveta Prokofyevna, having finished her lunch, announced that everyone was going out for a walk, directly, all together. The announcement was issued in the form of a command, curt, snappy, without a word of explanation. Everyone – that is, the young ladies and Prince S. – followed her out. She immediately struck off in the opposite direction to the one they followed daily. Everyone realized what the matter was and no one spoke for fear of upsetting the mother who, as though to forestall any possible opposition, strode ahead regardless, not turning to look back. Finally, Adelaida remarked that there was no need to be in such a hurry seeing as they were out for a leisurely stroll only, and they couldn't keep up with Mother.

"Now listen," Lizaveta Prokofyevna suddenly turned around and said, "we are now level with his house. Whatever ideas Aglaya may have on the subject and no matter how things turn out in the end, he is not a stranger to us, and besides all else he is in trouble and ill. At least I shall pop in to see how he is. If anyone wants to come with me, he's welcome, if not – let him go his own way. No one is under any obligation."

They all went in together of course. The Prince, as was to be expected, hastened to apologize once more for the vase and... for what happened.

"Well, that's nothing," Lizaveta Prokofyevna replied. "It's not the vase I'm sorry for, it's you. You can see for yourself now what happened. Now you know how it feels the morning after. But never mind that either, because it's no good holding you to account. Well, goodbye for now! Take a walk if you have the energy, and then back for a snooze – that's my advice. But if you feel like it, come and see us as before. Remember once and for all that whatever happens, whatever the consequences may be, you will always remain a friend of the family – of mine, anyway. At least no one can stop me speaking for myself..."

Everyone protested in like manner and confirmed Mother's sentiments. They left, but in this ingenuous urge to say something nice and encouraging, there was a very cruel sting, which had never even occurred to Lizaveta Prokofyevna. In the invitation "come and see us as before" and the words "of mine, anyway" there was again something ominous. The Prince cast his mind back to Aglaya. She had smiled at him sweetly when she came in and at parting, but she hadn't uttered a single word, even when everyone was pouring their hearts out, but she did glance at him intently a couple of times. Her face was paler than usual, as though she had had a bad night. The Prince definitely made up his mind to go and see them "as before", and looked nervously at the clock. Vera entered, exactly three minutes after the Yepanchins had left.

"Lev Nikolayevich, Aglaya Ivanovna has just asked me to pass a secret message to you."

The Prince fairly shuddered.

"A note?"

"No, a spoken one. She had barely time for that either. She wants you to stay at home all day today till seven or even nine in the evening, I didn't quite catch that last bit."

"But... what for? What could that mean?"

"I know nothing about that. Only she was adamant I had to pass the message to you!"

"Is that really what she said?"

"No, not quite, she only just had time to say the message quickly with her back to me. It was lucky I happened to be close by. But looking at her face, I knew if she was adamant or not. The way she looked at me, I nearly died..."

A few more questions and, without being any the wiser at the end, he succeeded in unnerving himself thoroughly. Left alone, he stretched himself out on the sofa and began to think. "Perhaps they're expecting someone before nine, and she is worried in case I disgrace myself yet again in front of other people," he reflected, and went on waiting anxiously for the evening to come, and looking the clock. But the solution came well before the evening, and also in the form of a call – a solution in the form of another, a painful riddle. Exactly half an hour after the Yepanchins had left, Ippolit turned up. He was so exhausted and worn out that without a single word he simply collapsed in a chair as though bereft of reason and immediately fell into an excruciating fit of coughing. He was coughing up blood. His eyes were glinting and the red spots had reappeared on his cheeks. The Prince muttered something, to which he did not respond and carried on in the same vein for a long time, waving his hand about frantically to be left alone for the time being. Finally he settled down.

"I can't stay, I'm leaving!" he brought out at long last in a rasping voice.

"Would you like me to accompany you?" the Prince asked, rising to his feet, but stopped abruptly on remembering that he had been told to stay put.

Ippolit burst out laughing.

"I didn't mean it that way," he continued, gasping for air and unable to clear his throat. "Quite the reverse, I came over especially, on a serious errand... else I'd not have bothered you. I'm leaving for the great hereafter, and this time, I surely mean it. *Kaput*! I'm not fishing for sympathy, believe me... I went to bed this morning, at ten, to stay there till doomsday, but I changed my mind and got up once more to come over to you... you see, I had my reasons."

"My heart aches just to look at you. Why didn't you just send for me, instead of dragging yourself over?"

"Well, that'll do. You've said what convention demands... Oh, I quite forgot, how is your health?"

"I'm all right. Last night I was... not very—"

"I heard, I heard all about it. The Chinese vase came to a sticky end, did it not? Pity I wasn't there! I came on a serious matter. First, I had the pleasure of seeing Gavrila Ardalionovich and Aglaya Ivanovna on a rendezvous by the green bench. I was well and truly struck by how silly some people can look at times. I informed Aglaya Ivanovna of this, after Gavrila Ardalionovich had left... You, Prince, appear not to be surprised by anything," he added, observing how calmly the Prince was taking all this. "Not to betray surprise, they say, is a mark of great intelligence. But the way I look at it, it could equally well be also a sign of great folly... To be sure, I'm not casting aspersions on you, I beg your pardon... My gift of the gab is letting me down today."

"I knew since yesterday that Gavrila Ardalionovich..." the Prince stopped short, visibly at a loss, despite Ippolit's exasperation at his lack of responsiveness.

"You knew! Well, I am surprised! To be sure, there's no need for you to go into it... And you didn't happen to witness the rendezvous, did you?"

"You saw I wasn't there, assuming you yourself were."

"Well, perhaps you were hiding under a bush somewhere. To be frank, however, I'm really glad, for you that is, otherwise I might have thought that preference had been accorded to – Gavrila Ardalionovich!"

"I must ask you not to speak to me of this, Ippolit, or to choose your words more carefully."

"What difference does it make if you know everything already?"

"You are mistaken. I know hardly anything, and Aglaya Ivanovna knows for certain that I know nothing. I knew nothing about the rendezvous either... You are telling me there was a rendezvous, are you not? Well, so be it, let's leave it at that then—"

"I don't understand, you knew and then you didn't know! You said, let's leave it at that? Well, you shouldn't be so gullible! Especially if you don't know anything. Your gullibility is the result of your ignorance. Do you realize what these two, brother and sister, are up to? Perhaps you have a shrewd idea?... All right, have it your way, I shan't go on about it..." he added, having noticed the Prince shift irritably. "But I came here on a personal matter and... have some explaining to do. Hell, one can't even die without having to explain oneself. I seem to be doing nothing else. Will you hear me out?"

"Go on! I'm listening."

"And, odd as it may appear, I want to change my mind yet again, and begin with Ganya. Would you believe it I too had been invited today to come to the green bench. However, I don't want to tell a lie, I insisted on the rendezvous myself, I talked my way into it, I promised to reveal a secret. I don't know if I came too early (I suspect I really did), but no sooner had I sat down next to Aglaya Ivanovna than Gavrila Ardalionovich and Varvara Ardalionovna turned up, arm in arm, as though out for a stroll. I had the feeling both were thoroughly astonished to see me there. They obviously hadn't expected it. They were in a shock. Aglaya Ivanovna flushed and, believe it or not, appeared a little flustered. I'm not sure if it was because I was there or simply because she happened to see Gavrila Ardalionovich, because let's face it, he is uncommonly handsome, is he not? The fact remains she flushed and put an end to the matter in no time. It actually was very funny. She got up, acknowledged Gavrila Ardalionovich's bow as well as Varvara Ardalionovna's smarmy smile and snapped, 'I only came to convey my personal thanks for your sincere and friendly sentiments, and should I ever stand in need of them, you can rest assured...' Here she curtsied and the two of them withdrew – feeling that they were made fools of, or else they felt triumphant; I couldn't tell which. Dear Ganya, bless him, was of course made to look a right fool but, naturally, he twigged nothing and just went as red as a beetroot (he pulls such funny faces at times!). But Varvara Ardalionovna, I think, realized they should make themselves scarce as soon as possible and that they'd get no more change out of Aglaya Ivanovna, and she left, with her brother in tow. She's more intelligent than he ever was, and I'm sure she's gloating now. The reason I had come was to agree with Aglaya Ivanovna on a meeting with Nastasya Filippovna."

"With Nastasya Filippovna!" the Prince exclaimed.

"I say, that's more like it! You're beginning to fight shy of your indifference and betray surprise! I'm delighted you want to be like other mortals. I shall tell you something amusing as a reward. It's what comes of being nice to haughty young ladies. For my pains I had my face slapped this morning."

"Mo-morally?" the Prince enquired, somewhat involuntarily.

"Yes, not physically. I don't think anyone's likely to raise his hand against such a one as I am, not even a woman. Not even Ganya would hit me! Though in truth there was a moment yesterday I thought he would attack me... I bet I know what you're thinking about now. 'There's no need to hit him – stifling him with a pillow or a wet rag in his sleep would do. It would serve him right!...' I can see it written on your face that that's what you're thinking this very instant."

"I have never thought that!" the Prince replied with disgust.

"I'm not sure about that. In the night I dreamt... someone... had stifled me to death with a wet rag... Shall I tell you who? Rogozhin, if you please! What do you think, is it possible to stifle someone with a wet rag?"

"I wouldn't know."

"I heard it was. All right, let's change the subject. So, why am I a gossip? Why did she call me a gossip today? And mark this, after she had heard me out to the last word and had even asked to repeat some parts... But that's women for you! It's for her sake I contacted Rogozhin, a fascinating character; it's for her sake I arranged a private meeting with Nastasya Filippovna for her. Perhaps I wounded her pride by suggesting she was glad to pick up Nastasya Filippovna's leftovers?

Of course I'd been trying to explain that to her in her own interests for ages, I admit that. I'd written her two letters on the subject, and now, thirdly, this rendezvous... When I first broached the subject, I said to her from the very start she was selling herself short... And, besides, the word 'leftovers' was not really mine at all. It was on everybody's lips at Ganya's, as she herself has confirmed. So, why then am I a gossip in her books? I can see it all, you're finding it most hilarious, and I bet my life you've already knocked up some silly rhyme to make up the picture:

> And maybe before I disappear for good
> Love'll smile on me in reward for all I stood.

Ha ha ha!" he burst into a hysterical paroxysm of laughter. "Remember though," he wheezed, choking himself with coughing, "Ganya's a right one! He talks of leftovers, and what else is it he himself wants to take advantage of now?"

The Prince took a long time before he answered. He was shocked.

"You mentioned a meeting with Nastasya Filippovna?" he muttered at last.

"Heh, did you really not know that Aglaya Ivanovna is due to meet Nastasya Filippovna today, for which end Nastasya Filippovna has been deliberately summoned from St Petersburg courtesy of Rogozhin and yours truly on the strength of Aglaya Ivanovna's personal invitation, and that the said person is at present ensconced with Rogozhin not a million versts from here in her former abode at Darya Alexeyevna's... her bosom pal, a rather dubious lady if you ask me. It is that dubious abode that Aglaya Ivanovna proposes to visit today for a sociable chat with Nastasya Filippovna, and to resolve various problems. Perhaps they want to chat about the weather? You don't mean to tell me you didn't know? Honestly?"

"This is unbelievable!"

"So much the better if it's unbelievable. On second thoughts, how indeed were you to know? For all that, if a fly should fly past here it's already common knowledge – that's Pavlovsk for you! Never mind, you've been warned and you can be grateful to me. Well, au revoir – in the next world perhaps. And another thing, if I clowned before you, it was because... well, why should I be the loser every time, tell me kindly! To keep your counsel and not my own? Look, I dedicated my 'Explanation' to her (you didn't know that?) And what was her reaction? He he! But there was no clowning on my part where she was concerned. I am perfectly innocent. It was she who shamed me and let me down... Come to that, I'm innocent as far as you're concerned too. Even if I did talk there of leftovers and suchlike things, I'm making up for it now by letting you know the day, the hour and the address of the meeting, and letting you in upon the whole of the game... out of irritation, and not any more noble sentiment, it goes without saying. So long, I talk too much like all stutterers and consumptives. Be on your guard, don't waste any time, if you know what's good for you. The meeting is tonight, that much is certain."

Ippolit headed for the door, but the Prince called out, and he stopped.

"So you are telling me Aglaya Ivanovna herself will go to see Nastasya Filippovna tonight?" the Prince asked. His face and forehead became covered in red blotches.

"I cannot be certain, but it very much looks like it," Ippolit answered, half-turning. "There really is no alternative. Nastasya Filippovna couldn't be expected to go to her, could she now? Nor could it be at Ganya's place within the earshot of a dying man. Do you know the state the General is in?"

"Look here, none of this is possible," the Prince argued, "simply because she could never leave the house even if she wanted to! You've no idea... what the rules of the house are. She could never go to see Nastasya Filippovna on her own. It's sheer nonsense!"

"There you are, Prince – no one jumps out of windows, but should there be a fire your most hoity-toity gentleman and your most finicky lady would jump. When up against it, and there's nowhere to turn, even a visit to Nastasya Filippovna may be on the cards. But are you sure they're so closely guarded, those young ladies of yours?"

"No, it's not that—"

"Not that? Well, all she has to do is descend the steps of the porch and keep going, regardless as to whether she ever wants to return home. There are cases when one does actually have to burn bridges and deny oneself the means of returning to base. Life isn't made up of just lunches, dinner parties and the presence of the likes of Prince S. It seems to me you take Aglaya Ivanovna for some fairy queen or a sheltered, innocent boarding-school girl. I mentioned this to her, and

I think she agreed. Keep your eyes peeled at about seven or eight...
If I were you, I'd send someone there to be on the lookout and catch
her just as she's coming down from the porch. Why not Kolya? He'd
be only too glad to be your spy, you can be assured of that, for you,
naturally... because, let's be frank, it's all relative really... Ha ha!"

Ippolit left. The Prince did not have to ask anyone to spy for him,
even if he were capable of such a request. Aglaya's injunction for him
to stay indoors had now become almost self-evident for him. Perhaps
she meant to come and pick him up? On the other hand, she may have
particularly not wanted him to be there, and therefore required him to
stay put... that was also a possibility. His head was spinning. He lay
down on the couch and shut his eyes.

However, be that as it may, things had come to a climax, to a final
resolution. No, he did not take Aglaya for a fairy queen or a schoolgirl.
He felt he had dreaded something like this for a long time now. But
why on earth did she want to see her? He was shivering all over. He was
again in a state of fever.

No, he did not take her for a child! He was aghast at some of her
views recently and at what she had said. It had seemed to him that
at times she'd taken excessive pains to put a brave face on things, to
keep herself in check, and he recalled that it had inspired fear in him.
True, he had forced himself not to dwell on this these past few days,
and had shunned all gloomy thoughts. But what was going on inside
that soul of hers? This question had been troubling him for a long
time now, even though his faith in that soul remained undiminished.
And now all this was finally to be revealed and exposed this very day.
A frightening prospect! And then again there was "that woman"! Why
was it he had always thought that woman would come precisely at the
very last moment and snap his fate like a piece of rotten thread? That
it had always seemed to him to be that way, he was ready to swear right
now even though he was only semi-conscious. If he had attempted to
forget *about her* lately, it was only because he was afraid of her. Well
then, did he love that woman or hate her? He had studiously avoided
asking himself this question today. He was innocent at heart in that
respect. He knew whom he loved... It was not so much their meeting he
was afraid of, or its incongruousness, or the reasons for it which were
certainly unknown to him, much less the final outcome, whatever shape
or form it took – he was afraid of Nastasya Filippovna herself. It came

to him several days later that in these traumatic hours he constantly raved about her eyes, the way she looked at him, he heard the words she spoke – strange words, even though precious little had stayed in his mind after these fever-ridden, soul-destroying hours. He had only vague memories for instance of Vera bringing him food and his eating it, with no recollection of whether he had slept after his meal or not. All he knew was that he had begun to see everything perfectly clearly only after Aglaya had suddenly entered on the terrace that evening and he had jumped off the couch and walked to the middle of the room to meet her. It was quarter-past seven. Aglaya was on her own. She was rather casually dressed, with a light hooded cloak over her shoulders. Her face was pale, as previously, and her eyes had a sharp dry lustre to them. He had never before seen such a look in her eyes. She surveyed him carefully up and down.

"You are completely ready," she observed softly, giving the impression of outer calm, "fully dressed, hat in hand. I take it someone has warned you, and I know who – Ippolit! Am I right?"

"Yes, he came to tell me—" the Prince muttered, more dead than alive.

"Let's go then. You know you must come with me whatever happens. I hope you can manage it. You can, can you not?"

"Yes, I can, but… is it possible?"

He stopped dead immediately, unable to say anything more. That was his one and only attempt to bring Aglaya to her senses; he then followed her slavishly. However disordered his thoughts were, he realized that nothing would stop her from going *there*, and consequently he was duty-bound to go with her. He could tell the strength of her resolve and how futile it would be for him to stand in her way. They walked in silence, hardly a word passed between them. He could not help noticing how well she knew the way, and when he suggested making a slight detour because it was less crowded along there, she heard him out as though under strain, and replied curtly, "Makes no difference!" As they drew level with Darya Alexeyevna's large old timber house, a splendidly attired lady in the company of a much younger woman emerged from the front door. They both got into a magnificent calash, which was waiting in the driveway, talking and laughing loudly, without so much as a glance at the two approaching figures as though they had not even noticed them. As soon as the calash had moved off, the door opened for a second time, and Rogozhin, who was already expecting them, let them in and shut it behind them.

"Apart from us four, there's no one else in the house now," he said in a loud voice and gave the Prince an odd look.

Nastasya Filippovna was waiting in the first room they entered. She too was dressed very plainly and completely in black. She stood up, but did not smile and did not even put out her hand to the Prince.

She looked directly at Aglaya, nervously and expectantly. They both sat down at a distance from each other, Aglaya in a corner of the room, Nastasya Filippovna at a window. The Prince and Rogozhin remained standing, nor had anyone offered either of them to take a seat. The Prince gave Rogozhin a baffled and somewhat pained glance, but the latter went on grinning as before. No one spoke for a few more seconds.

At last Nastasya Filippovna's features took on a vicious aspect. She continued to regard her visitor with steady, unblinking, almost hate-filled eyes, focused firmly on her. Aglaya was clearly ill at ease, but refused to be intimidated. On the way in she gave her rival a fleeting glance, and since then had sat, eyes to the ground, as though lost in thought. Once or twice she looked cursorily round the room in evident revulsion, as though afraid of being contaminated by the place. She was automatically adjusting the folds of her dress, and on one occasion shifted with distaste to the far end of the settee. She was hardly aware of her movements, but this only served to make them that much more offensive. At last she looked steadily and directly at Nastasya Filippovna, and recognized immediately the full extent of the hatred which glinted in her rival's eyes. Each knew what the other was thinking; Aglaya shuddered.

"I'm sure you know why I asked to meet you," she said at last, but very softly and, despite the brevity of the sentence, with a couple of halting pauses.

"No, I have no idea," Nastasya Filippovna returned in a clipped, matter-of-fact tone of voice.

Aglaya blushed. Perhaps it struck her as terribly odd and unbelievable that she should be sitting opposite "that woman", in the house of "that woman", awaiting her answer. The very first words Nastasya Filippovna spoke sent a shiver down Aglaya's spine. None of this of course escaped "that woman's" eyes.

"I'm sure you do... but you deliberately pretend you don't under-stand," Aglaya said in a subdued whisper, staring at the floor with grim intensity.

"Why should I do that?" Nastasya Filippovna asked with a faint smile.

"You want to take advantage of my situation... of the fact that I'm in your house," Aglaya replied with an ineptitude bordering on the ridiculous.

"You have only yourself to blame for the situation you're in, not me!" Nastasya Filippovna retorted suddenly. "I did not invite you. You invited yourself, and I still can't make out why."

Aglaya raised her head defiantly.

"Hold your tongue. I did not come to fight you on your terms—"

"Ah, so you did come to fight? As a matter of fact, I imagined that you... had more wit about you..."

The both looked at each other with open hostility. One of these women had only recently written emotionally charged letters to the other. And suddenly, at the first encounter and the first words, everything had gone up in smoke. What was the matter? At that moment it seemed no one of the four present in the room found this at all surprising. The Prince, who only the day before would not have credited the possibility of even dreaming of such an outcome, now stood and listened as though he had long been expecting all this. The most outlandish dream had turned into the starkest and most clearly delineated reality. One of these women detested the other so much at this instant, and was so eager to put it into words (perhaps that was the sole reason for her coming in the first place, as Rogozhin observed the next day) that, however wildly incensed her rival might have been with her disturbed mind and warped soul, it seemed there was no power on earth which could have resisted the venomous, truly feminine contempt for the woman opposite. The Prince was certain that Nastasya Filippovna would not be the first to bring up the letters. Her fiery looks told him what these letters might cost her now; but he was ready to die to stop Aglaya bringing them up too.

But Aglaya suddenly managed to take a hold on herself.

"You misunderstood me," she said. "I did not come... to quarrel with you, however much I dislike you. I... I came to hold a reasonable, sensible discussion with you. In calling upon you, I had already decided what I was going to say to you, and shall not deviate from my resolution even if you failed to understand me totally. It will be so much the worse for you, and not for me. I wanted to reply to what you wrote to me, and I wanted to reply in person, because it seemed to me to be the most appropriate thing to do. Please hear my reply to all your letters. I felt sorry for Prince Lev Nikolayevich the first time I got to know him and later when I found out what had happened at your soirée. I felt sorry for him because he is such a simple-hearted man, and in his simplicity had supposed he could be happy... with a woman... with such a character. What I feared would happen to him has happened. You could not fall in love with him. You made him suffer and then you left him. You could not love him, because you are too proud... no, not proud, my mistake, but because you are vain... perhaps not even that. You are selfish to the point of... insanity, and your letters addressed to me are proof enough of that. You could never have fallen in love with him, simple as he is, and perhaps deep down you even hated and mocked him. The only thing you could love was your own infamy and the ever-present realization that you'd been disgraced and insulted. Had you less infamy to contend with, or none at all, you'd have been more unhappy..." (Aglaya delighted in rolling off her tongue all these carefully considered and rehearsed charges, considered and rehearsed way back, at a time when in her wildest dreams she could not have foreseen the present encounter. With eyes brimming with venom, she observed the effect her words had on Nastasya Filippovna's pain-wracked features.) "You will recall," she continued, "he wrote me a letter then. He tells me you knew about the letter and had even read it. This letter made everything clear to me, and I was right. He recently confirmed it to me himself, that is, what I told you just now, word for word. After I received the letter, I began to wait. I was right in thinking you'd come here, because you'd miss St Petersburg too much. You are still too young and too beautiful for life in the provinces... Incidentally, these are not my words either," she added, blushing to the roots of her hair, and from this moment on her face remained flushed till the very end of her speech. "After I saw the Prince again, I felt a fresh wave of sorrow and pity for him. Do not laugh. If you laugh, it will make you unworthy of appreciating what I have—"

"Surely you can see I'm not laughing," Nastasya Filippovna said in a dejected, but severe tone of voice.

"It doesn't matter to me, you may laugh as much as you like. When I started questioning him myself, he told me he had stopped loving you long ago, that even the memory of you gave him pain, but that he pitied you and every time he thought of you his heart bled for you unbearably. I must say that for my part I had never before in my life come across anyone to equal him in generosity of spirit and boundless trustfulness. After all he said, I realized that anybody who wanted to take the trouble could easily deceive him, and whoever deceived him he would eventually pardon. It is for this that I fell in love with him…"

Aglaya halted for a second as though astonished, as though in disbelief that she could have said such a thing; but at the same time her eyes lit up with immense pride. It seemed she no longer cared even if "that woman" were to burst out laughing at the admission which had just escaped her.

"I have told you everything, and I'm sure you now realize what it is I want from you, or don't you?"

"I may well realize, but let me hear you say it all the same," Nastasya Filippovna said softly.

Aglaya's face flushed with anger.

"I wanted to know," she said firmly and distinctly, "by what right do you meddle in his feelings for me? By what right did you dare to write letters to me? By what right do you keep claiming to him and to me that you love him after you yourself had deserted him and run away from him, causing him such pain and… humiliation?"

"I didn't say anything about loving him either to you or to him," Nastasya Filippovna said with effort, "and… you are quite right, I did desert him…" she added, barely audibly.

"What do you mean you didn't say anything to me or to him?" Aglaya exclaimed. "What about your letters? Who asked you to be our go-between and try to persuade me to marry him? Isn't that enough? Why are you foisting yourself upon us? At first I had, on the contrary, the impression that by your answer you meant to set me up against him and that I should leave him. It was only later I realized what was going on. You imagine you're making some noble sacrifice with all this posturing… Could one whose first love is vanity possibly love him? Why didn't you simply go away, instead of writing these ridiculous letters to me? Why don't you marry a respectable gentleman, who loves you so much and has honoured you with offering you his hand?

The reason is all too obvious. If you were to marry Rogozhin, where would be your sense of having been hurt? He'd be doing you too much of an honour anyway. Yevgeny Pavlovich said about you that you've read too much poetry and that you're too educated for your... station, that you're bookish and indolent. Add vanity to it, and it all becomes clear—"

"And you're not indolent?"

This all came about too precipitately, too starkly, too unexpectedly, because, when setting out for Pavlovsk, Nastasya Filippovna, even though she anticipated the worst, still clung to a hope of sorts, though it was more likely to have been mischievous rather than harmless. As for Aglaya, she was prey to her momentary passions and hurtled headlong as though down a mountain, unable to resist the terrible pull of sweet revenge. Nastasya Filippovna was fairly taken aback; she looked at Aglaya and could hardly believe her senses. For a moment she was caught completely off-guard. Whether she was a woman who had read too many poems, as had been suggested by Yevgeny Pavlovich, or simply insane, as was the Prince's opinion of her, one thing was crystal clear – in spite of being cynical and provocative in her ways, she was in actual fact far more inhibited, gentle and trusting than one might have supposed. True, she was given to romanticizing, to solitary daydreaming, verging on the fantastic – but along with this she had strength and depth... The Prince was aware of this; he appeared thoroughly mortified. Aglaya noticed it and sensed his train of thought. She fairly shook with rage.

"How dare you speak to me like that?" she said with untold uppishness.

"You must have misheard me," Nastasya Filippovna returned with surprise. "How should I have spoken to you?"

"If you wanted to be an honest woman, why didn't you simply leave your seducer, Totsky, at the time... and spare yourself all those theatricals?" Aglaya suddenly blurted out with no rhyme or reason.

"What do you know about my circumstances to have the right to judge me?" Nastasya Filippovna asked with a shudder, going very pale.

"I know that you did not go out to work, but preferred to stay with the wealthy Rogozhin to act the fallen angel. I'm not surprised Totsky wanted to shoot himself because of this fallen angel!"

"Don't!" Nastasya Filippovna said with revulsion as though overcoming a painful recollection. "You demonstrated as much understanding of me, as... Darya Alexeyevna's chambermaid did, who'd recently sued her lover at the county court. In fact, she'd have had more sense—"

"No doubt an honest girl, making an honest living. Why are you so dismissive of a chambermaid?"

"I'm not dismissive of labour, I'm dismissive of you, when you talk about labour."

"If you wanted to be honest with yourself, you'd have gone out and worked as laundry woman."

They both stood up and glared at each other.

"Aglaya, stop it! You're being unfair," the Prince cried despairingly. Rogozhin had stopped grinning, but listened, tight-lipped, arms crossed on his chest.

"Just look at her," Nastasya Filippovna said, shaking with anger, "look at this young lady! And I thought of her as an angel! You came here without your governess, Aglaya Ivanovna, did you not?... And if you wish... if you wish, I'll tell you without any ado, why it is you came here? You took fright, and decided to come here!"

"Took fright of you?" Aglaya asked, incensed with naive arrogance that she should be spoken to thus.

"Of course – of me! If you dared come to see me, it is because you are afraid of me. Fear and hatred don't go together. To think that I could have respected you right up to this moment! And do you know why you are afraid of me and what your main purpose now is? You want to establish personally if he loves me more than you, because you are terribly jealous—"

"He told me already he hates you—" Aglaya muttered, utterly crestfallen.

"May well be! It may well be I'm not worthy of him, only... only I think it is a lie! He cannot hate me, and he could never have said such a thing! But let that pass, I'm ready to forgive you... in view of your situation... only I had a better opinion of you. I thought you were more intelligent, and even better-looking, honestly!... So, take your treasure... there he is, looking at you, starry-eyed! Take him with you, but on one condition – get out of here now! This very minute!..."

She fell back in her chair and burst into tears. But something new glinted in her eyes. She looked at Aglaya with hard intensity and rose to her feet:

"And if you want to know, I only have to give the order to him, do you hear me? And he'll leave you immediately and will stay with me for ever, and will marry me, and you will have to trot home on your own with your tail between your legs! Would you like me to, would you?" she cried like one demented, perhaps in disbelief that she could have come up with such a challenge.

Aglaya rushed for the door in panic, but she stopped and carried on listening, dumbstruck.

"Would you like me to kick Rogozhin out? You imagined I had already married Rogozhin for your pleasure. There, I'll call out, 'Get out of here, Rogozhin!' and I'll say to the Prince, 'Do you remember your promise?' My God, why did I humiliate myself so in front of them? Wasn't it you, Prince, who assured me that you'd marry me whatever might happen to me, and you'd never desert me, that you loved me and would forgive me everything, and that you re… respe… Yes, you said that too! And only not to be a burden to you, I ran away, but now I've changed my mind! Why did she treat me as though I was a loose woman? Am I a loose woman? Ask Rogozhin, he'll tell you! Now that she has disgraced me, and what's more, in your eyes, would you turn from me and walk away arm-in-arm with her? I'd curse you if you did, and that because you were the only one I had put my trust in. Rogozhin, get out, you're not needed any more!" she yelled, having lost all self-control, forcing out her words with effort, with strife-torn features, parched lips and probably with little idea of what she was raving about, but at the same time yearning for all she was worth to prolong her self-deception if only for a second more. Her abandon was so great, she could have died; at least that was the impression that the Prince formed. "Look, there he stands!" she shouted once more, pointing at the Prince. "If he doesn't come over to me now, if he doesn't take me and reject you, you can have him, he's yours, I don't need him!…"

She and Aglaya stood stock-still, and both stared at the Prince in wild expectation. But, as likely as not, he had probably no idea of the intensity of the challenge – in fact, assuredly not. All he saw was a desperate, sweet face, the sight of which, as he had once admitted to Aglaya, had pierced him to the quick. He could stand it no longer and he turned to Aglaya, pleadingly and reproachfully, as he pointed to Nastasya Filippovna. "Surely, this is impossible! Can you not see... how unhappy she is!"

But that was all he managed to say before he froze under Aglaya's outraged stare. In that stare there was so much suffering and at the same time so much hatred, that he threw up his hands in agony, and with a cry rushed towards her, but it was too late! She could not put up with even a moment's hesitation on his part, buried her face in her hands, and cried out, "Oh my God!" The next moment she was already out of the room, closely followed by Rogozhin, to unlatch the front door for her.

The Prince rushed after her too, but on the doorstep two arms suddenly entwined him in a tight embrace. Nastasya Filippovna's agonized, grief-stricken face was turned up at him pleadingly, her livid lips barely able to articulate her dismay:

"Are you running away with her, with her?..."

She collapsed senseless in his arms. He lifted her, laid her on a couch and stood over her in dumb expectation. On the table was a glass of water. Rogozhin, who was back directly, grabbed it and splashed some water in her face. She opened her eyes and for a minute did not know what was going on. But suddenly she looked around, shuddered, let out a cry and rushed towards the Prince.

"Mine! You are mine!" she cried. "The proud young lady has gone, hasn't she? Ha ha ha!" she laughed hysterically. "Ha ha ha! I was going to let her take him away! What for? What on earth for? I was mad! Mad!... Get out of here, Rogozhin, ha ha ha!"

Rogozhin looked at them intently, and without saying a word, picked up his hat and left the room. Ten minutes later the Prince was sitting next to Nastasya Filippovna, staring closely into her eyes and stroking her head and face with both hands as though she were a small child. He laughed when she laughed and was ready to cry when she cried. He did not say anything, but listened intently to her broken, excited and incoherent mutterings, understanding practically nothing, but smiling softly, and every time he thought she was beginning to look worried or began to cry, complain or scold him, he would immediately caress her head and her cheeks, trying to comfort and console her as though she were a small child.

9

TWO WEEKS HAVE ELAPSED since the events described in the last chapter, and the situation of the protagonists has changed to such an extent that we find it extremely difficult to continue our narrative unless we provide a number of specific explanations. And at the same time we feel we have to restrict ourselves to a simple exposition of the facts only, avoiding where possible all attempts at explaining, for the simple reason that in many instances we ourselves are at a loss to provide an explanation of what occurred. Such a reservation on our part must needs appear rather strange and puzzling, inasmuch as how can one continue recounting something of which one has neither a clear understanding nor a personal opinion? To avoid putting ourselves in an even more awkward position, let us try to clarify the above by way of an example, in the hope that the generous reader may understand our difficulty, the more so since this example will not be a digression, but on the contrary will present a direct and close sequel of the story.

Two weeks had elapsed, and it was the beginning of July. In the course of these two weeks our hero's story, especially the last episode, took a bizarre, rather amusing, almost incredible and at the same time extravagant turn, which little by little reverberated throughout all the streets adjoining the dachas of Lebedev, Ptitsyn, Darya Alexeyevna and the Yepanchins – in short, throughout the whole town and even its environs. Nearly all the inhabitants – the locals, the holidaymakers, the concert-goers – all began to tell one and the same story in a thousand different versions, namely how a prince, after causing a scene in a respectable, well-known family and after deserting the daughter of this family, to whom he had already proposed, had fallen for the charms of a popular strumpet, had broken off all former ties and, despite everything, despite all admonishments, despite the general indignation of the public, was determined to marry the disgraced woman in a matter of days, here in Pavlovsk, openly, publicly, his head held high and looking everybody directly in the eye. The affair was so embellished with various scandalous details, so many famous and influential people were implicated, so many unlikely and outlandish interpretations put upon the circumstances, and moreover, it was all presented in such factual and concrete terms, that universal curiosity and rumour-mongering were altogether quite excusable. The most subtle, clever and at the same time plausible interpretation came from the more sophisticated gossips, belonging to that contingent of level-headed people who always, in every society, consider it their mission to elucidate a given occurrence to others, while frequently deriving spiritual comfort themselves. By their lights, a young man of a good family, a prince, with hardly any Russian to speak of, allegedly wealthy, somewhat of a simpleton, a democrat to boot – fixated on nihilism, the latest fad, introduced courtesy of Mr Turgenev* – had fallen in love with the daughter of General Yepanchin and succeeded in gaining access to their house as an eligible husband-to-be. Just like that French seminarian, whose story had just recently done the rounds of all the papers – who had allowed himself to be ordained a priest, indeed purposely pleaded for it, and piously performed every ritual, every genuflection, obeisance and so on – all this in order to inform his bishop by letter on the very next day that, having no faith in God, he considered it dishonourable to mislead people and live at their expense on false pretences, and was therefore unfrocking himself and allowing his letter to be printed in the liberal press. Like that atheist, the Prince had, it would appear, performed a similar act of treachery. People spoke of how he had deliberately put off everything until the formal soirée at his in-laws', at which he was introduced to a great number of very distinguished persons, in order to proclaim loud and clear his way of thinking, abuse a number of dignitaries, renounce his fiancée – publicly and scurrilously – and, while resisting the servants, who were escorting him out, contrived to break a beautiful Chinese vase. To this was added, by way of an illustration of contemporary mores, that the befuddled young man really was in love with the General's daughter, his fiancée, but that he had rejected her purely out of nihilism and in anticipation of the ensuing outrage, so as not to forgo the pleasure of marrying in full view of the whole world a fallen woman and thereby proving that in his estimation there were neither fallen nor upright women, but only one type of woman – the emancipated woman; that he had no time for the traditional social categories, but believed only in the "woman question". Finally, in his eyes a fallen woman was even somewhat worthier than one who was not fallen. This explanation appeared to be the more likely and was accepted by the majority of the townspeople, the more so since it was corroborated by facts. True, many circumstances remained unexplained: it was rumoured that the poor girl loved her fiancé – to some, seducer – so much that she came running to him the very next day after he had deserted her and when he was ensconced with his mistress; others maintained on the contrary, that it was he who deliberately lured her to his mistress solely out of nihilist sentiments, wanting to dishonour and discredit her. Be that as it may, the interest in the affair grew by the day, the more so since no one was left in any doubt that the scandalous marriage really was on the cards.

And so, were we to be asked for an explanation – not of the nihilist overtones of the affair, but simply to what extent the prospective marriage would meet the Prince's real expectations; what was the real substance of his wishes at the time; how precisely was one to gauge our hero's actual state of mind at the given moment and so on, and so forth in this vein – we would be at a loss to respond. All we know was that the wedding really had been arranged and that the Prince had personally charged Lebedev, Keller and some acquaintance of Lebedev's, whom Lebedev had introduced to the Prince for the occasion, to take care of all the necessary preparations, in church as well as in the house; that money was not to be spared; that it was Nastasya Filippovna who had insisted on the wedding and urged everyone to proceed with all possible haste; that the groomsman was to be Keller in response to his own fervent pleadings for the honour; that Nastasya Filippovna was to be led to the altar by Burdovsky, who had simply jumped at the chance, and that the day itself was fixed for the beginning of July. But alongside these very precise facts, we were also aware of a number of others, which put us in an enormous quandary, simply because they were completely at variance with the preceding. For instance, we are very much inclined to suspect that, having charged Lebedev and others to take upon themselves the responsibilities for all the arrangements, the Prince had promptly, almost the very same day, all but forgotten that he had either a master of ceremonies, a groomsman or a wedding to come, and that even if he had issued instructions in haste for others to relieve him of all the arrangements, it was simply so as not to have to think about the matter any more and perhaps even to forget it altogether. So in that case, what did he think about, what did he want to remember and what did he strive for? There is also no doubt that he was under no coercion in the circumstances (for example, on the part of Nastasya Filippovna); that Nastasya Filippovna really had insisted on bringing the wedding day forward as much as possible and that the wedding itself was her idea, rather than the Prince's. But the Prince had agreed voluntarily, even somewhat absent-mindedly, as though he had been asked for some fairly matter-of-fact favour. We have a whole host of strange facts which not only do not shed light on the matter but, on the contrary, the more of them we take into account, the more they tend to obfuscate it. But, let us give another example.

We know for certain that in the course of this fortnight the Prince spent days and evenings with Nastasya Filippovna; that she took him for walks and concerts; that they both drove around in a calash every day; that he used to get worried if he missed an hour of her company (to all appearances he loved her sincerely); that he listened with a serene and submissive smile to whatever she might have been talking about for hours on end, without putting in a single word himself. But we also know that on these same days he would suddenly, without keeping it a secret from Nastasya Filippovna, try to see the Yepanchins, which drove her almost to despair. We know that while the Yepanchins remained in Pavlovsk, they would not see him, and access to Aglaya Ivanovna was constantly denied him; that he would leave them without saying a word and turn up the next day as though totally oblivious of the previous day's refusal, and would of course be turned away yet again. We also know that an hour, perhaps less, after Aglaya Ivanovna had stormed out of Nastasya Filippovna's, the Prince had already called on the Yepanchins fully expecting to find Aglaya there, and that his turning up at the Yepanchins had caused extreme consternation and dread, because Aglaya had not yet returned. It was from him that they first learnt that Aglaya and he had been to Nastasya Filippovna's. It was reported that Lizaveta Prokofyevna, her daughters and even Prince S. had given the Prince a very cold and unfriendly reception and had there and then in no uncertain terms barred him from the house and had withdrawn their friendship from him, especially after Varvara Ardalionovna had suddenly arrived to tell Lizaveta Prokofyevna that Aglaya Ivanovna has been with her in the house for the past hour in a dreadful state and appeared to have no wish to return home. This last communication astonished Lizaveta Prokofyevna more than anything, as was wholly understandable. On leaving Nastasya Filippovna's place, Aglaya would really have rather died than have faced her family, and therefore had rushed off to Nina Alexandrovna's. Varvara Ardalionovna

for her part had deemed it necessary to inform Lizaveta Prokofyevna
of this without delay. Mother and daughters immediately rushed off
to Nina Alexandrovna's, followed closely by the paterfamilias, Ivan
Fyodorovich, who had that very minute returned home; the rear was
made up by Prince Lev Nikolayevich himself, who came regardless of
the harsh words and admonitions to stay away. However, by orders of
Varvara Ardalionovna access to Aglaya was denied him there too. This
particular incident came to a close when Aglaya, seeing her mother and
sisters in tears and not rebuking her in any way, rushed into their arms
and returned home with them immediately. It was later reported, though
one could not be sure how accurately, that Gavrila Ardalionovich had
suffered a setback on this occasion too; that, taking advantage of his
sister's absence, after she had rushed off to Lizaveta Prokofyevna's,
and finding himself alone with Aglaya, he decided to talk of his love;
that, while listening to him, Aglaya, despite all her grief and tears, had
burst out laughing and had suddenly made a bizarre suggestion to him:
would he be prepared to prove his love to her by burning his finger
over a candle flame forthwith? It was said that Gavrila Ardalionovich
was so shocked, so bewildered by the suggestion, had betrayed so
much consternation, that Aglaya had burst out in a near hysterical fit
of laughter and rushed upstairs to Nina Alexandrovna's, where her
parents found her. This story reached the Prince courtesy of Ippolit
the next day. The by now totally bedridden Ippolit had purposely sent
for the Prince to tell it to him in so many words. How Ippolit had got
wind of it, we do not know, but after the Prince had heard about the
candle and the finger, he burst into such a fit of laughter that it took
Ippolit fairly by surprise; but then he suddenly began to shake all over
and burst into tears... On the whole, in these last few days he was
in an extraordinarily abstracted, confused and pained mood. Ippolit
declared openly that he judged him to be out of his mind; but for this
there was as yet no hard and fast evidence.

In presenting all these facts and yet fighting shy of offering a clarification, we do not wish on any account to exonerate our hero in the
eyes of our readers. Quite the reverse, we are well prepared to join in
the condemnation which he has provoked even amongst his friends.
Even Vera Lebedeva was indignant with him for a time; even Kolya
was indignant; Keller too was indignant – until he was appointed the
groomsman; as was Lebedev himself, who had even begun to wage a

campaign against the Prince also on the strength of quite the most righteous indignation. Of this we shall speak later. But it is with some of Yevgeny Pavlovich's very weighty and psychologically profound observations, which he had expressed to the Prince in a friendly conversation some six or seven days after the events at Nastasya Filippovna's, that we find ourselves in the greatest accord. Incidentally, it is worth noting that, not only the Yepanchins, but everyone directly or indirectly belonging to their household, had found it necessary to break all ties with the Prince. Prince S. for instance had even turned his back on him at a meeting, and had not acknowledged his salutation. But Yevgeny Pavlovich was not afraid of compromising himself by paying the Prince a visit, and this in spite of turning again into a daily visitor at the Yepanchins, where he was received with ever more goodwill. He came to see the Prince precisely two days after all the Yepanchins had left Pavlovsk. He knew, even as he entered, all the widespread rumours amongst the members of the public, to which he had perhaps in part contributed himself. The Prince was absolutely delighted to see him and immediately turned the conversation to the Yepanchins. Such a sincere and guileless approach also put Yevgeny Pavlovich completely at his ease, so that he got down to business without delay.

The Prince was not at all aware that the Yepanchins had left. The news caught him by surprise, and he went pale; but a minute later he shook his head, reflective and embarrassed, adding that that was to be expected, and then quickly followed by asking, "Where to?"

Yevgeny Pavlovich continued to observe him closely all the while, and everything taken together – that is, the rapidity of the Prince's questions, his embarrassment and at the same his rather curious openness, agitation and excitement – caused him a measure of surprise. By and by, he took pains to give the Prince a courteous and detailed account of all that had happened, which for the most part was quite new to the Prince as Yevgeny Pavlovich was his first contact with the Yepanchin house. Yevgeny Pavlovich confirmed that Aglaya really had been ill with fever and had not slept for three nights in a row; that she was better now and out of all danger, but in an unstable state, bordering on the hysterical... "At least it's good the family is at peace with itself! They all try not to bring up what had happened, even amongst themselves, let alone in front of Aglaya. The parents have already discussed a trip abroad, in autumn, immediately after

Adelaida's wedding. Aglaya had listened in silence when this was first mooted." He, Yevgeny Pavlovich, had also had a mind to take a trip abroad. Even Prince S., business commitments permitting, might perhaps take off for a month or two with Adelaida. The General himself would stay behind. For now the whole family had moved into a spacious country house in Kolmino, an estate of theirs about twenty versts from St Petersburg. Belokonskaya had still not left for Moscow and it appeared was putting off her departure deliberately. Lizaveta Prokofyevna was adamant that after all that had happened, it was not possible for them to remain in Pavlovsk. He, Yevgeny Pavlovich, had been making daily reports to her of the rumours circulating in town. The Yepanchins had not found it possible to move to their dacha on Yelagin Island.

"All things considered," Yevgeny Pavlovich added, "you must agree, they had no alternative... especially in view of all that is happening by the hour here in your house, Prince, and after your daily attempts to call on them, despite all the rebuffs—"

"Yes, yes, yes, you are quite right, I wanted to see Aglaya Ivanovna—" the Prince said, shaking his head again.

"Oh, my dear Prince," Yevgeny Pavlovich exclaimed suddenly with sad resignation, "how could you have let it all... come to this? Of course, of course it all happened so suddenly for you... I agree you could not help being totally confounded and... you could not have been expected to stop a frantic girl – that was beyond you! But you should have understood how serious, how strong was this girl's... attachment to you. She did not wish to share you with anyone else, and you... and you could abandon and destroy such a treasure!"

"Yes, yes, you are right, I am guilty," the Prince spoke with terrible anguish, "and do you know it was she, and she alone, Aglaya, who regarded Nastasya Filippovna in that light... the others, you know, did not."

"But that's exactly what is so annoying about the whole thing – that there was nothing serious!" Yevgeny Pavlovich exclaimed, getting thoroughly carried away. "Pardon me, Prince, but... I... I... I thought about it, Prince. I turned it over and over in my mind a lot. I know all that went on before, I know all that happened six months ago, everything, and – none of it was serious! It was all just an ideological infatuation, an illusion, a fantasy, nothing but smoke, and it was only the panicky jealousy of a completely inexperienced young girl who could have mistaken it for something serious!"

At this stage Yevgeny Pavlovich felt himself at liberty to give full vent to his pent-up indignation. In no uncertain terms, indeed with a depth of psychological insight, he unfolded before the Prince the entire canvas of his relationship with Nastasya Filippovna in the past. Yevgeny Pavlovich had always had the gift of the gab; now he positively excelled himself. "Everything from the very start," he announced, "was grounded on falsehood. That which starts on a false footing ends on a false footing. That is a law of nature. I hate it, it even incenses me, when... well, someone – calls you an idiot. You are too intelligent to be called so, but at the same time, you must agree, you are sufficiently out of the ordinary not to be like other people. I have come to the conclusion that the root cause of all that has occurred stems, first, from your so-to-speak congenital inexperience (note, Prince, this word 'congenital'), then from your extraordinary ingenuousness; further, from your phenomenal lack of a sense of proportion (something you owned up to yourself several times, Prince); and, finally from a massive onrush of ephemeral ideological convictions which, given your extraordinary sense of fairness, you have to this day been mistaking as genuine, natural and relevant! You must agree, Prince, that right from the start your relationship with Nastasya Filippovna was tinged with (for want of a better expression) some half-baked notions of democracy, that is to say, you were beguiled (to put it at its bluntest) by the 'woman question'. You see, I know full well the whole of that appallingly scandalous scene at Nastasya Filippovna's when Rogozhin brought his money. If you wish, I can analyse you in every particular and hold up the mirror to you to show just how sure I am of what's behind all this and why things have taken such a drastic turn! You're a young man who was pining in Switzerland for your native country, yearning to get back to Russia, a mysterious but promised land. You had read a pile of books about Russia – excellent books, no doubt – but for you, harmful. You returned home flushed with a fresh enthusiasm for action, and you plunged headlong into it! And lo and behold that same day you, a chaste and chivalrous knight, are informed of a sad and heart-rending story of a much wronged woman! You see her the same day. You are bewitched by her beauty – fantastic, demonic beauty (I fully agree she is a beauty). Add to this your nerves; add to this your falling sickness;

add to this our notorious, enervating St Petersburg thaw; add to this the whole of that day in an unfamiliar, almost ghostly city, a day of meetings and happenings, a day of unforeseen encounters, a day of the most unforeseen realizations, a day of the three beautiful Yepanchin sisters, amongst them Aglaya; add to this your exhaustion, your vertigo; add Nastasya Filippovna's drawing room and the atmosphere in that drawing room, and… what else could you have possibly expected from yourself, tell me?"

"Yes, yes, yes of course," the Prince said, shaking his head and getting flushed, "yes, this is almost all true. I really had hardly slept the previous night in the railway carriage and the night before that, and I was most upset—"

"Yes, of course, that's exactly what I'm driving at!" Yevgeny Pavlovich continued, getting more and more animated. "It's as clear as day that, buoyed by your passion, you rushed to make public a worthy sentiment, that you – a hereditary prince and a man of honour – refused to regard a woman as fallen not through any fault of her own but due to the immorality of a nefarious high-society profligate. Goodness, it's perfectly understandable! But that is not the point, my dear Prince: the point is whether your sentiments were grounded in truth, whether they were genuine or mere infatuation. Look here – a woman like that was once pardoned in the house of God, but she was not told that she did right, that she was worthy of all manner of praise and respect! Did not your own common sense tell you what was the matter three months later? Granted she may be innocent – I am not going to argue the case, I don't wish to – but could all her subsequent adventures have justified such an intolerable, satanic pride, such a brazen, intolerable egoism on her part, I ask you? I beg your pardon, Prince, I'm getting carried away, but—"

"Yes, that may all very well be so. You may well be right…" the Prince began to mutter. "She really is very irritable, and of course you are right, but—"

"She deserves pity? Is that what you want to say, my good Prince? But for the sake of pity and for the sake of doing her a good turn, was it right to insult another, a noble and spotless girl, to humiliate her in her rival's haughty, hate-filled eyes? What price pity after that? Isn't there a monstrous incongruity in all this? Could you really love a girl and so humiliate her in front of her rival, casting her aside for the other, before her rival's very eyes, after you had made her an honest proposal... for you did make her a proposal, did you not, in front of her parents and sisters at that! Can you call yourself an honourable man after that, allow me to ask you, Prince? And... did you not deceive an angel of a girl by assuring her of your love?"

"Yes, yes, you are right – oh, I feel I'm guilty!" the Prince said, wracked by unbearable anguish.

"But is that enough?" Yevgeny Pavlovich exclaimed furiously. "Is it really enough just to exclaim, 'Oh, it's my fault!' It's your fault, and yet you want to stand your ground! What about your fellow feeling, your oh-so 'Christian' fellow feeling, I mean? Surely you saw what she looked like at the time! Do you imagine she suffered any less than *the other one* did, that sweet temptress of *yours*? How could you stand by and let it all happen? How?"

"But... I did not—" the long-suffering Prince muttered.

"What do you mean, you did not?"

"Honest to goodness, I had no part in it. To this day I've no idea how it all came about... I – I ran after Aglaya Ivanovna, but Nastasya Filippovna fainted. And now I'm not allowed to see Aglaya Ivanovna."

"That makes no difference! You ought to have run after Aglaya Ivanovna even if the other one was lying senseless on the floor!"

"Yes... yes, I ought to have... but she would have died! She would have killed herself, you don't know her, and... I would have told Aglaya Ivanovna about it all later anyway and... You see, Yevgeny Pavlovich, it seems to me that you don't really know everything. Tell me, why won't they let me see Aglaya Ivanovna? I'd have explained everything to her. You see, both of them were talking at cross purposes at the time, completely at cross purposes, that's why it all ended the way it did... I can never explain it to you, but I could perhaps explain it to Aglaya... Oh my God, oh my God! You mentioned what she looked like at that moment when she ran out... oh my God, I remember!... Let's go, let's go!" he suddenly tugged at Yevgeny Pavlovich's sleeve, jumping to his feet.

"Go where?"

"To Aglaya Ivanovna, let's go now!..."

"But she's no longer here, I told you – and what on earth for?"

"She will understand, she will understand!" the Prince muttered, folding his hands in supplication. "She will realize it's all an awful misunderstanding, and that there's something else behind it all entirely."

"How do you mean something else? The fact remains you are getting married, are you not? It follows you insist on standing your ground... Are you getting married, or are you not?"

"Well, yes... I am. Yes, I'm getting married!"

"So how can it possibly be something else?"

"Yes, yes, it is, it is! It doesn't matter that I'm getting married, it really has nothing to do with it!"

"How do you mean it doesn't matter and has nothing to do with it? This is no laughing matter! You are getting married to a woman you love, to make her happy, and Aglaya Ivanovna has to stand by and see it all happen! How can you say it doesn't matter?"

"Make her happy? Oh, not at all! I'm just simply marrying her. She wants me to. And anyway, what of it if I am getting married – I... Well, it doesn't matter! I know only one thing, she definitely would have died. I can see now that this marriage with Rogozhin was utter madness! I now understand everything that I did not previously, and, you see, when the two stood opposite each other, I couldn't bear to look at Nastasya Filippovna's face... You don't know, Yevgeny Pavlovich" (he lowered his voice mysteriously) "I've never said this to anyone, not even to Aglaya, but I cannot bear Nastasya Filippovna's face... You were quite right when you spoke about that evening at Nastasya Filippovna's, but you missed one thing, because you have no idea. I was watching *her face*! I could not bear it the first time I saw her portrait that morning... You see Vera, Vera Lebedeva's eyes are quite different. I... I'm terrified of her face!" he added, completely overcome with fright.

"Terrified?"

"Yes! She is – insane!" he whispered, growing pale.

"Are you sure of that?" Yevgeny Pavlovich asked with mounting interest.

"Yes, I am – completely! These past few days have left no doubt whatever in my mind!"

"So what are you doing to yourself?" Yevgeny Pavlovich exclaimed in panic. "It would appear you are getting married out of some kind of fear? This beggars all understanding... You don't even love her, perhaps?"

"Oh no, I love her with all my heart! You see... she is nothing but a child right now – a total child! Oh, you don't know anything!"

"And this didn't stop you professing your love to Aglaya Ivanovna, did it?"

"No, no, it didn't!"

"How is that? Do you mean to say you want to love them both?"

"Oh, yes, yes!"

"Come, come, Prince, you cannot be serious, think what you are saying!"

"Without Aglaya I... I must see her, come what may! I... I shall soon die in my sleep. I know I shall die in my sleep tonight. Oh, if only Aglaya knew everything, if only she knew everything... and I mean everything! Because it must be everything, that's the first thing! Why is it we can never know *everything* about another person when we're up against it, and it's his fault!... There, I don't know what I'm talking about, I've lost the thread. You surprise me no end... And does she still look now like she did when she ran out? Oh yes, it is my fault all right! The likelihood is that I'm to blame for everything! I'm still not quite clear as to what exactly of, but I am to blame... There's something here I can't explain to you, Yevgeny Pavlovich, I haven't got the words, but Aglaya Ivanovna would understand! Oh, I always believed she'd understand."

"No, Prince, she wouldn't! Aglaya Ivanovna loved like a woman, like a living being, not like a... disembodied spirit. Do you know what, my hapless Prince? In all probability you loved neither the one nor the other!"

"I don't know... perhaps so, perhaps so. You are right about many things, Yevgeny Pavlovich. You are very clever, Yevgeny Pavlovich. Ah, my headache is coming back, let us go and see her! For God's sake, for God's sake!"

"I told you she has left Pavlovsk, she is in Kolmino."

"Let's go to Kolmino, let us go now!"

"That's not pos-si-ble!" Yevgeny Pavlovich said, stressing every syllable, and got up.

"Listen, I shall write a letter! Will you take it to her?"

"No, Prince, no! You mustn't ask me to run such errands, I cannot!"

They parted. Yevgeny Pavlovich left very puzzled. In his opinion also the Prince was somewhat mentally disturbed. And what was that about the *face* which the Prince feared and loved so much! Come to that, it really was possible he could die without Aglaya, and she would never find out that he had loved her so much! Ha ha! And how can one be in love with two women at the same time? A different kind of love for each, no doubt? That's very interesting... the poor idiot! And what will become of him now, I wonder?

10

CONTRARY TO HIS FOREBODINGS HOWEVER, the Prince did not die before his wedding either in his sleep or in his waking hours as he had predicted to Yevgeny Pavlovich. Perhaps he really did sleep badly and have bad dreams. But in the daytime he was perfectly normal and content, if only a little brooding, but this mostly when he was on his own. The preparations for the wedding went ahead apace. It took place about a week after Yevgeny Pavlovich's call on him. Given such haste, even the Prince's best friends, assuming he had any, would have had to admit defeat in their efforts to save the poor devil. Rumour had it that Yevgeny Pavlovich's call on him had taken place partly at the behest of General Ivan Fyodorovich and his spouse Lizaveta Prokofyevna. But even if these two, in the boundless goodness of their hearts, had indeed wished to save the madman from a fate worse than death, they would have had to stop at this one feeble attempt. Neither by their position, much less by their inclination (which was only natural), could they have been persuaded to more serious endeavour. We have mentioned that even those close to the Prince had opposed him in some measure. Vera Lebedeva, to be sure, did no more than shed some tears in private, keeping to her own room rather more than was her wont and visiting the Prince less often. It was also the time of the funeral of Kolya's father. The old man died from a second stroke, about eight days after the first. The Prince took a major part in the family's sorrow and during the first few days kept Nina Alexandrovna company for hours at a time. He attended the funeral mass and the burial. It was noticed that the Prince's arrival and departure was accompanied by involuntary whisperings by the congregation, similarly when he was out and about on the streets of the town or in the Gardens; every time he passed on foot or in a carriage there were subdued voices, his name was spoken, fingers were pointed, Nastasya Filippovna was mentioned. People looked around for her at the funeral, but she was not present. Neither was the Captain's widow, whom Lebedev had somehow managed to confine to her home and out of harm's way. The funeral ceremonies had a profound and painful effect upon the Prince. In reply to some question or other from Lebedev he whispered to him in the church that this was the first time that he had attended an Orthodox funeral liturgy – that is except for another occasion in a village church back in his childhood days.

"Yes indeed, it's strange to think the same person we had only recently voted in as our chairman, you remember, is now stretched out in a coffin," Lebedev whispered. "Are you looking for anyone?"

"No, it's nothing, I thought I—"

"Rogozhin?"

"Is he really here?"

"Yes indeed."

"That's what I thought. I was sure I saw his eyes," the Prince muttered, visibly shaken. "But... why is he here? Has he been invited?"

"Not at all. He doesn't even know the family. But all types beat a path here now. Why are you so surprised? I run into him quite often now – must be about four times in the past week, here in Pavlovsk."

"I have not seen him once... since that time," the Prince muttered.

Since Nastasya Filippovna had not mentioned either that she had met Rogozhin "since then", the Prince was certain that Rogozhin was lying low for some reason of his own. The rest of that day the Prince was completely immersed in his own thoughts. On the other hand, Nastasya Filippovna was in an unusually happy mood all that day and evening.

As time was fast running out, Kolya, who had made it up with the Prince before the death of his father, suggested the Prince take Keller and Burdovsky* for his groomsmen. He could vouch for Keller behaving properly, and indicated he might even come in "useful". As for Burdovsky – a discreet and reserved young man – there could be no qualms whatsoever about him. Nina Alexandrovna and Lebedev went out of their way to point out to the Prince that, seeing as the wedding had been decided upon, why hold it in Pavlovsk, especially at the height of the holiday season, of all times? Why make it all so public? Wouldn't St Petersburg have been better, or even at home? The Prince was only too well aware what was behind all these reservations, but he replied simply but firmly that it was at the express wish of Nastasya Filippovna.

Keller turned up the following day, bearing the news that he had been appointed groomsman. Before he entered the room, he stopped in the doorway and, as soon as he saw the Prince, raised his right hand with his index finger pointing upwards as though taking an oath.

"I shan't drink!"

Then he approached the Prince, shook both his hands vigorously and announced that he had, of course, been against it all initially and had said as much at the billiard table, and for no reason other than that he had always backed the Prince to the hilt and had daily, as a true friend, been advocating that he should marry Princess de Rohan* no less; but that it was now obvious the Prince was of an incomparably nobler ilk than all the rest of them put together! For what mattered to him was not glitter, not wealth and not even honours, but only – the truth! The sentiments of the elite did not come into question, and the Prince was much too well schooled not to be included in their number, speaking generally, that is! "But the bounders and all the rabble take a different view. In the town, in private houses, at gatherings, in dachas, at concerts, in taverns, in billiard rooms the talk is only of the forthcoming event. I even heard they were planning a charivari under your windows, and this, so to speak, on the wedding night! Should you need the services of an honest man armed with a pistol, Prince, I'm quite ready to discharge half a dozen or so well-aimed shots before you leave your marital bed on the morning after your wedding night." He also advised, in anticipation of a large crowd of enthusiasts emerging from the church, to set up a fire hose in the courtyard, but Lebedev would have none of it. "That would be like asking for the house to be torn down board by board."

"This fellow Lebedev is plotting against you, Prince, honestly! They want to put you in a mental home, can you imagine? Never mind the loss of your personal freedom and the unrestricted liberty to manage your own money, the two characteristics which distinguish us from our lesser, four-legged fellow creatures! I heard it, I swear I did! That's the honest truth!"

The Prince recalled that he had heard something of the kind himself, but, it goes without saying, had not paid any attention to any of it.

On this occasion too he merely laughed it all off, and thought no more about it. Lebedev had really been busy agitating something at one time; this man's schemes always seemed to emerge as though out of thin air and, fuelled by excessive fervour, they grew in complexity, expanded in all directions and became more and more divorced from the original concept; it is for this reason that he was seldom successful in life. When subsequently, almost on the wedding day itself, he came to the Prince to make a clean breast of it (he was forever in the habit of coming to those whom he was plotting against to make a clean breast of it, especially if he had failed), he announced he was born a Talleyrand,* but by a mysterious process had ended up a mere Lebedev. Then he came to the scheme he'd been plotting, which immediately roused the Prince's interest enormously. His story went that he had started by being on the lookout for some influential people to offer him patronage in case of need, and had turned to Ivan Fyodorovich. General Ivan Fyodorovich was flabbergasted, and however solicitous he was for the young man, "it would be most inappropriate for me to intervene at this stage to help him." Lizaveta Prokofyevna refused to have anything to do with him point-blank; Yevgeny Pavlovich and Prince S. would not hear of it. But he, Lebedev, would not be deterred, and had sought the counsel of a very shrewd lawyer, a venerable old man, his bosom pal and virtually his benefactor, who concluded that the matter was very feasible. All that was required were competent witnesses to the Prince's mental derangement, indeed insanity, supported above all by evidence from people in high places. Lebedev had taken heart at this stage, and had one day invited a fellow holidaymaker and doctor, also a venerable old man sporting the Order of St Anne round his neck, to come along and see the lie of the land, as it were; first, to get to know the Prince informally, and then, so to speak, make an off-the-record report on him. The Prince remembered this visit by the doctor; he remembered Lebedev pestering him beforehand, insisting he was ill, and after the Prince had firmly turned down all medical help, he suddenly turned up with the doctor in tow under the pretext that they were just back from Mr Terentyev, who was very poorly, and that the doctor wished to inform the Prince of something about the patient. The Prince had thanked Lebedev and had welcomed the doctor with extraordinary warmth. They immediately launched into discussion of the long-suffering Ippolit. The doctor asked to be told a little more of the suicide attempt, and the Prince totally captivated him with his version of the events and his comments. They touched upon the St Petersburg weather, on the Prince's own illness, on Switzerland and on Schneider. When it came to Schneider's clinical theories, the doctor was so absorbed that he spent an extra two hours listening to the Prince's accounts; in the process he smoked his host's excellent cigars, which were later supplemented by brandy, courtesy of Lebedev, and served by Vera. A small detail – the doctor, a happily married family man, immediately began paying her all manner of compliments which caused her to leave the room in a huff. They all parted friends. After the doctor had left the room, he informed Lebedev that if all such people were to be taken into care, who would the carers be? In response to Lebedev's impassioned reference to the impending event, the doctor just shook his head with a sly and mischievous leer, finally observing that, quite apart from "who marries whom, the seductive lady in question, as far as he heard anyway – never mind her extraordinary beauty, which alone could turn the head of any man – has riches galore from Totsky, from Rogozhin in the form of gems, diamonds, shawls and furniture, and that therefore this particular choice, far from being a sign of, as it were, crass stupidity on the part of the excellent Prince, was in fact an indication of the shrewd and sophisticated mindset of a calculating man of the world, and consequently would lead to a diametrically opposite and, as far as the good Prince was concerned, highly favourable outcome..." This had taken Lebedev completely by surprise, and that is how the matter was left at the time. At the end of his story Lebedev added, "As for now, you will see nothing from me save devotion and willingness to shed my blood for you, which is precisely what I came to pledge to you."

In the time remaining Ippolit also did his best to distract the Prince from his current preoccupations, and did not hesitate to send for him as he thought fit. His family lived in a small house close by. At least the children, Ippolit's brother and sister, were jolly glad because staying in the dacha gave them an opportunity to play in the garden, away from the patient. His unfortunate mother, on the other hand, had no such luck, and was for ever condemned to remain the victim of his caprices. The Prince found himself daily playing the part of an arbiter and peacemaker, for which Ippolit continued to call him his nanny, choosing at the same time not to forgo the opportunity to express his aversion to him for his role of conciliator. He was very cross with Kolya, who had latterly almost ceased visiting him, having first had to look after his dying father and subsequently take care of his widowed mother. Finally, Ippolit decided to turn the Prince's forthcoming marriage to Nastasya Filippovna into the butt of his jokes, and ended up by insulting and upsetting the Prince with the result that he too stopped coming to see him. One morning two days later the widow came to the Prince in tears, begging him to come to them, or else *he* would be the death of her. She added that he wanted to reveal a great secret. The Prince agreed. Ippolit wanted to make it up with him, burst into tears and, not surprisingly, after he had stopped crying, was even more vindictive, only being too cowardly to give vent to what was galling him. He was very poorly, and by all indications was not long for this world. He had no secret whatever to impart, managing only in his state of agitation (perhaps not altogether genuine) to utter some extraordinary breathless pleas to "beware of Rogozhin". "This is a man who will not yield an inch. We are no match for him, Prince. Once he has set his mind on something, he will not waver..." and so on, and so forth. The Prince began to question him more closely, wishing to evince some facts. But, apart from personal hunches and surmises, Ippolit could not offer any facts at all. He was, however, evidently over the moon to see that he had reduced the Prince to the state of a nervous wreck. At first the Prince was reluctant to respond to some of his more prying questions and only smiled at his suggestions "to flee, if need be, abroad. There are Russian priests everywhere and you can get married there." Finally Ippolit came up with the following opinion: "I'm concerned only for Aglaya Ivanovna. Rogozhin knows how much you love her – a love for a love. You took Nastasya Filippovna from him and he'll kill Aglaya Ivanovna. Even though she isn't yours yet, it'll be hard for you to live it down, won't it?" He had the satisfaction of seeing the Prince leave utterly upset.

These forewarnings about Rogozhin came on the eve of the wedding. That same evening, the Prince also saw Nastasya Filippovna for the last time before the ceremony. But Nastasya Filippovna was unable to put his mind at rest; quite the contrary, she herself had lately been the cause of his mounting anxiety. Just a few days earlier, whenever she saw him she had done her best to cheer him up; his sadness worried her. She had even tried to sing to him, but more often she told him all the humorous stories she could think of. Almost invariably the Prince pretended he found them funny, and from time to time his laughter really was genuine, brought on by her brilliant wit and the blithe spirit in which she recounted her stories, especially when inspiration took her, which was often enough. Seeing the Prince laugh, seeing what effect she had on him, she would be overcome with ecstasy and felt proud of herself. But just recently her sullenness and melancholy kept intensifying by the hour. His opinion of Nastasya Filippovna was pretty much settled, or else he would now naturally have found everything about her mysterious and incomprehensible. But he genuinely believed that she was not yet beyond salvation. He really meant it when he confessed to Yevgeny Pavlovich that he loved her deeply with all his heart, and in his love for her there really was something of the attraction one feels for a helpless and sickly child, whom it is difficult and even impossible to leave to its own devices. He did not try to justify his feelings for her to anyone and did not even like to talk about it, except when it was absolutely impossible to avoid the subject. One to one with Nastasya Filippovna they never talked of "feelings", as though by prior agreement. Anyone could participate in their happy and lively day-to-day conversation. Darya Alexeyevna subsequently recalled that all that time she had marvelled at them and admired them.

But his current view of Nastasya Filippovna's mental state absolved him in part from agonizing over many other perplexities. Now she was an altogether different person from the one he had known three months previously. He no longer pondered as to why for instance she had at the time fled from marrying him in tears, with reproaches and curses, whereas now she was insisting on getting it over and done with quickly. "It would seem she is no longer afraid of making me unhappy," he thought to himself. Such a sudden resurgence of self-confidence could not, in his view, have come about naturally. Neither, surely, could self-confidence of this kind have stemmed from her hatred of Aglaya alone. He credited Nastasya Filippovna with a somewhat deeper emotional sensitivity. Nor could it have been for fear of her fate with Rogozhin! In short, he admitted that all these considerations, along with many others, could well have been at work here; but the most likely explanation was the one he had long been suspecting, that one day her poor, strife-torn soul would simply give up the struggle. Though all these considerations to some extent absolved him from pondering over many unresolved questions, he was still far from enjoying either contentment or peace of mind throughout this period. Sometimes he sought to clear his mind of all thought. Indeed he appeared to regard the marriage as a kind of unimportant formality; for his own fate he had an altogether scant regard. As to divergence of opinion and discussions such as he had had with Yevgeny Pavlovich, he found himself completely at a loss and unable to contribute anything, and consequently did his best to avoid them entirely.

Incidentally, he observed that Nastasya Filippovna appreciated only too well how much he cared for Aglaya. True, she said nothing, but he noted the expression on her face whenever, even in the past, she saw him getting ready to visit the Yepanchins. As soon as the Yepanchins left, she fairly brightened up. However unobservant and slow on the uptake he was, he had been worried by the thought that Nastasya Filippovna would instigate some scandal to drive Aglaya from Pavlovsk. All the hoo-ha surrounding the wedding had been at least in part fomented in the dachas by Nastasya Filippovna in order to exasperate her rival. Since it was difficult to encounter the Yepanchins personally, Nastasya Filippovna, with the Prince seated next to her in her calash, had instructed her driver to drive right past the windows of their dacha. This came as a terrible shock to the Prince. As usual he realized what was happening only after it was already too late to do anything about it and the deed had been done. He said nothing, but was ill for two days following. Nastasya Filippovna never repeated the experiment again. In the few days just before the wedding she was often lost in deep thought, but she always ended up by overcoming her sorrows and picking herself up again; however, her melancholy increased each time round and she was never as cheerful as on the previous occasion. The Prince redoubled his vigilance. It struck him that she never spoke of Rogozhin with him. Only on one occasion, about five days before the wedding, a messenger arrived from Darya Alexeyevna asking him to come urgently, because there was something wrong with Nastasya Filippovna. He found her in a state close to delirium. She was shrieking in fits and starts, shaking, screaming and insisting that Rogozhin had hidden himself in the garden, that he was already in the house, that she'd seen him just then, that he would attack her in the night and… cut her throat! She was unable to calm down all day long. But that same evening, when the Prince popped in briefly to see Ippolit, the widow – who had just come back from the town where she'd gone on some minor business of hers – recounted that Rogozhin had visited her that same day at her place in St Petersburg and had showered her with questions about Pavlovsk. In reply to the Prince's question when precisely had Rogozhin called on her, the widow specified almost exactly the hour that Nastasya Filippovna claimed to have seen him. The matter was therefore put down to a case of simple hallucination. Nastasya Filippovna herself went to see the widow to check, and was thoroughly reassured.

On the eve of the wedding the Prince left Nastasya Filippovna in a state of high exuberance. Her wedding finery had arrived from her dressmaker in St Petersburg – her wedding gown, her headdress and so on and so forth. The Prince had no idea she would be so taken with her paraphernalia; for his own part he was full of praises, and his admiring comments made her even happier. But in the excitement she let slip something. She had heard there was hostility in the town, and that some local blades were really organizing a charivari with music and even songs for the occasion, and that all this was being done more or less with the blessing of the rest of the townsfolk; so, it was precisely because of this that she'd wanted to hold her head even higher in defiance, to dazzle everyone with the elegance and opulence of her attire – "let them shout their heads off, let them jeer, if they dare!" The very thought of this made her eyes sparkle. She harboured another, a secret expectation, but she did not divulge it: she hoped that Aglaya, or at least one of her emissaries, would be in the crowd, incognito, in the church, to observe and to marvel, and she was secretly making preparations for this. She parted from the Prince completely absorbed in these thoughts at about eleven in the evening; but it had not yet struck midnight when someone came running from Darya Alexeyevna with the message that he "ought come immediately, because there's trouble!" The Prince found his intended locked up in her bedroom, in tears, in a state of despair. For some considerable time she did not reply to anything that was said through the shut door; at long last she opened it to admit the Prince alone, locked it shut again and fell to her knees before him. (At least that was what Darya Alexeyevna, who had managed to spy something, reported later.)

"What am I doing! What am I doing! What am I doing to you!" she kept exclaiming, her arms wound tightly round his legs.

The Prince stayed a whole hour with her; we do not know what they talked about. According to Darya Alexeyevna they parted after an hour, reconciled to each other and happy. In the night the Prince sent someone round to enquire once more, but Nastasya Filippovna was already asleep. In the morning, before she had even woken up, there were two more messengers from the Prince to Darya Alexeyevna, and it was the third messenger who was charged with informing him that the place was now swarming with milliners and coiffeuses from St Petersburg, that there was no trace of yesterday's outburst and that Nastasya Filippovna was as preoccupied with her trousseau as could only be expected of such a beauty before her wedding. In fact at that very moment there was a most important consultation in progress to determine which of her jewels she should choose and how to wear them to the best advantage. The Prince calmed down completely.

The subsequent accounts of this wedding came from knowledgeable and, to all intents and purposes, trustworthy people.

The ceremony was to start at eight in the evening; Nastasya Filippovna was ready at seven. Crowds of idlers were beginning to gather at Lebedev's dacha as early as six, but mostly at Darya Alexeyevna's residence. The church began to fill up from seven onwards. Vera Lebedeva and Kolya were dying of anxiety for the Prince. However, their hands were full at home: they were busy in the Prince's rooms seeing the guests in and preparing the food. It must be said there was no reception planned after the ceremony. Apart from the obligatory persons, the only people whom Lebedev invited were Ptitsyn, Ganya, the doctor with the St Anne's Order and Darya Alexeyevna. When the Prince enquired as to why the doctor, who was an almost total stranger, had been invited, Lebedev replied archly, "He is decorated, a very distinguished person. To add lustre to the proceedings." The Prince found this highly amusing. Keller and Burdovsky, fitted out in tails and wearing gloves, looked very imposing, although it must be said the former gave the Prince and his entourage much unease by his all too evident bellicosity and the threatening looks he meted out to the loafers who were congregating round the house. Finally, come half-past seven, the Prince set off for the church in a carriage. Let us observe that he himself was anxious not to miss any of the more attractive and joyful rites and rituals; everything was performed openly, in plain view, demonstrably and – according to protocol. In the church, having somehow threaded his way through the crowd, braving uninterrupted muted gasps and whispering, and escorted by Keller who was casting threatening looks left and right, the Prince withdrew for a short while to the sanctuary, while Keller went to fetch the bride. At the entrance to Darya Alexeyevna's house he was met by a throng not only two or three times larger, but perhaps three times rowdier than at the Prince's place. As he was ascending the porch he caught such remarks as sorely tried his patience and was on the point of turning to the crowd with a few choice words, but was fortunately prevented from doing so by Burdovsky and Darya Alexeyevna herself, who made a timely appearance on the steps; they both grabbed him by the arms and forcibly dragged him into the house. Keller was incensed and refused to settle down. Nastasya Filippovna rose to her feet, looked at herself in the mirror once more, remarking, as Keller subsequently recounted, with a "wry" smile, that she was "as white as a corpse", bowed devoutly to the icon and proceeded out onto the porch. Her appearance was greeted with a dull murmur. Initially this was preceded by bursts of laughter, applause, isolated whistling; but a moment later by a series of exclamations.

"What a fine figure of a woman!" came a voice from the crowd.

"She's not the first, she won't be the last!"

"Nothing like a wedding to give a woman a good whitewash, you fools!"

"No, there's no beauty to match hers far and wide, hurrah!" voices resounded close by.

"A princess! I'd sell my soul for such a princess!" an office clerk yelled out. "'My life for just a single night!…'"*

Nastasya Filippovna really was as white as a sheet. But her large dark eyes flamed at the crowd like two hot embers; it was this intense gaze which proved too much for the gathering; indignation metamorphosed into cries of exaltation. The door of the carriage was already open, Keller had already offered the bride his arm, but suddenly she let out a cry and flung herself from the porch into the very thick of the crowd. All who were accompanying her froze in consternation. The crowd parted before her and five, six paces from the porch Rogozhin suddenly appeared. It was his gaze that Nastasya Filippovna had caught in the crowd. She ran towards him like one bereft of sense and grabbed hold of his hands.

"Rescue me! Take me away! No matter where, now!"

Rogozhin grabbed her in his arms and carried her bodily to the nearest carriage plying for hire. He then immediately produced his wallet, extracted a hundred-rouble note and handed it to the driver.

"To the railway station, and if you catch the train, a hundred more!"

He jumped into the carriage after Nastasya Filippovna and slammed the door shut. The driver did not hesitate a single second and whipped the horses into motion. Subsequently Keller excused himself that it all happened so unexpectedly. "One second more and I'd have known what to do, I'd have stopped them!" he assured to those who cared to listen to his story. Together with Burdovsky he grabbed another carriage that happened to be within reach and began to give chase, but along the way changed his mind, arguing that it was all too late! Nothing was to be achieved by force!

"And the Prince wouldn't have approved either!" Burdovsky concluded, shaken to the core.

As for Rogozhin and Nastasya Filippovna, they reached the station in good time. Having alighted from the carriage, just before boarding the train he still had time to stop a passing young girl with a fine headscarf and a dark, threadbare but still fitting mantilla round her shoulders.

"Would you please accept fifty roubles for your mantilla!" he said unexpectedly, offering the money to the girl. Before she had time to realize and appreciate what was happening, he had thrust a fifty-rouble note into the palm of her hand, stripped her off mantilla and headscarf, and draped it over Nastasya Filippovna's head and shoulders. Her striking attire was much too conspicuous and would have caused unwelcome attention on the train. It was only a little time later that the girl realized why the gentleman had bought her worthless apparel for such an exorbitant price.

The noise of the commotion reached the church in double quick time. As Keller was making his way towards the Prince, numerous people whom he had never seen before showered him with questions. Everybody was talking loudly; there was a lot of head-shaking, even guffaws of laughter here and there; no one was leaving the church, everyone was waiting to see how the bridegroom would take the news. He went pale, but accepted the news calmly, saying barely audibly, "I was afraid of something, all the same I did not expect it would be like this…" Then after a moment's silence he added, "Come to think of it… in her state… it could not have been otherwise." Subsequently Keller referred to this response as "ultra-philosophical". The Prince left the church apparently relaxed and in good spirits; at least that was the impression he created and how people reported it afterwards. He appeared anxious to get home and shut himself up on his own as soon as possible – but this was not to be. He was followed into his room by some of the guests, amongst them Ptitsyn, Gavrila Ardalionovich and the doctor, who gave no sign of wanting to leave. Besides, the whole house was virtually under siege from the idlers. He was still on the terrace when he heard Keller and Lebedev engage vigorously with a number of totally unfamiliar, though to look at quite respectable individuals, clamouring for all they were worth to be allowed onto the terrace. The Prince went up to them to enquire what was the matter and, having politely edged Lebedev and Keller out of the way, addressed in all courtesy one grey-haired stocky gentleman standing at the head of a number of other troublemakers, and asked him to do him the honour of joining the company. The gentleman was a little put out, nevertheless he agreed; he was followed by a second and a third. In all, half a dozen or more members of the crowd availed themselves of the opportunity which they did in as uninhibited a manner as possible; no others stepped forward however, and very soon those who had stayed behind began to berate the pushy ones. The newcomers were offered seats, a conversation got underway, tea was served – everything was done gracefully, properly, taking the visitors somewhat by surprise. There were of course some attempts to liven up the proceedings, attempts were made to veer the conversation towards the burning issue, pointed questions were asked, some indiscreet remarks were dropped. The Prince replied to all with such candour and simplicity and at the same time with such dignity, with such faith in the propriety of his guests that the indecorous questions ceased of their own accord. Little by little the conversation was becoming almost too serious. One querulous gentleman suddenly announced with an oath that he would not sell up his land whatever happened; that on the contrary he would sit on it and bide his time; that enterprise is better than dormant capital: "That, my dear sir, is the substance of my economic theory, let me tell you." Since he was addressing the Prince, the latter deferred to him eagerly despite the fact that Lebedev was at pains to whisper in his ear that this gentleman was as poor as a church mouse and had never owned a scrap of land in his life. About an hour passed. The tea-drinking came to an end, and the guests began at last to feel uncomfortable prolonging their stay. The doctor and the grey-haired gentleman took fervent leave of the Prince; the rest too were equally outgoing and noisy in bidding their respective farewells. Valedictions were pronounced as well as opinions on the lines that there was no need for regrets and that perhaps it was all for the best anyway, and so on. True, there were some attempts to ask for champagne, but the more senior of the guests managed to restrain the junior ones. After everybody had gone, Keller leant across to Lebedev and confided to him, "The likes of us two would have made a lot of fuss, started a fight, disgraced ourselves, called the police, but he has made new friends – excellent ones at that! I know them!" Lebedev, who was pretty bevvied up, sighed and said, "Thou hast hid these things from the wise and the prudent, and hast revealed them unto babes.* I've said it before about him, but would now add that the Lord has saved the babe himself, saved him from the abyss. Blessed be the Lord and all his saints!"

Finally by about half-past ten the Prince was left alone. He had a violent headache. Kolya, who had helped him to take off his bridegroom's suit and put on his everyday clothes, was the last to leave. They had a warm parting. Kolya did not go on about what had happened, but promised to call the next day reasonably early. Subsequently, he maintained that the Prince had not mentioned to him anything at that parting; consequently he had wanted to keep him too in the dark about his intentions. Soon there was hardly anyone left in the whole house: Burdovsky went to Ippolit's place; Lebedev and Keller went out somewhere in tandem. Vera Lebedeva alone stayed behind for some little while, taking down the decorations here and there and bringing the rooms more or less back to their everyday state. Before she left, she popped in to the Prince's room. He was sitting at the table, leaning on his elbows, his head buried in his hands. She approached him softly and touched him on the shoulder. The Prince looked at her blankly for about a minute, straining to remember something; then, snapping into full awareness and recollecting everything, he suddenly panicked dreadfully. However, it all ended with his impassioned plea to be woken up the next morning at seven, in time for the first train. Vera promised. The Prince implored her not to tell anyone about it; this too she promised. Finally, when she was already in the doorway on the way out, the Prince asked her to wait, approached her, took her by her hands and kissed them, then he kissed her on her forehead and said in a highly mysterious tone of voice, "Till tomorrow!" At least that's how Vera recounted it subsequently. She left the room, full of foreboding for him. Come the morning, she cheered up somewhat when, having knocked on his door just after seven as had been arranged, she informed him that the train for St Petersburg was to leave in a quarter of an hour. She recalled he was quite refreshed when he opened the door; he even managed a smile. It appeared he had not undressed for the night, but all the same he had slept. He said he might be back the same day. It was evident that at the time she was the only one whom he was able, or thought fit, to inform that he was setting out for the city.

11

AN HOUR LATER he was in St Petersburg, and shortly after nine he was already ringing Rogozhin's doorbell. He had come from the front entrance and for a long time no one opened up. At last the door to the apartment of the elderly Mrs Rogozhina opened and an old demure maidservant looked out.

"Parfyon Semyonych is not in," she announced from the doorstep. "Who do you want?"

"Parfyon Semyonych."

"He is out."

The woman was looking the Prince over with the utmost curiosity.

"Couldn't you at least tell me if he had spent the night here? And if he came... alone last night?"

The woman continued looking, but did not reply.

"He didn't have... Nastasya Filippovna here with him, last night, did he?"

"And if I may enquire, who would you yourself be, sir?"

"Prince Lev Nikolayevich Myshkin. He knows me very well."

The woman looked down.

"He is not at home."

"What about Nastasya Filippovna?"

"I wouldn't know anything about that."

"Wait, listen! When will he be back?"

"I don't know that either."

The door fell shut.

The Prince decided to call back in a quarter of an hour. He walked round to the backyard and ran into the caretaker.

"Is Parfyon Semyonych in?"

"He is."

"How is it I was told just now he wasn't?"

"At his door?"

"No, a servant of his mother's. When I rang at Parfyon Semyonych's, no one answered."

"Perhaps he's just gone for a walk," the caretaker surmised. "He never says when he does. He'll walk off with the key too sometimes and leave his rooms locked shut for days."

"Are you sure he was in last night?"

"He was. There were times he walked in at the front and I hadn't seen him."

"And did he have Nastasya Filippovna with him last night?"

"That I can't tell you. She doesn't call round that often. I suppose I'd have seen her if she had been with him."

The Prince left and for some time wandered up and down the pavement. The windows of Rogozhin's apartment were all shut; nearly all the windows of his mother's apartment were open. It was a bright, hot day. The Prince crossed to the other side of the street and stopped to have another look at the windows. Not only were they shut, but the white blinds were drawn down in each one.

He stood for about a minute, and – strangely – he had an idea that a corner of one blind was moved aside and for a split second he caught a glimpse of Rogozhin's face, which disappeared almost at once. He waited a little longer and was about to go and ring again, but changed his mind and decided to put it off for an hour. "Who knows, I might have been imagining things..."

Above all he had to hurry to the Izmailovsky District, to Nastasya Filippovna's former residence. He knew that on his advice, she had moved three weeks earlier from Pavlovsk, and taken rooms in the Izmailovsky District in the house of a respectable widowed teacher, an erstwhile good friend of hers, who had been letting a large furnished apartment, which constituted her principal means of subsistence. It was quite likely that on moving back to Pavlovsk she had kept this apartment; in any event it was reasonable to suppose that she had stayed the night in it after being dropped there by Rogozhin the previous evening. The Prince took a cab. On the way it struck him that that was where he ought to have started in the first place, because it was unlikely that she would have gone straight to Rogozhin's at night. Here he recalled the caretaker saying that Nastasya Filippovna didn't call round that often. If she did not call round often normally, why would she have stopped at Rogozhin's on this occasion? Comforting himself with these thoughts, the Prince finally arrived in the Izmailovsky District more dead than alive.

To his utter astonishment they not only had not seen Nastasya Filippovna either the day before or this day, but everyone poured out to stare at him as at a curiosity. The widowed teacher's whole numerous family, all girls born at yearly intervals from seven to fifteen, had followed their mother and surrounded him, open-mouthed. These were followed by their aunt, a lean, sallow-complexioned woman in a black dress, and finally by the grandmother, an aged lady in glasses. The widowed teacher begged the Prince to come in, and he obliged. He realized immediately that they knew exactly who he was and they also knew full well that his wedding was meant to have taken place yesterday, and were dying to question him not only about the wedding itself but why on earth was he now enquiring about the woman who had no business to be anywhere else except with him back in Pavlovsk, but were too embarrassed to do so. In a few brief words he satisfied their curiosity about the wedding. This provoked gasps and exclamations of surprise, so that he was obliged to recount almost all the rest too, in general terms, naturally. At last the counsel of the wise and solicitous ladies ruled that it was above all necessary to contact Rogozhin to find out all the details from him first-hand. Were he not at home (which ought to be ascertained definitively) or if he were reluctant to speak, the Prince ought to proceed to the Semyonovsky District to a certain German lady, an acquaintance of Nastasya Filippovna's, residing with her mother. It could well be that Nastasya Filippovna, in her emotional distress and desire to escape attention, had decided to stay overnight at their place. The Prince rose to his feet a broken man; subsequently they recounted that he was extraordinarily pale; truly, his legs were buckling under him. Finally, amidst an awful hubbub of voices he realized they were keen to act in unison with him and were asking for his contact address in town. He was unable to give one. They advised him to take a room somewhere in a hotel. The Prince thought a while and gave the address of his former hotel where about five weeks previously he had had his attack. Then he set off for Rogozhin's again.

This time not only did Rogozhin's door remain shut, but no one answered at his mother's door either. The Prince went down to look for the caretaker and found him with some difficulty in the yard. The caretaker was busy with something or other and answered most reluctantly, and for the most part even avoided looking at him; all the same he confirmed that Parfyon Semyonych had left for Pavlovsk early in the morning and would not be back for the rest of the day.

"I'll wait. Perhaps he'll be back in the evening?"

"Maybe not for the rest of the week, who knows."

"So he spent the night here after all, didn't he?"

"He did, yes he did..."

All this sounded very unconvincing and suspicious. It could well be that the caretaker had in the meantime received fresh instructions; previously he had been chatty, whereas right now he was simply turning his back on the Prince. But the Prince decided to come back again in a couple of hours and if necessary even to keep a lookout near the house for a while, but now there was still one more hope left at the German woman's place, and he hurried post-haste to the Semyonovsky District.

But at the German woman's place he was greeted with blank stares. By certain remarks dropped here and there he surmised that the beautiful German had quarrelled with Nastasya Filippovna about two weeks previously. As a result she had not heard anything about her all these days and was at pains to stress that she didn't care either, "not even if she married all the princes in the world". The Prince did not linger at her place. It occurred to him incidentally that she may have gone to Moscow as previously, and Rogozhin had naturally followed her, or had perhaps even gone together with her. "I must find some trace of her!" He recalled that he must book a room at the hotel and hurried to Liteiny Prospect. He got a room straight away. The waiter asked if Sir wanted to eat. Absent-mindedly he responded in the affirmative, and was later kicking himself that the meal had delayed him by half an hour; it had only later occurred to him that he could easily have left the meal untouched. A strange sensation had taken hold of him in that dingy and stifling hotel corridor, a sensation aching to metamorphose into a thought; but for the life of him he could do nothing to pin that nagging thought down. At last he left the hotel, hardly able to think straight; his head was spinning. But – where was he to go? He rushed to Rogozhin's again.

Rogozhin had not been back. No one answered the doorbell. He rang at his mother's door. The door was opened and he was told that Parfyon Semyonych was out and was not expected back for about three days. The Prince was particularly struck by the look of fierce curiosity with which the woman again regarded him. This time the caretaker was nowhere to be found. He crossed like before to the other side of the street, looked at the windows and for about half an hour, perhaps more, paced up and down in the intolerable heat; but this time nothing stirred; the windows did not open; the white blinds remained motionless. He became utterly convinced that in all probability it had only been a figment of his imagination before. By all appearances the windows were so dirty and hadn't been washed for so long that it would have been difficult at the best of times to distinguish anything even if anyone had actually peeped out through the glass panes. Taking heart from this thought, the Prince again set off for the Izmailovsky District to see the teacher.

He was expected there. The teacher had already been round to three or four addresses, and had even stopped over at Rogozhin's place: no sign of anyone. The Prince listened in silence; he went into the house, sat down on the sofa and stared about blankly as though in wonderment at what was being said to him. One strange thing: he could be extraordinarily attentive one moment, and impossibly absent-minded the next. The whole family subsequently maintained that on that occasion he behaved most oddly, so that it was very likely that "that was perhaps the precise moment of truth". Finally, he stood up and asked to see Nastasya Filippovna's accommodation. This comprised two spacious, well-lit rooms, very adequately furnished, and not cheap to rent. All the ladies reported subsequently that the Prince had surveyed every last thing in the rooms. Having spotted on a little side table an open library copy of the French novel *Madame Bovary*, he turned back a corner of the page at which it was open and asked for permission to take the book with him, and when it was pointed out that it was a library copy, he immediately thrust it in his pocket regardless. He sat down at an open window. His eyes fell on a gaming table, covered in chalk markings, and he asked who had been playing. They told him Nastasya Filippovna and Rogozhin had been playing "fools", "preference", "millers", "own trumps"* – all kinds of games, and that they had taken to playing cards very recently, after they had moved from Pavlosk to St Petersburg. In fact, Nastasya Filippovna had been complaining of boredom with Rogozhin, who would sit evenings on end without saying a word, not being able to maintain any kind of conversation, often driving her to tears. Suddenly, on the second evening Rogozhin produced a pack of cards from his pocket; Nastasya Filippovna fell about laughing, but agreed to play. The Prince asked for the cards with which they had been playing. But the cards were not to be found. Rogozhin had each time brought a new pack of cards in his pocket, and had always taken them back with him.

These ladies suggested he go to Rogozhin's once again and once again try knocking at the door, only louder this time, but not immediately – later that evening. "You never know!" they said. The teacher herself had offered to go before the day was out to Darya Alexeyevna's in Pavlovsk to see if she couldn't find out anything from her. They asked the Prince to call back at about ten in the evening so as at least to work out a plan of action for the following day. In spite of all the words of comfort and encouragement, the Prince's spirits were as low as could be. He reached his hotel on foot in utter despondency. The heat, the dust, the stifling midsummer air in St Petersburg held him like in a vice. He was pushed and jostled by humourless drunken passers-by; he stared without rhyme or reason into their faces, and walked in a needlessly roundabout way. It was late into the evening when he reached his hotel room. He decided to take a little rest, and then go back to Rogozhin's as he had been advised. He sat down on a couch, leant his elbows on a table and was lost in thought.

God only knows how long he stayed like that and what he thought about. There was much that inspired him with fear, and he was sensitive to this fear to the point of pain. Vera Lebedeva came to mind; then it occurred to him that perhaps Lebedev knew something of what was going on, and if he didn't, he could get to the bottom of it quicker and easier than he himself. Then he remembered Ippolit and that Rogozhin had called on Ippolit. Then he thought of Rogozhin: at the funeral, in the park, then – suddenly here in the corridor, where he had been lying in wait for him in the corner with a knife. He remembered his eyes, those eyes of his, staring at him in the dark. He shuddered. Yesterday's obsessive thought suddenly struck him forcefully. The essence of it was that if Rogozhin was in St Petersburg, then even if he had gone to ground for a time, he'd nevertheless end up by seeking him, the Prince, out, for good or for ill, as on the previous occasion. At least if Rogozhin had for some reason felt such a need, there was nowhere else for him to go except back to this same corridor. He had no other address, therefore he would probably come back to this same hotel... and would try to look for him here all right... if the need was that great. And, who knows, it could well be very great!

He thought along those lines, and the idea appeared to him perfectly plausible. But he would never have been able to account for his reasoning if he had thought about it deeper. For example, why should Rogozhin have suddenly felt such a need to see him, and why should it be unlikely that the two of them would not meet again in the end? But one realization weighed heavily upon him. "If things were going well for him, Rogozhin would not turn up," he argued. "He'd be much more likely to turn up if things had gone badly. And the odds are they have gone badly..."

Of course with this in mind the obvious thing would have been to stay put in the hotel and wait for Rogozhin, but he appeared to be unable to come to terms with this novel thought, grabbed his hat and dashed out. In the corridor it was by now almost totally dark. "What if he comes round the same corner and blocks my passage on the staircase?" the thought flashed through his mind as he approached the familiar spot. But no one was there. He reached the gate and walked out on the pavement. He was surprised to see how many people were out and about in the evening sunshine (a not uncommon sight in the St Petersburg dog days), and set off in the direction of Gorokhovaya Street. Some fifty paces on, at the first crossroads, someone in the crowd suddenly took him by the elbow and spoke into his ear in a hushed voice:

"Lev Nikolayevich, follow me, my friend. I need you."

It was Rogozhin.

Strangely, the Prince suddenly in an access of joy began to recount, nineteen to the dozen, that he'd been expecting him in the hotel corridor just now.

"I was there," Rogozhin replied unexpectedly. "Follow me!"

The reply took the Prince by surprise. But it took a full two minutes for the reply to sink in. When it did, the Prince shuddered and began to look closely at Rogozhin. But Rogozhin was striding half a pace ahead, not looking left or right and instinctively and adroitly avoiding the passers-by, to whom he did not give a second glance.

"Why didn't you ask for my room number... seeing as you've been to the hotel?" the Prince enquired all of a sudden.

Rogozhin stopped, looked at him, thought awhile, and replied completely wide of the question:

"Look here, Lev Nikolayevich, supposing you carry on straight, as far as the house, you understand? Whereas I'll walk over on the other side. But keep an eye on me, we don't want to get separated..."

With these words he crossed the street to the opposite pavement, looked at the Prince, and seeing that the latter was standing and just staring ahead blankly, he waved his arm in the direction of Gorokhovaya Street and began to walk, turning to look across at the Prince at regular intervals and signalling to him to keep going. He seemed satisfied to see that the Prince had understood that he should keep to his own side of the street. It occurred to the Prince that Rogozhin did not want to miss someone and that that was why he had crossed over to the other side. "But then why didn't he say whom to look out for?" They had walked about five hundred paces when suddenly the Prince began to shake for some reason. Rogozhin still kept looking over, though somewhat less frequently now. The Prince could bear it no longer, and motioned to Rogozhin to come over to him. Rogozhin crossed the street immediately.

"Is Nastasya Filippovna at your place?"

"She is."

"And was it you who looked out from behind the blind at me that time?"

"Yes..."

"So how come you?..."

But the Prince did not know what to say next or how to end the question; besides, his heart was pounding so heavily that he found it difficult to continue. Rogozhin did not say anything either and kept looking at him as before, slightly quizzically.

"Well, I'll go now," he said suddenly, preparing to cross over, "and you just carry on. Let's each keep to our own side... that'll be best... each to our own... you'll see."

When they finally turned from the two opposite pavements into Gorokhovaya Street and approached Rogozhin's house, the Prince's legs began to buckle under him again and he could hardly walk. It was about ten in the evening. The windows of the old lady's apartment were open as previously, Rogozhin's were shut, and in the dusk the white blinds stood out starker than ever. The Prince crossed the street and approached Rogozhin, who was waving from the porch to join him.

"Not even the caretaker knows I'm back. I told him I was going to Pavlovsk, and same at Mother's," Rogozhin said in a whisper, smiling slyly, almost smugly. "We'll go in and nobody will know."

He already had the key in his hand. As they were mounting the stairs, he turned and warned the Prince not to make a noise. He gently unlocked the door to his rooms, let the Prince enter, followed him softly, locked the door behind him and pocketed the key.

"Come," he said in a whisper.

He had been speaking in a whisper all the way from the Liteiny Prospect. Despite his outward calm, deep down he was in turmoil. When they stepped into the drawing room adjacent to his study, he approached a window and beckoned the Prince over mysteriously:

"When you started ringing the doorbell this morning, I knew immediately it was you. I tiptoed over to the door and heard you talking to old Pafnutyevna. And I'd told her at daybreak that if you, or anyone sent by you, or whoever, should come knocking at the door, to say she knew nothing at all, and especially if it happened to be you asking for me, and I gave her your name. And after you'd left, I thought to myself what if he's still there watching, or keeping a lookout from the street? I walked over to this same window, pulled the curtain aside, and there you were large as life, looking straight up at me... that's the long and the short of it."

"So where is... Nastasya Filippovna?" The Prince asked, gasping for air.

"She's... here," Rogozhin replied slowly after a short pause.

"Where then?"

Rogozhin raised his eyes at the Prince and looked hard at him:

"Come…"

He still spoke scarcely above a whisper, taking his time and, as before, seemed strangely abstracted. Even when he was telling how he'd moved the curtain aside, it was as though in mid-flow he had something else on his mind altogether.

They entered his study. There were changes in this room since the Prince's last visit. A green silk-lined curtain, with entrance flaps at either end, was hung across the room, dividing off the alcove where Rogozhin's bed stood from the rest of the study. The curtain hung heavily down to the floor, and the flaps were closed. It was very dark in the room; the white St Petersburg summer nights were beginning to draw in, and were it not for the full moon, it would have been difficult, with all the blinds pulled down, to identify anything in Rogozhin's dismal apartment. True, facial features could still be distinguished, albeit with difficulty. Rogozhin's face was pale, as usual. His eyes, glinting with a weird, immobile intensity, were fixed firmly on the Prince.

"Why don't you light a candle?" the Prince asked.

"No, no need," Rogozhin replied and, taking the Prince by the hand, pulled him down on a chair; he himself sat down opposite, their knees nearly touching; close by was a small table. "That's better. Let's just sit a while!" he said with a note of entreaty. There was a pause. "I knew you'd stay in that hotel," he began, as people are sometimes wont to begin with something extraneous before passing on to the main topic of conversation. "As soon as I walked into the corridor I thought, he's probably sitting there expecting me like I'm expecting him to show up this very moment! Did you go to the teacher?"

"Yes," the Prince said, his heart racing so fast he could hardly say a word.

"That crossed my mind too. People would start talking, I thought… and then I also thought, I'll bring him here so we could pass the night together…"

"Rogozhin! Where's Nastasya Filippovna?" the Prince brought out in a whisper and stood up suddenly, shaking in every limb. Rogozhin too rose to his feet.

"Over there," he said in a whisper, motioning with his head towards the curtain.

"Is she asleep?" the Prince whispered back.

Rogozhin looked hard at him again, as before.

"Shall we go and… Only, you… Never mind, come along!"

He lifted the curtain, stopped and turned to the Prince again.

"Go ahead!" he motioned towards the curtain and beckoned the Prince to go first. The Prince obeyed.

"It's dark here," he said.

"Not all that dark!" Rogozhin muttered.

"I can hardly see… the bed."

"Come closer," Rogozhin suggested softly.

The Prince took one step, then another one, and stopped. He stood trying to refocus his eyes for a minute or two; neither of them spoke at the bedside. The Prince's heart seemed to pound loud enough to shatter the dead silence of the room. But his eyes had already got used to the gloom and he could make out the whole of the bed – someone was asleep there, totally motionless; not a stir, not a breath reached his ears. The sleeping person was covered from head down with a white sheet with the contours of the outstretched body showing only indistinctly in relief. All around, on the bed, at the foot, on chairs close to the bed, even on the floor, were articles of clothing scattered pell-mell – the magnificent white silk wedding gown, flowers and ribbons. On the bedside table sparkled a string of diamonds thrown down anyhow. At the end of the bed on top of a bundle of some white lace protruded the toes of a foot from under the sheet; they seemed to be hewn out of marble and were frightfully rigid. The Prince stared and he felt that the longer he did, the deadlier the silence got in the room. Suddenly a fly flew off with a buzz to the head of the bed and vanished. The Prince shuddered.

"Come," Rogozhin said, touching his hand.

They drew back and sat down on the same chairs, facing each other. The Prince was shaking more and more and would not take his bewildered eyes off Rogozhin's face.

"I notice you tremble, Lev Nikolayevich," Rogozhin spoke finally, "as if you were about to go down with your ailment, remember, back in Moscow? Or as it once was before your fit. I can't think what to do with you now…"

The Prince was straining with all his might to make sense of what was being said, and could only sit and stare in bewilderment.

"It was you?" he brought out at last, motioning with his head towards the curtain.

"It… was me…" Rogozhin answered in a whisper and looked down.

They sat for about five minutes in silence.

"You see," Rogozhin continued as though he had not stopped, "you see, if in the course of your illness, you should have your fit, and start screaming your head off, someone might hear in the street or in the yard and realize that there are people staying the night up here. They'll start knocking and will come in… because they all think I'm away. I haven't lit the candles either or people might put two and two together. Because when I'm away, I take the key with me too, and no one comes in for three or four days even to tidy up, that's the rule of the house. So, to stop anyone knowing we're up here for the night—"

"Wait," the Prince said, "I've already asked the caretaker and the old lady if Nastasya Filippovna had stayed the night here… So they must already be on the alert."

"I know you asked. I told Pafnutyevna that Nastasya Filippovna had dropped in last night and had left for Pavlovsk the same night after only ten minutes with me. No one knows she spent the night here – no one. Yesterday she and I entered just as quietly as you and I did today. It had crossed my mind she wouldn't want to come in quietly, but – not a bit of it! She broke into a whisper, tiptoed all the way, gathered up her gown to stop it rustling, held the folds in her hands on the stairs and warned me with her finger herself – it was you she was scared of. On the train she was totally off her head with fright, and it was her idea to come here for the night. At first I thought I'd take her to that woman teacher's place – not a bit of it! 'He'll find me there before daylight,' she reckons, 'but you can hide me here, and tomorrow at first light we'll head for Moscow.' After that she wanted to go to Oryol, or something. And when she was getting into bed, she was going on about Oryol—"

"Wait! What is it you want to do now, Parfyon?"

"You worry me with all your trembling. We shall spend the night here, the two of us. There's no other bed apart from that one, but if we take the cushions from the two couches, I can spread them out here by the curtain, for you and me, to lie side by side. Because if they come, and start snooping around or looking for things, they'll see her and take her away just like that. They'll start questioning me, and I'll tell them it was me, and I'll be carted away at once. So why not just let her lie here for now, close by, close to you and me…"

"Yes, yes!" the Prince agreed readily.

"So, we don't admit it and we don't let them take her away?"

"Not on your life!" the Prince affirmed. "Never, never, never!"

"That's what I had in mind too, my boy, not to surrender her to anyone! We'll lie low here for the night. I left the house for one hour only in the morning, for the rest of the time I stayed with her. Come the evening, I went to fetch you over. One thing I'm worried about is the smell in this heat. Can you smell anything, or not?"

"Perhaps, I can't tell. It's bound to spread by morning."

"I covered her with an oilcloth, good quality, made in America, and placed the sheet over the oilcloth, and I put out four open jars of Zhdanov's solution, where they still are as I left them."

"Like that fellow… back in Moscow?"

"The smell gets everywhere, my friend. And she's just lying there… When it gets lighter in the morning, take a look. What's the matter, can't you get up?" Rogozhin asked with uneasy concern on seeing that the Prince was shaking so much that he was unable to get to his feet.

"My legs aren't up to it," the Prince muttered. "I know what it is, I'm just a bit frightened… It'll pass, and I'll be able to get up…"

"Wait now, I'll make up the bedding, and you can lie down… and me too… and we'll listen… because, my lad, I still don't know… I still don't know everything, my lad, so let me tell you from the start, so you know everything from the start…"

Mouthing these indistinct words, Rogozhin began to make the two beds. One could see he had probably worked it all out earlier in the morning. He had spent the previous night on his couch. But two people would not have fitted on it side by side, and he definitely wanted it to be side by side, which is why he had taken the different-sized cushions from the two couches and dragged them with much effort across the whole room to arrange them at the curtain, close by one of the flaps. At last the cushions were in place. He went up to the Prince and, supporting him gently and gingerly under his arm, led him to the improvised bed. But it turned out the Prince was well able to walk by himself, which would indicate that his fear was passing; and yet he continued to shake.

"You see, pal," Rogozhin began to speak suddenly after he had put the Prince down on the softer, left-hand-side cushion and had stretched himself fully clothed on the right, his hands under his head, "it's hot today, and that means a hell of a stench… I daren't open the windows.

Mother's got flowerpots with heaps of sweet-smelling flowers. I had a mind to bring them here, but Pafnutyevna would put two and two together, a nosy parker she is."

"Yes, she is," the Prince confirmed.

"Maybe I should buy bunches and bunches and cover her all over with flowers? But it struck me, my friend, it would break my heart seeing her heaped with flowers!"

"Listen…" the Prince asked in a faltering tone of voice, confused and groping for words, remembering and just as quickly forgetting what it was he wanted to say, "listen, tell me, what did you kill her with? A knife? The one that was here on the table?"

"That was the one."

"One more thing! There's something else I want to ask you, Parfyon… I'm going to ask you lots of questions… about all sorts of things… but I'd rather you told me straight away, right at the very start so that I can be quite clear about it – did you want to kill her with a knife before our wedding, before the ceremony started, at the church door? Did you, or didn't you?"

"I don't know if I did…" Rogozhin replied drily, slightly taken aback by the question and as though unable to make sense of it.

"Did you ever bring the knife to Pavlovsk with you?"

"Never. All I can tell you about this knife, Lev Nikolayevich, is this," he added after a pause. "I took it out of the locked drawer this morning, because it all happened early between three and four o'clock. I kept it between the pages of a book. And – what surprises me – it went in about three or four inches deep… here, right under her left breast… and just half a spoonful of blood trickled out on her shift, that's all there was…"

"That, that, that," the Prince muttered, propping himself up in terrible agitation, "I know all about that, I read about it… it's what's known as internal bleeding… Sometimes there's not even a drop, if the injury is straight to the heart—"

"Listen! What was that?" Rogozhin interrupted him abruptly, terrified, propping himself up on the makeshift bed. "Did you hear anything?"

"No!" the Prince returned, just as quickly and equally terrified, staring at Rogozhin.

"There's someone there! Can you hear? In the front room…"

They both pricked up their ears.

"I hear it," the Prince said resolutely in a whisper.

"Footsteps?"

"Footsteps."

"Should we lock the door?"

"Yes, we'd better..."

They locked the door and both settled down again. No one spoke for a long time.

"Oh, yes!" the Prince suddenly broke into his former distressed, panic-stricken whisper as though he'd thought of something else and was terrified out of his mind to lose the thread. He even sat up. "Yes... I meant to... these cards! Cards... I heard you'd played cards with her, hadn't you?"

"Yes," Rogozhin said after a pause.

"Where are they... these cards?"

"Here they are..." Rogozhin said after an even longer pause, "here..."

From his pocket he produced a used pack of cards wrapped in a piece of paper and offered it to the Prince. The Prince took them, but with a puzzled air. A novel, dreary and cheerless realization seized his heart. At that moment, and even much earlier, it suddenly came to him that he'd been way off the mark both in what he was saying and doing, and that these cards, which he was now holding in his hand and which he had been so eager to acquire, could be of no use, of no use whatsoever. He got up and wrung his hands in distress. Rogozhin was lying motionless and appeared not to have seen or heard his movements, but his eyes were glinting brightly in the dark, wide open and unblinking. The Prince sat down on a chair and began to look at him in terror. Half an hour or so went by. Suddenly Rogozhin yelled out loudly in disjointed bursts and roared with laughter, as though forgetting the need to keep his voice down.

"The officer, my word, the officer... d'you remember how she went with the whip for that officer at the bandstand, ha ha ha! And that young cadet... that cadet... that cadet who rushed forward..."

The Prince leapt to his feet in a new attack of fear. After Rogozhin had fallen silent (and he fell silent abruptly), the Prince hitched his chair closer, bent over him gently, and, his heart pounding, began to study the man on the floor. Rogozhin did not move his head towards him and appeared to be oblivious of his presence. The Prince stared and waited. Time was passing. Dawn was beginning to break. Every now and again Rogozhin would start to mutter something – loudly, brokenly and incoherently; between times he would cry out and burst into laughter; at such moments the Prince stretched out an unsteady hand to touch Rogozhin's head, his hair, to stroke them gently... he could do nothing more! He himself began to shake again, and again he appeared to lose all sensation in his legs. A completely new feeling of unspeakable hopelessness began to gnaw at his heart. In the meantime it had grown completely light. At last he lay down on his cushion, utterly exhausted and wretched, and pressed his face up against Rogozhin's, which was bloodless and rigid; his tears were running down Rogozhin's cheeks, but by then he himself did not feel them and was perhaps quite unaware of them...

At last, when, many hours later, the door opened, and people stepped into the room, they found the murderer totally insensible and in a fever. The Prince was sitting motionless close by on the bedding, and every time the ailing man let out a cry or began to rave, he would put out a shaking hand and stroke his hair and face as though for comfort and consolation. But he could no longer understand the questions that were put to him, or recognize any of the people who had entered the room and stood around him. And even if Schneider himself had arrived from Switzerland to have a look at his former pupil and patient, he too, thinking back what the Prince had been like at times in the first year of his treatment, would have just shaken his head and said, as then, "An idiot!"

12

Conclusion

THE TEACHER, having arrived in Pavlovsk post-haste, went straight to Darya Alexeyevna, who was still upset from the day before, and, telling her everything she knew, frightened her out of her wits. Both ladies decided to contact Lebedev immediately, who as the Prince's friend and landlord was also in a state of alarm. Vera Lebedeva recounted all she knew. On Lebedev's advice all three decided to go to St

Petersburg in order as soon as possible to forestall "that which could in all likelihood happen". Thus it was that the following morning at about eleven Rogozhin's apartment was forcibly entered by the police in the presence of Lebedev, the ladies and Rogozhin's brother, Semyon Semyonovich Rogozhin, who had his own apartment in another wing of the house. The decision to break in was prompted largely by the evidence of the caretaker, who had seen Parfyon Semyonych enter through the front door "quietly" with a companion the evening before. After this they no longer hesitated to break down the door, which no one came to open when the doorbell was rung.

Rogozhin was ill for two weeks with brain fever. After he recovered, he was examined and tried. He gave completely unmistakable, accurate and totally satisfactory evidence on all counts, on the strength of which the Prince was from the very start absolved from standing trial. Rogozhin spoke very little at the trial. He did not offer any objections when his defence counsel, a clever and articulate lawyer, made out a clear and logical case that the crime had been committed as a result of a brain fever, which had set in long before in consequence of all the distress suffered by the accused. But he did not add anything in support of this argument and, as previously, confirmed clearly and firmly all the details of what had happened. He was sentenced, in view of extenuating circumstances, to fifteen years' hard labour in Siberia. When the sentence was read out, he was grim-faced, taciturn and "lost in thought". His vast fortune, saving a small, comparatively speaking insignificant part spent in the early course of his merrymaking, passed to his brother, Semyon Semyonovich, to the latter's no small delight. Rogozhin's mother is still alive, and from time to time appears to recall her favourite son Parfyon, but only vaguely. God has spared her mind and heart from an awareness of the horror that had been visited upon her cheerless house.

Lebedev, Keller, Ganya, Ptitsyn and many other characters of our story live as before, have changed little, and there's hardly anything to say about them. Ippolit died in a terrible panic and somewhat earlier than he had calculated, about two weeks after the death of Nastasya Filippovna. Kolya was deeply shaken by all that had happened; he has grown very close to his mother. Nina Alexandrovna is very concerned that he is too serious for his age; he promises to turn into a very good man. Incidentally, it was partly due to his efforts that the

Prince's future was settled. He had from the start singled out Yevgeny Pavlovich Radomsky amongst all the people he had got to know in the recent past. He went to see him of his own accord, confided in him all the details of what had happened as he knew them and touched upon the Prince's present condition. He was not mistaken. Yevgeny Pavlovich was most solicitous for the fate of the unfortunate "idiot" and, thanks to his good offices, the Prince has found himself abroad again, back in Schneider's Swiss establishment. Yevgeny Pavlovich, having himself set out for a very extended sojourn in Western Europe and freely owning that, along with many other of his compatriots he is a "superfluous man"* in Russia, has been looking up his sick friend in Switzerland on a fairly regular basis, at least once every two or three months. But Schneider has been frowning and shaking his head more and more each time. He has been hinting at the total damage of all mental faculties; as yet he has not spoken of outright incurability, but his prognosis is most discouraging. Yevgeny Pavlovich takes all this very much to heart, and his heart is in the right place; to wit, he receives letters from Kolya and on occasion even writes back. But on top of that another unusual trait of his character has emerged, and since it is wholly positive, we shall hasten to reveal it. After each visit to Schneider's establishment Yevgeny Pavlovich, apart from writing to Kolya, sends a letter to another person in St Petersburg with the most detailed and sympathetic up-to-the-minute account of the Prince's condition. Besides assuring his correspondent of his never-ending devotion, Yevgeny Pavlovich has begun, and this more and more frequently and frankly, to allude in these letters to some of his personal views, ideas and feelings – amounting, in a word, to an attempt to establish something like a close and friendly relationship. The person with whom he maintains this correspondence, however infrequently, and who has merited his respect and attention is Vera Lebedeva. Try as hard as we may, we have not been able to ascertain how precisely such a relationship was engendered; but it must surely go back to that same affair with the Prince when Vera Lebedeva was so grief-stricken that she fell ill. But as to what the detailed circumstances in which the acquaintanceship and friendship took root were, we do not know. In truth, the reason we mentioned these letters is largely because some of them contained news of the Yepanchin family, and most importantly of Aglaya Ivanovna Yepanchina. In a rather confused letter from Paris,

Yevgeny Pavlovich informed Vera that Aglaya, after a brief and odd
fondness for an émigré Polish count, had unexpectedly married him
against the wishes of her parents. Even though they relented in the end,
it was only because there was the danger of a huge scandal breaking
out. Then, in another long and detailed missive after a silence of almost
six months, Yevgeny Pavlovich informed his correspondent that during
his most recent visit to Switzerland, he had fortuitously run into all the
Yepanchins at Schneider's clinic (excepting Ivan Fyodorovich who, of
course, had stayed behind in St Petersburg on business), and had seen
Prince S. as well. The meeting was rather odd. Everyone met Yevgeny
Pavlovich with unbounded enthusiasm. Adelaida and Alexandra for
some reason found it appropriate to thank him for his "angelic care for
the unfortunate Prince". On seeing the Prince in his sick and undignified
condition, Lizaveta Prokofyevna burst into a flood of the most heartfelt
tears. Apparently, all had been forgiven him. Prince S. came up with a
number of felicitous and wise observations on the occasion. Yevgeny
Pavlovich was under the impression that he and Adelaida were not yet
close enough to each other. But, for the future it seemed completely
on the cards that the fiery Adelaida would voluntarily and with all
her heart submit to the wisdom and experience of Prince S. Besides,
the lessons which the family had learnt had a very sobering effect on
her, especially Aglaya's latest adventure with her émigré count. All the
fears with which the family had surrendered Aglaya to this count had
materialized within six months, and new ones, such as no one could
ever have foreseen, were in the offing. It transpired that the man was
not even a count, and if he had emigrated to France, it was because
of something shady and obscure in his past. He had charmed Aglaya
with the extraordinary nobility of his long-suffering soul, pining for its
homeland, and had charmed her to such an extent that even before she
got married, she had joined some kind of a committee in exile for the
Liberation of Poland and, what's more, had ended up in the confessional
of a famous Catholic priest, who had gained an ascendancy over her
mind bordering on the maniacal. The huge fortune to which the count
had drawn Lizaveta Prokofyevna's and Prince S.'s attention proved to
be nonexistent. And, as if that were not enough, barely six months
after the wedding, the count and his friend, the famous confessor,
had succeeded in causing a total rift between Aglaya and her family,
so that she had not been heard of for several months... In a word,

there may have been lots to talk about, but Lizaveta Prokofyevna, her daughters and Prince S. were so shaken by all these happenings, that they were somewhat afraid to touch upon other matters in their conversation with Yevgeny Pavlovich, and in any case they knew full well that from other sources he was quite au fait with all the details of Aglaya Ivanovna's infatuations. Poor Lizaveta Prokofyevna was dying to get back to Russia and, according to Yevgeny Pavlovich, gave vent to bitter and prejudiced criticism of all that was foreign. "They can't even be trusted to bake a decent loaf of bread here, they can't. Come winter and they freeze like mice in a cellar," she said. "At least I've had a good cry the good old Russian way over this here poor devil," she added, bursting with emotion as she pointed towards the Prince, who did not recognize her at all. "We got carried away all right, time we came to our senses. All of it, all these foreign countries, the whole of this Western Europe of yours, is just a mirage, and all of us here abroad amount to no more than a mirage either... mark my words, you'll see for yourselves!" she concluded almost in a temper as she bade farewell to Yevgeny Pavlovich.

Note on the Text

This translation is based on the Russian text taken from Volume 8 (1973) of the *Complete Edition in Thirty Volumes* (*Polnoe sobranie sochineniy v tridtsati tomakh*) of Dostoevsky's works, edited by G.M. Fridlender, published in Leningrad in 1972–90 by the Nauka publishing company.

Notes

p. 6, *Eydtkuhnen*: Now Chernyshevskoye, a region in modern-day Kaliningrad, formerly a part of East Prussia.

p. 7, *gold napoleons*: Napoléon d'or, a French gold coin worth twenty francs, named after the Emperor Napoleon I.

p. 7, *fredericks*: Friedrich d'or, Prussian gold coin, 1750–1855.

p. 7, *Dutch ducats*: In the original, *arapchik*, a popular Russian name for a Dutch gold ducat, minted "illegally" in Russia from 1768 to 1868, originally to finance the war with Turkey (1768–74) and subsequently for other military operations as well as sundry state needs abroad.

p. 9, *Karamzin's History*: A reference to Nikolai Karamzin (1766–1826), novelist and author of the twelve-volume *History of the Russian State*.

p. 11, *Church Calendar*: The Russian Church Calendar (*Cheti Minei*) containing the lives of the Orthodox saints, homilies, descriptions of feast days and so on. In childhood, Dostoevsky was brought up on readings from the Church Calendar, and he held it in high esteem throughout his life, writing that, "for Russians these stories entail something reverential and purifying".

p. 11, *holy fools*: The holy fool (*yurodivy*) is a common religious motif in Russian literature, and is particularly significant in *The Idiot*. The holy fool typically led an unorthodox, itinerant life, was poorly dressed or half-naked, and spoke nonsensically or in riddles. The fool was also seen as a provocative figure and an outsider who was to be revered as one of God's chosen.

p. 17, *to serve sans servility*: A reference to the motto on the crest of Alexander Arakcheyev (1769–1834), Military Governor of St Petersburg – a loyal, but feared minister at the court of Emperor Paul I (1754–1801).

p. 17, *souls*: Bonded serfs on an estate.

p. 22, *we haven't got capital punishment*: Not quite accurate. Dostoevsky himself had been condemned to death in 1849, at the age of twenty-eight. This inclusion of this statement may have been to prevent intervention from censors.

p. 34, *Pogodin*: Mikhail Pogodin (1800–75), historian and archaeologist. In 1840–41 he published *Specimens of Ancient Slavonic-Russian Scripts*.

p. 55, *the Golden Horde*: Russian designation for the western part of the Mongol Empire, which thrived in the thirteenth and fourteenth centuries.

p. 60, *East and South... sung*: An approximate quote from a poem by Lermontov, 'Journalist, Reader and Writer' (1840).

p. 66, *one like that in Basle*: Probably *The Beheading of John the Baptist* by Hans Fries (1450–1520).

p. 79, *Holbein's Dresden Madonna*: *The Darmstadt Madonna* (1525–26) by Hans Holbein the Younger (1497–1543).

p. 94, *goatee... government employ*: Tsar Nicholas I, in a decree of 2nd April 1837, forbade civil servants to wear beards or moustaches.

p. 95, *Babette*: "Babette" is the French form of the Russian Varvara (or Varya); in English, Barbara.

p. 97, *Avis au lecteur*: "Note to the reader" (French). A caution.

p. 101, *Mon mari se trompe*: "My husband is mistaken" (French).

p. 108, *se non è vero*: Part of an Italian expression: "*se non è vero, è ben trovato*" ("even if it's a lie, it's a good one").

p. 112, *Athos, Portos and Aramis*: The three musketeers in the eponymous 1844 novel by Alexandre Dumas *père* (1802–70).

p. 112, *Kars*: A city in the north-east of Turkey. During the Crimean War (1853–56) it was under siege by the Russian forces from the end of May to 26th November 1855.

p. 112, *L'Indépendance*: *L'Indépendance belge*, a newspaper published in Brussels from 1830–1937, which Dostoevsky read while working on *The Idiot* (1867–68).

p. 129, *Rira bien... dernier*: "He who laughs last laughs loudest" (French).

p. 132, *Pirogov... briefly*: A fictitious account of actual events. The Russian surgeon Nikolai Ivanovich Pirogov (1810–81), chief medical officer at the siege of Sebastopol, left for St Petersburg on 1st June

1855, as a protest at the attitude of the Supreme Command for the needs of the casualties. He returned to Sebastopol in September.

p. 132, *Nélaton*: Auguste Nélaton (1807–73), famous French surgeon and member of the Paris Academy of Medicine, had never set foot in Russia.

p. 143, *The mighty... wane*: Opening lines of the fable *The Aged Lion*, by I.A. Krylov (1769–1844).

p. 156, *Marshal of the Nobility*: An elected post from among the more influential members of a district, deemed prestigious, but cumbersome. It was bound up with considerable private expenditure, predominantly for entertainment, and the task was to uphold the dignity and reputation of the gentry in the main by arbitrating in personal disputes and misunderstandings.

p. 157, *alternate... camellias*: Marguerite Gautier, the heroine of *La Dame aux camélias* by Alexandre Dumas *fils*, went out for walks carrying one day a bunch of red and the following day a bunch of white camellias.

p. 158, *de la vraie souche*: "Of the old stock" (French).

p. 171, *Third Guild of Merchants*: From 1775 merchants were divided into corporations or guilds according to the value of their capital: those of the Third Guild – the lowest – needed 500 to 1,000 roubles; those of the Second 1,000 to 10,000; those of the First 10,000 and more. In 1863 the Third Guild was phased out, leaving only two.

p. 175, *Ekaterinhof*: A palace and popular place of entertainment in south-west St Petersburg.

p. 192, *land-reform*: Land reforms in Russia were started in January 1864. They were administered by members of the nobility.

p. 193, *Izmailovsky Barracks*: A popular name for the district where the Izmaylovsky Imperial Guards Regiment had their barracks.

p. 194, *Tarasov's house*: Debtors' prison in the Izmaylovsky Barracks. In the spring of 1867, Dostoevsky himself was in danger of being confined there.

p. 197, *Peski*: Literally "The Sands" – so called because of the sandy soil – a working-class district in St Petersburg, now the Smolninsky Region.

p. 199, *a fit*: In the original *"rodimchik"*, Russian for children's eclampsy, popularly believed to be transmitted by occult means, hence Lebedev's vigorous reaction.

p. 200, *murder... papers*: Reported in *The Voice* (*Golos*), 10th March 1868.

p. 201, *Let mercy... justice*: From the manifesto proclaimed by Tsar Alexander II on 19th March 1856.

p. 202, *palki*: Literally "sticks", a game of cards.

p. 202, *kvas*: A popular traditional drink made from fermented bread.

p. 203, *Countess du Barry*: Jeanne Antoinette Bécu, Comtesse du Barry (1743–93), mistress of Louis XV of France and a victim of the Reign of Terror.

p. 207, *Nikolai Ardalionovich*: I.e. Kolya.

p. 208, *A measure... penny*: Revelation 6:6.

p. 208, *I... miserable*: Revelation 3:17.

p. 209, *Pavlosk*: In the nineteenth century, Pavlovsk was a resort outside St Petersburg popular with the upper classes from the capital.

p. 211, *Skopets*: The *skopets* (plural *skoptsy*), was a member of a heretical sect originating in eighteenth-century Imperial Russia, who sought salvation in castration. The concept derives from Matthew 19:12: " For there are eunuchs who have been so from birth, and there are eunuchs who have been made eunuchs by men, and there are eunuchs who have made themselves eunuchs for the sake of the Kingdom of Heaven. Let the one who is able to receive this receive it." The sect was persecuted, but those followers who merely expressed allegiance but did not actually practise mutilation were in no way restricted by the authorities. The Skoptsy became extremely efficient moneylenders and jewellers.

p. 214, *Solovyev's History*: *History of Russia from Ancient Times* by S.M. Solovyev (1820–79). The first volume was published in 1851, and by 1867 the *History* had reached seventeen volumes.

p. 215, *Old Believer*: The Old Believers, another persecuted sect, rejected the religious reforms (1650–1660) initiated by Patriarch Nikon (1605–81) and Tsar Alexei Mikhailovich Romanov (1629–76), which led to the schism of the seventeenth century.

p. 219, *verse... Pope*: The poem in question is probably Heinrich Heine's 'Heinrich', which describes the encounter between German Emperor Henry IV (1050–1106) and Pope Gregory VII (*c*.1015/1028–85) at Canossa.

p. 222, *arranged her fingers*: There are two basic finger formations for making the sign of the cross – with two fingers or with three.

The two-finger gesture, the more ancient of the two, is the only one acceptable to the Old Believers. The finger formation was a major issue in the history of the Orthodox Church. The Rogozhins were probably Old Believers originally, but had gradually "reformed"; however, underneath, they retained traditionalist sympathies.

p. 228, *God's every time... teaching*: See Luke 15:7, "there will be more joy in heaven over one sinner who repents than over ninety-nine righteous persons who need no repentance", and 15:10–32.

p. 235, *there should... longer*: See Revelation 10:6.

p. 237, *six people... madness*: Six people were found murdered in the merchant Zhemarin's residence: Zhemarin himself, his wife, his eleven-year-old son, his cousin, a caretaker and a cook. The murderer was one Witold Gorsky, an eighteen-year-old high-school student. He had drawn a kind of a flail (a medieval weapon consisting of a ball on a chain attached to a handle), and had it made in a smithy under the pretext that he needed it for gymnastic exercises.

p. 247, *Russia's Millennium celebrations*: Held on 8th September 1862.

p. 260, *Once there was a hapless knight*: A heavily edited version of Pushkin's 1829 ballad 'Once There Lived a Hapless Knight'.

p. 261, *A.M.D.*: An abbreviated form of "Ave, Mater Dei" ("Hail, Mother of God", Latin).

p. 261, *Lumen cœli, sancta Rosa*: "Heavenly light, holy rose" (Latin).

p. 267, *Gorsky and Danilov*: Gorsky has already been mentioned by Dostoevsky as the murderer of six people. A. Danilov, a nineteen-year-old student, was accused of murdering a pawnbroker. His case was widely reported from beginning of 1866 to the middle of 1868 and coincided with the publication of *Crime and Punishment*. Dostoevsky and many of his contemporaries drew obvious parallels between the murder and Dostoevsky's earlier novel.

p. 298, *B.*: Probably S.P. Botkin (1832–89), famous therapist. Dostoevsky was his patient in 1865.

p. 305, *Proudhon*: Pierre-Joseph Proudhon (1809–65), French philosopher and one of the leading lights of nineteenth-century socialism and anarchism, who propounded the slogan, "All property is theft". Proudhon was an inspiration to the Nihilist movement in nineteenth-century Russia, popularized by Ivan Turgenev in his groundbreaking novel *Fathers and Children*.

p. 308, *ha-ha*: In the original there is an oblique reference to Griboyedov's comedy *Woe from Wit*: "What would Princess Marya Alexeyevna have said!"

p. 317, *the star Wormwood of the Apocalypse*: See Revelation 8:10–11: "The third angel blew his trumpet, and a great star fell from heaven, blazing like a torch, and it fell on a third of the rivers and on the springs of water. The name of the star is Wormwood. A third of the waters became wormwood, and many people died from the water, because it had been made bitter."

p. 322, *Archbishop Bourdaloue*: Louis Bourdaloue (1632–1704), described as the "king of preachers and the preacher of kings".

p. 346, *Yelagin*: An island on the Neva.

p. 349, *Famusov*: A character in Griboyedov's *Woe from Wit*, symbolizing all that was ultra-traditional in the Russian landowning classes.

p. 360, *Pavlovsk Voksal*: A fashionable promenade-type concert hall, the "Vauxhall Pavilion", or Pavlovsk Voksal, where Johann Strauss II, Franz Liszt and Robert Schumann among many other celebrities gave concerts, and where Dostoevsky set some of the action described in his novel.

p. 376, *a duel*: Duels in Russia were strictly forbidden. Under the 1845 Criminal Code Keller risked a great deal if he were caught officiating at a duel.

p. 389, *The sun intones in heaven*: See Goethe's *Faust*: "*Die Sonne tönt nach alter Weise / In Brüdersphären Wettgesang...*" ("The sun intones in ancient fashion / With brother spheres contending...")

p. 390, *fonts of life*: See Revelation 21:6, 22:1, 22:17. Dostoevsky had marked out references to "the fonts of life" (more correctly "the water of life") in his copy of the Bible. "And let him that is athirst come. And whosoever will, let him take the water of life *freely*." (Dostoevsky's italics.)

p. 393, *Malthus*: Thomas Robert Malthus (1766–1834), an Anglican clergyman and highly influential political economist.

p. 401, *there should be time no longer*: Revelation 10:6.

p. 421, *Napoleon turned to England*: On 15th July 1815, Napoleon meant to take ship for America at Rochefort, but instead had to surrender to Captain Maitland of the *Bellerophon*.

p. 421, *the Gulf*: The Gulf of Finland.

p. 422, *an elderly gentleman*: Fyodor Petrovich Haase (1780–1853), a Moscow prison doctor and philanthropist.

p. 425, *les extrémités se touchent*: A reference to Blaise Pascal (1623–62), *Pensées*.

p. 427, *Christ's suffering… not symbolic*: The reference is to Docetism, an early Christian heresy which proclaimed that Jesus's body was incorporeal, and that Christ could not physically die.

p. 427, *Talitha cumi*: Mark 5:41: "Little girl, I say to you, arise."

p. 427, *Lazarus, come forth*: See John 11:43.

p. 427, *Those people*: See Matthew 27:54–62.

p. 432, *Millevoye's*: Charles-Hubert Millevoye (1782–1816). However, the verse quoted belongs to Nicolas Gilbert (1751–80).

p. 441, *Lacenaires*: Pierre François Lacenaire (1800–36), a French poet and murderer. Dostoevsky was deeply interested in his case, and he was probably the prototype for Raskolnikov in *Crime and Punishment*.

p. 450, *Paul de Kock's*: Paul de Kock (1793–1871), a French novelist.

p. 477, *razor… murderer*: The character of Rogozhin was based on V. Mazurin, a Moscow trader, whose murder of a jeweller, named Kalmykov, was widely reported at the end of November 1867. Like Rogozhin, Mazurin belonged to a well-known, well-established merchant family, had inherited a fortune and lived with his mother in their ancestral home, where the murder was committed. The murder weapon was a cut-throat razor, tightly wound with a piece of cord to stop it from folding. "Silk" is Dostoevsky's embellishment.

p. 477, *Zhdanov's solution*: A disinfectant deodorant first used in field hospitals, invented by N.I. Zhdanov.

p. 483, *Podkolesin*: A character in Gogol's play *The Marriage*: The bridegroom Podkolesin is about to tie the knot, but at the last moment, overwhelmed by the enormity of the commitment facing him and seeing all routes of escape cut, he makes a dash for freedom by jumping through a window.

p. 483, *Tu… Dandin*: *George Dandin ou Le Mari confondu* (1668), a comedy by Molière (1622–73) in which George Dandin, a long-suffering husband, discovers that the only solution to his failed morganatic marriage is suicide. The actual text reads *"Vous l'avez voulu… George Dandin…"*

p. 485, *Pirogov*: One of the protagonists in Gogol's 'Nevsky Prospekt' (1835).

p. 520, *RIP... resurrection*: From Nikolay Karamzin's *Epitaphs* (1792), this was Dostoevsky's favourite, and was inscribed on his mother's gravestone in 1837. An example of Dostoevsky's irrepressible penchant for parody at all costs.

p. 520, *Chernosvitov leg*: Rafail Chernosvitov (1810–68), designer of prosthetic limbs. He submitted his design of a prosthetic leg to the Invalid Committee in 1854.

p. 521, *The Archive*: Probably *The Russian Archive*, a monthly historical and literary journal published from 1863 to 1917.

p. 521, *One of our countrymen*: The reference is to Alexander Herzen (1812–70), who mentions this in *My Past and Thoughts* (1868).

p. 522, *boyars*: Russian feudal nobility, abolished by Peter the Great. General Ivolgin's anachronism is for comical effect.

p. 522, *Voilà un... père*: "Here's a sprightly lad! Who's your father?" (French).

p. 523, *Le fils... petit*: "The son of a boyar, and a brave one to boot. I love the boyars! Do you love me, my lad?" (French).

p. 523, *le petit boyard*: "The little boyar" (French).

p. 524, *giant in adversity*: The origin of the quotation is unknown.

p. 524, *Emperor Alexander's*: Emperor Alexander I (1777–1825).

p. 524, *Charras's book on Waterloo*: Jean-Baptiste Adolphe Charras (1810–65). *Histoire de la campagne de 1815. Waterloo.*

p. 525, *Davout*: Louis-Nicolas Davout, Marshal of France under Napoleon (1770–1823).

p. 525, *Mameluke Roustan*: Napoleon's Armenian bodyguard (1783–1845).

p. 525, *Constant*: Benjamin Constant (1767–1830), served as a tribune under Napoleon from 1799–1801.

p. 527, *le roi de Rome*: Napoleon II (1811–32), the son of Napoleon Bonaparte and his second wife, Marie Louise of Austria, was granted the title King of Rome by his father.

p. 527, *on the sweltering prison isle*: Reference to Pushkin's poem 'Napoleon' (1826).

p. 530, *St Anne's Cross*: The Order of St Anna, introduced in 1735, for bravery on the field of battle.

p. 530, *Nanny dear... who said that*: Nikolai Ogarev (1813–77), from his unfinished poem 'Humour' (1869).

p. 536, *Schlosser's*: Friedrich Christoph Schlosser (1776–1861), a German historian.

p. 548, *Stepan Glebov*: Stepan Glebov (*c*.1672–1718). Lover of Peter I's wife, Yevdokhiya Lopukhina – one of the charges for which he was condemned to death. The other was for allegedly being involved in a plot against Peter I. The manner of his death was exceptionally cruel. Prior to being impaled – a particularly long-drawn-out ordeal – he was for three days subjected to the knout, branding with hot irons and crucifixion with wooden pegs. He died completely unrepentant.

p. 548, *Osterman*: Andrei Ivanovich Osterman (1686–1747), a prominent German-born Russian statesman who, after an illustrious career under Peter I, fell into disfavour in the reign of Elizaveta when she ascended the throne in 1741. Osterman was initially to be broken on the wheel, but the sentence was commuted to lifelong banishment to Siberia.

p. 557, *Execute... Thomas More said*: More supposedly said to his executioner, "Be careful of my beard, it hath committed no treason."

p. 571, *Non possumus*: "We cannot" (Latin).

p. 573, *fraternité ou la mort*: "Fraternity or death" (French).

p. 573, *you will know... doings*: See Ezekiel 14:23 and Matthew 7:16.

p. 574, *Russians... self-flagellation*: This is possibly a reference to the Russian Khlyst sect, who believed in asceticism and self-flagellation.

p. 577, *C'est très curieux et c'est très sérieux*: "That's very curious and very serious" (French).

p. 579, *Laissez-le dire*: "Let him speak" (French).

p. 581, *Vraiment*: "You don't say!" (French).

p. 604, *nihilism... Turgenev*: The protagonist of Turgenev's *Fathers and Children* (1862), Bazarov, exemplified the type of the nihilist, as a character who rejected all conventional moral and social values. The word derives from the Latin "*nihil*".

p. 616, *Keller and Burdovsky*: There is an inconsistency here. Originally it was to be Keller only.

p. 617, *Rohan*: One of the most ancient and noble Houses of France.

p. 618, *a Talleyrand*: A reference to the famous French diplomat Charles Maurice de Talleyrand-Périgord (1754–1838), who served under the reigns of Louis XVI, Napoleon I, Louis XVIII, Charles X and Louis-Philippe and was instrumental in the success of various important European treaties.

p. 625, *My life for just a single night*: From Pushkin's *Egyptian Nights* (1837). Cleopatra offers to share her bed for one night with whoever agrees to die the morning after.

p. 628, *Thou hast... babes*: See Luke 10:21, Matthew 11:25.

p. 634, *fools... own trumps*: Nineteenth-century Russian card games.

p. 646, *superfluous man*: A romantic type, significant in nineteenth-century Russian literature, symbolizing a disillusioned, rebellious aristocrat, doomed to a never-ending quest for spiritual comfort. The most famous exponent is Eugene Onegin. With reference to the enigmatic Yevgeny Pavlovich, the characteristic is probably to be viewed as an affectation.

Extra Material

on

Fyodor Dostoevsky's

The Idiot

Fyodor Dostoevsky's Life

The family name Dostoevsky was derived from the village
Dostoev in the Minsk region. It was granted by the Prince of
Pinsk in perpetuity to the boyar Danil Ivanovich Rtishchev
in 1506 for services rendered. The city of Pinsk goes
back to the eleventh century and forms the heartland of
Belorussia. No fewer than four nationalities – Belorussian,
Russian, Ukrainian and Polish – go into the composition of
the Dostoevsky family tree, and the end result is about as
multinational as was possible at the time. The Rtishchevs
were Russian, the setting was Belorussian, the suffix "-sky"
is predominantly Polish, and over the years some of the
Dostoevskys moved and settled in the Ukraine, while others,
like the Fyodor Mikhailovich branch, ended up in Moscow.
Dostoevsky's father, Mikhail Andreyevich (1789–1839), was
the son of a Ukrainian Uniate priest, Andrei Dostoevsky.
Fyodor Mikhailovich himself, of course, never considered
himself anything other than Russian. The eminent Dostoevsky scholar, Lyudmila Saraskina, was recently asked if
the writer was not of Polish blood, and she responded:
"The Dostoevsky lineage presents a fascinating and unusual
mixture of nationalities: in a family where the father was
Lithuanian, the mother Ukrainian, there was a cult of Russian
literature and history, the cult of reading. The atmosphere
was one of devotion to the spoken word, and it is precisely
this which above all else shaped the author's creative make-
up. Hence, Dostoevsky's Russianness is a wholly cultural
rather than ethnic phenomenon." The concept "Lithuanian"
must, of course, be understood in the traditional sense, as in
the Grand Duchy of Lithuania, which has precious little to
do with modern Lithuania.

Birth and
Early Years

Fyodor Mikhailovich Dostoevsky was born in Moscow on 30th October 1821. In 1831, his father had bought a small estate, Darovoye, and two years later, the neighbouring Chermoshnya, which would acquire lasting fame as Chermashnya, in the violent murder plot of Karamazov senior in *The Karamazov Brothers*. Speaking of Darovoye, Dostoevsky confessed: "This small, insignificant place left in me the deepest and most memorable impression for life." Fyodor was the second in a family of six siblings. His mother, Maria Fyodorovna (née Nechayeva, 1800–37), a religious minded woman, came from a merchant family. She taught him to read from an edition of *One Hundred and Four Old and New Testament Stories*, and within the family circle there were readings from Karamzin's *The History of the Russian State*, as well as from the works of Derzhavin, Zhukovsky and Pushkin. Dostoevsky often sought the company of peasants, and his discussions with them proved to be a rich source of material for his future compositions.

Education

In 1832 Dostoevsky and his brother Mikhail were educated at home by visiting tutors, and from 1833 they were placed in various boarding schools. Dostoevsky found the atmosphere in these establishments oppressive and uncongenial, and his only solace was extensive and intensive reading. From late 1834 to early 1837 the two brothers attended one of Moscow's best private boarding schools, run by the Czech-born Leontiy Ivanovich Chermak, a man of little or no education, but a brilliant, intuitive pedagogue and a humane and understanding father figure. State-run schools, on the other hand, had an overall unflattering reputation for frequent application of the disciplinary rod and staple bad food. The teacher of Russian, Nikolai Ivanovich Bilevich, turned out to be something of a role model and has allegedly served as the prototype for Nikolai Semyonovich in *The Adolescent* (variously known as *Raw Youth* and *Accidental Family*), whom the hero Arkady picked at random as an appraiser of his autobiographical notes. "At long last I decided to seek someone's counsel. Having cast around, I chose this gentleman with purposeful deliberation. Nikolai Semyonovich was my former tutor in Moscow, and Marya Ivanovna's husband..." (*The Adolescent*, penultimate chapter.)

Parents' Death

By all accounts Dostoevsky's father, Mikhail Andreyevich, was an upstanding, hard-working family man – his one failing, however, being his touchy, short temper. After the death of his wife in 1837, he retired and settled in Darovoye, where he died on 6th June 1839. Officially the cause of death was recorded as apoplexy, but by all popular accounts he perished at the hands of his peasants, forming a possible clue to the origins of the plot involving the mysterious death of the head of the family in *The Karamazov Brothers*. The loss of his mother in 1837 coincided with the shattering news of Pushkin's fatal duel, which Dostoevsky perceived as a personal bereavement too. Dostoevsky's adulation of Pushkin continued all his life, and reached its apotheosis in 1880, only months before his own death.

In May 1837 he enrolled at the Koronad Filipovich Kosto-marov cramming institute, prior to applying to the Central Military Engineering Academy, where he got to know the highly colourful Ivan Nikolayevich Shidlovsky, subsequently a poet and church historian. Originally the name of the principal character in *The Idiot* was to be Shidlovsky, and when responding to Vladimir Solovyev's request in 1873 for some biographical material for an article, Dostoevsky enjoined him to mention his friend. "Make sure you mention him in your article. It does not matter that no one knows of him and that he has not left behind a literary legacy. I beg you, my dear chap, mention him – he was a *major* figure in my life, and deserves that his name should live on." Dostoevsky attended the Engineering Academy from January 1838; unfortunately his brother Mikhail had failed to qualify for entry. The gruelling, soul-destroying military regime was to a large extent relieved by the company of close and devoted friends, the writer Dmitry Vasilyevich Grigorovich being one of them. It was he who first noted Dostoevsky's reticence and unsociability, and who later recorded the tumultuous effect upon Dostoevsky of his rift with Belinsky and his circle, most particularly with Ivan Turgenev. *Central Military Engineering Academy*

The vast bulk of information on Dostoevsky's early life comes from the *Reminiscences* of his younger brother Andrei. He was an architect, and also a meticulously scrupulous and tidy worker in everything he undertook. His *Reminiscences* are well executed, detailed and informative. Quaintly, and for an architect not inappropriately, the book is conceived as a mansion, and the chapters are termed *rooms*.

Dostoevsky's first literary projects were conceived at the Engineering Academy. In 1841, at a soirée organized by his *Early Literary Works* brother Mikhail, Dostoevsky read out excerpts from some of his dramatic compositions – *Mary Stuart* and *Boris Godunov* – none of which have survived. On graduation, and having served just under a year in the St Petersburg Engineering Corps, he resigned with the rank of senior lieutenant (поручик) to devote himself entirely to literature.

His first published work was a translation of Balzac's *Eugènie Grandet*, which appeared in 1844. In the winter of the same year he started writing the epistolary novel *Poor Folk*. Dmitry Grigorovich and the poet Nikolai Nekrasov were so taken by it that they spent the night reading it in manuscript. They then headed for Belinsky's and on the doorstep announced, "We've a new Gogol!" to which Belinsky retorted, "Gogols sprout like mushrooms with you!" But having read the work, his enthusiasm knew no bounds: "The novel reveals such profundities of characters and of life in Russia as no one had ever dreamt of before." It was accepted for publication by the *St Petersburg Anthology*, edited by Nekrasov. The praise lavished on the novel obviously went to Dostoevsky's head, because he requested that each page should have a black border to make the work stand out; the astonished Nekrasov refused point blank, and it was published without the borders. It was an overnight success.

At the end of 1845 at a soirée at Belinsky's, Dostoevsky read out selected passages from *The Double*. Belinsky was quite interested at first, but later expressed his disapproval. This marked the beginning of the rift between the two men. Dostoevsky took it very badly and, stressed as he was, the very first symptoms of epilepsy, which were to plague him for the rest of his life, began to manifest themselves.

Arrest and Sentencing   In spring 1847 Dostoevsky began to attend (on a far from regular basis) the Friday meetings of the revolutionary and utopian socialist Mikhail Petrashevsky. The discussions, which included literary themes, bore on the whole a political and sociological slant – the emancipation of the serfs, judicial and censorship reforms, French socialist manifestos and Belinsky's banned letter to Gogol were typical subjects of debate. In 1848 Dostoevsky joined a special secret society, organized by the most radical member of the Petrashevsky Circle, one Nikolai Speshnev, by all accounts a colourful and demonic figure, whom Dostoevsky imagined to be his Mephistopheles. The society's goal was to organize an insurrection in Russia. On the morning of 23rd April 1849, the author, together with other members of the group, was arrested and confined in the Peter and Paul Fortress. Many of them, including Speshnev, found themselves depicted twenty-three years later in the pages of *Devils*.

After eight months in the fortress, where Dostoevsky wrote his story *The Little Hero*, he was found guilty of "plotting to subvert public order" and was initially sentenced to death by firing squad, which was at the last moment commuted to *mort civile*, amounting to four years of hard labour and subsequent conscription into the army. His experiences as a convict of the Omsk Fortress are poignantly recorded in *Notes from the House of the Dead* (1860–62) and the theme of execution itself is treated in some detail in *The Idiot*.

After January 1854 Dostoevsky served as a private in Semipalatinsk, eastern Kazakhstan. Even before his departure for the army, he wrote to Natalya Dmitrievna Fonvizina, the wife of one of the Decembrists (members of the ill-fated uprising in December 1825):

> I seem to be in some kind of an expectation of something; I can't help feeling I'm ill, and that soon, very soon something decisive will happen. I feel that I'm approaching a turning point in my life, that I've reached a state of maturity and am on the verge of something peaceful, blithe – perhaps awesome – but certainly inevitable.

These were prophetic words. Almost immediately on arrival in Semipalatinsk he made the acquaintance of a minor clerk, Alexander Ivanovich Isayev, an impoverished customs-and-excise officer and alcoholic, and his wife, Maria Dmitrievna. Mrs Isayeva was then twenty-nine years old. Dostoevsky fell head over heels for her, although his love was not always requited and she considered him to be "a man with no future". He was no doubt attracted by what he perceived to be her vulnerability and spiritual defencelessness. Dostoevsky's own life was not of the happiest, and the two revelled in bouts of self-pity. And then came a terrible blow: Isayev was transferred to Kuznetsk, some six hundred versts from Semipalatinsk. Dostoevsky took the parting indescribably badly.

Maria Dmitrievna

In August 1855 Maria Dmitrievna informed Dostoevsky that her husband had passed away. She was in dire straits – alone, without means, in an unfamiliar town, without relatives or

Marriage Proposals

friends to help her. Dostoevsky proposed to her immediately, but Maria Dmitrievna demurred. He realized, of course, that it was his own lowly status that was at the root of the problem. However, with the death of Nicholas I and the enthronement of Alexander II, there was hope in the improvement of the fate of the Petrashevsky convicts. In December 1855 he was made a warrant officer; this elated him so much that in early 1856 he wrote to his brother of his intention to tie the knot: "I've taken my decision and, should the ground collapse under me, I'll go through with it... without that, which for me is now the main thing in life, life itself is valueless..."

Dostoevsky was so desperately short of money that he implored his brother for a loan of 100 roubles or more, or as much as he could afford. Begging for money was to become a way of life for Dostoevsky. Almost in desperation, he made a daring move. Having obtained official leave to go to Barnaul, he took a secret trip to Kuznetsk. But, to his surprise, instead of being greeted with love and affection, he found himself in a situation such as is depicted in *White Nights* and *Humiliated and Insulted*. Maria Dmitrievna flung her arms round his neck and, crying bitterly and with passionate kisses, confessed that she had fallen in love with the schoolteacher Nikolai Borisovich Vergunov and was intending to get married to him. Dostoevsky listened in silence to what she had to say, and then sat down with her to discuss her prospective marriage to a man who had even less money than he, but had two incontestable advantages – he was young and handsome. Maria Dmitrievna insisted the two rivals should meet and, like the Dreamer in *White Nights* and Ivan Petrovich in *Humiliated and Insulted*, Dostoevsky decided to sacrifice his own love for the sake of others. This fairly bowled Maria Dmitrievna over: Dostoevsky wrote to Wrangel, quoting her words to him: "'Don't cry, don't be sad, nothing has yet been decided. You and I, and there's no one else.' These were positively her words. I spent two days in bliss and suffering! At the end of the second day I left full of hope..."

But he had scarcely returned to Semipalatinsk when Maria Dmitrievna wrote to him that she was "sad and in tears" and loved Vergunov more than him. Dostoevsky was again absolutely distraught, but still found it in him to continue to stand by the love of his life. He would seek to obtain for her an assistance grant on the basis of her deceased husband's government service record, try to enrol her son in the cadet corps and even assist Vergunov in securing a better position.

In those turbulent times, when Dostoevsky imagined he *Marriage to Maria and* had lost Maria Dmitrievna for ever, there was suddenly new *Return to St Petersburg* hope. On 1st October 1856 he was promoted to officer, and his dream of being able to return to St Petersburg became a distinct reality. It is unlikely that this was the only cause – Maria Dmitrievna had probably always loved him after a fashion, though obviously never as strongly as he loved her – but her resistance to him suddenly broke down to the extent that Vergunov simply melted into the background and was heard of no more. Later that month Dostoevsky went to Kuznetsk, sought and obtained Maria Dmitrievna's hand and was married to her on 6th February 1857.

His happiness knew no bounds, but a major blow was just round the corner. On their way back to Semipalatinsk, when the newly-weds had stopped in Barnaul, Dostoevsky, as a result of all the emotional upheaval, had a severe epileptic fit. This had a shattering effect on Maria Dmitrievna. The sight of her husband staring wildly ahead, foaming at the mouth and kicking convulsively on the floor must have been disconcerting and frightening in the extreme. She burst into tears and began to reproach him for concealing his ailment. He was actually innocent; he had been convinced that what he suffered from were ordinary nervous attacks, not epilepsy – at least that's what doctors had told him previously. All the same, he hadn't told her even that much.

They settled in St Petersburg, but the local climate was too uncongenial for her, and she moved to Tver. From then on they saw each other only sporadically, moving, as they did, from town to town and from flat to flat. On 7th June 1862 he made his first trip abroad – alone. He felt he had his own life to lead. Maria Dmitrievna had little to do with it, and she was fast approaching death, as she had contracted tuberculosis.

Dostoevsky returned to Russia in September. At the be- *Maria's Death* ginning of November 1863 the couple settled in Moscow. Maria Dmitrievna was fighting for her life, but on her deathbed she was getting more and more irritable and demanding. Dostoevsky looked after her assiduously, yet at the same time he was riveted to his writing desk. Her suffering and moodiness are reflected in the description of Marmeladov's wife in *Crime and Punishment* and of Ippolit in *The Idiot*. Maria Dmitrievna died on 14th April 1864.

More Literary Works On his return from Siberia in 1859 Dostoevsky published *Uncle's Dream* and *The Village of Stepanchikovo*, neither of which met with much success. *Notes from the House of the Dead* began its life in 1860 in the daily newspaper *The Russian World* (*Русский мир*), but only the introduction and the first chapter were printed, for Dostoevsky had to keep a wary eye on the censor, as he had pointed out to his brother Mikhail in a letter in 1859: "It could all turn out nasty... If they ban it, it can all be broken up into separate articles and published in journals serially... but that would be a calamity!" Chapters 2–4 were published in subsequent issues in 1861, but it was serialized no further in *The Russian World*. With some notable alterations, the early chapters were reprinted in the 1861 April issue of *Time* (*Время*), a journal he founded jointly with his brother, and the concluding chapter of Part II came out in May 1862. Certain passages, deemed subversive, were excised on the grounds that "morally regressive individuals, who are held back from crime by the severity of punishment alone, may be misled by the *Notes* to form a distorted impression as to the lack of efficacy of the legally prescribed sanctions" (Baron N.V. Medem, Chairman of the St Petersburg Board of Censors.) *Humiliated and Insulted* was also serialized in *Time* during 1861, and *Notes from the Underground* in *Epoch* (*Эпоха*), the second journal that the Dostoevsky brothers had founded in 1864.

In 1866 Dostoevsky was in dire financial straits and, in what could have been a moment of carelessness, but more likely for fear of being thrown in a debtors' jail, he concluded one of the most dishonest and unfavourable contracts in recorded literary history. The other contracting party was the publisher Fyodor Timofeyevich Stellovsky, by all accounts a ruthless and unprincipled money-grubber. According to the terms of the contract Dostoevsky had to deliver a brand-new novel by 1st November 1866, or lose all rights in all his subsequent compositions for a period of the next nine years. Dostoevsky was to receive three thousand roubles, but contingently on the new novel being completed and delivered within the prescribed period. Over half of this money was already spoken for; it was needed for the discharge of promissory notes, the irony being that most of these – unbeknown to Dostoevsky – were already in Stellovsky's hands. The wily Stellovsky knew perfectly well that Dostoevsky was a sick man and that the epileptic attacks, which occurred on a regular basis, made him unfit for work for days on end; besides, he was also aware that Dostoevsky was committed to completing *Crime and Punishment* and would be unable to write two novels simultaneously. It was very much in Stellovsky's interests that the contract was not fulfilled.

Right up to the end of September Dostoevsky worked flat out on *Crime and Punishment*. This was a novel on which many of his hopes were pinned. It was to be a heavyweight: most of the fiction he had written previously was shot through with humour and had a tongue-in-cheek quality about it, but for whatever reason his best efforts had failed to find wide acceptance, let alone a demand for more either from the public or the critics. He was not giving his readers what they wanted, so *Crime and Punishment* was to change all that. But then came the end of September, and not a word of the contractual novel had yet been penned. The significance of this suddenly hit him. The as yet non-existent – and very likely to remain such – novel was, not inappropriately, to be called *The Gambler*. His friend, the writer Alexander Milyukov, on hearing the sad story, suggested that a few of his fellow writers should pool their efforts and write a chapter or so each, the more so since Dostoevsky had already sketched out a plan; or, if he didn't wish to sacrifice that plan and wanted to keep it for his own use later, they'd work out something new themselves.

Dostoevsky declined, saying that he wouldn't put his name under anything he hadn't written himself. Milyukov then came up with the idea of using a stenographer. It was thus that the twenty-year-old Anna Grigoryevna Snitkina, who by chance had just recently completed a course in the new-fangled (for Russia, at all events) skill of stenography, came on the scene. They started work on 4th October 1866, and on 30th October the manuscript was ready for delivery, the deadline being midnight.

But Stellovsky had one more dastardly trick up his sleeve. He arranged to be out of his office on the day, and there was no one to receive the manuscript. On legal advice, they found out that it would be enough for the script to be lodged at a police station and signed for by a senior officer. Dostoevsky

Crime and Punishment and The Gambler

and Snitkina rushed to a police station, and luckily found an officer – usually, come the afternoon, senior officers were in the habit of disappearing without notice. Even so it was not till after 10 p.m. that they obtained the sought-after receipt. And so the novel – a manic, surcharged paean to reckless abandon and desperation – was finished from scratch in twenty-six days flat.

Marriage to Anna Snitkina   Dostoevsky married Anna Snitkina, twenty-five years his junior, on 15th February 1867. Exactly two months after their wedding, they both went abroad. Anna had taken charge of Dostoevsky's business affairs efficiently, and by and large successfully. She was proving herself indispensable on a second major front, making up for Dostoevsky's inadequacy in dealing with day-to-day practical affairs. But there was a limit even to her frugality, acumen and, above all, the positive influence she could exercise, when she encountered Dostoevsky's incurable penchant for gambling. This had manifested itself during his previous European tour with his mistress Apollinaria Suslova, immortalized as the enigmatic tease in *The Gambler*, whose story Anna was herself ironically obliged to set down on paper from the lips of her future husband.

While gambling with the devil-may-care Apollinaria had a romantic edge to it, indulging the habit on honeymoon with his level-headed, home-making wife Anna – impecunious as they were – became a cruel and pathetic, not to say sordid, human tragedy. He would find himself down to the last penny, dashing over to the tables, staking that very penny, losing it, running back home to pawn his cufflinks, his last remaining possessions, his wedding ring, his winter overcoat, his young wife's lace cloak, on his knees in front of her, beating his breast, with tears in his eyes accusing himself and imploring for forgiveness, and yet begging for just another louis or two from their common purse to go and break even. And it was in these circumstances, his frame continually convulsed by epilepsy, constantly on the move across Europe – like a veritable Flying Dutchman, flitting from one foreign resort to another – that he deliberated over, planned and eventually completed *The Idiot*. Not least of his handicaps was separation from Russia and its living language, which he himself considered essential in maintaining the momentum of his creative process.

On 5th March 1868 the couple experienced their first joys *Children*
of parenthood with the birth of their daughter Sofia, but two
months later followed the devastating blow of the infant's
death on 24th May. On 26th September 1869 their second
daughter Lyubov was born (*d.*1926). The Dostoevskys had
two more children: Fyodor, born 16th July 1871 (*d.*1922), and
Alexei, born 10th August 1875, who died before he reached the
age of three on 16th May 1878.

On their return from abroad to St Petersburg the Dostoevskys were beset by creditors for debts incurred before their
departure. Fortunately the plucky and quick-witted Anna
was able to fight them off, and the author went on to embark
upon and complete the last four of his great works more or
less undisturbed. *Devils* was published in 1871; *The Writer's
Diary* was begun in 1876 and, at intervals, continued till 1881;
The Adolescent came out in 1875, followed by *The Karamazov
Brothers* in 1880.

On 8th June 1880 Dostoevsky delivered his famous speech at *Address at the Pushkin*
the unveiling of the Pushkin memorial in Moscow organized *Memorial and Rivalry*
by the Society of the Friends of Russian Letters. It had a most *with Turgenev*
electrifying effect upon his audience, and has been subsequently
referred to as "well-nigh the most famous speech in Russian
history". Tolstoy declared it a farce, and point-blank refused to
attend. It therefore fell to the two remaining pillars of Russian
literature, the arch rivals Dostoevsky and Turgenev – who had
had it in for each other ever since they first met some thirty
years previously – to occupy the centre stage.

Of the two, his imposing, patrician-like physical presence
apart, it was Turgenev who, by dint of his reputation abroad,
coupled with his progressive, enlightened Western ideology at
home, felt that precedence to occupy the throne of Russian
literature should be accorded to him, rather than to the
reactionary, stick-in-the-mud Slavophile Dostoevsky. Moreover
the replies to such RSVP messages as had been received from
Western celebrities, notably Victor Hugo, Berthold Auerbach
and Alfred Lord Tennyson, were all addressed to Turgenev
– doubtless confirming him as the only Russian writer known
abroad – though it later transpired that all of the three prospective guests from abroad had politely declined the honour
to attend.

Still, home-grown honours were not to be spurned, and
the two writers, in true prize-fighter fashion, retired to their

respective camps to prepare and hone their speeches – Turgenev to his magnificent country seat Spasskoye-Lutovinovo, Dostoevsky to his modest house in Staraya Russa.

The festivities were spread over two days. Turgenev spoke on the seventh of June, Dostoevsky on the eighth. Of all the numerous speakers on the occasion, it was only Turgenev's and, above all, Dostoevsky's performances that have gone down in history. Turgenev, ever the aristocrat, did not indulge in any personal gibes in his speech. But what he did, as far as Dostoevsky was concerned, was equally hurtful. Having given Pushkin his rightful due, he permitted himself to express some doubt as to whether the author of *Eugene Onegin* may be regarded as a truly national and consequently world poet such as Homer, Shakespeare and Goethe. This question, Turgenev remarked, "we shall leave open by and by for now". Subsequently in his letter home to his wife, Dostoevsky remarked that Turgenev had humiliated Pushkin by depriving him of the title of national poet.

Dostoevsky himself was not present at this speech – he had been preparing his own. His famous speech took place the next day. He delivered an electrifying performance, passionately arguing for the greatness of Pushkin as *the* national writer. He claimed that Pushkin was not only an independent literary genius, but a prophet who marked the beginning of Russian self-consciousness and provided the paramount illustration of the archetypal Russian citizen as a wanderer and sufferer in his own land. Dostoevsky's speech culminated in a plea for universal brotherhood and was met with rapturous applause.

That evening, Anna Grigoryevna records in her *Reminiscences*, after Dostoevsky returned to his hotel late at night, utterly exhausted but happy, he took a short nap and then went out to catch a cab to the Pushkin Memorial. It was a warm June night. He placed the huge laurel wreath at the foot of the memorial and made a deep, reverential bow to his great mentor.

Later Works   On his return from Moscow in the summer of 1880, Dostoevsky embarked on a burst of writing activity that knows no precedent in Russian literature. There in a course of a few months he finished the bulk of *The Karamazov Brothers*, continued his *Writer's Diary* and kept up an intensive correspondence, while all this time suffering shattering, debilitating fits of epilepsy. But it was not all doom and gloom. The summer of 1880 was particularly warm, perhaps reminding him of gentler climates. His correspondence, going back to these balmy, final days, is characterized by being written in bursts – several letters at a time without a break – during strategic gaps in his work. On completion of *The Karamazov Brothers* in 1880, Dostoevsky made far-reaching plans for 1881–82 and beyond, the principal task being an ambitious sequel to the novel; yet at other moments at the end of that year, he confessed of a premonition that his days were numbered.

Tolstoy, says Igor Volgin, left the world defiantly, with a loud *Death* bang of the door, which reverberated throughout the world. By contrast, Dostoevsky's death was very low key. The author Boleslav Markovich, who came to see Dostoevsky just before he died, wrote: "He was lying on a sofa, his head propped up on a cushion, at the far end of an unpretentious, dismal room – his study. The light of a lamp, or candles, I can't remember, standing on a little table nearby, fell directly on his face, which was as white as a sheet, with a dark-red spot of blood that had not been wiped off his chin… His breath escaped from his throat with a soft whistle and a spasmodic opening and shutting of his lips." Dostoevsky died on 28th January 1881, at 8:36 p.m., according to Markovich's watch.

Dostoevsky's own universal legacy is, of course, indisputable, *Legacy* in the way that Shakespeare's is – meaning that, adulators apart, both have their eminent detractors too. Henry James, Joseph Conrad and D.H. Lawrence, to mention but three, famously disliked Dostoevsky.

Among the lesser known of Dostoevsky's legacies in the West is what is termed in Russian *достоевщина* (Dosto-evshchina). A dictionary definition of *достоевщина* would be: psychological analysis in the manner of Dostoevsky (in a deprecating sense); tendency to perversion, moral licence and degradation in society. This topic falls outside the scope of this account, but readers of his novels would see how in a traditional society, dominated by religion, such as was the case in nineteenth-century Russia, and also in the eyes of such fastidious arbiters as Turgenev, his repeated delving into the seedier aspects of human behaviour could easily attract severe censure. It is therefore fitting to end with the words – expressing Dostoevsky's essential ambiguity – of Innokenty Annensky, one of Russia's foremost Silver Age poets and literati: "Keep reading Dostoevsky, keep loving him, if you can – but if you can't, blame him for all you're worth, only keep reading him… and only him, mostly."

Fyodor Dostoevsky's Works

Poor Folk

Poor Folk (*Бедные люди*, 1846), Dostoevsky's debut epistolary novel, with which he conquered Belinsky's heart and entered upon the St Petersburg literary stage, is in choice of subject firmly rooted in Gogol. However, in emotional substance and character delineation it goes way beyond anything that the author of *The Overcoat* ever attempted. "People (Belinsky and others) have detected in me a radically new approach, of analysis rather than synthesis, that is, I dig deep and, delving to the level of the atoms, I reach further down to the heart of the matter, whereas Gogol's point of departure is the heart of the matter itself; consequently he is less profound." Although Dostoevsky's self-analysis may not be altogether convincing, the novel itself – an exchange of heart-rending letters between two lost souls – is artistically persuasive. It is set wholly in the stifling bureaucratic, class-ridden Russia of the early nineteenth century, but in spite of the passage of time has lost none of its universal appeal. The events could easily have been taking place in any epoch, in any society – a lowly official exchanging messages with some unfortunate, repressed female living in the house across the way – but the novel is inherently slow and short on action, which arguably limits its appeal to the reader.

The Double

Dostoevsky's next major work, *The Double* (*Двойник*, 1846) is by any standards a most unusual and inventive piece of novel writing. According to Dostoevsky's own evaluation, it was "ten times better than *Poor Folk*". This opinion, however, was not shared by the vast majority of contemporary critics, who had trouble accepting its blend of fantasy and realism. Mr Golyadkin, an ordinary, perfectly unremarkable, naive and helpless nineteenth-century man, is overwhelmed by the pace of progress in a modern metropolis with all the latest waterproof galoshes, open-plan offices, luxury soft-sprung carriages, dazzling gas streetlights and the hectic pace of social life all round, and begins to inhabit another world or, to put it in clinical terms, slowly but surely to lose his mind. The author does not state this in so many words – Mr Golyadkin's mental disintegration is never explained or accounted for. The reader is plunged into the *medias res* of a mad world from the word go. As a result Golyadkin's predicament gains in authenticity because specifics do not stand in the way of the reader identifying himself with the hero; each one of us can supply our own catalogue of examples that threaten our sanity and there is therefore a pervasive atmosphere of "there but for the grace of God go I".

The Double was hugely controversial, and on the whole was pronounced to be stylistically inadequate, a judgement with which Dostoyevsky himself tended to agree, though with important reservations. In 1846 he wrote to his brother: "absolutely everyone finds [*The Double*] a desperate and unexciting bore, and so long drawn out it's positively unreadable. But, funnily enough, though they berate me for bringing on tedium, they all, to a man, read it over and over again to the very end." This very early novel was already full of innovative, arresting characteristics: agitated, strained dialogue, always disordered, always rambling; madness predominating over method; a perplexed, pathetic soul cruelly disorientated amid confused perspectives of time and place; heart-rending tragedy compounded by a welter of manic Hollywood-type slapstick comedy – this off-the-wall tale of galloping schizophrenia took contemporary readers by storm and left them quite bewildered. Some critics hailed *The Double* as profound, others found it so permeated with the mentally aberrant spirit of Gogol's novella *Diary of a Madman* that it was no longer a question of influence, but of blatant imitation. However, if it was imitation, it was imitation of the highest order.

Like much in Dostoevsky, *The Double* was too far ahead of its time, and it would only find a reading public ready to appreciate and enjoy it to the full much later. For Vladimir Nabokov, who was no fan of Dostoevsky, *The Double* was "the best thing he ever wrote… a perfect work of art". Time and again Dostoevsky expressed, probably under the influence of outside pressures, his intention to "improve" *The Double*; a partially revised version appeared in 1866.

Netochka Nezvanova (*Неточка Незванова*, 1849), a novella originally conceived as a full-length novel, should be considered an unfinished work in the form we have it. Dostoevsky deals here with what was to become one of his favourite themes – the

Netochka Nezvanova

psychology and behaviour of an unusually precocious child. The plucky child-heroine Netochka has much in common with Nelly from *Humiliated and Insulted*, particularly in her capacity for boundless love, self-sacrifice and indomitable will-power. They are both fighters who refuse to succumb to life's vicissitudes whatever the odds.

Although the novella still captures the imagination today thanks to its dramatic intensity – which, for example, prompted a successful theatre adaptation at the New End Theatre in London in 2008 – it is generally considered to contain tedious and long-winded passages, which one outspoken contemporary critic, A. Druzhinin, characterized in 1849 as reeking of perspiration. These words must have rankled with Dostoevsky, because he recalls them with dramatic irony in the epilogue to *Humiliated and Insulted*.

The Village of Stepanchikovo   In *The Village of Stepanchikovo* (*Село Степанчиково*, 1859), Dostoevsky again found himself irresistibly drawn to Gogol, who had by then become an obsession. Set on a remote country estate, the story concerns a household completely dominated by the despotic charlatan and humbug Foma Fomich Opiskin, whose sententious utterance contains a good deal of satire on the reactionary Gogol. The owner of the estate, the retired Colonel Rostanev, is a meek, kind-hearted giant of a man, cruelly dominated by Opiskin. With deftly controlled suspense, the novel builds up to a confrontation between the two.

The chief asset of the work is its rich, dramatic dialogue – *The Village of Stepanchikovo* was in fact first conceived as a drama. It is through their words that Dostoevsky gives flesh and blood not only to the protagonists but also a host of unforgettable minor characters – the perspiringly loquacious and hypochondriac landowner Bakhcheyev, the literary valet Vidoplyasov, the dancing peasant household pet Falaley, the scheming poseur Mizinchikov and the unfortunate heiress Tatyana Ivanovna, touchingly confined in her fantasy world.

Humiliated and Insulted   Dostoevsky was thirty-nine when in January 1861 *Humiliated and Insulted* (*Униженные и оскорблённые*) began to be serialized in the first issue of *Vremya* (*Time*), the literary periodical which he founded jointly with his brother Mikhail. A much revised version came out in book form in autumn of the same year. It was his fourth novel to date after *Poor Folk* and *The Double* (1846), and *The Village of Stepanchikovo*

(1859), neither of the last two being originally designated as novels, but given the stylized titles of "poem" and "tale" (*повесть*) respectively. However, *The Village of Stepanchikovo* and *Humiliated and Insulted* have this in common: that they were written in close succession, straight after his return from the ten-year period of penal servitude and exile in Siberia, and were meant to serve as passports for re-entry to the literary scene from which he was debarred for so long.

Notes from the House of the Dead, literally and more accurately *Notes from the Dead House* (*Записки из мертвого дома*, 1862), is Dostoevsky's fictionalized record of four years of unremitting hardship and privation suffered as a convict in one of Tsar Nicholas I's Siberian penal institutions. In 1854 he wrote to his brother: "The different folk I met in the settlement! I lived amongst them and got to know them well. The stories I heard from the vagabonds and felons – about their nefarious deeds and gruelling way of life – would be enough to fill several tomes. What an amazing set of people!" Dostoevsky looked upon penal servitude with the eyes of an artist, making imaginative generalizations and giving the narrative a deliberately fictional intensity and tone. And yet its genre category is unclear. Without a coherent plot or storyline, it is hardly a novel. Attempts to call the work a memoir are fundamentally wrong. Dostoevsky had a particular penchant for "notes", which is perhaps the most appropriate term.

Notes from the House of the Dead

Tolstoy had read it three times, and in a letter to the critic Nikolai Strakhov, he wrote: "I was a bit under the weather the other day and reread *The Dead House*. I'd forgotten a lot... I know of no better work in the whole of modern literature, including Pushkin... If you see Dostoevsky, tell him I love him." In his response, Strakhov informed Tolstoy that Dostoevsky was very pleased to hear the words of praise and asked to be allowed to keep Tolstoy's letter, only he was taken a little aback at the implied note of disrespect for Pushkin.

Notes from the Underground (*Записки из подполья*, 1864) is a work which holds an enduring fascination for critics and readers. The opening words are, as in *Humiliated and Insulted*, a model of simplicity. But, instead of a calm, level-headed statement – "Last year, on the evening of 22nd March, I had a most unusual experience" – we have a burst of paranoid personal observations: "I am a sick man... I am a spiteful man. I am an unattractive man. I believe my liver

Notes from the Underground

is diseased", with no concern about whether the reader is prepared or interested.

At this stage one must of necessity note a certain lack of equivalence between *подполье* as in the original Russian title and "underground" – the nearest possible rendering of it into English. The Russian word is far more applicable to predominantly abstract conditions, from secretive, clandestine – in the political or criminal sense – to repressed, inhibited – in the psychological one. The book and its title were famously parodied in Woody Allen's *Notes from the Overfed* (1968): "I am fat. I am disgustingly fat. I am the fattest human I know, etc." Zany though this spin-off may appear, it is in the spirit of Dostoevsky himself, because *Notes from the Underground*, like most of his fiction, is itself full of madcap, riotous humour.

In pictorial terms the sinister side of the underground man is essentially Walter Sickert's figure in the black waistcoat and white shirt sitting with his head bowed beside the naked corpse of a woman. Dostoevsky did not go that far just then. The broody murderer – precisely as depicted in Sickert – came a little later, in *The Idiot*.

We don't know what motivated Jack the Ripper, or the Camden Town Murderer – Sickert doesn't tell us, and neither does Dostoevsky explain why his anonymous underground man harbours such hatred for the attractive young prostitute Liza, whom he ravishes, sermonizes, moves to the limits of self-pity and then rejects cruelly so that she leaves his lodgings in utter desperation. Dostoevsky was already groping his way towards formulating the aesthetics of crime. This would be fully accomplished in the later work, *Devils*.

The eminent critic Nikolai Mikhailovsky has pointed out that the novel is not artistically persuasive because of this lack of motive for the hero's antipathy towards the benighted prostitute Liza. "There is no reason for his spite towards her. The underground man foresees no results from his tormenting her. He abandons himself to his pastime out of love for the art." But perhaps absence of motive is the whole crux of the matter – supreme evil thrives on absence of motive.

Crime and Punishment (*Преступление и наказание*, 1866) is one of the four of Dostoevsky's major novels, which Nabokov referred to as "the *so-called* major novels" (my italics). The arguably much greater, but less well-known Nobel-Prize-winning author Ivan Bunin had a similarly low opinion of Dostoevsky's great novels, or novels of ideas, as they are also not infrequently referred to. Valentin Kataev recalls that Bunin raged over the hero, Raskolnikov: "Dostoevsky obliges you to witness impossible and inconceivable abominations and spiritual squalor. From here have come all Russia's ills – Decadence, Modernism, Revolution, young people who are infected to the marrow of their bones with *Dostoevshchina* – who are without direction in their lives, confused, spiritually and physically crippled by war, not knowing what to do with their strengths and their talents..."

At the heart of *Crime and Punishment* is the student Raskolnikov's premeditated murder of a miserable old woman moneylender with the manic idea that this act would somehow make him into a superman, raise him above the law and enable him to identify himself with Napoleon. Around this idea, Dostoevsky, armed with a marvellous title, manages to spin a truly fascinating tale. Issues of crime and punishment are always calculated to arouse interest, and he manages to score some significant firsts, to wit his creation of the detective Porfiry. "Wilkie Collins and Dickens portrayed Victorian detectives, but no one had yet shown the 'master' detective, capable of deducing facts from psychological observation: in the twentieth century the super-detective was a close rival of the criminal for the status of hero," writes Professor Richard Peace.

As mentioned above, Dostoevsky was addicted to gambling, *The Gambler* and he channelled this personal experience into his next novel, *The Gambler* (*Игрок*, 1866). The action takes place in the spoof town Roulettenburg, where a bunch of Russian prize idlers have fetched up to feed their habit and indulge in conspiracies and sterile romantic pursuits. As was to be expected, no one gets any richer, just the opposite, and all personal relationships end in frustration and heartache.

In a letter to his favourite niece Sofia Alexandrovna Ivanova, *The Idiot* to whom he dedicated *The Idiot* (*Идиот*, 1868), Dostoevsky wrote: "I have been nurturing the idea of this novel a long time now. It is a particular favourite of mine, but is so difficult that I have not dared to tackle it... The main aim is to portray a positively good man. There's nothing more difficult than this in the world, especially nowadays. All writers, not only ours, but even the European ones too, who tried, had to give up, for the simple reason that the task is measureless."

The hero of the novel, Prince Myshkin, is a Christ-like figure. He is mentally distinctly unstable, indeed he brands himself an idiot. The question arises, can saintliness survive in the real world? Russia being the real world, the novel's answer is no, because it is synonymous with some kind of mental deficiency, which is bound to lead to disaster. At the beginning of the novel Myshkin returns from a Swiss sanatorium after a lengthy treatment, hopefully on the way to complete recovery. Abroad he had witnessed public executions by guillotine, and the memories continue to haunt him, especially the gruesome ordinariness of the preparatory ritual. What goes through the condemned man's head as he hears the swish of the descending blade? In St Petersburg he finds no solace. On the day of his arrival, without a respite, he is thrown into a vortex of events that would have unsettled a much stronger man. Representing the darker side of humanity is the volatile, passionate, reckless merchant Rogozhin, whom Myshkin gets to know on the journey. It is a fateful meeting. As the action unravels both come to grief in their rivalry and quest for happiness, Rogozhin's fate being, if anything, the more heart-rending, because he ends up with blood on his hands beside the lifeless corpse of the woman they both loved to distraction. As for Myshkin, he returns to the sanatorium, we fear permanently.

The novel is conceived on a large scale with numerous sub-plots and a host of secondary characters. True to form they are all colourfully depicted, invariably with customary Dostoevskian humour and wit. However, some critics have found the structure of the novel problematic, and it is not the most popular choice among a wider readership.

Devils   In the work *Devils* (*Бесы*, 1871–72, also known as *The Possessed* and *Demons*), one of Dostoevsky's main concerns is nihilism: this is embodied in the novel to devastating effect through its memorable characters. The great Russian critic and novelist Dmitry Merezhkovsky argues in *Gogol and the Devil* that the suave, smooth-talking clownish con man Chichikov in Gogol's *Dead Souls* is the devil par excellence, because he is one of us who goes about deceiving people left, right and centre with impunity, hiding under his mask of normality and ordinariness – a point worth noting in relation to *Devils*.

The novel boasts some of the most blood-curdling episodes imaginable, but at the same time the translator Michael R. Katz writes: "*Devils* is without doubt Dostoevsky's most humorous work. It has more irony, more elements of burlesque and parody, more physical comedy and buffoonery, more exaggerated characterizations and ambiguous use of language than any of his other works." We are indeed not miles away from the Marx Brothers' *Night at the Opera*. Stepan Trofimovich Verkhovensky, with whom the novel opens and who continues to play a significant role to the very end, can, improbably enough, be seen as a Groucho Marx figure with a touch of Don Quixote thrown in. The picture is completed with the former's inimitable screen foil Margaret Dupont, who is represented in the novel by the grand and unapproachable Varvara Petrovna Stavrogina.

Dostoevsky based his story on a Russian press report of a brutal murder by a follower of the revolutionary anarchist Ivan Bakunin. He uses that as a paradigm for depicting a ruthless nationwide conspiracy, incidentally directed from abroad, to bring down the existing order in Russia. Acts of terrorism and extreme violence are used as political tools. But the events, despite being narrated by an apparently non-committal chronicler, are by no means a factual record of reality. The highly mysterious chronicler's very protestations of veracity are a novelist's ploy to draw the reader into a fantasy world that is blatantly of his own creation. At the centre of it are the demonically beguiling figures of Nicolas Stavrogin, a self-confessed paedophiliac and sadist, and his utterly unprincipled sidekick Pyotr Stepanovich Verkhovensky. Besides the motif of rampant terrorism, there is the theme of suicide, not as a desperate solution out of a psychological impasse, but as a supreme manifestation of one's will.

Dostoevsky had always been keenly interested in all aspects of publishing. Even his fictional characters are bitten by the bug. Vanya in *Humiliated and Insulted* talks to a publisher or entrepreneur, as he facetiously styles him, and appears to know his role and what motivates him; Liza Drozdova in *Devils* comes up with a serious proposal to bring out a digest, "an illuminating overview" of current affairs, and she waxes enthusiastic over the benefits and commercial viability of the prospective undertaking. Dostoevsky himself was a prolific journalist and the founder and editor of several periodicals. Liza's idea in fact goes back to Dostoevsky's plans of 1864–65 to found *Notebook* – a fortnightly periodical which failed to materialize – and looks forward to *Diary of a Writer*

Diary of a Writer

(*Дневник писателя*, 1873–81), which did materialize in 1873. In both cases Dostoevsky was to be the sole contributor. It is for this reason that *Diary of a Writer* can, indeed should, be regarded as a free-standing literary work. In essence it is a ground-breaking, wide-ranging amalgam of all types of literary genres, "an illuminating overview" of all that continued to preoccupy the writer till the end of his days, and some of the issues touched upon were further reflected in his Pushkin speech and in *The Karamazov Brothers*.

The Adolescent   In 1876 Dostoevsky wrote: "When, about a year and a half ago, Nikolai Alexeyevich Nekrasov asked me to write a novel for *The Notes of the Fatherland*, I was on the point of starting my version of *Fathers and Sons*, but held back, and thank God for that. I was not ready. All I've been able to come up with so far is my *The Adolescent*."

Just as in Turgenev's *Fathers and Sons*, the theme of the generation gap is at the heart of *The Adolescent* (*Подросток*, 1875). Incidentally the narrator-hero rejoices in the name of Arkady (Dolgoruky), the same as one of the principal characters, Arkady (Kirsanov), in Turgenev's story; the other – the more important of the two – being Evgeny Bazarov. The similarity does not end there. Both Arkady Dolgoruky and Evgeny Bazarov are kindred spirits, rebels at heart and ardent champions of liberalism and truth. This ideological confluence is quite remarkable because on most points the two authors could not see eye to eye at all.

Also, the theme of relationship with serf women is tackled head on by both authors, especially Dostoevsky, who of course extracts every ounce of drama from the controversy associated with such a liaison. Arkady is illegitimate: he is the son of the serf Sofia, wife of the bonded serf Makar Dolgoruky, and the gallivanting nobleman, Andrei Versilov. Dostoevsky is immediately on home ground – the trials and tribulations of a thoroughly dysfunctional family. After his wife had been taken away from him, Makar Dolgoruky leaves his village to wander off and walk the land as a penitent, surfacing only at the end of the story. Young Arkady, at nineteen – having been knocked all his life from pillar to post – is back with his biological father, whom he had hardly met since birth, eager to get to know him closely. It's a love-hate relationship from the start: Arkady is fascinated by Versilov, and is drawn to him inexorably. Versilov shares a good few characteristics with the devil of Ivan's nightmare in *The*

Karamazov Brothers, who, in line with Dostoevsky's intertwining of good and evil, is quite an affable, genial sort. Arkady wants to live up to his father, and in his young heart he nurtures a grand, but in his view eminently attainable and realistic idea. He lusts after money and, above all, power. As he says in the novel, he wants to become a Rothschild. Father and son also lust after the same woman almost to the point of committing murder. In the background there is the ever-present mother figure of the saintly, long-suffering Sofia, and what with Makar Dolgoruky bearing a strong resemblance to Father Zosima, the similarity between Dostoevsky's last two novels is striking. Yet the atmosphere is altogether different. Perhaps the chaotic, topsy-turvy, structurally unbalanced *Karamazov Brothers* is more action packed and stimulating, intellectually intriguing and humorous too, which is what counts with readers in the end, even the more sophisticated ones. *The Adolescent* is, in that case, arguably too sophisticated and refined for its own good. One way or another *The Adolescent* has been overshadowed by his other great novels both in Russia and the Anglophone West.

Sigmund Freud wrote that *The Karamazov Brothers* (Братья Карамазовы, 1879–80) was "the most magnificent novel ever written". Indeed, the novel played right into his hands, above all as regards the Oedipal connection. The work blends together literature, philosophy and entertainment in way that has held a strong appeal for many intellectual readers. *The Karamazov Brothers*

At the heart of the novel is a dysfunctional family, four sons – one illegitimate – and the father, a dissolute, cunning, mistrustful old man, who is in a running feud with the eldest over money and the favours of the local siren. The conflict gets out of hand and Dmitry Karamazov is accused of patricide. Bound up with this intense family drama is Dostoevsky's exploration of many of his most deeply cherished ideas. The novel is also richly comic and philosophically challenging. One chapter, entitled *The Legend of the Grand Inquisitor*, in which the churchman, in a confrontational dialogue with Christ, argues that freedom and happiness are incompatible, is styled a poem, and for its content and form occupies a unique place in literature.

This account of Dostoevsky's works is by no means exhaustive, but has had to be limited to some of the most famous and pivotal novels and novellas. During his career Dostoevsky wrote many other shorter works of fiction, not to mention articles, essays and travel writing, and among his short stories one could mention *Miscellaneous Short Fiction* the following, among many others: *White Nights* (*Белые ночи*, 1848), a story of isolation and heartbreak spanning four nights, during which the protagonist realizes his love for a young girl called Nastenka must always remain unfulfilled; *The Eternal Husband* (*Вечный туж*, 1870), which compellingly describes a recently widowed man's encounter with his dead wife's former lover; *A Gentle Creature* (*Кроткая*, 1876), the tale of a widowed pawnbroker's turbulent relationship with a young customer who eventually becomes his wife; *The Dream of a Ridiculous Man* (*Сон смешного человека*, 1877), which recounts the spiritual journey of its suicidal protagonist, who finds salvation in an encounter with a young girl and a subsequent dream.

Translator's Note

In 1868 Dostoevsky wrote in a letter, "The main aim of the novel is to depict a *wholly* virtuous man. There's nothing more difficult in the world, especially these days. All writers, not just our Russian ones, but even the Europeans, who attempted to depict a positively virtuous type – always gave up. The task is colossal. Virtue is an ideal, an ideal – be it our own or European – which is still very much in the making. There is only one positively virtuous man in the world, and that is Christ... of all the virtuous people in Christian literature, the most rounded off is Don Quixote. But he is virtuous solely because he is at the same time ridiculous. Dickens's Mr Pickwick (an incomparably weaker concept than Don Quixote, but prodigious nonetheless) is also ridiculous, and that is precisely why he's indomitable. We cannot help feeling protective towards the ludicrous and the naively odd amongst us, and our, the readers', sympathy goes out to them. This evocation of compassion is the very essence of humour."

Here Dostoevsky hits the nail on the head – goodness and humour go hand in hand. A good person has to be in some way funny, not necessarily funny-comical, but of necessity – funny-odd. That is the long and the short of Dostoevsky's great novel. The very title – *The Idiot* – says it all. Prince Myshkin, Dostoevsky's take on Christ, is an "idiot", and it is his unconventionality, his "idiocy" that makes him so Christ-like; neither can survive in the real world – they both perish, and at roughly the same age. The novel charts the life of a man whose goodness, probity, directness and absence of guile can be intensely funny, but is perceived by his fellows as a species of mental incapacity and oddity that ultimately calls for specialist medical intervention.

The novel opens with Myshkin returning to Russia from a Swiss clinic, and everything about him strikes the other passengers as distinctly odd, and provokes sarcastic comments, not to say crude mirth. His manner of speaking too – diffident and reserved, somewhat alien, lays him open to blunt and indiscreet questioning. "And did they cure you?" "No, not really." "Ha! I thought as much... but you paid through the nose..."

Everything about Myshkin is impractical, vulnerable, pathetic, odd and, of course, funny – and it is certainly this last characteristic which, while provoking mirth and ridicule, at the same time endears him to the most hardened of people that he encounters, and makes them involuntarily reach out to him. They soon learn to disregard his quirkiness and are drawn to seek his company and confide in him. Children too flock to him and adore him; a murderer-to-be exchanges crosses with him as a mark of fraternity and eternal friendship.

But he is not absolutely all sweetness, compliance and good cheer. His very goodness can also get up people's noses, and provoke open, violent resentment. In situations where his honour is impugned, while he does not give as good as he gets, neither does he automatically turn the other cheek as might have been expected of him. Suddenly, to our delight we discover that he is no Christ, and we applaud him and congratulate him. Well done, Myshkin! Go for it, Prince! We want action! We want blood and gore! At the drop of a hat we are part of the hooting, yelling crowd that cheered when the lions tore the Christians limb from limb...

Boundless saintliness can be an awful bore. This is surely what Dostoevsky meant by the extraordinary difficulty of portraying a *wholly* virtuous man – the fear of ending up by boring his readers! "I fear it'll turn out a bore. The novel is long," he wrote in the same letter. Like no one else, he knew that a writer must, above all, entertain and keep his readers happy, or perish.

And so to work. By looking through his notes, we see he made no end of false starts. The idiot he started with was nothing like the final one. It was a long and arduous search, culminating in frenetic bursts of dictation to his stenographer-

685

wife under impossibly difficult conditions; travelling from one country to another; going from casino to casino in which he lost every penny he had – mostly his wife's anyway – and when thus driven into a corner by himself, finding the necessary conditions in which to create his masterpiece.

Dostoevsky's final version of the character presents us with a question. As in the case of Hamlet, whose sanity is in doubt, so in the case of Myshkin. Is he mentally challenged, or not? Is he an idiot, or is he not? At times he does not appear at all as idiotic as he is made out to be. Some totally impartial and highly knowledgeable characters in the novel vouch for his unquestionable and exemplary good sense. In fact, in the end they pronounce him more level-headed than many another character who claims to be the very paragon of normality. But we soon conclude that Dostoevsky's world is so bizarre and convoluted that nothing can be taken for granted, least of all sanity and good sense.

Dostoevsky revels in peopling his novels with every kind of oddball imaginable. He may be accused of having taken the reader into a lunatic asylum, but never into a museum of waxworks. And in the treatment of them he is loving and compassionate throughout, or he would not have devoted so much attention to those that are spiritually and mentally unbalanced. From the almost permanently inebriated General Ivolgin with his endless cock-and-bull stories; to the incorrigible plotter, petty conspirator and congenital wheeler-dealer Lebedev who is yet interested in the Apocalypse; to Ferdyshchenko, the self-appointed clown and buffoon – Dostoevsky loves every single one of them. They are dear to his heart. They are his children, his holy fools, who not only know not what they say but who are often the mouthpieces of God, the bearers of eternal truths.

Dostoevsky's heroines are as hilarious as his men folk. For one thing, they refuse to play second fiddle. Whether in life or at the moment of death, they are always centre stage. The generous, open-hearted matriarch Lizaveta Prokofyevna is a towering, larger-than-life personality, who comes very close to obscuring Myshkin himself in her own distinctive brand of humour and quirkiness. The two are peculiarly complementary, and yet at times a foil to one another. They are distantly related by blood and their hearts beat in unison. They are the only two surviving members of the Myshkin family – significantly, the end of the line. Both are oddities, latter-day dinosaurs, square pegs in their respective round holes, or, to subvert the terminology of the times, "superfluous people". Their departure, which we will mourn, will herald a new dawn, which we hesitate to welcome.

Lizaveta Prokofyevna is another Christ-like figure, who has taken upon herself the sins of the world, in the shape of her family – that is, her three splendid but "impossibly unruly" daughters and her loving but roguishly errant husband. She is a spiritual hypochondriac par excellence, glorying in the role of a likeable and tyrannical domestic martyr, but as she herself points out, she has much in common with Prince Myshkin.

How different is the predatory, savagely beautiful and vindictively haughty Nastasya Filippovna! She too is possessed of humour, but of a vicious, sarcastic cast, which is corrosive and utterly destructive. She is the very devil of annihilation: she destroys the man who loves and cares for her – Myshkin – and the man who loves, but does not care for her – the darkly brooding, hot-tempered, uneducated but immensely shrewd and wealthy Rogozhin. The long-suffering Rogozhin, in his primitive, peasant uncouthness, feels he is surrounded on all sides by mocking, jeering clowns. But he is sufficiently self-possessed and thick-skinned not to have cared a jot for any of them, if only Nastasya Filippovna, whose feminine charms had ensnared him to absolute distraction, had not been at their head. She toys with him cruelly and mercilessly in private and in public, and he does not know how to handle her. And the worst of it is that he knows he doesn't know, which makes him all the wilder with frustration. Nastasya Filippovna is at the same time attracted and repelled by all that this dangerous man represents. And, however much time and effort Dostoevsky lavishes on depicting the good man, Myshkin, Rogozhin, by contrast, seems to burgeon formidably in stature almost by default; with every brush stroke applied to Myshkin, two seem to be added to Rogozhin.

Nastasya Filippovna is the very opposite of Desdemona, who is all feminine sweetness, submission and charm, yearning and desperately eager to quell her dear husband. And Othello will have none of it. Rogozhin is ready to spend all night on his knees, hoping his "queen" would let him kiss the hem of her dress. She makes light even of that, and instead of soothing her man, she provokes him. For her, comedy is tragedy that happens to others. She is in the Carmen mould. She makes Rogozhin dance to her tune, and in between the reels she is happy to make a fool of him, cast him aside and openly fall into his rival's, Myshkin's, arms. Not for fun, but in a mixture of fun and desperation. The two wildly contrasting men in her life are her undoing.

This is the flip side of humour; its injurious, hurtful, demonic side, which to a man of Rogozhin's dull, morose disposition, is like a red rag to a bull. It suddenly gets out of hand, overbalances into horribly unpleasant seriousness and comes crashing down about everyone's ears. *La commedia è finita! Ridi, Pagliaccio!* But did the sweet-tongued, docile, angelic Desdemona fare any better? There is but one story in the world, told in a thousand different ways!

* * *

Alexander Pushkin once said that translators are the post-horses of civilization. Never had a truer word been spoken – without translators the world would be in a cultural gridlock. But translators have always trodden a fraught path. Andrew Marvell wrote:

> He is translation's thief that addeth more
> As much as he that taketh from the store
> Of the first author.

This view is held more or less to this day, especially by the "warts and all" school. But the dangers of too slavish an adherence to the original were also noted long before the days of political correctness, in the form of the adage: "A translation is like a woman: if she's faithful, she's not beautiful, if she's beautiful, she's not faithful".

Dostoevsky is notorious for stretching language to its limits, often beyond. The reader in consequence sometimes wonders if he has not wandered into a lunatic asylum. The danger of the "warts and all" translations is that the characters, instead of sounding like native lunatics, which is exhilarating, sound merely like eccentric foreigners, which is unintentionally comical.

Abiding by the pronouncements of the wise, and with my hand on my heart, I would assure the reader that in my attempt to pass the camel through the eye of a needle – a metaphor for the act of translation – I have tried to be as faithful to the spirit of the original as possible, but always within the bounds of natural English.

– Ignat Avsey, 2010

Select Bibliography

Standard Edition:
The Russian text taken from Volume 8 (1973) of the *Complete Edition in Thirty Volumes* (*Polnoe sobranie sochineniy v tridtsati tomakh*) of Dostoevsky's works (Leningrad: Nauka, 1972–90) is the most authoritative to date.

Biographies:
Carr, Edward Hallett, *Dostoevsky, 1821–1881: A New Biography* (London: Allen & Unwin, 1931)
Dostoevsky, Anna, *Dostoevsky: Reminiscences*, tr. B. Stillman (Liveright, Dutton, 1974)
Frank, Joseph, *Dostoevsky*, vols. 1–5 (London: Robson, 1977–2002)
Grossman, Leonid Petrovich, *Dostoevsky: A Biography*, tr. Mary Mackler (London: Allen Lane, 1974)
Magarshack, David, *Dostoevsky* (London: Secker & Warburg, 1962)
Mochulsky, Konstantin, *Dostoevsky: His Life and Work* (Princeton, NJ: Princeton University Press, 1967)
Simmons, Ernest Joseph, *Dostoevsky: The Making of a Novelist* (London: John Lehmann, 1950)
Yarmolinsky, Avrahm, *Dostoevsky: A Life* (New York: Harcourt, Brace & Co., 1934)

On the Web:
www.petrsu.ru/~Dostoevsky
www.fyodordostoevsky.com

Acknowledgements

My grateful thanks go to all my friends for their unstinting help and warm encouragement in preparing the text and critical apparatus, namely to (in no particular order): Hugh Davidson, Joanna Wright, Peter Khoroche, John Moloney, Dr Virginie Avsejs, Dr Alexey Grigoriev, Leonid Feygin, Sergey and Natalia Toumakov and Daffni Percival.

The publisher, Alessandro Gallenzi, has always been immensely approachable, understanding and helpful. The editor, Alex Billington, supported by his able colleagues, has worked miracles on bringing my typescript up to scratch and moulding it into shape.

Last, but not least, I additionally wish to thank my friend John Moloney and my sister Virginie for their generous financial support at a very critical stage of the proceedings.

– Ignat Avsey

Dedication

To Anastasia

Ignat Avsey is a freelance independent scholar and translator. His published and commissioned translations include Dostoevsky's *The Village of Stepanchikovo*, *The Karamazov Brothers* and *Humiliated and Insulted*, as well as *Alzheimer's, the Plague of the Twenty-First Century* by Arkady Eisler.